MAFIA

MAFIA

THE GOVERNMENT'S SECRET FILE

ON ORGANIZED CRIME

Skyhorse Publishing

Skyhorse Publishing books may be purchased in bulk at special discounts for sales promotion, corporate gifts, fund-raising, or educational purposes. Special editions can also be created to specifications. For details, contact the Special Sales Department, Skyhorse Publishing, 555 Eighth Avenue, Suite 903, New York, NY 10018 or info@skyhorsepublishing.com.

www.skyhorsepublishing.com

10 9 8 7 6 5 4 3 2 1

Library of Congress Cataloging-in-Publication Data

Mafia : the government's secret file on organized crime / United States Treasury Department, Bureau of Narcotics.
    p. cm.
 ISBN 978-1-60239-668-5
1. Mafia--United States. 2. Organized crime--United States. I. United States. Dept. of the Treasury.
 HV6785.M294 2009
 364.1092'273--dc22

                    2009017805

Printed in Canada

FOREWORD

Under FBI Director J. Edgar Hoover's watch, the criminal organizations that would become known as La Cosa Nostra, the Mafia, and the Outfit were allowed to operate unimpeded for decades. Bureau resources focused instead on high-profile cases like the Lindbergh kidnapping and the apprehension of notorious bank robber John Dillinger—cases that were intended to elevate Hoover's stature, undeservedly, to that of America's quintessential crime buster. With *Mafia*, that myth will be dispelled once and for all.

In fact, the real story of law enforcement's war on organized crime during this period begins not with Hoover, but with the Treasury Department's Bureau of Narcotics. The thick, fascinating dossier you now hold in your hands, is the product of that bureau's groundbreaking investigation into an enormous league of Sicilian criminals and "crime families." From this compilation, Robert F. Kennedy,

after becoming attorney general in 1961, selected his "hit list" of criminals. This list—filled with profiles of men with strange nicknames and even stranger cultural mores—formed the backbone of what would become the nation's largest war on organized crime.

The 1950s heralded the formation of a number of Senate committees charged with investigating organized crime, but it was the Senate's McClellan Committee in 1957 that would spell the end of the honeymoon for Hoover's FBI.

Spearheaded by the ambitious young Kennedy, the Committee hearings became an instant media sensation. In all, fifteen hundred individuals, largely Sicilian and Italian Americans, were called to testify—among them my uncle and godfather, Chicago mob boss Sam Giancana. A sneering, arrogant, and uncooperative witness, Kennedy dubbed Giancana the "devil in a sharkskin suit."

Although the McClellan Committee hearings raised inescapable questions about the FBI's capabilities, Hoover insisted the witnesses were nothing more than *unorganized*, *local* criminals whose escapades were better addressed by local police. And unfortunately for Kennedy, during its early years, the Committee uncovered no irrefutable evidence of an organized crime cartel to demonstrate otherwise. Then, on November 14, 1957, fate intervened when local law enforcement stumbled upon a clandestine meeting of criminals in Apalachin, New York. The ensuing raid received national media attention, vindicating Robert Kennedy and confirming, once and for all, the existence of a national, organized criminal enterprise.

In the wake of this revelation, Hoover came under immense pressure to crack down on organized crime. Still, it wasn't until 1961—when Kennedy was named attorney general by his older brother, President John F. Kennedy— that the war on organized crime was formally declared. The new attorney general ordered Hoover to begin immediate investigations into eight hundred men. At the top of this list was Chicago's Sam Giancana.

Hoover finally caved and under his direction, over the following years,

the FBI made numerous scientific advances, from fingerprinting to forensic and ballistic tests. Pioneering modern investigative techniques, agents used wiretaps and relentless surveillance to compile highly accurate, detailed criminal profiles that built upon the Narcotics Bureau's initial, monumental work.

And yet—despite what was unquestionably the most ferocious domestic war in the history of the nation—it must be stated that even Kennedy's top target for prosecution, Sam Giancana, was never convicted of any crime. What this means in terms of the success or failure of this war can only be left to the truth of history, as it unfolds, over time.

What can be said with authority is that *Mafia* is an exact facsimile reproduction of the Treasury Department's original organized crime file, offering a rare and mesmerizing slice of American history, a journey to a very different time and place, and an unprecedented glimpse at the very roots of organized crime in this country.

As a cultural snapshot, *Mafia* is both prosaic—with its dates of birth and criminal records—and poetic, full of memorable nicknames and unforgettable faces. There are men here, like my uncle and his mentor Al Capone, who came to prominence during the "Roaring Twenties" and Prohibition and others, like Paul Castellano and Vinny "the Chin" Gigante, who would step into the limelight in the 1970s and '80s. Taken as a whole, *Mafia* is every bit as compelling as any hit TV series.

From international legends and bosses to street-corner bookies and thugs, they're all here—true American legends who are as much a part of the fabric of this nation as the hallowed threads of the red, white, and blue. They are who we are, and no American can afford to ignore them.

—Sam Giancana
January 20, 2009

MAFIA LIST INDEX

AMORUSO, Giuseppe	762	ATTRENTI, Vincenzo	764
AMORUSO, Nicholas	284	AVERSA, Thomas J.	187
ANACLERIO, Germaio	341	AVOLA, Mario	349
ANACLERIO, Jerry @	341	AVOLA, Marty @	349
ANASTASIO, Antonio	342		
ANCONA, Giacomo @	244	BABALU @	339
ANCONA, Jack	244	BABO @	673
ANDOLINO, Sam @	343	BABS, Joe @	359
ANDOLINO, Simone	343	BACILE, Vincent @	563
ANGELICA, Biagio	725	BACINO, Philip @	126
ANGELICO, Biaggio @	725	BACINO, Tony @	126
ANGELO, Big @	725	BADALAMENTE, Salvatore @	286
ANGERSOLA, George	80	BADALAMENTI, Gaetano	765
ANGERSOLA, John	81	BADALAMENTI, Salvatore	286
ANNALORO, Angelo @	70	BADALAMENTI, Sam @	286
ANNICHIARICO, Alfonso @	344	BADALAMENTI, Vito	766
ANNICCHIARICO, Anthony	344	BADALAMENTO, Salvatore @	286
ANSALDI, Marius J.	744	BAIONI, Larry @	198
ANSANI, Robert J. @	124	BALDY @	416
ANSELMO, Joseph	191	BALESTERI, Mario @	5
ANSONI, Robert J.	124	BALESTRERO, Mario @	5
ANTHONY, Paul @	13	BALISTRERI, Mario	5
ANZALONE, Giuseppe	763	BALLANCA, Sebastiano @	289
AQUILINA, Phillip @	418	BALSAMO, John M.	350
ARANCI, Marius A.	745	BALTO, Samuel @	118
ARDITO, John G.	345	BALZARINI, Ugo	767
ARMONA, Stefano @	347	BANANAS @	165
ARMONE, Joseph	346	BANANAS, Joe @	1
ARMONE, Stephen	347	BANANAS, Joe @	165
ARNAULT, Pierre @	748	BANANAS, Tony @	297
ARRA, Tom @	510	BANTI, Joe @	360
ARRESSA, Joe @	789	BARATTA, Peter	351
ARROSA, James @	789	BARATTO, Albert @	288
ARROSA, Joe @	789	BARBARA, Joseph M. Jr.	352
ATTARDI, Alfonso	348	BARBATO, Arnold	353
ATTARDI, Philip	285	BARBATO, Salvatore J.	354
ATTARTI, Phillip @	285	BARBERA, Joseph @	519
ATTRAENTE, Vincenzo	764	BARBERO, Jim @	781

BARBETO, Anthony @	353	BEANS, Louie @	448
BARCELLONA, Charles	355	BEATTIE, Ed @	328
BARCY, John @	128	BECK, Charlie @	430
BARESE, Carmine @	287	BECK, Joe @	431
BARESE, Ernesto	287	BECK, Joe @	492
BARI, Joe @	422	BECK, Petey @	432
BARILLA, Giovanni	768	BEHRMAN, Nathan	358
BARIS, Vincent @	6	BEJIN, Paul Marie @	755
BARISE, Vincent @	6	BELFONTE, Nick @	702
BARON @	688	BELLANCA, Benny @	289
BARON, The @	366	BELLANCA, Sebastiano	289
BARONE, Benny	273	BELLO, Anthony	126
BARONE, Bernard @	273	BELLO, Dominic @	139
BARONE, Joseph @	485	BELSAMO, John @	350
BARR, Al @	288	BENDA, Tony @	646
BARRA, Joseph J.	356	BENDENELLI, Joseph	359
BARRA, Morris	82	BENDER, Tony @	646
BARRA, Rocco	357	BENDINELLI, Joseph @	359
BARRASSE, Albert @	288	BENFANTE, Nick @	702
BARRASSO, Albert	288	BENFANTI, Nicholas	702
BARRASSO, Allessio @	288	BENFONTO, Nick @	702
BARRATTO, Albert @	288	BENNETT, John @	581
BARRIE, Ernie @	287	BENNY THE BUM @	420
BARRISA, Vincent J.	6	BENNY THE CRINGE @	481
BARRISE, Vincent J. @	6	BENNY THE SICILIAN @	289
BARTELLO, Michael @	200	BERATA, Pete @	351
BARTLET, John J. @	290	BERMAN, Nathan @	358
BARTOLOTTA, Domiano B.	7	BERMAN, Saul @	363
BARTOLOTTA, Matteo	200	BERTI, Enzo	769
BARZZIOLA, John @	230	▬▬▬▬▬▬▬▬▬▬	
BASBARINI, Daniel @	739	BIASE, Anthony J.	274
BATH, Johnny @	555	BIASE, Bernard B.	275
BATH BEACH, Johnny @	555	BIASE, Louis	276
BATTAGLIA, Albert @	594	BIASE, Samuel	277
BATTAGLIA, Samuel	125	BIASE, Tony @	297
BATTERS, Joe @	121	BIBBO, Nicholas	683
BAUASSO, Albert @	288	BIEGLER, Moe @	127
BAYONNE, Joe @	328	BIEGLER, Nathan	127

BIG AL @	108	BLANDO, Giovanni B. @	245
BIG DOMINICK @	319	BLANDO, John B.	245
BIG FRANK @	42	BLASIS, Alberto @	750
BIG FRANK @	759	BLOOM, Joseph @	647
BIG FREDDY @	441	BLOOM, Solomon	363
BIG JOHN @	560	BLUBBER @	363
BIG LARRY @	490	BLUBBERHEAD @	363
BIG MIKE @	229	BLUMETTI, Giuseppe T.	684
BIG MIKE @	337	BLUMETTI, Joseph @	684
BIG NOSE LARRY @	558	BOCCHICCHIO, Felix	290
BIG PAT @	565	BOIARDI, Richard	291
BIG PHIL @	283	BOIARDO, Diamond @	291
BIG SAM @	282	BOIARDO, Richie @	291
BIG SOL @	540	BOIARDI, Ruggerio @	291
BIG YOK @	324	BOMMARITO, Joseph	201
BILELLO, Tony @	246	BOMMARITO, Joseph	202
BILLECI, Salvatore C.	8	BOMMARITO, Long Joe @	202
BIONDA, Joe @	360	BOMPENSIERO, Frank	9
BIONDO, Joseph	360	BONADIO, Paul	292
BIONE, Larry @	198	BONANNO, Giuseppe @	369
BISOGNO, Joseph	361	BONANNO, Joseph	1
BISSANTI, Joe @	198	BONASERA, Anthony @	364
BISTONI, Albert @	746	BONASERA, Cassandros S.	364
BISTONI, Ansan A.	746	BONAVENTURA, Peter @	14
BISTONI, Joseph @	746	BONAVENTURE, John @	369
BIVONA, Joseph N.	362	BONDI, Joe @	360
BLACK BILL @	238	BONES, Tony @	387
BLACK, Frank @	111	BONFONTE, Nick @	702
BLACK, Joe @	362	BONGIORNO, Frank	365
BLACK, Louis @	111	BONGIORNO, Paul @	665
BLACK JIM @	64	BONINA, Nicholas	366
BLACK TONY @	236	BONINO, Antonio	246
BLACKIE @	66	BONITO, Salvatore	367
BLACKIE, Ray @	321	BONNANO, Joe @	1
BLACKIE @	649	BONO, Antonio Farina @	790
BLAH BLAH @	637	BONO, Joe @	608
BLAIR, George @	637	BONONNO, Joe @	1
BLANDA, Charles J.	63	BONPENSIERO, Harry @	9

BONS, Harry @	368	BRUNO, Angelo	703
BONSIGNORE, Harry	368	BRUNO, Danny	7
BONURA, Joseph	169	BRUNO, Enso @	682
BONURA, Nicholas J.	170	BRUNO, Enzo @	682
BONURA, Philip	171	BRUNO, Frank @	689
BONURE, Joe @	169	BRUNO, Joseph	130
BONVENTRA, John @	369	BRUNO, Michael @	401
BONVENTRE, Giovanni	369	BRUNO, Thomas @	453
BONVENTRE, Joe @	369	BRUNO, Vincent P.	10
BOOTS, Tony @	453	BRUNO, Vito	11
BORCIA, John P.	128	BUCALO, Phil @	771
BORELLI, Frank	370	BUCCI, Amato A.	685
BOTTLES @	735	BUCCOLA, Philip	771
BOUVENTRE, Joe @	1	BUCHER, Max @	99
BOVE, Joseph	371	BUCKALO @	447
BOVE, Nick @	250	BUCOLLO, Philip @	771
BOWEN, Frank @	60	BUFALINO, Rosario @	704
BOZZI, Angelo @	329	BUFALINO, Ross @	704
BRACCO, Ignazio	203	BUFALINO, Russell A.	704
BRACCO, Jack @	203	BUFALINO, William E.	204
BRANCATO, Dominick	129	BUFFA, Anthony	686
BRAZIOLA, John @	230	BUFFALINO, Russ @	704
BRESCIA, Lorenzo	372	BUFFALINO, William @	204
BRESCIO, Larry @	372	BUGS MEYER @	101
BRIANO, Joe @	53	BUIA, Angelo	373
BRITTON, Al @	425	BUIA, Matildo	374
BRODY, Charlie @	430	BULL, Charlie @	584
BROOKS, Bob @	77	BULL BROTHERS @	351
BROWN, Al @	149	BULLDOG NICK @	528
BROWN, Al @	630	BULLETS, Charlie @	333
BROWN, Frankie @	365	BUONASERA, Anthony @	364
BROWN, Paul @	748	BURNS, Joe @	191
BROWN, Tom @	510	BURNS, John @	827
BROWN, Willie @	501	BUSICK, James @	188
BRUCCOLA, Filippo @	771	BUSSERO, Philip @	375
BRUCKNER, Fred @	60	BUSTER @	345
BRUNO, Al @	405	BUSTER @	556
BRUNO, Albert @	149	BUZZEO, Fillippo	375

BUZZERO @	375	CAMPO, Vincenzo	172
BUZZIO, Phil @	375	CANDELMO, John	723
		CANDY @	723
CACCIATORE, Joseph M.	83	CANEBA, Ralph @	205
CADILLAC JOE @	231	CANEBA, Salvatore	774
CAESAR, Joey @	141	CANEBA, Ugo	775
CAFANO, Marshal @	131	CANGERO, Joe @	601
CAGO, Joe @	668	CANGRO, Joseph @	601
CAIFANO, Marshal	131	CANNARO, Ralph @	205
CALAMIA, Leonard	132	CANNAVO, Ralph	205
CALAMIS, Leonard @	132	CANNAVO, Sam @	205
CALASCIBETTA, Egidio	772	CANNONE, Ignatius J.	377
CALATABIANCA, Giuseppe	376	CANNONE, Nat @	377
CALECA, Ralph	247	CANNONE, Sonny @	377
CALECO, Ralph @	247	CANTALONOTI, Vincenzo @	779
CALICA, Ralph @	247	CANTILLO, Harry @	649
CALIDDU @	834	CAPALBO, Gaetano P.	13
CALIO, Antonio	705	CAPIZZI, Salvatore A.	378
CALLEO, Philip @	795	CAPONE, Albert @	288
CAMARA, Andrew @	682	CAPONE, Ermino John	133
CAMMARADO, Emanuel @	293	CAPONE, James Ralph	735
CAMMARATA, Emanuel R.	293	CAPONIGRO, Antonio R.	297
CAMMARATA, Francesco	773	CAPPER, Ralph @	735
CAMMERTO, Emanuel @	293	CAPPOLA, Frank @	781
CAMP, James @	172	CAPPOLA, Steve @	403
CAMPAGNA, Antonio	12	CAPTAIN FRANK @	695
CAMPBELL, Louis	294	CARBONE, Al @	405
CAMPE, Thomas @	296	CARBONE, Albert @	288
CAMPI, Albert @	296	CARBONETTI, Louis @	826
CAMPI, Charles @	295	CARELLO, Tony @	379
CAMPISE, Charles @	295	CAREY, Joe @	143
CAMPISE, Tom @	296	CARGO, Joe @	668
CAMPISI, Charles	295	CARILLO, Anthony	379
CAMPISI, Gasparo @	296	CARINE @	576
CAMPISI, Thomas	296	CARLISE, Rosario @	380
CAMPO, Frank @	385	CARLISI, Rosario	380
CAMPO, Jimmy @	172	CARLISI, Roy @	380
CAMPO, John @	304	CARLOS, Nicholas @	284

CARMINATE, Dominick	382	CASTELLANO, Paul C.	388
CARMINATI, Anthony	381	CASTELLO, Joe @	376
CARMINATI, Dominick	382	CASTIGLIA, Francisco @	409
CAROLLA, Anthony S.	173	CASTIGLIOLA, Dominick	14
CAROLLA, Sam @	776	CASTORINA, Vincenzo	389
CAROLLO, Anthony @	173	CASTRO, Joseph @	302
CAROLLO, Silva @	776	CATALANOTE, Joe @	780
CAROLLO, Silvestro	776	CATALANOTTE, Joe @	780
CARONA, James @	188	CATALANOTTE, Vincenzo	779
CARONA, Vincent @	188	CATALANOTTO, Joseph	780
CARONNA, Vincent	188	CATALDO, Joseph	390
CAROUA, Sam @	776	CATANIA, James C.	391
CARRADO, Lawrence @	209	CATANZARO, Paul	248
CARRAO, Vincent @	407	CATENA, Gerald @	299
CARRERIA, Vincent @	407	CATENA, Gerardo Vito	299
CARRILA, John @	581	CATONOA, Joe @	780
CARROLL, Frank @	462	CATRONE, Joe @	737
CARROLL, Joe @	396	CATRONE, Michael @	651
CARROLLO, Charles V.	777	CATRONE, Vincenzo @	738
CARRUBBA, Conrad @	383	CATRONI, Giuseppe @	737
CARRUBBA, Corrado	383	CATRONI, Vincenzo @	738
CARUSO @	406	CAURAVANA, Carl @	682
CARUSO, Anthony	384	CAVALIER, Charles @	687
CARUSO, Antonino	778	CAVALLARO, Charles	687
CARUSO, Frank @	192	CAVATAIO, Peter V.	206
CARUSO, Frank	385	CAVATAVIO, Pete @	206
CARUSO, Roy @	380	CECALA, Philip @	89
CARVOLA, John @	454	CELI, Arthur	392
CASABIANCA, Joseph @	756	CELLO, Tony @	126
CASABLANCA, James V.	386	CERITELLO, Mark @	551
CASELA, Pete @	298	CERONE, Jack	134
CASELLA, Peter	298	CERRITO, Joseph Xavier	15
CASINO, Arthur @	613	CHABOLLA, Eduardo D. @	755
CASINO, John @	570	CHACON, Enrique @	118
CASS, Sam @	484	CHAIM, Hyman @	647
CASTALDI, Anthony	387	CHALUPOWITZ, Abraham	16
CASTANGA, Mike @	37	CHAPMAN, Abe @	16
CASTELLANO, Constantine @	388	CHAPMAN, Larry @	372

CHAPPIE @	372	CIVELLO, Nicholas	250
CHARLIE FOUR CENTS @	619	CIVILLO, Joe @	726
CHARLIE MOUSE @	413	CLEMENTE, Joseph	397
CHARLIE THE BARBER @	306	CLEMENTE, Michael	398
CHARLIE THE BLADE @	116	CLEMENTE, William @	398
CHARLIE THE WOP @	355	CLUCO, Charles @	300
CHARLIE THE WOP @	451	COCKEYE BENNY @	518
CHARMONTE, Frank @	347	COCKEYED JOE @	780
CHECKERS @	69	COCKEYED PHIL @	505
CHEECH @	340	COCO @	649
CHEECH @	500	COCO, Eddie @	399
CHEECH @	829	COCO, Ettore	399
CHEESE, Tony @	317	COHEN, Martin	301
CHEZ, Tony @	317	COHEN, Max @	99
CHIAPETTA, Vincent	249	COHEN, Meyer Harris	17
CHIAPETTI, Vincent @	249	COHEN, Michael @	17
CHICK @	450	COHEN, Mickey @	17
CHICK, Joe @	427	COHEN, Morris @	301
CHIN CHIN @	468	COHEN, Phil @	133
CHINK @	394	COHEN, Solly @	615
CHINK @	495	COHN, Morris @	301
CHIRI, Charles S. @	300	COLA, Zio @	794
CHIRI, Salvatore	300	COLBY, Arthur @	133
CHOW @	519	COLLETTI, James @	64
CHUBBY @	382	COLLETTI, Vincenzo J.	64
CHUBBY @	517	COLLINS, Joe @	396
CHUT @	498	COLLONNA, Lucien @	753
CICCIO @	340	COLOMBO, Concetto @	18
CICCIO @	500	COLOMBO, Frank Monte	18
CICCONE, Anthony	393	COMMARATA, Francesco @	773
CIMINO, Paul	207	COMMARATS, Francesco @	773
CINQUEGRANA, Benedetto F.	394	CONDELMO, John @	723
CIRAULO, Vincent J.	395	CONFORTE, William	74
CIRELLA, Joe @	396	CONFORTI, Willie @	74
CIRELLI, Joseph	396	CONIGLIO, Benedetto	400
CIRILLO, Antonio @	762	CONIGLIO, Frank @	630
CIVELLA, Nick @	250	CONIGLIO, Thomas @	630
CIVELLO, Joseph F.	726	CONSOLO, Michael J.	401

CONTALDO, Thomas	402	COSTELLO, Larry @	670
CONTE, Charles @	748	COSTELLO, Mike @	398
CONTELANOTTE, Joe @	780	COSTIGLIA, Francisco	409
COPPOLA, Francesco Paolo	781	COTRONI, Giuseppe	737
COPPOLA, Michael	84	COTRONI, Pepe @	737
COPPOLA, Stephen F.	403	COTRONI, Vic @	738
CORALLO, Anthony	404	COTRONI, Vincenzo	738
CORALLUZZO, Earl	405	COTTONE, Giuseppe	784
CORALLUZZO, Orlando @	405	COTTONE, Vincenzo	785
CORBO, Paul John	85	COUDERT, Roger Antoine	748
CORDELLIANO, Antoine @	747	COVELLO, Antonio @	404
CORDOLERINI, Antoine @	747	COW @	20
CORDOLIANI, Antoine	747	COWBOY @	97
CORELLI, Joe @	328	CRAZY TOMMY @	402
CORNES, Eddie @	428	CRECO, Sal @	799
COROLLA, Anthony @	173	CRESCENZO, Charles @	333
CORONA, Anthony @	501	CRISCI, Anthony	410
CORONA, Frank	406	CRISCOLO, Alphonse @	411
CORRADO, Dominick	208	CRISCUOLI, Alfonso @	411
CORRADO, Lawrence C.	209	CRISCUOLO, Alfred	411
CORRALO, Tony @	404	CRISH, Tony @	410
CORRAO, Vincent	407	CROCE, Jean Baptiste	749
CORREALE, Paul	408	CUCCHIARA, Frank	192
CORSO, Giuseppe Jr.	782	CULANIA, Leonard @	132
CORSO, Giuseppe Sr.	783	CUOMO, Joe @	412
COSENZA, Anthony	19	CUOMO, Matthew	412
COSENZA, Frank	20	CURCIO, Charles	413
COSSMAN, Max J.	21	CURLEY, James @	652
COSTA, Anthony @	302	CURLY @	353
COSTA, Ed @	399	CUSAMANO, Joseph	251
COSTA, James @	386	CUSUMANO, Joe @	251
COSTA, Joseph Anthony	302	CUTANA, Jerry @	299
COSTA, Thomas @	384		
COSTELLI, Joe @	376	DABBENE, Frank	189
COSTELLO, Anthony @	140	DADDANO, William	135
COSTELLO, Frank @	349	DADO, William @	135
COSTELLO, Frank @	409	DAGO LOUIE @	55
COSTELLO, Jimmy @	472	D'AGOSTINO, Antoine	750

D'AGOSTINO, Dominick	414	DE GEORGE, James	419
DAGSTINO, Dominick @	414	DE GEORGE, Vincent @	419
D'ALESSIO, John	415	DEGRASSE, Rocky @	136
DANDIA, Joseph @	422	DE GRAZIA, Rocco	136
DANDIO, Joe @	422	DE GREGORY, Joseph @	4
D'ANDREA, John @	415	DEIPIERRO, Edward @	447
DANDY JACK @	716	DEITTO, Joe @	211
DANDY PHIL @	177	DEJOHN, Altroad @	348
DANIELLO, John	416	DE JOHN, Joseph @	427
DANIELLO, Jos. O'Neal @	416	DELANO, Joe @	153
DANIELS, Charles @	116	DE LARDO, Anthony	137
DANIELS, George @	220	DELLA, Pat @	677
DANIELS, Henry @	21	DEL MONICO, Charles @	659
DANIELS, Peter @	220	DEL MONTO, Thomas @	76
D'ANNA, Anthony John	210	DELMORE, Nicholas @	284
D'ARGENIO, Edward	417	DELRINO, Nicholas @	284
DATTA, Joe @	211	DELUCA, Biaggio @	511
DAVI, Pietro	786	DELUCA, Francesco @	252
DAVID, Jean	751	DELUCA, Frank	252
DAVIS, Roger @	748	DELUCA, Gefri @	511
DE BELLA, Dominic @	139	DELUCA, Giuseppe @	253
DE BELLA, Salvatore @	706	DELUCA, Joseph	253
DE BELLA, Samuel	706	DE LUCCA, Sam @	53
DE BELLA, Steven @	706	DELUCIA, Felice	138
DE BLASE, Sam @	38	DELUCIA, Paul @	138
DE BLOSE, Sam @	38	DEMAIO, Benny @	505
DEBRO, Joseph @	730	DEMARCO, Anthony @	718
DEBROW, James @	730	DEMARCO, James @	319
DE CARLO, Angelo	303	DE MARCO, John Anthony	688
DE CARLO, Ray @	303	DEMARTINI, Ben @	420
DECCA, Tony @	140	DE MARTINI, Theodore @	421
DECHARENTE, Anthony @	140	DE MARTINIE, James @	434
DECHARINTE, Anthony @	140	DE MARTINO, Benjamin	420
DECLARENTE, Anthony @	140	DE MARTINO, Theodore	421
DEE, Johnny @	415	DEMIO, Joe @	789
DEE, Tony @	140	DE NICOLA, Salvatore @	11
DE FEO, Peter	418	DENNIS THE MENACE @	509
DE GAETANO, George @	552	DENTICO, Joseph	422

DE PALERMO, Joe @	431	DI GIOVANNI, Joseph @	254
DE PAUL, Robert @	571	DI GIOVANNI, Peter @	255
DE PAULO, Frank @	207	DI GIOVANNI, Pietro	255
DE PIETRO, Jimmy @	434	DI GREGORIO, Antonio @	181
D'ERCOLE, Joseph	423	DI LICO, William @	222
DESIMONE, Frank	22	DI MAGGIO, Rosario	428
DESIMONIA, Frank @	22	D'INGIANNI, Vincent A.	727
DESMARAIS, Jacques @	755	DIO, Frankie @	89
DE STEFANO, Pierre @	814	DIO, Johnny @	429
DETULIO, Felice @	304	DIOGUARDI, Frank	89
DETULLIO, Felix John	304	DIOGUARDI, John Ignazio	429
DIAMOND, Joe @	443	DIOGUARDIA, Frank @	89
DIAO, John @	429	DIOGUARDIA, John @	429
DIATRO, Nicola @	212	DIOGUARDIO, Frank @	89
DI BELLA, Dominick A.	139	DIOGUARDIO, John @	429
DI BELLO, Carlo @	57	DIONISIO, Robert Victor @	65
DI BENE, Nicholas	424	DIONISIO, Rosario Vito	65
DI BIASE, Benny @	275	DI PALERMO, Charles	430
DI BIASE, Louis @	276	DI PALERMO, Joseph	431
DI BIASE, Tony @	274	DI PALERMO, Peter	432
DI BRISI, Alexander @	425	DI PALO, Benedetto @	394
DI BRIZZI, Alexander	425	DI PIETRA, Jimmy @	434
DI BRUZZI, Al @	425	DI PIETRO, Carlo	433
DI CARLO, Angelo	787	DI PIETRO, Charles @	433
DI CARLO, Anniello @	787	DI PIETRO, Cosmo @	433
DI CARLO, Calogero Lelio	426	DI PIETRO, Giovanni	788
DI CARLO, Joseph J.	86	DI PIETRO, James @	434
DI CARLO, Lilo @	426	DI PIETRO, John @	788
DICCI, Tony @	140	DI PIETRO, Vincent	434
DICHIARINTE, Anthony J.	140	DIPOLLITO, Joseph	23
DIE, John @	429	DIPPOLITO, Joseph @	23
DIECIDUE, Antonio	87	DI STEFANO, Francois @	812
DIECIDUE, Francesco @	88	DI STEFANO, Sal @	813
DIECIDUE, Frank	88	DI STEFANO, Vincent	435
DI FRANCESCO, Charles @	687	DITTA, Giuseppe	211
DI GIORGIO, Jimmy @	419	DITTA, Joe @	211
DI GIOVANNA, Joseph	427	DITTA, Nicola @	212
DI GIOVANNI, Giuseppe	254	DITTO, Joe @	211

		Eboli, Thomas	304 A
DIVARCO, Joseph	141	EDDIE THE WOP @	417
DODO @	203	EDER, Max	439
DOME, Louie @	562	EGGY @	477
DOMINO, Salvatore	174	ELVARADO, Aldo @	440
DOMINO, Sam	174	EMBARRATO, Alfred J.	440
DON ALFONSO @	104	EMILIO, Santo @	325
DON CARLO @	460	ENZO, Bruno @	682
DON CHEECH @	189	EPPOLITO, Alfred	441
DON CICCIO @	189	ERACE, Frank @	219
DON CICCIO @	781	ERICHSEN, Frank	442
DON CICCIO @	829	ERICKSON, Frank @	442
DON CICCIO @	835	ERIKSON, Frank @	442
DON COLA @	794	ERMINO, John @	133
DON PAOLO @	461	ERNANO, Frank @	827
DON STEFANO @	513	ERRA, Pasquale	90
DON TOTO @	61	ERRA, Patsy @	90
DON VINCENZO @	831	ESPOSITO, Ralph @	411
DON VITO @	842	EVOLA, Natale Joseph	443
DONATO, Anthony	436	EVOLA, Sabatore @	213
DONATO, Frank Louis	437	EVOLA, Salvatore	213
DONGARA, Charles @	438	EVOLA, Samuel @	213
DONGARRA, Charles @	438		
DONGARRA, Rosario @	438	FACCIA, Charles Henri @	759
DONGARRO, Charles	438	FALCO, Anthony @	448
DORNEY, Joe @	756	FALCONE, Joseph	91
DOTO, Giuseppe Antonio	789	FALCONE, Joseph	444
DOYLE, Jimmy @	107	FALCONE, Salvatore	92
DRAGNA, Frank Paul	24	FARGO, Henry @	197
DRAGNA, Frank Paul	25	FARINA, Antonio	790
DRAGNA, Gaetano @	27	FARRELL, Lou @	167
DRAGNA, Louis Tom	26	FARULLA, Rosario Airo	445
DRAGNA, Tom	27	FAT ARTIE @	605
DUANE, Clyde @	68	FAT FREDDIE @	621
DUARDI, James S. Jr.	28	FAT SONNY @	478
DUCKS, Tony @	404	FAT TONY @	620
DUJARDIN, Albert @	750	FATS @	354
DUKE @	8	FATS @	575

FATS @	613	FORGIONE, Joseph	305
FATS @	681	FORTE, John @	560
FEDESCO, Mike @	323	FOTI, Joseph	450
FEETS, Jimmy @	568	FOURTEENTH ST. STEVE @	347
FELDMAN, Morris @	326	FRACCACRETA, Charlie @	451
FELICE, Freddie @	93	FRACCACRETA, Paul (Paolo)	451
FELICI, Alfredo George	93	FRADELLA, Joseph @	243
FENO, Henry @	197	FRANCESE, John @	454
FERRARA, Anthony @	580	FRANCESE, O. @	104
FERRARA, Renaldo @	29	FRANCO, Cosmo	452
FERRARI, Renaldo	29	FRANCO, Fred @	93
FERRARO, Vito @	11	FRANCO, Gus @	452
FERRIGNO, Bartolo	446	FRANCOMANO, Anthony	453
FERRO, Antonio	447	FRANCONIA, Tony @	453
FIERRA, Anthony @	447	FRANGINO, @	593
FILARDO, Joseph	256	FRANK THE HAWK @	370
FINAZZO, Jimmy @	215	FRANK THE SPOON @	192
FINAZZO, Salvatore	214	FRANKIE T. @	525
FINAZZO, Sam @	214	FRANKIE THE BOSS @	541
FINAZZO, Vincent James	215	FRANKIE THE BUG @	385
FINNAZO, Sam @	214	FRANZESE, John	454
FINO, Floric @	483	FRASCA, Cosmo	455
FINO, William @	483	FRASCA, Gus @	455
FIORELLO, Frank Rocco	30	FRATTO, Louie @	167
FISCHETTE, Rocco @	142	FRATTO, Luigi	167
FISCHETTI, Joseph	94	FRAZESE, John @	454
FISCHETTI, Rocco	142	FREDDIE @	606
FISH, Frank @	137	FRENCHIE @	374
FISHER, Joseph @	94	FRENCHIE @	373
FISHER, Ralph @	142	FRENCHY @	753
FIUME, Armando	791	FRENO, Antonio @	404
FLIP FLOP @	68	FRIED, Harold @	46
FLORIS, Louis @	750	FRISCIA, Augustine	95
F. O. @	554	FRISCIA, Gus @	95
FOCERI, Louis	448	FUNZI @	653
FONTANA, August	449	FUNZUOLA @	653
FONTANA, Modestino @	449	FUNZY @	548
FONTANO, August @	449	FUSCO, Joseph Charles	143

GABY @	752	GELLITTE, George @	471
GAGALIANO, Frank @	316	GENESE, Pasquale	464
GAGLIANO, Frank @	316	GENNARO, Joseph	465
GALANTE, Carmine	456	GENNONE, George @	145
GALANTE, Salvatore @	470	GENOA @	661
GALANTI, Carmine @	456	GENOVESE, Antonio @	707
GALENTE, Camillo @	456	GENOVESE, Michael James	707
GALENTO, Carmine @	456	GENOVESE, Vito	307
GALLO, John J. @	49	GENTILE, Anthony S.	466
GALLO, Joseph	457	GENTILE, Cola @	794
GALLO, Lawrence	458	GENTILE, Nicola	794
GALLO, Pete @	582	GERNIE, John @	467
GALLO, Salvadore J.	175	GERNIE, Joseph	467
GALLO, Sam @	175	GESBERINI, Daniel @	739
GALLO, Vic @	176	GIACALONE, Anthony	217
GALLO, Vittorio Vincenzo	176	GIACALONE, Vito	218
GALLOWAY, Morris @	650	GIACALONE, William @	218
GALLUCCIO, Frank	459	GIANCANA, Sam	144
GAMBA, Constantino	792	GIANNONE, George @	145
GAMBINO, Carlo	460	GIAPONE, Robert @	478
GAMBINO, Paolo	461	GIARDANO, Anthony	257
GAMBRIENO, Carlo @	460	GIARDINI, Joe @	130
GAMBRINO, Carlo @	460	GIARRUSSO, Giacomo @	804
GARAFOLA, Frank @	462	GIEVA, Philip @	795
GARDINE, Joe @	130	GIGANTE, Vincent	468
GARINE, Joe @	130	GIGGY @	544
GAROFOLO, Frank	462	GIGI @	544
GARROME, Tony @	66	GI GI @	356
GARU, Charlie @	306	GIGLI, Salvatore @	470
GARUFI, Agatino	306	GIGLIO, Alexander	469
GASBARRINI, Daniel @	739	GIGLIO, Sal @	469
GASBARRINI, Dante	739	GIGLIO, Salvatore	470
GASSISI, Francesco	793	GIGLIO, Sandrino @	469
GAUDINO, Peter	216	GIGLIOTTI, Giorgio	471
GAZZOLA, John @	498	GIGS @	544
GELB, Saul @	463	GI JO @	356
GELB, Usche	463	GILLETTE, George C. @	471
GELD, Saul @	463	GINNONE, George	145

GIOIA, Philip @	795	GREEN, Lou @	16
GIONDINO, Joseph @	110	GRIBBS @	662
GIORDANO, Anthony·@	257	GRIECO, Peter @	798
GIORDANO, Salvatore	472	GRIO, Anthony @	667
GIOVA, Philip @	795	GUADINO, Peter @	216
GIOVE, Filippo	795	GUARNIERI, Anthony F.	475
GLIELMO, Joseph @	146	GUCCI, Bartallo @	476
GLIMCO, Giuseppe Paul	146	GUCCIA, Bartolo	476
GLIMCO, Joey @	146	GUIDO, Alfred	477
GOBEL, Tony @	607	GUIMENTO, Cappy @	708
GOIA, Philip @	795	GUIMENTO, Casper	708
GOLD, Joe @	148	GUINEA REDS @	187
GOLD, Morris @	650	GUIPPONE, Robert Angelo	478
GOLDEN, Harry @	99	GUV @	475
GOLDEN, Max @	99	GUY @	475
GOOCH, Joe @	96	GYP @	303
GOODLOOKING AL @	411		
GOODWIN, Steve @	60	HAMEL, Salvatore	479
GOOKS, Frankie @	370	HAMILTON, Paul @	408
GORDON, Abe @	16	HAMM, Paul @	408
GORDON, Max @	99	HAPPY @	9
GORDON, Solly @	463	HAPPY @	46
GOV @	475	HARDY, Joe @	826
GOVERNOR @	560	HARRIS, Charles @	326
GRAMPS @	136	HAUSER, Max @	99
GRANDI, Vincent @	394	HELM, Paulie @	13
GRANZA, Anthony	473	HERMAN, Pete @	827
GRASSO, Ben @	505	HIGGINS, Tony @	387
		HIRSCH, Harry @	46
		HOOKS, Georgie @	552
GREASEBALL @	73	HORSEFACE @	220
GRECO, Frank	474	HOUR, Paul @	408
GRECO, Joe @	521	HOWARD, Roy @	127
GRECO, Manlio Giuseppe	796	HUNCHBACK HARRY @	718
GRECO, Paolo	797	HUNT, Frank @	574
GRECO, Peter	798		
GRECO, Salvatore	799	IANNI, Giuseppe @	728
GRECO, Sam @	799	IANNI, Joseph	728
GREEN, Lenny @	132	IANNONE, Gregorio @	145

IAROSSI, Lawrence	480	JEVOLA, Salvatore @	213
IDA, Giuseppe @	308	JIMMIE THE WOP @	85
IDI, Giuseppe	308	JIMMIE BLUE EYES @	336
IGGY @	477	JIMMY NINETY TWO @	395
IGNARO, Lucien	753	JIMMY SECOND AVENUE @	395
IL TUNISIO @	807	JIMMY THE BAKER @	391
IMPASITATO, Vito @	147	JIMMY THE BLONDE @	407
IMPASTATO, Nicolo	800	JIMMY THE SNIFF @	674
IMPASTATO, Vito	147	J. L. @	193
IMPOSTATO, Frank @	800	JOE THE BLONDE @	457
IMPOSTATO, Vito @	147	JOE THE BOSS @	719
INDELICATO, Joseph	96	JOE THE GYP @	86
INDIVIELIA, Benny @	481	JOE THE WOP @	390
INDIVIGLIA, Benedetto @	481	JOE THE WOP @	465
INDIVIGLIA, John @	482	JOE Z @	328
INDIVIGLIO, Benjamin	481	JOE Z @	423
INDIVIGLIO, Cirino	482	JOHNNY THE BUG @	644
INTERNICOLA, Salvatore @	11	JOHNNY V @	271
IODINE, Frank @	437	JOHNS, Samuel @	586
IODINE, Tony @	436	JO JO @	522
IPPOLITO, Francesco @	97	JO JO @	83
IPPOLITO, Frank	97	JO JO @	302
IPPOLITO, Freddie @	441	JORDON, Edward S. A. @	463
IRACI, Francesco	219	JOSEY @	423
IRISH @	406		
ISABELLA, Flo @	483	KAPLAN, Solly @	615
ISABELLA, Florindo @	483	KASS, Samuel @	484
ISABELLA, Florio	483	KASSELLE, John @	56
ITALIANO, Red @	98	KASSOP, Samuel	484
ITALIANO, Salvatore	98	KASTEL, Philip Frank	177
ITALIANO, Vincenzo	801	KATO, Joe @	668
		KATZ, Phil @	330
JACKSON, Joe @	670	KELLY, Mike @	163
JAVOLA, Sam @	213	KILLER @	399
J. B. @	360	KING, George @	80
JEROME, Jimmy @	643	KING, John @	81
JEROME, Patsy @	464	KING, John @	688
JERRY-THE-WOLF @	86	KING, Salvatore @	470

KING, Saul @	463	LANZA, James Joseph	31
KLEIN, Abe @	16	LANZA, John @	630
KLEIN, Jack @	148	LANZA, Joseph	491
KLEIN, Jacob	148	LANZA, Socks @	491
KORNBLOOM, Max @	99	LAPADARUS, Angelo @	309
KORNHAUSER, Max	99	LAPADURA, Angelo	309
KRAEBER, Jean @	755	LAPADURA, Arcangelo @	309
KREISBERG, Saul @	463	LAPADURE, Angelo @	309
		LAPI, Joseph	492
LABAR, Joe @	485	LAPIDURA, Angelo @	309
LABARBA, Joe @	485	LAPPI, Joe @	492
LA BARBARA, Joseph	485	LA RASSO, Louis A.	310
LABARBERA, Joseph @	485	LA RASSO, Luciano A. @	310
LACASCIA, Charles	486	LARDINO, Daniel E.	150
LACERTA, Nick @	34	LARDINO, John	151
LA DUCA, James V.	487	LARGINO, Joseph @	151
LA DUCA, Vinny @	487	LA ROCCA, Alphonse C. @	32
LADUCO, Joe @	493	LA ROCCA, Alphonse J.	32
LAFATA, Salvatore	802	LA ROCCA, Francesco @	258
LAFATA, Vito	803	LA ROCCA, Frank	258
LAGATTUTA, Samuel	488	LA ROCCA, Lester @	709
LAGATTUTO, Sam @	488	LA ROCCA, Marty @	349
LAGET, Jean @	751	LA ROCCA, Sebastian John	709
LAGONARO, Giuseppe	804	LA ROCCO, John S. @	709
LAGUTTA, Samuel @	488	LA ROCCO, Mike @	633
LAINO, Frank J.	149	LA ROCK, Lester @	709
LA MANTIA, Francesco	805	LARRY NOSE @	480
LAMIDA, Frank @	221	LA SALA, James Vincent	33
LAMONICA, Peter	489	LA SALA, Vincent @	33
LAMOSS, Charles @	759	LASCOULA, Joseph	259
LANDI, Albert William	490	LASCOULA, Michael	260
L'ANGE @	754	LASCUOLA, Joe @	259
LANOLLI, Bud @	3	LATONA, Joseph	493
LANSKY, Jack	100	LATONE, Joe @	493
LANSKY, Jake @	100	LATONIA, Joe @	493
LANSKY, Meyer	101	LAZZARA, Augustine Primo	102
LANZA, Frank @	77	LAZZARA, Ernest	311
LANZA, Frank @	630	LAZZARO, Carmelo	494

LAZZARO, Carmine @	494	LITTLE ANGIE @	664
LAZZIA, Angelo @	120	LITTLE DAVY @	580
LEECH, William A. @	21	LITTLE HARRY @	718
LEFTY @	537	LITTLE JOE @	328
LEGNO, Joe @	54	LITTLE JOE @	631
LE GRAND @	759	LITTLE JOE @	684
LEGS, Paulie @	679	LITTLE LIBBY @	153
LEIS, Anthony @	499	LITTLE MAXIE @	439
LEMONS @	76	LITTLE MOE @	592
LENA, Pietro	806	LITTLE PATSY @	677
LEO, Anthony @	401	LITTLE PETE @	648
LEO, Arthur	495	LITTLE RABBITT @	360
LEONARD, Albert @	243	LITTLE SAM @	175
LEONARDI, Frank @	14	LITTLE T @	381
LESSA, Daniel	496	LITTLE TONY @	381
LEVY, Harry @	46	LIVOLSI, Frank @	500
LEWIS, Nathan @	358	LIVORSI, Frank S.	500
LIBERATORI, Ercoli @	153	LLOYD @	575
LICARI, Francesco @	807	LO CASCIA, Charles @	486
LICARI, Francois	807	LO CASCIO, Carmine	501
LICATA, Nicholas	34	LO CASCIO, Peter J.	502
LICATA, Pietro	497	LO CASCIO, Willie @	501
LICAVOLI, Peter	220	LOCASO, Mike @	401
LICCHI, Benjamin	312	LO COCO, Gaetano @	261
LICCHI, Joseph Anthony	313	LO COCO, Thomas @	261
LIEBERMAN, Morris @	101	LO COCO, Tano @	261
LIGUORI, Raffaele	808	LOFARO, Frank	503
LIGUORI, Ralph @	808	LOIACANO, Angelo M.	504
LIMA, Anthony J.	35	LOICONO, Frank @	781
LIMANDRI, Joseph	36	LOMBARDI, Joseph @	193
LIMANDRI, Marco	37	LOMBARDI, Joseph @	315
LIMANDRI, Michael @	37	LOMBARDI, Peter @	38
LINARDI, Joe @	328	LOMBARDINI, Andy @	314
LINARDI, John	498	LOMBARDINI, Paul @	315
LINARZI, John @	498	LOMBARDINO, Andrew	314
LIOLA, Don @	14	LOMBARDINO, Paul Mario	315
LISI, Anthony @	499	LOMBARDO, Carmine @	506
LISI, Gaetano	499	LOMBARDO, Joseph	193

LOMBARDO, Peter @	38	LUCIDO, Sam @	222
LOMBARDO, Philip	505	LUCKAS, Jack @	202
LOMBARDO, Pietro	38	LUCKY JOE @	665
LOMBARDO, Tony @	512	LUKE, Joe Peter @	729
LOMBARDOZZI, Alberto @	506	LUMBARDI, Peter @	38
LOMBARDOZZI, Carmine	506	LUMBATA, Carmelo @	506
LO MEDICO, Francesco	221	LUNETTES @	750
LO METICO, Frank @	221	LURASO, Luciano @	310
LOMONDE, Frank @	781	LUTTO, Sam @	222
LONDON, Bobby @	571		
LONG, Frank @	630	MACHINE GUN JOE @	259
LONG, Thomas @	331	MACI, Joe @	563
LONG, Tom @	529	MACRI, Sam @	57
LONGO, James	103	MADDI, Victor	730
LONGO, John @	630	MADDIE, Victor @	730
LONGO, Tommo @	529	MADRALENI, Paul @	755
LOPI, Joe @	492	MAGADDINO, Antonino	512
LOPICCOLO, Giuseppe	507	MAGADDINO, Stefano	513
LOPICCOLO, Joseph @	507	MAGANA, Antonio @	816
LO PICCOLO, Joseph Paul	508	MAGARDINO, Antonio @	512
LOPIPARO, Anthony J.	262	MAGARDINO, Stefano @	513
LO PROTO, Salvatore	509	MAGLIO, Paul @	138
LOQUASTO, Modesta	710	MAGLIOCCI, Joe @	514
LOQUASTO, Murphy @	710	MAGLIOCCO, Francesco	810
LUCANIA, Charles @	809	MAGLIOCCO, Giuseppe	514
LUCANIA, Salvatore C.	809	MAGLIOCCO, Joe @	514
LUCCA, Joseph	729	MAIMONE, Salvatore	515
LUCCHESE, Gaetano	510	MAIMONE, Saverio @	515
LUCCHESE, Tom @	510	MAINIONE, Saverio R. @	515
LUCCI, Bartu @	446	MAIORANA, Salvatore G.	516
LUCIANI, Ange Dominique	754	MAIORINO, Salvatore J.	517
LUCIANI, Mario @	754	MAIURI, Frank @	316
LUCIANO, Charles @	809	MAJURI, Frank T.	316
LUCIANO, Frank	511	MALIZIA, John Anthony	518
LUCIANO, Gefri @	511	MALONE, Joe @	328
LUCIANO, Lucky @	809	MALONE, Sam @	144
LUCIDO, Joe @	222	MALTESE, Vincent @	338
LUCIDO, Salvatore	222	MANCINO, Francesco J.	519

MANCINO, Frank @	519	MARCHESE, Benjamin @	75
MANCINO, Rosario	811	MARCHESE, Ignazio Carlo	75
MANCINO, Saro @	811	MARCHESE, Paul @	248
MANCINO, Sauro @	811	MARCHITTO, Anthony M.	317
MANCUSO, Anthony	520	MARCIANTE, Salvadore J.	179
MANCUSO, Antonio @	520	MARCO, Joe @	71
MANCUSO, Giuseppe	812	MARENO, Sam @	164
MANCUSO, Joseph @	812	MARESCA, Raymond	76
MANCUSO, Rosario @	521	MARI, Frank	525
MANCUSO, Russell @	521	MARIANO, Louis @	731
MANCUSO, Salvatore	813	MARINELLO, Joe @	347
MANCUSO, Serafino	814	MARINELLO, Peter A.	194
MANDALA, Nicolo	815	▮▮▮▮▮▮▮▮▮▮▮	
MANERA, Salvatore @	816	MARINO, Frank @	60
MANERI, Salvatore C.	816	MARINO, Frank @	397
MANERINE, Gabriel @	711	MARINO, Jimmy @	472
MANFREDI, Joseph	522	MARINO, Joe @	328
MANFREDONIA, Diego @	523	MARINO, Joe @	526
MANFREDONIA, Richard	523	MARINO, Lawrence T. @	180
MANGERI, Sam @	45	MARINO, Lorenzo	180
MANINI, Giuseppe @	818	MARINO, Louis	731
MANINO, Giuseppe @	818	MARINO, Mike @	84
MANIS, Sam @	543	MARINO, Salvatore	40
MANISCALCO, Nicolo	817	MARINO, Salvatore @	517
MANITO, Joe @	63	MARINO, Thomas @	516
MANNARINO, Archie @	524	MARINO, Thomas @	524
MANNARINO, Gabriel	711	MARINO, Toddo @	516
MANNARINO, Giacinto	524	MARINO, Toto @	516
MANNARINO, Kelly @	711	MARION, Louis @	731
MANNARINO, Salvatore	712	MARIONO, Joseph @	661
MANNARINO, Sam @	712	MARONE, Joseph	526
MANNERINO, Gabriel @	711	MARONI, Joe @	526
MANNINO, Giuseppe	818	MARRONE, Joe @	526
MANNO, John @	60	MARRONE, Nick @	528
MANZELLO, Giuseppe @	172	MARSALISI, Mariano	527
MARANO, Louis @	731	MARSHAL, John @	131
MARCELLA, Carlos @	178	MARTELLO, Nicholas	528
MARCELLO, Carlos	178	MARTIN, Frank @	85

MARTIN, Frank @	287	MAUGERI, Sam @	45
MARTIN, Frank @	316	MAURICE, John @	190
MARTIN, James @	642	MAURIELLO, Alfred V.	532
MARTIN, Jimmy @	472	MAURIO, Vincent @	533
MARTIN, John @	133	MAURO, Vincenzo F. A.	533
MARTIN, William @	9	MAZZA, Frank	66
MARTINE, Joseph @	561	MAZZANOBILE, Vito	821
MARTINI, Philip @	21	MAZZELLA, Giuseppe	822
MARTINO, Benny @	420	MAZZIE, Rocco	534
MARTINO, Gaetano	529	MC CARTHY, Steve @	60
MARTINO, Johnny @	530	MC NEESE, Allen @	46
MARTINO, Thomas @	529	MECILI, Anthony @	263
MARVONE, Salvatore @	515	MEDICO, Burgio @	713
MARVONE, Sibby @	515	MEDICO, William	713
MARZANO, Alfonso	104	MEING, Edward @	303
MARZUCCO, Joseph @	812	MELI, Angelo	223
MASON, Herbert @	46	MELI, Frank	224
MASON, Paul @	408	MELI, Vincent Angelo	225
MASSEI, Giuseppe @	105	MELIA, Frank @	224
MASSEI, Joseph	105	MELLO, Charles P. @	194
MASSI, James Leo	530	MELLO, Pete @	194
MASSI, Pasquale	318	MELO, Tony @	19
MASSI, Vincenzo @	793	MELTZER, Harold	46
MATRANCA, Pasquale @	531	MERCADANTE, Salvatore	804
MATRANGA, Francis @	42	MERLI, Louis @	55
MATRANGA, Frank	41	MESSINA, Antonio F. @	830
MATRANGA, Frank Isador	42	MESSINA, Frank @	397
MATRANGA, Gaspare	43	MEZZASALMA, Rosario S.	535
MATRANGA, Gaspare @	843	MEZZASALMA, Salvatore @	535
MATRANGA, Jasper @	43	MICELI, Anthony @	263
MATRANGA, Jaspere J.	843	MICELLI, Tony @	54
MATRANGA, Joseph Ernest	44	MICHAEL, John @	581
MATRANGA, Pasquale	531	MICILI, Anthony J.	263
MAUCERI, Corrado @	819	MICKEY MOUSE @	82
MAUCERI, Giovanni @	820	MIGLIARDI, Carlo	823
MAUGERI, Corrado	819	MIGOLENE @	800
MAUGERI, Giovanni	820	MIKE THE GEEP @	633
MAUGERI, Salvatore Angelo	45	MILANA, Anthony @	47

MILANO, Antonino	47	MONACHINO, Sam @	741
MILANO, Frank	48	MONACHINO, Saverio	741
MILANO, Frank Angelo	49	MONASTERSKY, Samuel	543
MILANO, John J.	50	MONDELLO, Sam	106
MILANO, Peter John	51	MONDOLINI, Paul @	755
MILL, Harold @	46	MONDOLONI, Paul Damien	755
MILLAN, John @	205	MONETTI, Michael J. @	131
MILLER, Charles @	142	MONFRE, Salvatore @	11
MILLER, Frank @	511	MONGRENO, Sam @	106
MILLER, Harry @	46	MONICA, Michael	544
MILLER, Joe @	21	MONK @	157
MILLER, John @	205	MONROE, Richard @	523
MILLO, James @	157	MONSIEUR ALBERT @	746
MILO, Thomas Sabbato, Jr.	536	MONTAGNA, John @	545
MILWAUKEE PHIL @	123	MONTANA, John Charles	545
MIMI @	37	MONTEMURRO, Samuel	546
MIMI @	529	MONTENEGRO, Charles @	451
MINACORE, Carlos @	178	MONTINO, John @	545
MINZAGEE @	496	MONZIGI @	496
MIRABILE, Paolo @	52	MOON, Tony @	393
MIRABILE, Paul	52	MOONEY, Sam @	144
MIRAGLIA, Lester	537	MORA, Lou @	190
MIRANDA, Michele	538	MORECIA, Sam @	773
MIRANDI, Mike @	538	MORELLI, Joe @	423
MIREAULT, Joseph @	748	MORICI, Louis	190
MIRRA, Anthony	539	MORREALE, Filippo Joseph	152
MIRRO, Anthony @	539	MORREALE, Philip @	152
MISERABLE, Tony @	672	MORRIO, Vincent J. @	533
MISSALE, Salvatore	540	MORRIS, Mickey @	82
MISURACA, Giorgio	824	MORROW, Vinnie @	533
MIX, Tom @	626	MORSELLINO, Vincenzo	547
MOCCARDI, Frank	541	MOSCA, Alfonso	548
MOCERI, Peter @	220	MOSCATO, Blasco @	725
MOGAVENO, Saro @	542	MOSSELLINO, James @	547
MOGAVERO, Rosario	542	MOUSIE @	495
MOGAVERO, Saro @	542	MR. BIG @	538
MONACHINO, Pasquale	740	MR. BREAD @	502
MONACHINO, Salvatore @	741	MR. BUD @	3

MR. HUGO @	616	NOYES, Henry @	197
MR. MIKE @	3	NUCCIO, Dominick	153
MR. TONY @	181	NUNCIO @	58
MUGAVERO, Saro @	542		
MUMMAIMI, Vinnie @	549	O'BRIEN, Joey @	122
MUMMIANI, Vincent	549	O'BRIEN, John @	688
MURIO, Vincent @	533	OCCHINO, Frank	554
MURPHY, Fats @	354	ODDO, John	555
MURRAY, John @	146	O'DONNELL, Martin L. @	688
MUSHKY @	496	OFRIA, Sebastian	556
MUTTON HEAD @	363	OKAY-BENNY @	75
		OLIVE, Joe @	265
NACLERIO, Jerry @	341	OLIVER, Joe @	265
NAGS @	129	OLIVETO, Dominick	319
NANI, Benny @	825	OLIVETT, Domenick @	319
NANI, Peter @	825	OLIVO, Joseph	265
NANI, Sebastiano	825	O'MADDALONESE @	325
NANZIO, Joe @	273	ONE EYE @	24
NAPALI, Frank @	264	ONTARIO, Joseph @	392
NAPOLI, Frank S.	264	ORLANDO, Calogero	557
NAPOLITANO, Anthony	550	ORLANDO, Charles @	557
NAPOLITANO, Frank @	550	ORLANDO, Ignazio Lawrence	558
NAPS, Tony @	550	ORLANDO, Joe @	147
NARDI, Edward @	151	ORLANDO, Lorenzo	559
NASONE, Michel @	625	ORLANDO, Willie @	501
NATALI, Frank @	264	ORMANDO, John @	560
NATALIE, Frank A. @	264	ORMENTO, John	560
NATARO, Joseph @	553	ORSINI, Francois @	756
NELLO @	293	ORSINI, Joseph	756
NEWMAN, Louis	304	ORZO, Freddy @	561
NICOLENE @	800	ORZO, Teddy @	561
NICOLINE, Michael	551	ORZO, Theodore Roosevelt	561
NICOLINI, Mike @	551	OSTICCO, Dave @	721
NICOLINO, Michael @	551	OSTICCO, James Anthony @	721
NIMO, Pete @	582	OSTICKO, Dave @	721
NOBILE, George	552	OSTICO, Dave @	721
NOBLE, George @	552	OSTICO, James @	721
NOTARO, Joseph Frank	553	OTTIERI, Joseph @	325

OZZIE @	161	PANZARINO, Vito Anthony	570
		PAOLACCI, Mariano	689
PACELLA, Louis	562	PAOLI, Orlando Delli	571
PACELLI, Vincent Joseph	563	PAPA, Fortunato	572
PACEY, Joe @	828	PAPADIO, Andimo @	573
PACINO, Joe @	688	PAPALARDO, Sam	690
PACOLI, Vincent @	563	PAPALARDO, Sylvester	691
PADRO, Tony @	795	PAPP, Sam @	690
PAGANO, Joseph Luco	564	PAPPADIA, Andinno	573
PAGANO, Pasquale Anthony	565	PAPPO, Jimmy @	472
PAGANO, Patsy @	565	PARDINI, Frank @	593
PAGANO, Salvatore @	156	PARENTE, Joseph John	279
PAGE, Frank @	574	PARENTI, Joe @	279
PAGNOTTI, Louis @	714	PARISE, Jack @	716
PAGNOTTI, Luigi	714	PARISI, Gioacchino	716
PAL @	550	PARISI, Jack @	716
PALACCI, Marian @	689	PARISI, Jackina @	716
PALADINO, Carmine	566	PAROUTIAN, Andre @	757
PALADINO, Rocco @	195	PAROUTIAN, Antronik	757
PALAZZOLA, Nick @	205	PARTIRO, Mike @	323
PALAZZOLA, Sam @	226	PASQUA, Frank Anthony	574
PALAZZOLO, Salvatore	226	PASQUALE, Frank @	574
PALERMO, Blinky @	715	PASSELLI, John @	56
PALERMO, Frank	715	PATATERNO, Mimi @	14
PALERMO, Joe @	431	PATRIACA, Raymond @	724
PALISADES, Joe @	614	PATRIARCA, Raymond	724
PALLADINO, Joseph @	566	PATTI, Santo	575
PALLADINO, Rocco	195	PAUL THE WAITER @	138
PALMER, Joe @	431	PAXTON, Sammy @	79
PALMER, Pete @	432	PAYNE, John @	636
PALMIERI, George	567	PEACH, Joe @	828
PANATERA, Frank Joseph	154	PEACHY @	137
PANCE, Anthony @	181	PEANUTS @	119
PANCI, Anthony	181	PECORA, Joe @	182
PANEBIANCO, Vincent J.	568	PECORA, Michael	53
PANICA, Victor	569	PECORA, Onofio @	183
PANSY @	567	PECORARA, Onofio @	183
PANSY @	570	PECORARO, John @	53

PECORARO, Joseph	182	PIERI, Salvatore	586
PECORARO, Michael	53	PIERI, Sam @	586
PECORARO, Onofio	183	PIGNETTI, Stephen T.	587
PELL, Carmine @	576	PINE, Grace	155
PELLEGRINO, Anthony @	826	PINELLI, Anthony R., Sr.	54
PELLEGRINO, Carmine	576	PINEY @	346
PELLEGRINO, Giuseppe	826	PINTO, Anthony	588
PELLEGRINO, Peter (Pietro)	577	PIRICO, Francesco	829
PELLEGRINO, Rocco	578	PIRRONE, Gaspare @	227
PELLIGRINO, Joseph @	826	PISANO, Joe @	828
PELOSA, Tony @	579	PISANO, Salvatore	156
PELOSO, Anthony	579	PISANO, Sol @	156
PELSA, Tony @	579	PISCIOTTA, Anthony	589
PEPINO, Don @	376	PISCIOTTA, Francesco @	266
PERAZIOLA, John @	230	PISCIOTTA, Frank	266
PERETTO, Joseph @	184	PISCIOTTA, George @	590
PERILLO, Armando	827	PISCIOTTA, Rosario	590
PERILLO, Herman @	827	PISCIOTTA, Sally @	590
PERRI, James @	270	PISCOPO, Louis @	55
PERRITO, Joseph @	94	PISCOPO, Salvatore	55
PERRONE, Espano Gaspare	227	PIZZO, Frank @	347
PERRONE, Jasper @	227	PIZZOLO, Sam @	226
PERRONE, Sam @	228	PLUMER, James D. @	107
PERRONE, Santo	228	PLUMERI, James Dominick	107
PETILLO, David	580	POLIAFICO, Salvatore F.	692
PETROLLI, Ralph @	477	POLIAFICO, Sylvester @	692
PETRONE, John Michael	581	POLICASTRO, Guy @	320
PHILLIPS, Sal @	470	POLICASTRO, Peter Joseph	320
PIACENTI, Peter John	582	POLICHERI, James	157
PIAZZA, Salvatore @	816	POLIZZANO, Ralph	591
PICCARELLI, James	583	POLIZZI, Alfonso @	108
PICCARELLI, Joseph Chas.	584	POLIZZI, Alfred	108
PICCI, Joe @	828	POLIZZI, Michael	229
PICCOLO, Frank Louis	77	POLLADINO, Rocco @	195
PICELLI, Vincent @	563	POLLINA, Antonio @	717
PICI, Giuseppe	828	POLLINA, Dominick @	717
PICONA, Matthew @	585	POLLINO, Dominick	717
PICONE, Michael	585	POLLINO, Nick @	717

POLO, Sam @	692	QUASARANO, Jimmy @	231
PONCI, Harry @	368	QUASARANO, Joseph R.	231
PONTIAC BROTHERS @	518	QUASARANO, Raffaele	232
POPE, Fortunato @	572	QUASARANO, Ralph @	232
POPE, Fortune @	572	QUELLO, Herbert @	580
POPURA, Joe @	109		
PORETTO, Joseph @	184	RADIO RED @	394
PORKY @	551	RAFT, George @	367
PORRETTO, Joseph	184	RAGONE, Joseph	599
PRESINZANO, Angelo	592	RAIO, Joe @	601
PRESINZANO, Moey @	592	RALPH THE PIMP @	808
PRESTA, Alexander Joseph	267	RAM @	67
PRESTA, Mario	185	RANDAZO, Jimmy @	233
PRESTON, Alex @	267	RANDAZZO, James @	233
PRIMAVERA, Giuseppe @	146	RANDAZZO, Vincenzo	233
PRISINZANO, Frank	593	RANDO, Joe @	729
PRISIOLA, John @	230	RANDO, Thomas @	427
PRIVATEER, Anthony @	594	RANZINO, Anthony	186
PRIVATERA, Anthony J.	594	RAO, Calogero	600
PRIZIOLA, John	230	RAO, Charles @	600
PRIZIOLA, Papa John	230	RAO, Joseph	601
PROFACE, Joe @	596	RAO, Vincenzo John	602
PROFACI, Frank	595	RAVA, Armand Thomas	603
PROFACI, Giuseppe	596	RAVO, Armand @	603
PROJETTO, Giuseppe @	444	RAVO, Thomas @	603
PROJETTO, Salvatore @	92	RAYMOND, Frank @	324
PUCCIARELLI, James @	583	RAYMOND, Mike @	163
PUCO, Daniel @	597	RAYMOND, Yock @	324
PUCO, Stephen Martini	597	RED @	29
PUGGINO, Angelo @	504	REDS @	187
PUGGY @	504	REID, Charles @	809
PUNCHY @	620	REINA, Giacomo	604
PURPURA, Joseph	109	REINA, Henry @	604
		REINA, Jack @	604
QUARTIERO, Lawrence	598	REINA, Ray @	321
QUASAMONI, James @	232	REINO, Rinaldo	321
QUASARANO, Gino @	232	RELLI, Charlie @	584
QUASARANO, James @	232	RELLIE, James @	583

REPOLA, Arthur	605	RIZZOTTI, Louis Tom @	26
RESTUCCIA, Francesco	830	RIZZOTTI, Tom	27
RICARDI, Chester @	828	RIZZUTO, Anthony	612
RICCA, Jack @	604	RIZZUTO, Nino @	612
RICCA, Paul @	138	ROBERTO, Domenico	832
RICCARDULLI, John J.	606	ROBERTO, John	833
RICCI, Anthony	607	ROBERTS, Dan @	832
RICCI, Antonio @	607	ROBERTS, John @	60
RICCI, Gaetano @	607	ROBINO, Calogero	834
RICCIARDI, Joe @	608	ROCCA, Alfred @	411
RICCIO, Joseph Vincent	110	ROCCO, Arthur @	495
RICCO, Arthur	626	ROCCO, Frank @	30
RICCOBENE, Harry	718	ROCK, Joe @	125
RICCOBONA, Joe @	608	ROCKY @	357
RICCOBONO, Joseph S.	608	ROGER, Roy @	748
RICE, Sam @	125	ROGIE @	534
RICH, John @	119	ROMA, John @	724
RIELA, Anthony Peter	322	ROMANO, Eugene @	661
RIGLEY, Peter @	220	ROMANO, Frank @	219
RIMI, Vincenzo	831	ROMANO, Frank @	411
RINALDI, Joe @	131	ROMANO, Frank @	455
RINALDI, Rosario	609	ROMANO, John @	160
RINALDI, Samuel @	609	ROMANO, Josie @	423
RINALDO, Sam @	609	ROMANO, Nunzio	613
RIVERA, Charlie	584	RONDOZZO, James @	233
RIZZO, Albert @	333	RONNIE @	606
RIZZO, Angelo	610	ROSA, David @	580
RIZZO, Charles @	333	ROSATO, Joseph	614
RIZZO, Frank @	610	ROSE, Frank @	684
RIZZO, Jack	158	ROSE, Joe @	580
RIZZO, Joe @	552	ROSELLI, Giovanni	56
RIZZO, John @	474	ROSELLI, John @	56
RIZZO, Lawrence @	559	ROSEN, David @	580
RIZZO, Lorenzo @	559	ROSEN, Harry @	647
RIZZO, Salvatore Peter	611	ROSEN, Nig @	647
RIZZO, Sam @	611	ROSEN, Sol @	363
RIZZO, Tony @	610	ROSEN, Solomon	615
RIZZOTTI, Frank @	25	ROSENBLOOM, Max @	99

ROSS, Charles @	613	RUSSO, Frank @	437
ROSS, Charles @	809	RUSSO, Frank	525
ROSS, Frank @	197	RUSSO, Gaetano	617
ROSS, Frank @	385	RUSSO, Guy @	617
ROSS, Frank @	670	RUSSO, James @	502
ROSS, Mike @	84	RUSSO, James V.	159
ROSS, Tony @	742	RUSSO, Jimmy @	188
ROSSI, Charles @	413	RUSSO, Jimmy @	472
ROSSI, Hugo @	616	RUSSO, Joe @	131
ROSSI, Louis @	55	RUSSO, Joe @	202
ROSSI, Ugo	616	RUSSO, Joe @	537
ROSSI, William @	60	RUSSO, Joe @	645
ROSSIN, William @	60	RUSSO, John @	493
ROTHMAN, Solly @	615	RUSSO, John @	502
RUBERTO, Dominic @	832	RUSSO, Joseph @	359
RUBERTO, Giovanni @	833	RUSSO, Michael	323
RUBERTO, John @	833	RUSSO, Mike @	84
RUBINO, Calogero @	834	RUSSO, Pasquale @	160
RUBINO, Michael	234	RUSSO, Patrick	160
RUBINO, Michele @	234	RUSSO, Patsy @	160
RUGIERO, Gabriel @	711	RUSSO, Pete @	465
RUGIERO, Salvatore @	712	RUSSO, Sam @	207
RUGNETTA, Giuseppe	719	RUSSO, Tommy @	617
RUGNETTI, Joseph @	719	RUSSO, Tony @	159
RUSH, Jimmy @	583	RUSSO, Tony @	359
RUSHE, Jimmy @	583	RUSSO, Tony @	436
RUSS, Sam @	205	RUSSO, Tony @	447
RUSSELL, Joseph @	456	RUSSO, William @	135
RUSSELLI, John @	56	RUSSO, William @	428
RUSSI, Frank @	538	RYAN, Tommy @	402
RUSSO, Alfred @	411		
RUSSO, Angelo @	373	SABELLA, James	618
RUSSO, Buck @	160	SABELLA, Vincenzo @	618
RUSSO, Dominick @	453	SABIE @	536
RUSSO, Frank @	85	SACCAROMA, Blackie @	111
RUSSO, Frank @	192	SACCAROMA, Louis	111
RUSSO, Frank	268	SAL THE BEAK	640
RUSSO, Frank @	385	SALADINO, Joe @	67

SALARDINO, Joseph	67	SASSO, Angelo	619
SALERNO, Angelo Charles	619	SAUSARITO @	445
SALERNO, Anthony Michael	620	SAUSEETZ @	400
SALERNO, Ferdinando J.	621	SAVALLA, Onofrio @	3
SALERNO, Fred @	621	SAVARINO, William Biaggio	112
SALLI, Salvatore	622	SAVELLI, Mike @	3
SALLI, Sam @	622	SAVERIA, Frank @	409
SALLY BLUE EYES @	509	SAVERINO, Francesco Paolo	835
SALLY THE BLONDE @	509	SAVERIO, Frank @	409
SALLY THE SHEIK @	555	SCAGLIONE, Joseph	113
SALVADOR, Don @	98	SCAGLIONE, Salvatore	114
SALVIN, Sam @	642	SCAL, Joseph @	392
SALVO, Bart @	623	SCALICE, Jack @	627
SALVO, Battisto	623	SCALICE, John @	836
SALVO, John B. @	623	SCALICE, Sam @	628
SALVO, Sam @	38	SCALICH, John @	693
SALVY @	642	SCALICI, Giacomo	627
SAMMY THE JEW @	484	SCALICI, Giovanni	693
SANCINELLA, Rocco	624	SCALICI, Giovanni	836
SAN GIACOMA, Carmine	324	SCALICI, Jack @	627
SAN GIACOMO, Yock @	324	SCALICI, Salvatore	628
SANGUINO, Fiore @	635	SCALISE, Giovanni @	836
SANSONE, Carmelo	625	SCALISE, Jack @	627
SANTAGATA, Aniello	325	SCALISE, John @	693
SANTAGATO, Aniello @	325	SCALISE, John @	836
SANTANELLO, Anthony @	196	SCALISE, Sam @	628
SANTANIELLO, Albert @	196	SCALISH, John @	693
SANTANIELLO, Anthony	196	SCALISI, Alfred @	440
SANTELLO, Peter @	351	SCALISI, Sam @	628
SANTENELLI, Antonio @	196	SCALLO, Tony @	473
SANTIELLO, Jimmy @	570	SCARCELLI, Paul @	185
SANTORA, Salvatore	626	SCARFACE JOE @	201
SANTORE, Frank	161	SCARFONI, Antoine @	750
SANTORO, Salvatore T.	626	SCARPELLE, Tony @	269
SANTOS, Louis @	118	SCARPELLI, Anthony	269
SANTOS, Paul @	53	SCARPELLI, James	270
SARNO, Philip @	120	SCARPULLA, Giacomino @	629
SASEETZ @	400	SCARPULLA, Jack @	629

SCARPULLA, Michele Giacomo	629	SIANO, Joseph @	668
SCHIFFMAN, Charles	326	SICA, Alfred Gerardo	58
SCHILLACI, Giovanni	630	SICA, Fred @	58
SCHIPANI, Joseph F.	631	SICA, Joseph	59
SCHIPPMAN, Charles @	326	SILK SHIRT JIMMY @	652
SCHLITZ, Johnny @	606	SILVER FOX @	751
SCHNOZZOLA @	625	SILVERTELLI, Henry @	197
SCHOOL, Joe @	259	SILVESTRI, Gaspare	837
SCHOOL, Mike @	260	SIMEONE, Vincent @	57
SCIALLO, Frank @	826	SIMONE, Joseph @	397
SCIANDRA, Angelo Joseph	720	SIMONI, Pierre Dominique	758
SCIATA, Mario @	3	SINAZZO, Sam @	214
SCIBILIO, Peter @	38	SISCO, Michel @	750
SCIORTINA, Pat @	632	SKINNY RAZOR @	304
SCIORTINO, Joe @	362	SKUNGE, Tony @	473
SCIORTINO, Pasquale	632	SLIM @	585
SCOOCH, Joe @	96	SLITS @	606
SCOSSE, Sam @	57	SMALDONE, Clyde George	68
SCOTTY @	71	SMALDONE, Eugene	69
SCOZZARI, Simone	57	SMALL, George @	637
SEDETTO, Mike @	633	SMARRA, George @	637
SEDOTTO, Michael	633	SMITH, David	636
SELVEITELLO, Henry @	197	SMITH, Pop @	636
SELVITELLA, Henry A.	197	SMURRA, George	637
SELVITELLI, Henry @	197	SOLLY @	540
SENDER, Max @	323	SOLLY ONE EYE @	156
SENNA, John @	142	SONNY @	454
SENNA, Rocco @	142	SONNY @	478
SERRITELLA, Sam	162	SORCI, Antonino	838
SERRITELLA, Tony @	162	SORCI, Pietro	839
SETTIMO, Salvatore S.	634	SORGE, Santo	638
SETTIMO, Sam @	634	SORRENTINO, Stephen	60
SEVERINO, F. @	835	SORRENTINO, Thomas S. @	60
SHIPMAN, Charles @	326	SPADARO, Joseph	639
SHORTY @	335	SPARKY @	208
SHORTY ARMONE @	346	SPECIALE, Benny @	640
SHORTY RALPH @	247	SPECIALE, Salvatore	640
SIANO, Fiore	635	SPERANDEO, John @	774

SPICA, Giovanni Rosario	235	STRETCH, Joe @	645
SPICA, John @	235	STROLLO, Anthony C.	646
SPIGA, Giovanni @	235	STROMBERG, Chaim @	647
SPIGA, John @	235	STROMBERG, Harry	647
SPIGA, Rosario @	235	STROMBERG, Hyman @	647
SPINA, Pasquale	641	STUDO @	691
SPINELLA, James @	70	STUTZ, Joe @	658
SPINELLA, Michael	840	SUCHOWLANSKY, Meyer @	101
SPINELLA, Vincenzo @	70	SUGAR @	568
SPINELLI, James	70	SUGARHOUSE PETE @	255
SPINELLI, Jim @	70	SUMIRRE, George @	637
SPINUZZI, Joseph	71	SUTERA, Frank @	89
SPIRITO, Francois	759	SWATTY @	566
SPITALE, Salvatore	642	SWIMMY @	706
SPITALIERI, Anthony J.	694	SWORD, Walter @	60
SPRANDO, James @	122	SYLVESTRO, Antonio	742
SPRANGE, Mike @	163		
SPRANZA, Michael	163	TALLONE, Len	132
SPRANZE, Michael @	163	TAMBONE, Peter Salvatore	648
SQUILLANTE, Vincent J.	643	TANNINO @	765
SQUINT @	405	TANO @	765
STACEY, Mike @	164	TANTILLO, Enrico Nicolo	649
STASI, Michael Andrew	164	TANTILLO, Harry @	649
STEEL, Martin @	840	TARRY @	344
STEFANO, Frank @	812	TARRYTOWN @	344
STEFANO, Pierre @	814	TAUBMAN, Moische	650
STEIN, M. @	650	TAUBMAN, Morris @	650
STELLA, Harry @	452	TAYLOR, Bobby @	124
STELLA, Ralph @	374	TEA BAGS @	588
STELLANO, Tommy @	402	TEDDY THE BUM @	421
STEVE THE BUG @	597	TEE ZEE @	678
STICCO, Vincenzo @	721	TEETS @	125
STIRONE, Joseph @	722	TELLI, James @	392
STIRONE, Nicholas	722	TENNENBAUM, Morris @	650
STOPELLI, Innocenzio	644	TENTE, Alfred @	411
STOPPELLI, John @	644	TERAMINE, Anthony	236
STRACCI, Joseph	645	TERIACA, Terry @	115
STREET, Joseph @	645	TERIACA, Vincent	115

TERMAIN, Tony	236	TOCCO, Pietro	240
TERMINE, Tony @	236	TOCCO, Vito @	238
TERRANOVA, John J.	651	TOCCO, William @	238
TESSALONA, Vincenzo @	652	TODARO, Charles @	733
TESSALONE, James	652	TODARO, Frank @	733
TESSALONE, Vincent @	652	TODARO, Vincent James	733
T. H. @	387	TOLENTINO, Nicholas	656
THE BALD HEAD @	289	TOMMY JR. @	536
THE BLIMP @	273	TONY "D" @	140
THE BOMP @	9	TONY "G" @	257
THE BRUSH @	329	TONY NOSE @	520
THE CAPTAIN @	787	TONY PIE @	381
THE CHAMP @	449	TONY SPIT @	694
THE CHIEF @	364	TONY THE CHUMP @	199
THE CHIN @	468	TONY THE PIP @	262
THE EYE @	655	TONY THE SHEIK @	379
THE FOX @	384	TORREGIANO, Giuseppe @	665
THE GREEK @	642	TORREGROSSA, Andrea	657
THE MAHOFF @	647	TORREGROSSA, Andrew @	657
THE OLD MAN @	307	TORRIDO @	628
THE OLD MAN @	578	TORTORICI, Joseph	658
THE OLD MAN @	780	TOTO @	378
THE SHORT ONE @	61	TOTO @	634
THREE FINGER BROWN @	510	TOTO @	774
THREE FINGER PANSY @	567	TOTO @	799
TIERI, Frank Alfonso	653	TOTO-L'Ingegnere @	799
TIMPA, Erasimo	237	TOUGH TOMMY @	402
TIMPA, Sam @	237	TOUGH TONY @	342
TIPA, Giuseppe Jr.	654	TOURINE, Charles Jr.	659
TIPA, Joseph @	654	TOURINE, Charles Sr.	116
TITA, Nick @	212	TOURINO, Charlie @	116
TITTA, Joe @	211	TRAFFICANTE, Francesco C.@	117
TITTA, Nick @	212	TRAFFICANTE, Frank C.	117
TOBOZZI, Vincent @	618	TRAFFICANTE, Santo Jr.	118
TOCCO, Guglielmo	238	TRAFICANTE, Santos @	118
TOCCO, Joseph	655	TRAINA, Giuseppe	660
TOCCO, Pete @	240	TRAMAGLINO, Eugene	661
TOCCO, Peter	239	TRAMAGLINO, Gino @	661

TRAMUNTI, Carmine @	662	VECCHIO, Giuseppe	327
TRAUMAGLINO, Eugene @	661	VECCHIO, Joe @	327
TRAUMUNTI, Carmine Paul	662	VECIA, Bartolo @	476
TRAVERS, William Arthur @	290	VELLUCCI, Anthony J.	672
TRIGGER MIKE @	84	VELLUCCIA, Anthony @	672
TRONOLONE, John Pasquale	119	VENEZIA, Giorgio	841
TRONOLONE, Salvatore @	119	VENTO, Joseph A.	673
TROPICANO, Joe @	687	VENTO, Sebastiano @	673
TROTTA, John @	677	VICIO, Bartalo @	476
TRUPIA, Carlo @	663	VICTOR, Russell @	521
TRUPIA, Charles Vincent	663	VIELA, Paul @	138
TUCKER, Frank @	85	VILLANO, Mike @	69
TUMENSIO, Angelo @	664	VINTALORA, James @	674
TUMINARO, Angelo	664	VINTALORO, James	674
TURPIN, Ben @	505	VIRUSSO, Santo	120
TURRICIANO, Pasquale @	666	VISCONTI, Frank	695
TURRIDU, Salvatore @	799	VITALE, John Joseph	271
TURRIGIANO, Giuseppe	665	VITALE, Joseph @	843
TURRIGIANO, Pasquale	666	VITALE, Michaelangelo	675
TURSO, Nick @	14	VITALE, Salvadore @	676
TUTTIE @	685	VITALE, Salvatore	61
TUTTSON, Tony @	236	VITALE, Salvatore	676
TWO EYE @	25	VITALE, Sam @	676
T. Z. @	678	VITALE, Toto @	61
		VITALE, Vito	842
U CAPITANO @	787	VITALI, John @	271
URBINATI, Carlo	165	VITALORA, James @	674
		VITOLE, Salvatore @	676
		VITONE, Don @	307
VADALA, Anthony	667	VIZZINI, Calogero	696
VALACHI, Joseph	668	VIZZINI, Charles @	696
VALENTE, Anthony @	827	VOLPE, Louis @	456
VALENTE, Frank @	670	VOTA, Angelo @	781
VALENTE, Stanley @	669		
VALENTI, Costenza Peter	669	WALKER, Al @	440
VALENTI, Stanley P. @	669	WARD, Jimmy @	530
VALENTI, Frank Joseph	670	WASH @	353
VALENTINO, Mike @	323	WEATHERBIRD @	268
VALLE, Alarico	671		

WEBER, Max @	21	ZACCARO, Patsy	677
WHITE, Charlie @	116	ZAGARI, Vincent @	205
WHITE, Charlie Jr. @	659	ZANGOGLIA, Anthony F.,Jr.	678
WHITE, Patsy @	677	ZANNINO, Ilario A.	198
WHITEY @	751	ZANNINO, Larry @	198
WILKINS, Sam @	21	ZAZA @	428
WILLIAMS, George @	294	ZERBO, Ippolito @	679
WILLIAMS, George @	304	ZERBO, Paul	679
WILLIE POTATOES @	135	ZERELLO, Joe @	241
WILLIE THE CREEP @	74	ZERILLI, Joseph	241
WILLIE THE WOP @	501	ZERILLO, Joe @	241
WINTERS, Gus @	452	ZICARELLI, Joseph	328
WOP JENKINS @	187	ZICARI, Emanuel	680
WORTMAN, Buster @	272	ZINGALE, Joseph	697
WORTMAN, Frank Leonard	272	ZINGALE, Thomas Joseph	698
		ZIP @	73
YANNI, Joseph @	467	ZITO, Frank	166
YOCK, John @	324	ZOTZ, Joe @	491
		ZUPIE @	162

ARIZONA

Died on May 11, 2002 of heart failure at age 97 in his
Tuscon, AZ home.

NAME   : Joseph BONANNO

ALIASES   : Joe Bananas, Joe Bononno,
                  Joe Bonnano, Joe Bouventre

DESCRIPTION   : Born 1-18-1905 Castellammare,
                  Sicily, 5'9", 190 lbs, brown
                  eyes, brown-grey hair, natur-
                  alized 5-17-45, Brooklyn, NY.

LOCALITIES   : Resides 1847 East Elm Street,
FREQUENTED   Tucson, Arizona. Travels ex-
                  tensively about U.S. & makes
                  frequent trips to Italy.

FAMILY   : Married Filippa LaBruzzo; daughter: Catherine; sons:
BACKGROUND   Salvatore (married to Rosalie Profaci, niece of
                  Giuseppe Profaci) and Joseph: father: Salvatore;
                  mother: Catherine Bouventre; both parents deceased.

CRIMINAL   : Lucky Luciano, Francisco Costiglia, Giuseppe Profaci,
ASSOCIATES   Anthony Corallo, Thomas Lucchese, Carmine Galante.

CRIMINAL   : FBI #2534540 NYCPD #B-85172 I&NS #C-6602167 Record
HISTORY   dating from 1930 includes arrests for grand larceny,
                  possession of gun, transportation of machine guns,
                  obstruction of justice.

BUSINESS   : Has interests in Grande Cheese Co., Fond du Lac, Wis.;
                  Alliance Realty & Insurance, Tucson, Arizona; and
                  Brunswick Laundry Service, Brooklyn, N.Y.

MODUS   : Attended 1957 Apalachin Mafia meeting and Binghamton,
OPERANDI   NY, meeting 1956. One of the most important Mafia
                  leaders in U.S. and attends all top-level Mafia
                  meetings. Makes trips to Italy to confer with Mafia
                  leaders there and to negotiate for international
                  narcotic trafficking.

1

CALIFORNIA

He was deported to Italy on July 8, 1961, and died on September 5, 1962 of natural causes after only fourteen months there.

NAME : Michael ABATI

ALIASES : Mario Sciata, Mike Savelli, Mr. Mike, Mr. Bud, Onofrio Savalla, Bud Lanolli, Lanolli Amofrio

DESCRIPTION : Born 5-1-1900, Monte San Guiliano, Trapani, Sicily, 5'7½", 177 lbs, brown eyes, grey-black hair, medium ruddy complexion, mole on point of chin. Deportation warrant pending (1960).

LOCALITIES FREQUENTED : Resides in factory of Oro Olive Co., Oroville, Cal.

FAMILY BACKGROUND : Married Maria Abati (also nee Abati) who does not live with him. Wife resides Castellammare Del Golfo, Trapani. No children. Father: Antonino; mother: Marie Scudera.

CRIMINAL ASSOCIATES : Sam Lima, Phillip Maita, Mario Balistreri, James Lanza, Vince LaRocca, Alfonse LaRocca, Anthony Lima.

CRIMINAL HISTORY : FBI #1716819, San Francisco PD# 76271, 1st arrest in 1935 in Penna., for investigation; arrested in Penna., 1939 for Armed Robbery; arrested Penna., in 1944 for violation Interstate Commerce; arrested 1948 in San Francisco, Calif., and indicted along with Frank Scappatura for the Nick De John Murder.

BUSINESS : Presently manages the Oroville, Calif., plant named Oro Olive Co., owned by James and Anthony Lanza.

MODUS OPERANDI : Has been known as a racketeer and has been involved in crimes of violence; a long standing member of the Mafia in the San Francisco area.

NAME	: Giuseppe ADAMO
ALIASES	: Joseph Adamo and Joseph Degregory.
DESCRIPTION	: Born 11-21-02 Alcamo, Sicily 5'6½", 155 lbs., brown-greying hair, brown eyes, wears glasses, has 2 moles, one on right side of face and other on left side of face, an alien.

LOCALITIES FREQUENTED	: Residence, 4010 Hempstead Circle, San Diego, Calif., Subject resided in Los Angeles area prior to his relocation to San Diego.
FAMILY BACKGROUND	: Parents, Ignacio Adamo and Rosaria De Gregorio, married to Maria Greco; two children, Ignacia J. and Roselia Marie; also has 4 sisters and 2 brothers in Italy.
CRIMINAL ASSOCIATES	: "MOMO" Adamo (dead brother); Frank DeSimone; Matranga Family; Dragna Family; Greco Family; ▮▮▮▮▮▮▮▮▮▮ Li Mandri Family; ▮▮▮▮▮▮ ▮▮▮▮▮▮ Nick Licata, all of Calif.
CRIMINAL HISTORY	: FBI #1060177, Los Angeles PD# A-30222, convicted in 1935 for Federal liquor violation; I.&N.S. currently working on deportation proceedings against him.
BUSINESS	: Owns the Arizona and Panama Clubs in San Diego in partnership with Peter Montana.
MODUS OPERANDI	: Together with his deceased brother (Momo), he was one of the leaders of the Mafia in the San Diego area.

NAME	: Mario BALISTRERI
ALIASES	: Mario Balesteri, Mario Balestrero
DESCRIPTION	: Born 11-20-1901 San Francisco, Cal., 5'8", 175 lbs, blue eyes, brown hair, bald pate, walks with limp (right foot).
LOCALITIES FREQUENTED	: Resides Route 2, Box 605, Homestead Road, Santa Clara, Cal., frequents San Jose, Cal. and Kansas City, Mo.

FAMILY
BACKGROUND
: Married Delia Olivo (sister of Joseph Olivo, of Kansas City, Missouri); sons: Carl & Marco; father: Salvatore (deceased); mother: Jennie (remarried).

CRIMINAL
ASSOCIATES
: ███████████████████████ Abraham Chalupowitz, ████████████ of California, Arturo Leyvas of Phoenix, Sebastiano Nani (deportee) and Charles Schiffman, of New Jersey.

CRIMINAL
HISTORY
: FBI #93064 San Francisco PD #P-302 Record dating from 1924 includes arrests for counterfeiting and narcotic trafficking. Three Federal Narcotic con- victions.

BUSINESS
: Deals in scrap metal and real estate.

MODUS
OPERANDI
: Persistent large scale Mafia narcotic trafficker, operating in association with important smugglers and traffickers who are members of the Mafia in the San Francisco Bay area.

NAME	: Vincent Joseph BARRISA
ALIASES	: Vincent Joseph Barrise, Vincent Baris, Barise.
DESCRIPTION	: Born 6-27-03 in San Francisco, Calif., 5'10½", 200 lbs., brown eyes, brown-grey hair, ruddy complexion, stocky build.
LOCALITIES FREQUENTED	: Resides at 308 Precita, San Francisco, Calif., under name Vincent Baris.
FAMILY BACKGROUND	: Wife, Carmel Alterei Barrisa three daughters
CRIMINAL ASSOCIATES	: ███████████████████ (missing) and other racketeers in San Francisco area.
CRIMINAL HISTORY	: FBI #829216, San Francisco PD# 36195, 6 months, suspended in 1925 for violation gun law; 2 years and 2 days 1938 at McNeil, possession of still.
BUSINESS	: Drives truck.
MODUS OPERANDI	: Named as "Gun" for the Mafia in the San Francisco area.

NAME   : Domiano Bruno BARTOLOTTA

ALIASES   : Danny Bruno (which he com-
                  monly uses)

DESCRIPTION : Born 3-22-19 Detroit, Mich.,
                  5'10", 150 lbs, medium build
                  black hair, brown eyes.

LOCALITIES   : Now in California area.
FREQUENTED   When in Detroit resides with
                  mother at 3888 Lakewood,
                  Detroit, or with uncle,
                  Michael Rubino, 1068 Bedford,
                  Grosse Pte. Park, Mich.

FAMILY   : Single; father: Rosalino; mother: Anna Rubino;
BACKGROUND   brothers: Matteo & Samuel, in Detroit, John, Sidney
                  & James in California; sisters: Phyllis Messini &
                  Grace La Salle, (both in California).

CRIMINAL   : Sam Lucido, Michael Rubino, Matteo Bartolotta,
ASSOCIATES   ███████████████ Anthony Giacalone, ███████

CRIMINAL   : FBI #3739742, Detroit PD #82615, LA PD# 181189.
HISTORY   Record dates from 1937 and includes arrests for
                  assault with deadly weapon, conspiracy (gambling),
                  interference with police officer & armed robbery.

BUSINESS   : No known legitimate business enterprise.

MODUS   : Lower level minor Mafia hoodlum who engages in
OPERANDI   bookmaking and armed robbery. Well acquainted with
                  top level Mafiosi through his uncle Michael Rubino.

NAME   : Salvatore Ciro BILLECI

ALIASES   : Duke

DESCRIPTION   : Born 11-17-1914 Pittsburg,
                    Cal. 5'9½", 180 lbs, brown
                    eyes, black hair, dark com-
                    plexion, medium build.

LOCALITIES   : Resides 262 Cutter Street,
FREQUENTED   Pittsburg, Cal., with his
                    parents.

FAMILY   : Separated from wife, Gina;
BACKGROUND   father: Ciro; mother: Pietra
                    Cardinalli.

CRIMINAL   : ██████████████ Vincent Bruno, Reynaldo Ferrari,
ASSOCIATES   ████████████████████████████████ Anthony
                    Marcella.

CRIMINAL   : FBI #4575075   San Francisco PD #160966
HISTORY   Record consists solely of arrests for narcotic
                    law violations. Served ten years on Federal
                    Narcotic conviction and has another Federal
                    Narcotic case pending (1960).

BUSINESS   : Owns and operates commercial fishing boat.

MODUS   : With Mafia associates is actively engaged in
OPERANDI   the wholesale distribution of narcotics in the
                    San Francisco, Santa Cruz and Monterey, California,
                    areas.

In 1955, he went to jail for five years for bribery. In 1967, he became an FBI informant. Bompensiero was shot on February 10, 1975 by L.A. mob gunman, Thomas Ricciardi, at a telephone booth.

NAME   : Frank BOMPENSIERO

ALIASES   : The Bomp, Happy, William Martin, Harry Bonpensiero

DESCRIPTION   : Born 9-29-1905, Milwaukee, Wis., 5'6", 190 lbs, brown hair, balding, brown eyes, stocky build.

LOCALITIES   : Resided 5878 Estelle Street,
FREQUENTED   San Diego, Cal. Currently (1960) incarcerated.

FAMILY   : Married Thelma Jan San-
BACKGROUND   felippe; daughter: Mary Ann; brother: Salvatore.

CRIMINAL   : ███████████████ Dragna family, Adamo family, Frank
ASSOCIATES   DeSimone, Matranga family, Nicholas Licata, all of California, and Peter Licavoli, of Detroit.

CRIMINAL   : FBI #337240 SanDiego PD #16337 Record dating from
HISTORY   1928 includes arrests for prohibition violation, possession of firearms, gambling, kidnapping, murder and bribery. 1955 sentenced to 18 mos. to 42 years in San Quentin State Prison for bribery.

BUSINESS   : Owned Southland Music Co. of San Diego with Gaspare Matranga, and the Trans-America Wire Service in San Diego.

MODUS   : A capable organizer and one of the most important
OPERANDI   Mafia members in the San Diego area. Is a Mafia killer and held in great fear by the underworld. Suspect in three murders since 1938.

NAME	: Vincent Peter BRUNO
ALIASES	: Vince
DESCRIPTION	: Born 7-5-08, Pittsburg, Cal., 5'8", 165 lbs., brown eyes, grey brown hair, medium complexion and medium build.
LOCALITIES FREQUENTED	: Resides at 307 Monroe St., Monterey, California.
FAMILY BACKGROUND	: Marital status unknown; has a brother Joseph Bruno @ "Corky".
CRIMINAL ASSOCIATES	: Salvatore Billeci, Renaldo Ferrari, Stephen Sorrentino, ▮▮▮▮▮▮ Joe Parente, ▮▮▮▮
CRIMINAL HISTORY	: FBI #2307656, San Francisco PD# 64501, criminal history dates to 1937, and includes convictions for violations of State and Federal Narcotic Laws and obscene letters.
BUSINESS	: Owns and operates two commercial fishing boats with brother, Joseph Bruno.
MODUS OPERANDI	: With Mafia associates is actively engaged in the wholesale distribution of narcotics in Stockton and San Francisco, Calif., areas.

NAME   : Vito BRUNO

ALIASES   : Salvatore Monfre, Salvatore
                  Internicola, Vito Ferraro,
                  Salvatore De Nicola.

DESCRIPTION   : Born 12-28-95 Trapani,
                  Sicily, 5'6", 164 lbs.,
                  brown eyes, grey hair,
                  alien registration number
                  A 5616068.

LOCALITIES   : Resides 1449 Powell St.,
FREQUENTED   Apt 33, San Francisco, Cal.
                  Frequents Tropical Grill
                  and Lanza Olive Oil Co., both in San Francisco.

FAMILY   : Single, father: Vito, mother: Calogera Leo, (both
BACKGROUND   dead), had brother Joseph and sisters Frances and
                  Vita, all of whom are dead.

CRIMINAL   : Lanza brothers, Michael Abati, Philip Maita, Joe
ASSOCIATES   Cerrito, all of California.

CRIMINAL   : FBI #451367, several arrests for violation of the
HISTORY   prohibition laws; currently under deportation pro-
                  ceedings at San Francisco, California.

BUSINESS   : None

MODUS   : Closely associated with all upper echelon Mafia
OPERANDI   members in San Francisco Bay area; and also with
                  known narcotic traffickers.

NAME	: Antonio CAMPAGNA

ALIASES : Tony Campagna

DESCRIPTION : Born 7-27-1884 San Procopio, Reggio, Italy, 5'2", 160 lbs, brown eyes, grey hair, fair complexion, wears glasses. Naturalized So Dist. Calif., 10-22-43.

LOCALITIES FREQUENTED : Resides at 12409 San Fernando Rd., San Fernando, Calif., Liquor and grocery store attached to home.

FAMILY BACKGROUND : Wife: Rosa; has two married daughters.

CRIMINAL ASSOCIATES : Salvatore Maugeri, ███████████████ Joseph Tocco, Charles Albero, Joe Marone and Jasper Matranga.

CRIMINAL HISTORY : FBI #1119995, Los Angeles PD# 45986. Record dating from 1931 includes arrests for violation of Prohibition Act, assault with a deadly weapon, attempted murder, and violation of Federal Narcotic Laws.

BUSINESS : Owns Liquor-grocery store at 12409 San Fernando Rd., San Fernando, Calif. This store is operated by his two married daughters and he and his wife live in the rear of the store.

MODUS OPERANDI : Formerly financed large scale narcotic smuggling from Mexico and China and distributed the contraband in Calif., and interstate. Due to advanced age and heart ailment has retired from active criminal activity and from participation in Mafia affairs beyond acting as advisor.

NAME : Gaetano Paul CAPALBO

ALIASES : Paul Anthony, Paulie Helm

DESCRIPTION : Born March 14, 1914, N.Y.C.
5'5", 160 lbs, medium build,
dark brown-grey hair, brown
eyes, ruddy complexion,
often wears glasses.

LOCALITIES : Resided at 476 38th Ave.,
FREQUENTED   SanFrancisco; frequented
the Pup Bar,201 Columbus
Ave.,S.F.; prior to 1955
lived in East Harlem section
of New York City.

FAMILY : Was married to Clara Giuliano; at time of arrest in
BACKGROUND   1958 was living in common law with Mrs. Ruth Berry
Arana; father: Joseph; mother: Antoinette; brother:
Frank; sisters: Dorothy Petrullo & Rose Antoncelli.

CRIMINAL :
ASSOCIATES   ██████████████████ Rocco Mazzie, Joseph Barra, Harry
Tantillo.

CRIMINAL : FBI #2340720. NYCPD B#200313. Has criminal record
HISTORY   dating back to 1933, including grand larceny and
narcotic law violations. Has two convictions for
Federal narcotic law violations, in connection with
one of which he is now serving a ten`year sentence.

BUSINESS : Claims to be a laborer, but has never been gainfully employed.

MODUS : Has been a large-scale narcotic trafficker for over
OPERANDI   25 years; associated with and respected by the
Mafia element of NYC and California.

NAME : Dominick CASTIGLIOLA

ALIASES : Nick Turso, Mimi Pataterno,
Frank Leonardi, Peter Bona-
ventura, Don Liola

DESCRIPTION : Born 6-1-1908 NYC, 5'5½",
200 lbs, brown eyes, brown
hair, tattoo right forearm

LOCALITIES : Resided 425 W. 99th St., Los
FREQUENTED   Angeles, Cal. & previously
3901 Derbigny St., New Orleans,
La. Current whereabouts
unknown. Frequents Texas,
NYC, New Orleans & California.

FAMILY : Married; has one son and one daughter.
BACKGROUND

CRIMINAL : Salvatore Vitale, John Farino, Salvatore Domino,
ASSOCIATES   Carlos Marcello, Anthony Panci, Joseph DeNicola.

CRIMINAL : FBI #3357343   New Orleans PD #58007 Record
HISTORY   dating from 1931 includes arrests for robbery,
swindling, abuse of child and sex perversion.

BUSINESS : Has operated bar and used car lot.

MODUS : A middle echelon Mafia racketeer who is closely
OPERANDI   associated with some of the top Mafiosi in all
parts of the U.S. He engages in swindling, narcotic trafficking and other illicit enterprises.

14

In 1968, *LIFE* magazine identified Cerrito as the crime boss of San Jose, CA. Cerrito sued for libel, but the case was eventually dismissed. He died on September 8, 1978, from natual causes.

NAME : Joseph Xavier CERRITO

ALIASES : Joe Cerrito

DESCRIPTION : Born 1-25-11, Palermo, Sicily, 5'5", 190 lbs., brown eyes, black-grey hair, wears glasses, stocky build.

LOCALITIES FREQUENTED : Resides 421 San Jose Ave., Los Gatos, Calif., frequents Detroit and NYC and San Francisco Bay area.

FAMILY BACKGROUND : Married to Elizabeth Agnes Ardizone, daughter: Elizabeth; sons: Stephan Rosario, Roy, Salvatore Anthony; father: Stefano; mother: Paola, brothers: Salvatore and Gaetano; sister: Mary Benevenita.

CRIMINAL ASSOCIATES : Sebastiano Nani (deportee) Peter Piacenti, Vito Bruno, ▬▬▬▬▬▬▬▬ and Philip Maita, all of California.

CRIMINAL HISTORY : FBI #822488 C, assigned in answer to query by State Bureau, Sacramento, California.

BUSINESS : Owns Lincoln-Mercury Sales Co; 614 N. San Jose Ave., Los Gatos, California.

MODUS OPERANDI : Attended Apalachin Mafia meeting 1957 with James J. Lanza representing the organization from the San Francisco Bay area.

NAME	: Abraham CHALUPOWITZ

ALIASES : Abe Chapman, Abe Klein, Abe Gordon, Lou Green

DESCRIPTION : Born 7-3-04, Poland, Jewish, 5'6", 150 lbs, brown hair, brown eyes, medium build, rough skin. Alien, to be deported on release from prison.

LOCALITIES FREQUENTED : Prior to incarceration resided San Mateo, Calif., & frequented San Francisco gambling houses. Has been in Alcatraz & McNeil Island Pen., since 1951. Due for release October 1960.

FAMILY BACKGROUND : Divorced from Zalia Chapman. Mother resided at Chicago under name of Alta Chacht.

CRIMINAL ASSOCIATES : Sebastiano Nani, ▮▮▮▮▮▮ Mario Balistreri of California, Charles Schiffman, Samuel Kassop and the late Waxey Gordon of NY.

CRIMINAL HISTORY : FBI #264265. Record dating from 1928 includes arrests for theft & immigration violation. Three Federal narcotic convictions.

BUSINESS : No legitimate occupation.

MODUS OPERANDI : A one-time member of the murder, Inc., mob in Brooklyn, NY. He has operated over the years with the approval and cooperation of important Mafiosi in all parts of the country. A persistent large scale narcotic trafficker.

Cohen was convicted for tax evasion in 1961, served part of his sentence in Alcatraz, and was released from the Atlanta Federal Penitentiary in 1972. He died on July 29, 1976 in his sleep.

NAME : Meyer Harris COHEN

ALIASES : Michael Cohen, Mickey Cohen

DESCRIPTION : Born 9-4-13 NYC, Jewish, 5'6", 163 lbs, brown-grey hair, brown eyes, medium to stocky build, has bullet wound in right shoulder.

LOCALITIES FREQUENTED : Resides 705-C Barrington Rd, West Los Angeles, Calif. In recent years has primarily stayed around Los Angeles area.

FAMILY BACKGROUND : Married LaVonne Weaver in 1940, divorced 1959, no children; father: Max, born in Russia and died in NYC 1914; mother: Fannie, born in Russia; has two sisters and three step-brothers.

CRIMINAL ASSOCIATES : Harold Meltzer, Sica Brothers, Battaglia Brothers, Harry Rudolph, ███████████ Joe DiCarlo, James Fratianno, Sam F. LoCigno, & George Piscitelle, all of Los Angeles, California.

CRIMINAL HISTORY : FBI #755912. Los Angeles PD #178743-C. Since 1933 he has had over 20 arrests for offenses ranging from failure to register as an ex-con to suspicion of murder. Has been convicted on embezzlement, bookmaking, violation of Federal Income Tax Laws, & disturbing the peace.

BUSINESS : Reputed to own Carousel Ice Cream Parlor, 11719 San Vincente, West Los Angeles, Calif.

MODUS OPERANDI : Though non-Italian he has strong ties with influential Mafiosi and is reputed to be behind the scenes controller of Los Angeles area boxing and bookmaking.

NAME	: Frank Monte COLOMBO
ALIASES	: Concetto Colombo (Born as)
DESCRIPTION	: Born 11-2-08, Pozzollo, Sicily, Italy, 5'7½", 148 lbs brown eyes, dark brown-grey hair, fair complexion, medium build, "shield & anchor" tattoo upper left arm. Naturalized San Francisco 9-2-39, petition #45229.

LOCALITIES FREQUENTED	: Resides at Polynesian Hotel, Honolulu, Hawaii; in San Francisco resided at 50 Turk Street.
FAMILY BACKGROUND	: Divorced from Adelia in 1953; father: Antonio; mother: Cecelia (both born Italy, now deceased).
CRIMINAL ASSOCIATES	: Salvatore Maugeri, ███████████ ████████
CRIMINAL HISTORY	: FBI #904323, San Francisco PD#52314. Record dating from 1931 includes arrests for counterfeiting and gambling.
BUSINESS	: Co-owner Polynesian Hotel. Was a seaman from 1925-1939.
MODUS OPERANDI	: Engaged in organized counterfeiting racket in association with other Mafia members.

NAME	:	Anthony COSENZA

ALIASES : Tony Cosenza, Tony Melo

DESCRIPTION : Born 10-8-03 at Philadelphia Penna., 5'4", 170 lbs., eyes brown, hair black and grey, dark complexion and stout build.

LOCALITIES FREQUENTED : Resides at 1230 Kearny St., San Francisco, Calif.

FAMILY BACKGROUND : Wife is named Ann, they have no children; subject is a brother of Frank Cosenza alias "The Cow" and a sister Rose is Mrs. Sam Maugeri.

CRIMINAL ASSOCIATES : Frank Cosenza (brother), ████████████ and Mario Balistreri.

CRIMINAL HISTORY : FBI #1303631, San Francisco PD# 38842, criminal record dates to 1926 when he was arrested for manslaughter at San Francisco, Cal., subject has one conviction for violation of the narcotic laws.

BUSINESS : Occupation, bartender.

MODUS OPERANDI : An underling in the Mafia who directs prospective wholesale purchasers of narcotics to the organization's distributors.

NAME   : Frank COSENZA

ALIASES   : "Cow"

DESCRIPTION   : Born 6-13-05 at San Fran-
                 cisco, Calif., 5'4½", 169
                 lbs., light brown eyes, grey
                 black hair, dark complexion,
                 stout build, ring finger and
                 little finger of left hand
                 amputated.

LOCALITIES   : Resides at 1515 - 25th Ave.,
FREQUENTED   San Francisco, Calif., fre-
                 quents news stands in the
                 Bay area of San Francisco.

FAMILY   : Subject is a brother of Anthony Cosenza @ Tony Melo,
BACKGROUND   and a sister Rose is Mrs. Sam Maugeri.

CRIMINAL   : Anthony Cosenza (brother), ███████████████
ASSOCIATES   Sam Maugeri, Mario Balistreri and ███████████

CRIMINAL   : FBI #368211, San Francisco PD# 1423, criminal record
HISTORY   dates from 1931 and includes arrests for manslaughter
                 and drugs; prior convictions for both the Federal
                 Narcotic Laws and Calif., State Narcotic Laws.

BUSINESS   : Wholesale news paper route for the Call-Bulletin
                 in San Francisco, Calif.

MODUS   : With Mafia associates engages in the smuggling and
OPERANDI   wholesale distribution of narcotics in the San Fran-
                 cisco, Calif., area.

NAME	: Max J. COSSMAN
ALIASES	: Max Weber, Joe Miller, Sam Wilkins, William A. Leech, Henry Daniels, Philip Martini
DESCRIPTION	: Born 2-22-1895 Pittsburgh, Pa, Jewish, 5'4½", 140 lbs, slight build, brown eyes, grey hair, sallow olive complexion, neat dresser.
LOCALITIES FREQUENTED	: Now serving a 24 yr penitentiary sentence at a Federal Institution in Mexico City, D.F.; prior to confinement, generally resided in the Los Angeles area. Visited San Francisco, Baja Calif., & Mexico City.
FAMILY BACKGROUND	: Present Wife, Maria Moctezuma de Cossman, resides Tasmania 314, Mexico City, D.F. Divorced from Ida Cossman 1937 after three children, Harold Theodore & Florence; father: Jacob.
CRIMINAL ASSOCIATES	: Mickey Cohen, ████████ Gustavo Alvarado, Joseph Sica, Harry Meltzer.
CRIMINAL HISTORY	: FBI #576020. LAPD #30226M5. Record dating from 1919 includes arrests for larceny, bootlegging, parole violation, Federal narcotic conviction. Suspected of murdering two Mexican police officers.
BUSINESS	: No legitimate occupation.
MODUS OPERANDI	: A master criminal who has associates among opium growers, clandestine chemists & traffickers, including top level Mafiosi. Even though incarcerated he has been carrying on large scale transactions by mail and by using wife as intermediary.

21

He was de-barred because of his criminal activity.
DeSimone died of a heart attack at age 57 on August 4,
1967.

NAME : Frank DeSIMONE

ALIASES : Frank DeSimonia

DESCRIPTION : Born 7-17-1909 Pueblo, Colo.,
5'11", 174 lbs, brown hair,
brown eyes, 1½" cut scar on
chin, defective right eye,
wears glasses.

LOCALITIES : Resides 7838 Adore St.,
FREQUENTED   Downey, Cal., with his mother.
Frequents Perino's Restaurant
and Moulin Rouge Night Club,
both Los Angeles, Cal.

FAMILY : Single; father: Rosario (deceased); mother: Rosalia
BACKGROUND   Cordo; brother: Joseph (dentist); sisters: Josephine
and Towina.

CRIMINAL : Joseph and Fred Sica, Nicholas Licata, Anthony Pin-
ASSOCIATES   elli, John Roselli, Dragna brothers and ███████
███████ of California, Diecidue brothers of Tampa.

CRIMINAL : FBI #770726-C Los Angeles Sheriff's #B-610574
HISTORY   Arrested 1959 for contempt of court and conspiracy
to obstruct justice. 1960 sentenced to 4 years on
the latter charge.

BUSINESS : Is an attorney. Represents and advises Mafia
members in the California area.

MODUS : Attended 1957 Apalachin Mafia meeting as head of the
OPERANDI   Mafia in the California area, succeeding the deceased Jack Dragna, and as legal advisor.

22

> Dipollito died in January, 1974, of a heart attack.

NAME	: Joseph DIPOLLITO
ALIASES	: Joseph Dippolito
DESCRIPTION	: Born 12-28-1914, California, 5'11½", 240 lbs, black hair, brown eyes, heavy build.
LOCALITIES FREQUENTED	: Resides 3193 Mayfield Ave., San Bernardino, Calif.
FAMILY BACKGROUND	: Father: Charles.
CRIMINAL ASSOCIATES	: Louis Dragna, Angelo Polizzi, Marco and Joseph LiMandri, Louis Piscopo, Giuseppe Adamo, Jasper Matranga, Nicholas Licata and Frank Fiorello.
CRIMINAL HISTORY	: FBI #1413807 Los Angeles Co. Sheriffs #241443 Record dating from 1937 includes arrests for violation Internal Revenue Laws, for which he was convicted twice.
BUSINESS	: Associated with his father, Charles Dipollito, in the operation of the Dipollito Vineyards, San Bernardino, California. Manager of the Arrowhead Liquor Store, San Bernardino, Calif.
MODUS OPERANDI	: High ranking member of the Mafia in the San Bernardino area, having taken the position relinquished by his father, who has had to curtail his activities because of advanced age.

NAME : Frank Paul DRAGNA

ALIASES : "One Eye"

DESCRIPTION : Born 8-11-24 at Los Angeles, Calif., 5'10", 195 lbs., brown eyes (glass right eye) black hair, ruddy complexion, stout build.

LOCALITIES FREQUENTED : Resides at 4757 Kensington Ave., San Diego, Calif., frequents the Gold Rail Bar and various bookmaking establishments at San Diego, Calif.

FAMILY BACKGROUND : Son of Jack Dragna, nephew of Tom Dragna, cousin to Louis Tom Dragna and Frank Paul Dragna, @ Two Eye; has a sister Anna (Mrs. Stephen G. Niotta); is married to Nadine Rose Wiley.

CRIMINAL ASSOCIATES : Tom Dragna (uncle); Frank Paul and Louis Tom Dragna (cousins); Frank Bompensiero, ███████ Harold Meltzer, ███████████████ and Simone Scozzari.

CRIMINAL HISTORY : FBI #4677210, Los Angeles PD# 144978, arrested at Los Angeles, Calif., on 2-14-50 for conspiracy to commit murder.

BUSINESS : Manager of the Gold Rail Bar, San Diego, Calif.

MODUS OPERANDI : A younger member of the Mafia element who is assisting Frank Bompensiero in the operation of the organization's rackets in the San Diego, Calif., area.

Dragna died April 2, 1993.

NAME   : Frank Paul DRAGNA

ALIASES   : "Two Eye". Frank Rizzotti.

DESCRIPTION   : Born 11-18-18 Los Angeles,
                 Calif. 5'9½", 199 lbs, brown
                 eyes, dark brown hair.

LOCALITIES   : Resides 339 N. Hartley,
FREQUENTED   West Covina, Calif. Frequents
                 Los Angeles area and Las
                 Vegas, Nevada.

FAMILY   : Wife's name is Vivian,
BACKGROUND   brother: Louis Tom, father:
                 Tom; is nephew of deceased Jack Dragna.

CRIMINAL   : Tom Dragna (father), Louis Tom Dragna (brother),
ASSOCIATES   Frank P. Dragna @ One Eye (cousin), John Roselli,
                 Simone Scozzari, Frank Bompensiero, all of the
                 southern California area.

CRIMINAL   : FBI# 1489319. Los Angeles PD# 32506M13. Arrests
HISTORY   since 1938 include bookmaking, burglary, con-
                 spiracy to commit murder.

BUSINESS   : Formerly operated Trans-American Wire Service in
                 Los Angeles for his deceased uncle Jack Dragna.

MODUS   : A younger member of the Mafia, who, with his
OPERANDI   brother Louis Tom & his cousin Frank Paul @ One
                 Eye, is actively taking over control of the Mafia
                 rackets in southern California from his aging
                 father Tom and his late uncle Jack Dragna.

In 1980, he was convicted of extortion charges, and was ordered to spend a year in a community treatment center. He was also fined $50,000.

NAME : Louis Tom DRAGNA

ALIASES : Louis Tom Rizzotti

DESCRIPTION : Born 7-18-20 Los Angeles, Calif., 6'0", 180 lbs., brown eyes, black-grey hair wears glasses.

LOCALITIES FREQUENTED : Resides 1429 E. Thelborn, West Covina, Calif., frequents Las Vegas, Nev., Los Angeles and San Diego, Cal.

FAMILY BACKGROUND : Married to Doris Norton, has adopted child; father: Tom, brother: Frank Paul @ "Two Eye".

CRIMINAL ASSOCIATES : Tom Dragna (father), Frank Paul Dragna (brother), ▬▬ and Joe ▬▬, Frank Bompensiero, John Roselli, Harold Meltzer, ▬▬▬▬▬ all of Calif., Tony Accardo (Chicago), Pete Licavoli (Detroit).

CRIMINAL HISTORY : FBI #4677209, Los Angeles PD# 107427, arrests since 1946 deal mainly with bookmaking.

BUSINESS : Owns Save-On Fashions, 216 Rowland, West Covina, Calif., and has interest in Brand Motors Co., Los Angeles.

MODUS OPERANDI : With brother Frank Paul @"Two Eye" and cousin Frank Paul @ "One Eye", he is taking over leadership of the Mafia in Southern Calif., from his aging father Tom and uncle Jack Dragna (dead). Dragna clan is associated with all types of organized crime in Southern California area.

NAME   : Tom DRAGNA

ALIASES   : Born Gaetano Adragna,
                 Tom Allen, Gaetano Dragna,
                 Tom Rizzotti

DESCRIPTION   : Born 11-25-88 Corleone,
                 Palermo, Sicily, 5'4" 162
                 lbs, brown eyes, grey hair,
                 prominent nose, naturalized
                 Los Angeles, Cal., 11-10-39.

LOCALITIES   : Resides 649 N. Hartley, W.
FREQUENTED   Covina, Calif., frequents
                 Los Angeles, Calif, area and
                 Las Vegas, Nevada.

FAMILY   : Married Julia Torisco; brother: Jack (dead); sons:
BACKGROUND   Louis Tom and Frank Paul @ "Two Eye"; mistress:
                 Mildred Gilreath; daughter: Anna.

CRIMINAL   : ████ and Joe ████, his sons Louis Tom and Frank
ASSOCIATES   Paul, Nick Licata, ██████████ Joe Adamo,
                 John Roselli, ██████████ Harold Meltzer, all of
                 California.

CRIMINAL   : FBI #463258, Los Angeles PD# 30188-M-15, record
HISTORY   dating from 1932 includes arrests for violation
                 deadly weapons act, national firearms act, conspir-
                 acy to commit murder.

BUSINESS   : Retired.

MODUS   : Dragna and his deceased brother, Jack were leaders of
OPERANDI   the Mafia in Southern Calif., area and controlled most
                 organized illegal rackets. Was also a major suspect in
                 narcotic smuggling. Retired and turned over leadership
                 of Mafia to his two sons Louis Tom and Frank Paul
                 @ "Two Eye", and a nephew Frank Paul @ "One Eye."

Duardi was sentenced, in 1985, to 8 years in federal prison for extortion. He is suspected in the Binaggio/ Giargotta hit in 1950, and he is still alive today at the age of 88.

NAME : James Salvatore DUARDI, JR.

ALIASES : Jimmy

DESCRIPTION : Born 3-11-21 in Kansas City, Mo., 6'1", 187 lbs., black hair, brown eyes, husky build.

LOCALITIES FREQUENTED : Resides at 336 Cottonwood Drive, Vallejo, Calif.

FAMILY BACKGROUND : Wife Norma Ruth Duardi, also known as "Leslie"; two children; Uncle, Gaetano Lococo.

CRIMINAL ASSOCIATES : Anthony Marcella, Gaetano Lococo, Joe and Mike LaScoula, Nick and Carl Civello of Kansas City, Mo.

CRIMINAL HISTORY : FBI #5092078, Kansas City PD# 61571, arrested 6-8-52 for the murder of George W. Weavers; was a suspect in the Binaggio killing in 1950, (both crimes in Kansas City, Mo.), numerous arrests for drinking and investigation.

BUSINESS : Bartender at Eddie's Bar, 1324 Hi Way 40, Vallejo, Calif.

MODUS OPERANDI : Is constantly in possession of loaded firearms and is alleged to be a vicious killer; being used by the Mafia in this respect.

NAME   : Renaldo FERRARI

ALIASES   : Renaldo Ferrara, "Red".

DESCRIPTION   : Born 10-4-11 San Francisco,
                   Calif, 5'10½", 175 lbs,
                   brown eyes, reddish hair,
                   thinning out on top, fair
                   complexion.

LOCALITIES   : Resided 645 Geary St., San
FREQUENTED   Francisco, Calif., frequented
                   "Tenderloin" district of
                   San Francisco.

FAMILY   : Married Carmilla Arias 1930. Divorced 1953; son:
BACKGROUND   Richard; father: Louis, (deceased); mother: Jennie
                   Gandini.

CRIMINAL   : Vincent Bruno, Joe Parente, ███████████████
ASSOCIATES   ██
                   ███████████████, all of San Francisco area.

CRIMINAL   : FBI #1354180. San Francisco PD# 134644. Arrests
HISTORY   since 1936 include robbery, convictions for both
                   State & Federal Narcotic Laws. Sentenced 7-3-56
                   to 5 years for Federal Narcotic Laws.

BUSINESS   : Operated Ciro's Bar, 645 Geary St, San Francisco,
                   Calif., till his arrest in 1956.

MODUS   : A major narcotic trafficker in the San Francisco
OPERANDI   area for many years; also involved in pandering
                   & receiving stolen goods. Is trusted by & deals
                   with known Mafia members in the area.

29

NAME : Frank Rocco FIORELLO

ALIASES : Frank Rocco

DESCRIPTION : Born 6-30-07 NYC, 5'7", 185
lbs, heavy build, dark brown
hair, brown eyes.

LOCALITIES : Resides at 757 W. Crescent,
FREQUENTED Redlands, Calif. Frequents
Fiorello-LiMandri Grape
Ranch, Mira Loma, Calif, 4111
Archibald Ave, Ontario, Cal.

FAMILY : Wife: Helen LiMandri, (dau-
BACKGROUND ghter of Marco LiMandri); father: Sabato; mother:
Maria Lucia Turco.

CRIMINAL : Marco LiMandri, Joseph LiMandri, Theodore DeMartino,
ASSOCIATES ████████████████████████████████, Joseph
D'Ipollito and Michael Coppola.

CRIMINAL : FBI #1937638. Record dates from 1940 and includes
HISTORY arrests for the violation of State and Federal
Alcohol Laws.

BUSINESS : Co-owner of Fiorello-LiMandri Grape Ranch.

MODUS : Over the past years has been a bootlegger and a
OPERANDI chemist engaged in the clandestine conversion to
heroin of opium smuggled from Mexico. Is an important figure in the Mafia, partly through influence of father in law.

He was convicted in 1952 of failing to report nearly $1 million in unpaid taxes. Lanza died of natural
causes at the age of 73 on June 19, 1989.

NAME : James Joseph LANZA

ALIASES : Jimmy Lanza

DESCRIPTION : Born 10-25-02 Palermo, Sicily
5'8", 175 lbs, brown eyes,
brown hair (balding on top),
wears glasses. Claims derivative citizenship I&NS #A-
11-422-437.

LOCALITIES : Resides 19 Wildwood, San
FREQUENTED   Mateo, Calif, frequents NYC,
Scranton, Pa, & San Francisco
Bay area.

FAMILY : Married Josephine Naso; son: Frank (married);
BACKGROUND   father: Francesco; mother: Catarine Albanese; brothers: Anthony and Grazia; sister: Rosina.

CRIMINAL : Michael Abati, Philip Maita, Vito Bruno, Marino
ASSOCIATES   brothers, ████████████████, █████████ and
Nick Licata all of Calif., Nick Stirone (Pitts-
burgh).

CRIMINAL : FBI #832684C assigned in answer to query by State
HISTORY   Bureau, Sacramento, Calif. No criminal record.
Citizenship under examination.

BUSINESS : Operates Lanza Olive Oil Co., 559 Washington St.,
San Francisco, Calif., with brother Anthony as a
partner. Is also a real estate and insurance dealer.

MODUS : Attended Apalachin Mafia meeting 1957 with Joseph X.
OPERANDI   Cerrito representing the organization from the San
Francisco Bay area.

NAME	: Alphonse J. LaROCCA
ALIASES	: Alphonse Charles LaRocca

DESCRIPTION : Born 2-9-12, San Francisco, Calif, 6'1", 228 lbs, brown eyes, black hair, swarthy complexion and heavy build.

LOCALITIES FREQUENTED : Resides at 260 Cayuga Ave., San Francisco, Cal. Frequents business establishment at 2350 Taylor St., San Francisco, California.

FAMILY BACKGROUND : Wife: Vera LaRocca; son: Leo; brother: Pasquale; father: Accursio (Leo) deceased.

CRIMINAL ASSOCIATES : Tony and ▓▓▓▓▓▓ Phillip Maiti, and James Lanza.

CRIMINAL HISTORY : Arrested by San Francisco Police Department for investigation on June 27, 1939, and subsequently discharged. No further arrest record is known.

BUSINESS : Owns LaRocca & Sons, a seafood business at San Francisco, Calif., with his brother Pasquale. Together with other members of the LaRocca Family, subject has an interest in a number of commercial fishing boats.

MODUS OPERANDI : Subject is an important member of the Mafia in Calif., and a suspected narcotic smuggler.

Arrested in 1954 and convicted of drug trafficking, he recieved a long prison sentence.

NAME : James Vincent LASALA

ALIASES : Jimmie LaSala, Vincent LaSala

DESCRIPTION : Born 6-4-04 at Brooklyn, NY, 5'7", 190 lbs., brown eyes, grey hair, complexion dark and build stout.

LOCALITIES FREQUENTED : Resides at 3645 Fletcher Dr., Los Angeles, Calif., makes frequent trips between Los Angeles and San Francisco, Calif.

FAMILY BACKGROUND : Marital status unknown. His consort is Mrs. Leona Mann; has son, Frank LaSala; a sister Mrs. Grace Busterno, nephews, Mike Kaleel, Antonio and Thomas Busterno and a niece, Joan Busterno.

CRIMINAL ASSOCIATES : ▮▮▮▮▮▮▮ (son), ▮▮▮▮▮▮▮, ▮▮▮▮▮▮▮, Frank Messina, ▮▮▮▮▮▮▮, Anthony Caruso and ▮▮▮▮▮▮▮, all of Calif., and Joseph DiGiovanna of New York City.

CRIMINAL HISTORY : FBI #690454, Los Angeles PD# 82171, has record of arrests dating from 1933, on such charges as narcotics, counterfeiting and bookmaking, with one conviction for violation of the Federal Narcotic Laws.

BUSINESS : No legitimate business known.

MODUS OPERANDI : Is an active member in the Mafia's organization for the wholesale distribution of narcotics on the West Coast.

He retained the title of Boss until his death on
October 19, 1974.

NAME : Nicholas LICATA

ALIASES : Nick Lacerta

DESCRIPTION : Born 2-20-1896 Camporeale,
Sicily, 5'6", 172 lbs, stocky
build, eyes brown, brown
greying hair, wears glasses,
Italian accent. Naturalized
Los Angeles 3-25-32 #C-3-577-
606.

LOCALITIES : Resides at 427 W. Queen,
FREQUENTED   Inglewood, Calif., Apt #1.

FAMILY : Married Serafina Cracchiolo; father: Colagero;
BACKGROUND   mother: Vita Mustacchia; children: Carlo, (married
daughter of William Tocco of Detroit), Vitani and
Francesca; brothers: Valdassare, Domenico, Vincent,
Leonardo, Anthony, Colagero; sisters: Antonina and
Vincenza.

CRIMINAL : All upper echelon Mafiosi in Southern Calif., such
ASSOCIATES   as the Dragna, Adamo, Desimone, Sica, Matranga and
LiMandri families, the ███████████████████,
Battaglia Brothers and Simone Scozzari.

CRIMINAL : FBI #2585380. Los Angeles PD#170490. One arrest in
HISTORY   1945 for refilling liquor containers, also arrested
in Tony Brancata & Tony Trombino murders, in Los
Angeles, during early 1950's.

BUSINESS : Owns apartment houses in the Inglewood, Calif.,
area including the apartment house where he resides.

MODUS : One of the top members of the Mafia in California
OPERANDI   and former front man for the deceased Jack Dragna.

April 27, 1953, Lima was sentenced to the California
State Prison for grand theft.

NAME : Anthony J. LIMA

ALIASES : Tony

DESCRIPTION : Born 10-13-1905, Johnstown,
Pa. 5'5", 145 lbs, brown
eyes, dark hair, receding.

LOCALITIES : Resides with Helen Henour
FREQUENTED at 110 Carl Street, San
Francisco, Cal. and visits
another woman residing at
112A Carl St.,San Francisco.

FAMILY : Married Teresa Lima, daughter
BACKGROUND of Salvatore Lima, his uncle; has three children;
brother: Dominick.

CRIMINAL : Alphonse LaRocca, Anthony Abbate, James Franzone,
ASSOCIATES Michael Abati, Sebastiano Nani (deportee) and
Salvatore Taramino.

CRIMINAL : FBI #103403A San Francisco PD #38265 Indicted and
HISTORY tried for murder in Pennsylvania 1928, and in 1951
was sentenced at San Francisco for grand theft and
conspiracy, paroled 10-29-56 from San Quentin Prison.
Parole runs to 4-27-60.

BUSINESS : For parole purposes works at fruit stand owned by
his brother Dominick at 1676 Market St., San Francisco.

MODUS : A Mafia killer who is greatly feared by the Italian
OPERANDI residents of the Stockton-Lodi, California, area.
He specializes in extortion and fraud.

NAME   : Joseph LI MANDRI

ALIASES   : None

DESCRIPTION   : Born 10-5-1913, NYC, 5'7",
                  195 lbs, brown eyes, brown
                  hair, ruddy complexion,
                  stocky build.

LOCALITIES   : Resides 4588 Alamo Drive,
FREQUENTED   San Diego, Cal. Frequents
                  liquor stores, night clubs
                  & farms owned by his in-laws,
                  the Dippolito Family, in San
                  Diego and San Bernardino
                  County, California.

FAMILY   : Married Florence Dippolito in 1946; father: Marco,
BACKGROUND   alias "Mimi"; mother: Mary; sister: Helen (wife of
                  Frank Rocco Fiorello); father-in-law: Salvatore
                  Charles Dippolito.

CRIMINAL   : Dippolito Family, Dragna Family, Jasper and Frank
ASSOCIATES   Matranga, Angelo Polizzi, ██████████████ and all
                  higher echelon West Coast Mafiosi.

CRIMINAL   : FBI #927552 NYCPD #B-134084 Has record of four
HISTORY   arrests dating from 1935, with one conviction for
                  violation of the Federal Narcotic Laws.

BUSINESS   : Owns and operates a grape farm in San Bernardino
                  County, California.

MODUS   : An influential member of the Mafia in Southern
OPERANDI   California and a director for the organization's
                  activities in the labor union racket.

NAME   : Marco Li MANDRI

ALIASES   : Mimi, Michael, Mike Castanga

DESCRIPTION : Born 4-14-91, Palermo,
                  Sicily, 5'6", 170 lbs., hair
                  brown-grey, bald on top,
                  brown eyes and ruddy complex-
                  ion, is in ill health.

LOCALITIES   : Marco and his wife Mary
FREQUENTED   reside at 4879 Austin Drive
                  San Diego, Calif.

FAMILY   : Parents, Joseph and Helen
BACKGROUND   Pecoraro, Wife, Mary, son,
                  Joseph.

CRIMINAL   : Frank Fiorello (son-in-law), Joseph Li Mandri (son),
ASSOCIATES   Charles Dippolito and son Joseph, Dragna Family,
                  ██████████████, ██████████████, Simone Scozzari,
                  Frank Desimone, Adamo Family, all of Calif.

CRIMINAL   : FBI #967752, NYC, PD# B137172, in 1935, LiMandri
HISTORY   was arrested in connection with shipment through
                  the mails of morphine and counterfeit money, also
                  arrested 1942 NYC for violation Federal Liquor Laws.

BUSINESS   : The Li Mandris own a 9 unit apartment house at 335
                  East 55th St., NYC and a grape ranch with son-in-
                  law Frank Fiorello F.&L. Ranch, Etiwanda Road, Mira
                  Loma, Calif.

MODUS   : Is reputed to have been one of the largest narcotic
OPERANDI   distributors in the U.S., with connections in both
                  Italy and N.Y., and a top Mafia figure in NYC and
                  Southern Calif.

NAME   : Pietro LOMBARDO

ALIASES   : Peter Lombardo, Lombardi,
                  Lumbardi, Sam DeBlose, Sam
                  Salvo, Peter Scibilio, Sam
                  DeBlase.

DESCRIPTION   : Born 12-17-1901 Alcamo,
                  Trapani, Sicily, 5'5", 145 lbs
                  black-greying hair, brown
                  eyes, bullet scars both
                  cheeks. Naturalized Detroit,
                  Mich. 4-14-1947.

LOCALITIES   : Resides 903 LaBrea Drive,
FREQUENTED   Inglewood, Calif. Has made trips in recent years to
                  Italy, Detroit and New York City.

FAMILY   : Married Jennie Palazzolo; son: Mithcell, daughter:
BACKGROUND   Marie; father: Melchiorre; mother: Maria Scibilia;
                  brothers: Joseph, Frank & Anthony; sisters: Marie
                  & Mrs. Providence Sgroi.

CRIMINAL   : Angelo Meli, Raffaele Quasarano & John Priziola, of
ASSOCIATES   Detroit, Francesco Coppola & Giuseppe Catalanotto,
                  of Italy, and the Matranga Family, of Los Angeles.

CRIMINAL   : FBI #372032 Los Angeles SO #B-595347 Record dating
HISTORY   back to 1922 includes arrests for robbery, gambling,
                  disorderly conduct, burglary, assault with a deadly
                  weapon, interstate auto theft and counterfeiting.

BUSINESS   : No known legitimate occupation.

MODUS   : An important Mafia member in both Michigan and
                  California. Engages in all types of commercial
                  crime.

38

He was indicted in October 1977, for the murders of Orlando and Peter Catelli. On October 12, 1980, he and his father, Salvatore, were convicted of 2nd degree murder and attempted murder. Angelo died of congestive heart failure due to diabetes in February 1983.

NAME : Angelo Anthony ████████

ALIASES : None

DESCRIPTION : Born ████████ Sharon, Pa.,
6'0", 201 lbs, brown eyes,
black hair, ruddy complexion.

LOCALITIES : Resides ████████████████████,
FREQUENTED San Jose, Calif. Frequents
Calif., Cheese Co., 295 W.
San Carlos, San Jose, Calif.

FAMILY : ████████████████████;
BACKGROUND ████████████████:
████████████████████:
████████.

CRIMINAL : ████████████, James Lanza, Salvatore Marino ████████
ASSOCIATES

CRIMINAL : Only known arrest was in Santa Clara County, Calif.,
HISTORY 3-8-52 for a misdemeanor.

BUSINESS : ████████████████████████

MODUS : Influential in Mafia through ████████████████
OPERANDI a former numbers racketeer who invested his illicit
gains in the cheese business and in recent years
has not been known to commit any overt criminal
acts.

NAME   : Salvatore MARINO

ALIASES   : None

DESCRIPTION   : Born 4-14-1898 Portocello,
                Santa Flavia, Palermo,
                Sicily, 5'9", 160 lbs, grey
                hair, brown eyes, medium
                build, hole in end of nose.
                Naturalized Mercer, Penna.,
                5-2-28.

LOCALITIES   : Resides 755 Willow Glen Way,
FREQUENTED   San Jose, Calif., frequents
                Calif., Cheese Co., 295 W.
                San Carlos, San Jose, California.

FAMILY   : Married Josephine Palumbo; sons: Angelo & Joseph;
BACKGROUND   daughter: Antoinette.

CRIMINAL   : Settimo Accardo, Frank Desimone, John LaRocca,
ASSOCIATES   Peter Piacenti, ████████████████████

CRIMINAL   : No FBI # assigned. Only known arrest was for in-
HISTORY   vestigation in Buffalo, NY, 1942.

BUSINESS   : Co-owner, with son Angelo, of California Cheese Co.

MODUS   : Former head of the numbers racket in the Sharon, Pa.,
OPERANDI   area, he invested his illicit gains in the cheese
                business and apparently no longer commits overt
                criminal acts. However he maintains his Mafia
                connections and is influential in Mafia affairs.

NAME   : Frank MATRANGA

ALIASES   : None

DESCRIPTION   : Born 4-11-11, Chicago, Ill.;
                 6'0", 225 lbs., hazel eyes,
                 dark brown hair, medium com-
                 plexion and heavy build.

LOCALITIES   : Resides at 1859 W. 78th St.,
FREQUENTED   Los Angeles, Cal. Frequents
                 the Sierra Dist. Co., Los
                 Angeles, Cal., and the vari-
                 ous bars in that city.

FAMILY   : Son of Filippa and Antonio Matranga; brother,
BACKGROUND   Francis; two sisters, Katherine and Mary; married
                 to Maxine Agnes Hanson; son, Frank Anthony.

CRIMINAL   : ███████████, ███████████ and ████████
ASSOCIATES   ████████ of Los Angeles, Cal.; ████████████
                 ████████ and Frank I. ████████ (cousins), Joseph
                 Adamo and Paul Mirabile, of San Diego, California.

CRIMINAL   : FBI #1079136, Los Angeles PD #29838M21. Has a
HISTORY   record of four arrests dating from 6-22-31, with
                 one felony conviction for violation of liquor laws.

BUSINESS   : With son Anthony Frank Matranga owns the Sierra
                 Dist. Co., (coin machine distributorship) and
                 several taverns in Los Angeles, California.

MODUS   : An active member of the Mafia in the State of Cal.
OPERANDI   with associates in both the Los Angeles and San
                 Diego areas.

NAME   : Frank Isador MATRANGA

ALIASES   : "Big Frank", Francis Matranga

DESCRIPTION   : Born 8-21-13 Balestrati,
                    Sicily. 5'8½", 147 lbs,
                    black hair, brown eyes, dark
                    complexion, naturalized.

LOCALITIES   : Resides 5316 East Palisades
FREQUENTED   Road, San Diego, Calif. Fre-
                    quents Cuckoo Club, Hula Hut,
                    Java Club, all in San Diego.

FAMILY   : Married to Frances Priziola;
BACKGROUND   brothers: Joseph E., Gaspare, Liberante; sister: Mrs.
                    Catherine Vitale; father: Isador; mother: Mary.

CRIMINAL   : Joe Adamo, Frank Bompensiero, Paul Mirabile, Louis
ASSOCIATES   T. Dragna, Joseph & Marco LiMandri, all of Calif.,
                    Mike Polizzi, John Priziola (father-in-law), of
                    Detroit; Salvatore Vitale (missing deportee brother-
                    in-law).

CRIMINAL   : FBI# 412019B. San Diego, Calif., PD# 77593. Has
HISTORY   only one arrest for a traffic violation.

BUSINESS   : With other members of his family has interests in
                    several bars in downtown area of San Diego.

MODUS   : An international narcotic trafficker and one of
OPERANDI   the most powerful younger members of the Mafia in
                    the San Diego area.

He died of natural causes, at the age of 73, in 1993.

NAME : Gaspare MATRANGA

ALIASES : Jasper Matranga

DESCRIPTION : Born 4-18-1920, Balestrati, Sicily, 5'11", 160 lbs, brown eyes, dark brown hair, naturalized 10/30/42 Florida

LOCALITIES FREQUENTED : Resides 4805 Biona Drive, San Diego, Cal. Frequents Cuckoo Club and other bars & restaurants owned by his brothers & cousins in San Diego. Made trips to Italy 1946 & 1954.

FAMILY BACKGROUND : Married Marie Giuseppa Rita Peri; father: Isidor; mother: Mariana Parrino; sister: Catherine (married to Salvatore Vitale); brothers: Frank Isador, Joseph Ernest and Liberante.

CRIMINAL ASSOCIATES : His brothers, Joseph, Frank & ▓▓▓▓▓▓ his cousin, Frank Matranga, Joseph Adamo, Paul Mirabile, Frank & ▓▓▓▓▓▓, all of San Diego, Cal., another cousin, Frank Matranga, of Los Angeles, and ▓▓▓▓▓▓ of Mexico and Italy.

CRIMINAL HISTORY : FBI #672563 San Diego Sheriff's Office #GP6954 Arrested at San Diego on two occasions in 1954 for assault with a deadly weapon.

BUSINESS : With his brother Liberante he operates the Cuckoo Club, 1040 3rd Street, San Diego, California.

MODUS OPERANDI : Member of a leading Mafia family and himself a professional assassin for the Mafia.

NAME : Joseph Ernest MATRANGA

ALIASES :

DESCRIPTION : Born 3-25-22, Balestrati, Sicily. 5'9", 165 lbs, brown eyes, black hair, dark complexion, naturalized.

LOCALITIES FREQUENTED : Resides 4006 Hempstead Circle, San Diego, Calif. Frequents Cuckoo Club, Java Hut, & Hula Hut, all in San Diego, Calif.

FAMILY BACKGROUND : Married to Josephine Priziola; brothers: Gaspare, Frank I., Liberante; sister: Mrs. Catherine Vitale (wife of missing deportee Salvatore Vitale); father: Isador; mother: Mary.

CRIMINAL ASSOCIATES : Joe Adamo, Frank Bompensiero, Paul Mirabile, Marco LiMandri, Louis T. Dragna, all of Calif., Mike Polizzi, John Priziola (father-in-law), of Detroit, Mich., Salvatore Vitale (missing brother-in-law).

CRIMINAL HISTORY : FBI# 4582298. SO San Diego, Calif. #97380. Arrest record includes possession of brass knuckles.

BUSINESS : Together with other members of his family he has interests in several bars in the downtown area of San Diego, Calif.

MODUS OPERANDI : A powerful figure among the younger Mafia members in the San Diego area, who is considered the possible successor to the late Mafia leader Anthony Mirabile.

NAME	: Salvatore Angelo MAUGERI
ALIASES	: Sam Maugeri, Sam Mangeri
DESCRIPTION	: Born 12-16-1897 Catania, Sicily, 5'7", 195 lbs, grey hair, brown eyes, medium complexion, stout build, naturalized 5-17-29 at NYC.

LOCALITIES
FREQUENTED : Resides 350 30th St., San Francisco, Cal. Frequents residences of children and other relatives in Santa Cruz and San Francisco, Cal.

FAMILY
BACKGROUND : Married Rosalina Cosenza and they have four children, Mildred, Joan, Sebastino, & Salvatore, Jr.; brothers: Vincent & Michael; father: Dominic; mother: Maria Anugiato (both deceased).

CRIMINAL
ASSOCIATES : ███████, Joe Dentico, Philip Maita, James Lanza, Tony Campagna.

CRIMINAL
HISTORY : FBI #285165. San Francisco PD#35238. Arrests since 1924 include violation of National Prohibition Ace, counterfeiting, and conviction for Federal Narcotic Laws.

BUSINESS : No legitimate business known.

MODUS
OPERANDI : An influential member of the Mafia in the State of California, and a major interstate narcotic trafficker.

NAME   : Harold MELTZER

ALIASES   : Harold Fried, Harold Mill,
                  "Happy", Herbert Mason,
                  Harry Levy, Allen McNeese
                  Harry Miller, Harry Hirsch

DESCRIPTION   : Born 1-16-1908 NYC 5'7",160
                  lbs, brown hair, brown eyes,
                  walks with slight limp.

LOCALITIES   : Resides 355 S. New Hampshire.
FREQUENTED   Los Angeles, Cal. Frequents
                  Enid, Okla., Laredo, Texas,
                  Baltimore, Miami, Las Vegas, N.Y.C., Boston, Canada,
                  Mexico, Cuba, Hong Kong, Japan, Hawaii & Phillipines.

FAMILY   : Married Dolores Fuller Moutner; two sons; father:
BACKGROUND   David; mother: Celia Mason; brothers: Samuel & James.

CRIMINAL   : Mickey Cohen, Meyer Lansky, John Ormento, Louis Tom
ASSOCIATES   Dragna, Max Cossman, ███████████.

CRIMINAL   : FBI #113017, LosAngeles PD #96472, NYCPD #B115520
HISTORY   Since 1920 he has been arrested for disorderly con-
                  duct, larceny, homicide, assault with intent to
                  kill, possession of dangerous weapon, escape, gamb-
                  ling and violation of Federal Narcotic and Customs
                  Laws. Two Federal narcotic convictions.

BUSINESS   : Partner with Louis Tom Dragna in California Sports-
                  wear Co., 1024 So. Maple, Los Angeles, Calif.

MODUS   : An International drug trafficker closely allied with
OPERANDI   top Mafia racketeers. Smuggled narcotics in large
                  quantities from Mexico & Cuba to California & N.Y.
                  Head of large bookmaking and prostitution syndicate
                  in Calif. Associated with top labor organizers.

He died in 1958.

NAME : Antonino MILANO

ALIASES : Anthony Milana, Tony

DESCRIPTION : Born 12-5-1888, Milanesi,
Reggio Calabria, Italy.
5'6", 175 lbs, brown eyes,
grey hair, dark complexion,
stout. Naturalized Cleveland
Ohio 6-27-1924, #C-2-072835

LOCALITIES : Resides 1538 North Crescent
FREQUENTED Heights, Hollywood, Cal.

FAMILY : Married Josephine DiSanto;
BACKGROUND sons: Peter John, Frank Angelo, John J. & Carmello;
father: Pietro; mother: Grazia Mazza; brother: Frank

CRIMINAL : Anthony Pinelli, Frank Milano (brother), Simone
ASSOCIATES Scozzari, Nicholas Licata, ████████, Sam
LoCigno and Milano's sons.

CRIMINAL : FBI #433240   Cleveland PD #11100   Record dates
HISTORY from 1912 and includes arrests for suspicious
person, "black hand" suspect, counterfeiting.

BUSINESS : Owns savings and lean company and other business
establishments in Cleveland, Ohio.

MODUS : For many years a high echelon Mafia member, he is
OPERANDI now in poor health and relinquishing his position
and power to his sons.

47

He was indicted for tax evasion in 1935 but avoided the case by fleeing to Mexico. He died in a Los Angeles hospital in 1990.

NAME : Frank MILANO

ALIASES : None

DESCRIPTION : Born 2-27-1891 San Roberto, Reggio, Calabria, Italy, 5'7½", 185 lbs, black-grey hair, balding, stocky build, blue-grey eyes.

LOCALITIES FREQUENTED : Resides Los Angeles, Calif., formerly 375 N. Hawkins Ave, Akron, Ohio.

FAMILY BACKGROUND : Father: Pietro; mother: Grazia Mazza; brother: Anthony Milano.

CRIMINAL ASSOCIATES : Alfred Polizzi, John Angersola, George Angersola, all of Miami, Florida; Mickey Cohen of Los Angeles, Calif., John Scalish, of Cleveland, Ohio and Lucky Luciano.

CRIMINAL HISTORY : FBI #4687. Akron PD# 26868. Record dating from 1913 includes arrests for counterfeiting, murder and liquor violations.

BUSINESS : Has extensive interests and property holdings in Mexico, Los Angeles, Miami and Akron.

MODUS OPERANDI : Top echelon Mafia racketeer. Accumulated great wealth during prohibition era. Finances various illicit operations but activities curtailed because of poor health.

NAME   : Frank Angelo MILANO

ALIASES   : John J. Gallo

DESCRIPTION   : Born 7-17-27, Cleveland,
                  Ohio, 5'8½", 175 lbs, hair
                  black, brown eyes, dark com-
                  plexion, medium build.

LOCALITIES   : Resides 846 Palm Ave, West
FREQUENTED   Hollywood, Calif, also re-
                  sides at times at 3338
                  Watseka, Culver City, Calif.,
                  (home of brother Peter), fre-
                  quents the Roman Candle Bar,
                  Los Angeles, Calif, which his brother Peter owns;
                  also frequents the clubs on the "Strip" in Holly-
                  wood, Calif.

FAMILY   : Father: Anthony Milano; mother: Josephine DiSanto;
BACKGROUND   brothers: Peter John, John J. and Carmello Milano;
                  Uncle: Frank Milano.

CRIMINAL   : Members of the Milano family, ██████████, █████
ASSOCIATES   ████████, ████████████████████, Simone
                  Scozzari and Nick Licata.

CRIMINAL   : FBI #906688A, L.A. Sheriff's Office #B604423,
HISTORY   arrests for lottery, grand theft and bookmaking.

BUSINESS   : Works as bartender at the Roman Candle Bar, 5571
                  Sepulveda, Los Angeles, Calif., this bar is owned
                  by his brother Peter John Milano.

MODUS   : Subject is active in bookmaking and lotteries and
OPERANDI   is also reported to be taking over some of his
                  father's duties in the Mafia.

NAME : John J. MILANO

ALIASES : None

DESCRIPTION : Born 8-20-31 Cleveland, Ohio,
6'2", 195 lbs, brown eyes,
brown hair, wears glasses.

LOCALITIES : Resides 846 Palm Ave, W.
FREQUENTED   Hollywood, Calif. Frequents
Roman Candle Bar, 5571 Sepul-
veda, Los Angeles, Cal,
which his brother Peter John
owns. John J. also works at
this bar as a bar tender. He
also frequents the clubs on the "Strip" in Hollywood, Calif.

FAMILY : Father: Anthony Milano; mother: Josephine DiSanto;
BACKGROUND   brothers: Peter John, Frank Angelo and Carmello
Milano; Uncle: Frank Milano.

CRIMINAL : Members of family, ███████████, █████████████
ASSOCIATES ██.

CRIMINAL : No known criminal record.
HISTORY

BUSINESS : Works as bartender at the Roman Candle Bar, 5571
Sepulveda, Los Angeles, Calif. This bar is owned
by his brother Peter John.

MODUS : Active in bookmaking and lotteries and is also
OPERANDI   reported to be taking over some of his father's
duties in the Mafia.

Acting boss for the L.A. Crime Family from 1979 to 1984, he's currently believed to be the official boss of the family and owns the Rome Vending Company.

NAME : Peter John MILANO

ALIASES : None

DESCRIPTION : Born 12-22-25 Cleveland, Ohio, 5'10", 195 lbs, brown hair, brown eyes.

LOCALITIES : Resides 3338 Watseka Ave,
FREQUENTED   Culver City, Calif., frequents Roman Candle Bar, 5571 Sepulveda, Los Angeles Calif., owns this bar; also reported to frequent clubs on the "Strip" in Hollywood, California.

FAMILY : Wife: Concetta; father: Anthony; mother: Josephine
BACKGROUND   DiSanto; brothers: John J., Frank Angelo and Carmello; uncle: Frank Milano.

CRIMINAL : Members of family, ███████, ███████████,
ASSOCIATES   ████████████████████████████████.

CRIMINAL : No known criminal record.
HISTORY

BUSINESS : Owns and operates the Roman Candle Bar, 5571 Sepulveda, Los Angeles, California.

MODUS : Active in bookmaking and lotteries and reported
OPERANDI   to be taking over his father's duties in the Mafia.

51

NAME : Paul MIRABILE

ALIASES : Paolo Mirabile

DESCRIPTION : Born 1-12-96 Trapani, Sicily. 6'0", 175 lbs., grey hair, brown eyes, medium build, dark complexion, naturalized 3-1-20 Detroit, Mich.

LOCALITIES FREQUENTED : Resides Balboa Apartments, 2206 6th St., San Diego, California.

FAMILY BACKGROUND : Marital status unknown; father: Liborio; mother: Josephine Rizzo; brothers: Pietro, Vincenzo, Anthony (deceased), & Joseph (deceased).

CRIMINAL ASSOCIATES : ███████, Frank DeSimone, Adamo family, █████ ██████, Matranga family, & Dragna family, all of California.

CRIMINAL HISTORY : FBI#574937. San Diego PD#13542M19. Arrested 10-29-22 at Detroit, Mich. (PD#19269) for grand larceny. Applicant inquiries at Los Angeles and San Diego, California.

BUSINESS : No legitimate business known.

MODUS OPERANDI : Is alleged to have taken over the position of his brother, the late Tony Mirabile, as head of the Mafia in San Diego County. A man of great influence in the California organization.

NAME	: Michael PECORARO
ALIASES	: Pecora, Joe Briano, John Pecoraro, Sam DeLucca, Paul Santos.
DESCRIPTION	: Born 10-11-1898, Palermo, Sicily, 5'4½", 135 lbs, brown eyes, grey hair, mole below right eye.
LOCALITIES FREQUENTED	: Last known address 5326 Marlborough Dr., San Diego, Cal. Frequents Southern Cal., NYC and Englewood, NJ.
FAMILY BACKGROUND	: Separated from wife Rose; lives with Gloria Molinaro ● Edith; 2 daughters with Gloria; father: Giovanni; mother: Vincenza Galatta (both parents deceased); sister: Mary (wife of Dominick LiMandri).
CRIMINAL ASSOCIATES	: Lucky Luciano, ██████████████████, Salvatore Mezzasalma, Paul & Carlo Gambino, Joseph Orsini.
CRIMINAL HISTORY	: FBI #1111205 NYCPD #B-107273 Nassau Co. PD #22636 Has a lengthy record dating from 1917, including arrests for receiving stolen property, grand larceny, conspiracy, fraud in obtaining FHA loans, bootlegging. Currently (1960) fugitive from Nassau County P.D., having jumped bond after pleading guilty to forgery.
BUSINESS	: Has operated food packing and importing companies.
MODUS OPERANDI	: Uses his Mafia connections from coast to coast and around the world to further his illegal enterprises. Sets up business fronts to carry on smuggling, forgery, swindling and other crimes.

NAME   : Anthony R. PINELLI, SR.

ALIASES   : Joe Legno, Tony Micelli

DESCRIPTION : Born 10-28-1899 at Calascibetta, Sicily, 5'5", 180 lbs,
brown eyes, grey hair, dark
complexion and stout build,
alien, U.S. I&NS File A-517
7225.

LOCALITIES : Owns homes at 481 Sierra Mad-
FREQUENTED   re Blvd, and 500 Monte Cito
Blvd, Sierra Madre, Calif.,
has his own airplane and fre-
quents Chicago, Ill., NYC, and Puerto Rico.

FAMILY   : Married Madeline Micelli, five children; Anthony R.,
BACKGROUND   Salvatore, Josephine T., Catherine C., and Mary Ann;
father: Anthony; mother: Madeline Trigone; has been
living with Josephine Melton.

CRIMINAL   : Tony Accardo, Joe Sica, Angelo Polizzi, Joseph
ASSOCIATES   Riccio, Frank DeSimone, Sam Giancana, Dragna Brothers.

CRIMINAL   : FBI #2678506, A&TT D# X3113, has record of numerous
HISTORY   arrests for liquor law violations dating to 1927;
1960 arrested for evasion of California State income
tax. Deportation proceedings pending.

BUSINESS   : Has large real estate holdings and is a produce
broker, olive oil importer, restaurant and motel owner.

MODUS   : Very influential member of the Mafia in Calif., Ill.,
OPERANDI   and Indiana. Considered by law enforcement agencies
as being Southern California's number one hoodlum.

NAME	: Salvatore PISCOPO
ALIASES	: Louis Piscopo, Louis Merli, Louis Rossi, "Dago Louie"
DESCRIPTION	: Born 10-10-93 Naples, Italy 5'7", 190 lbs, brown eyes, grey hair, naturalized 4-22-38 Los Angeles, Calif.

LOCALITIES FREQUENTED	: Resides 1318 Hayworth, Apt #3, Los Angeles, Calif., frequents "Strip" clubs in Hollywood and gambling clubs in Las Vegas.
FAMILY BACKGROUND	: Wife's name is Evelyn, has 3 grown children: Nanilla, William, and Evelyn. (Parents names unavailable)
CRIMINAL ASSOCIATES	: Dragna Family, Sica brothers, James Iannone, ████████, ████████, Johnny Roselli, ████████████, Nick Licata all of California.
CRIMINAL HISTORY	: FBI #1491870, Los Angeles PD# 29988-M-7, arrests from 1926 include concealed weapons, burglary, homicide, conspiracy to commit murder.
BUSINESS	: No legitimate business.
MODUS OPERANDI	: Worked for deceased Mafia leader Jack Dragna; now a gambler in large scale Mafia connected operations.

Some conspiracy theorists think that he took part in the 1963 assassination of JFK. In 1976, he was called to testify about this conspiracy but was found to have been missing for five months. On August 9, 1976, his decomposed body was found in a steel fuel drum, floating in a bay near Miami—he'd been shot, strangled, and his legs were sawed off.

NAME : Giovanni ROSELLI

ALIASES : John Roselli, John Russelli, John Kasselle, John Passelli

DESCRIPTION : Born 7-4-04 Chicago, Ill, 5'8", 171 lbs, brown-grey hair, blue eyes.

LOCALITIES FREQUENTED : Resides 1251 No. Crescent Hts., Hollywood, Cal. Frequents gambling casinos at Las Vegas where he has room at Tropicana Hotel. Travels frequently all parts U.S.

FAMILY BACKGROUND : Divorced from movie actress June Lang; father: Vincenzo; mother: Maria Russo (both deceased); cousin: Joseph Evangelista.

CRIMINAL ASSOCIATES : Dragna family, Philip Kastel, Harold Meltzer, Francisco Costiglia, Charles Fischetti, Louis Piscopo.

CRIMINAL HISTORY : FBI #3339986. L.A. Sheriff's Office #51247. Record dating from 1926 includes arrests for suspicion of robbery, vagrancy, interfering with trade, mail fraud & violation of parole.

BUSINESS : Vice-President Monte Prosser Productions and varied other interests.

MODUS OPERANDI : A top Mafia figure at Los Angeles and Las Vegas. Active in labor racketeering and control of gambling.

The second underboss to Desimone, he was deported
to Italy in 1962 after scrutiny from the cops post-
Apalachian Convention.

NAME : Simone SCOZZARI

ALIASES : Carlo DiBello, Sam Scosse,
Sam Macri, Vincent Simeone

DESCRIPTION : Born 1-7-1900, Palermo, Sicily, 5'9", 155 lbs, brown
eyes, grey hair, bald pate,
fair complexion, glasses.
Alien, I&NS #A-5135558.

LOCALITIES : Resides 3056 Sullivan Ave.,
FREQUENTED Rosemeade, Calif. Frequents
Orange Hotel, Ontario, Cal.
& California Race Tracks.

FAMILY : Married Theresa Macri in 1958; brother: Frank;
BACKGROUND sisters: Anna & Josephine (all in Sicily); father:
Salvatore; mother: Rosa Megna (both deceased).

CRIMINAL : Nicholas Licata, Anthony Milano, Dragna brothers,
ASSOCIATES ████████████, Paul Mirabile, John Roselli, Joseph
Sica & Giuseppe Adamo, all of California area.

CRIMINAL : FBI #497230-B Los Angeles PD #53870 Has had several
HISTORY arrests for bookmaking and one for conspiracy to obstruct justice (for which sentenced 1960 to 5 years
and $10,000). Deportation proceedings pending.

BUSINESS : Operated Venetian Club, Los Angeles, until it was
forced to close in 1958. Large real estate holdings.

MODUS : Attended 1957 Apalachin Mafia meeting as a leader
OPERANDI from the Southern California area, representing
the Mafia-controlled rackets in that area.

57

He died in 1987.

NAME : Alfred Gerardo SICA

ALIASES : Fred Sica, "Nuncio"

DESCRIPTION : Born 2-19-15, N.J., 5'8",
180 lbs., brown eyes, brown
hair, swarthy complexion and
stout build.

LOCALITIES : Resides 627 N. Griffith Park
FREQUENTED Drive and also maintains an
apartment at 805 N. Lincoln
St., both in Burbank Calif.,
frequents the Capitol Shoe
Co., and Carousel Ice Cream
Parlor, both of Los Angeles,
Calif.

FAMILY : Subject is a brother of Joseph, Angelo and Frank
BACKGROUND Sica, he is divorced and is reported to be consorting with a Mrs. Dixie Doherty.

CRIMINAL : Joseph, ███████████████████ (brothers), ███████
ASSOCIATES ███████, Thomas, Frank P. and Louis T. Dragna
and Micky Cohen, all of Calif.

CRIMINAL : FBI #839704, Los Angeles PD #46894, has record
HISTORY of arrests dating to 1933, on such charges as
assault and robbery; in 1950 was arrested for narcotic violation but was not prosecuted due to the
murder of chief government witness.

BUSINESS : Owns and operates the Capitol Shoe Co., Los Angeles,
Calif.

MODUS : A bookmaker and extortionist who acts as a "muscle"
OPERANDI for the Mafia in the Los Angeles area.

NAME	: Joseph SICA
ALIASES	: None
DESCRIPTION	: Born 8-20-11, Newark, N.J. 5'8", 190 lbs., black eyes, brown hair, stocky build, dark complexion and rough.
LOCALITIES FREQUENTED	: Resides at 10219 La Tuna Canyon Road, Sun Valley, Calif., frequents "Strip Clubs" in Hollywood area.
FAMILY BACKGROUND	: Subject is brother of Alfred Frank and Angelo Sica.
CRIMINAL ASSOCIATES	: Alfred, ███████████████, (brothers), Thomas DeMayo, Mickey Cohen, Salvatore Iannone, James Iannone and is well known to all racketeers in Southern Calif.
CRIMINAL HISTORY	: FBI #343378, Los Angeles PD# 32483M12, dates from 1926 and includes arrests for larceny, grand larceny robbery, violation of Mann Act and violation of Federal Narcotic Laws.
BUSINESS	: Unknown.
MODUS OPERANDI	: Important Mafia leader who maintains organization through strong arm methods and extreme violence; is known as a killer; travels with bodyguard and is reported to deal in wholesale quantities of heroin.

NAME	: Stephen SORRENTINO

ALIASES : William Rossin, Thomas
Stephen Sorrentino, William
Rossi, Frank Marino, John
Manno, Steve Goodwin, John
Roberts, Fred Bruckner,
Steve McCarthy, Walter Sword
Frank Bowen.

DESCRIPTION : Born 7-6-06, San Francisco,
Calif., 5'8", 157 lbs.,
brown-grey hair, brown eyes,
dark complexion, medium
build.

LOCALITIES : Presently incarcerated in Folsom prison; formerly
FREQUENTED   resided at 285 Santa Clara Ave., Brisbane, Calif.

FAMILY : Sisters, Celia Nelson and Catherine Mayes, 285
BACKGROUND Santa Clara Ave., Brisbane, Calif.

CRIMINAL : ███████, ████████, ████████, John Stoppelli,
ASSOCIATES ████████████, ███████████████, John Rizzo, ████
            ██████, ████████.

CRIMINAL : FBI #228777, San Francisco PD# 34961, includes
HISTORY   arrests for pimping, burglary, robbery, assault
           with a dangerous weapon, possession of dynamite,
           as well as narcotics charges; is now in Folsom
           Prison on a robbery charge.

BUSINESS : Former Occupation, Motel manager.

MODUS : A hoodlum type Mafioso; was engaged in the large
OPERANDI scale traffic of narcotics in the San Francisco
          and Oakland areas for many years; alleged to have
          source of supply in Mexico.

NAME	: Salvatore VITALE
ALIASES	: Toto, Don Toto, the Short One.
DESCRIPTION	: Born 10-1-02 Partinico, Sicily, Italy, 5'6", 140 lbs, black hair, sharp features, long nose. Illegal Alien.
LOCALITIES FREQUENTED	: Resided 5670 Mary Lane Dr, San Diego, Calif., disappeared May 1956, and has not since been located. Frequented Detroit & Southern California.

FAMILY
BACKGROUND
: Married Katherine Matranga; daughter: Rose Marie DeGregorio; son: Salvatore, Jr.; father: Francesco Paolo; mother: Rosa Arculeo.

CRIMINAL
ASSOCIATES
: Francesco Paolo Coppola, Lucky Luciano, Matranga family, Ralph Caneba, ▇▇▇▇▇▇▇▇.

CRIMINAL
HISTORY
: FBI #1209612. Detroit PD #53442. Criminal history dates from 1936, when convicted of Federal narcotics & liquor violations. Sentenced to 15 yrs, 1937 sentence commuted and permitted to depart U.S. voluntarily. Returned illegally, arrested and returned to prison 1952. Released 1954 on a technicality and was awaiting both new trial and deportation when he disappeared.

BUSINESS
: Formerly operated Tropics Cafe, 122 B'way San Diego, Calif., owned by corporation consisting of his wife and brothers-in-law Joseph and Gaspare Matranga.

MODUS
OPERANDI
: A top level Mafia narcotics violator who smuggled large quantities of heroin into the U.S., for distribution in Detroit, Calif., & New Orleans.

COLORADO

He succeeded to leadership of the Pueblo faction
in Colorado in 1931, after the deaths of Pete & Sam
Carlino. The date of his death is unknown.

NAME : Charles J. BLANDA

ALIASES : Charlie Blanda, Joe Manito

DESCRIPTION : Born 11-2-99, Amesville,
Iowa, 5'5", 180 lbs., build
stocky, brown eyes, brown-
grey hair, swarthy complexion

LOCALITIES : Resides, 1104 Carteret St.,
FREQUENTED Pueblo, Colo., frequents
Five Queens Nite Club,
Coffee Pot Cafe, Holiday
Drive Inn, all at Pueblo,
Colorado.

FAMILY : Wife is Cora E. Blanda; they have one son; subjects
BACKGROUND parents are Josephine and Joseph Blanda, Los Angeles,
California.

CRIMINAL : Joseph J. Spinuzzi, Frank Mazza, James Colletti,
ASSOCIATES Robert Dionisio, Paul Incarto, all of Pueblo and
Trinidad, Colo., ████████████, James Spinelli, Clyde
and Eugene Smaldone, Joe Salardino, all of Denver,
Colorado.

CRIMINAL : FBI #379778, Denver PD# 14562, 1st arrested in 1915
HISTORY for burglary; numerous subsequent arrests for grand
larceny, burglary, etc; in 1953 convicted of Income
Tax evasion; released from Federal penitentiary in
1956.

BUSINESS : Has interest in Spinuzzi Brothers Plumbing Co.,
Pueblo, Colo., Blanda is also alleged to own interest
in the Jiffy Car Wash, Pueblo, Colo., he is the co-
owner, with Joseph Spinuzzi and Joseph Salardino of
the Five Queens Nite Club in Pueblo, Colorado.

MODUS : Is alleged to be the second in command of the Mafia
OPERANDI in Colo., and assists in the control of gambling and
other rackets throughout the state.

NAME   : Vincenzo James COLLETTI

ALIASES   : James Colletti, Black Jim

DESCRIPTION : Born 10-3-1897 Lucca Sicula,
                   Sicily, Italy, 5'7", 194 lbs,
                   black hair, brown eyes, false
                   teeth, partial amputation
                   left little finger, natural-
                   ized NYC 2-17-1920.

LOCALITIES : Resides 1415 Carteret,
FREQUENTED   Pueblo, Colo. Frequents 806
                   E. 2 St., Pueblo, Trinidad
                   Colo. Cheese Co., Trinidad,
                   Col., and towns of Aguilar & Walsenberg, Colorado.

FAMILY   : Married Mary Castiglia 1942; former wives: Josephine
BACKGROUND   Pispico and Raffiela Fazio, both deceased; son:
                   Frank; father: Vito; mother: Pasquala Parlapiano
                   (both deceased).

CRIMINAL   : Rosario Dionisio, Frank Garafolo, Joseph Bonanno,
ASSOCIATES   Giuseppe Spadaro, Anthony Valenti, Joseph Spinuzzi.

CRIMINAL   : FBI #761291C, Denver, Colo. PD#66949. Record dating
HISTORY   from 1933 includes arrests for disorderly conduct,
                   drunkenness & vagrancy.

BUSINESS   : Former liquor store & bar owner. Now part owner of
                   Colorado Cheese Co., Trinidad, Colorado.

MODUS   : Attended 1957 Mafia meeting at Apalachin, NY.
OPERANDI   Top level Mafia member in Colorado area with strong
                   control of the gambling racket there. Active in
                   large scale narcotic traffic with his close asso-
                   ciate, Joseph Bonanno.

NAME	: Rosario Vito DIONISIO
ALIASES	: Robert Victor Dionisio
DESCRIPTION	: Born 12-13-94 at Lucca, Sicula, Sicily, 5'8", 228 lbs, blue eyes, grey-brown hair, florid complexion and heavy build, naturalized 9-7-21 at Trinidad, Colo.

LOCALITIES FREQUENTED	: Resides at 1002 Arizona St., Trinidad, Colo., frequents Denver, Pueblo, and Walsenburg, Colo., in addition to various establishments in Trinidad.
FAMILY BACKGROUND	: Married in Wyoming in 1916, wife's name is Nina, they have five children; father: Rosario V. Dionisio Sr., is deceased.
CRIMINAL ASSOCIATES	: James Colletti, ██████████, Nick Bisulco and Frank Garofolo, all of Trinidad; Clyde and Eugene Smaldone, James Spinelli, ██████████ and Joseph Salardino, all of Denver, Colo., and ██████████ of NYC.
CRIMINAL HISTORY	: FBI #4445105, Colorado SP# 20822, convicted at Trinidad, Colo., on 10-21-38 for obtaining money under false pretenses; sentenced 3-5 years in the Colorado State Prison.
BUSINESS	: Retired. Subject was the former owner of the Colorado Cheese Co., Trinidad, Colo.
MODUS OPERANDI	: This subject is the most influential member of the Mafia in Colorado; is the supervisor of the organization's gambling and bookmaking operations throughout the State.

> He was the principal enforcer for the Smaldone gang
> and a slot-machine man.

NAME : Frank MAZZA

ALIASES : "Blackie", Tony Garrome

DESCRIPTION : Born 1-11-12 Denver, Colo.,
5'10", 160 lbs, black-grey
hair, brown eyes, medium
build.

LOCALITIES : Resides 2835 Vallejo St.,
FREQUENTED   Denver, Colo. Frequents Sun-
set Pool Hall, Denver, Colo,
Five Queens Nite Club,
Pueblo, Colorado.

FAMILY : Married Martha Narajo; three children; previously
BACKGROUND   married to Julie Short; father: Antonio; mother
Rosina Rota.

CRIMINAL : Clyde and Eugene Smaldone, ███████, ███████,
ASSOCIATES   ███████, ███████, John Routa, all of
Denver, Colo. Joseph Spinuzzi, James Colletti,
Charles Blanda, Pueblo, Colorado.

CRIMINAL : FBI #314757, Denver PD# 13085. Record dating from
HISTORY   1928 includes arrests for violation of prohibition
laws, burglary, highjacking, armed robbery, and
income tax evasion.

BUSINESS : Currently employed as laborer by Webb & Knapp Co.

MODUS : Known as the "enforcer" for the Smaldone brothers,
OPERANDI   Denver, Colorado, Mafia Bosses. Has a "tough"
reputation among the Italian element in Colorado.

He operated the Paradise Club with his brother, Gus Salardino.

NAME : Joseph SALARDINO

ALIASES : Joe Saladino, Ram

DESCRIPTION : Born 7-5-05 at Monroe, La., 5'8", 175 lbs., black hair, brown eyes, medium heavy build, dark complexion.

LOCALITIES FREQUENTED : Resides 2430 West 41st Ave., Denver, Colorado, frequents Sunset Pool Hall, Gaetano's Tavern, Denver, Colo., and Five Queens Nite Club in Pueblo, Colo.

FAMILY BACKGROUND : Married to the former Rose Josephine Cellino of Buffalo, New York, has one son.

CRIMINAL ASSOCIATES : Clyde and Eugene Smaldone of Denver, Colo., Robert Victor Dionisio, Trinidad, Colo., James Colletti, ███ ███████ and Joseph Spinuzzi of Pueblo, Colo.

CRIMINAL HISTORY : FBI #294130, Denver PD 23154, has been arrested for violation of the Prohibition act and also for armed robbery, no felony convictions.

BUSINESS : Has interest in several "vending machine" operations in Denver, is a partner with Joseph Spinuzzi in the Five Queens Nite Club, Pueblo, Colo.

MODUS OPERANDI : Currently is running the gambling operations in Denver, Colo., for the Smaldone Brothers while they are in prison, is an important member of the Mafia in Colo.

He passed away in January 1998, at the age of 91.

NAME : Clyde George SMALDONE

ALIASES : "Flip Flop", Clyde Duane

DESCRIPTION : Born 8-27-06 at Denver, Colo,
5'6", 160 lbs., dark brown
eyes, grey-black hair, dark
complexion and stout build.

LOCALITIES : Resides at 3042 W. 41st Ave.,
FREQUENTED   Denver, Colo., frequents
Gaetano's Lounge, 38th and
Tejon, Denver, Colorado.

FAMILY : Wife's name is Mildred, they
BACKGROUND   have two children. Father's
name is Ralph and his brother is Eugene Smaldone.

CRIMINAL : Eugene Smaldone (brother); ██████████, James
ASSOCIATES   Spinelli, Robert Victor Dionisio, Joseph Spinuzzi,
Charles Blanda, James Colletti, Joseph Salardino,
all of Colorado; and Joseph Sica of Los Angeles, Cal.

CRIMINAL : FBI #672372, Denver PD# 9333, arrest record dates
HISTORY   to 1919, on charges of violation of National Prohibition Act, hi-jacking, murder, assault and grand
larceny. On 8-22-55 was sentenced to 12 years in
Federal prison for obstruction of justice.

BUSINESS : Partner in the ownership of Gaetano's Lounge, 38th
and Tejon, Denver, Colorado.

MODUS : With his brother, Eugene Smaldone, controls gambling
OPERANDI   in and around Denver, is acquainted with major criminals throughout the U.S., and is an influential
member of the Mafia in Colorado.

He was the head of the Smaldone crime family in Denver until March 1992, when he died of a heart attack.

NAME : Eugene SMALDONE

ALIASES : Mike Villano, "Checkers"

DESCRIPTION : Born 7-8-10, Denver, Colo.,
5'7½", 200 lbs., black hair,
brown eyes, heavy build,
medium complexion.

LOCALITIES : Resides 3314 W. 37th Ave.,
FREQUENTED Denver, Colo., frequents
Gaetano's Lounge 38th and
Tejon, Denver, Colo.

FAMILY : Married (wife's name Frances
BACKGROUND M.) with one child, father's name is Ralph and his
brother is Clyde George Smaldone.

CRIMINAL : Clyde George Smaldone (brother), ███████████, James
ASSOCIATES Spinelli, Robert Victor Dionisio, Joseph Spinuzzi,
Charles Blanda, James Colletti, Joseph Salardino, all
of Colorado, Joseph Sica, Los Angeles, Calif.

CRIMINAL : FBI #539866, Denver PD #B-2833, 1st arrest 1926 viol-
HISTORY ation prohibition act, convicted in 1933 violation
liquor statutes, 1937 to 7-10 years for bombing, 1954
convicted Federal Court for Jury Tampering, presently
(1959) in Leavenworth Penitentiary, has been arrested
for almost every type of crime including murder.

BUSINESS : Partner in the ownership of Gaetano's Lounge, 38th &
Tejon, Denver, Colo.

MODUS : With his brother, Clyde George Smaldone, controls
OPERANDI gambling in and around Denver, is acquainted with
major criminals throughout the U.S., and is an influential member of the Mafia in Colo.

NAME	: James SPINELLI
ALIASES	: Vincenzo Spinella, James Spinella, Jim Spinelli.
DESCRIPTION	: Born 4-3-1895 Vena Maida, Catanzaro, Calabria, Italy, 5'3½", 160 lbs, blue eyes, grey hair, naturalized 12-18-18 Ft. Houston, Texas.
LOCALITIES FREQUENTED	: Resides 4501 W 34th Ave, Denver, Colorado. Frequents the Circus Bar in Denver.
FAMILY BACKGROUND	: Married Irene Walker; sons: James & Jerry; father: Giuseppe; mother: Maria Mauro.
CRIMINAL ASSOCIATES	: Jerry Raso (deceased), Clyde and Eugene Smaldone, Robert V. Dionisio, Joseph Spinuzzi, James Colletti, all from Colorado; Joseph Sica from California.
CRIMINAL HISTORY	: FBI #73132. Denver PD #7661. Arrests since 1921 include investigation of murder, violation of the Prohibition Laws, carrying concealed weapons, reckless driving, and two convictions of Federal Narcotic Law violation.
BUSINESS	: Is the owner of the Circus Bar at 5400 Morrison Road, Denver, Colorado.
MODUS OPERANDI	: Together with Robert V. Dionisio and James Colletti he is considered one of the leaders of the Mafia in Colorado. Has been an enforcer for the Mafia and a prime suspect in murders in the Denver area. Also engaged in illegal gambling activities.

He took over running the Colorado family from James
Colletti in 1969 and ran it until his death on
September 6, 1975.

NAME : Joseph James SPINUZZI

ALIASES : Scotty, Joe Marco, Jos. E.
Spinuzzi, Jos. D. Spinuzzi

DESCRIPTION : Born 1-19-09 Pueblo, Colo.,
5'8½", 175 lbs, black hair,
brown eyes, stocky build.

LOCALITIES : Resides 2139 E Orman, Pueblo
FREQUENTED   Colo., frequents 5 queens &
Coffee Pot Cafe, Pueblo,
Colo. Also Walsenberg &
Trinidad, Colo., & Las Vegas,
Nevada.

FAMILY : Wife: Frances Clementi; one son; father: Salvatore;
BACKGROUND   mother: Giuseppa De Gioia, (both deceased).

CRIMINAL : Robert V. Dionisio, Joseph Salardino, Clyde &
ASSOCIATES   Eugene Smaldone, James Colletti, James Spinelli,
██████████████.

CRIMINAL : FBI #940085, Colo. State Prison #20258. Record
HISTORY   dates from 1931 and includes arrests for prohibition law violation, receiving stolen property, safe
cracking, burglary & extortion.

BUSINESS : Owns Coffee Pot Cafe, Pueblo, Colo. Co-Owner with
Jos. Salardino, of Five Queens Nite Club, Pueblo,
Colorado.

MODUS : One of the Mafiosi who control gambling & other
OPERANDI   rackets in Pueblo, Colo. In 1952 ventured into
the narcotic traffic but was unsuccessful in distribution and discontinued.

CONNECTICUT

NAME	: Ippolito Paolo AGRESTA
ALIASES	: Paul Agresto, "Greaseball", "Zip".
DESCRIPTION	: Born 6-18-06 Gioia Tauro, Calabria, Italy, 5'6", 155 lbs., black-grey hair, brown eyes, naturalized 6-20-45 Bridgeport, Conn.

LOCALITIES FREQUENTED	: Resides 85 Steuben St., Bridgeport, Conn. Frequents Hotel Savoy, Mento's Service Station, Ocean Sea Grill, all Bridgeport, Conn.
FAMILY BACKGROUND	: Married to Francesca Corica; brothers: Joseph, Vincent, Anthony, & Rocco; has several sisters also.
CRIMINAL ASSOCIATES	: Frank Piccolo, ███████████, ███████████, all of Bridgeport; Sam Accardi & John Ormento of N.Y. area; Joe Doto & ████████████ of Italy.
CRIMINAL HISTORY	: FBI#4882273. Arrested 1947 at Milford, Conn., for idleness, later changed to extortion, for which he received an 8 months sentence.
BUSINESS	: Salesman for Columbia Motors (used cars), Bridgeport, Conn., which is owned by Frank Piccolo.
MODUS OPERANDI	: A trusted associate of known Mafia traffickers in N.Y.C. Makes trips to Italy in connection with narcotic transactions. With Frank Piccolo he controls a good deal of the illegal gambling in Bridgeport area.

NAME   : William CONFORTE

ALIASES   : Willie Conforti, Willie the
                 Creep.

DESCRIPTION   : Born 1-7-09 New Haven, Conn.
                 5'5", 180 lbs., hazel eyes,
                 hair is greying, heavy build.

LOCALITIES   : Resides 872 Campbell Ave.,
FREQUENTED   West Haven, Conn. Frequents
                 Carson's Restaurant & Lip's
                 Bar, both in New Haven.

FAMILY   : Married to Mary King;
BACKGROUND   father: Alfonso; mother: Maria Tolomeo; brother:
                 James.

CRIMINAL   : ███████████ (brother), Raymond Maresca, Frank
ASSOCIATES   Piccolo, Paolo Agresta, all of Conn.; Paul Zerbo
                 of N.Y.C.

CRIMINAL   : FBI#686025. New Haven PD#4220. Arrests since 1933
HISTORY   include counterfeiting, robbery with violence,
                 maintaining gambling premises.

BUSINESS   : No legitimate business known.

MODUS   : With brother James & Raymond Maresca has been
OPERANDI   engaged in the narcotic traffic, with Mafia
                 traffickers in N.Y.C. as the source of supply.

NAME : Ignazio Carlo MARCHESE

ALIASES : Benjamin Marchese, "Okay Benny"

DESCRIPTION : Born 2-12-03 Palma, Italy. 5'9", 195 lbs., brown eyes, hair is greying, naturalized 2-2-44 in Conn.

LOCALITIES FREQUENTED : Resides 97 Myrtle Ave., Ansonia, Conn. Frequented lower east side (Little Italy) section of Manhattan. Currently (1959) incarcerated for Federal Narcotic Laws.

FAMILY BACKGROUND : Married to Theresa DiMarche; daughter: Grace; sons: Michael & Carlo; brother: Michele.

CRIMINAL ASSOCIATES : Frank Piccolo, Raymond Maresca, Paul Agresta, ████████████, all of Conn.; ██████████ (brother) of Los Angeles; Anthony Castaldi & Vincent Corrao of N.Y.C.

CRIMINAL HISTORY : FBI#4612703. Conn. State Police #49778. Arrests since 1930 include carrying concealed weapon, robbery with violence, and conviction for Federal Narcotic Laws.

BUSINESS : Occasional employment as a tailor.

MODUS OPERANDI : An interstate narcotic trafficker who obtained his supply from known Mafia traffickers in N.Y.C.

NAME   : Raymond MARESCA

ALIASES   : "Lemons", Thomas Del Monto

DESCRIPTION   : Born 1-19-03 New Haven, Conn.
                  5'7", 160 lbs., brown eyes,
                  grey-black hair, middle
                  finger left hand amputated.

LOCALITIES   : Resides 549 Valley St., New
FREQUENTED   Haven, Conn. Frequents
                  Carson's Restaurant, Lip's
                  Bar & Grill, & parking lot
                  at 1172 Chapel St., all in
                  New Haven.

FAMILY   : Married to Concetta DePalma, has a daughter.
BACKGROUND   father: Leonard; mother: Felice; sisters: Alice
                  & Anna; brother: Eugene.

CRIMINAL   : Carmine Locascio, Vincent Squillante, ███████
ASSOCIATES   ███████, all of NYC; ██████ & William ███████
                  of New Haven, Conn.

CRIMINAL   : FBI#26808. New Haven PD#2696. Arrests since 1923
HISTORY   include breaking & entering, robbery with violence,
                  carrying concealed weapons, and convictions for
                  Federal Narcotic Laws.

BUSINESS   : Employed at 1172 Chapel St. (parking lot), New
                  Haven, Conn. Also believed to have interest in
                  Valley Supermarket, New Haven, Conn.

MODUS   : Major distributor of narcotics in New Haven area
OPERANDI   & close associate of known Mafia traffickers in
                  N.Y.C. from whom he obtained narcotics. Also
                  engaged in loan shark business & any illegal
                  activity available.

Frank was killed on September 19, 1981, probably on order of Paul Castellano (the Gambino family boss).

NAME   : Frank Louis PICCOLO

ALIASES   : Frank Lanza, Bob Brooks

DESCRIPTION   : Born 7-2-21 N.Y.C., 6'0",
                  200 lbs., black hair, brown
                  eyes, husky build.

LOCALITIES   : Resides 188 Peace St.,
FREQUENTED   Stratford, Conn. Frequents
                  Columbia Motors, Ocean Sea
                  Grill, Hotel Savoy, all in
                  Bridgeport, Conn.

FAMILY   : Married to Virginia
BACKGROUND   Paglinco & has 4 children; father is Francesco;
                  mother is Fannie Lanza.

CRIMINAL   : Paolo Agresta, Ignazio C. Marchese, ███████████,
ASSOCIATES   ███████████, all of Bridgeport area; ███████
                  ███████ of Los Angeles; Anthony Castaldi & Rocco
                  Mazzie of N.Y.C.

CRIMINAL   : FBI#428348A. Bridgeport PD#7637. Arrests since
HISTORY   1947 include gambling, assault, income tax evasion.

BUSINESS   : Has interest in Columbia Motors (used car lot),
                  Bridgeport, Conn.

MODUS   : Associated with major Mafia traffickers from New
OPERANDI   York's East Harlem area; believed to be engaged
                  in interstate traffic; also engaged in all
                  illegal gambling rackets in Bridgeport area.

FLORIDA

NAME   : Salvatore AMARENA

ALIASES   : Sammy Paxton

DESCRIPTION   : Born 7-14-20, NYC, 5'9½", 175
                  lbs, medium build, blue eyes,
                  black hair.

LOCALITIES   : Havana, Cuba. At Tampa fre-
FREQUENTED   quents "Guys and Dolls Club",
                  last Tampa address 4707 Bay
                  View Ave, and 2307 N. Dundee.
                  Street.

FAMILY   :
BACKGROUND

CRIMINAL   : Santo Trafficante, Jr., ███████████, Charles
ASSOCIATES   Tourine, Jr., Meyer Lansky, Diecidue Brothers.

CRIMINAL   : FBI #167160B. Tampa, Florida Police Identification
HISTORY   #14008. Arrested Tampa, Fla, 4-2-57 for fighting
                  with a police officer, May 6, 1957 threatening a
                  cab driver with a gun at airport, Tampa.

BUSINESS   : Gambling club manager.

MODUS   : Trusted associate of international hoodlum and
OPERANDI   Mafia leader Santo Trafficante, Jr., at Havana.

NAME	: George ANGERSOLA
ALIASES	: George King
DESCRIPTION	: Born 8-7-02 at NYC, 5'11", 232 lbs, brown eyes, grey hair, complexion florid and stout build.

LOCALITIES FREQUENTED	: Known to have residences in both Miami, Fla., and Cleveland, Ohio, frequents the Carib Hotel and vicinity at Miami Beach, Fla., and night clubs on Short Vincent St., Cleveland, Ohio.
FAMILY BACKGROUND	: Married. Brother of John Angersola and deceased Fre Angersola.
CRIMINAL ASSOCIATES	: John Angersola (brother), Alfred Polizzi, Joseph Massey and Mike Coppola, all of Miami, Fla., John DeMarco and John Scalish of Cleveland, Ohio; Frank Milano, Akron, Ohio; Joseph DiCarlo, Youngstown, Ohio; and Charles Fischetti, Chicago, Ill.
CRIMINAL HISTORY	: FBI #560579, Cleveland PD#36152, has arrest record dating to 1926, for extortion, murder, robbery and liquor, convictions for extortion and liquor.
BUSINESS	: Has interests in the Carib Hotel, Wofford Hotel and other properties at Miami, Fla.
MODUS OPERANDI	: Financial Backer of major gambling enterprises at Miami, Fla., and Cleveland, Ohio, and a high ranking Mafia member.

He owned the Grand Hotel in Miami Beach.

NAME : John ANGERSOLA

ALIASES : John King

DESCRIPTION : Born 5-1-98, NYC, 5'9", 200 lbs., brown eyes, grey hair, (balding), dark complexion, stout build.

LOCALITIES FREQUENTED : Resides at 1424 W. 28th St., Miami Beach, Fla., frequents the Carib and Wofford Hotels Miami, Florida.

FAMILY BACKGROUND : Wife is Amy Angersola, they have three children, a brother to George Angersola and deceased Fred Angersola.

CRIMINAL ASSOCIATES : George Angersola (brother), Joe Massei, Alfred Polizzi and Mike Coppola, all of Miami, Florida, John Scalish and John DeMarco of Cleveland, Ohio, and Charles Fischetti, Chicago, Illinois.

CRIMINAL HISTORY : FBI #98146, Cleveland PD#20240, has arrest record dating to 1921, for murder, extortion and robbery.

BUSINESS : Owns interest in Carib Hotel, Wofford Hotel and other properties at Miami, Florida.

MODUS OPERANDI : With George Angersola, finances large scale gambling enterprises at Miami, Fla., and Cleveland, Ohio; a leader of the Mafia in both Cleveland and Miami.

NAME	: Morris BARRA
ALIASES	: Mickey Mouse, Mickey Morris
DESCRIPTION	: Born 9-25-06, Bronx, N.Y. 5'8", 180 lbs, brown eyes, brown-grey hair, ruddy complexion, medium build.

LOCALITIES FREQUENTED	: Resides 3152 Nailer Drive, Ft. Pierce, Fla. Frequents his construction projects at Ft. Pierce and when in NYC frequents Jomor Amusement Co. & Artuso's Pastry Shop, both in the Bronx.
FAMILY BACKGROUND	: Married Margarite Sabato; sons: Joseph & Rocco; daughter: Theresa; brother: Joseph; nephew: Nicholas Giulianti of Miami Beach, Fla.
CRIMINAL ASSOCIATES	: ▓▓▓▓▓▓▓▓, of Ft. Pierce, Fla., his sons ▓▓▓▓ ▓▓▓▓, his brother ▓▓▓▓, ▓▓▓▓▓▓▓▓, Frank Luciano, ▓▓▓▓▓▓▓ & ▓▓▓▓▓▓▓▓ all of NYC.
CRIMINAL HISTORY	: FBI #196697 NYCPD #61356 Record dating from 1923 includes arrests for assault, grand larceny and counterfeiting. Two counterfeiting convictions.
BUSINESS	: With brother Joseph owns the Jomor Amusement Co., Bronx, NY, and has interest in a colony of small homes at Ft. Pierce, Fla.
MODUS OPERANDI	: A high level member of the Mafia's organization for the importation and distribution of narcotic drugs.

NAME   : Joseph M. CACCIATORE

ALIASES   : "JO JO"

DESCRIPTION   : Born 11-25-02 at Tampa, Fla.
                 5'6½", 110 lbs., brown eyes,
                 grey hair, dark complexion,
                 slender build.

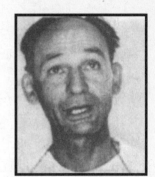

LOCALITIES   : Resides at 5810 Buffalo Rd,
FREQUENTED   Tampa, Fla., frequents the
                 Columbia Restaurant and
                 various taverns in Ybor City
                 section of Tampa, Florida.

FAMILY   : The son of Salvatore and Maria Cacciatore, both
BACKGROUND   deceased; has a brother Charles and four nephews,
                 Francesco, Salvatore, Epifanio and Enrico Trafficante
                 all residing in Tampa, Fla., another nephew, Santo
                 Trafficante Jr., resides in Havana, Cuba.

CRIMINAL   : Sam Mondello, Trafficante Brothers, ███████████,
ASSOCIATES   Salvatore Italiano and Augustine Friscia, all of
                 Tampa, Florida.

CRIMINAL   : FBI #273579, Tampa PD# 4653, arrest record dates
HISTORY   to 1925 on such charges as bolita and gambling with
                 two prior convictions for violation of the narcotic
                 laws.

BUSINESS   : Operates produce market on Buffalo Rd., Tampa, Fla.

MODUS   : With Mafia associates engaged in the smuggling and
OPERANDI   wholesale distribution of narcotic drugs.

He died in 1966 of natural causes.

NAME : Michael COPPOLA

ALIASES : Trigger Mike, Mike Ross, Mike Russo, Mike Marino

DESCRIPTION : Born 7-20-1900 Salerno, Italy. 5'5", 155 lbs., brown eyes, black-grey hair, I&NS file A 10292316.

LOCALITIES FREQUENTED : Resides 4431 Alton Road, Miami Beach, Florida. Frequents Collins Avenue and 23rd St., Miami Beach, and makes occasional trips to East Harlem area in Manhattan.

FAMILY BACKGROUND : Parents: Giuseppe & Angelina (both dead), brothers: Ralph, John, Vincent, Louis, sisters: Mrs. Helen Multitillo, Mrs. Amelia Gallo, Mrs. Josephine Tufaro, Mrs. Mary Frediroso.

CRIMINAL ASSOCIATES : Joe Rao, Joe Stracci, Tom Lucchese, Frank Costello, Tony Strollo, Meyer Lansky, all of NYC, Joe Massei, Fred Felice, Patsy Erra, all of Miami Beach, Fla.

CRIMINAL HISTORY : FBI #677976, NYCPD-B #54988. Arrests since 1914 include burglary, felonious assault, homicide, and Federal Narcotic Laws.

BUSINESS : Believed to have interest in Midtown Social Club, 21st Street and Collins Ave., Miami Beach, Fla.

MODUS OPERANDI : Currently involved in gambling activities in Miami Beach. Has been a feared and powerful racketeer from East Harlem area NYC, and has engaged in narcotic smuggling and distributing with top Mafia associates.

NAME   : Paul John CORBO

ALIASES   : Frankie Carbo, Frank Russo,
                  Frank Tucker, "Jimmie the
                  Wop," Frank Martin.

DESCRIPTION: Born 8-10-04 NYC, 5'8", 180
                  lbs, grey hair, brown eyes,

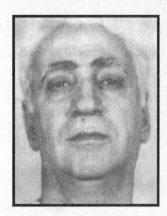

LOCALITIES   : Resides 2637 Taft St.,
FREQUENTED   Hollywood, Fla. Frequents
                  Miami Beach and well known
                  midtown bars & night clubs
                  in NYC. Also attends all
                  major prize fights.

FAMILY   : Divorced from Catherine Connelly in 1955, daughter:
BACKGROUND   Carol Ann; father: Angelo; mother: Clementine
                  Petrono (both deceased); sisters: Mrs. Julia Vastano,
                  Mrs. Josephine Bayer, Mary; brothers: Anthony,
                  Alfonso, and Nick (deceased).

CRIMINAL   : Russell Bufalino, ████████████████, Blinky Palermo,
ASSOCIATES   Sica brothers, James Plumeri, Harry Stromberg.

CRIMINAL   : FBI# 187972. NYCPD B#95838. Arrests since 1922 in-
HISTORY   clude felonious assault, murder, robbery with gun,
                  extortion.

BUSINESS   : Sports promoter and fight manager.

MODUS   : Acts as "front man" for Mafia associates who are
OPERANDI   muscling in the fight racket.

He earned the title of Public Enemy Number One in
Buffalo, NY.

NAME : Joseph J. DI CARLO

ALIASES : Joe DeCarlo, Jerry the Wolf,
Joe the Gyp.

DESCRIPTION : Born 11-8-1899, Vallelunga,
Sicily, Italy. 5'6", 175
lbs, brown eyes, black-grey
hair. Derivative citizenship.

LOCALITIES : Resides 530 So. Shore Drive,
FREQUENTED Miami Beach, Fla. Frequents
Esquire Smoke Shop, Carib
Hotel, Tahiti Bar & Grand
Barber Shop, all in Miami
Beach. Makes trips to Youngstown, Ohio and Utica-
Rochester area of New York State.

FAMILY : Married Elsie Pieri (sister of narcotic violator
BACKGROUND Salvatore Pieri); daughter: Vinnie; father: Joseph
P.; mother Florence Palmeri.

CRIMINAL : Stefano & Antonino Magaddino, Salvatore Pieri, Sal-
ASSOCIATES vatore Rizzo, Anthony Strollo, Cassandras Bonasera
(brother-in-law), Joseph Massei, Angersola Brothers.

CRIMINAL : FBI #286967 Buffalo PD# 14592 Record dating from
HISTORY 1920 includes arrests for assault, coercion, intim-
idating witness and violation Federal Narcotic Laws.

BUSINESS : No known legitimate occupation.

MODUS : A feared Mafioso, utilized as a killer by the Mag-
OPERANDI addino Brothers of Buffalo, NY. Forced to leave the
Buffalo area by police and is currently engaged in
Mafia controlled illegal gambling in the Greater
Miami area.

NAME	: Antonio DIECIDUE
ALIASES	: Tony
DESCRIPTION	: Born 5-12-1896, Gianciana, Agrigento, Sicily, Italy. 5'6½", 175 lbs, medium build, receding grey-black hair.

LOCALITIES FREQUENTED	: Resides 4600 E. Broadway, Tampa, Fla. Frequents Ybor City area and the Italian Club, East Broadway, Tampa, Florida.
FAMILY BACKGROUND	: Married: Giuseppina Guestella; father: Alphonso; mother: Antonina Arcuri; (both parents born Italy); brother: Frank.
CRIMINAL ASSOCIATES	: Salvatore Falcone, Augustine Primo Lazzara, brother Frank Diecidue, Trafficante Brothers.
CRIMINAL HISTORY	: FBI #804567B Tampa PD #53182 Has only one known arrest, for investigation of bolita operation.
BUSINESS	: In partnership with his brother Frank in the Diecidue Produce Co., Tampa, Fla.
MODUS OPERANDI	: Member of Tampa's leading Mafia family. He, his brother, Frank, and Augustine Primo Lazzara are bankers in the bookmaking and lottery operations in Tampa, Florida.

He was convicted of conspiracy in November 1976.
"Daddy Frank" died on October 19, 1994.

NAME : Frank DIECIDUE

ALIASES : Francesco Diecidue

DESCRIPTION : Born 2-20-15 Tampa, Florida, 5'5½", 171 lbs, medium-heavy build, black hair, brown eyes.

LOCALITIES FREQUENTED : Resides 4501 10th Ave, Tampa, Fla. Frequents Ybor City area, Columbia Rest., Italian Club, E. Broadway, Yellow House Bar, all in Tampa, Fla.

FAMILY BACKGROUND : Single; father: Alfonso Diecidue; mother: Antonina Arcuri, both born Italy; brother: Antonio Diecidue.

CRIMINAL ASSOCIATES : Salvatore Falcone, Italiano Brothers: Frank & Santo Trafficante, Jr., Augustine Primo Lazzara, Frank Ippolito.

CRIMINAL HISTORY : FBI #764739-B. Tampa PD #53176. Since 1944 this subject has been arrested 4 times for violation of the lottery laws. 10-20-58 convicted of conducting a lottery operation and received a sentence of 5 years at Tampa, Fla. Currently out on an appeal bond.

BUSINESS : Partner with brother Antonio in the Diecidue Produce Co., Tampa, Fla. He is also the manager of the Italian Club, E. Broadway, Tampa.

MODUS OPERANDI : Frank Diecidue is one of the top lieutenants of the Tampa Mafia mob. He is a close associate of the Trafficante brothers and Augustine Lazzara as banker in the lottery bookmaking and bolita operations of Tampa.

NAME	: Frank DIOGUARDI
ALIASES	: Frank Sutera, Philip Cecala, Frank Dioguardio, Frankie Dio, Frank Dioguardia.
DESCRIPTION	: Born 9-13-1917, NYC, 5'6", 160 lbs, brown eyes, brown hair, stocky build.
LOCALITIES FREQUENTED	: Resides 1021 N.E. 162nd St., No. Miami Beach, Fla. Frequents Sky View Lounge and Little Napoli Restaurant in Miami. Makes trips to NYC and Montreal, Canada.

FAMILY BACKGROUND	: Married Carmela Sutera; father: Dominick; mother: Rose Plumeri; brothers: John & Thomas; uncles: William, Joseph & James Plumeri.
CRIMINAL ASSOCIATES	: John Dioguardi, George Nobile, ▮▮▮▮▮▮▮, Locascio Brothers, all of NYC, Pasquale Erra, Alfred Felice, Michael Coppola & James Plumeri, all of Miami.
CRIMINAL HISTORY	: FBI #863979 NYCPD #B-121379 Record dating from 1934 includes arrests for rape, concealed weapon, unregistered still, theft from interstate shipment.
BUSINESS	: Has juke boxes and cigarette machines in the Greater Miami area; has interest in Palange's Restaurant, North Miami Beach, Florida.
MODUS OPERANDI	: A powerful Mafia figure in the Miami area. Major interstate narcotic trafficker and labor union racketeer.

```
NAME            : Pasquale  ERRA

ALIASES         : Pat Erra, Patsy Erra

DESCRIPTION     : Born 11-29-15, NYC, 5'5",
                  140 lbs., brown eyes, black
                  hair, mole at side of chin,
                  dark complexion, and medium
                  build.
```

```
LOCALITIES      : Resides at 3720 Chase Ave.,
FREQUENTED        Miami Beach, Fla., fre-
                  quents the Dream Bar, Hotel
                  Albian, Hotel Fountainbleau,
                  and Club LaRue, all of Miami
                  Beach, Florida.

FAMILY          : Separated from wife and child, father is Rocco Erra,
BACKGROUND        mother's name is Assunta; has two brothers, Mike and
                  Rocco Jr., his family resides at Astoria, Long Island,
                  New York.

CRIMINAL        : Joe Massei, Mike Coppola, Joseph Indelicato, Charles
ASSOCIATES        Tourino, Fred Felice, and Terry Teriaca, of Miami,
                  Fla., Joe Rao and Joe Valachi of NYC.

CRIMINAL        : FBI #1593543, NYC PD# B151752, arrest record dates
HISTORY           from 1936, with convictions for auto theft and vio-
                  lations of the Federal Narcotic Laws.

BUSINESS        : Is a partner in the Dream Bar and owns other Miami
                  Beach real estate.

MODUS           : Is the enforcer and right hand man for Mike Coppola
OPERANDI          and an important member of the Mafia in NYC and
                  Miami, Florida.
```

NAME   : Joseph FALCONE

ALIASES   : Joe Falcone

DESCRIPTION   : Born 11-6-25 Utica, NY, 5'7½"
                  190 lbs, stocky build, blue
                  eyes.

LOCALITIES   : Resides 5609 N. W. 7th Ave,
FREQUENTED   Miami, Fla. Frequents N.W.,
                  7th Ave, Italian neighbor-
                  hood of Miami & travels to
                  Tampa, Fla.

FAMILY   : Father: Salvatore (1957
BACKGROUND   Apalachin delegate); mother: Josephine Provenzano;
                  son: Joseph Salvatoro Falcone.

CRIMINAL   : Diecidue Family of Tampa, Fla. Father, Salvatore
ASSOCIATES   Falcone.

CRIMINAL   : No FBI # Assigned. Was arrested on 5-27-59, Miami,
HISTORY   Fla, charged with harboring his fugitive father
                  Salvatore Falcone.

BUSINESS   : Operates the Falcone & Sons Wholesale & Retail
                  Italian Grocery, 5609 N.W. 7th Ave, Miami, Fla.

MODUS   : Joseph Falcone has no criminal record and is
OPERANDI   ostensibly a respectable business man. He is,
                  however, undoubtedly cognizant of his fathers
                  activities in the Mafia and is considered a threat
                  because of potential Mafia influence through his
                  father, one of the 1957 Apalachin delegates.

NAME   : Salvatore FALCONE

ALIASES   : Salvatore Projetto

DESCRIPTION : Born 8-17-91 Sciacca, Sicily
                  naturalized 7-21-25 Utica,
                  NY, 5'6", 180 lbs., heavy
                  build, stoop-shouldered,
                  brown eyes, grey hair.

LOCALITIES   : Resides 1652 N.W. 62nd St.,
FREQUENTED   Miami, Fla., frequents Utica
                  Rome, N.Y., area, Tampa,
                  Fla., and NYC.

FAMILY   : Married to Josephine Provenzano, sons are Anthony S.,
BACKGROUND   Joseph, Victor A., and Salvatore Jr., daughter is
                  Clara A., parents Antonio and Maria (both dead),
                  brother: Joseph.

CRIMINAL   : ███████████ and Joe Falcone (brother) of Utica, NY
ASSOCIATES   area, Vincent Carrao and Salvatore Ameli of NYC,
                  Diecidue brothers of Tampa, Nicola Gentile (deportee).

CRIMINAL   : FBI #1697794, has arrest for violation Federal
HISTORY   Liquor Laws. Indicted (1959) for 18 USC 371 (pend-
                  ing).

BUSINESS   : Operates Italian-American grocery business at 5609
                  N.W. 7th Ave., Miami, Fla., with his son Joseph.

MODUS   : Attended Apalachin Mafia meeting 1957 with brother
OPERANDI   Joe representing the organization from the Utica-
                  Rome area NY., moved to Florida in 1946 leaving
                  active control of the organization to his brother
                  Joe.

NAME	: Alfredo George FELICI
ALIASES	: Freddie Felice, Fred Franco
DESCRIPTION	: Born 10-15-12, N.Y.C., N.Y.; 5'8", 170 lbs., brown eyes, brown hair, dark complexion, and medium build.
LOCALITIES FREQUENTED	: Resides at 1770 Normandie Dr., Miami Beach, Fla. Frequents the vicinity of 23rd and Collins Ave., Miami Beach, Fla., and the Turf Restaurant, 47th St. and Broadway Avenue, New York City, New York.

FAMILY BACKGROUND	: Subject is the son of Giovanni and Mary Felici, nee Caparo. Has a sister Geraldine.
CRIMINAL ASSOCIATES	: Pasquale Erra, Mike Coppola, Joe Vento, Pasquale Genese, Frank DioGuardio, Vincent Mauro, ███████ ███████, Charles Tourino, Theodore, Benjamin and ███████████, Joe Bendenelli, John Ormento and Salvatore Santoro.
CRIMINAL HISTORY	: FBI #951876, NYC PD #B132768, Miami Beach PD #A14019. Arrest record dates from 1931, on such charges as vagrancy, carrying concealed weapon, gambling and narcotics with one felony conviction for violation of the Federal Narcotic Laws.
BUSINESS	: Owns interest in the LaRue Club, 23rd and Collins Ave., Miami Beach, Florida.
MODUS OPERANDI	: Associated with other Mafia members in the organization's gambling and bookmaking activities in the Miami Beach area.

NAME	: Joseph FISCHETTI

ALIASES : Joseph Fisher, Joseph Perrito

DESCRIPTION : Born 4-3-10 Brooklyn, N.Y. 5'8", 170 lbs., hazel eyes, grey-brown hair, medium build, fair complexion.

LOCALITIES FREQUENTED : Resides 6701 Miami View Dr., Miami Beach, Fla. Frequents the Bonfire Restaurant, Dream Bar, & Ted's Grotto, all in Miami Beach, Fla.

FAMILY BACKGROUND : Single, resides with divorcee Lee Pollack. father: Nicola (deceased); mother: Mary; brothers: Nicholas & Rocco; sisters: Mildred, Mrs. Mary Monoaco, Mrs. Rose Mareno, & Mrs. Helen Salvaggio. Is a cousin to the notorious Capone family of Chicago, Ill.

CRIMINAL ASSOCIATES : Paul DeLucia, Tony Accardo, ███████████, Rocco DeGrazia, & the Capone brothers, all of Chicago, Ill.; Joe Massei, ████████████, Anthony Carfano, & Joseph and Angelo DiCarlo, all of Miami Beach.

CRIMINAL HISTORY : FBI#448736. Miami PD#7914. Arrests since 1932 includes investigation of activities and violation of the White Slave Act.

BUSINESS : Has interest in the Fount-Wip Corp., Miami, Fla.

MODUS OPERANDI : With Mafia associates controls extensive gambling interests in the State of Florida.

He died April 17, 1960.

NAME : Augustine FRISCIA

ALIASES : Gus

DESCRIPTION : Born 2-2-05 Tampa, Fla, 5'7",
173 lbs, medium build, grey-
black hair, brown eyes.

LOCALITIES : Resides 2302 Ridgewood St,
FREQUENTED Tampa, Fla. Frequents Colum-
bia Rest., Yellow House Bar,
Gene's Bar, Tampa, Fla.

FAMILY : Married Visitation Rodriguez;
BACKGROUND father: Francesco; mother:
Rosalia Cicura, (both born Italy); uncle: Henry
Ciccerello.

CRIMINAL : Frank Diecidue, Augustine Primo Lazzara, Angelo
ASSOCIATES Bedami, Frank Ippolito, Frank Trafficante.

CRIMINAL : FBI #689739. Tampa PD #11094. Record dates from
HISTORY 1933 and includes arrests for using mails to defraud,
assault and intent to kill.

BUSINESS : Unemployed, no legitimate source of income.

MODUS : Friscia is considered a lesser member of the Tampa
OPERANDI Mafia mob. He is associated with Frank Diecidue
and Augustine Lazzara in the bolita and lottery
operations in Tampa. He is also an arson specialist.

NAME   : Joseph INDELICATO

ALIASES   : Joe Scooch, Joe Gooch.

DESCRIPTION   : Born 6-10-10 NYC, 5'9",
                225 lbs, grey eyes, brown
                hair, heavy build, dark
                complexion.

LOCALITIES   : Resides 385 82nd Street,
FREQUENTED   Apt. 25, Miami Beach, Fla.
                Frequents Cavendish Card
                Club, The Esquire Smoke
                Shop, and The South Florida
                U-Drive-It Co., all located
                in Miami Beach, Fla.

FAMILY   : Married to Gussie Seiler, has a sister, Mrs. Jennie
BACKGROUND   Melori of Brooklyn, N.Y.; he is a cousin of the
                notorious Salvatore Falcone.

CRIMINAL   : Salvatore Falcone, Mike Coppola, Freddie Felice,
ASSOCIATES   Angersola brothers, Mannarino brothers, Joseph
                DiCarlo, Angelo DeCarlo.

CRIMINAL   : FBI # 561964. NYCPD-B # 102684. Arrests since
HISTORY   1932 include robbery, policy, and a felony con-
                viction in NYC for a jewel robbery.

BUSINESS   : Owns the South Florida U-Drive-It Co., and the
                Sunshine State Transport Co., both located at
                169 Lincoln Road, Miami Beach, Fla.

MODUS   : A feared and influential member of the Mafia in
OPERANDI   Florida, and a director in the organization's
                gambling and labor racketeering activities in
                Florida.

NAME : Frank IPPOLITO

ALIASES : Cowboy, Francesco Ippolito

DESCRIPTION : Born 4-16-21 Tampa, Fla,
5'10", 195 lbs, medium build,
balding black hair, brown
eyes.

LOCALITIES : Resides 2412 9th Ave, Tampa,
FREQUENTED Fla. Frequents a poolroom at
1120 Grand Central Ave, Columbia Rest., & Yellow House
Bar, Tampa.

FAMILY : Married Esther Jacqueline Ward; father: Francesco;
BACKGROUND mother: Mattia Cacciatore; brother: Carl.

CRIMINAL : Augustine Primo Lazzara, Frank Diecidue, Frank &
ASSOCIATES Santo Trafficante, Jr., William Savarino.

CRIMINAL : FBI #3631483. Tampa SO #65949. Record dates from
HISTORY 1943 and includes arrests for assault & battery,
vagrancy, breaking & entering, failure to assist
police officer & conducting a lottery.

BUSINESS : No legitimate occupation known.

MODUS : Ippolito is involved in the large scale bookmaking
OPERANDI lottery and bolita operation of the Tampa Mafia mob.
He takes direct orders from Frank Diecidue. He is
also known to be the sometime body guard of Henry
Trafficante.

NAME	: Salvatore ITALIANO

ALIASES   : "Red" Italiano, Don Salvador

DESCRIPTION   : Born 10-19-96 at Belmonte, Sicily, 5'8", 185 lbs., eyes blue, hair reddish-grey, ruddy complexion, stout build naturalized on 1-14-47 at Tampa, Fla.

LOCALITIES   : Resides at 906 Homere Ave.,
FREQUENTED   Mexico City, D.F. Mexico; when in Tampa, Fla., resides at 3413 Beach drive; frequents Anthony Distributors, Inc., Tampa, Fla.

FAMILY   : Married Maria Spoto on 6-24-17, at Tampa, Fla., they
BACKGROUND   have two children, Anthony S. and Eleanor (Mrs. Charles Cumbo); his father was Anthony and his mother Nora, both are deceased.

CRIMINAL   : Diecidue Brothers, ███████████████ (son), Primo
ASSOCIATES   Lazzara, Joe V. Provenzano, Augustine Friscia, ██████ ████████ and the Trafficante Brothers, all of Tampa, Florida.

CRIMINAL   : FBI #449467, criminal history dates from 1925 and con-
HISTORY   sists of arrests for liquor, smuggling, violation of narcotic laws and perjury, with two felony convictions.

BUSINESS   : Has controlling stock in Anthony Distributors, Inc., a wholesale liquor distributorship at Tampa, Fla., has gross income of $2,200 per month from rental properties at Tampa and St. Petersburg, Fla.

MODUS   : An internationally known smuggler of narcotics and
OPERANDI   aliens and an influential Inner Council Mafioso.

NAME	: Max KORNHAUSER
ALIASES	: Max Golden, Max Kornbloom, Max Hauser, Max Rosenbloom, Max Cohen, Max Gordon, Harry Golden, Max Bucher.
DESCRIPTION	: Born 12-25-1890 NYC, 5'6", 160 lbs, brown eyes, bald, sallow complexion, medium build, sniffs heroin,
LOCALITIES FREQUENTED	: Resides Cotillion Arms Apts, 6930 Rue Versailles, Miami Beach, Fla.
FAMILY BACKGROUND	: Wife: Ann Bucher, former wife Rose King.
CRIMINAL ASSOCIATES	: Joseph Miller, ██████████, ████████, ███ ███.
CRIMINAL HISTORY	: FBI #81960. NYCPD #B58619. Arrests date from 1915 for disorderly conduct, vagrancy, pickpocketing, and grand larceny; four convictions for violation of Federal Narcotic Laws.
BUSINESS	: Manager Cotillion Arms Apts., Miami Beach, Fla.
MODUS OPERANDI	: In the past has been a large scale narcotic trafficker in Chicago, Detroit & Kansas City. Since release from prison in 1952 has managed hotels in Miami Beach and apparently refrained from criminal activities. Numbers important Mafia racketeers among his associates and could return to criminal activity at any time.

NAME	: Jack LANSKY
ALIASES	: Born Jacob Suchowlansky, Jake.
DESCRIPTION	: Born 2-17-05, Grodno, Poland. Jewish, 5'11", 180 lbs, brown eyes, brown-grey hair, fair complexion, medium build, wears glasses.
LOCALITIES FREQUENTED	: Resides 1146 Harrison St., Hollywood, Fla. Frequents Gold Coast Lounge, Hollywood, Fla., & Miami, NYC, Las Vegas.
FAMILY BACKGROUND	: Wife: Anne; daughter: Roberta; mother: Fenke; brother: Meyer.
CRIMINAL ASSOCIATES	: Meyer Lansky, Santos Trafficante Jr., Francisco Costiglia, Anthony Accardo.
CRIMINAL HISTORY	: No known criminal record.
BUSINESS	: No legitimate occupation. Owns land and building of New Plantation Restaurant, Hallandale, Fla., from which he has an income.
MODUS OPERANDI	: An underling of his brother, Meyer Lansky, in the operation of large scale Mafia-controlled gambling and other illicit enterprises.

He died in Miami on January 15, 1983 of lung cancer.

NAME : Meyer LANSKY

ALIASES : Born Meyer Suchowlansky, bugs Meyer, Morris Lieberman

DESCRIPTION : Born 7-4-02 Grodno, Poland, Jewish, 5'5", 145 lbs, brown eyes, grey brown hair. Naturalized Brooklyn, NY, 9-27-1928.

LOCALITIES FREQUENTED : Resides 612 Hibiscus Drive, Hallandale, Fla. Frequents Gold Coast Lounge, Hollywood, Florida, Miami, NY, & Las Vegas.

FAMILY BACKGROUND : Divorced from Anna Citron; children from first marriage; Bernard, Sandra, Paul; second wife: Thelma Schwartz; mother: Fenke (deceased); brother: Jack.

CRIMINAL ASSOCIATES : Lucky Luciano, Giuseppe Doto, Francisco Saveria, Anthony Accardo, Santo Trafficante, Jr., Jack Lansky.

CRIMINAL HISTORY : FBI #791783. NYCPD #B70258. Record dates from 1918 and includes arrests for petty larceny, felonious assault, bootlegging, gambling, narcotics.

BUSINESS : Has interests in Havana Riviera, Capri Hotel and Sans Souci Gambling Casino, all in Havana, Cuba, & Flamingo Hotel, Las Vegas, Nevada.

MODUS OPERANDI : One of the top non-Italian associates of the Mafia. Controls gambling in partnership with leading Mafiosi. Finances large scale narcotic smuggling and other illicit ventures.

He died on April 8, 1968.

NAME : Augustine Primo LAZZARA

ALIASES : None

DESCRIPTION : Born 9-10-06 Tampa, Fla,
5'11", 250 lbs, medium-heavy
build, dark brown hair,
brown eyes.

LOCALITIES : Resides at 1017 10th Ave,
FREQUENTED Tampa, Fla. Frequents the
Ybor City area of Tampa,
the Columbia Rest., Yellow
House Bar, Gene's Bar.

FAMILY : Married Alice Alonso; daughter: Angelina, (married
BACKGROUND to Ruddy L. Heiny); brothers: Joseph Lazzara, Nelson
Lazzara.

CRIMINAL : Frank Trafficante, Santo Trafficante, Jr., Frank &
ASSOCIATES Antonio Diecidue, Frank Ippolito, Joseph & ▉▉▉▉▉
▉▉▉▉▉.

CRIMINAL : FBI #210604A, Tampa SO #38335. Record dating from
HISTORY 1949 includes arrests for assault to commit murder,
bribery and conspiracy to operate bolita gambling
ring.

BUSINESS : Owns & operates Yellow House Bar, 2201 15th St,
Tampa, Fla. Owns Gene's Bar, 2932 22nd St, Tampa,
which is in the name of son-in-law Ruddy L. Heiny.

MODUS : Lazzara is one of the top Mafia leaders in the
OPERANDI Tampa area. He is involved in large scale gambling
& bolita operations as a banker with other members
of the Tampa mob, such as the Trafficante & Diecidue
brothers.

He was once a bodyguard for Santo Jr. He died on June 15, 1992.

NAME : James LONGO

ALIASES : James Costa Longo, Jimmy

DESCRIPTION : Born 11-28-1910 Wilkes Barre, Penna., 5'8", 182 lbs, brown hair, brown eyes, heavy build ruddy complexion.

LOCALITIES FREQUENTED : When in Tampa resides at 2119 Beach St. For the past few years has resided mostly at Havana, Cuba where he worked for Santos Trafficante, Jr., at the Sans Souci Club.

FAMILY BACKGROUND :

CRIMINAL ASSOCIATES : Santos Trafficante, Jr., Meyer Lansky, Jack Lansky.

CRIMINAL HISTORY : FBI #4454459. Tampa SO #22089. Record dating from 1944 includes arrests for aggravated assault, reckless driving, possession of bolita & vagrancy.

BUSINESS : Works at gambling casino.

MODUS OPERANDI : A Lieutenant and "enforcer" for Tampa Mafia leader Santos Trafficante, Jr.; he looks after Trafficante's gambling interests in Cuba and travels to various parts of U.S., and Cuba for the Trafficante organization.

NAME	: Alfonso MARZANO
ALIASES	: Don Alfonso, O. Francese, Alfonso Albano.
DESCRIPTION	: Born 6-26-1890, Naples, Italy; 5'3", 160 lbs, brown eyes, grey hair, fair complexion, naturalized 4-8-29 Newark, New Jersey.
LOCALITIES FREQUENTED	: Resides 729 N.E. 3rd St., Hallandale, Fla. Frequents area of Gulfstream Race Track, Hallandale, Florida.

FAMILY BACKGROUND	: Wife: Margaret; daughter: Mary; father: Salvatore.
CRIMINAL ASSOCIATES	: Vincent Tessalone, ██████████, ██████████, ██████████, Joe Orsini, Jean Laget, Joe Profaci, all of NYC; John Sperandeo of Italy.
CRIMINAL HISTORY	: FBI #488033. NYC PD# B96462. Arrests since 1929 include possession of a gun, counterfeiting, and Federal Narcotic Laws.
BUSINESS	: Has interests in Saratoga Turf Mineral Waters Corp., 177 Chrystie St., NYC, which is run by his son-in-law.
MODUS OPERANDI	: Has been engaged both in narcotic trafficking and counterfeiting in close association with known Mafia traffickers from the "Little Italy" section of lower Manhattan.

NAME : Joseph MASSEI

ALIASES : Joe Massei, Giuseppe Massei

DESCRIPTION : Born 2-2-99 at Wyandotte, Mich., 5'5½", 160 lbs., eyes hazel, brown hair, medium complexion, stout build.

LOCALITIES FREQUENTED : Resides at 520 Lakeview Dr., (Flamingo Bay) Miami Beach, Fla., owns yacht "Vergo", frequents the Carib Hotel, Tahiti Bar & Club LaRue of Miami, Florida.

FAMILY BACKGROUND : Married to Vera Heal, has no children and no known living relatives; father, Daniel Massei born in Italy and mother Margaret Daley Massei was born in Iceland.

CRIMINAL ASSOCIATES : Pete Licavoli, Joe "Scarface" Bommarito, Angelo Meli William Tocco, Mike Rubino, and Santo Perrone, all of Detroit, Mich., Al Polizzi, Joe DeCarlo, Mike Cappola and Fred and John Angersola of Miami, Fla.

CRIMINAL HISTORY : FBI #597894, Detroit PD# 13808, has an extensive arrest record with only two convictions, one for bribery and the other for contempt of court.

BUSINESS : Has financial interests in the following: Miami Provision Co., Grand Hotel, Sands Hotel of Miami, Fla., the Tellman Casting Co., Hamtrack Motor Co., of Detroit, Mich., the Club Elwood, Webster Inn and Victory Club of Toledo, Ohio.

MODUS OPERANDI : Is the business man type Maffioso, active in gambling and bookmaking and an influential member of the organization in Mich., and Florida.

NAME	: Sam MONDELLO

ALIASES : Sam Mongreno

DESCRIPTION : Born 9-25-07 Tampa, Fla.,
5'6", 175 lbs, stocky build,
brown eyes, receding grey-
black hair. NOTE: Police
records show D.O.B. 1-2-02,
Bur. Vital Statistics shows
9-25-07, but birth notifica-
tion not filed until 1927.

LOCALITIES : Resides 308 Howard St.,
FREQUENTED Tampa, Fla. Frequents Ybor
City area of Tampa, Italian Club, E. Broadway, Ybor
City, Yellow House Bar.

FAMILY : Married Rosaria Gonzales; son: Sam Mondello, Jr.;
BACKGROUND father: Vincenzo, (born Italy); mother: Giacomina
Premori.

CRIMINAL : Augustine Primo Lazzara, Trafficante brothers,
ASSOCIATES Antonio and Frank Diecidue, ███████████████.

CRIMINAL : FBI #3589797. Hillsboro County Sheriff's #16553.
HISTORY Record dates from 1942 and includes arrests for
vagrancy, reckless driving, operating gambling
house, possession Bolita & liquor law violations.

BUSINESS : Owns and operates the Causeway Market, S. 2nd St,
Tampa, Fla.

MODUS : Mondello has long been associated with Lazzara and
OPERANDI Bedami as a banker in the bolita and lottery activities of Tampa. In the past two years he seems to
have dropped to the background of these rackets,
but is still an important Mafia figure in the Tampa
area.

> On September 17, 1971, Plumeri was found strangled to death.

NAME : James Dominick PLUMERI

ALIASES : Jimmy Doyle, James D. Plumer

DESCRIPTION : Born 4-14-03 Regalbuto, Sicily. 5'7", 175 lbs, brown eyes, black-grey hair balding on top, naturalized 7-29-26 NYC, I&NS #C2321487.

LOCALITIES FREQUENTED : Resides 9224 Dickens Ave., Surfside, Fla. Frequents Miami Beach, Midtown Manhattan area, and most prize fights.

FAMILY BACKGROUND : Married Mary Orapollo; son: Thomas; father: Gaetano; mother: Giuseppina Granazi; brothers: Vito, Joseph; sisters: Angelina, Rosa, Mrs. Viola Serina, Mrs. Catherine Contine.

CRIMINAL ASSOCIATES : Johnny Dio (nephew), Joe Stracci, Joe Rao, Dominick Alaimo, Russell Bufalino, █████████, Frank Carbo, Harry Stromberg, ████████.

CRIMINAL HISTORY : FBI #672798. NYCPD B#114266. Arrests since 1923 include felonious assault, extortion, homicide.

BUSINESS : Has interests in Seam Binding Co., & Ell Gee Carriers Corp., both located at 218 W. 35th St., NYC, also has interests in trucking concerns & dress factories in NYC & Allentown, Penna.

MODUS OPERANDI : A Mafia member, who, with other Mafiosi in NYC, has through terroristic methods, gained control of most of the trucking in the garment industry in Manhattan.

He died in 1994.

NAME : Alfred POLIZZI

ALIASES : Albert Allen, Al Polizzi, Alfonso Polizzi, Big Al.

DESCRIPTION : Born 3-15-1900 Siculiana, Sicily, naturalized 6-8-28, Cleveland, 5'10", 170 lbs, brown eyes, black-grey hair.

LOCALITIES FREQUENTED : Resides 6857 Granada Blvd., Coral Gables, Fla. Frequents area of 23rd St, and Collins Ave., Miami Beach, Fla.

FAMILY BACKGROUND : Married to Philomena Valentino; daughter: Joanne; sons: Raymond A., Nicholas G; father: Alphonse; mother: Giovanna Indelica.

CRIMINAL ASSOCIATES : Angersola brothers & Joe Massei of Miami, Joe Doto & Lucky Luciano of Italy, Frank Costello & Joe Profaci of NYC, John DeMarco & John Scalish of Cleveland, Frank Milano of California.

CRIMINAL HISTORY : FBI #118357. Cleveland PD #32332. Arrests since 1920 include robbery, prohibition act, Internal Revenue Act, suspicion of murder.

BUSINESS : Has an interest in the Thompson- Polizzi Construction Co., Coral Gables, Fla.

MODUS OPERANDI : One of the most influential members of the Mafia in the U.S. Was leader of the Mafia in Cleveland before moving to Fla. Is associated with international narcotic traffickers; and engaged in illicit gambling activities in the Miami area.

NAME   : Joseph PURPURA

ALIASES   : Joe Purpora, Joe Popura

DESCRIPTION   : Born 5-16-1897, Palermo,
                  Sicily, 5'6", 160 lbs, brown
                  eyes, grey hair, wears glass-
                  es, naturalized 11-29-43
                  Chicago, Ill.

LOCALITIES   : Resides 1325 Bird Rd, Coral
FREQUENTED   Gables, Fla. Also has resi-
                  dence in Revere, Mass. Fre-
                  quents all major race tracks
                  in Eastern U.S. and makes
                  trips to Italy.

FAMILY   : Married to Elina Ticina and has one daughter: father:
BACKGROUND   Francesco (dead); mother: Santa Gambero (residing in
                  Palermo).

CRIMINAL   : Philip Buccola, Rocco Palladino, Henry Selvitella,
ASSOCIATES   Frank Cucchiara, Raymond Patriarca, all of Boston
                  area. Salvatore Falcone.

CRIMINAL   : No FBI # assigned. No criminal record known.
HISTORY

BUSINESS   : Horse trainer.

MODUS   : Has trained race horses for Mafia racketeers, now
OPERANDI   training for stable owned ostensibly by his wife.
                  Engaged in crooked race activities.

NAME   : Joseph Vincent RICCIO

ALIASES   : Joseph Giondino

DESCRIPTION   : Born 9-6-08 B'klyn, NY, 5'7",
                  197 lbs, stocky build, black
                  hair-balding, brown eyes,
                  tattoo right arm.

LOCALITIES   : Resides 7900 NE 10 Ave,
FREQUENTED   Miami, Fla. Frequents Riccio's
                  Rest., 991 NE 79th St, & the
                  23rd St, area of Miami Beach.

FAMILY   : Married Ruth Meadow (de-
BACKGROUND   ceased 1957); father: Vincenzo; mother: Maria
                  Cimmaruta; sister: Josephine A.; brothers: Anthony J,
                  & Henry A.

CRIMINAL   : Frank DioGuardi, Charles Tourine, Sr, Salvatore
ASSOCIATES   Falcone, Angersola Brothers, ███████████████.

CRIMINAL   : FBI #285783. Miami PD #31677. Record dating from
HISTORY   1930 includes arrests for rape, vagrancy, grand
                  larceny, operating gambling house, dangerous wea-
                  pon, etc.

BUSINESS   : Is the undisclosed owner of Riccio's Italian-
                  American Rest., 991 NE 79th St, Miami, Fla.

MODUS   : Closely associated with other important Mafia
OPERANDI   figures in the operation of large scale bookmaking
                  and gambling in Miami area.

NAME	: Louis SACCAROMA
ALIASES	: Louis Black, Frank Black, Blackie Saccaroma.

DESCRIPTION	: Born 4-25-1895 N.Y.C. 5'4", 170 lbs, brown eyes, grey hair balding on top, wears glasses.
LOCALITIES FREQUENTED	: Resides 805 NW 109th St., Miami, Fla. Frequents Biscayne Boulevard & 79th St in Miami, and the Esquire Smoke Shop, Miami Beach.
FAMILY BACKGROUND	: Married, wife's name is Rose.
CRIMINAL ASSOCIATES	: Andrew Alberti, Steve Armone, Salvatore Falcone, Mike Coppola, George & John Angersola, Joe Rao, Patsy Erra, Frank Carbo.
CRIMINAL HISTORY	: FBI #252901. NYCPD B# 78226. Arrests since 1916 include robbery, felonious assault, conviction for Federal Narcotic Laws.
BUSINESS	: Has interest in Surf Restaurant, 7417 Collins Ave., Miami Beach; and also in prize fighters.
MODUS OPERANDI	: When living in NYC he was a major narcotic trafficker closely associated with Mafia traffickers. Since moving to Florida he became engaged in illegal gambling, and trying to promote "fixed" boxing matches and horse races; working closely with Mafiosi from the Miami area.

NAME   : William Biaggio SAVARINO

ALIASES   : None

DESCRIPTION   : Born 4-22-06, Houston, Tex.,
                 5'9", 140 lbs, slender build,
                 balding grey-black hair,
                 brown eyes.

LOCALITIES   : Resides 1014 E. North St,
FREQUENTED   Tampa, Fla. Frequents Ybor
                 City area of Tampa, Colum-
                 bia Rest., Lido Bar, Sands
                 Bar.

FAMILY   : Married Adla Alonso.
BACKGROUND

CRIMINAL   : Frank Ippolito, Frank Diecidue, Joseph and █████
ASSOCIATES   ██████████, ██████████.

CRIMINAL   : FBI #139602D. Tampa PD #73525. Record dates from
HISTORY   1958 and includes arrests for lottery & child
                 molestation.

BUSINESS   : Bartender at the Sands Bar, 208 E. Lafayette St,
                 Tampa, Florida.

MODUS   : Savarino is a lesser member of the Tampa Mafia mob
OPERANDI   and is involved with such individuals as Frank
                 Diecidue and Frank Ippolito in the bookmaking and
                 lottery operations in Tampa.

NAME : Joseph SCAGLIONE

ALIASES : None

DESCRIPTION : Born 9-3-1899 Tampa, Fla.,
5'6", 210 lbs, heavy build,
brown eyes, brown hair, balding, medium complexion.

LOCALITIES : Resides at 2101½ 8th Ave,
FREQUENTED   Tampa, Fla. Frequents the
Ybor City area of Tampa, the
Columbia Rest., and the Kom-
In Bar, 1813 21st St, Tampa.

FAMILY : Married Josephine Partanna; brother: Basil Scaglione.
BACKGROUND

CRIMINAL : Primo Lazzara, Frank Diecidue, ███████████████,
ASSOCIATES   Frank Ippolito, and ██████████.

CRIMINAL : FBI #2907967. Tampa S.O. #13753. Record dating from
HISTORY   1932 includes numerous arrests for violation of
lottery laws & violation of liquor laws.

BUSINESS : He is alleged to have silent interest with his brother Basil in the Kom-In Bar, 1813 21st St, Tampa.
His name does not appear on the license for this
establishment because his record makes him inelig-
ible in Tampa to operate a bar.

MODUS : For many years Scaglione was associated with other
OPERANDI   members of the Tampa Mafia mob in large scale bookmaking and lottery activities, however, in recent
yrs, he has broken away from this mob and is believed,
with his brother Basil, to bank lottery operations a-
mong the Spanish speaking elements of Tampa. It is believed Eddie Blanco, a Cuban-American, is his top
Lieutenant.

113

Reportedly a Mafia boss in Tampa from the late 1940s until about 1950. He died in 1964.

NAME : Salvatore SCAGLIONE

ALIASES : None

DESCRIPTION : Born 11-12-1891 Rosario, Santa Fe, Argentina, 5'4", 183 lbs, grey hair, brown eyes. Naturalized Tampa, Fla, 3-6-36.

LOCALITIES FREQUENTED : Resides 2303 10th Ave, Tampa, Fla. Frequents various bars, cafes, etc Yber area, Tampa.

FAMILY BACKGROUND : Wife: Maria; children: Stefano, Tom, Rosina, Onofria (all born Alessandria, Italy); father: Stefano; mother: Rosa Bonanno.

CRIMINAL ASSOCIATES : Santos Trafficante Jr., ███████████, ███████ ████████, Diecidue Brothers, Salvatore Falcone.

CRIMINAL HISTORY : FBI #355220B, Tampa SO #51472. Arrested and tried in county court, Tampa, 1953 in attempted claw-hammer murder of another racketeer, Joseph Castellano.

BUSINESS : Operates Grocery Store.

MODUS OPERANDI : One of the leaders of the Mafia in Tampa.

NAME : Vincent TERIACA

ALIASES : Terry Teriaca

DESCRIPTION : Born 10-5-17 USA, 5'8", 165
lbs, stocky build, brown eyes
black hair.

LOCALITIES : Resides at 10290 E. Bay Har-
FREQUENTED bor Dr, Miami Beach, Florida.
Frequents Dream Bar, Ciro's,
5 O'Clock Club, LaRue Club &
Little Napoli Rest., all
Miami Beach or Miami, Fla.
Formerly frequented midtown
area of New York City.

FAMILY : Wife: Lucille.
BACKGROUND

CRIMINAL : Max Eder, ████████████, Pasquale Erra, John Dio-
ASSOCIATES Guardia, Frank DioGuardio, Freddy Felice, Joe
Riccio, ████████████ and ████████████████.

CRIMINAL : No FBI # assigned. Only record is gambling arrest
HISTORY in New York.

BUSINESS : Manages Dream Bar, Miami Beach, Florida.

MODUS : Operates "Gyp" night clubs in Miami area in
OPERANDI association with other Mafia racketeers.

NAME   : Charles TOURINE, SR.

ALIASES   : Charlie Tourino, Charlie
                  the Blade, Charlie White,
                  Daniels.

DESCRIPTION   : Born 3-19-06 Mattewan, N.J.,
                  5'6", 160 lbs., brown eyes,
                  black grey hair, illiterate.

LOCALITIES   : Resides 9101 E. Bay Harbor
FREQUENTED   Drive, Miami Beach, Fla.,
                  frequents Treasure Isle
                  Motel, Casablanca Hotel,
                  Albion Hotel, Carib Hotel,
                  all in Miami Beach.

FAMILY   : Married to Erena Victoria Pierina Rodriquez (a Cuban)
BACKGROUND   son is Charles Jr. (by 1st wife).

CRIMINAL   : Mike Coppola, Santo Trafficante, Patsy Erra, Meyer
ASSOCIATES   Lansky, Sam Accardi, Angelo DeCarlo, ███████████,
                  Joe Doto, Joe Pici, Mike Miranda.

CRIMINAL   : FBI #695716, Miami Beach PD# A-1783, numerous
HISTORY   arrests since 1933 including murder, holdup, obstruc-
                  ting justice, liquor laws, conspiracy.

BUSINESS   : Believed to have interests in Treasure Isle Motel,
                  Miami, and gambling at the Casablanca Hotel, Miami
                  Beach.

MODUS   : Considered an international narcotic trafficker in
OPERANDI   association with his son Charles Jr., and deportee
                  Joe Pici. Operated gambling establishment in Havana,
                  Cuba, during Batista regime, with other Mafia asso-
                  ciates; suspected of being used as a professional
                  gun-man by Mafia associates in various section of
                  U.S.A.

116

NAME	: Frank Cacciatore TRAFFICANTE
ALIASES	: Francesco Cacciatore Trafficante.
DESCRIPTION	: Born 11-15-14, Tampa, Fla., 5'7½", 220 lbs., brown eyes, brown-grey hair, medium complexion and stocky build.
LOCALITIES FREQUENTED	: Resides at 705 W. Alford St. Tampa, Fla., frequents Colombia Restaurant and various gambling establishments in Ybor City section of Tampa, Florida.

FAMILY BACKGROUND : Wife is named Violet; father was Santo Trafficante Sr. (deceased), mother's name is Maria; has four brothers Santo Jr., Sam, Epifanio and Enrico; also has uncle Epifanio Trafficante residing in San Francisco, Cal.

CRIMINAL ASSOCIATES : ▆▆▆▆, ▆▆▆▆, Sam and Santo ▆▆▆▆▆ Jr., (brothers); the Diecidue Brothers, Salvatore Italiano, Primo Lazzara, ▆▆▆▆▆▆▆, and Augustine Friscia, all of Tampa, Florida.

CRIMINAL HISTORY : FBI # unassigned, Pinellas County, Fla., SO #17993; has record of only one arrest, on 6-5-59 at Clearwater, Fla., for bribery and conspiracy to violate lottery laws.

BUSINESS : Owns produce market at Tampa, Florida.

MODUS OPERANDI : A veteran gambler and bolita operator and a prominent member of the Mafia at Tampa, Florida.

117

He died 3 hours after undergoing a triple-bypass in Houston, TX on March 17, 1987.

NAME : Santo TRAFFICANTE JR.

ALIASES : Louis Santos, Enrique Chacon Samuel Balto, Santos Traficante.

DESCRIPTION : Born 4-16-10 Tampa, Fla., 5'11", 180 lbs., brown eyes, brown-greying hair, wears glasses.

LOCALITIES FREQUENTED : Resides 2505 Bristol Ave., Tampa, Florida, frequented Havana, Cuba, and Miami, Fla.

FAMILY BACKGROUND : Parents: Santo Sr., and Maria Giuseppe; brothers: Frank, Salvatore, Enrico, Epifanio, uncle Joe M. Cacciatore (convicted trafficker).

CRIMINAL ASSOCIATES : Meyer Lansky, Dino Cellini, Diecidue Brothers, Salvatore Italiano, August P. Lazzara, Sam Mannarino, Jack Lansky, Joe Catalanotte.

CRIMINAL HISTORY : FBI #482531 B, Tampa PD# 50366, arrests since 1946 include bribery, bolita, conspiracy (wagering act).

BUSINESS : Has interests in Columbia Restaurant, Nebraska, Tangerine, and Sands Bars all in Tampa; had gambling interests in Sans Souci Hotel Havana, during Batista regime.

MODUS OPERANDI : Attended Apalachin Mafia meeting 1957, representing the Mafia gambling interests in both Tampa and Havana; a leader of the Mafia in Tampa, succeeding his deceased father; is also an international drug trafficker.

He died on May 29, 1991 in Miami Beach from cardiac complications.

NAME : John Pasquale TRONOLONE

ALIASES : Salvatore Tronolone, John Rich, Peanuts

DESCRIPTION : Born 12-12-10, Buffalo, N.Y. 5'10½", 195 lbs., brown eyes brown hair and greying, complexion dark, stout build.

LOCALITIES FREQUENTED : Resides at 8090 Hawthorne Ave., Miami Beach, Fla., frequents the Tahiti Bar, the Carib Hotel and Wofford Hotel, Miami, Fla.

FAMILY BACKGROUND : Marital status unknown, his mother and brother Ceasar reside at Buffalo, N.Y.

CRIMINAL ASSOCIATES : Frank Caruso, Joe Massey, John and George Angersola, Joseph DiCarlo and Fred Felice.

CRIMINAL HISTORY : FBI #370314, Buffalo PD #26713, has arrest record dating to 1925, on such charges as assault, burglary and robbery.

BUSINESS : Manager of the Tahiti Bar, Miami Beach, Fla.

MODUS OPERANDI : Subject is a gambler and bookmaker who acts as an enforcer for the Mafia in the Miami area.

NAME	: Santo VIRUSSO
ALIASES	: Santo Virruso, Philip Sarno, Angelo Lazzia.

DESCRIPTION : Born 11-1-94 Pietraperzia,
Sicily, 5'8½", 155 lbs,
hazel eyes, grey hair, medium build, sallow complexion. Naturalized 11-6-31
Chicago.

LOCALITIES   : Resides Shorecrest Apart-
FREQUENTED   ments, 2750 N. Surf Rd.,
Hollywood, Fla. Frequents
Chicago, Ill., & Miami Beach, Florida, area.

FAMILY   : Wife is Gena Virusso. Has divorced wife Rosaria
BACKGROUND   Arcodijane & 3 daughters, Lucia, Antoinette &
Vincenzina, all residing in Italy. Stepson: Rocco;
mother: Lucia Puzzo; brothers: Michael & Salvatore.

CRIMINAL   : Louis Campagna (deceased), ███████████, █████
ASSOCIATES   ████, ████████, ████████, ████████,
████████████████.

CRIMINAL   : FBI #1032557. Chicago PD#C-71438. Arrests since 1922
HISTORY   include murder (Sicily) and in 1935 & 1945 in the
U.S. also for murder.

BUSINESS   : Owns and operates the Shorecrest Apartments, 2750
N. Surf Road, Hollywood, Fla.

MODUS   : Subject is an influential member of the Mafia in
OPERANDI   both Florida and Illinois.

He served as Al Capone's bodyguard. At the age of 86, on May 27, 1992, he died of congestive heart failure.

NAME : Anthony Joseph ACCARDO

ALIASES : Joe Batters, Tony Accardo

DESCRIPTION : Born 4-28-06, Chicago, Ill., 5'9½", 195 lbs., heavy build dark brown and grey hair, hazel eyes, swarthy complexion.

LOCALITIES FREQUENTED : Resides at 915 Franklin St., River Forest, Ill., frequents Meo's Norwood House, Chicago, Ill., and Pedicones Restaurant, Lyons, Ill.

FAMILY BACKGROUND : Married to Clarice Evelyn Porter and has 3 children, Anthony, Marie and Lindy Lee; sister, Rose, brothers are Martin and John.

CRIMINAL ASSOCIATES : Paul Ricca, Jack Cerone, Murray Humphreys, Sam Giancana, Jack Guzik, Rocco Fischette, James DeGeorge; he knows most of the major racketeers in the U.S.

CRIMINAL HISTORY : FBI #1410106, Chicago PD# D-83436, criminal record dates back to 3-22-22, includes arrests for gambling, carrying a concealed weapon, disorderly conduct and murder investigation.

BUSINESS : He claims to be a salesman for Premium Beer Sales Inc., 2555 W. Armitage Ave., Chicago, Ill.

MODUS OPERANDI : A Mafia leader who controls the major organized racketeering in Chicago and Cook County; former member of old Capone mob.

In 1986, he was convicted of taking profits from Las Vegas casinos and was in prison until 1996. He died of natural causes on February 22, 1997.

NAME : Joseph AIUPPA

ALIASES : Joey O'Brien, James Sprando

DESCRIPTION : Born 12-1-07 Chicago, Ill, 5'7", 185 lbs, black-grey hair, brown eyes, wears glasses.

LOCALITIES FREQUENTED : Resides 4 Yorkshire Drive, Elmhurst, Ill., frequents Turf Club, 22nd & Cicero, Cicero, Ill., a gambling club.

FAMILY BACKGROUND : Married Rosalia Tonari; father: Simone; mother: Rose Greco.

CRIMINAL ASSOCIATES : Anthony Accardo, Robert J. Ansoni, Joseph DiVarco, ████████████████, Giuseppe Glimco.

CRIMINAL HISTORY : FBI #951184. Record dating from 1935 includes arrests for assault to kill, refusal to testify before Senate committee, shipping gambling devices interstate & refusal to register as gambling devices dealer.

BUSINESS : A partner with Robert J. Ansoni & others in Taylor & Co., manufacturers of gambling equipment. One of the directors of Local 450, Bartender's Union Cicero, Illinois.

MODUS OPERANDI : In control of Mafia gambling operations in Cicero area, of Chicago.

He was acting boss of the Chicago Outfit in the late 1960s, before going to jail for extortion. He died in the Marion, IL state prison from natural causes on September 25, 1971.

NAME   : Felix A. ALDERISIO

ALIASES   : Phillip Alderisio,
                "Milwaukee Phil"

DESCRIPTION   : Born 4-26-10 Chicago, Ill.
                5'9½", 189 lbs., hazel eyes,
                brown hair, medium build,
                dark complexion.

LOCALITIES   : Resides 515 Longcommon Rd.,
FREQUENTED   Riverside, Ill. Frequents
                Armory Lounge, Forest Park,
                Ill., and Hickory House,
                Chicago, Ill.

FAMILY   : Married to Molly and they have one son.
BACKGROUND

CRIMINAL   : Tony Accardo, Patrick Russo, ▮▮▮▮▮▮▮▮▮▮,
ASSOCIATES   Albert Frabotta, Sam Giancana, Fiore Buccieri,
                & Marshal Caifano, all of Chicago, Ill.

CRIMINAL   : FBI#1021382. Chicago PD#D-62062. Arrests since
HISTORY   1933 include liquor law violations and auto
                theft.

BUSINESS   : Partner with Albert Frabotta in the ownership
                of the Hickory House, 750 N. Rush St., Chicago,
                Ill.

MODUS   : With Mafia associates is alleged to finance large
OPERANDI   scale narcotic transactions and is reputed to be
                an "enforcer" in the organizations labor activities.

NAME   : Robert J. ANSONI

ALIASES   : Robert J. Ansani, Bobby
                  Taylor.

DESCRIPTION   : Born 1-12-04 Chicago, Ill.,
                  5'9", 160 lbs, has brown eyes
                  and brown hair.

LOCALITIES   : Resides at 3320 Olmstead Rd,
FREQUENTED   Riverside, Ill.

FAMILY   : Wife: Grace.
BACKGROUND

CRIMINAL   : Anthony Accardo, Joseph Aiuppa.
ASSOCIATES

CRIMINAL   : FBI #178416. Record dates from 1922 and includes
HISTORY   arrests for rape, speeding and interstate shipment
                  of gambling devices.

BUSINESS   : A partner with Joseph Aiuppa and others in Taylor
                  and Co., manufacturers of gambling equipment.

MODUS   : One of top Mafiosi controlling syndicated gambling
OPERANDI   in Cicero, Illinois, area.

He was convicted of extortion in 1967 and sent to jail. He was released in 1972 and died from natural causes soon after.

NAME : Samuel BATTAGLIA

ALIASES : Teets, Joe Rock, Sam Rice

DESCRIPTION : Born 11-5-06, Kenosha, Wis.; 5'8", 140 lbs., blue eyes, gray-brown hair, fair complexion and medium build.

LOCALITIES FREQUENTED : Resides at 114 N. Ridgeland Ave., Oak Park, Ill. Frequents the Armory Lounge, Forest Park, Ill.

FAMILY BACKGROUND : Wife, Angela Rose; father, Salvatore; mother, Guiseppa nee Scaletta; sisters, Mary and Sarah; brothers, James, Anthony, Joseph, and August Battaglia.

CRIMINAL ASSOCIATES : Paul DeLucia, Marshal Caifano, Frank Laino, ███████████, █████████, Lewis Fratto and Sam Giancana, all of Chicago, Illinois.

CRIMINAL HISTORY : FBI #320614, Chicago PD #D-20339. Dates from 1924 and includes burglary, larceny, robbery, murder and possession of firearms.

BUSINESS : No legitimate business or employment.

MODUS OPERANDI : An influential member of the Mafia and a dominant figure in the organization's gambling activities on Chicago's west side.

NAME	: Anthony BELLO

ALIASES   : Philip Bacino, Tony Bacino,
                 Tony Cello

DESCRIPTION   : Born 1-4-02 Ribera, Sicily,
                 5'5½", 178 lbs, light brown
                 eyes, black-grey hair.

LOCALITIES   : Resides 14 163rd St, Calumet
FREQUENTED   City, Illinois.

FAMILY   : Married Jennie Bacino.
BACKGROUND

CRIMINAL   : Paul DeLucia, Tony Accardo, of Chicago area; Joe
ASSOCIATES   Profaci, Joe Magliocco, Andrew Lombardino, ███████
                 ███████, Emanuele Cammerata, of NY, NJ, area;
                 Anthony Pinelli, Paul Mirabile, Tony Mirabile (dead),
                 Frank Bompensiero, of Southern Calif., area.

CRIMINAL   : FBI #2020359. Cleveland PD# 32767. Arrests since 1928
HISTORY   include homicide and violation Internal Revenue Laws
                 (liquor).

BUSINESS   : Operates John's Pizzeria, 121 State St, Calumet City,
                 Indiana.

MODUS   : Attended Cleveland Mafia meeting 1928. One of the
OPERANDI   higher ranking Mafia members in the U.S. Controls
                 several large gambling operations in Chicago &
                 Calumet City, Indiana.

NAME : Nathan BIEGLER

ALIASES : Roy Howard, "Moe", "Moey"

DESCRIPTION : Born 8-21-04 NYC, Jewish,
5'7", 140 lbs, slender build,
grey hair (thinning), ruddy
complexion.

LOCALITIES : Resides at Pratt Lane Hotel,
FREQUENTED 1246 Pratt Blvd, Chicago,
Ill. Frequents Lake Side
Tavern, 4675 South Lake Park,
Chicago, Ill.

FAMILY : Married; father: David; mother: Sarah; sisters:
BACKGROUND Betty Biegler, Jane Kalish, Rae Becker; brothers:
Joseph, Reuben, Samuel and William.

CRIMINAL : Moische Taubman, Jacob Klein, ██████████████,
ASSOCIATES ████████████, ████████████.

CRIMINAL : FBI #587489. Chicago PD #D-22718. Since 1932 subject
HISTORY has three previous convictions for violation of the
Federal Narcotic Laws.

BUSINESS : Owns part interest and operates Lake Side Tavern,
4675 South Lake Park, Chicago, Illinois.

MODUS : At one time considered one of the most important
OPERANDI narcotic traffickers in the Midwest. Currently
capable of wholesale narcotic transactions through
previous association with important Italian and
Jewish sources of supply. Is well known to and
trusted by important Mafia members.

NAME   : John Patrick BORCIA

ALIASES   : John Barcy

DESCRIPTION   : Born 4-5-95 Chicago, Ill.
                 5'8", 220 lbs., brown eyes,
                 grey hair, ruddy complexion,
                 stout build.

LOCALITIES   : Resides 958 N. Hamilin Ave.,
FREQUENTED   Chicago, Ill. Frequents
                 Nielsen's Restaurant,
                 Chicago, Ill.

FAMILY   : Married to Lillian.
BACKGROUND

CRIMINAL   : ████████, ██████████, & ████████████, all
ASSOCIATES   of Chicago, Ill.

CRIMINAL   : FBI#519191. Chicago PD#D-15414. Arrests since
HISTORY   1915 include burglary, robbery, larceny, contempt
                 of court, possession of firearms, carrying concealed
                 weapon, assault with weapon, & violation of
                 California State Narcotic Laws.

BUSINESS   : No legitimate business or employment.

MODUS   : With Mafia associates is engaged in labor activities
OPERANDI   in the Chicago area.

```
NAME            : Dominick BRANCATO

ALIASES         : "Nags"

DESCRIPTION     : Born 2-26-06 New Orleans,
                  La., 5'8", 175 lbs, brown
                  eyes, dark brown hair.

LOCALITIES      : Resides at Commonwealth
FREQUENTED        Hotel, Chicago, Ill.  Fre-
                  quents Wrightwood Tavern &
                  Leader Cigar Store, both in
                  Chicago.
```

```
FAMILY          : Father: Dominick; mother:
BACKGROUND        Anna; brother: Cosmo; sister: Antoinette.

CRIMINAL        : Dominick Nuccio, Dominick DeBello, Rocco DeGrazia,
ASSOCIATES        Frank Laino, Sam Giancana, Leonard Calamia, all of
                  Chicago area.

CRIMINAL        : FBI #732118.  Chicago PD# C-26383.  Arrests since
HISTORY           1928 include burglary, suspicion of murder, armed
                  robbery.

BUSINESS        : No legitimate business or employment known.

MODUS           : Operates handbooks on Chicago's near north side;
OPERANDI          collects tribute from other handbook operators,
                  dice games, prostitutes; with Dominick DeBello
                  & Dominick Nuccio he is known as the 3 Doms in
                  Mafia circles in Chicago.  They were enforcers
                  and strong arm men in the old Capone mob.
```

NAME   : Joseph BRUNO

ALIASES   : Joe Giardini, Joe Gardine,
                  Joe Garine.

DESCRIPTION   : Born 11-22-12 Boston, Mass.,
                  5'10", 210 lbs., brown eyes,
                  black hair.

LOCALITIES   : Resided 3540 N. Newcastle,
FREQUENTED   Chicago, Ill. Frequented
                  Pioneer Lounge & Stella
                  Auto Sales, Elmwood Park,
                  Ill. Currently (1959)
                  incarcerated for Federal
                  Narcotic Laws.

FAMILY   : Wife is Mary, has 2 children; brothers: Charles &
BACKGROUND   Salvatore; sister: Josephine; father is dead;
                  mother: Mary Bruno.

CRIMINAL   : Carlo Urbinati, ███████████████, ██████████████,
ASSOCIATES   Patrick J. Russo, all of Chicago area, Vito
                  Genovese of N.Y.C.

CRIMINAL   : FBI#1828913, Chicago PD#35804. Arrests since 1939
HISTORY   include Federal Liquor Laws and 2 convictions for
                  Federal Narcotic Laws.

BUSINESS   : Had interests in Stella Auto Sales (used cars) at
                  7355 W. Grand, Elmwood Park, Ill.

MODUS   : A major narcotic trafficker in the Chicago area
OPERANDI   obtaining his supply from known Mafia traffickers
                  in N.Y.C. Is known to be a strong-arm man.

Caifano died of natural causes in 2003.

NAME : Marshal CAIFANO

ALIASES : John Marshal, Joe Rinaldi, Michael J. Monetti, Marshal Cafano, Joe Russo.

DESCRIPTION : Born 7-19-11 Chicago, Ill. 5'6", 160 lbs., brown eyes, grey-brown hair, medium build, dark complexion.

LOCALITIES FREQUENTED : Resides 415 Aldine St., Apt. 6-D, Chicago, Ill., under name of Monetti. Frequents Armory Lounge, Forest Park, Ill., and various night clubs in area Rush Street, Chicago.

FAMILY BACKGROUND : Married to Sue Darline Vaughan; brother: Leonard "Fat" Caifano (murdered in 1951).

CRIMINAL ASSOCIATES : Tony Accardo, Felix Alderisio, Sam Giancana, Fiore Buccieri, Albert Frabotta, all of Chicago area; Louis T. Dragna of Los Angeles area.

CRIMINAL HISTORY : FBI#552863. Chicago PD#C-30104. Arrests since 1929 include burglary, compounding a felony, larceny.

BUSINESS : No known legitimate business or employment.

MODUS OPERANDI : Associated with other Mafia members in a gambling syndicate operating in Chicago & Las Vegas. Suspected interstate narcotic trafficker and reputed "killer" and "muscle man" for Mafia gambling syndicate.

He was charged with the 1947 murder of Nicholas DeJohn but was later acquitted.

NAME : Leonard CALAMIA

ALIASES : Leonard Calamis, Lenny Green Len Tallone, Leonard Culania

DESCRIPTION : Born 1-11-10, Kansas City, Mo., 5'4", 142 lbs, black hair, blue eyes, fair complexion and small build.

LOCALITIES FREQUENTED : Resides 1119 W. Drummond St, Chicago, Ill., frequents gambling establishments in Ill., and Wisc., when in San Francisco, Calif., frequents the Poodle Dog Restaurant at 1121 Polk Street.

FAMILY BACKGROUND : Wife: Catherine F. Tallone; brother: Joseph; father: Pasquale; mother: Guiseppa Dursa, (now Mrs. Frank Turanello).

CRIMINAL ASSOCIATES : ████████, ████████, Al LaRocca, ████ ████, all of San Francisco, Dominick Nuccio, ████ ████, ████████, ████ ████, all of Chicago.

CRIMINAL HISTORY : FBI #366116, Chicago PD# C35054, arrests include highway robbery, murder and narcotics; is believed to have been the finger man in the assassination of Mike DeJohn at San Francisco, Calif., in 1948.

BUSINESS : No legitimate business known.

MODUS OPERANDI : A professional "killer" for the Mafia and a wholesale dealer of narcotics between Chicago and Calif.

His date of death is unknown.

NAME : Ermino John CAPONE

ALIASES : Arthur Colby, John Martin, John Ermino, Phil Cohen

DESCRIPTION : Born 4-12-04 Brooklyn, NY, 5'10½", 200 lbs, brown eyes, brown-grey hair, (balding on top), wears glasses.

LOCALITIES FREQUENTED : Resides 5423 Hyde Park Blvd, Chicago, Ill. Frequents Trade Winds Bar in Chicago, & spends considerable time at Miami Beach, Florida.

FAMILY BACKGROUND : Lives with a woman named Mary & they have a son Michael; brothers: James Ralph, Matthew, Albert J., & the notorious Al (deceased); sister: Mrs. Mafalda Maritote; father: Gabriel; mother: Theresa Rialo, (both deceased).

CRIMINAL ASSOCIATES : Rocco & Joe Fischetti, Joe Fusco, Sam Giancana, Pat Manno, James Allegretti, Jake Guzik, Murray Humphries, all of Chicago area.

CRIMINAL HISTORY : FBI #282094. Chicago PD# D93525. Arrests since 1922 include investigation & suspicion of robbery.

BUSINESS : Has interests in Steelco Drilling Co., Chicago, Ill., & the Ocean Inn, Miami, Fla.

MODUS OPERANDI : Close associate of leading Mafia members in Chicago area. Is associated with them in illegal gambling operations both in Chicago & Miami.

NAME : Jack CERONE

ALIASES : Jackie

DESCRIPTION : Born 7-7-14 Chicago, Ill.,
5'6½", 195 lbs, brown eyes,
brown hair, dark complexion,
stout build.

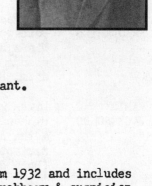

LOCALITIES : Resides 2000 N 77th Ave,
FREQUENTED Elmwood Park, Ill. Frequents
Casa Madrid, Melrose Park,
Illinois.

FAMILY : Father: John; mother: Rose Valant.
BACKGROUND

CRIMINAL : Anthony Accardo, John DeBiase
ASSOCIATES

CRIMINAL : FBI #627727A. Record dates from 1932 and includes
HISTORY arrests for traffic offenses, robbery & suspicion
of a Mafia murder.

BUSINESS : Affiliated with Premium Beer Sales, Incorporated,
Chicago, Ill.

MODUS : Controls beer distribution for the Mafia syndicate
OPERANDI in Chicago through muscle tactics.

He was a loan shark for the Chicago Outfit. He was
sentenced to 15 years imprisonment in May 1966 for
conspiracy to rob a bank. He died of natural causes
in prison on September 9, 1975.

NAME : William DADDANO

ALIASES : William Dado, William Russo,
"Willie Potatoes"

DESCRIPTION : Born 12-28-12 Chicago, Ill.,
5'5", 140 lbs, dark brown
hair (balding), brown eyes,
medium build.

LOCALITIES : Resides 8109 26th St, North
FREQUENTED Riverside, Ill., frequents
Armory Lounge, Forest Park,
Illinois.

FAMILY : Married to Mary and has 5 children; father: Anthony.
BACKGROUND

CRIMINAL : Tony Accardo, Frank La Porte, James Allegretti,
ASSOCIATES Patrick Russo, Joseph Amato, ███████, █████
████.

CRIMINAL : FBI #1922776, Chicago PD# D-30878. Arrests since
HISTORY 1936 include burglary, bank robbery, larceny.

BUSINESS : No known legitimate employment or business known.

MODUS : Has reputation as torturer and murderer. Rapidly
OPERANDI rising in Mafia, believed to be wresting the number
two Chicago Mafia position from Sam Giancana.

NAME   : Rocco DeGRAZIA

ALIASES   : Rocky DeGrasse, "Gramps"

DESCRIPTION   : Born 12-8-97, Melrose Park,
                  Ill.; 5'8", 175 lbs., hazel
                  eyes, grey hair, dark com-
                  plexion and medium build.

LOCALITIES   : Resides at 171 25th Ave.,
FREQUENTED   Melrose Park, Ill. Fre-
                  quents the gambling estab-
                  lishment which he operates
                  on the first floor of the
                  building where he resides.

FAMILY   : Wife is named Margaret. They have no children.
BACKGROUND   His mistress is Etta Fisher and he has one son,
                  Nicky, by her. Brothers are Nick, Joseph, Tony
                  and Andrew DeGrazia, the latter being deceased.

CRIMINAL   : Rocco Fischetti, ████████, Tony Capezio, ██████
ASSOCIATES   ████████, Sam Battaglia, Claude Maddox and Louis
                  Stacy.

CRIMINAL   : FBI #389499, Chicago PD #D-26847. Subject has
HISTORY   a record of nine arrests dating from Dec. 30,
                  1914, on such charges as burglary, larceny,
                  narcotics and income tax evasion with one felony
                  conviction on the latter charge.

BUSINESS   : Owns and operates the Casa Madrid Club, a gambl-
                  ing establishment located at 171 25th Ave.,
                  Melrose Park, Ill.

MODUS   : An influential member of the Mafia in the State
OPERANDI   of Illinois and a director in the organization's
                  gambling activities in the Chicago area.

NAME   : Anthony DE LARDO

ALIASES   : Frank Fish, "Peachy"

DESCRIPTION   : Born 2-17-07 Chicago, Ill.
                   5'8", 165 lbs., grey eyes,
                   grey hair, ruddy complexion,
                   medium build.

LOCALITIES   : Resides 6914 S. Marshfield,
FREQUENTED   Chicago, Ill. Frequents
                   Lewis George's Restaurant &
                   Coletti's Celebrity Inn,
                   both on South Ashland Ave.,
                   Chicago, Ill.

FAMILY   : Wife: Joanne; son: Randall; father: Vito (dead);
BACKGROUND   mother: Sylvia DeLardo is remarried to a man named
                   Fish; half-sister: Anna; half-brothers: James,
                   Floyd, & Frank.

CRIMINAL   : Frank LaPorte, ████████, ████████████████,
ASSOCIATES   ████████████, & ████████████, all of Chicago.

CRIMINAL   : Chicago PD#C-17630. Tried and acquitted for the
HISTORY   gangland murder of Martin (Sunny Boy) Quick. Also
                   tried and acquitted for assault and intent to
                   murder Police Officer James Kelly in June, 1929.
                   Convicted in 1933 of conspiracy to intimidate State's
                   witnesses and sentenced to 8 years imprisonment.

BUSINESS   : Owns sizable block of stock in the Mercury Record
                   Corp., 35 E. Wacker Dr., Chicago, Ill.

MODUS   : With other Mafia members controls gambling in
OPERANDI   Chicago's south side.

> He died of a heart attack on October 11, 1972.

NAME : Felice DeLUCIA

ALIASES : Paul DeLucia, Ricca, Maglio, Viela, Paul the Waiter

DESCRIPTION : Born 7-10-1898, Naples, Italy, 5'8¼", 179 lbs, hazel eyes, grey hair. Denaturalized and currently fighting deportation order.

LOCALITIES FREQUENTED : Resides 1515 Bonnie Brae Place, River Forrest, Ill. Currently (1959) serving 3 yrs Federal prison for income tax evasion.

FAMILY BACKGROUND : Wife: Nancy; son: Paul Jr.; daughter: Mrs. Mary Ponzio; father: Antonio; mother: Maria Annunziata; sisters: Emilia Beatrice, Mrs. Anna Robustelli, Mrs. Clementina Iervolino, Mrs. Luisa Chiaccio.

CRIMINAL ASSOCIATES : Anthony Accardo, Rocco Fischetti, Sam Giancana, Jack Guzik, Charlie English, Eddie Vogel, Sam Hunt, all of Chicago area.

CRIMINAL HISTORY : FBI #832514. Chicago PD# D78267. Arrests since 1943 include extortion, anti-racketeering act, and currently (1959) incarcerated for Federal income tax evasion.

BUSINESS : No legitimate business known.

MODUS OPERANDI : A ranking Mafia member in the Chicago area who has been engaged in illegal gambling, extortion, racketeering of all types.

NAME   : Dominick A. DiBELLA

ALIASES   : Dominic Bello, Dominic
                 DeBella.

DESCRIPTION   : Born 5-10-02 Franklin, La.,
                 5'7", 170 lbs, brown eyes,
                 brown hair, medium build,
                 ruddy complexion.

LOCALITIES   : Resides 918 Wellington Ave.,
FREQUENTED   Chicago, Ill. Frequents the
                 Berkshire Hotel and various
                 night clubs around State &
                 Division Sts in Chicago.

FAMILY   : Wife is named Debra.
BACKGROUND

CRIMINAL   : ▮▮▮▮▮▮▮, Dominick Brancato, Dominick Nuccio,
ASSOCIATES   ▮▮▮▮▮▮▮, Lawrence Mangano, ▮▮▮▮▮▮▮▮▮▮▮,
                 ▮▮▮▮▮▮▮▮▮, all of Chicago area.

CRIMINAL   : FBI # 305340. Chicago PD # 24186. Has a record of
HISTORY   eight arrests since 1923, including auto theft,
                 murder, manslaughter, and carrying concealed
                 weapons.

BUSINESS   : No legitimate business known.

MODUS   : A "strong-arm" type Mafioso and a remnant of the
OPERANDI   old Capone organization. Is very active in illegal
                 gambling activities in Chicago, and is a specialist
                 on shake-down tactics. With Dominick Brancato and
                 Dominick Nuccio he is known as one of the feared
                 and notorious 3 D's.

NAME : Anthony Joseph DICHIARINTE

ALIASES : Tony Dee, Tony "D", Tony
Decca, Tony Dicci, Anthony
DeCharinte, Declarente,
Decharente, Anthony Costello

DESCRIPTION : Born 5-5-18, St. Paul, Minn.
5'10", 200 lbs, hazel eyes,
dark chestnut hair.

LOCALITIES : Resides 6455 Longmeadow Dr.,
FREQUENTED Lincolnwood, Ill. Frequents
Eat-A-Bite Snack Shop, 6001
W Grand Ave., Gateway Bowl-
ing Alleys, 6432 W North Ave, Chicago, Illinois.

FAMILY : Married Margaret DelGuidice; son: Anthony, Jr.;
BACKGROUND daughter: Diane; father: Joseph; mother: Anna
Costello; brothers: Leonard & Frank; sisters:
Felicia Albrecht & Carmelia Pace.

CRIMINAL : ████████████, Salvatore Pisano, ████████████,
ASSOCIATES ████████████, Joseph Vecchio, Carlo Urbanati.

CRIMINAL : FBI #1797682, Chicago PD# C-87471. Dates from 1939
HISTORY with felony convictions for robbery and theft from
interstate shipment. Federal narcotic case pending
1960.

BUSINESS : Owns and operates the A&S Auto Sales Co., 601
W Madison, Oak Park, Illinois.

MODUS : With Mafia associates in Chicago, Ill., and NYC,
OPERANDI NY., is engaged in the interstate traffic in heroin
on a large scale.

Divarco's involvement in the Chicago Outfit was learned of by the FBI through surveillance and informants. He was convicted of RICO Act violations in 1985 and died in prison in 1986.

NAME : Joseph DIVARCO

ALIASES : Joey Caesar

DESCRIPTION : Born 12-17-10 Chicago, Ill, 5'5½", 170 lbs, dark chestnut hair, brown eyes, olive complexion, medium-stout build.

LOCALITIES : Resides 4275 Jarvis, Lincoln-
FREQUENTED wood, Ill, frequents the Snack Bar, 1220 N. Clark St, Chicago, & the Sunshine Restaurant, Niles, Illinois.

FAMILY : Wife,Pat; father: Salvatore; mother: Virginia
BACKGROUND LaSchulter.

CRIMINAL : Anthony Accardo, James Allegretti, Dominick DeBello,
ASSOCIATES all of Chicago, and Joseph Sica of Los Angeles.

CRIMINAL : FBI #1095466, Chicago PD #E33232. Record dates back
HISTORY to 1937 conviction for counterfeiting.

BUSINESS : Owns and controls glassware and glasswasher distributorship, 405 N. State Street,Chicago.

MODUS : One of the top Mafiosi on Chicago's North Side, con-
OPERANDI trolling night club & restaurant operations through muscle tactics.

> He was friends with Frank Sinatra. He died of a heart
> attack in New York in 1964. He was 60 years old.

NAME : Rocco FISCHETTI

ALIASES : Ralph Fisher, John Senna,
Charles Miller, Rocco Senna,
Rocco Fischette.

DESCRIPTION : Born 3-17-04 NYC, 5'11", 175
lbs, medium build, grey hair,
hazel eyes, wears glasses,
ruddy complexion.

LOCALITIES : Resides 3100 Sheridan Rd,
FREQUENTED Chicago and/or 9356 Forest
View, Evanston, Ill. Fre-
quents Singapore Barbecue,
1011 N. Rush St., Chicago, Illinois.

FAMILY : Lived with sister-in-law Dorothy Fagen; father:
BACKGROUND Nicola; mother: Mary; brothers: Nicholas, Joseph,
Charles (deceased).

CRIMINAL : Anthony Accardo, Frank Costello, Joseph Fischetti
ASSOCIATES (brother), Meyer Lansky, Jake Guzik, Paul DeLucia.

CRIMINAL : FBI #3854015. Record dating from 1943 includes
HISTORY arrests for conspiracy, refusal to testify and
gambling.

BUSINESS : Believed to have silent interest in Vernon Club,
Lake County, Illinois.

MODUS : For a number of years was chief of gambling oper-
OPERANDI ations for the Mafia in Chicago area. One of top
six Mafiosi in Chicago.

He left the world of organized crime after Prohibition
and died on December 5, 1976 in Chicago.

NAME   : Joseph Charles FUSCO

ALIASES   : Joe Fusco, Joe Carey

DESCRIPTION : Born 5-6-02 Chicago, Ill.
               5'10 3/4", 213 lbs., brown
               eyes, grey hair, stout build,
               dark complexion.

LOCALITIES   : Resides 8011 Loomis St.,
FREQUENTED   Chicago, Ill. Frequents
               Merit Liquor Co., Kusper
               Liquor Co., Fort Dearborn
               Wholesale Liquors, and
               Casey & Evans Wholesale
               Liquors, all of Chicago, Ill.

FAMILY   : Marital status unknown; father: Charles; mother:
BACKGROUND   Josephine; sister: Josephine.

CRIMINAL   : ████████, Joseph Fischetti, Tony Accardo, Jack
ASSOCIATES   Guzick & Murray Humphreys, all of Chicago, Ill.

CRIMINAL   : FBI#854516. Chicago Crime Commission reports that
HISTORY   subject's criminal records disappeared from the
               files of the Chicago Police Dept. in the late
               thirties. Is known to have had at least two con-
               victions for violation of the National Prohibition
               Act while affiliated with the Capone Syndicate
               during the Prohibition Era.

BUSINESS   : President of Merit Liquor Co., 372 W. Ontario St.,
               Chicago, Ill. During 1959 has taken over control
               of Kusper Liquor Co., Fort Dearborn Wholesale
               Liquors, and the Casey & Evans Wholesale Liquors,
               all of which are now located at 36th & Racine Sts.,
               Chicago, Ill.

MODUS   : An influential member of the Mafia at Chicago, Ill.
OPERANDI

He earned enemies in the outfit for not sharing pay and being too high profile and was living in exile in Mexico. Upon returning to the U.S., he was shot in the back of the head in the basement of his home on June 19, 1975. After falling over, he was shot 6 more times in the face.

NAME : Sam GIANCANA

ALIASES : Sam Mooney, Sam Malone

DESCRIPTION : Born 7-16-08, Chicago, Ill.; 5'9", 175 lbs., hazel eyes, dark chestnut hair, fair complexion and medium build.

LOCALITIES FREQUENTED : Resides at 1147 Wenonah Ave. Oak Park, Ill. Frequents the Army Lounge, Norwood House, Villa Venice, all of Chicago, Illinois.

FAMILY BACKGROUND : Wife, Angeline DeTolve, died in 1954. Has three daughters, Annette, Bonita Lou and Francine. Mother deceased, father is Tony Giancana, and sisters are Mary, Josephine and Victoria. Sam's consort is Ladana Collins, 20 E. Delaware, Chicago, Illinois.

CRIMINAL ASSOCIATES : Tony Accardo, ███████, ████████, ████ ████████, Sam Battaglia and Leonard Gianola, all of Chicago, Illinois.

CRIMINAL HISTORY : FBI #58437, Chicago PD #E-27465. Subject has record of 13 arrests dating from Sept. 1925, on such charges as murder, grand larceny, auto theft, burglary and liquor law violations with two felony convictions.

BUSINESS : Owns the Forest Lounge, the R & S Liquor Co., the Lohmar Dist. Co., Chicago, Ill., and has gambling interests and an interest in the shrimp business in Cuba.

MODUS OPERANDI : A top ranking member of the Mafia in the State of Ill. and a director of the organization's activities in Chicago and vicinity.

NAME	: George GINNONE
ALIASES	: Gennone, Giannone, Gregorio Iannone
DESCRIPTION	: Born 7-12-04 Staletti, Catanzaro, Calabria, Italy, 182 lbs, black hair, brown eyes, stocky build, scar on left cheek. Naturalized Chicago 3-2-31.
LOCALITIES FREQUENTED	: Resides 3250 W Palmer, Chicago, Ill.

FAMILY BACKGROUND	: Divorced from wife. Has daughter living at 5355 W. Iowa, Chicago; father: Camizo; mother: Mary.
CRIMINAL ASSOCIATES	: Solly Pisano, Danny Princippi, Anthony Castaldi.
CRIMINAL HISTORY	: FBI #1359607. Cicero, Ill, PD#2548. Convicted violation Federal liquor laws in 1943. Convicted violation Federal narcotic laws in 1951, received consecutive five year sentences on two counts, paroled 1-18-58. On parole until 6-19-61.
BUSINESS	: Glass cutter.
MODUS OPERANDI	: Middle echelon Mafioso who formerly operated illicit stills on Chicago's west side. More recently he has been associated with Solly Pisano in wholesale distribution of narcotic drugs.

NAME   : Giuseppe Paul GLIMCO

ALIASES   : Joey Glimco, Joseph Glielmo,
                 John Murray, Giuseppe
                 Primavera.

DESCRIPTION   : Born 1-14-09, Campagna,
                 Salerno, Italy, 5'6", 175 lbs
                 brown eyes, grey hair, nat-
                 uralized 6-23-43, Chicago,
                 Illinois.

LOCALITIES   : Resides 628 Selbourne Rd,
FREQUENTED   Riverside, Ill. Frequents
                 Esquire Lounge, Melrose Park,
                 Ill, also the Fulton St, Market section of Chicago.

FAMILY   : Wife: Lena; son: Joseph Jr.; daughter: Joan; father:
BACKGROUND   Vito; mother: Paulina Primavera, (deceased); bro-
                 thers: Anthony, Frank, James, Carl & John, Jr., all
                 of Chicago; sister: Mrs. Rose Plescia, Chicago;
                 paramour: Laverne Murray.

CRIMINAL   : Anthony Accardo, Frank LaPorte, William Daddano,
ASSOCIATES   ███████████████, ███████████, ████████████,
                 ███████████.

CRIMINAL   : FBI #233623. Numerous arrests ranging from disorderly
HISTORY   conduct to murder with no convictions. Efforts to
                 deport him for falsifying naturalization application
                 so far unsuccessful.

BUSINESS   : President of Local 777, Chicago Taxi Driver's Union
                 and also affiliated with Automatic Phonograph Dis-
                 tributing Co., at 806 Milwaukee Ave, Chicago, Ill.

MODUS   : A top Mafia syndicate figure in Chicago who has
OPERANDI   used muscle tactics to hold control in labor & juke
                 box racketeering.

146

NAME   : Vito IMPASTATO

ALIASES   : Vito Impostato, Joe Orlando,
                  Vito Impasitato

DESCRIPTION   : Born 6-26-1904, Cinisi,
                  Palermo, Sicily, Italy.
                  5'8", 140 lbs, black-grey
                  hair, brown eyes, natural-
                  ized Springfield, Ill. 9-11-45.

LOCALITIES   : Resides 1940 Wiggins Avenue,
FREQUENTED   Springfield, Ill. Frequents
                  Supper Club, Springfield, Ill.

FAMILY   : Married Edith Jannazzo; son: Faro Vito; daughter:
BACKGROUND   Lena Kathryn; father: Faro; mother: Katrina Orlando;
                  brothers: Jack (Springfield) & Pietro (Cinisi, Italy);
                  mistress: Margaret Henry.

CRIMINAL   : Frank Zito,
ASSOCIATES

CRIMINAL   : FBI #100248   Springfield, Ill. PD #4493
HISTORY   Record dating from 1926 includes arrests for kid-
                  napping, robbery and murder.

BUSINESS   : Owns Supper Club, 2641 So. 6th St., Springfield,
                  Ill., in partnership with his mistress, Margaret
                  Henry.

MODUS   : Powerful Mafia figure in Springfield area, having
OPERANDI   gained his position through operating as a strong-
                  arm man and killer for Frank Zito (1957 Apalachin
                  Mafia meeting delegate) during the 1930's & 40's.
                  His club is a rendezvous for local and out-of-state
                  racketeers.

NAME	: Jacob KLEIN

ALIASES : Jake Klein, Joe Gold, Jack Klein.

DESCRIPTION : Born 6-6-03 B'klyn, NY, Jewish, 5'5", 190 lbs, balding, grey hair on sides, heavy build, brown eyes.

LOCALITIES FREQUENTED : Resides 1128 Pratt Boulevard, Chicago, Ill. Frequents Flamingo Motel, Wheeling, Ill, Joy Auto Mart, 1220 N. Cicero Ave, Chicago, Ill. Also frequents Sheridan Bar & Rest., Sheridan Rd, and Irving Park, Chicago, Illinois.

FAMILY BACKGROUND : Married; father: Louis; sister: Mrs. (Nettie) Ann Landon; sister-in-law: Miss Ruth E. Neilson.

CRIMINAL ASSOCIATES : Moische Taubman, Nathan Biegler (cousin), ████ █████, ██████████, Isadore Cohen, Sam Seritella, ██████████████████ and ████████████.

CRIMINAL HISTORY : FBI # 554296. Record dating from 1931 consists of convictions of Federal prohibition & narcotic laws.

BUSINESS : Part interests in the Flamingo Motel, Wheeling, Ill, and the Lake Side Tavern, 4675 South Lake Park, Chicago, Illinois.

MODUS OPERANDI : An associate of wholesale narcotic traffickers including important Mafia racketeers, in NYC, Chicago. Through contacts capable of providing illicit narcotics in kilogram lots.

NAME : Frank J. LAINO

ALIASES : Al Brown, Albert Bruno

DESCRIPTION : Born 11-16-08, Chicago, Ill,
5'10", 244 lbs., dark hair,
Hazel eyes, heavy build and
ruddy complexion.

LOCALITIES : Resides 4649 West Lexington
FREQUENTED   St., Chicago, Ill., frequents "Gardens Tavern" and
other drinking establish-
ments in Melrose Park, Ill.

FAMILY : Father: Joe Laino, mother: Rose Laino nee LaMonda,
BACKGROUND   both deceased; half brother, Joe Lobes, Sister,
Isabelle Scardin, both of Chicago, Illinois.

CRIMINAL : Rocco De Grazia, Patrick Russo, Frank Santore,
ASSOCIATES   ▓▓▓▓▓▓▓▓, ▓▓▓▓▓▓▓▓, ▓▓▓▓▓▓▓▓,
▓▓▓▓▓▓▓▓, ▓▓▓▓▓▓▓▓, William Daddano.

CRIMINAL : FBI 256733, Chicago PD# C-20378, arrested Pontiac
HISTORY   Mich., 1925 for grand larceny, sentenced 1 to 10
years; numerous arrests on such charges as assault,
murder and investigation.

BUSINESS : A bartender.

MODUS : Distributor of heroin for Rocco De Grazia and other
OPERANDI   Mafia associates; has been considered a strong arm
man.

NAME	: Daniel E. LARDINO
ALIASES	: Dan
DESCRIPTION	: Born 10-24-14, Chicago, Ill, 6'0", 155 lbs, slim build, dark chestnut hair, hazel eyes, medium complexion.
LOCALITIES FREQUENTED	: Resides at 2853 W Congress St, Chicago, Ill.
FAMILY BACKGROUND	: Wife: Joanne; father: Joseph; mother: Anna Tishman; brother: John (also labor racketeer).
CRIMINAL ASSOCIATES	: Anthony Accardo, John Russo, ██████████, Joseph Aiuppa, ██████████.
CRIMINAL HISTORY	: FBI #4145696. Record dates from 1943 and includes arrests for burglary, malicious mischief, drunken driving and disorderly conduct.
BUSINESS	: Business agent for local 593, Hotel and Apartment Employees Union.
MODUS OPERANDI	: Mafia labor racketeer who employs muscle tactics against druggists and hotels on Chicago's North Side.

NAME	: John LARDINO
ALIASES	: Joseph Largino, Edward Nardi
DESCRIPTION	: Born 2-27-07 Chicago, Ill, 5'10½", 190 lbs, blue eyes, dark brown-grey hair.
LOCALITIES FREQUENTED	: Resides 1201 Belleporte, Oak Park, Ill, also believed to own residence at 901 N. Hamlin, Chicago.
FAMILY BACKGROUND	: Wife: Angela; father: Joseph; mother: Anna Tishman; brother: Daniel Lardino, another labor racketeer.
CRIMINAL ASSOCIATES	: Anthony Accardo, ███████████, Jack Cerone, Joseph Glielmo, Salvatore Battaglia.
CRIMINAL HISTORY	: FBI #994524. Record dates from 1927 & includes arrests for robbery & investigation.
BUSINESS	: Business Agent for Local 593, Hotel & Apartment Employees Union, a Capone syndicate dominated Union.
MODUS OPERANDI	: Mafia labor racketeer and strong arm man.

NAME	: Filippo Joseph MORREALE
ALIASES	: Philip Morreale.
DESCRIPTION	: Born 2-27-13 Chicago, Ill. 5'8½", 165 lbs, hazel eyes, dark brown hair, medium build, dark complexion.
LOCALITIES FREQUENTED	: Resides 2901 West Congress Ave., Chicago, Illinois. Frequents 455 W. Evergreen Ave., & 451 W. Oak St., both in Chicago, Ill.

FAMILY BACKGROUND	: Married to Frances Presto, father is Vincenzo, mother is Rose Carramusa.
CRIMINAL ASSOCIATES	: ████████████, ████████████, ████████████, ████████████, all of Chicago area.
CRIMINAL HISTORY	: FBI # 103509A. Chicago PD # C-39295. Arrests from 1930 include robbery, auto theft, contributing to the delinquency of a minor. In July 1945 he was questioned as a suspect in the murder of his cousin, Carl Carramusa.
BUSINESS	: Owns and operates P.J. Morreale Home Appliances, 3742 West Chicago Ave., Chicago, Ill.
MODUS OPERANDI	: Is closely associated with members of the Mafia in the Chicago area.

NAME	: Dominick NUCCIO

ALIASES : Joe Delano, Little Libby, Ercoli Liberatori.

DESCRIPTION : Born 4-9-1895 Chicago, Ill. 5'4½", 135 lbs, brown eyes, black-grey hair, has three small moles on right cheek.

LOCALITIES FREQUENTED : Resides 602 North Park Hotel Chicago, Ill. Frequents the "Loop" area and near north side in Chicago.

FAMILY BACKGROUND : Wife's name is Inez; son: Philip Joseph; other son Dominick Jr deceased; father: Filippo; mother: Maria Calata (both deceased).

CRIMINAL ASSOCIATES : Dominick DeBello, Dominick Brancato, Tony Accardo, Rocco Fischetti, Rocco DeGrazia, Sam Giacana, Leonard Calamia, ███████████, all of Chicago.

CRIMINAL HISTORY : FBI# 559718. Chicago PD #D-15232. Arrests since 1918 include burglary, assault to murder, murder, Internal Revenue Laws.

BUSINESS : No known legitimate business or employment; formerly operated a tavern.

MODUS OPERANDI : Engaged in handbook operations on Chicago's near north side. A member of the old Capone mob. Is one of the more important members of the Mafia in the Chicago area. Dominick Nuccio, Dominick Brancato & Dominick DeBello are known as the 3 Doms among the Chicago Mafia and are considered "enforcers" and "strong-arm" men.

NAME   : Frank Joseph PANATERA

ALIASES   : None

DESCRIPTION   : Born 8-24-26, Chicago, Ill.;
                 5'8", 200 lbs., brown eyes,
                 black hair, dark complexion
                 and stocky build.

LOCALITIES   : Resides at 2956 S. Wallace
FREQUENTED   St., Chicago, Ill. Fre-
                 quents Phil's Tavern, Spot-
                 lite Tavern, Silver Bar
                 Club, and Ciro's Cocktail
                 Lounge, Chicago, Illinois.

FAMILY   : Wife is named Ann; father is Phillip and mother is
BACKGROUND   Loretta, all residing at 2956 S. Wallace St.,
                 Chicago, Illinois.

CRIMINAL   : ███████████, ████████████, Jack Rizzo, ███████
ASSOCIATES   ████████, ████████████████, ████████████████,
                 Joseph DiCarlo and ████████████████████, all of
                 Chicago, Illinois.

CRIMINAL   : FBI #301396B, Chicago PD #E-458. Arrest record
HISTORY   dates from 1952 and includes conviction for vio-
                 lation of the Federal Narcotic Laws.

BUSINESS   : Employed as a bartender at Phil's Tavern (owned
                 by his sister) at 2958 S. Wallace St., Chicago, Ill.

MODUS   : With Mafia associates is engaged in the wholesale
OPERANDI   distribution of heroin in Chicago, Illinois.

```
NAME            : Grace PINE

ALIASES         : None

DESCRIPTION     : Born 7-24-08, Chicago, Ill.,
                  White-female, 5'4", 130 lbs,
                  black-grey hair, brown eyes,
                  medium complexion, medium
                  build.

LOCALITIES      : Resides 2130 North Lincoln
FREQUENTED        Park West, Chicago, Ill.

FAMILY          : Former husband: Mike Condic;
BACKGROUND        daughter: Mrs. Delight
                  Mitchell Marko; grandson: Michael Mitchell; father:
                  Jack Pine; mother: Elizabeth: sisters: Cecil Sweeney
                  and Adeline Pine.

CRIMINAL        : Joseph Bruno, ███████████████ and ███████████
ASSOCIATES        ██████████.

CRIMINAL        : None
HISTORY

BUSINESS        : Owns and operates Drexel Drug Company, 4300 S.
                  Drexel Ave, Chicago, Illinois.

MODUS           : Close friend of Joseph Bruno and alleged to
OPERANDI          have his narcotic connections in Montreal, Canada.
                  Knows most of the important hoodlums and racketeers
                  in the Chicago area and works in close conjunction
                  with Mafia racketeers in both bookmaking and narcotic
                  trafficking.
```

NAME : Salvatore PISANO

ALIASES : Sol, Solly, Solly one eye, Salvatore Pagano

DESCRIPTION : Born 11-13-06 Chicago, Ill, 5'3½", 325 lbs, obese, brown hair, brown eyes, dark complexion, artificial left eye.

LOCALITIES FREQUENTED : Resides 5417 West Jackson St., Chicago, Ill., frequents Eat-A-Bite Grill at 6001 West Grand Ave., Chicago, Illinois.

FAMILY BACKGROUND : Single; father: Louis (deceased); mother: Mary; brother: Ralph (deceased); sisters: Theresa Dinicao and Agnes Pisano.

CRIMINAL ASSOCIATES : ██████████, Anthony Dichiarinte, George Ginnone, ██████████, ██████████, ██████████, ██████████, ██████████.

CRIMINAL HISTORY : FBI #765916, Chicago PD# C56886, arrested 1933 for burglary, numerous subsequent arrests on various charges; three convictions for violation of narcotic laws, Federal narcotic case pending 1960.

BUSINESS : Operates fruit store, 4660 So. Pulaski, Chicago, Illinois.

MODUS OPERANDI : With Mafia associates is engaged in the interstate narcotic traffic.

NAME : James POLICHERI

ALIASES : Monk, James Allegretti,
James Millo

DESCRIPTION : Born 5-31-05 Oliveto Citra,
Salerno, Italy, 5'8½", 180
lbs, grey hair, brown eyes,
ruddy complexion, stout build
diabetic. Resident Alien
I&NS #A-5551562.

LOCALITIES : Resides 21 East Cedar St,
FREQUENTED Chicago. Frequents Berkshire
Hotel, Chicago, and Sunshine
Restaurant, Niles, Illinois.

FAMILY : Married Florence Ramsey; father: Dominic; mother:
BACKGROUND Lucia Reo; brothers: Anthony & Benny; sisters: Susie,
Mary, Dora; step-sister: Lucille Calabrese.

CRIMINAL : Paul Ricca, William Daddano, Frank LaPorte, Joseph
ASSOCIATES DiVarco, John Capone, ████████████████, Joseph Amato,
all of Chicago, and Joe Sica of Los Angeles, Calif.

CRIMINAL : FBI #1500264. Record dating from 1934 includes
HISTORY arrests for counterfeiting and violation National
Prohibition Act.

BUSINESS : Owns Ciro's Night Club, 816 N. Rush St., Chicago,
and is believed to own several other night clubs
in Chicago. Secret partner in Las Vegas gambling
casinos.

MODUS : A Mafia "bag-man" for bookmaker collections and
OPERANDI policy pay-offs. Also fronts for the Mafia in the
operation of Chicago taverns.

NAME   : Jack RIZZO

ALIASES   : None

DESCRIPTION   : Born 9-18-23, Chicago, Ill.;
                5'10", 175 lbs., brown eyes,
                black hair, swarthy complex-
                ion and medium build.

LOCALITIES   : Resides at 2748 W. Belmont,
FREQUENTED   Chicago, Ill. Frequents
                Kelly's Lounge, Racine and
                Wilson Sts.; Harry's New
                Yorker Bar, 900 Rush St.;
                The Fountainebleau Tavern,
                624 W. Division St.; and the Spotlight Tap Room,
                3113 N. Broadway Ave., all of Chicago, Illinois.

FAMILY   : Marital status, single.
BACKGROUND

CRIMINAL   : Patrick Russo, ███████████, ███████████,
ASSOCIATES   ███████████ and Frank Panatera, all of Chicago,
                Ill.; and Frank Pasqua of New York City, N.Y.

CRIMINAL   : FBI #281857B. This subject has a record of one
HISTORY   felony conviction for violation of the Federal
                Narcotic Laws.

BUSINESS   : Reportedly owns an interest in Kelly's Lounge,
                The Fountainebleau Tavern and Harry's New Yorker
                Bar, all of Chicago, Illinois.

MODUS   : With Mafia associates is engaged in the wholesale
OPERANDI   distribution of heroin in Chicago, Illinois.

NAME   : James V. RUSSO

ALIASES   : Jimmie, Tony Russo

DESCRIPTION : Born 3-12-15, Chicago, Ill.;
               5'4", 174 lbs., brown eyes,
               gray-black hair, walks with
               limp in left leg, complex-
               ion ruddy and build stout.

LOCALITIES   : Resides at 249 W. 24th St.,
FREQUENTED   Chicago, Ill. Frequents
               Cermack and Wentworth Ave.,
               and Chinatown, both in
               Chicago, Illinois.

FAMILY   : Marital status unknown. Brother, Joseph Russo,
BACKGROUND   resides at 2522 S. Lowe St., Chicago, Illinois.

CRIMINAL   : Sam Serritella, ███████████████, ███████████████,
ASSOCIATES   ███████████, ███████████ and ███████████,
               all of Chicago, Illinois.

CRIMINAL   : FBI #3811016, Chicago PD #D-74854. Arrest re-
HISTORY   cord dates from 1938 and includes disorderly con-
               duct, robbery, violation of liquor laws, and
               violation of the Federal Narcotic Laws with felony
               convictions on both of the latter charges.

BUSINESS   : No legitimate business known.

MODUS   : Associated with other Mafia members in the whole-
OPERANDI   sale distribution of narcotics in Chicago's South
               Side.

NAME	: Patrick RUSSO
ALIASES	: Patsy, Buck, John Romano, Pasquale Russo
DESCRIPTION	: Born 5-17-04 Chicago, Ill, 5'9", 255 lbs, brown-grey hair, hazel eyes, dark olive complexion, alleged diabetic, two fingers on right hand partially paralyzed.
LOCALITIES FREQUENTED	: Resides 435 Wrightwood, Chicago, Ill. Frequents the Hub Lounge, 512 W. Diversey.
FAMILY BACKGROUND	: Father: Anthony; mother: Anna; brothers: Victor, Richard, Rocco, Carmen; sister: Genevieve.
CRIMINAL ASSOCIATES	: Joe Bruno, Jack Rizzo, Frank Panatera, William Daddano and other top Chicago hoodlums, John Ormento of NYC.
CRIMINAL HISTORY	: FBI #690068, Chicago PD #C- 50547. Record dates from 1924 and includes arrests for larceny, robbery and violation of the narcotic laws.
BUSINESS	: Owner and operator of the Hub Lounge, 512 West Diversey, Chicago.
MODUS OPERANDI	: Wholesale narcotic trafficker supplying heroin to the interstate traffic and locally in Chicago. Has sources of supply for pure heroin among NYC Mafiosi.

160

NAME   : Frank SANTORE

ALIAS   : Ozzie

DESCRIPTION : Born 1-23-15, Melrose Park,
                Ill.; 5'9", 162 lbs., brown
                eyes, dark brown hair,
                swarthy complexion and
                medium build.

LOCALITIES : Resides at 7508 W. Harrison
FREQUENTED   St., Forest Park, Ill. Fre-
                quents the Casa Madrid and
                Lumber Gardens, both in
                Melrose Park, Illinois.

FAMILY   : Marital status unknown. Brothers, Anthony, John
BACKGROUND   and Victor Santore, all reside in Melrose Park,
                Ill. A brother Patrick and sister Marion both
                reside in Forest Park, Ill. Another brother,
                Peter, lives in Chicago, Illinois.

CRIMINAL   : ██████████████ (brother), Rocco DeGrazia, Patrick
ASSOCIATES   Russo, and ██████████████████, all of Chicago, Ill.

CRIMINAL   : FBI #731130A. Dates from 1951 and includes arrests
HISTORY   for violation of the Federal Narcotic Laws.

BUSINESS   : No legitimate business known.

MODUS   : With Mafia associates is engaged as a wholesale
OPERANDI   distributor and interstate trafficker in narcotic
                drugs.

NAME   : Sam SERRITELLA

ALIASES   : Zupie, Tony

DESCRIPTION   : Born 7-21-22, Chicago, Ill.;
                6'0", 190 lbs., brown eyes,
                black hair, dark complexion
                and medium build.

LOCALITIES   : Currently serving a ten year
FREQUENTED   sentence for violation of
                the Federal Narcotic laws.
                Formerly frequented 22nd
                and Wentworth Ave., and
                Curley's Tavern, Canal and
                Cermack Road, both in Chicago, Ill.

FAMILY   : Wife is Jean Serritella, nee Larson, residing at
BACKGROUND   2803 Lexington Dr., Hazelcrest, Ill. Mother,
                Antonia and father, Vito reside at 2918 Prince-
                ton, Chicago, Ill., with sister Ruth and a brother
                Frank. Another brother, Daniel, resides at 2716
                Princeton, Chicago, Illinois.

CRIMINAL   : James V. Russo, ██████████████, ████████████,
ASSOCIATES   ██████████████, ████████████████, all
                of Chicago, Ill., and ████████████ of N.Y.C., N.Y.

CRIMINAL   : FBI #2677927, Chicago PD #D-57540. Dates from
HISTORY   1942 and includes convictions for violations of
                liquor laws and the Federal Narcotic Laws.

BUSINESS   : No legitimate business known.

MODUS   : With Mafia associates was engaged in the local
OPERANDI   wholesale distribution and the interstate traffic
                in heroin on a large scale.

162

NAME   : Michael SPRANZA

ALIASES   : Mike Kelly, Mike Raymond,
                  Michael Spranze, Mike Sprange

DESCRIPTION   : Born 3-3-05 Chicago, Ill,
                  5'8", 210 lbs, brown eyes,
                  black hair, stout build,
                  ruddy complexion.

LOCALITIES   : Resides 1317 W. Monroe Ave,
FREQUENTED   River Forest, Illinois.

FAMILY   : Wife: Sophia; father: Michael;
BACKGROUND   mother: Helen.

CRIMINAL   : Anthony Accardo, Sam Hunt, John Russo, ▮▮▮▮
ASSOCIATES   ▮▮▮▮▮▮▮, ▮▮▮▮▮▮▮▮▮▮▮, Claude Maddox, Ralph Pierce,
                  John Lardino.

CRIMINAL   : FBI #145661, Chicago PD #C91203. Picked up twice by
HISTORY   the Chicago PD for investigation. No other known
                  arrests.

BUSINESS   : Owns Gould Coal Co., in partnership with John
                  Lardino.

MODUS   : Old time Capone mobster and Mafia racketeer. Be-
OPERANDI   cause of ill health has curtailed his active
                  participation in Mafia affairs.

NAME   : Michael Andrew STASI

ALIASES   : Sam Mareno, Mike Stacey

DESCRIPTION   : Born 8-1-04 Chicago, Ill.,
                  5'5", 150 lbs., brown eyes,
                  grey hair, medium complexion
                  and medium build.

LOCALITIES   : Resides 1319 N. 14th St.,
FREQUENTED   Melrose Park, Ill., also
                  maintains residence at Miami.
                  Florida.

FAMILY   : His wife Maria Stasi, from
BACKGROUND   whom he is separated resides
                  at 117 N. 14th St., Melrose Park, Ill., has three
                  children, Lois Ann and Rose Marie Stasi and a son
                  who uses the name Sam Mareno Jr.

CRIMINAL   : Rocco De Grazia, Salvatore Pisano, George Ginnone
ASSOCIATES   and Joe Bruno, all of Chicago, Illinois.

CRIMINAL   : FBI #4558587, Detroit PD# 33968, arrest record dates
HISTORY   to 1928 on such charges as narcotics and armed
                  robbery.

BUSINESS   : No legitimate business or occupation.

MODUS   : Associated with other Mafia members in bookmaking,
OPERANDI   gambling and the interstate traffic in narcotics.

NAME	: Carlo URBINATI
ALIASES	: Bananas, Joe Bananas
DESCRIPTION	: Born 1-21-17, Chicago, Ill., 5'11", 175 lbs., hazel eyes, black-graying hair, olive complexion and medium build.
LOCALITIES FREQUENTED	: Currently serving five year sentence at U.S. Penitentiary, Leavenworth, Kan., for violation of Narcotic Laws. Resided at 2930 Montclaire Ave., Melrose Park, Ill. Frequented the Pioneer Lounge in Melrose Park, Ill.
FAMILY BACKGROUND	: Wife, Grace English Urbinati is a sister of the notorious Charles Carmen English, juke box racketeer and close associate of Tony Accardo.
CRIMINAL ASSOCIATES	: Joe Bruno, ███████, ███████████ and Patrick Russo, all of Chicago, Ill., and Vito Genovese of New York City, New York.
CRIMINAL HISTORY	: FBI #1065767, Chicago PD #C-69016. Arrest record dates from 1935 and includes grand larceny, hijacking, liquor, assaulting Federal officer and violation of the Federal Narcotic Laws with two felony convictions.
BUSINESS	: No legitimate business.
MODUS OPERANDI	: With Mafia associates was engaged in the wholesale interstate traffic in narcotic drugs.

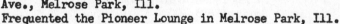

He was indicted in an FBI investigation for mafia activities in the Midwest but maintained power into the 1970s. He died on August 22, 1974 of natural causes.

NAME : Frank ZITO

ALIASES :

DESCRIPTION : Born 2-24-1893, Palermo, Sicily, 5'6", 185 lbs, brown eyes, grey hair, bald pate, wears glasses, naturalized 9-11-45, Springfield, Ill.

LOCALITIES FREQUENTED : Resides 1801 Illini Road, Springfield, Ill. Frequents Cloverleaf Pool Room and Schoenle's Tavern, both in Springfield.

FAMILY BACKGROUND : Married Lena Sgro; brothers: Pietro, Phil & Carl (who live in Italy) Sam & Tony (Springfield, Ill.); sisters: Mrs. Rosa Simonetta, Mrs. Benedict Fecarrota, Mrs. Florencia Galo (all in Italy); father: Giuseppe; mother: Lorenza Salomona.

CRIMINAL ASSOCIATES : Frank & ██████████, ██████████ (his brothers-in-law), ██████████ and ██████ ████ (his brother) all of Springfield, Ill.

CRIMINAL HISTORY : FBI #1777995 Record dating from 1931 includes arrests for murder investigation and conviction for Federal Liquor Law violation.

BUSINESS : Has interests in tavern operations, cigarette machines and juke boxes in Springfield area.

MODUS OPERANDI : Attended 1957 Apalachin Mafia meeting, representing the organization's interests in gambling, prostitution & bookmaking in the Springfield and Sangamon, Illinois, areas.

He served as Des Moines, Iowa's crime boss from 1940
until his death from cancer on November 24, 1967.

NAME	: Luigi FRATTO
ALIASES	: Louie Fratto, Lou Farrell
DESCRIPTION	: Born 7-17-08 at Chicago, Ill, 5'3½", 173 lbs., brown eyes, grey hair, heavy build and wears glasses.
LOCALITIES FREQUENTED	: Resides at 115 Caulder Ave., Des Moines, Iowa, frequents Superior Distributing Co., Des Moines, Iowa.
FAMILY BACKGROUND	: Married. Mother, Bianca and father, Thomas Fratto; brother, Carmen Fratto, and sister Lillian Stelleto, all of Chicago, Ill.
CRIMINAL ASSOCIATES	: Fischetti Brothers, Sam Giancana, and Tony Accardo, all of Chicago, Illinois.
CRIMINAL HISTORY	: FBI #1194703, Chicago PD# C77091, arrest record dates to 1933, on charges of violation of postal laws and conspiracy.
BUSINESS	: Owns the Superior Distributing Co., 618 E. 2nd St., Des Moines, Iowa.
MODUS OPERANDI	: A labor racketeer and close associate of remnants of the Capone Syndicate. This subject is the most influential member of the Mafia in the State of Iowa.

NAME	: Joseph BONURA
ALIASES	: Joseph John Bonura, Joe Bonure.
DESCRIPTION	: Born 2-8-06 New Orleans, La. 5'5½", 135 lbs., brown hair, brown eyes, sallow complexion.
LOCALITIES FREQUENTED	: Resides 625 S. Genois St., New Orleans, La. Frequents Tulane Restaurant & Bar, Rumpus Bar, & St. Charles Ave., all in New Orleans.

FAMILY BACKGROUND	: Married to Rose; brothers: Philip, Sam, Nicholas, & Louis. Father: Andrea; mother: Marie Lala.
CRIMINAL ASSOCIATES	: Anthony S. Carolla, ███████, ████████, & brothers Philip, ███, Nicholas, & ██████.
CRIMINAL HISTORY	: FBI#213240. New Orleans PD#7644 & 31637. Arrests since 1925 include auto theft, robbery, Dyer Act, OPA violation, and convictions for Federal Narcotic Laws.
BUSINESS	: Owns & operates Tulane Restaurant & Bar, 3601 Tulane Ave., New Orleans, La.
MODUS OPERANDI	: A major narcotic trafficker in Louisiana & Texas area. Is a close associate of Mafia leaders in New Orleans, La.

NAME : Nicholas J. BONURA

ALIASES : Nick Bonura, Nicholas
Joseph Bonura

DESCRIPTION : Born 2-19-13 New Orleans, La.
5'8", 145 lbs, brown hair,
brown eyes, mole right temple

LOCALITIES : Resides 3629 Bruxelles St.,
FREQUENTED New Orleans, La. Frequents
Tulane Restaurant & Bar in
New Orleans.

FAMILY : Wife: Inez; father: Andrea;
BACKGROUND mother: Marie Lala; brothers: Joseph, Philip, Sam
and Louis.

CRIMINAL : Joseph, Philip, ▇▇▇▇▇▇▇ (brothers), ▇▇▇
ASSOCIATES ▇▇▇▇, Frank Ragusa & ▇▇▇▇▇▇, all of New Orleans,
Louisiana area.

CRIMINAL : FBI #1369641. New Orleans PD# 60220 arrests since
HISTORY 1937 include gambling and conviction for Federal
Narcotic Laws.

BUSINESS : Plumber.

MODUS : Member of the notorious Bonura Family, important
OPERANDI Mafia members in Texas-Louisiana area. Through the
years has been an important distributor of narcotics
and is currently operating a horse race handbook.

NAME   : Philip BONURA

ALIASES   : Phillips Bonura, Phil Bonura,
                  Phillip Bonura.

DESCRIPTION   : Born 7-4-08 Kenner, La.,
                  5'6½", 132 lbs, black hair,
                  brown eyes, tattoo "P.B." on
                  right forearm, slim build,
                  sallow complexion.

LOCALITIES   : Resides 222 Nursery Ave.,
FREQUENTED   Metairie, La. Frequents
                  Bonura's Auto Service in
                  Metairie, La, & Tulane
                  Restaurant & Bar in New Orleans, La.

FAMILY   : Married Annie B. Vangrada; brothers: Joseph, Sam
BACKGROUND   Nicholas, & Louis, all of New Orleans; father:
                  Andrea; mother: Marie Lala.

CRIMINAL   : Anthony S. Carolla, ██████████, ██████████,
ASSOCIATES   ██████████, and brothers Joseph, ███, Nicholas,
                  & ██████████.

CRIMINAL   : FBI #317438. New Orleans PD#7643. Arrests since 1925
HISTORY   include grand larceny, bank robbery holdup, armed
                  robbery, & convictions for Federal Narcotic Laws.

BUSINESS   : Owns & operates Bonura's Auto Service, 1618 Veteran's
                  Memorial Highway, Metairie, La.

MODUS   : A major narcotic trafficker in Louisiana & Texas
OPERANDI   area. Is a close associate of Mafia leaders in
                  New Orleans, La.

NAME : Vincenzo CAMPO

ALIASES : Jimmy Campo, Giuseppe
Manzello, James Camp.

DESCRIPTION : Born 6-11-05 Siculiana,
Sicily, 5' 1 3/4", 135 lbs,
blue eyes, dark brown hair,
naturalized New Orleans, La,
2-20-42.

LOCALITIES : Resides 4725 S. Carrollton
FREQUENTED Ave., New Orleans, La.
Frequents Big Hat Restaurant
Bar & Campo's Florist shop,
both in New Orleans.

FAMILY : Married Josephine Frances Catalanato; four children;
BACKGROUND father: Stefano (deceased); mother: Anna Bissi;
sister: Mrs. Antonina Campozambito (Italy), brothers:
Charles (New Orleans), Paul (Boston), Stefan, (Canada).

CRIMINAL : Anthony Ranzino, Anthony Panci, Onofio and Joe
ASSOCIATES Pecoraro, Carlos Marcello, Anthony S. Carolla, all of
New Orleans area, Salvatore Vitale and Silvestro
Carolla of Italy.

CRIMINAL : FBI #452303. New Orleans PD #30398. Arrests since 1924
HISTORY include vagrancy, marihuana laws, operator house of
prostitution.

BUSINESS : Owns and operates Campo Florist, 4723 S. Carrollton
Ave., New Orleans, La.

MODUS : A member of the Mafia in the New Orleans area,
OPERANDI having engaged in narcotic trafficking and operating
house of prostitution.

His marriage to Maria Zaniatta, niece of Carlos Marcello, joined the Carolla & Marcello families. He became boss of the New Orleans crime family in 1993.

NAME : Anthony S. CAROLLA

ALIASES : Tony Carolla, Anthony Corolla, Anthony Carollo

DESCRIPTION : Born 11-24-23 New Orleans, La. 5'11½", 228 lbs, brown eyes, black hair, heavy build, ruddy complexion.

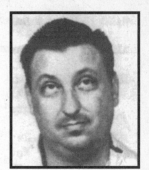

LOCALITIES FREQUENTED : Resides 5500 Vermillion Blvd, New Orleans, La. Frequents Town Bar in New Orleans and Town & Country Rest., & Lounge, Jefferson Parish, La.

FAMILY BACKGROUND : Married to Marie; father: Silvestro (deportee); mother: Caterina Carollo; brother: Salvatore.

CRIMINAL ASSOCIATES : Joseph & Onofio Pecoraro, Joseph Poretto, Carlos Marcello, Anthony Panci, & Bonura brothers, all of New Orleans.

CRIMINAL HISTORY : New Orleans PD#72294 shows an arrest in 1954 for gambling.

BUSINESS : Owns and operates Town Bar, 820 St. Charles Ave., New Orleans, La.

MODUS OPERANDI : An up and coming Mafia leader in New Orleans which position he inherited from his father Silvestro, who was deported. Also engaged in illegal gambling ventures with Carlos Marcello in New Orleans area.

NAME	: Salvatore DOMINO
ALIASES	: Sam Domino
DESCRIPTION	: Born 1-28-06 Franklin, La, 5'7¼", 218 lbs, grey eyes, grey hair, heavy build.
LOCALITIES FREQUENTED	: Resides 6326 Cartwright Dr, New Orleans, La. Frequents Domino's Pizzeria & Bar, New Orleans, La.
FAMILY BACKGROUND	: Married Mary Howard; daughter: Patricia; father: Calogero; mother: Giuseppa Maria Calabressa.
CRIMINAL ASSOCIATES	: Carlos Marcello, Anthony Carolla, Joe Bonura, ████ ██████, █████████████, all of New Orleans area; Joseph Gagliano and Salvatore (Sam) Vitale of Italy.
CRIMINAL HISTORY	: FBI #902582B. New Orleans PD# 86927. Arrests since 1933 include vagrancy, indecent exposure, disturbing the peace by threats.
BUSINESS	: Owns and operates Domino's Pizzeria and Bar, 701 St., Charles St., New Orleans, La.
MODUS OPERANDI	: Close associate of known narcotic traffickers in New Orleans; also engaged in illegal gambling operations under the control of the Mafia organization in the New Orleans area.

NAME	: Salvadore J. GALLO
ALIASES	: Sam Gallo, Little Sam
DESCRIPTION	: Born 11-14-1899 New Orleans, La, 5'4", 244 lbs, brown hair (bald), grey eyes, heavy build.
LOCALITIES FREQUENTED	: Resides 2721 Mithra St, New Orleans, La. Frequents French Market area in New Orleans & Jefferson Parrish, La.

FAMILY BACKGROUND	: Married Katherine Cadaro; father: Joseph; mother: Rose Lacana.
CRIMINAL ASSOCIATES	: ▇▇▇▇▇▇▇, Victor Gallo, Joseph Marcello Jr., Joseph Poretto, ▇▇▇▇▇▇▇, ▇▇▇▇▇▇▇.
CRIMINAL HISTORY	: FBI #938078B. New Orleans PD#75894. Arrests since 1945 include OPA violation (black marketeering) and gambling.
BUSINESS	: Has interests in Nola News, Jefferson Parrish, La, a race wire service.
MODUS OPERANDI	: An important member of the Mafia gambling syndicate in the New Orleans area. Also known as pay-off man.

NAME	: Vittorio Vincenzo GALLO

ALIASES   : Vic Gallo

DESCRIPTION : Born 1-10-1895 NYC, 5'4",
               145 lbs, heavy build, brown
               eyes, black-grey hair.

LOCALITIES   : Resides 230 W. Wm. David
FREQUENTED   Parkway, Metairie, La. Fre-
               quents 1-2-3-Club, New
               Orleans, La., and Chester-
               field Club, Jefferson Parrish
               Louisiana.

FAMILY   : Separated from wife, Jane; mother: Angelina Frione;
BACKGROUND   brothers: Ross, Vincent, Albert.

CRIMINAL   : Salvador J. Gallo, ███████████████████,
ASSOCIATES   ██████████████ & ████████.

CRIMINAL   : FBI #1804397. Cleveland PD#50836. Record dating from
HISTORY   1939 includes arrests for sodomy and contributing to
               delinquency of minor.

BUSINESS   : Manages the Chesterfield Club, Jefferson Parrish,
               Louisiana.

MODUS   : An important member of the Mafia gambling syndicate
OPERANDI   in New Orleans and Jefferson Parrish, La. Influ-
               ential in political circles.

In the 1950s, Kastel opened the Tropicana with partner Frank Costello. He died August 16, 1962, reportedly taking his own life, with a gun shot wound to the head.

NAME : Philip Frank KASTEL

ALIASES : Dandy Phil

DESCRIPTION : Born 4-2-1893 NYC, Jewish, 5'7", 165 lbs, grey hair, brown eyes, ruddy complexion, medium build.

LOCALITIES FREQUENTED : Resides 119 S Claiborne, New Orleans, La.; frequents Beverly Club, 217 La Barre Rd, & Town & Country Rest., Jefferson Parish, La.

FAMILY BACKGROUND : Divorced Elsie Conner 1940 & married Margaret Dennis; father: Solomon; mother; Rachel Rosenthal; brother: Allen Kastel; sisters: Florence, Ida Kastel Steinberg and Rose Kastel Walter.

CRIMINAL ASSOCIATES : Frank Costello, Meyer Lansky, Carlos Marcello, Joseph Poretto.

CRIMINAL HISTORY : FBI #188908. San Francisco PD# 37758. Record dating from 1926 includes arrests for mail fraud & income tax evasion.

BUSINESS : Operates Beverly Club, 217 La Barre Rd, Jefferson Parish, Louisiana.

MODUS OPERANDI : One of the controllers of gambling in the New Orleans area. Though not Italian he operates with approval of and in affiliation with top echelon Mafia racketeers.

He was deported to Guatemala in 1961. In 1989, he started suffering from strokes and he died on March 3, 1993.

NAME : Carlos MARCELLO

ALIASES : Carlos Minacore, Carlos Marcella

DESCRIPTION : Born 2-6-10, Tunis, Africa, 5'4½", 173 lbs., black-grey hair, brown eyes, heavy build.

LOCALITIES FREQUENTED : Resides 577 Woodvine Ave., Metairie, La., frequents Town and Country Club, Jefferson Music Co., Beverly Club, all in Jefferson Parish, La.

FAMILY BACKGROUND : Wife: Jacquelyn, brothers: Vincent J., Joseph P., Peter, Pascal, Samuel J., father: Giuseppe, mother: Luigia Faruggia.

CRIMINAL ASSOCIATES : Anthony Panci, Anthony S. Carolla, Phil Kastel, all of New Orleans, Frank Costello of NYC, Frank Coppola and Silvestro Carolla of Italy (deportees).

CRIMINAL HISTORY : FBI #292542, New Orleans PD# 13471, Arrests since 1929 include assault and robbery, liquor law violations, and conviction for Federal Marihuana Laws.

BUSINESS : Owns Town & Country Motel; has interests in Jefferson Music Co., and Nola News Co., all in Jefferson Parish, Louisiana.

MODUS OPERANDI : Is considered the top ranking member of the Mafia in New Orleans area. Controls distribution of coin machines and racing wire service in New Orleans area. Gained reputation through terroristic activities. Currently engaged in legal fight to prevent deportation.

NAME   : Salvadore J. MARCIANTE

ALIASES   : None

DESCRIPTION   : Born 7-14-17 New Orleans,
                   La, 5'10", 235 lbs, black
                   hair, brown eyes, heavy
                   build, cut scar on left hand
                   palm & wrist. U.S. Coast
                   Guard Seaman Document Z# 99-
                   0228.

LOCALITIES   : Resides 1522 Hancock, Gretna,
FREQUENTED   Louisiana.

FAMILY   : Married & has 2 children; father: Peter; mother:
BACKGROUND   Florence Finazzo.

CRIMINAL   : Carlos Marcello, Anthony Panci, Anthony Carolla.
ASSOCIATES

CRIMINAL   : FBI #940290A. New Orleans PD# 44692. Record dating
HISTORY   from 1945 includes arrests for aggravated assault &
                   black marketing gas ration stamps.

BUSINESS   : Employed as butcher by Jefferson Packing Co., New
                   Orleans, La. Formerly a seaman.

MODUS   : Underling of New Orleans Mafia chief Carlos Marcello.
OPERANDI

NAME   : Lorenzo MARINO

ALIASES   : Lawrence T. Marino, Larry
                 Marino.

DESCRIPTION   : Born 9-5-04 Siculiana,
                 Sicily. 5'11", 180 lbs.,
                 black-grey hair, grey eyes,
                 has artificial leg, citizen
                 by derivation from father
                 Garlando.

LOCALITIES   : Resides 4855 Government St.,
FREQUENTED   Baton Rouge, La. Frequents
                 Bologna Brothers Wholesale
                 Co. (liquor dealers), Baton Rouge, La., & makes
                 trips to Italy.

FAMILY   : Married to Mamie Clesi; father: Garlando; mother:
BACKGROUND   Croce Siracusa (both deceased); sister: Mrs.
                 Carmela Sidote; brother: Joseph.

CRIMINAL   : Anthony Ranzino, Vincent Campo, Anthony S. Carolla,
ASSOCIATES   all of New Orleans; Salvatore Italiano of Tampa;
                 Joe Gagliano & Silvestro Carollo of Italy.

CRIMINAL   : No criminal record known or available.
HISTORY

BUSINESS   : Liquor salesman for Bologna Brothers Wholesale
                 Co., Baton Rouge, La.

MODUS   : Close associate of major Mafia narcotic traffickers
OPERANDI   in New Orleans area, and occasionally visits Mafia
                 deportee traffickers in Italy.

NAME   : Anthony PANCI

ALIASES   : Mr. Tony, Antonio DiGregorio
                  Anthony Pance.

DESCRIPTION   : Born 8-1-07 Garfield, NJ,
                  5'10", 195 lbs., brown eyes,
                  black hair, speaks with
                  foreign accent.

LOCALITIES   : Resides 2938 Derbigny St.,
FREQUENTED   Metairie, La., frequents
                  French market and 2nd &
                  Claiborn sts., in New
                  Orleans, La.

FAMILY   : Married to Kate Bounds.
BACKGROUND

CRIMINAL   : Carlos Marcello, Anthony Ranzino, Vincenzo Campo,
ASSOCIATES   Joseph A. Giardina, all of New Orleans; Joseph
                  Gagliano of Italy (deportee).

CRIMINAL   : FBI #90544A, New Orleans PD# 53300, arrests since
HISTORY   1953 include conviction for Federal narcotic laws.

BUSINESS   : Owns and operates Tony's Bar-B-Q, 2428 S. Claiborne
                  Ave., New Orleans, La.

MODUS   : An important member of the Mafia narcotic traffick-
OPERANDI   ing group in New Orleans area, dealing in wholesale
                  quantities, and having sources of supply in NYC from
                  Mafia traffickers.

NAME	: Joseph PECORARO

ALIASES : Joe Pecora

DESCRIPTION : Born 3-22-16, New Orleans, La., 6'1", 170 lbs., black hair, brown eyes, dark complexion, slender build.

LOCALITIES FREQUENTED : Resides 3631 Elysian Fields Ave., New Orleans, La. Frequents French Market area, Idle Hour Bar, & Town Bar, all in New Orleans.

FAMILY BACKGROUND : Married to Marie Charello, father: Baptiste (deceased, former Mafia leader in New Orleans area), brothers: George and Onofio.

CRIMINAL ASSOCIATES : Onofio Pecoraro (brother), Anthony S. Carolla, Anthony Panci, Carlos Marcello, Anthony Ranzino, all of New Orleans area.

CRIMINAL HISTORY : FBI #2810861, New Orleans PD #33757. Arrests since 1933 include auto theft and possession of stolen property.

BUSINESS : Owns and operates Idle Hour Bar, 1800 St. Philip St., New Orleans, La.

MODUS OPERANDI : Engaged in Mafia controlled gambling and handbook operations in New Orleans area. Close associate of known Mafia narcotic traffickers in New Orleans area.

NAME   : Onofio PECORARO

ALIASES   : Onofio Pecora, Onofio
                  Pecorara

DESCRIPTION   : Born 4-25-06, New Orleans,
                  La., 5'9", 157 lbs., brown
                  eyes, black hair, has cut-
                  scar in center of upper lip.

LOCALITIES   : Resides 6027 Chef Menteur
FREQUENTED   Highway, New Orleans, La.,
                  frequents Jacks Barber Shop,
                  Town Bar, and French market
                  area in New Orleans.

FAMILY   : Wife's name is Frances, brothers are Joseph and
BACKGROUND   George, father is Baptiste (dead).

CRIMINAL   : Nick and Philip Bomura, Joseph Pecoraro (brother),
ASSOCIATES   Vincenzo Campo, all of New Orleans, Joseph
                  Gagliano of Italy (deportee).

CRIMINAL   : FBI #897585, New Orleans PD# 8970, arrests since
HISTORY   1926 include robbery and conviction for Federal
                  narcotic laws.

BUSINESS   : Operates Tropical Tourist Court and Trailer Park,
                  Chef Menteur Highway, New Orleans, La.

MODUS   : Was an important source of supply for narcotics in
OPERANDI   New Orleans area, obtaining and distributing the
                  narcotics through Mafia affiliates.

NAME   : Joseph PORRETTO

ALIASES   : Joseph Peretto, Poretto

DESCRIPTION : Born 3-21-06 New Orleans, La,
                  5'8½", 267 lbs, black hair,
                  brown eyes, fair complexion,
                  stout build.

LOCALITIES   : Resided 509 St. Louis St.,
FREQUENTED   New Orleans. Frequents Jef-
                  ferson Parrish, La., & rac-
                  ing & gambling establish-
                  ments in Hot Springs, Ark.

FAMILY   : Married & divorced from Bell Marie Bernard Shyer
BACKGROUND   (well known New Orleans Madam); father: Charles;
                  mother: Maria Frisco.

CRIMINAL   : Carlos Marcello, Phil Kastel, ▆▆▆▆▆▆▆▆, Onofrio
ASSOCIATES   and Joseph Pecoraro, Joseph Marcello Jr., Anthony
                  Carolla, ▆▆▆▆▆▆▆, all of New Orleans area; and
                  Frank Costello of NYC.

CRIMINAL   : FBI #1799932. Louisiana B of I #160446. Record dates
HISTORY   from 1936 and includes arrests for operating lottery,
                  price control violation and refusal to testify be-
                  fore a Senate Committee.

BUSINESS   : Manages Town & Country Rest., & Lounge, Jefferson
                  Parrish, La. Has interests in Nola News in Jefferson
                  Parrish, a horse race wire service.

MODUS   : In association with other important Mafia members
OPERANDI   has large scale gambling and prostitution operations
                  in New Orleans and Jefferson Parish, La.

184

NAME   : Mario PRESTA

ALIASES   : Paul Scarcelli

DESCRIPTION   : Born 7-28-1898 Mendicino,
                  Cosenza, Calabria, Italy,
                  5'11", 170 lbs, black hair,
                  brown eyes, medium build,
                  alien - I&NS #A-1156907.

LOCALITIES   : Resides 1140 Jackson Ave.,
FREQUENTED   New Orleans, La., frequents
                  520 S. Alexander, New Or-
                  leans, and Shell Beach, La.

FAMILY   : Wife: Francesca Panza; step-daughter: Lena Dan
BACKGROUND   Esteoz; father: Anthony; mother: Tomassina Stinghi;
                  brothers: Alfredo (Naples, Italy) & Albert Presta
                  (Paterson, NJ.); half-brother: Charles Leon Presta
                  (New Orleans); sister: Albina Caputa, Naples, Italy.

CRIMINAL   : Frank Costello, Phil Kastel, Meyer Lansky, Jos Civello
ASSOCIATES   (Dallas, Texas), Carlos Marcello (New Orleans).

CRIMINAL   : FBI #4310005, New Orleans PD# 43457. Arrested New
HISTORY   Orleans 1945 for shooting & dangerously wounding.
                  Deportation proceedings pending (1960).

BUSINESS   : Employed as "salesman & contact man" by Gold Seal
                  Creamery, 520 S. Alexander, New Orleans.

MODUS   : New Orleans representative of Mafia chief Frank
OPERANDI   Costello, controlling gambling in that area. At
                  the time of the 1957 Mafia meeting at Apalachin, NY,
                  Presta was stopped by state police six miles from
                  the scene of the meeting, although it could not
                  be proven that he attended the meeting it is almost
                  certain that he did.

NAME   : Anthony RANZINO

ALIASES   : Tony Ranzino

DESCRIPTION   : Born 2-12-1899, Cefalu,
                  Sicily, 5'5½", 193 lbs,
                  brown eyes, black-grey hair,
                  wears glasses, I&NS #A-355-
                  4140.

LOCALITIES   : Resides 1221 North Gayoso,
FREQUENTED   New Orleans, La. Frequents
                  2822 Florida Ave, and the
                  French Market area, both in
                  New Orleans.

FAMILY   : Married Mary Michel; son: Joseph; daughter: Phillipa;
BACKGROUND   father: Giuseppe; mother: Filippa Mormino; brothers:
                  Giacindo, Salvatore, Gaetano.

CRIMINAL   : Sam Vitale (Sicily), Jimmy Campo, Anthony Panci,
ASSOCIATES   Joseph & Onofrio Pecoraro, all of New Orleans area.

CRIMINAL   : No FBI #assigned. New Orleans PD #41521. Arrested
HISTORY   11-28-43 at New Orleans for investigation of
                  murder and swindling.

BUSINESS   : Owns Ranzino Terrazo Co., 2822 Florida Ave, New
                  Orleans, Louisiana.

MODUS   : An important Mafia member in the New Orleans area,
OPERANDI   closely associated with known Mafia narcotic traf-
                  fickers. Specialized in swindling.

NAME	: Thomas J. AVERSA

ALIASES : Thomas Laversa, Wop Jenkins, Reds, Guinea Reds.

DESCRIPTION : Born 11-26-03 Ragusa, Sicily 5'8", 175 lbs, light complexion, grey eyes, chestnut greying hair.

LOCALITIES FREQUENTED : Resides 403 Marlow Road, Baltimore, Md., frequents Chanticleer Nite Club and Cross Street Market area, both in Baltimore.

FAMILY BACKGROUND : Married to Bertha Werner. Father's name is Joseph and mother's name is Fillipina Guarnera.

CRIMINAL ASSOCIATES : ██████████████, James Caronna, ██████████, ████████, Louis Morici, ███████████, ██████████████, ████████████████, all of Baltimore.

CRIMINAL HISTORY : Baltimore, Md., P.D.#4773. Numerous arrests in Baltimore since 1934, principally on gambling charges.

BUSINESS : Owns Chanticleer Nite Club, Baltimore, Md.

MODUS OPERANDI : One of the heads of the Mafia in Baltimore area, rumored to be a silent partner in several small bars in Baltimore; finances attorney fees and bail bonds for local Italian racketeers.

NAME   : Vincent CARONNA

ALIASES   : Vincent Carona, James Carona
                  Jimmy Russo, James Busick

DESCRIPTION   : Born 3-5-04, Bisacquino,
                  Sicily, USI&NS Alien #
                  A5463839C, 5'7", 185 lbs.,
                  black greying hair, brown
                  eyes, ruddy complexion,
                  wears glasses.

LOCALITIES   : Resides 2900 Smith Ave.,
FREQUENTED   Baltimore Md., frequents
                  Trocadero Democratic Club,
                  Dixie Diner, bars in Belair Market area, all in
                  Baltimore.

FAMILY   : Married twice, present wife Gertrude Barshop; has
BACKGROUND   son Joseph by 1st marriage and son Michael by 2nd;
                  father is Joseph J. and mother is Genevieve
                  Occhipinti.

CRIMINAL   : Louis Morici, ███████████, Frank Dabbene, █████
ASSOCIATES   ████████████████, all of Baltimore, Benny
                  Bellanca and Frank Scalice (deceased) of NYC.

CRIMINAL   : FBI #355701, Baltimore, Md., PD#44409, numerous
HISTORY   arrests since 1925 including petit larceny, loaded
                  gun, gambling, operating bookie joints.

BUSINESS   : Salesman for Weather-Tite Corp., Baltimore, which
                  firm is run by his son Joseph.

MODUS   : Is considered an international drug trafficker;
OPERANDI   makes trips to Italy; is one of the heads of the
                  Mafia in the Baltimore area.

NAME	: Frank DABBENE
ALIASES	: Don, Don Cheech, Don Ciccio

DESCRIPTION : Born 1-10-1897, Reggio di
Calabria, Italy, naturalized
11-14-33 Utica, NY, 5'7",
165 lbs., brown hair balding
brown eyes, fair complexion.

LOCALITIES : Resides 6416 Frederick Road,
FREQUENTED   Catonsville, Md., frequents
              Trocadero Democratic Club,
              Baltimore, and night clubs
              on East Baltimore St.

FAMILY   : Single, father is John and mother is Providenza
BACKGROUND   Poretto (both dead), has nephew Stephen Provenza.

CRIMINAL   : Vincent Caronna, Louis Morici, ██████████████,
ASSOCIATES   █████████████████████, all of Baltimore,
              Frank Scalice (dead) of New York.

CRIMINAL   : FBI #4661856, Baltimore PD#65061, numerous arrests
HISTORY   for suspicion of murder, lottery.

BUSINESS   : Assists nephew Stephen Provenza in running the
              Carry-Out beverage store, Baltimore.

MODUS   : Finances bookmakers and operates gambling games in
OPERANDI   Baltimore county; is a suspect in international
              trafficking of narcotics; important member of the
              Baltimore area Mafia.

NAME	: Louis MORICI
ALIASES	: Lou Mora, John Maurice
DESCRIPTION	: Born 4-18-96, Palermo, Sicily, naturalized, 5'5", 160 lbs., blue eyes, brown greying hair.
LOCALITIES FREQUENTED	: Resides 5638 Clearspring Rd, Baltimore, Md., frequents Trocadero Democratic Club, Bernie's Coin Machine Co., Dodge Coin Machine Co., Trocadero nite club, all in Baltimore.

FAMILY BACKGROUND	: Married to Lillian Blakely, has one son, father is Serafino and mother is Mattea Grasso (both dead), brothers Joe, Peter, John, all in Italy.
CRIMINAL ASSOCIATES	: Vincent Caromma, Frank Dabbene, Tom Aversa, ███ and █████, ████████, ████████, █████████ ███████, all of Baltimore; also ████████████ and ████████████ of Canada; also Thomas Marino, Sebastian Nani, ████████████, Leonard Calamia.
CRIMINAL HISTORY	: FBI #815473C, Baltimore, PD #34741, convicted in Italy for Possession of deadly weapon; many arrests in Baltimore for questioning and investigation of various crimes.
BUSINESS	: Silent partner in Annello Construction Co., Baltimore, Md.
MODUS OPERANDI	: Is considered the head of the Mafia in the Baltimore area, and a suspected international drug trafficker; is the banker for several number lottery organizations in Baltimore.

MASSACHUSETTS

NAME	: Joseph ANSELMO
ALIASES	: Joe Burns
DESCRIPTION	: Born 10-13-09 N.Y.C., 5'10", 205 lbs., brown eyes, black-grey hair, stocky build.
LOCALITIES FREQUENTED	: Resides 12 Langely Road, Arlington, Mass. Frequents north end section of Boston & makes trips to Cleveland, Detroit, & Pittsburgh.
FAMILY BACKGROUND	: Married to Mildred Hudson; father is Angelo; mother is Rosa Lombardo.
CRIMINAL ASSOCIATES	: Frank Cucchiara, Joe Lombardo, Henry Selvitella, Anthony Santaniello, ███████, all of Boston area.
CRIMINAL HISTORY	: FBI#556313. Boston PD#28491. Arrests since 1931 include breaking & entering, carrying concealed weapon, receiving stolen goods.
BUSINESS	: Has been operating a restaurant in Boston; in May 1959 his application for license as a "second" was approved by the Mass. Boxing Commission.
MODUS OPERANDI	: Has considerable influence with leading Mafia members in Boston-Providence area, and acts with authority. Engaged in bookmaking activities.

> Cucchiara killed his wife and then killed himself
> with a shotgun at their home in Belmont, MA on
> January 23, 1976.

NAME : Frank CUCCHIARA

ALIASES : Frank Caruso, Frank Russo,
Frank the Spoon

DESCRIPTION : Born 3-29-1895 Salemi,
Sicily, naturalized 8-10-31
Boston, Mass., 5'3½", 156
lbs, stocky build, brown eyes
hair brown & greying, has 6"
scar in palm of left hand.

LOCALITIES : Resides 282 Common St.,
FREQUENTED Watertown, Mass., frequents
Purity Cheese Co., European
Restaurant, Giro's Cafe, Florentine Cafe, all in
Boston.

FAMILY : Wife: Santa Lucy Giordano; no children; brother:
BACKGROUND Peter (Boston); sister in Italy; father: Vito;
mother: Antonia Cardonna.

CRIMINAL : Philip Buccola, Raymond Patriarca, ███████████,
ASSOCIATES Rocco Palladino, Henry Selvitella, Albert Santaniello,
Frank Morelli.

CRIMINAL : FBI #4477, Boston PD#19057. Arrested 1925 Boston
HISTORY possession of morphine and dynamite, arrested again
1932 Boston suspicion of murder.

BUSINESS : Owns Purity Cheese Co., 55-57 Endicott St., Boston.

MODUS : Attended Apalachin meeting 1957 as representative
OPERANDI of the Mafia from the New England area; operates
gambling joints in North End of Boston; finances
narcotic transactions.

NAME : Joseph LOMBARDO

ALIASES : Joseph Lombardi, J.L.

DESCRIPTION : Born 9-1-95 in Italy,
naturalized, 5'9", 160 lbs,
medium build, hair is grey
and balding, brown eyes,
medium complexion.

LOCALITIES : Resides 100 Lawrence St.,
FREQUENTED   Medford, Mass. Frequents
Giro's Cafe and Suffolk
Downs Race Track (Boston).

FAMILY : Father is Joseph and mother is Carmen Felician both
BACKGROUND   of Italy. Has two brothers, Pasquale and Vincent.

CRIMINAL : Philip Buccola, Frank Cucchiara, Raymond Patriarca,
ASSOCIATES   Rocco and Joseph Palladino, Albert Santaniello,
████████████, Henry Selvitella, all of Boston area.

CRIMINAL : FBI #520374, Mass. State Police #18464, 1st arrest
HISTORY   in 1917, for assault with intent to kill, a 1925
arrest for possession of morphine, other arrests
for bribery, murder, lottery, possession of revolver, assault with intent to kill.

BUSINESS : With brothers Vincent and Pasquale, and nephew
Paul Intisio, owns Giro's Cafe, 464 Hanover St.,
Boston, meeting place of all known racketeers.
Also a bookmaker.

MODUS : Is a member of the top hierachy of the Mafia in
OPERANDI   the Mass. area.

NAME	: Peter Anthony MARINELLO
ALIASES	: Pete Mello, Charles P. Mello
DESCRIPTION	: Born 4-20-11 Boston, Mass. 5'8", 170 lbs., brown eyes, black hair.
LOCALITIES FREQUENTED	: Currently (1959) a fugitive. Used to frequent Malden, Revere, & Boston, Mass., area, also carnivals & race tracks.
FAMILY BACKGROUND	: Married to Carolyn Copson; father: Leo (dead); mother: Victoria Zittola; sisters: Mrs. Mary Capello & Mrs. Rose Giachinta; brothers: Louis, Dominick, Anthony, Michael, & Frank.
CRIMINAL ASSOCIATES	: Florio Isabella, ████████, Tony Vellucci, Nathan Behrman, all of N.Y.C.; Wady David, ██████, ████, ████████, ████████, all of Boston area.
CRIMINAL HISTORY	: FBI#1432750. Boston PD#48953. Arrests since 1927 include grand larceny, assault & battery, breaking & entering. Currently (1959) wanted for violation Federal Narcotic Laws.
BUSINESS	: No legitimate business known.
MODUS OPERANDI	: Engaged in illegal activities most of his life. A wholesale distributor of narcotics for the Mafia controlled Behrman-Vellucci organization of N.Y.C.

194

NAME	: Rocco PALLADINO
ALIASES	: Rocco Paladino, Rocco Polladino
DESCRIPTION	: Born 4-20-06 Boston, Mass. 5'5½", 175 lbs., brown eyes, dark brown hair.
LOCALITIES FREQUENTED	: Resides 232 Orient Ave., East Boston, Mass. Frequents Day Square area in Boston & New England race tracks.
FAMILY BACKGROUND	: Married to Louise Cassetta & has 1 son & 2 daughters; brothers: Joseph & Anthony; father: Nunzio; mother: Letteria Larosa.
CRIMINAL ASSOCIATES	: Joe Lombardo, Anthony Santaniello, Raymond Patriarca, Henry Selvitella, Frank Cucchiara, Philip Buccola, all of Boston-Providence area.
CRIMINAL HISTORY	: FBI#1904814. Mass. State Police #46793. Arrests since 1914 include breaking & entering, Prohibition Act, suspicion of manslaughter.
BUSINESS	: Financially connected with Dock Square Grill in Boston, and the Burlington Sand & Gravel Co., Burlington, Mass.
MODUS OPERANDI	: One of the leaders of the Mafia in the Mass. area. With Mafia associates controls bookmaking operations in East Boston, Mass., area.

NAME	: Anthony SANTANIELLO
ALIASES	: Albert Santaniello, Anthony Santanello, Antonio Santenelli.
DESCRIPTION	: Born 6-9-03 Boston, Mass., 5'7", 140 lbs., medium build fair complexion, dark brown eyes, hair is greying, wears eye glasses, sickly looking.
LOCALITIES FREQUENTED	: Resides 245 Tappan St., Brookline, Mass., frequents Paddock Cafe, Giro's Cafe and the North End District of Boston.

FAMILY BACKGROUND	: Related to Leo Santaniello a North Shore Bookie, and to Amato Santaniello hoodlum and strong arm man.
CRIMINAL ASSOCIATES	: Frank Cucchiara, Joseph Lombardo, Larry Bione, Frank Morelli, Raymond Patriarca, ████████, Henry Selvitella, Philip Buccola.
CRIMINAL HISTORY	: FBI #1467159, Mass. State Police #65030, arrested Federal Narcotic Laws in 1938 (dismissed).
BUSINESS	: Operates the Paddock Bar 255 Tremont St., Boston, Mass., is also a shylock and a bookie.
MODUS OPERANDI	: Is called "the old man" and "the arbitrator" by other members of the Mafia in the New England area.

NAME   : Henry A. SELVITELLA

ALIASES   : Henry Noyes, Henry Fargo,
                  Henry Feno, Frank Ross,
                  Selvitelli, Silvertelli,
                  Selveitello.

DESCRIPTION   : Born 3-15-02 Boston, Mass.,
                  5'3", 225 lbs; grey hair,
                  heavy build, brown eyes,
                  dark complexion.

LOCALITIES   : Resides 24 Yeamans St.,
FREQUENTED   Revere, Mass. Frequents
                  Noyes Dry Cleaning Salon,
                  Paddock Bar, Giro's Cafe, all in Boston, Mass.

FAMILY   Married twice, present wife's name is Rosania; his
BACKGROUND   : father is named Louis, and his mother is named
                  Esther Caggiano.

CRIMINAL   : Philip Buccola, Raymond Patriarca, ███████████,
ASSOCIATES   Frank Cucchiara, Albert Santaniello, Joseph Lombardo,
                  all known racketeers in the Boston area.

CRIMINAL   : FBI #810055, Mass. State Police #21624, criminal
HISTORY   record from 1915 including larceny as a juvenile,
                  rape, larceny, gambling, liquor violations, con-
                  spiracy to commit murder.

BUSINESS   : Listed as sole owner of Noyes Dry Cleaning Salon,
                  300 Hanover St., Boston, Mass., which he operates
                  with his son George.

MODUS   : Is considered a top member of the Mafia in the
OPERANDI   Mass., area.

On February 27, 1996, Zannino died in a Springfield, MO prison of natural causes.

NAME : Ilario A. ZANNINO

ALIASES : Larry Zannino, Larry Bione, Larry Baioni, Joe Bissanti.

DESCRIPTION : Born 6-15-20 Boston, Mass. 5'7", 160 lbs., brown eyes, dark brown hair.

LOCALITIES FREQUENTED : Resides 17 Morraine St., Jamaica Plain, Boston, Mass. Frequents Paddock Bar, El Morocco Cafe, & Giro's Cafe, all in Boston.

FAMILY BACKGROUND : Married to Isabella Tawa; father: Joseph; mother: Isabella LaGrada.

CRIMINAL ASSOCIATES : Anthony Santaniello, Henry Selvitella, Frank Cucchiara, Raymond Patriarca, Joe Lombardo, all of Boston area.

CRIMINAL HISTORY : FBI#5122703. Boston PD#63865. Arrests since 1941 include assault & battery, armed robbery, murder, bookmaking.

BUSINESS : No legitimate business or employment known.

MODUS OPERANDI : Associated with Mafioso Anthony Santaniello in illegal gambling operations. An enforcer for the Mafia in the Boston area, taking the place of deceased Mafia leader Anthony Cortese.

NAME   : Antonino ABATE

ALIASES   : Tony Abate, Tony The Chump,
                  Anthony Abbate.

DESCRIPTION   : Born 1-2-04 Balestrati,
                  Sicily, 5'6", 180 lbs,
                  black hair, brown eyes,
                  cut scar on left cheekbone,
                  I&NS # 1418454.

LOCALITIES   : Resides 22020 Louise, St.
FREQUENTED   Clair Shores, Michigan.
                  Frequents Surf & Sands
                  Motel, Caseville, Michigan.

FAMILY   : Has son Angelo & daughter Beatrice by 1st wife. Now
BACKGROUND   married to Eleanore Palazzola and has 3 children,
                  Angelo, Michael, and Mary Margaret; father: Angelo;
                  mother: Maria Fiori.

CRIMINAL   : John Priziola, Pete Licavoli, Angelo Meli, Joseph
ASSOCIATES   Zerilli, Mike Rubino, all of Detroit area; John
                  Ormento of N.Y.C.

CRIMINAL   : FBI # 695623. Detroit PD # 35019. Arrests since
HISTORY   1920 include armed robbery, burglary, murder, lar-
                  ceny, and gambling.

BUSINESS   : Owns and operates Surf & Sands Motel, Caseville,
                  Michigan.

MODUS   : A Mafia member from the Detroit area engaged in
OPERANDI   illegal gambling activities controlled by the
                  Mafia in the Detroit area.

NAME	: Matteo BARTOLOTTA
ALIASES	: Michael Bartello (which he commonly uses), Michael Bruno Bartello.
DESCRIPTION	: Born 7-26-17 Detroit, Mich., 5'7", 210 lbs, heavy build, black hair, brown eyes.
LOCALITIES FREQUENTED	: Resides 3888 Lakewood, Detroit, Mich., frequents residence of uncle, Michael Rubino, at 1068 Bedford, Grosse Pte Park, Mich., & Dream Bar, Detroit; also Los Angeles, Calif., (Pica Club) & Miami, Florida.
FAMILY BACKGROUND	: Single; father: Rosalino; mother: Anna Rubino; brothers: Domiano, John, Sidney & James in Calif., Samuel in Detroit; sisters: Phyllis Messini & Grace La Salle, both in California.
CRIMINAL ASSOCIATES	: Sam Lucido, Michael Rubino, Domiano Bartolotta, ████████████, ████████████.
CRIMINAL HISTORY	: FBI #4630310, Detroit PD# 82619, LA PD# A89796. Record dates from 1946 and includes arrests for robbery, gambling & liquor law violations.
BUSINESS	: No known legitimate business enterprise.
MODUS OPERANDI	: Lower echelon Mafia hoodlum who engages in bootlegging and gambling. Well acquainted with top Detroit Mafiosi through his uncle, Michael Rubino.

He was killed while resisting arrest.

NAME : Joseph BOMMARITO

ALIASES : Scarface Joe

DESCRIPTION : Born 5-26-03, St. Louis, Mo., 5'8", 185 lbs, black-grey hair, which is thinning, eyes brown, medium complexion, cut scar on right corner of mouth and upper lip.

LOCALITIES FREQUENTED : Resides 7540 W. Seven Mile Rd., Detroit, Mich., frequents residence of Pete Licavoli, 1154 Balfour, Grosse Pointe Park, Michigan.

FAMILY BACKGROUND : Wife: Ruth Fowler; father: Giuseppe; mother: Lina.

CRIMINAL ASSOCIATES : Pete Licavoli, John Priziola, Mike Rubino, Tony Abate, Joseph Bommarito @ Long-Joe, ██████████ all of Detroit; ██████████, Cleveland, Ohio.

CRIMINAL HISTORY : FBI #145941, Detroit PD# 37496, 1st arrest 1926 for armed robbery, numerous subsequent arrests for assault, murder, extortion, carrying concealed weapons prohibition and State gambling laws.

BUSINESS : Has interests in Longfellow and Emerson Apartments, P&T Oil Co., Torosian Oil Co., Michigan Mutual Distributing Co., Aurora Gasoline Royalties, all in the Detroit area.

MODUS OPERANDI : Considered most prominent "Numbers" operator in the Detroit and down-river area of Michigan; associated with Pete Licavoli in this operation.

NAME	: Joseph BOMMARITO

ALIASES : Long Joe Bommarito, Jack Luckas, Joe Russo.

DESCRIPTION : Born 2-17-09 Palermo, Italy, naturalized 7-7-58 Detroit, 5'11", 190 lbs., medium build medium complexion, brown hair brown eyes, scar right eyebrow, scar on left side of upper lip.

LOCALITIES FREQUENTED : Resides at 4117 Kensington, Detroit, Mich., frequents Al Green's Restaurant and Rooster Tail Supper Club.

FAMILY BACKGROUND : Wife's name Marie, married 2-13-47, has three children; Theodore, Grace and Geraldine; brother-in-law of Peter Licavoli; father: Isadore; mother: Grace Lucido.

CRIMINAL ASSOCIATES : Joseph "Scar Face" Bommarito, Angelo Meli, Mike Rubino, William Tocco, Peter Licavoli, John Priziola, Joe Zerilli, Joe Massei, Tony Teramaini, Sam Lucido, and Mike Polizzi.

CRIMINAL HISTORY : FBI #563534, Detroit PD #29317, 1st arrest in 1927 for robbery armed, numerous subsequent arrests for Violation U.S. Tarriff Act, National Prohibition Act, Kidnapping, Violation of the State Gambling Laws, and murder.

BUSINESS : Prince Michigan Manufacturing Co., and Del Ray Scrap Co., Detroit.

MODUS OPERANDI : Status in the Mafia in Detroit, Mich., is on a par with Mike Rubino, Mike Polizzi, and Joe Massei; A Chief-Lieutenant in the Licavoli-Scar Face Bommarito gambling combine at Detroit.

NAME : Ignazio BRACCO

ALIASES : Jack Bracco, Dodo.

DESCRIPTION : Born 4-14-14 Brooklyn, N.Y.
5'10½", 175 lbs, brown eyes,
black wavy hair, sharp pro-
truding nose.

LOCALITIES : Resides 22955 Lakeshore
FREQUENTED Drive, St. Clair Shores,
Mich. Frequents Fort Wayne
Hotel in Detroit.

FAMILY : Married to Marie Madeleine
BACKGROUND Lutz and has no children; brother: Charles (dead);
sister: Mrs. Anna Mattia; father: Gaetano;
mother: Giovannina Lombardo.

CRIMINAL : Anthony Teramine, Mike Rubino, Peter Gaudino,
ASSOCIATES Raffaele Quasarano, ███████████, all of Detroit,
Giuseppe Catalanotte of Italy, Dominique Albertini
of Marseilles, France.

CRIMINAL : FBI# 1645652. Detroit PD# J-17443. Arrests since
HISTORY 1933 include armed robbery, larceny, breaking and
entering.

BUSINESS : Employed as bartender at Housey Maison Riviera,
8900 East Jefferson Ave., Detroit, Mich.

MODUS : An important member of the Mafia in the Detroit
OPERANDI area who took over the narcotic trafficking activities of his deceased brother Charles. Makes
trips to France to arrange for international
narcotic trafficking.

NAME   : William Eugene BUFALINO

ALIASES   : William Buffalino

DESCRIPTION : Born 4-13-1918 Pittston, Pa.
                6'0", 215 lbs, heavy build,
                black hair, brown eyes, glasses.

LOCALITIES   : Resides 12353 Wilshire, Det.,
FREQUENTED   Mich., also maintains residence
                at 47 E. Railroad St., Pittston
                Pa. Frequents Michigan Confer-
                ence of Teamsters, 2801
                Trumbull, Detroit, Mich.

FAMILY   : Married Marie Antoinette Meli, daughter of Frank
BACKGROUND   Meli; has 1 son and 2 daughters; father: Salvatore;
                mother: Louise Galante; cousin: Russell Bufalino,
                of Pittston, Pennsylvania.

CRIMINAL   : Salvatore Finazzo, ███████████████, Vincent Meli,
ASSOCIATES   Wm. Tocco, Frank Meli, Angelo Meli, James R. Hoffa.

CRIMINAL   : FBI #430478B Detroit PD #110617 Arrested Detroit
HISTORY   1953 for conspiracy to extort, St. Louis 1954 for
                investigation of murder, witness before Kefauver
                Committee 1951 and before N.Y. Grand Jury in James
                Hoffa wiretap case in 1957.

BUSINESS   : Pres. of Teamsters Loc. 985 & co-owner E. W. Bliss
                Motors, both Detroit. Attorney, member Mich. Bar Ass'n

MODUS   : Specializes in labor racketeering. Consultant to
OPERANDI   Mafia members in labor rackets. Considered un-
                official "legal mind" in illegal activities such
                as extortion and other related activities.

NAME   : Ralph CANNAVO

ALIASES   : Cannaro, Caneba, Nick
                  Palazzola, Sam Cannavo,
                  Vincent Zagari, John Miller,
                  John Millan, Sam Russ.

DESCRIPTION   : Born 10-30-12 Partinico,
                  Palermo, Sicily, Italy, 5'8"
                  150 lbs, blue eyes, dark
                  brown hair, slender build,
                  fair complexion. Not a U.S.
                  citizen, Alien Reg #1933530.

LOCALITIES   : Last known address 4814
FREQUENTED   Farmbrook Ave, Detroit, Mich. (1950). Has been de-
                  ported from U.S. on three occasions. Now believed to
                  have again illegally entered U.S., but whereabouts un-
                  known.

FAMILY   : Married Jeanette Finn; father: Salvatore; mother:
BACKGROUND   Marcantonia Zigari (both deceased); brothers: Dominic
                  & Frank; sisters: Mary Safina & Pietrina Mendola.

CRIMINAL   : Salvatore Vitale, Salvatore Mancuso, ███████████
ASSOCIATES   ██████████████████████████, of Italy, Nick Ditta, ████
                  ██████.

CRIMINAL   : FBI #342863. Detroit PD# 38979, I&NS #4141-0-76.
HISTORY   Record dates from 1930 and includes arrests for in-
                  vestigation, violation immigration laws and Federal
                  Narcotic conviction.

BUSINESS   : No legitimate occupation.

MODUS   : A hardened Mafia criminal who has never had a legit-
OPERANDI   imate source of income; with other Mafiosi here and
                  in Italy has engaged in counterfeiting and narcotic
                  trafficking for many years.

```
NAME          : Peter Victor CAVATAIO

ALIASES       : Pete Cavatavio

DESCRIPTION   : Born 5-19-30 Detroit, Mich.,
                5'9", 187 lbs, black hair,
                brown eyes, medium complex-
                ion, expensive dresser.

LOCALITIES    : Resides 765 Middlesex,
FREQUENTED      Grosse Pointe Park, Mich.,
                frequents Erie Baking Co.,
                Windsor, Canada; Surplus
                Bake Store, Carson's Rest-
                aurant & City Wide Cleaners,
                all Detroit, Mich.

FAMILY        : Wife: Pietrina Carrado; son: Dominic; daughters:
BACKGROUND      Patrina & Rose; father: Dominic; mother: Rose Salvato.

CRIMINAL      : Sam Finazzo, Michael Rubino, ███████████████, ██████████
ASSOCIATES      ████████, ██████████████████, ███████████████, █████████
                ███████, ████████████████.

CRIMINAL      : No FBI # assigned.  Detroit, Mich., PD# 175509.
HISTORY         Record consists only of misdemeanor & gambling
                arrests.

BUSINESS      : Operates Erie Baking Co., Windsor, Canada.  Also
                has income from City Wide Cleaners & Wide City
                Cleaners (both corporations controlled by his
                father.  Reports income in excess of $15,000 per
                year.

MODUS         : Although relatively young he is well respected in
OPERANDI        Detroit Mafia circles.  Is considered an adept stu-
                dent of Mafia aims under the tutelage of Salvatore
                (Sam) Finazzo one of Detroit's Mafia leaders.
```

206

NAME   : Paul CIMINO

ALIASES   : Sam Russo, Frank De Paulo,

DESCRIPTION : Born 9-14-98, San Biagio,
                  Platani, Sicily, 5'6", 135
                  lbs., brown hair, brown eyes
                  receding hair line, small
                  mole on nose.

LOCALITIES   : Formerly resided at 4133
FREQUENTED   Iroquois St., Detroit, Mich.
                  frequents Detroit Race Tracks
                  Vulcano Pizzeria, 6520 Mich-
                  igan Ave., and Al Green's,
                  Detroit; at the present time
                  is missing.

FAMILY   : Divorced from his second wife, Rose Bruno (2-26-52),
BACKGROUND   has three children from this marriage. First wife
                  deceased (Ignacia Bongiovanni), one child by common-
                  law wife Antonia Panariso, child deceased. Father
                  (Girolamo Cimino - deceased), mother Mattia Biod-
                  olillo, both born in Italy.

CRIMINAL   : Sam Caruso, Peter Gaudino, Joe Catalanotte, Frank
ASSOCIATES   Coppola, ████████, Joseph LoPiccolo, Anthony
                  Giordano, Dominique Albertini, ████████, Frank
                  Cammarata.

CRIMINAL   : FBI #623852, Detroit PD #84727, reported to have
HISTORY   eight arrests in Italy before coming to the U.S., in
                  1923; has two arrests in the U.S., for numbers in
                  1944 and 1948.

BUSINESS   : No legitimate employment.

MODUS   : An international drug trafficker and member of the
OPERANDI   Mafia in the Detroit area.

NAME	: Dominick CORRADO
ALIASES	: "Sparky", Domonic Corrado
DESCRIPTION	: Born 11-18-14 Detroit, Mich. 5'8", 160 lbs., brown eyes, black-grey hair.
LOCALITIES FREQUENTED	: Resides 5542 Nottingham Ave., Detroit, Mich. Frequents T.D. Music Co., 1013 St. Antoine St., Detroit.
FAMILY BACKGROUND	: Married to Frances Milazzo & has 4 children; father: Marco; mother: Antonina Elnia; brothers: James A. & Peter.
CRIMINAL ASSOCIATES	: ▓▓▓▓▓▓▓▓▓, ▓▓▓▓▓▓▓▓, Joe "Scarface" Bommarito, Lawrence Corrado, William Bufalino, all of Detroit area.
CRIMINAL HISTORY	: FBI#988732A. Detroit PD#96265. Arrests since 1939 include gambling, carrying concealed weapon, assault with intent to kill.
BUSINESS-	: Has interest in T.D. Music Co., 1013 St. Antoine St., Detroit, Mich.
MODUS OPERANDI	: A cousin of the notorious deceased Mafia leader Pete Corrado. Engaged in illegal gambling activities and is a strong arm man.

208

NAME	: Lawrence C. CORRADO
ALIASES	: Lawrence Carrado
DESCRIPTION	: Born 8-5-13 Detroit, Mich. 5'5", 208 lbs., black hair, brown eyes, heavy build.
LOCALITIES FREQUENTED	: Resides 4381 Drexel St., Detroit, Michigan.
FAMILY BACKGROUND	: Married to Rose Mitchell; father: Salvatore; mother: Angela Pitti.
CRIMINAL ASSOCIATES	: Dominick Corrado, Joe "Scarface" Bommarito, Joe Zerilli, Mike Rubino, all of Detroit.
CRIMINAL HISTORY	: FBI#574314. Detroit PD#57778. Arrests since 1930 include carrying concealed weapons, armed robbery, investigation for murder.
BUSINESS	: No legitimate employment or business known.
MODUS OPERANDI	: A nephew of the notorious deceased Mafia leader Pete Corrado. Maintains a reputation as a strong arm man and has been linked with 2 gangland slayings in the Detroit area.

He died of natural causes on May 27, 1984.

NAME : Anthony John D'ANNA

ALIASES : Tony Danna, Antonio D'Anna

DESCRIPTION : Born 12-10-99, Terrasini, Sicily, 5'7", 160 lbs, medium build, dark complexion, black greying hair, naturalized in Detroit, Michigan 11-9-31.

LOCALITIES FREQUENTED : Resides at 712 Berkshire, Grosse Pointe Park, Mich.

FAMILY BACKGROUND : Married Maria Barrace; daughter, Katherine is married to Anthony Bagnasco; daughter, Letitia Jane; mother: Kathryn Giannola; father: Pasquale, became involved in the Giannola gangland feud and was shot and killed in 1917 or 1918 as he was walking with Sam Giannola.

CRIMINAL ASSOCIATES : Peter and Yonnie Licavoli, now in prison; William Tocco, ███████, Mike Rubino, ███████, Angelo Meli, Joe Zerilli, Joe Bommarito, Santo Perrone of Detroit; Joe Massei of Florida.

CRIMINAL HISTORY : Detroit PD# 17275, arrests since 1921 include attempting to bribe a witness to a murder, prohibition law violation and armed robbery; was associated with Joe Massei in the bootlegging racket.

BUSINESS : Realizes huge annual income from the E & L Transport Co., of Detroit, the E & L Transport Co., of Indiana, and from rental property.

MODUS OPERANDI : A close associate of all top Mafia members in Detroit area; formerly a bootlegger.

NAME   : Giuseppe DITTA

ALIASES   : Joe Ditta, Joe Ditto, Joe
                  Datta, Joe Deitto, Joe Titta.

DESCRIPTION   : Born 3-28-1895 Paceco, Italy,
                  5'5", 150 lbs, brown eyes,
                  brown hair, circular scar on
                  right cheekbone. Naturalized
                  8-7-44 at Detroit, Mich.

LOCALITIES   : Resides 6087 Harrel, Detroit,
FREQUENTED   Mich. Frequents grocery store
                  at 9908 Connors & at 4398
                  Coplin St, (residence of
                  brother Nick) both in Detroit.

FAMILY   : Married Brigida; sons: Sam & Filippo; daughters:
BACKGROUND   Paulina & Francis; father: Filippo; mother: Paolo
                  Ochipinti (both deceased); brothers: Frank & Nick.

CRIMINAL   : Nick Ditta (brother), ████████████, Joe Catalno,
ASSOCIATES   ████████████████.

CRIMINAL   : No FBI # assigned. Detroit PD #15924. Arrests since
HISTORY   1921 include extortion, violation of prohibition
                  laws, & violation of the Postal Laws.

BUSINESS   : Retired. Formerly owned Ditta's Market 9908 Connors,
                  Detroit, Mich.

MODUS   : Has been an accomplice of his brother Nicola, an
OPERANDI   important Detroit Mafioso, in safecracking, ex-
                  tortion, gambling & narcotic rackets. Now believed
                  to be retired from active participation in such
                  crimes, but still active in Mafia affairs.

NAME   : Nicola DITTA

ALIASES   : Nick Titta, Nick Tita,
                 Nicola Diatro.

DESCRIPTION   : Born 8-11-05 Paceco, Sicily,
                 5'6", 160 lbs, brown hair,
                 blue eyes, receding hair
                 line, naturalized in 1941
                 at Detroit, Mich.

LOCALITIES   : Resides 4398 Coplin Street,
FREQUENTED   Detroit, Mich. Frequents
                 Alicia Bar & V.O. Bar, both
                 Detroit; also makes trips
                 to Muskegon & Grand Rapids, Mich., and Youngstown,
                 Ohio.

FAMILY   : Wife's name is Angelina; sons: Philip, Benny, and
BACKGROUND   Vito; daughter: Pauline; brothers: Frank, Joseph;
                 father: Filippo; mother: Paola Occhipinti.

CRIMINAL   : Pete Licavoli, Mike Rubino, William Bufalino,
ASSOCIATES   Joe "Scarface" Bommarito, ███████, Vincent Meli,
                 all of Detroit area, Steve Armone of NYC, and
                 Giuseppe Catalanotte of Italy.

CRIMINAL   : FBI #802867. Detroit PD# 23328. Arrests since 1924
HISTORY   include armed robbery, murder, extortion.

BUSINESS   : Employed as a real estate salesman by the Abdoo
                 Realty Co., Detroit, Mich.

MODUS   : An important member of the Mafia in Detroit area.
OPERANDI   Has reputation of numbers racketeer, safe burglar,
                 extortion; and has been involved in the narcotic
                 traffic with known Mafia traffickers in Detroit.

He was shot in 1919 and survived. In 1987, he pled
guilty at the Pizza Connection Trial and received 15
years in jail.

NAME : Salvatore EVOLA

ALIASES : Sabatore Evola, Sam Evola,
Sam Javola, Salvatore Jevola,
Samuel Evola.

DESCRIPTION : Born 12-4-1895 Palermo,
Sicily, 5'5½", 160 lbs,
brown-grey hair, blue eyes,
medium build.

LOCALITIES : Resides 22501 Avalon, St.
FREQUENTED Clair Shores, Mich. Frequents
U&M Cheese Mfg. Co, Port
Huron, Michigan & Detroit,
Mich., area.

FAMILY : Married Margaret Cucurru; sons: Salvatore & Joseph;
BACKGROUND daughter: Joan; father: Salvatore; mother: Josephine;
brothers: John & Jack.

CRIMINAL : Giuseppe Catalanotte (deportee), Nick & Joe Ditta,
ASSOCIATES Wm. Tocco, Salvatore Finazzo, ████████████, Giuseppe
Zerilli, Santo Perrone, Pete Lombardo and Raffaele
Quasarano; Pietro Davi & Rosario Mancino, of Italy.

CRIMINAL : FBI #46204. Detroit PD#10172. Arrests since 1920
HISTORY include robbery, burglary, felonious assault,
attempted rape, counterfeiting.

BUSINESS : Owns & operates U&M Cheese Manufacturing Co., 3733
N. River Rd, Port Huron, Mich.

MODUS : Middle echelon Detroit Mafioso closely associated
OPERANDI with top Mafia racketeers.

NAME   : Salvatore FINAZZO

ALIASES   : Sam Finazzo, Sam Sinazzo,
             Sam Finnazo

DESCRIPTION : Born 11-5-08 St. Louis, Mo.,
             5'5", 165 lbs., heavy build,
             brown eyes, black hair with
             receding hairline.

LOCALITIES : Resides at 18655 Gina Court,
FREQUENTED   Clinton Township, Mich.,
             frequents surplus bake shops
             at 8000 W. 8 mile and 9106
             Woodward, former residence
             at 781 Lakewood, all in
             Detroit, Mich.

FAMILY   : Married to Josephine Genna in 1929 at Detroit, has two
BACKGROUND   children, Vincent James, and Anna Milano, both residing
             in Detroit.

CRIMINAL   : Rafaele Quasarano, John Priziola, Peter Cavataio, Tony
ASSOCIATES   Randazzo, ███████, ████████████, and other Detroit
             hoodlums.

CRIMINAL   : FBI #1766946, Detroit PD #48219; arrest record dates
HISTORY   from 1926 in Detroit; one conviction for conspiracy
             to violate State gambling law in 1940; several fines
             for misdemeanors and several arrests for crimes rang-
             ing from robbery-armed to murder.

BUSINESS   : Owner of two surplus bake shops in Detroit; also owns
             interest in Greenfield Furniture Co., Detroit, Mich.

MODUS   : A close associate with Rafaele Quasarano in both
OPERANDI   pseudo-legitimate businesses and in the inter-
             national drug traffic; a major figure in the Detroit
             Mafia.

NAME	: Vincent James FINAZZO
ALIASES	: Jimmy Finazzo

DESCRIPTION : Born 4-28-31 Detroit, Mich.
5'6", 170 lbs, brown eyes,
black wavy hair, stocky
build.

LOCALITIES   : Resides 2502 Newport, De-
FREQUENTED   troit, Mich. Frequents
surplus baked goods stores
at 8000 W. Eight Mile Road
& 9106 Woodward, Detroit.

FAMILY   : Wife: Yvonne; daughters: Josephine and Louise;
BACKGROUND   father: Salvatore; mother: Josephine Genna;
sister: Anna Marie Milano.

CRIMINAL   : Salvatore Finazzo (father), Raffaele Quasarano,
ASSOCIATES   Michael Polizzi, Peter Cavataio, Peter Tocco, Angelo
Meli, Giuseppe "Long Joe" Bommarito, all of Detroit.

CRIMINAL   : FBI #428323B Detroit PD #110381 Record dating from
HISTORY   1948 includes arrests for assault & battery, armed
robbery, disturbing the peace. Federal narcotic conviction 1960.

BUSINESS   : Before 1960 narcotic arrest was employed at Michigan
Conference of Teamsters, 2801 Trumbull, Detroit, Mich.

MODUS   : An up and coming young Mafioso, following closely in
OPERANDI   the footsteps of his father. Will engage in any
illegal activity which is lucrative and has engaged
in large scale narcotic trafficking.

NAME   : Peter GAUDINO

ALIASES   : Peter Guadino

DESCRIPTION   : Born 4-1-00 Marsala, Sicily,
                5'4", 140 lbs., small build,
                brown eyes, grey-black hair,
                medium complexion, natural-
                ized 4-5-46.

LOCALITIES   : Resides 19944 Woodmont St.,
FREQUENTED   Harper Woods, Mich., fre-
                quents Gaudino Imported and
                Domestic Groceries, 13201
                Mack Ave., Detroit Race
                Tracks, Al Green's Restaurant
                Rooster Tail Restaurant all of Detroit.

FAMILY   : Married to Josephine Gaudino and has two children;
BACKGROUND   father is Domenico (deceased), Mother is Maria Valenti,
                Brother, Dr. Nicolo Gaudino of Marsala; Brother, Casper
                of Casablanca; Sister, Mrs. Mary Culickia of Marsala.

CRIMINAL   : Paul Cimino, ████████████, Joseph Lo Piccolo, Sam
ASSOCIATES   Caruso, Anthony Giordano, Dominique Albertini, Joe
                Catalanotte, ████████, ████████████████, Frank
                Cammarata.

CRIMINAL   : FBI #149718, convicted in 1934 and sentenced to a
HISTORY   term of three to twenty years for malicious threats,
                paroled 11-3-36.

BUSINESS   : Retired from and past owner of Gaudino Imported
                and Domestic Groceries, 13201 Mack Ave., this business
                now owned by Gaudino's son.

MODUS   : Believed to be an international drug trafficker; also
OPERANDI   a top member of the Mafia in the Detroit area.

216

He was supposed to be meeting Jimmy Hoffa at the time
of Hoffa's disappearance. He died in 2001, at the age
of 82.

NAME : Anthony GIACALONE

ALIASES : Tony Giacalone

DESCRIPTICN : Born 1-9-19 Detroit, Mich.,
6'0", 230 lbs, brown hair,
brown eyes, large build.

LOCALITIES : Resides 701 Balfour, Grosse
FREQUENTED Pte. Park, Mich., frequents
Old Corner Bar, Navaho Bar,
New Moon Bar and Back Stage
Bar, all Detroit.

FAMILY : Married to Jennie; father:
BACKGROUND Giacomo; mother: Antonina Ciaramitaro; brothers:
Vito and Charles; sister: Rose Provengano.

CRIMINAL : Sam Lucido, ████████████, George Massu, ███████
ASSOCIATES █████, ████████████, ████████████, Mike Rubino
and ████████████.

CRIMINAL : FBI #748689A, Detroit PD# 59837. Arrests since 1937
HISTORY include stripping cars, rape, armed robbery, firearms, bribery of police officer and gambling.

BUSINESS : Occasionally employed as bartender and also engaged
in real estate business.

MODUS : Operates policy racket in Detroit area as part of
OPERANDI the Peter Licavoli Mafia gang.

NAME	: VITO GIACALONE

ALIASES : William Giacalone

DESCRIPTION : Born 4-16-1923 Detroit, Mich.
5'8", 216 lbs, black hair,
hazel eyes, heavy build.

LOCALITIES : Resides 951 Nottingham, Grosse
FREQUENTED   Pointe, Mich. Frequents Old
Corner Bar, New Moon Bar, Back
Stage Bar and DeMichaele's Bar
and Bowling Alley, all in
Detroit, Mich.

FAMILY : Married Rose Stellino; son: Jack; father: Giacomo;
BACKGROUND   mother: Antonina Ciaramitaro; sister: Rose
Provengano; brothers: Anthony & Charles.

CRIMINAL : Salvatore Lucido, Michael Rubino, Peter Vitale,
ASSOCIATES   ███████████, ███████████, Anthony &
███████████ (his brothers).

CRIMINAL : FBI #748906A Detroit PD #82622   Record dates
HISTORY   from 1940 and includes arrests for gambling,
concealed weapons, loitering and traffic warrants.

BUSINESS : Reported to have interest in Old Corner Bar,
8857 Gratiot, Detroit, Michigan.

MODUS : Gambling controller in the Greek section of
OPERANDI   Detroit, representing the interests of the organization formerly headed by the late Pietro
Corrado, who was a top ranking Detroit Mafia
member.

NAME	: Francesco IRACI
ALIASES	: Frank Erace, Frank Romano
DESCRIPTION	: Born 11-20-03 Augusta, Sicily, 5'6", 168 lbs, black grey hair, brown eyes, medium build, dark complexion. Naturalized Detroit 9-24-28.
LOCALITIES FREQUENTED	: Resides 14221 Wilshire, Detroit, Mich. Frequents Eastown News Stand, Detroit, Mich.

FAMILY BACKGROUND	: Married to Anita; son: John; father: Giovanni; mother: Emmanuala Romano; brothers: Sebastian & Salvatore.
CRIMINAL ASSOCIATES	: Salvatore Finazzo, Giuseppe Moceri, Raffaele Quasarano, Mike Rubino, Anthony & ███████.
CRIMINAL HISTORY	: FBI #34523. Detroit PD# 23397. Arrests since 1924 for armed robbery, jewel theft, operating policy house.
BUSINESS	: Owns & operates Eastown News Stand, 8051 Harper, Detroit, Michigan.
MODUS OPERANDI	: Middle echelon Mafioso engaged mainly in bookmaking operations.

> He was a member of the Council of Dons in Detroit. He died on January 11, 1984.

NAME : Peter LICAVOLI

ALIASES : Peter Moceri, Pete Liccavoli Peter Rigley, Peter Daniels, George Daniels, "Horseface".

DESCRIPTION : Born 7-2-02 St. Louis, Mo., 5'6 3/4", 195 lbs, stout build, black wavy hair, brown eyes, scar on left wrist.

LOCALITIES FREQUENTED : Resides at 1154 Balfour Rd, Grosse Pte, Park, Mich., winter home at Grace Ranch, Tucson, Ariz. Frequents Tucson, Ariz., Cortez Hotel, San Diego, Cal., Al Green's Rest., Grosse Pte Park, Mich., currently incarcerated.

FAMILY BACKGROUND : Married Grace Bommarito; sons: Michael, Theodore & Peter; daughters: Geraldine & Kathy.

CRIMINAL ASSOCIATES : Joseph Bonanno, ████████████████ & Anthony Spagnola of Tucson; Joseph Bommarito, William Tocco, Joseph Zerilli of Detroit, Michigan.

CRIMINAL HISTORY : FBI #237021. Detroit PD# 30787. Record dates from 1912 & includes arrests for juvenile delinquency, robbery, kidnapping, bootlegging, murder, auto theft, assault & battery, bribery, gambling & extortion. Currently serving 30 months for tax violation.

BUSINESS : Owns Apache Realty & Development Co. of Detroit and Tucson and the Tucson Printing Co. Part owner of Skyroom of Tucson, a night club.

MODUS OPERANDI : A vicious Mafia criminal and killer who will stop at nothing. With Joseph Bommarito has taken control of bootlegging and gambling in Detroit area.

NAME   : Francesco LO MEDICO

ALIASES   : Frank Lamida, Frank LoMetico

DESCRIPTION   : Born 7-20-90 Partinico,
                  Sicily, 5'6", 175 lbs, brown
                  eyes, dark brown-grey hair.

LOCALITIES   : Resides 2225 Lakewood Ave.,
FREQUENTED   Detroit, Mich. Makes fre-
                  quent trips to Sicily.

FAMILY   : Married to Rachel Lazzano;
BACKGROUND   daughter: Margherita; bro-
                  thers: Gaspare, Vito,
                  Salvatore; father: Salvatore; mother: Margherita
                  Daidone (both deceased).

CRIMINAL   : John Priziola, Angelo Meli, John Spica, Joe Zerilli,
ASSOCIATES   Raffaele Quasarano, Pete Licavoli, all of Detroit
                  area, Salvatore Vitale (missing), Francesco P.
                  Coppola (deportee).

CRIMINAL   : FBI #4697345. Detroit PD# 11047. Arrests since
HISTORY   1919 include shooting with intent to kill, carrying
                  concealed weapon.

BUSINESS   : Former tavern owner. No current known legitimate
                  business or employment.

MODUS   : A powerful & influential leader of the faction of the
OPERANDI   Mafia in Detroit which hails from Partinico, Sicily.
                  Makes frequent trips to Sicily & arranges for inter-
                  national smuggling of narcotics.

He died in 1985 at the age of 79.

NAME : Salvatore LUCIDO

ALIASES : Sam Lucido, Sam Lutto, Joe
Lucido, William Di Lico

DESCRIPTION : Born 3-11-06 Detroit, Mich.,
5'8", 200 lbs, brown eyes,
black-grey hair, stout build

LOCALITIES : Resides 1507 Sunningdale Dr,
FREQUENTED Grosse Pt. Park, Mich. Fre-
quents S&B Hardware, 19341
Mack, Grosse Pt, Mich.

FAMILY : Married Rose Moceri; son:
BACKGROUND Jack; daughters: Vincenzia and Marilyn; father:
Giacomo; mother: Vincenzia Moceri.

CRIMINAL : Matteo Bartolotta, Domiano Bartolotta (California),
ASSOCIATES Joe & ████████████, Anthony & Vito Giacalone,
Mike Rubino all of Detroit.

CRIMINAL : FBI #1286583, Detroit PD# 20235. Arrests since 1923
HISTORY include armed robbery, murder, kidnapping, birbery,
gambling, possession of unregistered gun.

BUSINESS : Owns & operates with Sebastian Lucido, the S&B
Hardware, 19341 Mack, Grosse Pte., Mich.

MODUS : With other Mafiosi has engaged in bootlegging and
OPERANDI gambling operations in Detroit area. Controlling
figure in numbers operation in Detroit's East Side.

Meli was a member of the "Partnership" in Detroit. He died December 1, 1969 in Ft. Lauderdale, FL at the age of 72.

NAME : Angelo MELI

ALIASES :

DESCRIPTION : Born 2-10-1897 San Cataldo, Sicily, naturalized 7-29-29, Brooklyn, N.Y., 5'9", 185 lbs., grey hair, bald, dark complexion, brown eyes.

LOCALITIES FREQUENTED : Resides at 1326 Devonshire St., Grosse Pointe, Mich., has summer home and farm at 8129 Riverside Drive, Marine City, Mich.; frequents Hillcrest Country Club, Detroit.

FAMILY BACKGROUND : Wife: Vincenza DiMercurio; son: Vincent (married Pauline Perrone); daughter: Marie Antoinette (married to Jack Tocco, son of Wm. Tocco); daughter: Angela; brother: Frank; father: Vincent; mother: Maria Antoinia Ingaglio.

CRIMINAL ASSOCIATES : John Priziola, Joe Bommarito, Rafaele Quasarano, Pete Licavoli, Wm. Tocco, William Bufalino, John Ormento, Frank Livorsi, Onofrio Minaudo, Frank Coppola.

CRIMINAL HISTORY : FBI #3263518, Detroit PD#12264. Arrests date back to 1919, ranging from murder to disorderly conduct. Meli was so notorious in the 1930's that he was listed by Detroit Police as Public Enemy No. 1.

BUSINESS : Has interests in Flint Cold Storage, gas-station @ McDougall and Vernor Highway, Bilvin Dist. Co., Dallor Dry Cleaners, Federal Auto Supply of Detroit.

MODUS OPERANDI : One of the leaders of the Mafia and organized crime in the Detroit area.

NAME   : Frank MELI

ALIASES   : Frank Melia

DESCRIPTION : Born 8-25-1894 San Cataldo,
              Caltanissetta, Sicily, black-
              grey hair, brown eyes, med-
              ium heavy build, dark comp-
              lexion, naturalized 7-30-29
              Brooklyn, New York.

LOCALITIES   : Resides 12601 Wilshire,
FREQUENTED   Detroit, Mich. Frequents
               Meltone Music Co., & White
               Music Co, both at 2600 Grand
               River, Detroit, Michigan.

FAMILY   : Married Grazia Panzica; son: Vincent Angelo; daugh-
BACKGROUND   ter: Marie Antoinette; father: Vincent; mother:
               Maria Antonia Incaglio; brother: Angelo.

CRIMINAL   : Angelo Meli (brother), Mike Polizzi, Joe Zerilli,
ASSOCIATES   William Tocco, Joe Bommarito, Pete Licavoli, Mike
               Rubino & William Bufalino all of Detroit.

CRIMINAL   : Michigan State Police #18191. Detroit PD# 2210.
HISTORY   Record dates from 1924 and includes arrests for
               murder and armed robbery.

BUSINESS   : With son Vincent Angelo Meli, owns & operates
               Meltone Music Co, & White Music Co, 2600 Grand
               River, Detroit, Michigan.

MODUS   : Brother of Detroit Mafia leader Angelo Meli and
OPERANDI   himself an important Mafia figure active in the
               juke box racket.

> He died of bone cancer at the age of 87 in January 2008.

NAME : Vincent Angelo MELI

ALIASES : None

DESCRIPTION : Born 1-2-21 San Cataldo,
Caltanissetta, Sicily, Italy,
5'9", 190 lbs, black hair,
brown eyes, medium heavy
build, Denver U.S. citizenship from father.

LOCALITIES : Resides 1683 Newcastle,
FREQUENTED Grosse Pte. Woods, Mich.,
frequents 2600 Grand River,
Detroit, Mich, & Saginaw,
Michigan.

FAMILY : Married Grace M. DiMecurio; father: Frank; mother:
BACKGROUND Grazia Panzica; sister: Marie Antoinette.

CRIMINAL : Angelo Meli (uncle), Frank Meli (father), William
ASSOCIATES Tocco, William Bufalino, Santo Perrone, Raffaele
Quasarano, all Detroit, Michigan.

CRIMINAL : FBI #80299C. Detroit PD# 96842. Show arrest in 1950
HISTORY for investigation of gambling laws which case was
dismissed.

BUSINESS : With father Frank Meli, owns & operates Meltone
Music Co, & White Music Co, both at 2600 Grand River,
Detroit, Mich. Also owns Ace Automatic Co, & Bel-
Aire Lodge both in Saginaw, Michigan.

MODUS : Father & Uncle are important Detroit area Maifa
OPERANDI leaders. Active with his father in the Mafia controlled juke box racket.

225

```
NAME           : Salvatore PALAZZOLO

ALIASES        : Sam, Palazzola, Pizzolo

DESCRIPTION    : Born 7-6-02 Cinisi, Palermo,
                 Sicily, 5'11", 175 lbs, grey-
                 black hair, brown eyes, na-
                 turalized Detroit 12-3-28.

LOCALITIES     : Resides 440 Riverview Ave.,
FREQUENTED       Monroe, Mich. Frequents
                 Detroit's "Down River Area."

FAMILY         : Married Nicolina Bommarito,
BACKGROUND       father: Salvatore; mother:
                 Felice Galati.

CRIMINAL       : Angelo Meli, Giuseppe Bommarito, Frank Meli, Peter
ASSOCIATES       Licavoli, ███████████████ .

CRIMINAL       : FBI #1321. Detroit PD #45215. Record dating from
HISTORY          1925 includes arrests for indecent exposure, Inv.,
                 of violation of immigration laws, petit larceny,
                 carrying concealed weapons, breach of excise tax
                 (Canada).

BUSINESS       : No legitimate occupation known. Lists self as
                 "merchant".

MODUS          : Old time bootlegger and influential Mafioso who
OPERANDI         controls gambling in Detroit's "Down River Area" in
                 association with Emmanuel Badalamenti
```

NAME	: Espano Gaspare PERRONE
ALIASES	: Jasper Perrone, Gaspare Pirrone.
DESCRIPTION	: Born 2-21-93 Alcamo, Sicily, naturalized 2-13-28 Detroit. 5'5", 180 lbs., brown eyes, thinning grey hair, heavy build.
LOCALITIES FREQUENTED	: Resides both in Mt. Clemens, Mich., & Hollywood, Fla. Frequents Detroit, Mich., & Hollywood, Fla.
FAMILY BACKGROUND	: Married to Louise Calcagno & has 2 children; father: Melchiarre; mother: Maria (both dead); brothers: Santo & Mathew.
CRIMINAL ASSOCIATES	: Angelo Meli, Frank Meli, John Priziola, Santo Perrone (brother), all of Detroit; Pete Lombardo of California; Joe Catalanotte (deportee)
CRIMINAL HISTORY	: FBI#1023186. Detroit PD#12997. Arrests since 1918 include violation of Draft Laws, Firearms Act, Liquor Laws.
BUSINESS	: Has interests in real estate in Hollywood, Fla.
MODUS OPERANDI	: Associated with his brother Santo who is a "strong arm man" & "enforcer" for the Mafia in the Detroit area.

On January 19, 1962, Perrone's right leg was destroyed when a bomb exploded in his car. He was murdered on March 11, 1968 by Frank Mari.

NAME : Santo PERRONE

ALIASES : Sam Perrone

DESCRIPTION : Born 12-24-95 Alcamo, Sicily, 5'7", 165 lbs., Medium build, grey-black hair, brown eyes, right eye crossed, wears glasses, naturalized 11-13-34, Detroit.

LOCALITIES FREQUENTED : Resides currently on transient bases with sons-in-law Vincent Meli, Carl Renda and Augustino Orlando, all of Detroit, Mich., frequents AAA Auto Wash at 12825 Gratiot, Detroit, and the Italian-American Club of Detroit.

FAMILY BACKGROUND : Married to Agosta (Ida) Calcagno, has 3 daughters, brother of Gasper and Mathew Perrone, father-in-law of Carl Renda, Vincent Meli, and Augustino Orlando. Father's name Melchiarre, mother's name Maria, both deceased.

CRIMINAL ASSOCIATES : Angelo Meli, Frank Meli, ███████████, Gasper Perrone Joe Catalanotte, Pete Lombardo, ███████████.

CRIMINAL HISTORY : FBI #334934, Detroit PD# 12837, arrest record dates back to 1919, convictions for violation Liquor Laws, Internal Revenue Laws, Labor Laws; several other arrests from concealed weapons to murder; prime suspect in Walter Ruether shooting in 1945.

BUSINESS : Only known current business operation is AAA Auto Wash at 12825 Gratiot in Detroit.

MODUS OPERANDI : Known strike-breaker, alien smuggler, financier for any illegal enterprises, considered as "enforcer" for Mafia in Detroit.

NAME	: Michael POLIZZI
ALIASES	: Big Mike.
DESCRIPTION	: Born 1-2-24 San Cataldo, Sicily; 5'11", 230 lbs, brown eyes, brown hair, graduate of Syracuse University.
LOCALITIES FREQUENTED	: Resides 17304 Juliana Ave., East Detroit, Mich. Frequents Valley Plater's Inc., Detroit.

FAMILY BACKGROUND	: Married to Angeline Priziola & has 2 children; father: Angelo (dead); mother: Assunta.
CRIMINAL ASSOCIATES	: Joe "Scarface" Bommarito, Raffaele Quasarano, John Priziola (father-in-law), Pete Licavoli, ██████ ██████, Mike Rubino, all of Detroit area; John Ormento, Salvatore Santoro, of NYC; Frank and Joseph Matranga of San Diego area.
CRIMINAL HISTORY	: FBI# 842609B. Detroit PD# 98381. Only arrest in 1950 at Detroit for armed robbery.
BUSINESS	: Has substantial interests in Torasion Oil Co., Valley Plater's Inc., and Moravian Acres, all in Detroit area.
MODUS OPERANDI	: One of the most prominent younger members of the Detroit Mafia who is taking over the place in the organization formerly held by his deceased father Angelo.

Priziola, one of the five members of the Council of
Dons, attempted to seize control of Detroit after the
death of Joseph Zerilli in 1978. His reign ended nearly
a year later with his death on April 14, 1979.

NAME   : John PRIZIOLA

ALIASES   : Papa John Priziola, John
                  Braziola, John Barzziola,
                  John Prisiola, John Peraziola

DESCRIPTION   : Born 1-12-1893, Partinico,
                  Sicily, Italy. 5'3½", 165
                  lbs, brown-eyes, grey-brown
                  hair, balding, wears glasses.

LOCALITIES   : Resides 1349 Devonshire St.,
FREQUENTED   Grosse Pointe, Michigan

FAMILY   : First wife, Thomasina, de-
BACKGROUND   ceased, mother of Ninette (Mrs. Peter Tocco), Frances
                  (Mrs. Frank Matranga), Angeline (Mrs. Michael Polizzi)
                  and Josephine (Mrs. Joseph Matranga); second wife,
                  Francesca, mother of Thomasina (Mrs. James D. Camma-
                  rata); father: Giuseppe; mother: Antonina Sciacchitana.

CRIMINAL   : All top ranking Detroit Mafiosi; Ralph Caleca and
ASSOCIATES   Anthony Giordano of St. Louis; John Ormento & Salva-
                  tore Santoro of NYC; Frank & Joseph Matranga of Cal-
                  ifornia; Salvatore Vitale, Francesco Coppola and
                  Serafino Mancuso of Italy.

CRIMINAL   : FBI #783659-C Detroit PD #10171 Record dating from
HISTORY   1917 includes arrests for grand larceny, prohibition
                  law violation, concealed weapons and murder.

BUSINESS   : St. Clair Terrace Corp., royalties from P&T Oil Co.,
                  rentals from 16906 Harper, Detroit; Jon Car Homes.

MODUS   : One of the heads of the Mafia in the Detroit area.
OPERANDI   Engaged in large scale narcotic smuggling and
                  distribution.

NAME   : Joseph R. QUASARANO

ALIASES   : Jimmy, Cadillac Joe

DESCRIPTION   : Born 4-4-1898 Partinico,
                    Sicily, Italy. 5'4", 150 lbs,
                    brown eyes, brown-grey hair.

LOCALITIES   : Resides 459 Bournemouth,
FREQUENTED   Grosse Pointe, Mich. Fre-
                    quents residences of married
                    sons Joseph & Anthony.

FAMILY   : Wife: Grace; sons: Anthony
BACKGROUND   & Joseph; father: Anthony;
                    mother: Mary Cippola.

CRIMINAL   : Raffaele Quasarano, Michael Polizzi, Salvatore
ASSOCIATES   Finazzo, Angelo Meli, John Priziola, Peter Gaudino.

CRIMINAL   : Detroit PD #11212 Record dating from 1929 includes
HISTORY   arrests for bribery and obstructing justice.

BUSINESS   : He and his sons own Eastown (Beer) Distributors,
                    14725 Gratiot, Detroit, Michigan.

MODUS   : Middle echelon Detroit Mafia member. No recent
OPERANDI   overt criminal activities, but is rather influ-
                    ential in a group of Detroit Mafiosi who origin-
                    ated in Partinico, Sicily.

NAME : Raffaele QUASARANO

ALIASES : Ralph, Gino & James Quasarano, James Quasamoni.

DESCRIPTION : Born 12-20-1910 Mauch Chunk,
Pa., 5'8", 160 lbs, medium
build, black hair, blue eyes,
glasses, numerous cyst scars
on back of neck.

LOCALITIES : Resides 20143 Doyle Court,
FREQUENTED   Grosse Pte. Woods, Michigan.
Frequents Michigan Mutual
Distributing Co., Detroit, Mich.

FAMILY : Married Giovanna Vitale; two children; father: Vin-
BACKGROUND   cenzo (deceased); mother: Francesca; brother: Diego
(resides Italy); father-in-law: Vito Vitale.

CRIMINAL : Angelo Meli, John Priziola, Angelo Polizzi, Pietro
ASSOCIATES   Gaudino, Michael Polizzi & Salvatore Finazzo, of
Detroit; John Ormento, Frank Livorsi, Francisco
Costiglia, of N.Y.; Lucky Luciano, Francisco P.
Coppola, Giuseppe Corso & Vito Vitale of Italy.

CRIMINAL : FBI #736238 Detroit PD #40868 Record dating from
HISTORY   1931 includes arrests for disorderly conduct, armed
robbery, shooting, wire tapping, gambling and violation of Federal Narcotic Laws.

BUSINESS : Owns Motor City Barber Supply, Greenfield Furniture,
Moravian Acres & Motor City Arena & Gym, Detroit.

MODUS : A top level Detroit Mafia member and international
OPERANDI   narcotic trafficker. His father-in-law, Vito Vitale,
is a Mafia leader in Italy.

232

NAME : Vincenzo RANDAZZO

ALIASES : James Randazzo, Jimmy Randazo, James Rondozzo

DESCRIPTION: Born 12-5-03 Campo Franco, Sicily, 5'5", 165 lbs, grey hair, brown eyes, naturalized 7-5-39 Detroit, Mich.

LOCALITIES : Resides 2234 Edwin, Hamtramck, Mich. Frequents bars and pool rooms in Hamtramck area.
FREQUENTED

FAMILY : Wife is Angeline, has a daughter Mary Ann and a son; brother: Gaspare; father: Joseph; mother: Maria Gianno.
BACKGROUND

CRIMINAL : Sam Finazzo, Rafaele Quasarano, Joe "Scarface" Bommarito, Mike Rubino, Pete Licavoli, all of Detroit area.
ASSOCIATES

CRIMINAL : FBI# 196145. Detroit PD# 35024. Arrests since 1928 include armed robbery, maintaining gambling place.
HISTORY

BUSINESS : Owner of Jim's Soda Bar, 2713 E. Davison Street, Detroit, Michigan.

MODUS : A Mafia member from the Detroit area currently engaged in Mafia controlled illegal gambling in the Detroit area.
OPERANDI

NAME   : Michael RUBINO

ALIASES   : Michele Rubino

DESCRIPTION   : Born 2-26-11 Detroit, Mich.,
                 5'4", 165 lbs., stock build,
                 grey-black hair, brown eyes,
                 ruddy complexion.

LOCALITIES   : Resides at 1068 Bedford,
FREQUENTED   Grosse Pointe Park, Mich.,
                 frequents Al Green's Rest-
                 aurant, Rooster Tail Supper
                 Club in Detroit and Lom-
                 bardi's Horse Ranch, Algonac
                 Mich.

FAMILY   : Married to Marie Helen Moore; has two children,
BACKGROUND   Daniel and Diane; both parents are deceased.

CRIMINAL   : Mike Polizzi, Angelo Meli, John Priziola, Rafaele
ASSOCIATES   Quasarano, ████████████, Santo Perrone, ████████████,
                 Joe (Scarface) Bommarito.

CRIMINAL   : FBI #275030, Detroit PD #37506, convicted for vio-
HISTORY   lation of Federal Narcotic Law in case, Mich-2725 in
                 1941; sentenced to 18 months; convicted for counter-
                 feiting in 1934 in Detroit and sentenced to 7 years;
                 several arrests in Detroit for gambling with no con-
                 victions.

BUSINESS   : Has interests in City-Wide Cleaners, P & J Oil Co.,
                 Torosian Oil Co., all in Detroit; is associated with
                 Mike Polizzi, George (Moses) Massu, Joe (Scarface)
                 Bommarito, and Ed. Torosian in the above businesses.

MODUS   : The "Enforcer" for the gambling operations in Detroit;
OPERANDI   reported to control all gambling in the "down-river"
                 suburban area of Detroit; Mafia "expert" on organized
                 gambling operations.

NAME	: Giovanni Rosario SPICA

ALIASES : John Spica, Giovanni Spiga,
John Spiga, Rosario Spiga

DESCRIPTION : Born 4-2-1888, Montelepre,
Palermo, Sicily, Italy.
5'6", 150 lbs, brown eyes,
dark brown hair-bald.
Naturalized Detroit 1-9-50

LOCALITIES : Resides 3926 Field Street,
FREQUENTED   Detroit, Mich.

FAMILY : Married Vincenza Palermo;
BACKGROUND   sons: James & Thomas; daughter: Rosalie (Mrs.
Antonio Terranova).

CRIMINAL : John Priziola, Frank Meli, Angelo Polizzi, James
ASSOCIATES   Quasarano, John Ormento, Raffael Quasarano,
████████████.

CRIMINAL : FBI #294166   Detroit PD #18696   Record dating
HISTORY   from 1926 includes arrests for prohibition law
violation, extortion, disorderly conduct, Federal
Narcotic conviction. Deported from U.S. 1938 and
later readmitted because married to U.S. citizen.

BUSINESS : Retired from trucking business.

MODUS : Top level Detroit Mafia member. Engages in narcotic
OPERANDI   smuggling and wholesale trafficking in cooperation
with other Mafiosi.

NAME	: Anthony TERAMINE
ALIASES	: Tony Termain, Tony Termine, Black Tony, Tony Tuttson.

DESCRIPTION	: Born 2-16-06 Detroit, Mich., 5'8½", 160 lbs, black hair, brown eyes, heavy build, ruddy complexion.
LOCALITIES FREQUENTED	: Resided 3948 Harvard, Detroit Mich. Frequents Gratiot Central Market, Tuller Hotel, 5847 Mitchell, all in Detroit & also visits Chicago, Ill., and California.
FAMILY BACKGROUND	: Divorced from Mrs. Lillian Einkorn and has son Irvin; father: Savillio; mother: Mary; brother: Joseph; sister: Mrs. Mamie Puglia; girl-friend: Grace Slater, 5847 Mitchell; all of Detroit; & common-law-wife: Joyce Tollis of Chicago, Ill.
CRIMINAL ASSOCIATES	: Frank LoMedico, Raffaele Quasarano, Toto DiGiovanni, Joe Russelli, all of Detroit; Frank & Joseph Matranga of California; & Joe Catalanotte.
CRIMINAL HISTORY	: FBI #649176. Detroit PD#24030. Arrests since 1922 include armed robbery, gambling, defrauding hotel, State Liquor Laws, & 2 convictions for Federal Narcotic Laws.
BUSINESS	: No legitimate employment or business known. On occasion works with brother Joseph with fruit business at Gratiot Central Market in Detroit.
MODUS OPERANDI	: A major violator of the narcotic laws and is closely associated with Mafia leaders in Detroit.

NAME	: Erasimo TIMPA
ALIASES	: Sam Timpa
DESCRIPTION	: Born 4-9-14 Detroit, Mich., 5'3", 150 lbs, black hair, brown eyes, dark complexion, stocky build.
LOCALITIES FREQUENTED	: Resides 19155 Woodmont, Harper Woods, Mich., frequents Motor City Barber & Beauty Supplies, 3457 Gratiot, Detroit, Michigan.
FAMILY BACKGROUND	: Father: Vincenzo; mother: Concetta Accetta, both born Italy; married to Ann, no known children.
CRIMINAL ASSOCIATES	: Raffaele Quasarano, Angelo Meli, John Priziola, Angelo Polizzi, Frank Meli, and Paolo Cimino, all of Detroit, Michigan.
CRIMINAL HISTORY	: FBI #3370455, Detroit PD#60614. Has arrests from 1939 thru 1945 for investigation of stench bombing, conspiracy to commit extortion, gambling, abortion, possession and sale of counterfeit meat ration stamps. Received full presidential pardon 1956.
BUSINESS	: With co-owners Mario Oddo and Raffaele Quasarano, he operates the Motor City Barber and Beauty Supplies Co., 3457 Gratiot, Detroit, Michigan.
MODUS OPERANDI	: With other Detroit Mafiosi has been engaged for many years in labor racketeering.

237

> Tocco retired to Florida in 1963 and died May 28, 1972.

NAME : Guglielmo TOCCO

ALIASES : William Tocco, Vito Tocco, "Black Bill".

DESCRIPTION : Born 1897 Terrasini, Sicily. 5'7", 160 lbs, brown eyes, grey wavy hair.

LOCALITIES FREQUENTED : Resides 781 Middlesex, Grosse Pointe, Mich., frequents Rooster Tail & Al Green's Restaurants in Greater Detroit area.

FAMILY BACKGROUND : Married to Rosalie Zerilli; sons: Jack & Anthony; daughters: Mrs. Evelyn Sperazza, Mrs. Mary Bagnasco, Mrs. Josephine Tocco, Mrs. Rosalie Tocco, Mrs. Grace Licata.

CRIMINAL ASSOCIATES : Angelo Meli, Joe Zerilli, John Priziola, Pete Tocco, Pete Licavoli, Joe "scarface" Bommarito, all from Detroit area; Joe Profaci & John Ormento of NYC.

CRIMINAL HISTORY : FBI# 534742. Detroit PD# 13817. Arrests since 1920 include armed robbery, prohibition laws, gambling, and investigation of murder.

BUSINESS : Together with brother-in-law Joe Zerilli he owns Detroit Italian Baking Co., Pfeiffer Macomb Distributors of Detroit, Lake Shore Coach Lines of Grosse Pointe, and also has an interest in the Jarson & Zerilli Produce Co., Detroit.

MODUS OPERANDI : Together with Joe Zerilli he heads the branch of the Mafia in Detroit who emigrated from Terrasini, Sicily. Acts as "judge" in arbitrations of the gambling combine in Detroit headed by Licavoli-Bommarito combine.

NAME   : Peter TOCCO

ALIASES   : Pete Tocco

DESCRIPTION   : Born 6-30-15, N.Y.C., 5'9",
                 180 lbs., medium build,
                 black hair, grey eyes, dark
                 complexion, has operation
                 scar on right ankle.

LOCALITIES   : Resides at 19974 E. Doyle
FREQUENTED   Court, Grosse Pointe, Mich.,
                 frequents DiLorenzo-Tocco
                 Importing & Wholesale Co.,
                 at 13200 Mack, Detroit, of
                 which he is part owner,
                 also frequents the Rooster Tail Restaurant.

FAMILY   : Married to Antoinette Priziola, daughter of John
BACKGROUND   Priziola; no relation to William "Black Bill" Tocco
                 or Pete Tocco of Detroit.

CRIMINAL   : John Priziola, William Tocco, Pete Tocco, Angelo Meli,
ASSOCIATES   Pete Licavoli, Joe Bommarito, all of Detroit.

CRIMINAL   : Criminal record dates back to 1949 when he was arrested
HISTORY   for violation State gambling laws; he was not convicted
                 on this charge; has no other arrests; Detroit PD #160860.

BUSINESS   : Part owner of the DiLorenzo-Tocco Fish and Poultry Co.,
                 Detroit; part owner of DiLorenzo-Tocco Importing &
                 Wholesale Food Co., also of Detroit.

MODUS   : A younger member of the Detroit Mafia; is a member of
OPERANDI   the Licavoli-Bommarito gambling syndicate.

239

NAME   : Pietro TOCCO

ALIASES   : Pete Tocco

DESCRIPTION   : Born 6-8-1892 Terrasini,
                 Palermo, Sicily, Italy, 5'9",
                 157 lbs, blue eyes, grey
                 hair, medium build, natural-
                 ized.

LOCALITIES   : Resides 710 Joseph Campau
FREQUENTED   St, Detroit, Michigan.

FAMILY   : Married Fillipenia Cusmano;
BACKGROUND   sons: Samuel J. & Anthony P;
                 daughter: Grace; father: Salvatore; mother: Grace
                 Palazzolo; brothers: John (Boston), Joseph (B'klyn),
                 Salvatore (Italy); sister: Grace Tocco, (Detroit),
                 and Jenny Tocco, (Italy).

CRIMINAL   : Joseph Matranga, John Priziola, ███████████, █████
ASSOCIATES   █████, █████████, █████████.

CRIMINAL   : FBI #378737. Detroit, Mich. PD #16268. Record dates
HISTORY   from 1921 and includes arrests for murder and narcotic
                 law violations. Federal narcotic conviction.

BUSINESS   : Owns Tocco's Market 700 Joe Campau St., Detroit, which
                 is operated by his son Anthony P. Tocco.

MODUS   : An influential Detroit Mafia member who dominated
OPERANDI   the narcotic traffic in that area until his arrest
                 in 1940, after which time he appears to have with-
                 drawn from active participation in Mafia crimes.

In the 1960s, Zerilli was named one of the ruling members of Detroit's mafia. He died October 30, 1977, of natural causes.

NAME : Joseph ZERILLI

ALIASES : Joe Zerello, Joe Zerillo

DESCRIPTION : Born 12-11-1897 Terrasini, Sicily, 5'5", 175 lbs, brown eyes, black-grey hair, naturalized 1936 in Detroit.

LOCALITIES FREQUENTED : Resides 702 Middlesex, Grosse Pointe, Mich. Frequents Al Green's & Rooster Tail Restaurants in Detroit, also Detroit area race tracks

FAMILY BACKGROUND : Wife: Josephine Orlando; son: Anthony, married to Frances Profaci (daughter of Joe Profaci); daughters: Mrs. Josephine Licavoli, Mrs. Rosalie Tocco; father: Anthony; mother: Rosalie Tocco.

CRIMINAL ASSOCIATES : William Tocco, Pete Licavoli, William Bufalino, Angelo Meli, Joe "Scarface" Bommarito, Peter Tocco all of Detroit area, Joe Profaci, Joe Magliocco, John Ormento, all of NYC area.

CRIMINAL HISTORY : FBI #795171C, Detroit PD# 11413. Record indicates one arrest in 1919 for carrying concealed weapons.

BUSINESS : Owns Jarson & Zerilli Produce Co., Detroit, & is partners with William Tocco in Pfeiffer Macomb Distributors & Lake Shore Coach Lines in Grosse Pointe, Mich.

MODUS OPERANDI : A leader of the Mafia in Detroit. Was a bootlegger during Prohibition and now acts as judge & arbitrator of the Licavoli-Bommarito gambling syndicate in Detroit.

NAME   : Leonard AFFRONTI

ALIASES   : Lonnie, Albert Leonard,
                  Joseph Fradella.

DESCRIPTION   : Born 5-24-98, Canada, 5'7",
                  155 lbs., brown eyes, grey
                  hair, dark complexion, stout
                  build.

LOCALITIES   : Resided at 514 Gillis,
FREQUENTED   Kansas City, Mo., currently
                  incarcerated U.S. Peniten-
                  tiary, Leavenworth, Kansas.

FAMILY   : Married to Billie Leroy,
BACKGROUND   Father, Antonio, mother, Antonina Fradella, five
                  sisters, all married, one of them to Tudie Lascuola.

CRIMINAL   : ████, ███, ██████████████, Joe Olivo, ██████████,
ASSOCIATES   Jack Ancona, Frank Crapisi, all of Kansas City.

CRIMINAL   : FBI #189847, Kansas City PD#66036, numerous arrests
HISTORY   since 1919 including, highway robbery, murder and
                  two convictions Federal Narcotic Laws; currently
                  serving 20 year sentence (narcotics), possible re-
                  lease in 1968.

BUSINESS   : None.

MODUS   : Interstate narcotic trafficker; a killer and strong
OPERANDI   arm man for the Mafia in the Missouri area.

NAME   : Jack ANCONA

ALIASES   : Giacomo Ancona,

DESCRIPTION   : Born 1-10-1889, Castelve-
                    trano, Trapani, Sicily, 5'7",
                    165 lbs, brown eyes, grey
                    hair, fair complexion. Res-
                    ident Alien I&NS #A-321406.

LOCALITIES   : Resides at 2826 E. 8th St, &
FREQUENTED   frequents Roma Bakery Co.,
                    both Kansas City, Mo.

FAMILY   : Wife Jennie Ancona deceased;
BACKGROUND   children: Joseph, John, Samuel J., Rosie (now Mrs.
                    John Sorrentino) and Genevieve (now Mrs. Charles
                    Gerber); father: Giovanni; mother: Rosa Conte.

CRIMINAL   : Joseph Olivo, ███████████, █████████████, Joseph
ASSOCIATES   and Frank DeLuca, Carl and Nicholas Civello, Joseph
                    and Michael Lascoula and Joseph Filardo, all of
                    Kansas City, Missouri.

CRIMINAL   : FBI #1683880. The files of the Kansas City, PD re-
HISTORY   flect that Ancona's file was destroyed in March
                    1929, by order of Director of Police; on 9-18-39,
                    was sentenced to seven years imprisonment for vio-
                    lation of the narcotic laws.

BUSINESS   : No legitimate occupation known.

MODUS   : From 1930 up until his conviction in 1939, Ancona
OPERANDI   had charge of distribution for the narcotic syndicate
                    operated by the Mafia; since his release, he has been
                    inactive in the rackets, but receives a share in the
                    proceeds of all illicit income of the local organ-
                    ization.

NAME : John B. BLANDO

ALIASES : Giovanni Battista Blando

DESCRIPTION : Born 6-12-1897, Bagheria,
Sicily, 5'7½", 175 lbs,
brown eyes, grey hair, olive
complexion and stout build,
naturalized 10-10-27, Kansas
City, Mo.

LOCALITIES : Resides 637 E. 74th St.,
FREQUENTED Kansas City, Mo., frequents
Superior Wines & Liquor Co.,
The Roma Baking Co., and
5th St., Drug Store, all of Kansas City, Mo.

FAMILY : Married Maria Balistrere, has three children,
BACKGROUND Emanuel R., Antonio, and Grace L. Blando.

CRIMINAL : James Balestrere (uncle), Joseph Filardo, Joseph
ASSOCIATES Cusamano, Nicholas Civello, ████, ███████, Pete and
Joseph DiGiovanni, Gaetano Lococo, Alex, ██████████
██████████████, all of Kansas City, Mo; also associated
with prominent members of the Mafia throughout the
U.S., and Europe.

CRIMINAL : No FBI # assigned. Arrested Kansas City, Mo., 1924,
HISTORY for bootlegging.

BUSINESS : Has the Superior Wines & Liquor Co., Inc., Kansas
City, Mo., which controls the Schenley liquor
franchise; he and his children own the stock of this
corporation.

MODUS : Replaced his uncle James Balestrere as head of the
OPERANDI Mafia in Kansas City, Mo., when the latter retired
in 1950.

NAME   : Antonio BONINO

ALIASES   : Tony Bilello.

DESCRIPTION   : Born 3-9-05 Gibellina, Sic-
                ily; 5'4", 165 lbs, brown
                eyes, black hair, natural-
                ized 9-27-43 Kansas City.

LOCALITIES   : Resides 3620 Gladstone Blvd,
FREQUENTED   Kansas City, Mo. Frequents
                Quaff Buffet, Roma Baking
                Co., 5th St Drug Store, Pom-
                peian Room, Antonio's Piz-
                zeria, all in Kansas City.

FAMILY   : Married to Vincenza Solito; daughter: Virginia;
BACKGROUND   son: Nunzio.

CRIMINAL   : Nick & Carl Civello, Joe & Mike Lascoula, ████
ASSOCIATES   ██████, ███████████, ████████████, █
                ██████████, ███████████████, all of Kansas City.

CRIMINAL   : FBI# 595763. Kansas City, Mo., PD# 34069.
HISTORY   Arrests since 1932 include violation of the
                National Prohibition Act.

BUSINESS   : Owns and operates the Quaff Buffet Tavern in
                Kansas City, Mo.

MODUS   : During the late thirties he was a "runner" for
OPERANDI   the Kansas City Mafia controlled narcotic syn-
                dicate. Later he worked as a croupier at several
                dice games operated by the organization; is used
                as an underling to carry out orders of his Mafia
                superiors.

NAME	: Ralph CALECA

ALIASES : Caleco, Calica, Shorty Ralph

DESCRIPTION : Born 5-21-00 Partinico, Sicily, 5'3", 145 lbs., medium build, brown hair, turning grey, brown eyes, wears glasses, tattoo right forearm, naturalized at St. Louis in 1944.

LOCALITIES FREQUENTED : Resides 7323 Devonshire Ave, St. Louis, Mo., frequents Anthony Novelty and Vending Co., St. Louis County, Mo.

FAMILY BACKGROUND : Wife, Lena (nee Bologna), 52, married in St. Louis, in 1934, son, Dominick, and daughter, Joann (Penny), father, Dominick and mother, Anna both deceased, sisters Anna, Josie Graga, Jennie Talie, Angelina Crawel, Mary Bono, Rose Viviano, and Laura Schmidt, Dominica Biondo, and brother, Pete Caleca, all of St. Louis, Mo.

CRIMINAL ASSOCIATES : John J. Vitale, Anthony Giardano, Anthony Lopiparo, ███████████, and ███████████.

CRIMINAL HISTORY : FBI #665472, St. Louis PD #19526, has record dating to 1923 with arrests for suspicion of murder, convicted in September 1958, began sentence 10-13-58, evading income-tax (3 years).

BUSINESS : Partner in the Twin-City Distributing Co., with Anthony Giardano and Anthony Lopiparo.

MODUS OPERANDI : A trusted member of the local Mafia with racket associates throughout U.S.

NAME	: Paul CATANZARO
ALIASES	: Paolo Catanzaro, Paul Marchese
DESCRIPTION	: Born 11-9-84, Gibellina, Sicily, 5'2", 145 lbs., eyes brown, hair grey, complexion dark, short build, naturalized 7-7-24, Kansas City, Mo.

LOCALITIES
FREQUENTED : Resides alone at 538 Olive St., Kansas City, Mo., frequents Roma Bakery, 5th St., Drug Store, both in Kansas City, Mo.

FAMILY
BACKGROUND : Wife deceased. Has two daughters, Francisca, now Mrs. Pete Mendicini and Nicoletta, now Mrs. Jack Ross, both residing in Kansas City, Missouri.

CRIMINAL
ASSOCIATES : Joseph and Pete DiGiovanni, Joseph Filardo, Joseph Cusamano, Joseph and Frank DeLuca, James Balestrere and ██████████.

CRIMINAL
HISTORY : Kansas City PD #52189, arrested 7-29-15, again on 3-23-19 for "Black Hand" activities, 8-23-15 for arson, 4-30-20 for murder of 12 year old Frank Carramusa, and two subsequent arrests for violation of liquor laws; no felony convictions.

BUSINESS : Retired. Was formerly a so-called watchman for the Midwest Distributing Co., Kansas City, Mo., but in reality was a bodyguard and handyman for the owners, Joseph and Pete DiGiovanni.

MODUS
OPERANDI : Assists in carrying out the edicts of the local Mafia organization, Kansas City area.

NAME   : Vincent CHIAPETTA

ALIASES   : Vincenzo Chiapetta, Vincent
                  Chiapetti

DESCRIPTION   : Born 11-23-86, Poggioriale,
                  Italy, 5'11", 170 lbs.,
                  slender build, blue eyes,
                  grey hair, complexion fair,
                  naturalized 5-28-19, Pitts-
                  burgh, Penna.

LOCALITIES   : Resides at 21 York Hills Dr.,
FREQUENTED   Brentwood, St. Louis, Mo.

FAMILY   : Wife Maria died in 1952.
BACKGROUND   They have two children, Carmela (born 2-20-14), and
                  Orsolina (born 8-18-15), the latter lives in St. Louis,
                  and Carmela resides in Kansas City, Mo.

CRIMINAL   : John B. Blando, James Balestrere, Joseph, Pete, ███████
ASSOCIATES   ████████████████, Joseph Filardo, Joseph Cusamano,
                  Frank and Joseph DeLuca, all of Kansas City, Mo.,
                  Anthony Miceli, John Vitale, and Anthony Giordano, all
                  of St. Louis, Mo., Nicolo Gentile, ████████████ and
                  Nicolo Impostato, all of Italy.

CRIMINAL   : Kansas City PD #9047, files of Kansas City Police Dept.,
HISTORY   reflect only two arrests, one in 1911 for investigation
                  and a traffic arrest in 1940.

BUSINESS   : Vice President of the Medical Arts Building, Inc., 5899
                  Delmar Blvd., St. Louis, Mo.

MODUS   : Subject is an influential member of the Mafia, he is
OPERANDI   reported to have replaced Pasquale Miceli as head of
                  the organization at St. Louis, Mo.

His skimming from the Stardust casino led him to be one of the first ten people named in the Nevada Gaming Comission's Exclusion List in 1960. Civello died March 12, 1983, from lung cancer.

NAME : Nicholas CIVELLO

ALIASES : Nick Civella, Nick Bove

DESCRIPTION : Born 3-19-12, Kansas City, Mo., 5'8", 180 lbs., brown eyes, black hair (thinning) dark complexion.

LOCALITIES FREQUENTED : Resides 401 Maple Blvd., Kansas City, Mo., frequents Roma Baking Co., 5th St., Drug Store, Pompeian Room & Antonio's Pizzeria, all in Kansas City, Mo.

FAMILY BACKGROUND : Parents: Antonio & Antonia Bove, Wife, Kathryn Anzalone, brothers, Carl & Steve.

CRIMINAL ASSOCIATES : James Balestrere, John B. Blando, Pete & Joe DiGiovanni, Frank & Joe DeLuca, Joe & Mike Lascoula, of Kansas City, Mo., Nicola Impostato & ███████ ██████████ (deportees).

CRIMINAL HISTORY : FBI #1224024, Kansas City PD# 22672, arrests start in 1932 including theft, prohibition act, larceny, robbery with firearms.

BUSINESS : Owns interests in Pompeian Room, Gallucci Real Estate Co., and a trucking business, all in Kansas City, Mo.

MODUS OPERANDI : Attended the Apalachin Mafia meeting 1957 with Joe Filardo, representing the Mafia interests from Kansas City, Mo., area; is known as an "enforcer" for the Mafia in Kansas City.

NAME : Joseph CUSAMANO

ALIASES : Joe Cusumano

DESCRIPTION : Born 1-25-1900, Castelvetrano
Sicily, 5'7", 190 lbs, brown
eyes, grey hair, stout build,
naturalized Kansas City, Mo,
12-18-44.

LOCALITIES : Resides at 101 S. Van Brunt
FREQUENTED   Blvd., Kansas City, Mo., frequents Roma Bakery, 1301 Independence Ave, 5th St, Drug
Store, 1050 E. 5th St, &
5421 Brooklyn Ave, all in Kansas City, Missouri.

FAMILY : Married Carmela Mentesano at Kansas City, Mo.,
BACKGROUND   10-9-29, has three children, Rose (Mrs. Samuel
Brancato), Josephine (Mrs. Joseph H. Ferrentelle),
and Frances Cusamano.

CRIMINAL : Joseph Filardo, James Balestrere, John B. Blando,
ASSOCIATES   Joseph and Frank DeLuca, Joseph and Pete DiGiovanni,
Nicholas Civella, and Alex Presta, of Kansas City,
Mo., and Vincent Chiapotta of St. Louis, Mo.

CRIMINAL : FBI #828237B, record dates from 1940 & includes
HISTORY   arrests for failure to register under Alien Registration Act and violation of Food & Drug laws.

BUSINESS : Partner in the Roma Bakery Co., Kansas City, Mo.

MODUS : Has never actively engaged in the rackets at Kansas
OPERANDI   City, Mo; he is the business man type Mafioso and is
a director in the local organization.

De Luca died in May, 1967.

NAME : Frank DE LUCA

ALIASES : Francesco Deluca

DESCRIPTION : Born 4-1-1898, Giordinello, Sicily, 5'8", 185 lbs, brown eyes, grey hair, dark complexion, noticeable twitching of left eye & face. Resident Alien, I&NS #A-5-570413.

LOCALITIES FREQUENTED : Resides at 1320 Admiral Blvd, Kansas City, Mo, frequents Roma Baking Co., 1301 Independence Ave, 6133 Rockhill Rd, 5th St, Drug Store and 5421 Brooklyn Ave, all Kansas City, Missouri.

FAMILY BACKGROUND : Married Lillian Cora Buckner; father: Antonio; mother: Antonio Buzzetta; brothers: Salvatore & Joseph.

CRIMINAL ASSOCIATES : James Balestrere, Joseph Filardo, Joseph Cusamano, John B. Blando, Pete and Joseph DiGiovanni, Joseph and Michael Lascoula of Kansas City, Mo; John Vitale and Anthony Lopiparo of St. Louis, Mo; Nicolo Impostato and ███████████ of Italy.

CRIMINAL HISTORY : FBI #1820551, Kansas City PD #30610. Arrests since 1930 for murder, carrying concealed weapons and violation of the Alien Enemy Registration Act.

BUSINESS : No legitimate occupation.

MODUS OPERANDI : This former narcotic wholesaler is a director in the Mafia for the Kansas City area.

He died March 20, 1952.

NAME   : Joseph DE LUCA

ALIASES   : Giuseppe DeLuca, Joe DeLuca

DESCRIPTION : Born 4-17-1893, Giordinello,
               Sicily, 5'8½", 210 lbs,
               brown eyes, grey hair, dark
               complexion, stout build.
               Resident Alien I&NS #A-1360-
               946.

LOCALITIES   : Resides at 6133 Rockhill Rd,
FREQUENTED   Kansas City, Mo., frequents
               the Roma Baking Co., and
               5421 Brooklyn, Ave, both of
               Kansas City, Mo.

FAMILY   : Married Frances C. Perry; father: Antonio; mother:
BACKGROUND   Antonia Buzzetta; brothers: Salvatore & Frank.

CRIMINAL   : James Balestrere, John B. Blando, Pete and Joseph
ASSOCIATES   DiGiovanni, Frank DeLuca, Joseph Filardo, Joseph
               Cusamano, Thomas Lococo, Joseph Spalito, ██████████,
               Sr., and Anthony Lopiparo of St. Louis, Mo., Nicolo
               Impostato and ████████████ of Sicily.

CRIMINAL   : FBI #338-2583, Kansas City PD#40870. Arrested for
HISTORY   violation of the National Prohibition Act 12-16-30;
               one conviction for violation of the Narcotic Laws.

BUSINESS   : No legitimate occupation.

MODUS   : No longer active in the rackets at Kansas City, Mo.,
OPERANDI   is an influential man in the local Mafia and receives
               a share of the proceeds from all illegal enterprises
               in which the organization is engaged.

He earned the nickname "Scarface" after a botched attempt at insurance fraud left him with a permanent scar.

NAME : Giuseppe DI GIOVANNI

ALIASES : Joseph DiGiovanni

DESCRIPTION : Born 4-23-1888 Chiusa Scla-
fani, Palermo, Sicily, Italy.
5'5", 170 lbs, brown eyes,
grey hair, extensive burn
scar right side face. Naturalized Kansas City 10-1-1924.

LOCALITIES : Resides 1217 W. 70 Terrace,
FREQUENTED Kansas City and frequents
5th St. Drug Store & Roma
Bakery, all in Kansas City, Mo.

FAMILY : Married Vincenzina (Jenny) Fasone; children: Paul
BACKGROUND Anthony, Salvatore and Susie; brothers: Pete, Paul
and Vincent, all of Kansas City, Mo.; father: Salvatore.

CRIMINAL : Pete, ███████████████████████, James Balestrere,
ASSOCIATES John B. Blando, Joseph Filardo, Joseph Cusamano,
████████████████ and Vincent Chiapetta.

CRIMINAL : FBI #1007227 Kansas City PD #7079 Record dating
HISTORY from 1915 includes arrests for kidnapping, resisting
arrest, "Black Hand" activities, bootlegging and
murder.

BUSINESS : Retired 1953. He & brother Peter sold the Midwest
Dist. Co. to their sons, Sam & Paul, for $2500.
This Seagrams franchise and liquor stock valued
in excess of a half million dollars.

MODUS : Head of the Mafia for the State of Missouri for
OPERANDI many years. Due to advanced age has stepped down
from that position, but still wields great influence in the Mafia.

He died of natural causes in August, 1929 at the age
of 54.

NAME   : Pietro DI GIOVANNI

ALIASES   : Peter DiGiovanni, Sugar-
house Pete.

DESCRIPTION : Born 6-28-1886, Chiusa Scla-
fani, Palermo, Sicily, Italy
5'10", 185 lbs, brown eyes,
grey hair, stout. Naturalized Kansas City 7-8-1924.

LOCALITIES : Resides 502 Campbell Street,
FREQUENTED frequents K. C. Wholesale
Liquor Co. & Roma Bakery Co.,
all in KansasCity, Mo.

FAMILY   : Married Mary Olivo (sister of Jos. Olivo; children:
BACKGROUND Sadie (Mrs. Patsy Ventola), Salvatore & Paul Marco;
brothers: Joseph, Vincent, Paul; father: Salvatore.

CRIMINAL   : Joseph, ███████████████████████, James Balistrere,
ASSOCIATES Paul Catanzaro, John B. Blando & ████████████████.

CRIMINAL   : FBI #4007370 Kansas City PD #69179   Record dating
HISTORY   from 1915 includes arrests for violation National
Prohibition Act, "Black Hand" activities & murder.

BUSINESS   : Retired in 1953, when he and brother Giuseppe sold
the Midwest Dist. Co. to their sons Sam & Paul for
$2500. This liquor stock and Seagrams franchise
valued in excess of half a million dollars.

MODUS   : Due to his advanced age he has discontinued active
OPERANDI   participation in the rackets, but is a director
of the Mafia for the Kansas City area.

NAME : Joseph FILARDO

ALIASES : Joe Filardo

DESCRIPTION : Born 8-10-1898, Castelvetrano Sicily, 5'7½", 160 lbs, brown eyes, grey hair, dark complexion, medium build. Naturalized Kansas City, Mo., 10-4-40.

LOCALITIES FREQUENTED : Resides 103 S. Van Brunt Blvd., Kansas City, Mo., frequents Roma Baking Co., & 5th St. Drug Store, both in Kansas City, Mo.

FAMILY BACKGROUND : Married Carmela Capo DiAntonino, two children, Michael and Antoinetta (Mrs. Victor J. Vogliardo).

CRIMINAL ASSOCIATES : John B. Blando, James Balestrere, Joseph Cusamano, Pete and Joseph DiGiovanni, Frank & Joseph DeLuca, Carl Civello and Alex Presta, all of Kansas City, Vincent Chiapetta & John Vitale of St. Louis, Nicola Impostato & ▓▓▓▓▓▓▓▓▓▓ of Sicily.

CRIMINAL HISTORY : FBI #753474C, Kansas City PD #89990, arrests since 1922 include blackmail, murder, Federal liquor laws, and 3 convictions for Food and Drug laws.

BUSINESS : Is President of the Roma Baking Co., Kansas City, Mo.

MODUS OPERANDI : Attended Apalachin Mafia meeting 1957 with Nick Civello, representing the Mafia interests in Kansas City, Mo.; a very influential Mafia member.

In 1941, the chief of police of Collinsville, IL was fired after it was discovered that he released Giardano before the L.A. authorities arrived with extradition papers.

NAME : Anthony GIARDANO

ALIASES : Tony, Anthony Giordano, Tony G.

DESCRIPTION : Born 6-24-14, St. Louis, Mo. 5'8½", 182 lbs., black hair, blue eyes, medium build, dark complexion, tattoo on right arm.

LOCALITIES : Resides at 6901 Roland Blvd.
FREQUENTED St. Louis County, Mo.

FAMILY : Wife, Catherine, father,
BACKGROUND Vincent, mother, Mary, brothers, Joseph, and Sam, sisters, Pearl Tocco, Josephine Trupiana, all of St. Louis, Mo., Phyllis Fontana, another sister of Detroit, Mich.

CRIMINAL : John J. Vitale, Anthony Lopiparo, ███████████,
ASSOCIATES Ralph Caleca, Anthony Rizzo, ███████████, ███████████, and ███████████, all of St. Louis, Mo., Sam Vitale, New Orleans, La., and Ralph Quasarano, Detroit, Mich., Frank Coppola of Sicily.

CRIMINAL : FBI # 1624141, St. Louis PD #43407, dates back to
HISTORY 1938, and includes arrests for carrying concealed weapon, robbery, hold-up, income tax evasion and counterfeit tax stamps, sentenced to 4 years imprisonment on the latter charge on 9-28-56.

BUSINESS : Anthony Novelty Co., 3401 Kienlen, St. Louis County; Anthony Discount Co., same address; Greene Fluorspar Mining Co., Elizabethtown, Ill., Twin-City Distributing Co., St. Louis, Mo.

MODUS : One of the trusted members of the St. Louis Mafia
OPERANDI with associates in New Orleans, La., Detroit, Mich., and Sicily.

NAME	: Frank LA ROCCA

ALIASES	: Born Francesco Franco and legally changed.

DESCRIPTION	: Born 2-14-1889 Lucca Sicula, Agrigento, Sicily, Italy, 5'10", 185 lbs, brown eyes, dark complexion, medium build naturalized 11-10-44, Kansas City, Mo.

LOCALITIES FREQUENTED	: Resides 136 S. Spruce Ave, Kansas City, Mo, frequents the LaRocca Wholesale Grocery Co, and the Roma Baking Co., Kansas City, Mo.

FAMILY BACKGROUND	: Married Josephine F. Cherrito; sons: Salvatore J. & Joseph T.; daughter: Josephine (Mrs. Joseph J. Dolei).

CRIMINAL ASSOCIATES	: James Balestrere, John B. Blando, Joseph Filardo, Joseph Cusumano, Thomas Lococo, Frank and Joseph DeLuca, Pete, Joseph, ███████████████████, Nick Civella.

CRIMINAL HISTORY	: FBI #64795. Kansas City PD #10734. Was arrested on two occasions in 1920 for murder, and in 1921 for investigation of another murder. All records relating to this subject have been removed from files of the police department and county prosecutor's office at Kansas City.

BUSINESS	: Owns LaRocca Wholesale Grocery Co., Kansas City, Mo.

MODUS OPERANDI	: Is an influential member of the Mafia and receives a share of the proceeds from all of the illicit activities in which the local organization is engaged.

258

NAME	: Joseph LASCOULA
ALIASES	: Joe School, Joe Lascuola, Machine Gun Joe
DESCRIPTION	: Born 1-1-1897 Termini, Palermo, Sicily, 5'8", 190 lbs, grey hair, brown eyes.
LOCALITIES FREQUENTED	: Resides 1910 E. 72nd Street, Kansas City, Mo. Frequents North Side Democratic Club, Bridge Club & Artcraft Store Equipment Co., Kansas City.

FAMILY BACKGROUND	: Wife: Pauline; father: Giacomo; mother: Saveria Sansone; brothers: Michael, Philip, Henry & James.
CRIMINAL ASSOCIATES	: Michael Lascoula (brother), ▮▮▮▮▮▮▮▮ (cousin), Joe Oliver, Carl & Nick Civella, Joe Filardo, all of Kansas City, John Vitale & Anthony Giordano, of St. Louis, and Nick Impastato, of Italy.
CRIMINAL HISTORY	: FBI #467361 Kansas City PD #9257 Arrests since 1919 include National Prohibition Act, carrying concealed weapon, trafficking in narcotics & associating with thieves.
BUSINESS	: With brother, Michael, operates clubs at 121½ E 5th St. & 4229 Main Street and has interest in Artcraft Store Equipment Co., all in Kansas City, Missouri.
MODUS	: A prominent member of the Mafia organization in Kansas City which distributed narcotics in the midwest. Is respected and feared by the underworld in Kansas City. Has acted as "fence" for stolen jewelry.

NAME : Michael LASCOULA

ALIASES : Mike School

DESCRIPTION : Born 5-19-06, Kansas City,
Mo., 5'8", 168 lbs, brown
eyes, black grey hair, dark
complexion.

LOCALITIES : Resides at 6744 Montgall Ave,
FREQUENTED Kansas City, Mo., frequents
The Artcraft Store Equipment
Co., Inc., the 5th St. Drug
Store, both of Kansas City.

FAMILY : Married Clara O. Monsen; father: Giacomo; mother:
BACKGROUND Saveria Sansone; brothers: Joseph, Phillip, Henry &
James.

CRIMINAL : Joseph Lascoula (brother), ▮▮▮▮▮▮▮▮ (cousin),
ASSOCIATES Joseph Olivo, Carl and Nicholas Civello, Joseph
Filardo, all of Kansas City, Mo., John Vitale, of
St. Louis, Mo., Nicolo Impostato and ▮▮▮▮▮▮▮,
both of Italy.

CRIMINAL : FBI #1806821. Kansas City PD# 17588. Record dates
HISTORY from 1929 and includes arrests for gambling, armed
robbery and violation of the Narcotics Laws.

BUSINESS : Operates gambling casino at 121½ E. 5th St, Kansas
City, Mo., has interest in gambling place called the
"Bridge Club," owns stock in the Artcraft Store Equip-
ment Co., Inc., Kansas City, Missouri.

MODUS : A member of the Mafia organization for distribution
OPERANDI of narcotics throughout the Midwest with sources of
supply in NYC, NY, Chicago, Ill., and New Orleans,
La.

He died in the late 1990s of natural causes.

NAME   : Thomas LOCOCO

ALIASES   : Gaetano Lococo, Tono, Tano.

DESCRIPTION   : Born 1-3-95, Kansas City, Mo.
                  5'7½", 150 lbs., brown eyes,
                  grey hair, complexion medium
                  small build.

LOCALITIES   : Resides at 346 S. Jackson
                  Ave., Kansas City, Mo., fre-
                  quents Gaetano's Restaurant
                  & Cocktail Lounge, Roma Bak-
                  ing Co., 5th St., Drug Store,
                  all of Kansas City, Mo.

FAMILY   : Subject is one of seven children born to immigrant
BACKGROUND   Sicilian parents; married to Edith Gargotta; has
                  two daughters, Carolina (Mrs. Paul Scaglia), and
                  Santa (Mrs. Edward J. Bruni).

CRIMINAL   : James Balestrere, John B. Blando, Joseph and Pete
ASSOCIATES   DiGiovanni, Joseph and Frank DeLuca, Joseph Cusamano
                  Joseph Filardo, Nicholas and Carl Civello, and ▮▮▮▮
                  ▮▮▮▮▮▮▮▮▮▮, all of Kansas City, Mo.

CRIMINAL   : FBI #278541, Kansas City PD# 9640, has been asso-
HISTORY   ciated with the Kansas City underworld since 1913;
                  has been arrested on nine occasions on such charges
                  as murder, stolen property, grand larceny and in-
                  come tax evasion, for which he was sentenced to two
                  years imprisonment on 9-11-50.

BUSINESS   : Owns and operates Gaetano's Restaurant and Cocktail
                  Lounge at Kansas City, Mo., his son-in-law, Edward
                  J. Bruni, is manager of this establishment.

MODUS   : Was a stockholder in Kansas City drug syndicate with
OPERANDI   other members of the Mafia; is an influential member
                  of the local organization and receives a share of the
                  proceeds from the rackets in which they are interested.

NAME	: Anthony Joseph LOPIPARO
ALIASES	: Tony Lopiparo, "Tony the Pip"
DESCRIPTION	: Born 1-19-14, St. Louis, Mo. 5'11", 190 lbs., muscular build, brown hair, greying, bald in front, brown eyes, prominent round nose, bushy eyebrows.
LOCALITIES FREQUENTED	: Resides 5881 Highland, St. Louis, Mo., frequents Anthony Novelty & Vending Co., Anthony Discount Co., both at 3401 Kienlen, St. Louis County, Greene Fluorspar Mining Co., of Elizabethtown, Ill.
FAMILY BACKGROUND	: Married Rose Marie Migini, Jan. 21, 1947, and divorced 9-21-49, Lopiparo adopted two children of Rose, James Anthony and Jovena; married Bonnie D. Cardwell, 10-21-49, Yuma, Ariz., divorced second wife and remarried first wife, Rose; father, Joseph and mother, Catherine both deceased; brothers, Nick and Sam; sisters, Mary Dailey and Mamie Dailey; in addition to two adopted children Lopiparo has two sons, Joseph 4, and Sam, 5 months.
CRIMINAL ASSOCIATES	: John J. Vitale, St. Louis, Vincent Todaro of Va., Joseph LoPiccolo of N.Y., Anthony Giardano, Ralph Caleca and ▄▄▄▄▄▄▄▄, of St. Louis.
CRIMINAL HISTORY	: FBI #710969, St. Louis PD #32943, has a lengthy arrest record dating back to 1931, and has served sentences for criminal contempt, and evasion of income-tax.
BUSINESS	: Associated with John Vitale and Anthony Giardano in the Anthony Novelty & Vending Co., and the Anthony Discount Co., St. Louis; has an interest in the Greene Fluorspar Mining Co., Elizabethtown, Ill.
MODUS OPERANDI	: An important member of the St. Louis Mafia

NAME : Anthony J. MICILI

ALIASES : Anthony Mecili, Miceli

DESCRIPTION : Born 5-27-1920 Chicago, Ill.
5'9", 170 lbs, brown eyes,
black hair, thinning on top,
olive complexion, flashy
dresser.

LOCALITIES : Resides 9449 Engel Lane,
FREQUENTED Olivette, Mo. Frequents
Micili & Sons Funeral Home,
1150 N. Kingshighway, St.
Louis, Mo.

FAMILY : Widowed; father: Pasquale; mother: Margaretta
BACKGROUND Maniscolo; brother: Phillip A. Micili; sister:
Rosalie, married to Vito Cusumano.

CRIMINAL : ████████████, John J. Vitale, ████████████,
ASSOCIATES Anthony Lopiparo.

CRIMINAL : No known arrests.
HISTORY

BUSINESS : President of Micili & Sons Funeral Home, 1150 N.
Kingshighway, and has part interest in Standard
Service Station, Lindburgh & Olive Streets, both
in St. Louis, Missouri.

MODUS : Is an influential member of the Mafia, having
OPERANDI taken over some of the authority of his late father,
Pasquale Micili, who was one of the leaders of the
organization in the St. Louis area.

```
NAME            : Frank S. NAPOLI

ALIASES         : Frank A. Natalie, Natali,
                  Napali

DESCRIPTION     : Born 1-5-00, Siculiana,
                  Sicily, 5'7", 165 lbs., eyes
                  brown, greyish hair, medium
                  build, naturalized in St.
                  Louis, Mo., (1926).

LOCALITIES      : Resides 4633 Carter, St.
FREQUENTED        Louis, Mo.

FAMILY          : Father, Mike Napoli and
BACKGROUND        mother, Maria Napoli both
                  deceased, Brothers, Joseph, St. Louis, Mo., and
                  James, San Francisco, Calif., Sisters, Catherine
                  DiAngelo and Marie Catalana both of St. Louis, Mo.,
                  Wife, Marie H. Napoli nee Dickmann.

CRIMINAL        : John J. Vitale, Frank Russo, and racketeers of the
ASSOCIATES        St. Louis area.

CRIMINAL        : FBI #2114185, St. Louis PD# 48749, arrested in 1940
HISTORY           at St. Louis, violation of the Federal Narcotic Law
                  (John Vitale, et al), dismissed before the U.S.
                  Commissioner, 2-10-41.

BUSINESS        : Presently a salesman with Bilgere Chevrolet Co.,
                  2820 N. Grand Ave., St. Louis, Mo.

MODUS           : An underling who carries out the orders of his Mafia
OPERANDI          superiors in the St. Louis area.
```

NAME	: Joseph OLIVO
ALIASES	: Joe Oliver, Joe Olive

DESCRIPTION : Born 2-14-1899, Kansas City,
Mo., 5'9", 170 lbs, brown
eyes, grey hair, medium
build, dark complexion.

LOCALITIES : Resides 3035 N. 18 St.,Kansas
FREQUENTED   City, Kansas. Frequents the
Olympic Stadium, Fifth Street
Drug Store & Nigro Service
Sta., all Kansas City, Mo.

FAMILY : Father: Giuseppe; mother: Louise; brother: Stephen;
BACKGROUND   sisters: Mary (Mrs. Peter DiGiovanni), Fannie (widow
of James Arnone) and Delia (Mrs. Mario Balistreri,
of Santa Clara, California).

CRIMINAL : ▬▬▬▬▬▬▬▬▬▬▬▬▬, Michael & Joseph
ASSOCIATES   Lascoula, Nicholas & Carl Civello, all of Kansas
City, Mo., John Vitale, Anthony Lopiparo & Anthony
Giordano of St. Louis, Nicolo Impastato of Italy.

CRIMINAL : FBI #81060 Kansas City PD #10971 Record dating
HISTORY   from 1921 includes arrests for burglary, robbery,
and grand larceny and three narcotic convictions.

BUSINESS : Owns a one fourth interest in the Olympic Stadium,
Kansas City, Missouri.

MODUS : A trusted member of the Mafia narcotic distributing
OPERANDI   organization operating in the Midwest with sources
of supply in New York City and Europe.

NAME   : Frank PISCIOTTA

ALIASES   : Francesco Pisciotta

DESCRIPTION   : Born 7-2-1892, Montelepre,
                  Sicily, 5'6", 160 lbs, grey
                  hair, brown eyes, naturalized
                  St. Louis, Mo., 4-13-56.

LOCALITIES   : Resides 5585a Lansdowne,
FREQUENTED   St. Louis, Mo.

FAMILY   : Married Josephine Balonzo;
BACKGROUND   sons: Joseph and Leo;
                  daughters; Fern & Mary Ann;
                  father: Joseph (deceased); mother: Niefa; sisters:
                  Frances (Mrs. Sam Margese), Rosa (Mrs. Joe Lolonegea),
                  Maddie (Mrs. Joe Randazzo), Mary (Mrs. Onofrio Polo-
                  lezza) and Janie Pisciotta.

CRIMINAL   : John J. Vitale, James Scarpelli, Frank Natale, Ralph
ASSOCIATES   Caleca, Frank Russo and Anthony Lopiparo, all of St.
                  Louis, Mo.

CRIMINAL   : FBI #590807 St. Louis PD #31746 Record dating from
HISTORY   1930 includes arrests for suspicion of robbery at St.
                  Louis, violation of U.S. Customs laws at Ft. Worth,
                  and conviction for counterfeit ration stamps.

BUSINESS   : No legitimate occupation.

MODUS   : A lesser member of the Mafia in the St. Louis area.

NAME	: Alexander Joseph PRESTA

ALIASES   : Alex Presta, Alex Preston

DESCRIPTION : Born 7-9-02, Kansas City, Mo., 5'6½", 175 lbs, brown eyes, black-grey hair, dark complexion, stout build.

LOCALITIES   : Resides at 1048 E 5th St.,
FREQUENTED   Kansas City, Mo., frequents 5th St., Drug Store, Presta Real Estate & Insurance Co., Roma Baking Co., all of Kansas City, Missouri.

FAMILY   : Is one of six children born to Sicilian immigrant
BACKGROUND   parents. Sisters and brothers are: Mary Migliazzo, widow of Sam; Angelina, (Mrs. Joseph J. Capra), Rose (Mrs. Giovanni Blondo), Minnie (Mrs. Joseph Tutorino) Louis and Chester Presta; married Millie Nasello, June 1924, at Independence, Missouri.

CRIMINAL   : █████████████████████████, Nicholas and
ASSOCIATES   Carl Civello, Joseph Filardo and James Balestrere all of Kansas City, Missouri.

CRIMINAL   : FBI #205947, Kansas City PD#14319; has record of
HISTORY   arrests dating to 1923, on such charges as burglary, bootlegging and extortion with two felony convictions for violation of the National Prohibition Act.

BUSINESS   : Is a partner in the Bridge Club, a gambling casino; owns an interest in the Presta Real Estate & Insurance Co., both of Kansas City, Missouri.

MODUS   : Is political front and liason man for the Kansas
OPERANDI   City Mafia.

NAME	: Frank RUSSO
ALIASES	: Weatherbird

DESCRIPTION : Born 1-31-01, St. Louis, Mo. 5'6 3/4", 155 lbs., medium build, swarthy complexion, brown eyes, brown hair, high forehead, almost bald.

LOCALITIES FREQUENTED : New "DeSoto Hotel", 11th & Pine Sts., St. Louis, Mo., permanent guest (1959..verified).

FAMILY BACKGROUND : Marital Status, Single. Mother and Father, deceased, sister Josephine Cira, 4106 San Francisco, St. Louis, Mo., brother, Michael Russo, whereabouts unknown.

CRIMINAL ASSOCIATES : John J. Vitale, Tony Lopiparo, Anthony Giordano and Ralph Caleca.

CRIMINAL HISTORY : FBI #2113995, and St. Louis PD# 48744, arrested in 1940, St. Louis, Mo., narcotic charge, with John J. Vitale, et al -- charge dismissed; other arrests for gambling and investigation.

BUSINESS : Operated a fruit and produce stand, 6501 Manchester, St. Louis, Mo., (1957); operated stand in Union Market; still in such business, location unknown.

MODUS OPERANDI : A trusted associate of the St. Louis Mafia and an interstate narcotic trafficker.

NAME	: Anthony SCARPELLI

ALIASES : Tony Scarpelle

DESCRIPTION : Born 7-22-99 in Penna.,
6'0", 250 lbs, brown eyes,
grey hair, stout build,
swarthy complexion.

LOCALITIES : Resides 4737 Terrace Ave.,
FREQUENTED St. Louis, Mo. Frequents
Anthony Novelty & Vending
Co., St. Louis County, Mo.

FAMILY : Wife's name is Lillian;
BACKGROUND brothers: William and James; sister: Mrs. Amelia
Zumparo.

CRIMINAL : John J. Vitale, James Scarpelli (brother), Ralph
ASSOCIATES Caleca, Frank Russo, Frank Natalie, all of St.
Louis, Mo., Joe & Mike Lascoula, Joe Oliver, of
Kansas City, Mo., Nick Impastato of Italy.

CRIMINAL : FBI# 3375832. St. Louis PD# 54551. Arrests since
HISTORY 1921 include armed robbery and violation of the
liquor laws.

BUSINESS : Employed by Mico-Mining & Milling Co., St. Louis,
also receives fees from Missouri Smelting Co.,
St. Louis, Mo.

MODUS : Is a member of the Mafia organization in St. Louis
OPERANDI and closely associated with known Mafia narcotic
traffickers there.

NAME : James SCARPELLI

ALIASES : James Perri

DESCRIPTION : Born 6-21-1896 Easton, Pa.,
5'8", 250 lbs, brown eyes,
grey hair, swarthy complexion, heavy build, scar on
right side of face, and on
left hand.

LOCALITIES : Resides 5330 Jamieson Ave,
FREQUENTED St. Louis, Mo., frequents
the Anthony Novelty & Vending Co., and Anthony Discount Co., of St. Louis, Missouri.

FAMILY : Wife, Catherine; father: Francesco; mother: Rosa
BACKGROUND Castiglione; brothers: William and Anthony; sister:
Emelia Zumpano.

CRIMINAL : John J. Vitale, Anthony Scarpelli, ███████████████,
ASSOCIATES ███████████████████████████.

CRIMINAL : FBI #87428. St. Louis PD #18289. Dates back to 1921
HISTORY and includes arrests for robbery, liquor violation,
murder and gambling.

BUSINESS : Was employed as a salesman at Auffenberg Motors, 820
N. Kingshighway, St. Louis, Mo., operated Delmar
Motor and Transmission Overhaul Co., St. Louis, Mo.,
with Anthony Giammanco and Frank Scarpelli.

MODUS : A bookmaker for racing and sports events at St.
OPERANDI Louis, Mo., and a member of the local Mafia organization.

NAME : John Joseph VITALE

ALIASES : Johnny V, John Vitali

DESCRIPTION : Born 5-17-09, St. Louis, Mo.
5'11", 208 lbs., heavy build
ruddy complexion, black-grey
hair, (balding), brown eyes.

LOCALITIES : Resides 3725 Avondale Ave.,
FREQUENTED Arbor Terrace, St. Louis Co,
Mo., frequents Anthony Nov-
elty & Vending Co., 3401
Kienlen, Pine Lawn, St. Louis
Co., Mo.

FAMILY : Married to Fannie, has 4 children, Joseph, Mary Ann,
BACKGROUND (Mrs. Robert Phillips) of Wabash, Ind., John Jr., and
Rosetta, (Mrs. George V. Harrison; Father, Joseph,
(deceased), Mother, Mary Vitale, nee Bovaconti; Brothers,
Joseph, Charles, William, Nick, Phillip; Sisters, Theresa,
and Rosemarie, all of St. Louis, Mo.

CRIMINAL : Anthony Giardano, Anthony Lopiparo, Ralph Caleca, ▮▮▮▮
ASSOCIATES ▮▮
all of St. Louis, and Michael Lascoula, and Joe Olivero
of Kansas City, Mo., Sam Vitale (cousin), of New Orleans,
La., and Nicolo Impostato of Sicily.

CRIMINAL : FBI #793259, St. Louis PD #36177, dates back to 1920
HISTORY and includes arrests for robbery, with firearms, concealed weapons, forgery, murder, receiving stolen property, and Federal Narcotic Law (1940).

BUSINESS : Anthony Novelty & Vending Co., and Anthony Discount
Corp., both of St. Louis, Mo.

MODUS : A leading member of the St. Louis Mafia, and inter-
OPERANDI national Narcotic Trafficker.

He died of complications from larynx cancer surgery on August 3, 1968.

NAME : Frank Leonard WORTMAN

ALIASES : Buster Wortman

DESCRIPTION : Born 12-4-04 East St. Louis, Ill, 5'9", 180 lbs, brown-grey hair, brown eyes.

LOCALITIES FREQUENTED : Resides Lebanon Rd, Collins-ville, Ill. Frequents Gorman Bricklaying Co, Plaza Amuse-ment Co, & W.R. Cigarette Vending Co., St. Louis & Paddock Catering Co, E. St. Louis, Ill.

FAMILY BACKGROUND : Divorced from Dorothy; 4 young children; living with Sylvia Shaw @ Chi Chi; father: Edward; mother: Grace; brother: Edward.

CRIMINAL ASSOCIATES : ███████████, Elmer Dowling, ███████████ ██████, ███████████.

CRIMINAL HISTORY : FBI #739186. St. Louis PD #22901. Record dating from 1926 includes arrests for interstate auto theft, assaulting government officer, contempt of court & income tax evasion.

BUSINESS : Owns in whole or part companies listed under "Localities Frequented."

MODUS OPERANDI : In control of all organized crime in St. Louis area. Though he and his organization are non-Italian they operate in alliance with Mafia groups in all parts of the country.

NAME	: Benny BARONE
ALIASES	: The Blimp, Bernard Barone, Joe Nanzio
DESCRIPTION	: Born 1-29-12 Omaha, Nebr., 5'7", 365 lbs, obese build, dark brown hair, bald on top, dark complexion, brown eyes.
LOCALITIES FREQUENTED	: Resides with sister at 1314 S 24th St, Omaha, Nebr, frequents Carter Lake Social Club, Carter Lake, Iowa; Herman's Cigar Store, Rocket Bar & Grill, all of Omaha; PeeDee's Club, Council Bluffs, Iowa.
FAMILY BACKGROUND	: Single; father: Ben Barone; mother: Theresa Pistilla; brothers: John F. Barone, Louis Barone, Joe Barone (deceased); sister: Mrs. Sam J. (Marie) Pistillo.
CRIMINAL ASSOCIATES	: Biase Brothers, Omaha; ▆▆▆▆▆▆▆▆▆▆▆▆▆, ▆▆▆▆▆▆▆▆, ▆▆▆▆▆▆▆▆, Council Bluffs, Iowa and Omaha, Nebraska; and numerous Chicago, Calif., Las Vegas and New York hoodlums. ▆▆▆▆▆▆▆ of Tulsa.
CRIMINAL HISTORY	: FBI #500634. Served 4 terms in Federal and State Penitentiaries for Prohibition Act, Dyer Act, receiving stolen property and accessory after the fact, bank robbery.
BUSINESS	: No legitimate employment.
MODUS OPERANDI	: Contact man and Mafia leader in Omaha area. Primarily gambling and liquor violator, but is known to be associated with narcotic traffickers from New York City.

He died of natural causes on September 21, 1991.

NAME : Anthony Joseph BIASE

ALIASES : Tony Biase, Tony DiBiase

DESCRIPTION : Born 9-6-08, Omaha, Neb.,
5'3", 160 lbs., heavy build,
black-grey hair, waves and
thinning in front, hazel
eyes, dark complexion, 3"
diagonal scar on right cheek

LOCALITIES : Resides at 2207 Mason St.,
FREQUENTED Omaha, Neb., frequents Owl
Smoke Shop, 610 S. 16th St.,
Omaha, Neb.

FAMILY : Marital status unknown, is a brother of Sam, Benny
BACKGROUND and Louis, of Omaha, Neb.

CRIMINAL : Sam, Louis, and Benny (brothers), ███████████████,
ASSOCIATES ███████████, ███████████, ███████████, ████████
████████, Benny Barone, all of Omaha, Neb., Samuel
Carrollo, Kansas City, Mo., Anthony Marcella, ██████
████████, Calif.

CRIMINAL : FBI #36521, Omaha PD #9839, has been arrested for
HISTORY burglary, theft and numerous times for bookmaking.

BUSINESS : Partner in Owl Smoke Shop, 610 S. 16th St., Omaha, Neb.

MODUS : Interstate narcotic trafficker, bookmaker and gambler
OPERANDI and an influential member of the Mafia at Omaha, Neb.

NAME	: Bernard Benjamin BIASE
ALIASES	: Benny Biase, Benny DiBiase
DESCRIPTION	: Born 11-12-11, Omaha, Neb., 5'7", 185 lbs., brown eyes, black hair, complexion medium and heavy build.
LOCALITIES FREQUENTED	: Resides at 4215 Pinkney St., Omaha, Neb., frequents the Owl Smoke Shop and Newhall Hotel, Omaha, Neb.
FAMILY BACKGROUND	: Married. Is a brother of Anthony, Samuel and Louis of Omaha, Neb.
CRIMINAL ASSOCIATES	: Tony, Sam and Louis (brothers), ▓▓▓▓▓▓▓, ▓▓▓▓ ▓▓▓▓▓, ▓▓▓▓▓▓▓▓▓, Benny Barone and ▓▓▓▓▓▓▓▓▓, all of Omaha, Neb., Samuel Carrollo, Kansas City, Mo., ▓▓▓▓▓▓▓▓▓▓▓, Milwaukee, Wisc., Anthony F. Marcella and ▓▓▓▓▓▓▓▓ of Calif.
CRIMINAL HISTORY	: FBI #1749112, Omaha PD #15527, arrest record dates from 1931 with one felony conviction for robbery.
BUSINESS	: Partner in the Owl Smoke Shop, 610 S. 16th St., Omaha, Neb.
MODUS OPERANDI	: Interstate narcotic trafficker, bookmaker and fence; an important member of the Mafia at Omaha, Neb.

NAME   : Louis BIASE

ALIASES   : Louie Biase, Louis DiBiase

DESCRIPTION   : Born 2-1-16, Omaha, Neb.;
                  5'4", 180 lbs., brown eyes,
                  black wavy hair, dark com-
                  plexion and stout build.

LOCALITIES   : No permanent address. Trav-
FREQUENTED   els throughout the United
                  States attending horse races
                  at the various tracks. Fre-
                  quents the Owl Smoke Shop
                  and the Newhall Hotel when
                  in Omaha, Nebraska.

FAMILY   : Marital status unknown. Subject is a brother of
HISTORY   Tony, Sam and Benny Biase of Omaha, Nebraska.

CRIMINAL   : Tony, Sam and Benny Biase (brothers), ███████
ASSOCIATES   ███████, ████████████, ████████, Benny
                  Barone and ████████████, all of Omaha, Neb.;
                  Samuel Carrollo, Kansas City, Mo.; ████████
                  ████, Las Vegas, Nev.; Anthony F. Marcella and
                  ████████████████ of California.

CRIMINAL   : FBI #1298537, Omaha PD #16921. Dates from 1932
HISTORY   and includes robbery, possession of burglar
                  tools, resisting arrest, and operation of bunco
                  game.

BUSINESS   : Not engaged in legitimate business.

MODUS   : Interstate narcotic trafficker, bookmaker and
OPERANDI   horse race enthusiast. A member of the Mafia
                  organization at Omaha, Nebraska.

NAME   : Samuel BIASE

ALISES   : Sam Biase

DESCRIPTION : Born 11-6-13, Omaha, Neb.,
                 5'6½", 150 lbs., brown eyes,
                 brown wavy hair, and dark
                 complexion.

LOCALITIES   : Resides at 1014 S. 27th St.,
FREQUENTED   Omaha, Neb., frequents Owl
                 Smoke Shop and Newhall Hotel
                 Omaha, Neb.

FAMILY   : Married. Is a brother of
BACKGROUND   Anthony, Benny and Louis
                 Biase of Omaha, Neb.

CRIMINAL   : Anthony, Benny and Louis Biase, (brothers); ▓▓▓▓▓
ASSOCIATES   ▓▓▓▓▓▓, ▓▓▓▓▓▓▓▓, ▓▓▓▓▓▓▓▓▓, Benny Barone
                 and ▓▓▓▓▓▓▓▓▓, all of Omaha, Neb., Samuel
                 Carrollo, Kansas City, Mo., ▓▓▓▓▓▓▓▓▓▓▓,
                 Milwaukee, Wisc., Anthony Marcella and ▓▓▓▓▓
                 ▓▓▓▓▓▓ of Calif.

CRIMINAL   : FBI #157566, Omaha PD #12338, record reflects 24
HISTORY   arrests dating to 1924 with two felony convictions
                 for robbery.

BUSINESS   : Partner in Owl Smoke Shop, 610 S. 16th St., Omaha, Neb.,

MODUS   : Interstate narcotic trafficker, bookmaker and fence;
OPERANDI   an important member of the Mafia at Omaha, Neb.

NEVADA

NAME	: Joseph John PARENTE

ALIASES : Joe Parente, Joe Parenti

DESCRIPTION : Born 1-23-91 San Francisco,
Calif., 5'5½", 185 lbs.,
eyes brown, hair black-grey,
olive complexion, left small
finger crooked at third joint

LOCALITIES : Resides at 2535½ Meadows St.,
FREQUENTED Las Vegas, Nevada; owns
property at 51 Gold Hill
Grade, San Rafael, Calif.,
(wife lives at this address).

FAMILY : Wife is named Madeline.
BACKGROUND

CRIMINAL : ██████,Roger Coudert, Renaldo Ferrari, Vincent
ASSOCIATES Bruno and ██████████.

CRIMINAL : FBI #183381, San Francisco PD# 21229, 1st arrest
HISTORY was in 1913 for forgery for which he was sentenced
to seven years in San Quentin Prison; numerous subsequent arrests for liquor law violations; sentenced to four years at McNeil Island for violation
of the narcotic laws and is presently on parole.

BUSINESS : He is an owner of the Eirie Silica Sand & Flagstone
Corp., in Las Vegas, Nevada.

MODUS : An interstate narcotic trafficker and an important
OPERANDI member of the Mafia on the West Coast.

NAME	: Onofrio ABATE
ALIASES	: None

DESCRIPTION : Born 3-10-1899 Trapani, Sicily, Italy, 5'10", 195 lbs, stocky build, black-grey hair, brown eyes. Left leg amputated (auto accident in Europe). Arrived in US, from Tunisia 1946. Legal resident alien I&NS #A6428516.

LOCALITIES FREQUENTED : Resides 157 Walker Rd, W. Orange, NJ. Frequents 14th Ave, sect., of Newark, NJ, also NYC, Phila, & Atlantic Highlands, NJ. Formerly resided 18 Rue Chiero, Tunis, Tunisia.

FAMILY BACKGROUND : Married in Tunisia 1928 to Pietra Accardo, sister of Settimo Accardo; sons: Francesco Nicola & Salvatore Daniel; daughter: Franca Alba Maria; sister: Pasqualina Abate; father: Nicola; mother: Rosa Bocina.

CRIMINAL ASSOCIATES : Settimo Accardo, Vito Genovese, Charles & Thomas Campisi, Aniello Santagata.

CRIMINAL HISTORY : FBI #579877A. NJSBI #418644. One arrest in U.S., conspiracy to operate lottery.

BUSINESS : No legitimate occupation known.

MODUS OPERANDI : Close associate and right hand man of Settimo Accardo, important Mafioso, who is now a fugitive from Federal narcotics prosecution. Assisted Accardo in gambling, narcotic & alcohol rackets.

He died in December, 1997.

NAME : Settimo ACCARDO

ALIASES : Sam Accardi, Big Sam,
Giuseppe Accarobi

DESCRIPTION : Born 10-23-02, Vita, Sicily,
5'9½", 200 lbs, brown eyes,
heavy build, black hair greying and receding.

LOCALITIES : Family resides at 188 Frank-
FREQUENTED lin St., Bloomfield, N.J.,
he is currently (1959) a
fugitive for violation Federal Narcotic Laws.

FAMILY : Married to Teresa Menio, has 3 sons, Salvatore,
BACKGROUND Carmine and Joseph, parents (dead) were Salvatore
and Francesca Avila, sister is Pietra and brothers
Joseph and Frank (dead).

CRIMINAL : Lucky Luciano, Tom and Charles Campisi, Carmine
ASSOCIATES Lo Cascio, Joe Doto, Frank Costello, Tony Corallo,
Tony Strollo, Cristoforo Rubino (dead) and all top
Mafia leaders in NY and NJ.

CRIMINAL : FBI #683907, Newark PD# 17577, arrests since 1928
HISTORY include atrocious assault and battery, violation
Federal Narcotic Laws (1955), is fugitive in this
case, having jumped $92,500 bond.

BUSINESS : Was engaged in real estate and building construction in Newark, NJ area.

MODUS : A very important top echelon Mafia leader from
OPERANDI Newark area, who was engaged in international narcotic trafficking.

He died in 1957.

NAME : Filippo AMARI

ALIASES : Big Phil, Philip Amari

DESCRIPTION : Born 12-16-1899, Ribera, Agrigento, Sicily, 6'0", 200 lbs, stocky build, gray hair, brown eyes.

LOCALITIES FREQUENTED : Formerly resided at 15 Q Betty Anne Drive, Raritan Township, NJ, now reported to be Ribera, Sicily. Passport lists permanent address as Mt. Pleasant Road, Edison, NJ. Frequents Elizabeth, NJ, Newark, NJ, New York, NY, and Miami, Florida.

FAMILY BACKGROUND : Married Maria Masapolli; daughters: Carmela Confortino and Sara; father: Giuseppe; mother: Carmela Truncale.

CRIMINAL ASSOCIATES : ███████████, Frank Majuri, ███████████.

CRIMINAL HISTORY : No known criminal record.

BUSINESS : Claims to own liquor store in NJ. Active in construction union activities.

MODUS OPERANDI : Important Mafia figure who backs Union County, NJ, gambling activities and through his union connections obtains employment for legal and illegal immigrants.

Amoruso stood trial for the murder of a prohibition agent.

NAME : Nicholas AMORUSO

ALIASES : Nicholas Delmore, Nicholas Carlos, Nicholas Delrino.

DESCRIPTION : Claims born 9-24-1888 San Francisco, Calif., 5'6", 160 lbs, light brown hair-greying medium build, ruddy complexion. Birth details were questioned by I&NS but Delmore was declared a citizen 1-30-53 by 3rd Circ., Ct. of Appeals.

LOCALITIES FREQUENTED : Resides 340 Westwood Ave, Long Branch, NJ, frequents DiMartino's Lounge, Elizabeth, NJ, Riberia Social Club, Union, NJ, Old Orchard Country Club, Eatontown, New Jersey.

FAMILY BACKGROUND : Married Ernestine Wakefield; son: Frank Delmore; father: Luigi; mother: Providenza.

CRIMINAL ASSOCIATES : Frank Costello, Vincent Alo, ███████████, Frank Majuri.

CRIMINAL HISTORY : FBI #319465. NJSP #35457. Record dates from 1933 & includes arrests for murder, violations of prohibition act and resisting Federal officer.

BUSINESS : "Advisor" to Local 394 NJ Shippers Ass'n; real estate holdings in NJ and Florida.

MODUS OPERANDI : Top level Mafioso, formerly a bootlegger, who has retired from violent crime to the quasi-legitimate field of labor unions. Obtains "kick-backs" from Italian emigrants for whom he obtains employment through his power in the labor unions.

NAME   : Philip ATTARDI

ALIASES   : Phillip Attarti

DESCRIPTION   : Born 6-15-1891 Italy, 5'7",
                  180 lbs, grey-black hair,
                  brown eyes, heavy build,
                  I&NS-A#5549773.

LOCALITIES   : Resides 804 S. 4th St., Cam-
FREQUENTED   den, NJ, frequents 4th & Roy-
                  den Sts., Camden, NJ & Phila-
                  delphia, Penna.

FAMILY   : Wife: Rose Marcozzi; sons:
BACKGROUND   Lawrence & William; daughter: Rose; father: Antonio;
                  mother: Rosa.

CRIMINAL   : Pasquale Massi, Louis Campbell & the late Philip
ASSOCIATES   De Pietra, all of Camden, New Jersey.

CRIMINAL   : FBI #282893, Camden PD# 3080. Arrests since 1927
HISTORY   include assault & battery, liquor law violations,
                  Internal Revenue Laws, murder, carrying a gun and
                  passing counterfeit money.

BUSINESS   : No legitimate business or employment known.

MODUS   : Old time Mafia bootlegger and counterfeiter. Be-
OPERANDI   cause of age and ill health no longer takes part
                  in Mafia activities beyond acting in advisory
                  capacity.

285

NAME   : Salvatore BADALAMENTI

ALIASES   : Sammy, Badalamente, Badalamento.

DESCRIPTION : Born 12-26-17 NYC, 5'7", 150 lbs, brown hair, brown eyes.

LOCALITIES : Resides 244 McElroy Ave,
FREQUENTED   Palisades, NJ, summer home
92 Hewlett Ave, Point Lookout
L.I. Frequents Greenwich
Village, NYC.

FAMILY   : Married Lucy Balun; father:
BACKGROUND   Charles; mother: Ann Rizzo; alleged to be related to
Anthony Strollo.

CRIMINAL   : Anthony Strollo, Joseph Profaci, Sebastiano Nani,
ASSOCIATES Vincent Mauro, John Dio Guardia.

CRIMINAL   : FBI #2847522. NYCPD #B135053. Record dates from 1935
HISTORY   and includes arrests for burglary, grand larceny,
petit larceny and bookmaking.

BUSINESS   : Partner in Barnett Transport Co., 211 W 36th St,
NYC and in Caruso Music Co., Rego Park, L.I.

MODUS   : Mafia strong arm man in New York's garment district.
OPERANDI   Chief Lieutenant in charge of gambling for Anthony
Strollo.

NAME	: Ernesto BARESE
ALIASES	: Frank Martin, Carmine Barese, Ernie Barrie
DESCRIPTION	: Born 5-10-20 Naples, Italy, 5'7", 135 lbs, brown hair, greying, brown eyes, tattoo right forearm.
LOCALITIES FREQUENTED	: Resides 1563 Anderson Ave., Ft. Lee, N.J., frequents Ft. Lee, N.J., lower East Side (NYC) and New Haven, Conn.
FAMILY BACKGROUND	: Married 1943 to Gladys Lyden. Divorced 1947. Daughter: Sandra; married Anna Schulman 1949, divorced 1952; daughter: Dianne; father: Salvatore, (deceased); mother: Marie Tudisco; sister: Maria.
CRIMINAL ASSOCIATES	: Lucky Luciano, ███████████████, Michael Spinella, Gabriel Graziani, Santo Trafficante.
CRIMINAL HISTORY	: FBI# 1621338, NYCPD# B275664, record dates from 1935 and includes arrests for auto theft, breaking and entering, possession of pistol, grand larceny, burglary and interstate transportation of stolen goods. Currently (1959) awaiting deportation to Italy.
BUSINESS	: No legitimate source of income known.
MODUS OPERANDI	: A top Mafia member. While taking part in every type of illicit enterprise his main work for the organization was that of a courier travelling between the U.S. and Italy carrying narcotics and making arrangements for the transportation of and payment for same.

NAME	: Albert BARRASSO
ALIASES	: Baratto, Barratto, Barrasse, Bauasso, Capone, Carbone, Alessio Barrasso, Al Barr
DESCRIPTION	: Born 5-5-08, Newark, NJ, 5'5", 160 lbs, grey black hair, brown eyes, good teeth, stocky build.
LOCALITIES FREQUENTED	: Resides at 113 Willard Ave., Bloomfield, NJ. Has lived in Miami, Fla., and Kearny, NJ.
FAMILY BACKGROUND	: Married Maria Del Presto in 1927 has two children by that marriage, Maria and Theresa; divorced in 1943 and married Marian Carbone, has two children by this marriage, Alberta and Donna; is a brother-in-law to narcotic trafficker Aniello Santagata; father: Biagio; mother: Cesarina Mazzarola.
CRIMINAL ASSOCIATES	: Aniello Santagata, ███████████, Onofrio Abate, Joseph Gagliano, Settimo Accardo, Paul Lombardino
CRIMINAL HISTORY	: FBI #1860669 NJ State B of I #214011, Newark NJ PD #66002. Record dates from 1934 and includes arrests for gambling, automobile violations & illegal sale of firearms.
BUSINESS	: No legitimate occupation known.
MODUS OPERANDI	: Once a prize fighter, he is considered to be a tough person and is well liked in the Mafia with which he has been associated for many years.

NAME : Sebastiano BELLANCA

ALIASES : Sebastiano Ballanca, Benny Bellanca "The Bald Head", "Benny the Sicilian".

DESCRIPTION : Born 1-6-04, Cattolica, Sicily, naturalized, 1-8-31, NYC, 5'4", 165 lbs, build stocky, brown hair, (greying) almost completely bald, eyes blue, medium complexion, scar on right cheek sometimes wears glasses.

LOCALITIES FREQUENTED : Currently a fugitive, last known address 209 Tremont Ave., Fort Lee, NJ. Frequented Guy's Restaurant, Astoria, NY, Montreal, P.Q. and Windsor, Ontario.

FAMILY BACKGROUND : Father was Pasquale, his mother Josephine Renda, wife is Jennie, has grown children.

CRIMINAL ASSOCIATES : Frank Scalise (dead), Joe Pici, Peter Beddia, Jack Scarpulla and Albert Anastasia (dead), Michele Sisco, ▮▮▮▮▮▮▮▮▮▮, Sam Accardi.

CRIMINAL HISTORY : FBI #797788, Bellanca has been convicted for violation of the Federal Narcotic Laws.

BUSINESS : Last known business; owner of Guy's Restaurant, Astoria, Long Island.

MODUS OPERANDI : One of the most important international smugglers in the U.S., and a top ranking Mafioso from the NY area; was originally a partner of Jack Scarpulla and Frank Scalise, he received narcotic supplies from the Coudert-Sisco Combination of Montreal & France.

```
NAME          : Felix BOCCHICCHIO

ALIASES       : William Arthur Travers,
                John J. Bartlet.

DESCRIPTION   : Born 1907, U.S., 5'7½",
                145 lbs., slender build,
                dark brown hair, brown eyes,
                dark complexion, has stiff
                right leg, old bullet wound.

LOCALITIES    : Resides 16 Black Horse Pike,
FREQUENTED      Mount Ephraim, N.J., fre-
                quents 500 Club, Atlantic
                City, N.J., Bo-Bet Motel,
                Mount Ephraim, N.J.

FAMILY        : Married, wife's name Elizabeth; brother's name
BACKGROUND      Anthony.

CRIMINAL      : ████████████, Angelo Bruno, Peter Casella,
ASSOCIATES      Pasquale Massi, Dominick Pollino, Louis Campbell,
                Dominick Olivetto, ████████████, all of the
                Philadelphia, Camden area.  Lucky Luciano, Italy.

CRIMINAL      : FBI #359540, Camden PD# 5577; arrests since 1925
HISTORY         including larceny, murder suspect, holdup, white
                slave traffic act, escape and breaking prison,
                assault and battery, state liquor violations.

BUSINESS      : Fight manager, owns Bo-Bet Motel and K.O. Car Wash,
                Mount Ephraim, N.J., Co-owner with brother Anthony
                in City Liquor Co., 4 West Kings Highway, Mount
                Ephraim, N.J.

MODUS         : Gambler in underworld, Philadelphia-South Jersey
OPERANDI        area; alleged master mind behind many burglaries
                and robberies in Camden and Philadelphia area.
                Close associate of Mafia leaders in Camden area.
```

At the age of 95, in 1984, Boiardi died of natural causes.

NAME   : Richard BOIARDI

ALIASES   : Richie Boiardo, Ruggerio
                  Boiardi, Diamond Boiardo.

DESCRIPTION   : Born 11-8-1890 Naples, Italy.
                  5'7", 210 lbs., brown eyes,
                  grey hair, bullet scar on
                  left cheek.

LOCALITIES   : Has residences in Newark,
FREQUENTED   N.J., and Havana, Cuba.
                  Frequents Newark, N.Y.C.,
                  & gambling houses in Havana.

FAMILY   : Married to Jenny Manfro (deceased); son: Anthony;
BACKGROUND   daughters: Marie & Rose.

CRIMINAL   : Sam Accardi, Gerard Catena, Tom Campisi, Charles
ASSOCIATES   Campisi, Charles Tourine, Paul Lombardino, Anthony
                  Caponegro, all of Newark, N.J., area.

CRIMINAL   : FBI#330595. Newark PD#9315. Arrests since 1921
HISTORY   include manslaughter, assault & battery, & carrying
                  concealed weapons.

BUSINESS   : Reputed to have interest in Sea Gull Hotel, Miami
                  Beach, Fla.

MODUS   : One of the Mafia leaders from the Newark, N.J.,
OPERANDI   area engaged in all types of illegal rackets; also
                  active in gambling activities in Havana, Cuba.

```
NAME          : Paul BONADIO

ALIASES       : None

DESCRIPTION   : Born 6-7-03 NYC, 5'9", 160
                lbs, medium build, black
                hair, brown eyes, wears
                glasses.

LOCALITIES    : Resides at 326 Cross St,
FREQUENTED      Fort Lee, NJ, frequents
                Stage Coach, Little Ferry,
                NJ, Gene Boyle's, Clifton,
                NJ, Fiesta Cocktail Lounge,
                Woodridge, NJ, The Hangar,
                34 Forest Ave, Paramus, NJ.

FAMILY        : Not married; father: Nicola; mother: Margaret Monaco,
BACKGROUND      both born in Italy, both dead; brothers: Salvatore,
                Joseph and Nicola.

CRIMINAL      : Giuseppe Doto, Charles Chiri, ███████████████
ASSOCIATES      ██████████████████████████████, Anthony Strollo.

CRIMINAL      : No known arrests.
HISTORY

BUSINESS      : President of the Automotive Conveying Co., Inc., 800
                Fairview Ave, Fair View, NJ.

MODUS         : A top ranking member of the Mafia in the NY, & NJ, area,
OPERANDI        with connections in every major city in the U.S.
                Giuseppe Doto's front man before Doto was deported
                and still represents Doto's interests.
```

Cammarata was brutally murdered in 1972 while coming out of a Miami bistro. He was mowed down with 8 rounds from a .30 caliber carbine.

NAME   : Emanuel Rovere CAMMARATA

ALIASES   : Emanuel Cammarado, Cammerto, "Nello"

DESCRIPTION   : Born 10-9-03, Villabate, Palermo, Sicily, 5'6", 175 lbs, brown eyes, black hair, pocked marked face. Naturalized Newark, NJ 7-14-47.

LOCALITIES   : Resides 1050 N.E. 107th St.,
FREQUENTED   Miami Shores, Fla., and 13 Prospect Place, West Orange, New Jersey.

FAMILY   : Married to Giuseppa Messina; no children; father:
BACKGROUND   Giovanni; mother: Antonia Miono; brothers: Alfonso and Rosario; sister: Providenza DiChiara.

CRIMINAL   : ▮▮▮▮▮▮▮▮▮▮▮, Rinaldo Reino, Joseph Profaci, ▮▮▮▮▮
ASSOCIATES   ▮▮▮▮▮, Settimo Accardo.

CRIMINAL   : FBI #1458593. Cleveland, Ohio PD #32755. Arrests since
HISTORY   1927 include auto theft, suspicious person and investigation.

BUSINESS   : Owns Club Harmony, 184 N.E. 79th St., Miami, Fla.

MODUS   : Attended the 1928 Mafia meeting at Cleveland, Ohio.
OPERANDI   Is one of the leading Mafia figures in the north jersey area.

NAME	: Louis Edward CAMPBELL
ALIASES	: Louis D. Campbell, George Williams.
DESCRIPTION	: Born 10-17-97 Phila., Pa., 5'9", 170 lbs, dark chestnut hair, chestnut eyes, dark complexion, medium build.
LOCALITIES FREQUENTED	: Resides 639 Randolph St, Camden, NJ. Frequents 500 Club, Atlantic City, NJ; vicinity of 4th and Royden Sts, Camden, NJ.
FAMILY BACKGROUND	: Married Lenore Deturo; no children; father: William; mother: Jessie Cianfrana.
CRIMINAL ASSOCIATES	: Felix DeTullio, Joseph Rugnetta, Harry Riccobene, Peter Casella, ████████████, Dominick Pollino, Pasquale Massi, Felix Bocchicchio, ████████████, Angelo Bruno, all of the Philadelphia-Camden area.
CRIMINAL HISTORY	: FBI #340330, Philadelphia PD# 76932. Record dating from 1917 includes arrests for assault and battery, larceny, carrying a concealed deadly weapon, robbery, murder, illegal possession and use of drugs, disorderly conduct, lottery, counterfeiting, gambling.
BUSINESS	: No legitimate business known.
MODUS OPERANDI	: Professional gambler. Former Lieutenant of the late Marco Reginelli, Mafia leader of the Philadelphia-South Jersey area.

NAME   : Charles CAMPISI

ALIASES   : Campi, Charles Campise

DESCRIPTION : Born 10-16-12 Newark, N.J.,
               5'4", 160 lbs., brown hair,
               grey eyes, stocky build.

LOCALITIES   : Resides 118 Tuxedo Parkway,
FREQUENTED   Newark, N.J., frequents
               Atlantic City and Ventnor,
               NJ, and Miami, Florida.

FAMILY   : Father: Pietro, Mother:
BACKGROUND   Fortunata Longo, Wife: Rose,
               Children: Peter, Mrs. Lois
               Sanitate, Brothers: Tom, Gus, Salvatore, Biagio,
               Louis and Anthony.

CRIMINAL   : Lucky Luciano, Tom (brother), Sam Accardi, Vito
ASSOCIATES   Genovese, and other well known Mafia members in
               Newark, New Jersey area.

CRIMINAL   : FBI #652456, Newark New Jersey PD# 17122. Arrests
HISTORY   Since 1932 include carnal abuse, grand larceny,
               aggravated assault, Federal Liquor Laws, and convic-
               tion for Federal Narcotic Laws.

BUSINESS   : No legitimate business known.

MODUS   : With brother Tom was one of the top echelon operators
OPERANDI   in the Mafia narcotic smuggling and distributing or-
               ganization headed by Sam Accardi. One of the top hood-
               lums in the northern New Jersey area.

NAME   : Thomas CAMPISI

ALIASES   : Gasparo Campisi, Albert
                  Campi, Thomas Campe, Tom
                  Campise

DESCRIPTION   : Born 5-12-11, Newark, N.J.,
                  5'4", 185 lbs., grey eyes,
                  wavy light brown hair, stocky
                  build.

LOCALITIES   : Resides 265 14th Ave., Newark
FREQUENTED   N.J., frequents major race
                  tracks in NYC, Atlantic City
                  and Miami.

FAMILY   : Father: Pietro, Mother: Fortunata Longo, Wife:
BACKGROUND   Christine, Children: Fay, Lois, Connie, Peter,
                  Thomas Jr., Brothers: Gus, Charles, Salvatore, Biagio,
                  Louis, Tony.

CRIMINAL   : Lucky Luciano, Sam Accardi, Joe Doto, Vito Genovese,
ASSOCIATES   George Scalise, Frank Borelli, Vincent Carrao.

CRIMINAL   : FBI #148998, Newark New Jersey PD# 10658. Arrests
HISTORY   since 1928 include assault, kidnapping, liquor laws,
                  and conviction for Federal Narcotic Laws.

BUSINESS   : No legitimate business known.

MODUS   : A leader in the Mafia narcotic smuggling and dist-
OPERANDI   ributing organization headed by Sam Accardi of
                  Newark, N.J., with brother Charles is considered one
                  of top hoodlums in northern New Jersey area.

It is believed that Antonio played a part in the murder of Angelo Bruno. Caponigro's body was found in a trunk of a car in the Bronx on April 18, 1980. He had been stripped of his clothes, shot 14 times, and had multiple stab wounds.

NAME : Antonio Rocco CAPONIGRO

ALIASES : Tony Bananas, Tony Biase, Tony Caponigro

DESCRIPTION : Born 6-22-12 Chicago, Ill., 5'10", 185 lbs, black hair, brown eyes, receding hairline.

LOCALITIES FREQUENTED : Resides 124 Silver Spring Rd., Short Hills, NJ. Frequents NY, Chicago, Miami, Las Vegas, Mexico and Canada

FAMILY BACKGROUND : Married Katheen Cox; son: Victor; daughters: Ann, Katheen & Susan; father: Rocco; mother: Rosine Squarzzi; brother: Anthony (recently released from life sentence for armed robbery).

CRIMINAL ASSOCIATES : ██████████, Dominic Luciano, Alfred Salerno, ██████████, Gerardo Catena, Settimo Accardo.

CRIMINAL HISTORY : FBI #389561. Newark PD #13923. Record dating from 1927 includes arrests for auto theft, burglary, robbery, adultery, atrocious assault, suspicion of murder and assault on government reservation. On probation until 9-20-60.

BUSINESS : Owns a motel, a bar, restaurants & vending machine companies.

MODUS OPERANDI : Influential Mafioso who has amassed a great amount of money from bootlegging and gambling;now the largest lottery operator in NJ. A dangerous Racketeer and killer.

He's thought to be responsible for the bomb that exploded in Philip Testa's house on March 15, 1981. He was forced into retirement for lying about his involvement in the bombing.

NAME : Peter CASELLA

ALIASES : Pete Casela

DESCRIPTION : Born 8-28-07 St. Louis, Mo., 5'9", 220 lbs, heavy build, brown hair, hazel eyes, scar under right eyebrow.

LOCALITIES FREQUENTED : Resides 105 S. Dorset Ave., Ventnor, N.J., frequented J & R Flower Shop, Phila., Pa., and Bamboo Club, Atlantic City, N.J.

FAMILY BACKGROUND : Married to Julia Greenjack, has two brothers, Anthony and Sam; has one daughter.

CRIMINAL ASSOCIATES : ▮▮▮▮▮▮, ▮▮▮▮▮▮, Frank Palermo, Felix DeTullio, ▮▮▮▮▮▮, Felix Bocchicchio, James Massi, Joseph Lo Piccolo, Lawrence Orlando, Vincent Todaro, Marco Reginelli (dead).

CRIMINAL HISTORY : FBI #894604, Phila., P.D. #74700, several arrests since 1927 including larceny, lottery, homicide; currently serving 40 years for violation Federal Narcotic Laws.

BUSINESS : Was part owner of Ticket Grill, Phila., Pa., and Bamboo Club, Atlantic City, N.J.

MODUS OPERANDI : Interstate narcotic trafficker; was a lieutenant of deceased Mafia head, Marco Reginelli, in Phila., Camden area.

He died in Florida, in 2000, of natural causes at the age of 98.

NAME : Gerardo Vito CATENA

ALIASES : Gerald Catena, Jerry Allen, Jerry Cutana, Jerry Catena.

DESCRIPTION : Born 1-2-02 Newark, N.J. 5'7", 185 lbs, blue eyes, brown-grey hair.

LOCALITIES : Resides 21 Overhill Road,
FREQUENTED South Orange, NJ. Frequents El Sorrento Cafe, Bleeker Club, Old Colonial Inn, all in Newark, & La Martinique Cafe on Route 29, Mountainside, N.J.

FAMILY : Married to Catherine McNally; daughters: Patricia,
BACKGROUND Geraldine, Donna, Vicki; son: Richard; sisters: Mrs. Mary Frederico, Mrs. Sadie Dellasante; father: Francesco; mother: Donata Speziale.

CRIMINAL : Lucky Luciano & Joe Doto of Italy, Frank Costello,
ASSOCIATES Anthony Strollo, Michael Lascari, Angelo DeCarlo, Sam Accardi, Nick Delmore, Charles Tourine.

CRIMINAL : FBI# 144036. Newark PD# 9636. I&NS# A11086977.
HISTORY Arrests since 1923 include robbery, hijacking, bribing a Federal juror, suspicion of murder.

BUSINESS : Has interests in People's Express Co., Advance Vending Co., Runyon Vending Sales Co., Kool-Vent Awning Co., all in Newark, N.J.

MODUS : Attended Apalachin Mafia meeting 1957 with other
OPERANDI Mafia members representing the interests of the Mafia controlled rackets in northern N.J. Used strong-arm methods to gain control of vending machine industry in northern N.J.

NAME : Salvatore CHIRI

ALIASES : Charles Cluco, Charles
Salvatore Chiri

DESCRIPTION : Born 8-9-1888 Villa Scalia,
Palermo, Sicily, 5'6", 185
lbs, brown eyes, white hair,
heavy build, alien I&NS #A5-
167880.

LOCALITIES : Resides 2 Bridle Way,
FREQUENTED   Palisades, NJ. Frequents
I&C Dress Co., 341 W. 38th
St, NYC, El Sorrento Rest.,
Newark, N.J., & La Martinique Rest., Mountainside,
NJ.

FAMILY : Married Mary Graziano; daughters: Rose & Joan;
BACKGROUND   father: Giovanni Antonio; mother: Rosalia Cataldo.

CRIMINAL : Giuseppe Biondo, Anthony Strollo, Gaetano Lucchese,
ASSOCIATES   Charles Dongarra, Anthony Accardo, Giuseppe Doto,
Salvatore Caneba.

CRIMINAL : FBI #774935C. Only record shows alien registration
HISTORY   on 12-26-40 as Salvatore Chiri #5167880.

BUSINESS : Has interests in Automotive Conveying Co., located
in both Cliffside, NJ, & Mahwah, NJ, is partner
in I&C Dress Co., 341 W. 38th NYC.

MODUS : Attended Apalachin Mafia meeting 1957 in behalf of
OPERANDI   deported Mafia leader Joe Doto. Is now an elderly
and well respected Mafioso whose guidance is often
sought by the younger Mafiosi.

NAME   : Martin COHEN

ALIASES   : Marty, Morris, Morris Cohn

DESCRIPTION   : Born 1-12-11 Newark, NJ,
                  Jewish, 6'0", 246 lbs, brown
                  eyes, brown hair, heavy
                  build, ruddy complexion.

LOCALITIES   : Resides 10 Marshall St, Irv-
FREQUENTED   ington, NJ; previously re-
                  sided with his sister Mrs.
                  H. Schwartz 18 Marshall St,
                  Irvington, NJ. Frequents
                  various areas in Irvington
                  and Newark, NJ and also Midtown area of NYC.

FAMILY   : Father: Joseph; mother: Lizzie Fishman; divorced;
BACKGROUND   currently living with a Lillian Pennuchio.

CRIMINAL   : Anthony Castaldi, Carmine & Peter Locascio, Thomas
ASSOCIATES   Mancuso, William Margo, Anthony Pinto, Samuel Kassop,
                  ███████████ & ███████████████ of Miami Beach,
                  Florida, Settimo Accardo.

CRIMINAL   : FBI #749781. Newark PD #16859. Record dates from
HISTORY   1929 and includes arrests for attroc. assault and
                  battery; gambling; selling gas ration coupons, pos-
                  session of counterfeit gas coupons and nylons. Fed-
                  eral narcotic conviction.

BUSINESS   : No legitimate occupation.

MODUS   : Wholesale distributor of narcotics in NYC and
OPERANDI   interstate. Has many associates among the top
                  echelon of the Mafia. Also engaged in large
                  scale numbers operation in Newark, New Jersey.

NAME	:	Joseph Anthony COSTA
ALIASES	:	Jo Jo, Anthony Costa, Joseph Castro
DESCRIPTION	:	Born 10-21-07 NYC, 5'6", 180 lbs, brown hair, brown eyes, wears glasses, appearance of an ex-fighter.
LOCALITIES FREQUENTED	:	Resides 385 Fairview Ave., Paramus, NJ. Frequents Hillside Cleaners, Lodi, NJ, Stage Coach Inn, S. Hackensack, NJ; Petrullo's Rest., Hackensack, NJ, Gene Boyle's Lounge, Clifton, NJ.
FAMILY BACKGROUND	:	Married Helen Larzo; daughter: Melanie; father: Guiseppe; mother: Francesca Moglia; brother: Anthony.
CRIMINAL ASSOCIATES	:	Joseph Manfredi, Angelo LaPadura, Salvatore Santora, Philip Lombardo.
CRIMINAL HISTORY	:	FBI #259583B, NJ State Police #273291. Record dating from 1942 includes arrests for wage act violation, employment of minor without certificate, bootlegging and conspiracy.
BUSINESS	:	Co-owner of the Hillside Cleaners, 15 Hillside Place, Lodi, NJ with his brother Anthony.
MODUS OPERANDI	:	Operates stills for Mafia racketeers in northern NJ. Currently conducting bookmaking operations at the above mentioned cleaning store.

DeCarlo was sentenced to 12 years in prison for extortion related to the poisoning of Louis Saperstein. He died in Mountainside, NJ on October 20, 1973, less than a year after his release.

NAME : Angelo DeCARLO

ALIASES : Ray DeCarlo, "Gyp" DeCarlo, Edward Meing

DESCRIPTION : Born 2-28-02, Hoboken, N.J., 5'8", 200 lbs., brown eyes, black-grey hair.

LOCALITIES FREQUENTED : Resides on Route 22, Mountainside, N.J. Frequents Newark, N.J. and Miami, Fla.

FAMILY BACKGROUND : Wife believed to be Frances Ryan, has two children, father is Joseph, mother is Anne Pantalino, both born in Italy.

CRIMINAL ASSOCIATES : Jerry Catena, Abner Zwillman (dead), Richard Boiardi, Anthony Caponegro, ███████████, all of Newark area; Lucky Luciano of Italy.

CRIMINAL HISTORY : FBI #29873. Neward PD #8670. Arrests since 1923 include breaking and entering, counterfeiting, robbery, federal liquor laws and income tax evasion.

BUSINESS : Operates La Martinique Tavern, Route 22, Mountainside, New Jersey.

MODUS OPERANDI : Close associate of Mafia members in Newark area. Is active with them in illegal gambling activities and waterfront union activities in Hoboken and Jersey City, New Jersey areas.

NAME	: Felix John DETULLIO
ALIASES	: Felice Detulio, John Campo, Skinny Razor, Louis Newman, George Williams.
DESCRIPTION	: Born 8-2-07 Phila., Pa. 5'11", 179 lbs, dark brown hair, brown eyes.
LOCALITIES FREQUENTED	: Resides 2367 Baird Blvd., Camden, N.J. Frequents Television Bar in Phila., and 500 Club in Atlantic City.

FAMILY BACKGROUND	: Wife's name is Hildegard; sons: Dominick, John M., Marco.
CRIMINAL ASSOCIATES	: Angelo Bruno, Harry Riccobene, Dominick Pollino, Peter Casella, Joseph Rugnetta, all of Phila., area, Pasquale Massi and ███████████ of the Camden area.
CRIMINAL HISTORY	: FBI# 928463. Phila., PD# 68570. Arrests since 1924 include larceny, possession of untaxed liquor, sus - picion of murder, lottery.
BUSINESS	: Part owner of Television Bar, 8th & Washington Ave, Universal Exterminating Co, Rheingold Beer Distributors, all in Phila., Pa.
MODUS OPERANDI	: One of the higher ranking Mafia members in the Philadelphia-Camden area. Is closely associated with other Mafia members engaged in interstate narcotic trafficking.

> Eboli was assassinated at his girlfriend's home in Brooklyn on July 16, 1972. He died from 5 gunshot wounds to his body.

NAME : Thomas Vito Michael EBOLI

ALIASES : Tom DiRosa, Tommy Ryan, Tommy Rye, Tom Eberle

DESCRIPTION : Born 6-13-1911, Scisciano, Naples, Italy, 5'10¼", 165, brown-grey hair, brown eyes, dark comp., tattoo right arm. Naturalized NYC 8-27-1960 INS# C-8216086

LOCALITIES FREQUENTED : Resides 379 Forrest Drive, Englewood Cliffs, NJ, frequents Greenwich Village, NYC, particularly Tommy's Bar 171 Bleecker St, Noble's 33 W 8th St, Obie's 313 6 Ave. Frequently visits Italy.

FAMILY BACKGROUND : Legal wife, Anna Ariola, resides Melrose Park, Ill. She is mother of sons Louis (26) & Thomas (25). Eboli lives with Mary Percello, mother of his daughters, Madelena Masterson (22) & Mary Ann (14) & son Saverio (21); father: Louis; mother: Madalena Maddalone (deceased); brother: Pasquale, alias Patty Ryan.

CRIMINAL ASSOCIATES : Vito & Michael Genovese, Salvatore Lucania, Anthony Strollo, Francisco Costiglia, Vincenzo Mauro.

CRIMINAL HISTORY : FBI #3061565   NYCPD #B-144093
Record dating from 1933 includes arrests for assault, disorderly conduct, vagrancy & gambling.

BUSINESS : Interest in several restaurants, including those frequented, and Tryan Cigarette Vending Service, Inc.

MODUS OPERANDI : Has been a high ranking member of the Anthony Strollo Mafia group and is believed to have now taken over full control of that group from Strollo.

NAME   : Joseph FORGIONE

ALIASES   : Joe

DESCRIPTION : Born 5-20-1900 Newark, NJ,
                  5'8", 170 lbs, medium build,
                  brown eyes, brown-grey hair.

LOCALITIES   : Resides at 2559 Burns Ave.,
FREQUENTED   Union, NJ, frequents Passaic,
                  Elizabeth, Newark, NJ., NYC
                  and Miami, Florida.

FAMILY   : Wife: Louise; son: Joseph;
BACKGROUND   daughters: Constance, Joan
                  and Louisa; father: Giovanni; mother: Constenza
                  Maricondo.

CRIMINAL   : Lucky Luciano, Ray DeCarlo, Anthony Russo.
ASSOCIATES

CRIMINAL   : FBI #12668A. NJ SP#80191. Record dates from 1927
HISTORY   includes arrests for receiving stolen goods, dis-
                  orderly conduct, and gambling.

BUSINESS   : Associated with Willner Auctioneers, 11 Commerce
                  St., Newark, NJ, was formerly active on the Newark,
                  NJ, waterfront where he worked as a cargo checker.

MODUS   : Active in Mafia gambling activities in the Newark,
OPERANDI   NJ, area. Also involved in North Jersey waterfront
                  union activities.

NAME : Vito GENOVESE

ALIASES : Don Vitone, "The Old Man"

DESCRIPTION : Born 11-21-1897 Roccarainola,
Naples, Italy. 5'7", 160
lbs, brown eyes, black-grey
hair, wears glasses.
Naturalized 11-25-36, NYC

LOCALITIES : Resides 68 W. Highland Ave.,
FREQUENTED Atlantic Highlands, N.J.
Frequents Greenwich Village
area of NYC, Old Orchard
Country Club and Piano Bar,
Atlantic Highlands, N.J.

FAMILY : Separated from wife, Anna Petillo; son: Philip;
BACKGROUND step-daughter: Mrs. Anna Simonetti; brothers:
Michael and Carmine; father: Felice; mother:
Nunziata (both deceased).

CRIMINAL : Frank Costello, Tony Strollo, Tom Lucchese, Joe
ASSOCIATES Biondo, Joe Stracci, Joe Doto, Lucky Luciano.

CRIMINAL : FBI #861267. NYCPD B#59993. Extensive arrest
HISTORY record since 1917, including burglary, concealed
weapons, auto homicide and murder; has conviction
for violation of Federal narcotic laws.

BUSINESS : Has interests in Colonial Trading Co., Waste Paper
Removal Co., Erb Strapping Co., Tryon Cigarette
Service Co. and many night clubs, all in N.Y.C.

MODUS : Attended Apalachin Mafia meeting 1957. Financial
OPERANDI backer for international narcotic smuggling. Is
reputed Mafia head of N.Y.C. rackets, shares in
gambling and other interstate rackets with deportee
Lucky Luciano.

NAME   : Giuseppe IDI

ALIASES   : Giuseppe Ida, Giuseppe Aida

DESCRIPTION   : Born 6-14-1890 Fiumare Di
                Muro, Calabria, Italy, 5'6",
                145 lbs, brown eyes, grey
                hair, naturalized 5-2-19
                Phila., Penna.

LOCALITIES   : Resides 108 Lincoln Ave.,
FREQUENTED   Highland Park, NJ. Frequents
                area of Broome & Mulberry
                Sts., Manhattan.

FAMILY   : Wife's name is Mamie; adopted son: John T. Sondonato
BACKGROUND   (who is a nephew); father: Gaetano (dead); mother:
                Angela Pensabene.

CRIMINAL   : Rocco Pelligrino, Vito Genovese, Sam Accardi, Jerry
ASSOCIATES   Catena, Dominick Olivetti, Joe Doto, Anthony Riela.

CRIMINAL   : No FBI # assigned. 1959 indicted for conspiracy to
HISTORY   obstruct justice. Currently (1960) a fugitive on
                this charge.

BUSINESS   : Has been a salesman for DeAngelis Buick Agency,
                New Brunswick, New Jersey.

MODUS   : Attended Apalachin Mafia meeting 1957 as a leader
OPERANDI   from the New Brunswick, NJ, area. With Mafia asso-
                ciates he controlled bookmaking activities, illegal
                alcohol, & all types of gambling in New Brunswick
                area.

NAME : Angelo LAPADURA

ALIASES : Angelo Lapadure, Angelo
Lapadarus, Arcangelo Lapadura,
Angelo Lapidura.

DESCRIPTION : Born 8-1-1891, San Cataldo,
Caltanissetta, Sicily, 5'5",
165 lbs, grey hair, brown
eyes. Alien Reg #5227532.

LOCALITIES : Resides 382 Oak St, Passaic,
FREQUENTED NJ, frequents Roma Gardens,
and Nick's Pizzeria, Paterson,
New Jersey.

FAMILY : Married to Vida Monalo (died 1955); children Lucy,
BACKGROUND Fanny, Sadie, Josephine, Samuel, Rose, Angelina;
father: Salvatore; mother: Lucy Prezia both born
Sicily; brothers: Salvatore and Joseph.

CRIMINAL : William Locascio, Michael and Joseph Limandri,
ASSOCIATES ████████████████, Angelo Polizzi.

CRIMINAL : FBI #303879, Newark, NJ PD#21421. Record dates from
HISTORY 1929 and includes arrests for kidnapping, numerous
violations of the U.S. Liquor Laws and carrying a
concealed weapon.

BUSINESS : Worked for Andrew Manufacturing Co., Passaic, NJ,
but at the present time is unemployed. In 1947
operated Motel in Glendale, Arizona.

MODUS : A member of the NJ Mafia group. His criminal act-
OPERANDI ivities have consisted mostly of bootlegging &
gambling.

"Fat Lou" was a longtime Underboss of the DeCavalcante crime family. He was reported "missing" in the summer of 1991, failing to show up for his 65th birthday party. Though his body has never been found, Vincent Palermo confessed to his murder, along with three other "shooters."

NAME	: Louis A. LaRASSO
ALIASES	: Luciano Luraso, Luciano Anthony LaRasso.
DESCRIPTION	: Born 11-13-1926, Elizabeth, NJ, 5'7", 206 lbs, brown eyes, dark brown hair.
LOCALITIES FREQUENTED	: Resides 2711 Bradbury St., Linden, NJ. Frequents Int'l Hod Carriers & Common Laborers Union, Local 394, Elizabeth, NJ.
FAMILY BACKGROUND	: Married Stephanie Idec; daughters: Maria, Lois and Johanna; brother: Albert; sister: Mrs. Catherine Signorelli; father: Alfonso; mother: Maria Lobritto.
CRIMINAL ASSOCIATES	: Anthony Riela, Frank Majuri, Vito Genovese, Giuseppe Idi, Dominick Olivetto, Emanuel Riggi, Richard Boiardi.
CRIMINAL HISTORY	: FBI #745765-C Only known arrest was for conspiracy to obstruct justice, for which sentenced in 1960 to 4 years imprisonment.
BUSINESS	: Operates a Sinclair Service Station in Elizabeth,NJ. Is a trustee of International Hod Carriers and Common Laborers Union, Local 394, Elizabeth, NJ.
MODUS OPERANDI	: Attended 1957 Apalachin Mafia meeting. An up and coming younger Mafia leader from the northern New Jersey area who has engaged as a strong-arm man in labor union racketeering.

NAME   : Ernest LAZZARA

ALIASES   : Ernie

DESCRIPTION   : Born 9-22-14 Passaic, NJ,
                   5'11", 200 lbs, stocky build,
                   black hair, brown eyes, mou-
                   stache, wears glasses.

LOCALITIES   : Resides Buffa Drive, Franklin
FREQUENTED   Township, NJ. Frequents Pas-
                   saic, Irvington, Newark &
                   Elizabeth, NJ & NYC.

FAMILY   : Wife: Vivian; daughter: Lynn;
BACKGROUND   father: Emielo; mother: Congattina Maricondo; brother:
                   Louis.

CRIMINAL   : Sam Accardi, Martin Cohen, Samuel Kass, ████████████,
ASSOCIATES   Anthony Castaldi.

CRIMINAL   : FBI #4224372, Newark PD# 52225, Passaic County, NJ #
HISTORY   7433. Criminal Record dates from 1939, includes one
                   arrest for violation of the Federal Narcotic Laws.

BUSINESS   : Operates a bakery at 459 Somerset Ave, New Brunswick,
                   New Jersey.

MODUS   : In association with other Mafiosi carries on large
OPERANDI   scale gambling activities in north jersey area;
                   finances narcotic transactions.

NAME	: Benjamin LICCHI
ALIASES	: Benny
DESCRIPTION	: Born 1-2-13 NYC, 5'10", 222 lbs, heavy build, grey-brown hair, balding, brown eyes, dark complexion, tattoos both forearms.
LOCALITIES FREQUENTED	: Resides 429 Parker Ave., Hackensack, NJ. Frequents 107th St., & 2nd Ave, 116th St, & Pleasant Ave, both NYC & Fairlawn, NJ. Currently incarcerated.

FAMILY BACKGROUND	: Wife: Marie Grantino; daughters: Marie Mayo, Mamie Borelli; father: Salvatore; mother: Marie Magistro; brothers: Joseph & Anthony; sister: Bessie Casimenti
CRIMINAL ASSOCIATES	: Joseph Licchi, Frank Borelli, Charles Curcio, Rocco Mazzie, Vincent Squillante, Nicholas Tolentino
CRIMINAL HISTORY	: FBI #614023, NYCPD #B103186. Record dates from 1932 and includes arrests for robbery, assault & robbery, grand larceny & violation of Federal Narcotic Laws.
BUSINESS	: Operated small contracting business from residence. Is a plumber & mechanic by trade.
MODUS OPERANDI	: Part of the Mafia organization, headed by Frank Borelli, which produced heroin in large quantities in a clandestine laboratory in NJ. This heroin was then distributed in NY and Chicago, Ill.

NAME : Joseph Anthony LICCHI

ALIASES :

DESCRIPTION : Born 4-9-19 NYC, 5'6", 146 lbs, black receding hair, brown eyes, dark complexion, moustache, deformed right little finger.

LOCALITIES FREQUENTED : Resides 12-63 3rd St., Fairlawn, NJ, frequents Hackensack, NJ, 1st Ave, & 107th St, NYC, 116th St, & Pleasant Ave, NYC, currently incarcerated.

FAMILY BACKGROUND : Wife: Marie Pisanelo; no children; father: Salvatore; mother: Marie Magistro; sister: Bessie Casimenti; brothers: Benjamin & Anthony.

CRIMINAL ASSOCIATES : Benjamin Licchi, Frank Borelli, Charles Curcio, Rocco Mazzie, Vincent Squillante, Nicholas Tolentino

CRIMINAL HISTORY : FBI #1182170, NYCPD #B 144035. Record dates from 1936 and includes arrests for assault & robbery. NJ State narcotic conviction 1957 sentenced to 5-7 years NJ State Prison.

BUSINESS : Carpenter & mechanic. Worked for brother, Benjamin, in contracting business.

MODUS OPERANDI : Part of the Mafia organization, headed by Frank Borelli, which produced heroin in large quantities in a clandestine laboratory in NJ. This heroin was then distributed in NY and Chicago, Ill.

NAME	: Andrew LOMBARDINO
ALIASES	: Andy Lombardini
DESCRIPTION	: Born 1-24-05 Newark, NJ, 5'6", 190 lbs, brown eyes, black-grey hair balding on top.
LOCALITIES FREQUENTED	: Resides 76 Riverside Drive, Florham Park, NJ. Frequents major cities in South New Jersey area.

FAMILY BACKGROUND	: Married; sons: Louis & Andrew Jr; daughters: Mary & Martha; father: Luigi; mother: Licari Maltia (both deceased); wifes parents: Mary & Louis Fidemi.
CRIMINAL ASSOCIATES	: Giuseppe Profaci, Giuseppe Magliocco, Salvatore Lombardino, Vincent Mangano, Charles Campisi, Settimo Accardo, ▬▬▬▬▬.
CRIMINAL HISTORY	: FBI #609609. Newark PD#19883. Arrests since 1928 include vagrancy, assault & battery, threat to kill.
BUSINESS	: Construction business.
MODUS OPERANDI	: Attended Cleveland Mafia meeting in 1928 and is closely associated with Giuseppe Profaci & Giuseppe Magliocco.

NAME	: Paul Mario LOMBARDINO

ALIASES : Paul Lombardini, Joseph
Lombardi.

DESCRIPTION : Born 2-20-1912, Gibellina,
Trapani, Sicily, 5'8½", 195
lbs, brown eyes, black hair.
I&NS file #A-5686663 (Alien).

LOCALITIES : Resides 11 Seventh Avenue,
FREQUENTED   Newark, NJ Frequents Newark
area and Lower East Side,NYC

FAMILY : Divorced from Antoinette
BACKGROUND   Alberti, who bore him three children, Rose, Grace
and Paul; now married to Irene Alice Davidson;
mother: Gracia Musso (now Mrs. Cologero LaPlaca).
Father died in Italy before Lombardino & mother
came to U.S.

CRIMINAL : Settimo Accardo, Rinaldo Reino, ███████████████,
ASSOCIATES   Charles Tourine & Richard Boiardi.

CRIMINAL : FBI #4697254 Newark PD #30274 Record dating from
HISTORY   1940 includes arrests for vagrancy, larceny &
conviction for violation Federal Narcotic Laws.

BUSINESS : Painting contractor.

MODUS : Lower echelon member of a Mafia narcotic smuggling
group in northern New Jersey. This group was
formerly headed by Settimo Accardo, who fled to
Italy in 1955 to escape Federal Narcotic prosecution.

315

Majuri died in 1983.

NAME	: Frank T. MAJURI
ALIASES	: Frank Maiuri, Frank Gagliano, Frank Martin, Frank Gagaliano.
DESCRIPTION	: Born 4-18-1909, NYC, 5'10" 229 lbs, dark brown hair, brown eyes, heavy build.
LOCALITIES FREQUENTED	: Resides 629 S. Broad Street, Elizabeth, N.J.
FAMILY BACKGROUND	: Married Carmela Camiano; son: Charles; daughter: Marie; brothers: John, Vincent, Anthony, Louis; sister: Mrs. Bessie Scapara.
CRIMINAL ASSOCIATES	: Louis LaRasso, Anthony Riela, Dominick Olivetto, Vito Genovese, Frank Carbo, James Plumeri, Richard Boiardi, Filippo Amari.
CRIMINAL HISTORY	: FBI #1102386 Record dating from 1935 includes arrests for illegal manufacture of alcohol, bookmaking, violation of probation and conspiracy to obstruct justice (for which sentenced 1960 to 5 years).
BUSINESS	: Labor foreman for C. F. Braun & Co., Tromley Point, Linden, N.J.
MODUS OPERANDI	: Attended 1957 Apalachin Mafia meeting with other members from northern New Jersey area. Engages in extortion from Italian illegal immigrant laborers in the Newark-Elizabeth area.

NAME   : Anthony Michael MARCHITTO

ALIASES   : Tony Cheese, Tony Chez.

DESCRIPTION   : Born 8-31-11 Jersey City, NJ,
                  5'8½", 180 lbs, stocky build,
                  medium complexion, brown
                  eyes, light brown hair, re-
                  ceding hairline.

LOCALITIES   : Resides 130 Greenville Ave.,
FREQUENTED   Jersey City, NJ. Frequents
                  New Ocean Tavern, 269 Ocean
                  Ave., Jersey City, Local
                  1478 ILA Warehousemen, 1312
                  Washington St., Hoboken, Local 1823 Industrial Em-
                  ployees Union and the Hoboken and Jersey City piers.

FAMILY   : Married Rose DeAngeles; son: Anthony; father:
BACKGROUND   Fortunato; mother: Anna Marie Pompei; brothers:
                  Fortunato and Dominick; sisters: Marie Isabella,
                  Isabella and Marie Theresa.

CRIMINAL   : ███████████████, ████████████████, ████████████
ASSOCIATES   ████████, ████████████.

CRIMINAL   : FBI #26242B. Jersey City PD# 13057. Record dates
RECORD   from 1951 and includes arrests for attrocious as-
                  sault, material witness and conspiracy to commit
                  birbery.

BUSINESS   : Owns the New Ocean Tavern, Jersey City, NJ, or-
                  ganizer of Local 1478 ILA Warehousemen, Secretary
                  and Business Agent for Local 1823, Indust., Em-
                  ployees Union.

MODUS   : Powerful Mafia figure in the control of NJ, docks,
OPERANDI   union strongarm man and extortionist.

317

NAME	: Pasquale MASSI
ALIASES	: Pat
DESCRIPTION	: Born 11-7-03 Mosciano S. Angelo, Abruzzi, Italy, naturalized 8-22-47, Camden, N.J, 5'6", 230 lbs, heavy build, black hair, brown eyes, scar on chin, tattoos on right and left forearms.
LOCALITIES FREQUENTED	: Resides 1420 Park Blvd., Camden, N.J, frequents Casa Blanca Night Club, Marlton Pike, Camden, N.J.
FAMILY BACKGROUND	: Married to Laura Filipkoski, has son Jerry, daughter Constance, brothers Jerry, Frank, Umberto, father Pangrazio, mother Concetta Battestini (both dead).
CRIMINAL ASSOCIATES	: Lucky Luciano, Joseph Rugnetta, Dominick and ████, Frank Palermo, Pete Casella, Louis Campbell, Dominick Oliveto.
CRIMINAL HISTORY	: FBI #336243, N.J. State Police #24345, several arrests since 1922 including rape, robbery, firearms act.
BUSINESS	: Operates St. George Motel, Route 70, Camden, N.J.
MODUS OPERANDI	: An important member of the Mafia in the Phila., Camden area; makes trips to Italy where he meets with Lucky Luciano.

"Big Dom" was arrested at the Apalachin Conference in November 1957. He died in January 1969.

NAME : Dominick OLIVETO

ALIASES : Domenick Olivett, James DeMarco, "Big Dominick".

DESCRIPTION : Born 1-6-07 Camden, N.J. 5'9", 180 lbs, brown eyes, dark brown hair.

LOCALITIES FREQUENTED : Resides 1157 Magnolia Ave., Camden, N.J. Frequents area of Philadelphia and Camden.

FAMILY BACKGROUND : Married to Marie Del Ficco; sons: Anthony & Robert; brothers: Daniel, William, Felice; sisters: Mrs. Lucy Serto, Mrs. Rose DeRose, Mrs. Lena Paioletti; father: Antonio; mother Maria Sanzone (both dead).

CRIMINAL ASSOCIATES : Felix DeTullio, Angelo Bruno, Richard Boiardi, Joe Ida, Jerry Catena, Pasquale Massi, ▆▆▆▆▆▆▆▆, ▆▆▆▆▆▆▆▆, Frank Palermo.

CRIMINAL HISTORY : FBI #2935549. Camden PD #694. Arrests since 1937 include larceny, gambling, bootlegging.

BUSINESS : Has interests in Forrest Products Co., Runnemede, N.J., Vogue Manufacturing Co., Vineland, N.J., and Quality Liquor Co., Camden, N.J.

MODUS OPERANDI : Attended Apalachin Mafia meeting 1957 representing the interests of the Mafia controlled rackets in the Camden area. Took over leadership of the Mafia in the Camden area after the death of Mafia leader Marco Reginelli in 1956.

319

NAME   : Peter Joseph POLICASTRO

ALIASES   : Guy

DESCRIPTION   : Born 1-30-17 Jersey City, NJ,
                 5'10", 210 lbs, black hair,
                 brown eyes, heavy build,
                 large ears, double chin.

LOCALITIES   : Resides 6108 Tyler Place,
FREQUENTED   West NY, NJ. Frequents Union
                 City, Jersey City, Hoboken
                 and NYC.

FAMILY   : Married and has three child-
BACKGROUND   ren; father: Charles; mother: Bessie Amobile.

CRIMINAL   : Carmine Galente, Joseph Zicarelli, ███████████,
ASSOCIATES   Salvatore Giglio, Angelo Presinzano.

CRIMINAL   : No FBI # assigned. Hudson Co., Sheriff's Office #
HISTORY   46900. No previous criminal history; is currently
                 (1959) under indictment on charges of misconduct
                 in office, (that of sergeant of West New York, N.J.,
                 Police Dept.). Was suspended but now has been re-
                 instated pending trial.

BUSINESS   : Detective Sgt., Hudson County Police, also does
                 private detective work for N.Y. divorce lawyers.

MODUS   : Reputed to be a "front man" for the Mafia, inter-
OPERANDI   ceding on behalf of criminals arrested by various
                 police agencies. The misconduct charge was in
                 connection with his having performed this duty
                 for Mafia bigwig Carmine Galente in 1959.

NAME : Rinaldo REINO

ALIASES : Blackie, Ray, Reynold

DESCRIPTION : Born 11-4-1923, NYC, 5'10",
150 lbs, slender, black hair,
brown eyes, mustache, constantly troubled with arth-
ritis & rheumatic fever.

LOCALITIES : Resides 410 13th Avenue,
FREQUENTED   Newark, NJ. Frequents
Newark night clubs and the
Holiday Club in NYC.

FAMILY : Married Rita Gata; four children; father: Carmine;
BACKGROUND   mother: Helen Alberti; brothers: Joseph & Salvatore;
sisters: Annette Laskoski, Marie DeStefinas & Julia.

CRIMINAL : Settimo Accardo, Joseph Accardo, ███████████████,
ASSOCIATES   Paul Lombardino, Campisi brothers.

CRIMINAL : FBI #2556339 Newark PD #45008 Record dating from
HISTORY   1939 includes arrests for robbery, assault & battery,
attrocious assault & Federal Narcotic conviction.

BUSINESS : Currently employed as bus driver.

MODUS : Part of a north Jersey Mafia group which carries on
OPERANDI   large scale gambling, illicit alcohol and narcotics
operations.

NAME	: Anthony Peter RIELA

ALIASES : None

DESCRIPTION : Born 8-22-1896, Terranova, Sicily, 5'6½", 180 lbs, grey eyes, black-grey hair, naturalized Brooklyn, NY, 8-2-33.

LOCALITIES FREQUENTED : Resides 7 Benvenue Avenue, West Orange, NJ, frequents Airport Motel, Newark, NJ.

FAMILY BACKGROUND : Wife: Josephine; son: Andrew; father: Andrea; mother: Maria Polizzi.

CRIMINAL ASSOCIATES : Frank Majuri, Gerardo Catena, Giuseppe Bonanno, Frank Zito, James Colletti, Louis LaRasso, Vito Genovese.

CRIMINAL HISTORY : FBI #796624-C Newark NJ PD #67510 Record dating from 1955 includes arrest for maintaining nuisance, permitting prostitution, conspiracy to obstruct justice (for which sentenced 1960 to 4 years and $10,000 fine). Suspect in two murders in Rockford, Illinois, in 1944.

BUSINESS : Owns Airport Motel and Newarker Motel, both in Newark, N.J.

MODUS OPERANDI : Attended 1957 Apalachin Mafia meeting as a leader from the Newark area. With other Mafia associates he is engaged in illegal gambling and strong-arm rackets in Newark and vicinity.

NAME	: Michael RUSSO
ALIASES	: Mike Valentino, Mike Fedesco, Mike Partiro, Max Sender
DESCRIPTION	: Born 11-23-1893 Cerda, Sicily, 5'9", 150 lbs, brown eyes, black-grey hair.
LOCALITIES FREQUENTED	: Resides 105 Ridgely Ave., Iselin, NJ, frequented Boston, Mass, Buffalo, NY, Cleveland, Ohio, & Florida.

FAMILY BACKGROUND	: Married to Mary Almasi, son: Charles; father: Giuseppe; mother: Francesca (both dead).
CRIMINAL ASSOCIATES	: Vito Genovese, Sam Accardi, Andrew Lombardino, Joe Profaci, Joe Magliocco, Emanuel Cammarata, Charles Tourine Sr.
CRIMINAL HISTORY	: FBI #88259. Cleveland PD#32775. Arrests since 1911 include assault, burglary, swindling, homicide, embezzlement.
BUSINESS	: No legitimate business or employment known.
MODUS OPERANDI	: Attended Cleveland Mafia meeting 1928. Has been a powerful influence in the Mafia for many years. In his younger days was an "enforcer." Currently is less active and in semi-retirement.

NAME   : Carmine San GIACOMA

ALIASES   : Big Yok, John Yock, Yock
                  San Giacomo, Raymond, Yock
                  Raymond, Frank Raymond.

DESCRIPTION   : Born 7-26-1896 Newark, NJ,
                  6'0", 210 lbs, brown eyes,
                  black-grey hair.

LOCALITIES   : Resides with his son Frank,
FREQUENTED   at 50 Cottage Place, Long
                  Branch, NJ. Formerly lived
                  for many years in Newark, NJ.
                  Has been in Elizabeth, NJ,
                  Florida and New York.

FAMILY   : Wife deceased; children: Frank and Lucy San Giacomo;
BACKGROUND   father: Vito; mother: Lucia Veiniera both deceased.

CRIMINAL   : Paul Lombardino, Andrew Lombardino, Settimo Accardo,
ASSOCIATES   ███████████, and the late Abner Zwillman.

CRIMINAL   : FBI #808899. NJSP #126398. Record dating from 1924
HISTORY   includes arrests for highway robbery & assault and
                  battery.

BUSINESS   : Owned the San Giacomo Paper Corp., and the Cornwall
                  Paper Mill Co., in Newark, and also had a waste
                  paper company. Is partially retired at this time.

MODUS   : A one-time Mafia enforcer working for the late Abner
OPERANDI   "Longie" Zwillman, Quarico Moretti and other North
                  Jersey Mafia leaders. He is still influential in
                  Mafia affairs although he appears to have retired
                  from active participation in crime.

NAME   : Aniello SANTAGATA

ALIASES   : Santagato, Joseph Ottieri,
                  O'Maddalonese, Emmet Agato,
                  Santo Emilio, Santiago Amella

DESCRIPTION   : Born 1-13-1888 Maddaloni,
                  Caserta, Italy, 5'6", 198
                  lbs, grey hair, brown eyes,
                  dark complexion, naturalized
                  newark, NJ 10-3-1928 No.
                  C-493304.

LOCALITIES   : Resides 1 Kearney Ave,
FREQUENTED   Kearney, NJ. Frequents 14th
                  Ave, section of Newark, NJ, lower east side of NYC,
                  Wilson Ave, section of B'klyn, NY, NY area race
                  tracks, Mexico.

FAMILY   : Married Grace Carbone 1952 and she divorced him
BACKGROUND   after he went to prison in 1955. He is again liv-
                  ing with her; father: Raphael; mother: Giovanna
                  Della Rocco; sister: Lucille Carrolo.

CRIMINAL   : ███████████████ (Mexico), ███████████, Campisi
ASSOCIATES   Brothers, Angelo Buia, Settimo Accardo.

CRIMINAL   : FBI #1671607. NYCPD #B22389. Record dating from 1909
HISTORY   includes arrests for pickpocket, larceny, kidnapping,
                  bastardy, fornication, assault & battery, disorderly
                  conduct, gambling, bootlegging. Federal narcotics
                  conviction.

BUSINESS   : Retired barber. Collecting social security.

MODUS   : An old time Mafioso who is highly regarded by other
OPERANDI   members. Has sources for narcotics in Italy, Mexico
                  & Canada and has been responsible for the smuggling
                  & distribution of untold quantities of heroin. Re-
                  cently (1960) perjured himself before a Grand Jury
                  in an attempt to protect another Mafia member and
                  narcotic trafficker.

NAME : Charles SCHIFFMAN

ALIASES : Charles Shipman, Schippman, Morris Feldman, Charles Harris

DESCRIPTION : Born 9-14-1903, Wallington, NJ, Jewish, 5'6", 156 lbs, brown-grey hair, brown eyes.

LOCALITIES FREQUENTED : Resides 79 Van Buren Street, Passaic, NJ, frequents mid-town NYC and northern New Jersey.

FAMILY BACKGROUND : Single; father: Samuel; mother: Sarah Feldman (both deceased); sisters: Eva Sternberg, Esther Schiffman & Ann Floff; brothers: Barney & Arthur.

CRIMINAL ASSOCIATES : John Ormento, Salvatore Santoro, Moische Taubman, ██████████, Abraham Chalupowitz, Joseph Littman.

CRIMINAL HISTORY : FBI #313781 NYCPD #B-123114 Newark NJ PD #6034 Record dating from 1921 includes arrests for burglary, breaking & entering, drunkenness, robbery, concealed weapon, highway robbery & three Federal Narcotic convictions.

BUSINESS : No legitimate occupation.

MODUS OPERANDI : A confirmed and vicious criminal who for many years headed a gang of racketeers who engaged in every type of illicit enterprise in the northern New Jersey area. Is known to and allied with top Mafia criminals from all parts of the U.S. Large scale narcotic trafficker.

NAME	: Giuseppe VECCHIO
ALIASES	: Joe Vecchio
DESCRIPTION	: Born 6-26-1917 in N.Y.C. 5'6", 170 lbs, black hair, brown eyes, heavy build, scar over left eye.
LOCALITIES FREQUENTED	: Resides 86 Bloomfield Ave., Nutley, NJ. Frequents Palm Beach, Fla., and Montreal, Canada.

FAMILY BACKGROUND	: Married Susan Genovese; sons: Jerry & Michael; father: Carmine; mother: Antoinetta Tuchorana.
CRIMINAL ASSOCIATES	: Settimo Accardo, ███████████, Giuseppe Cotroni, Henri Samson, ███████████.
CRIMINAL HISTORY	: FBI #1258494 NYCPD #B-154898 Record dating from 1934 includes arrests for disorderly conduct and burglary.
BUSINESS	: Owns All State Asphalt Co., Nutley, N.J.
MODUS OPERANDI	: Courier for the Cotroni brothers narcotic smuggling organization of Montreal, Canada. Vecchio has transported large quantities of heroin to the U.S. for delivery to Mafia narcotic distribution organizations.

Zicarelli was an eyewitness to a triple murder of fellow capos in Brooklyn in 1981. He was most likely "bait" to reassure the three before they were murdered. "Bayonne Joe" passed away in August 1983, at the age of 1971, from natural causes.

NAME : Joseph ZICARELLI

ALIASES : Joe Marino, Ed Beattie, Joe Malone, Joe Corelli, Joe Linardi, Little Joe, Joe Z., Bayonne Joe.

DESCRIPTION : Born 10-9-12 Bayonne, NJ, 5'6", 175 lbs, medium build, black-grey hair, brown eyes.

LOCALITIES FREQUENTED : Resides 255 Ave, B, Bayonne, NJ. Frequents Modern Motor Sales, Union City, NJ, night clubs in Union City & North Bergen, NJ, NY, & NJ, racetracks.

FAMILY BACKGROUND : Married Mari Regna; son: Joseph; father: Maurice; mother: Rose Linardi; brother: John.

CRIMINAL ASSOCIATES : Carmine Galente, ███████, ███████, Vito Genovese, Anthony Strollo, Anthony Caponigro.

CRIMINAL HISTORY : FBI #1107492. NYSP #142776. Record dates from 1930 and includes arrests for grand larceny, bootlegging and gambling.

BUSINESS : Partner of Carmine Galante in Latimer Shipping Co., an import export firm at 10 E 49 St, NYC. Also owns cigarette vending machine business at West NY, NJ.

MODUS OPERANDI : One of the Mafia leaders in the NJ, area. An international arms smuggler and controls all organized gambling in North Jersey area, operates a loan shark business with Louis LaPore and Sam Guiarusso in Hudson County, New Jersey.

```
NAME          : Angelo ABBRESCIA

ALIASES       : Angelo Bozzi, The Brush,
                Angelo Abruscia, Arcangelo
                Abbrescia.

DESCRIPTION   : Born 3-11-1900 Bari, Italy,
                5'3", 163 lbs, grey eyes,
                grey hair (balding), walks
                with a limp.

LOCALITIES    : Resides 23-56 31st Ave.,
FREQUENTED      Astoria, L.I., NY, frequents
                area 117th St. & 3rd Ave.,
                Canal & Mott Sts, both in
                Manhattan.

FAMILY        : Married to Mary DeStefano; daughter: Rose; father:
BACKGROUND      Joseph; mother: Rose Pelella (both dead); brother:
                Pietro.

CRIMINAL      : ████████, Sam Kass, ████████████, Charles Curcio,
ASSOCIATES      John Ormento, Salvatore Santoro, ████████████████,
                all of NYC, Ugo Mariani (Deportee).

CRIMINAL      : FBI #201962.  NYCPD B#73752.  Arrests since 1929
HISTORY         include assault 2nd, Federal Liquor Laws, convic-
                tion for Federal Narcotic Laws.

BUSINESS      : No legitimate business or employment known.

MODUS         : A Mafiosi & major narcotic trafficker for many
OPERANDI        years who supplied narcotics to dealers both local-
                ly & interstate.  Had his own smuggling source of
                supply & also dealt with other Mafia traffickers.
```

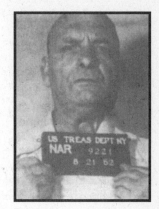

NAME : Philip Joseph ALBANESE

ALIASES : Phil Katz, Philly

DESCRIPTION : Born 11-7-07, NYC, NY; 5'9",
180 lbs., brown eyes, dark
brown hair, sallow complexion and stocky build.

LOCALITIES : Resides at 1108 Philip Court
FREQUENTED   Valley Stream, Long Island,
NY. Frequents 121 Mulberry
St., 124th St. and First Ave
and Pier 28, North River,
all in NYC.

FAMILY : Divorced from Lillian Cappola in 1931. Currently
BACKGROUND   married to Rose Russo. They have two children.
Brothers, Joseph, Dominick, Anthony and Rosario;
and sister, Nancy; all residing in NYC.

CRIMINAL : George Nobile, Joe Marone, Vito Tozzi, Eugene
ASSOCIATES   Uricola, ███████████████ and Frank Donato.

CRIMINAL : FBI #4042881, NYC PD #B-282814. Dates from 1925
HISTORY   and includes robbery, income tax evasion and
violations of the narcotics laws.

BUSINESS : A public loader on the North River piers, NYC, NY.

MODUS : A "strong-arm man" for the Mafia and reputed boss
OPERANDI   of New York City's 4th Ward for this organization.

NAME : John ALBASI

ALIASES : Thomas Long

DESCRIPTION : Born 6-18-10 NYC, 5'6", 155 lbs, hazel eyes, grey hair thinning out on top.

LOCALITIES FREQUENTED : Resides 334 E. 105th St., NYC. Frequents Jennie's Restaurant 2036 2nd Ave., New York City.

FAMILY BACKGROUND : Married to Tessie Scondizzo; sons: Virgil & John; sisters: Mrs. Louise Delardi, Mrs. Elsie Lidolsi, Mrs. Sadie Rebitz; father: Virgil; mother: Maria Alberice.

CRIMINAL ASSOCIATES : Anthony Castaldi, Edward D'Argenio, John Ormento, Arthur Leo, Angelo Salerno, Alfred Salerno, Harry Tantillo, all of NYC.

CRIMINAL HISTORY : FBI #562959. NYCPD B#84696. Arrests from 1930 include burglary, unregistered still, conviction for Federal Narcotic Laws.

BUSINESS : Superintendent of apartment building at 2953 Barnes Ave., Bronx, New York.

MODUS OPERANDI : A wholesale distributor of narcotics who is closely associated with known Mafia traffickers from whom he obtains his supply of narcotics.

NAME   : Charles M. ALBATE

ALIASES   : Charley

DESCRIPTION : Born 2-19-23, NYC, 5'11½",
               200 lbs, brown wavy hair,
               blue eyes, wears glasses,
               light complexion, moles on
               nose, chin & left cheek,
               heavy build.

LOCALITIES   : Resides 1080 Wheeler Ave,
FREQUENTED   Bronx, NY, frequents 1751 E
               172nd St, 1473 Hoe Ave, &
               1326 Noble Ave, Bronx, NY.

FAMILY   : Single; father: Joseph, (deceased); mother: Rose
BACKGROUND   Scafeti (deceased); brother: Joseph; sisters: Mary
               Prisco, Agnes Vieidomini & Carmella Collica.

CRIMINAL   : Anthony Carminati, John Ardito, Rocco Sancinello,
ASSOCIATES   Frank Mancino, Angelo Loiacano, Stephen Puco.

CRIMINAL   : FBI #291120A, NYCPD B#277236. Record dates from
HISTORY   1949 and includes arrests for burglary & unlawful
               entry.

BUSINESS   : Truck driver for Jaco Plumbing Co., 1751 E 172nd
               St., Bronx, NY.

MODUS   : A member of the Mafia of lesser importance, who is
OPERANDI   associated with members of the Bronx Mob in the
               distribution of large quantities of narcotics.

NAME	: Charles ALBERO
ALIASES	: Charlie Bullets, Charles Rizzo, Albert Rizzo, Charles Crescenzo
DESCRIPTION	: Born 4-26-02, NYC, 5'7½", 170 lbs., medium build, dark brown hair, brown eyes.
LOCALITIES FREQUENTED	: Resides 2390 Tiebout Ave., Bronx, N.Y., frequents Vinnie's Restaurant, Midnight Cafe and Jenny's Restaurant, Bronx, N.Y., also Race Tracks.

FAMILY BACKGROUND	: Wife's name Dorothy, children are Charles Jr., Franklin and Madeline, is brother-in-law of Charles "Four Cents" Salerno.
CRIMINAL ASSOCIATES	: Joe Rao, Joe Marone, Mike Coppola, Joe Tocco, Joe Dentico, Steve Armone, Frank Livarsi, John Ormento and all top hoodlums in East Harlem area NYC.
CRIMINAL HISTORY	: FBI #59088, NYC PD# 49903, arrests commence in 1941 and include concealed weapons, narcotics (NY State) grand larceny, rape and conviction for Federal Narcotic Laws.
BUSINESS	: Employed at Melrose Salvage Co., and Bridge Motors Inc., both in Bronx.
MODUS OPERANDI	: Interstate and International narcotic trafficker, a leader of the Mafia traffickers from N.Y's., East Harlem area.

NAME   : Andrew ALBERTI

ALIASES   : Andy

DESCRIPTION: Born 10-15-20 NYC, 5'5",
             175 lbs, dark brown hair,
             brown eyes, stocky build.

LOCALITIES : Resides 2675 Henry Hudson
FREQUENTED   Parkway, Bronx, NY, frequents
             area E. 12th St. & 1st Ave.
             & most prize fights in NYC.
             Makes trips to Italy.

FAMILY   : Married to Adele Serpentini,
BACKGROUND   daughter: Marilyn, son: Andrew Jr; brother: James;
               father: Frank; mother: Domenica Cammarata (both dead)

CRIMINAL   : Steve Armone, John Laget, Hugo Rossi, John Ormento,
ASSOCIATES   Joe DiPalermo, Frank J. Valenti, Peter C. Valenti,
               Louis Saccaroma, Salvatore Mezzasalma.

CRIMINAL   : FBI# 345652B. Only arrest on 4-23-53 on a com-
HISTORY   plaint for violation Federal Narcotic Laws, which
               was dismissed.

BUSINESS   : Operates the Alberti Baking Co; 441 E. 12th St.,
               NYC., with his brother James. Also has interests in
               prize fighters.

MODUS   : Has taken over position of his deceased father in
OPERANDI   the Mafia from the area of E. 12th St. & 1st Ave.
               Makes trips to Italy in connection with narcotic
               smuggling operations & together with Jean Laget &
               Steve Armone, constitutes a major source of supply
               for wholesale dealers in New York City.

NAME   : Dominick ALLOCCO

ALIASES   : Shorty

DESCRIPTION   : Born 9-20-13 NYC, 5'7", 192
                  lbs, black-greying hair,
                  brown eyes, heavy build.

LOCALITIES   : Last resided 737 Southern
FREQUENTED   Blvd., wife now resides 2955
                  Pearson Ave., both Bronx, NY.
                  Frequents 1760 Watson Ave &
                  Fordham & Westchester Ave.,
                  Bronx. Also Detroit, Cleve-
                  land & Chicago. Currently
                  incarcerated.

FAMILY   : Wife: Margaret DePasqua; daughter: Lois; father:
BACKGROUND   Gaetano; mother: Rose Terricano (both deceased);
                  brothers: Salvatore, John, Frank, Anthony & Phillip;
                  sisters: Tessie, Betty Sedotto & Mary Regnetta.

CRIMINAL   : Saro Mogavero, Salvatore Santoro, Rosario Rinaldi,
ASSOCIATES   ███████, ███████.

CRIMINAL   : FBI #5130074, NYCPD E# 19941. Record dating from
HISTORY   1948 consists entirely of arrests by Federal Bureau
                  of Narcotics, convicted in 1948, 1951 & 1955. Now
                  (1959) serving 10 year term on 1955 conviction.

BUSINESS   : No sustained legitimate employment.

MODUS   : An important Mafia member who supplies heroin in
OPERANDI   wholesale quantities to distributors in NY, Detroit,
                  Cleveland & Chicago. Reputed to be trigger man in
                  Mafia killings including that of narcotic trafficker
                  Joe Franco in 1948.

Alo died of natural causes on March 9, 2001 in Florida at age 96. He's buried in Woodlawn Cemetery in the Bronx, NY.

NAME : Vincent ALO

ALIASES : Jimmy Blue Eyes, James Allen

DESCRIPTION : Born 5-26-04, NYC, 5'7", 160 lbs, black grey hair balding, blue eyes, dark complexion, sharp features, neat dresser.

LOCALITIES FREQUENTED : Resides 315 Riverside Dr, NYC & 1248 Monroe St, Hollywood, Fla., frequents Ziegfield Rest., 55th St. & 6th Ave, Hotel Picadilly, 45th St, & 8th Ave, in NYC, Colonial Inn, Miami, Fla, Chicago, Detroit, Cuba.

FAMILY BACKGROUND : Wife: Florence Galinus; sons: Lawrence & William by wifes previous marriage to Lawrence Miller; father: Salvatore; mother: Julia Colzo; brothers: Frank & Joseph; sisters: Isabel & Angelia.

CRIMINAL ASSOCIATES : Frank Costello, Joseph Doto, Vito Genovese, Charles Bernoff, Augie Pisano (deceased), Frank Erickson.

CRIMINAL HISTORY : FBI #554810, NYCPD B#58781. Record dates from 1923 and includes arrests for robbery and possession of gun.

BUSINESS : No known legitimate means of support.

MODUS OPERANDI : Notorious top echelon Mafia member. Financier of gambling in the U.S. & Cuba & Puerto Rico.

NAME   : Michael Peter ALTIMARI

ALIASES   : Mike, Big Mike

DESCRIPTION : Born 11-1-1913, NYC, 5'5½",
                215 lbs, heavy build, blue
                eyes, black-grey receding
                hair, cleft in chin, double
                chin, fair complexion.

LOCALITIES   : Resided 186 Brinsmade Avenue,
FREQUENTED   Bronx, NY, & frequented the
                Fountain Blue Bar, Playhouse
                Bar, Opera Inn and Ten Pin
                Bar, all in NYC. Currently (1960) incarcerated.

FAMILY   : Single; father: Frank; mother: Mary; both parents de-
BACKGROUND   ceased; brothers: John, Joseph, Ernest and Paul.

CRIMINAL   : Nicholas Bonina, Nicholas Martello, Anthony Marcella,
ASSOCIATES   ███████████, Victor Panica, Frank Borelli, Anthony
                Pisciotta, Joseph Valachi & Anthony Carminati.

CRIMINAL   : FBI #2603611 NYCPD #B-202795 Record dating from
HISTORY   1937 includes arrests for murder, gambling and three
                convictions for Federal Narcotic Law violation.
                Sentenced to 12 years in 1959 for Federal Narcotic
                violation.

BUSINESS   : No legitimate employment.

MODUS   : A trusted Mafioso who has engaged in large scale
OPERANDI   local and interstate narcotic trafficking all of
                his adult life.

337

NAME   : Vincent AMALFITANO

ALIASES   : Vincent Maltese, Jimmie

DESCRIPTION   : Born 1-1-16 NYC, 5'9", 195
                lbs, brown hair, brown eyes,
                dark complexion.

LOCALITIES   : Resides 4301 21st Ave.,
FREQUENTED   Astoria, NY, formerly resided
                Babylon, NY and Brooklyn, NY.
                Frequents Gun Hill Tavern,
                720 E 214th St & Holland Ave.
                both Bronx.

FAMILY   : Wife: Margaret Duffy; no children; father: Francesco;
BACKGROUND   mother: Angelina Maltese (both born Italy).

CRIMINAL   : Robert Guippone, ███████████, ██████████,
ASSOCIATES   ███████████, Michael Nicoline, Anthony Carminati.

CRIMINAL   : FBI #131501 C, NYCPD# B138465, record dates from
HISTORY   1935 and includes arrests for assault & robbery &
                gambling.

BUSINESS   : No legitimate employment known.

MODUS   : With other Mafiosi engages in wholesale narcotic
OPERANDI   trafficking.

NAME   : Alexander AMAROSA

ALIASES   : Babalu, Amorosa, Bobby

DESCRIPTION   : Born 6-29-30 Brooklyn, NY,
                 5'6", 120 lbs, dark brown
                 hair, brown eyes, dark com-
                 plexion, slender build, tat-
                 toos both arms classified
                 4-F in draft because of in-
                 fantile paralysis.

LOCALITIES   : Resides 34 So. Oxford St,
FREQUENTED   Brooklyn, NY. Before incar-
                 ceration 1955 frequented
                 Myrtle Ave, & Skillman St, Lafayette Ave, & So., Ash-
                 land Pl, Brooklyn & midtown area of Manhattan, NYC.

FAMILY   : Married Rhoda Markowitz; sons: Alexander & Eugene;
BACKGROUND   father: Leonard; mother: Mary Treglio; sister: Connie;
                 brothers: Paul, John, Richard, Anthony.

CRIMINAL   : FBI #4816067. NYCPD #B251702. Record dating from 1947
ASSOCIATES   includes arrests for theft of government checks, rape,
                 burglary, unlawful entry. Federal narcotic conviction
                 on which conditionally released September 1959. Under
                 parole supervision until July 1960.

BUSINESS   : Laborer, now unemployed & collecting relief from
                 NYC Department of Welfare.

MODUS   : Was a lesser member of the narcotic smuggling &
OPERANDI   distributing organization headed by the late Mafia
                 chief Cristofaro Robino.

NAME   : Frank AMENDOLA

ALIASES   : Cheech, Ciccio

DESCRIPTION   : Born 3-7-99, Salerno, Italy,
                  5'6½", 170 lbs., brown eyes,
                  brown hair (mostly bald), &
                  a ruddy complexion.

LOCALITIES   : Resides at 3220 Campbell Dr.,
FREQUENTED   Bronx, N.Y., frequents bars
                  in East Bronx and East Harlem
                  sections of NYC.

FAMILY   : Wife's name is Fannie, has
BACKGROUND   one daughter named Theresa who is married to
                  Theodore Bonano.

CRIMINAL   : Joseph Marone, Gregory Ardito, Joseph Dentico,
ASSOCIATES   John Ormento, Salvatore Santora, Charles Albero.

CRIMINAL   : FBI #487684, NYC, PD# B96360, dates back to 1916
HISTORY   when he was arrested for grand larceny; numerous
                  arrests for robbery, possession of a revolver and
                  conviction for Federal Narcotic Laws.

BUSINESS   : None.

MODUS   : Receives large shipments of heroin direct from over-
OPERANDI   sea sources of supply; is in charge of distribution
                  among the more important sources of supply in the
                  East Harlem and Bronx sections of New York City;
                  associate of well known Mafia traffickers in East
                  Harlem area NYC.

NAME   : Germaio ANACLERIO

ALIASES   : Jerry Anaclerio, Jerry
                  Naclerio.

DESCRIPTION   : Born 1-2-17 N.Y.C., 5'4½",
                  200 lbs., brown eyes, black
                  hair, heavy build, sallow
                  complexion.

LOCALITIES   : Resides 167 E.103rd St.,
FREQUENTED   N.Y.C. Frequents area of
                  E.103rd St. & 3rd Ave.,
                  E.86th St. & Lexington Ave.,
                  & a club at 340 E.73rd St.,
                  all in Manhattan.

FAMILY   : Married to Diane Fuchs; daughters: Angelina and
BACKGROUND   Phyllis; brothers: Louis & Frank; sister: Mrs.
                  Rachel Vitrullo; father: Gaspare; mother: Angelina
                  Castellano.

CRIMINAL   : Benny Coniglio, Michael Altimari, Nick Bonina,
ASSOCIATES   Charles Barcelona, Bartolo Ferrigno, Harry Tantillo,
                  Rosario Rinaldi, all of N.Y.C.

CRIMINAL   : FBI#753191, NYC PD-B#116101. Arrests since 1931
HISTORY   include rape, grand larceny, auto theft, felonious
                  assault, & conviction for Federal Narcotic Laws.

BUSINESS   : No legitimate business or employment known.

MODUS   : A major narcotic trafficker from upper east side
OPERANDI   N.Y.C.; obtains his supply from known Mafia
                  associates.

His brother Albert was murdered (possibly by Vito Genovese) in 1957, and "Tough Tony" retained control of the Brooklyn docks until he died of natural causes on March 1, 1963.

NAME : Antonio ANASTASIO

ALIASES : Tough Tony

DESCRIPTION : Born 2-24-06 Catanzaro, Italy, became U.S. citizen in the Eastern Dist., of NY, on 6-11-40, 5'6", 175 lbs, grey hair, brown eyes, stocky build.

LOCALITIES FREQUENTED : Resides 8220 11th Ave, B'klyn NY. Frequents Alto-Knight Social Club, Mulberry & Kenmare Sts, NYC, Union Office, 343-Court St, B'klyn, NY.

FAMILY BACKGROUND : Wife: Rose Iacqua, (deceased); daughter: Marian Scotto; son-in-law: Anthony Scotto; father: Bartolemeo, (deceased); mother: Marian Polistena (deceased); brothers: Albert, Jerry & Joseph (all deceased); Frank, Ralph & Louis in Italy, Rev. Salvatore Anastasio in the U.S.

CRIMINAL ASSOCIATES : Carmine Lombardozzi, Joseph Profaci, George Noble, John & Frank Dio Guardi, Anthony Bonasera, John Oddo.

CRIMINAL HISTORY : FBI #4743827, NYCPD B#232495. Record dates from 1925 and includes arrests for homicide investigation, felonious assault & assault.

BUSINESS : Business Manager Local 1814, I.L.A., 343-Court St, Brooklyn, NY.

MODUS OPERANDI : Top echelon Mafia leader & "Boss" of the B'klyn waterfront.

342

NAME : Simone ANDOLINO

ALIASES : Sam

DESCRIPTION : Born 3-13-07, New Castle,
Penna, 5'8", 154 lbs, brown
hair, brown eyes.

LOCALITIES : Resides 132 Avenue V, Brook-
FREQUENTED lyn, NY. Frequents 651
Liberty Ave, Brooklyn, NY,
also bars and gambling establishments in Bensonhurst,
Bath Beach and Gravesend
sections of Brooklyn.

FAMILY : Wife: Mary; daughter: Theresa; parents, deceased.
BACKGROUND

CRIMINAL : Joe Profaci, Frank Livorsi, Thomas Dioguardia,
ASSOCIATES John Dioguardia, John Oddo, Anthony Anastasia, Vito
Genovese, Mike Mirandi, John Ormento, ███████████,
Anthony Tocco, Dominick Corrado.

CRIMINAL : FBI #5064655, NYCPD E#14667, dates from 1935 with
HISTORY numerous arrests for gambling, bookmaking and policy.

BUSINESS : Partner in Andolino and D'Amico Bakery, 651 Liberty
Ave., Brooklyn, NY.

MODUS : Influential Mafia member. Closely associated with
OPERANDI top level NY Mafiosi. Operates gambling & bookmaking
establishments in Brooklyn's Bath Beach section.

NAME	: Anthony ANNICCHIARICO
ALIASES	: Terry, Tarry, Tarrytown, Tony, Alfonso
DESCRIPTION	: Born 11-23-20 Brooklyn, NY, 5'6", 145 lbs, medium build, black hair, brown eyes, prominent nose, receding hairline, sometimes has mustache.
LOCALITIES FREQUENTED	: Resides 128 Union St, Brooklyn, NY. Before incarceration in 1955 frequented Red Hook section of Brooklyn, Luxor Baths, midtown night clubs & hotels, all NYC.
FAMILY BACKGROUND	: Married Antoinette Susino 1941 was separated from her 5 years but they have rejoined since his release from prison; daughters: Carmela & Nancy; father: Alfred; mother: Carmela Esposito; brother: Charles; sisters: Mrs. Rose Long, Mrs. Mary Bielike.
CRIMINAL ASSOCIATES	: Alexander Amarosa, Peter Tambone, Giacento Mannarino, Cristofaro Robino (deceased), ▮▮▮▮▮▮▮▮▮▮▮.
CRIMINAL HISTORY	: FBI #3968879. NYCPD #B335625. Record dates from 1944 and includes arrests for theft of government property & assault. Federal Narcotic conviction on which conditionally released September 1959. Under parole supervision until July 1960.
BUSINESS	: Currently unemployed.
MODUS OPERANDI	: Before incarceration was part of the narcotic smuggling & distributing organization headed by the late Mafia chief Cristofaro Robino.

"Buster" was charged with racketeering in 2006 and, in December of that year, was released on bail while awaiting trial. He died on December 31, 2006 from pancreatic cancer.

NAME : John Gregory ARDITO

ALIASES : Buster

DESCRIPTION : Born 10-28-19, NYC, 5'8½", 185 lbs., stocky build, eyes brown, straight brown hair, sallow complexion, mole on right side of chin.

LOCALITIES FREQUENTED : Resides at 20-37 154th St., Whitestone, NY, frequents the Alto Knights Social Club Kenmare and Mulberry Sts., NYC; Evergreen Ave., and E. 156th St., Bronx.

FAMILY BACKGROUND : Married to Fay Cervasi and the father of two children, John and Annette.

CRIMINAL ASSOCIATES : Thomas Luchese, Vincent Mauro, Charles Albero, Joe Marone, Joe Bendenelli, Anthony Castaldi, and most hoodlums in East Harlem area.

CRIMINAL HISTORY : FBI #1763382, NYC PD #B161139, criminal record dates back to 1937 and includes arrests for seduction, possession of counterfeit money, and conviction for Federal Narcotic Laws.

BUSINESS : Part owner of a butcher shop at 590 East 156th St., Bronx, NY.

MODUS OPERANDI : Associated with major Mafia leaders in the New York area; a source for large quantities of heroin in the local and interstate traffic.

Armone became the Gambino family underboss in 1986 but was arrested and imprisoned for racketeering in Florida soon after. He died, while in prison, of natural causes in 1992.

NAME : Joseph ARMONE

ALIASES : Piney, Shorty Armone

DESCRIPTION : Born 9-13-17 N.Y.C., 5'5", 140 lbs., brown hair, grey eyes, medium complexion, small build.

LOCALITIES FREQUENTED : Resided 148 Jefferson St., Brooklyn, N.Y. Frequented Lulu's Bar, 2nd Ave. & 13th St., and area of E. 14th St. & 1st. Ave. Currently (1959) incarcerated for N.Y. State parole violation.

FAMILY BACKGROUND : Married to Josephine DiQuarto & they have 2 children; father: Teri; mother: Anna (both dead); brothers: Steve, Frank, & Angelo; sisters: Angela, Florence, & Margarita.

CRIMINAL ASSOCIATES : Steve Armone (brother), Andrew Alberti, Angelo Meli, George Nobile, Eugene Tramaglino, Arnold Romano, all of N.Y.C.

CRIMINAL HISTORY : FBI#798682. NYC PD-B#125181. Arrests since 1933 include robbery, felonious assault, homicide, and conviction of Federal Narcotic Laws.

BUSINESS : No legitimate business or employment known.

MODUS OPERANDI : A member of the Mafia trafficking organization in the vicinity of E. 14th St. & 1st Ave., N.Y.C., which is headed by his brother Steve & Arnold Romano. Is a dangerous hoodlum.

He died in 1960.

NAME	: Stephen ARMONE
ALIASES	: Stefano Armona, Frank Pizzo, Joe Marinello, 14 St. Steve, Frank Charmonte
DESCRIPTION	: Born 11-17-1899 Palermo, Sicily. 5'4", 163 lbs, brown eyes, black-grey hair, limps due to fracture of left hip.
LOCALITIES FREQUENTED	: Resides 98-05 63rd Road, Queens, NY. Frequents East 14th St., 1st to 3rd Avenues, and the Alberti Baking Co., 441 East 12th Street, all NYC.
FAMILY BACKGROUND	: Father: Terenzio; mother: Anna Grammauta (both deceased); brothers: Joseph, Frank, Angelo; sisters: Angela, Florence & Margarita.
CRIMINAL ASSOCIATES	: Andrew Alberti, Joseph Marone, Joseph Valachi, Arnold Romano, Eugene Tramaglino, Joseph Armone, Charles Albero, Anthony Strollo.
CRIMINAL HISTORY	: FBI #320538 NYCPD #B-86090 Arrests since 1918 include assault & battery with intent to kill, burglary, Federal Narcotic Law conviction.
BUSINESS	: No legitimate business or employment known.
MODUS OPERANDI	: A Mafia leader in N.Y.C.'s East 14th Street area. With Arnold Romano and other Mafiosi has been engaged in large scale narcotic smuggling and wholesale distribution for many years.

NAME : Alfonso ATTARDI

ALIASES : Alphonso Attardi, L. L. Altroad, Altroad DeJohn.

DESCRIPTION : Born 9-12-1900 Sciacca, Sicily. 5'4", 160 lbs., brown eyes, black-grey hair, I&NS-A#11812051.

LOCALITIES FREQUENTED : Resided 14 E. 23rd St., New York, N.Y. Frequented area of 1st Ave. & E. 12th St., 159 Chrystie St., both in Manhattan. Also made trips to New Orleans & Texas.

FAMILY BACKGROUND : Married to Josephine Carroseta (dead); daughter: Beatrice; son: Joseph; brother: Girlando; sisters: Grace, Rose, & Margaret.

CRIMINAL ASSOCIATES : Steve Armone, Joe Armone, Eddie D'Argenio, Hugo Rossi, Jack Scarpulla, all of N.Y.C.; Biagio Angelica of Texas; ▅▅▅▅▅▅▅▅ & Lucky Luciano of Italy.

CRIMINAL HISTORY : FBI#1378150. Arrests since 1938 include conviction for Federal Narcotic Laws.

BUSINESS : No legitimate business or employment known.

MODUS OPERANDI : With Mafia associates has been engaged in the interstate narcotic traffic.

NAME   : Mario Joseph AVOLA

ALIASES   : Frank Costello, Joseph
                  Aiello, Marty Avola, Mario
                  Pasquale Avola, Marty Larocca

DESCRIPTION   : Born 11-2-12, NYC, 5'11",
                  190 lbs, grey hair, brown
                  eyes, medium build, mole
                  left side of nose, scars on
                  left ankle, walks with a
                  limp, has arthritis.

LOCALITIES   : Resides 2460 Tiebout Ave.,
FREQUENTED   Bronx, NY. Frequents East
                  Harlem area, 113th St., 2nd Ave, NYC, East Tremont
                  Ave., Bruckner Boulevard & Tiebout Ave, of the Bronx,
                  NY, also Hoboken, N.J. Currently incarcerated.

FAMILY   : Divorced from Lena Jacobson; father: Joseph (de-
BACKGROUND   ceased); mother: Josephine Santora; brother: Joseph;
                  sisters: Frances McGrath & Josephine Larocco.

CRIMINAL   : Michael Altimari, ███████████████, Sam Liguori,
ASSOCIATES   ███████████████, Joseph Manfredi.

CRIMINAL   : FBI #336950, NYCPD #88607. Record dates back to
HISTORY   1929 & includes arrests for burglary, grand larceny,
                  resisting Federal Agent with a dangerous weapon,
                  interstate transportation of stolen automobile.
                  Federal Narcotic Law conviction for which now
                  (1959) doing 3 years. Due for release 11/60.

BUSINESS   : No legitimate means of support.

MODUS   : A member of the Mafia of lesser importance, who
OPERANDI   will venture into any illegal activity.

NAME : John Michael BALSAMO

ALIASES : John Belsamo

DESCRIPTION : Born 3-21-06 Brooklyn, N.Y.,
6'1", 185 lbs, grey eyes,
black-grey hair practically
bald on top.

LOCALITIES : Resides 4502 Avenue M,
FREQUENTED Brooklyn, N.Y. Often makes
trips to Italy.

FAMILY : Wife's name is Mary, has 2
BACKGROUND children; sisters: Mrs. Ann
Avvenire, Mrs. Frances Giliberto; father: Giacchino;
mother: Josephine Cusimano (both deceased).

CRIMINAL : Joe Profaci, Joe Magliocco, Sam ████ Accardi,
ASSOCIATES Sebastiano Nani, Lucky Luciano, Santo Sorge.

CRIMINAL : No criminal history with the FBI or NYCPD.
HISTORY

BUSINESS : Has been employed as salesman by Sunland Beverage
Co., Brooklyn, N.Y., which is owned by Joe Magliocco.
Also employed as a salesman for Encyclopedia Brit-
tannica.

MODUS : Used as a "front" man by other Mafia associates.
OPERANDI Usually acts as courier for important messages and
dealings between them; particularly when he makes
trips to Italy.

```
NAME          : Peter BARATTA

ALIASES       : Pete Berata, Bull (Bull
                Brothers), Peter Santello

DESCRIPTION   : Born 11-23-11 NYC, 5'6", 170
                lbs, blue eyes, black hair
                greying, medium build, olive
                complexion.

LOCALITIES    : Resides 1957 Gleason Ave.,
FREQUENTED      Bronx, NY. Frequents East
                Harlem area of NYC from 110th
                to 118th St.

FAMILY        : Wife: Carmela Cusano; two children: Evelyn & Joseph;
BACKGROUND      father: Rosario; mother: Agata Gelardi (both born
                Italy); brothers: Anthony, Michael, Thomas.

CRIMINAL      : His brothers, Anthony, ██████ & ████, also
ASSOCIATES      Charles Albero, ██████████, Alfonse Mosca.

CRIMINAL      : FBI #2012035, NYCPD #B 190199. Arrested 1940 for
HISTORY         assault & robbery. Two subsequent arrests for
                gambling.

BUSINESS      : Operates junk yard, 406 E 110th St.

MODUS         : With other Mafiosi trafficks in narcotics, handling
OPERANDI        kilogram quantities, also has gambling interests &
                participates in holdups, hijacking, etc.
```

NAME	: Joseph Mario BARBARA, Jr.
ALIASES	: None
DESCRIPTION	: Born 5-24-1936, Endicott, NY, 5'10", 280 lbs, black hair, brown eyes, heavy build.
LOCALITIES FREQUENTED	: Resides Castle Gardens, Vestal, NY, frequents Red Barn Restaurant and Vestal Steak House, Vestal, NY.

FAMILY BACKGROUND	: Father: Joseph, Sr. (deceased); mother: Josephine Vivona; brother: Peter; sister: Angela.
CRIMINAL ASSOCIATES	: Salvatore Monachino, Pasquale Turrigiano, Ignatius Cannone, Bartolo Guccia, Joseph & Salvatore Falcone, Anthony Guarnieri, Santo Volpe, ██████████████.
CRIMINAL HISTORY	: No FBI # assigned NYCPD #B-431573 Pleaded guilty to contempt of court 1959, received a suspended sentence 1960 and placed on probation until December 17, 1962. No other arrests.
BUSINESS	: Planning to enter the construction business with a large amount of money left to him by his father.
MODUS OPERANDI	: Personally made all of the preparations for the 1957 Apalachin Mafia meeting, at which his late father was the host. In assisting his father he became acquainted with many of the top ranking Mafia racketeers in the nation. He has become a trusted confidant in Mafia circles as a result of his steadfast refusal to divulge any particulars of the Apalachin meeting to law officials.

NAME   : Arnold BARBATO

ALIASES   : Wash, Curly, Anthony Barbeto

DESCRIPTION   : Born 1-30-11, NYC, 5'7",
                  140 lbs, black-grey hair,
                  brown eyes, slim build, med-
                  ium complexion.

LOCALITIES   : Resides 2350 Beaumont Ave.,
FREQUENTED   Bronx, N.Y., frequents East
                  Harlem Section of NYC, prim-
                  arily the Blue Moon Bar,
                  115th St., & 1st Ave.

FAMILY   : Married Dorothy Sacco; children: Maria & Anthony;
BACKGROUND   father: Anthony; mother: Maria Desimone; brothers:
                  Sam, Michael, Joseph; sisters: Nettie Calvelli &
                  Angela Barbato.

CRIMINAL   : ███████████████, Joseph Marone, Joseph Rao, Michael
ASSOCIATES   Coppola, ████████████████.

CRIMINAL   : FBI #751203, NYCPD #B107915. Record dates from
HISTORY   1932 and includes arrests for robbery, assault,
                  alcohol violations and Federal Narcotic Law viola-
                  tions.

BUSINESS   : No legitimate occupation known.

MODUS   : A member of the Mafia, particularly the "107th
OPERANDI   Street Mob" supplies narcotics locally and inter-
                  state.

NAME : Salvatore Joseph BARBATO

ALIASES : Fats Murphy

DESCRIPTION : Born 8-13-13 NYC, 5'4", 180
lbs, dark brown hair, brown
eyes, 1" scar upper lip, 3"
scar left cheek.

LOCALITIES : Resided 2128 Virgil Place,
FREQUENTED Bronx, NY. Frequented
Dick's Diner, 138 & Bruckner, Blue Bird Bar, 2890
Buhre Ave, Bronx, 112th &
2nd, NYC. Currently (1959)
incarcerated.

FAMILY : Wife: Lucille DeFillippis; sons: Christopher,
BACKGROUND Salvatore & Anthony; father: Michael; mother:
Carolina Immato (both deceased); brothers: Anthony,
Michael, Frank; sisters: Tessie Furilla, Mary
Germine, Lucille Riccardo, Anna Cassano.

CRIMINAL : Paul DeVillo, James V. Casablanca, ▮▮▮▮▮▮▮▮▮,
ASSOCIATES Vincent Squillante, Rocco Mazzie, Anthony Castaldi.

CRIMINAL : FBI #382288, NYCPD #B84770. Record dates from 1930
HISTORY and includes arrests for armed robbery, disorderly
conduct & violation of State & Federal Narcotic
Laws. 1957 sentenced to 12 years for Federal
Narcotic violation.

BUSINESS : Co-owner of DiLisi's Bakery, 411 E 63 St, NYC.

MODUS : An important Mafia member and narcotic trafficker,
OPERANDI dealing in wholesale quantities of heroin. Was a
major source of supply for heroin going to Puerto
Rico.

```
NAME           : Charles BARCELLONA

ALIASES        : Charlie-the-Wop

DESCRIPTION    : Born 12-15-15 in Licata,
                 Sicily, Italy, 5'7", 175 lbs,
                 black hair, brown eyes, med-
                 ium build, naturalized
                 1-30-47 Southern District of
                 NY. Cert. # 6703036.

LOCALITIES     : Resided 162 E 107th St.,
FREQUENTED       frequented 116th St.& Pala-
                 dino, Cove Bar, 3rd Ave., &
                 103rd St., & Mid-town area,
                 NYC.  Currently (1959) incarcerated.

FAMILY         : Married Pauline Provenzano; adopted son Jackie,
BACKGROUND       father: Phillip; mother: Maria Liboria, (both de-
                 ceased), brothers: Anthony, Joseph, Frank; sisters:
                 Lucy Virggino, Tessie Degennero.

CRIMINAL       : Joseph DiPalermo, Ralph Polizzano, Carmine Polizzano,
ASSOCIATES       Germaio Anaclerio, John Ormento, Peter Contes,
                 Carmine Galante.

CRIMINAL       : FBI #699414, NYCPD #116817.  Arrests dating back to
HISTORY          1927 include robbery, assault and violation of Fed-
                 eral & State Narcotic Laws.  In 1959 while serving
                 a 4-5 year state narcotic sentence, he received an
                 additional consecutive 5 year sentence for narcotic
                 conspiracy.

BUSINESS       : Has worked as restaurant manager & credit collector.

MODUS          : A trusted Mafia member who has gained prominence in
OPERANDI         the organization in the past several years.  Was
                 supplying large quantities of narcotics to dealers
                 in New York's midtown area and out of state.
```

```
NAME            : Joseph J. BARRA

ALIASES         : GiGi, GiJo

DESCRIPTION     : Born 5-27-1928, Portchester,
                  NY, 5'7½", 170 lbs, straight
                  black hair, hazel eyes, neat
                  dresser.

LOCALITIES      : Resides 110 Ward Drive, New
FREQUENTED        Rochelle, NY.  Frequents 187
                  & Crescent, Capri Lounge,
                  Blue Moon Bar & Monterey Club,
                  all in Bronx, NY.  Visits
                  Ft. Pierce, Florida.

FAMILY          : Wife: Frances; two sons; father: Morris; mother:
BACKGROUND        Margarite Sabato; brother: Joseph; sister: Theresa.

CRIMINAL        : His father and brother, his uncle Joseph Barra,
ASSOCIATES        Nicholas DiBene, Giacomo Scarpulla, Pisciotta
                  Brothers, ██████████, ██████████, ██████████.

CRIMINAL        : FBI #164400-A   NYCPD #B-299256   Record dating from
HISTORY           1943 includes arrests for juvenile delinquency,
                  assault, perjury and conspiracy to violate Federal
                  Narcotic Laws.

BUSINESS        : No legitimate occupation.

MODUS           : A young, but influential, Mafia member.  Part of a
OPERANDI          Bronx wholesale narcotic distribution organization.
                  Also engages on a large scale in the bookmaking and
                  loan shark rackets.
```

NAME	: Rocco BARRA

ALIASES   : Rocky

DESCRIPTION : Born 5-6-27, NYC, 5'7", 185
               lbs, brown hair, brown eyes,
               medium build, sallow com-
               plexion.

LOCALITIES   : Resides 810 Lydig St., Bronx,
FREQUENTED   NY, frequents 187 & Crescent,
               Capri Lounge, Blue Moon Bar
               & Monterey Club all in Bronx.
               Frequently visits Ft. Pierce
               Fla.

FAMILY   : Married to Roslyn Lockwich; children: Ronald &
BACKGROUND   Margaret; father: Morris; mother: Margarite Sabato;
               brother: Joseph; sister: Theresa.

CRIMINAL   : Morris Barra, Joseph Barra (brother), Joseph Barra
ASSOCIATES   (uncle), Nick Dibene, Jack Scarpulla, Pisciotta
               Brothers, Frank Scalise (deceased).

CRIMINAL   : FBI #4219535, NYCPD #B265601. Criminal record
HISTORY   dates back to 1944 & arrests include assault, un-
               lawful entry, grand larceny and felonious assault.

BUSINESS   : No legitimate occupation known.

MODUS   : A trusted Mafia member & former Lieutenant of the
OPERANDI   late Frank Scalise in narcotic trafficking. Is a
               wholesale distributor of narcotics locally & inter-
               state, also has gambling & loan shark interests.

NAME	: Nathan BEHRMAN
ALIASES	: Nathan Berman, Nathan Lewis, Natie
DESCRIPTION	: Born 7-29-13 NYC, Jewish, 5'7", 170 lbs, black hair, brown eyes, heavy, glasses.
LOCALITIES FREQUENTED	: Last resided 64-34 102nd St, Queens, NY. Frequented 316 W 90th St, Tony's Bar & Grill Milady's Rest., & Mulberry & Kenmare Sts, all in NYC. Currently incarcerated.

FAMILY BACKGROUND : Married Joan Hoffman; children: Maxine, Sherry; father: Harry; mother: Jennie Frieberg Behrman Dashefsky (both deceased); brothers: George, Hyman, & half brother Norman Dashefsky; sisters: Nettie Shratter, Hattie Massive, & half sister Marian Fine.

CRIMINAL ASSOCIATES : Harry Stromberg, ██████████████, █████████████, Stephen Puco, Anthony Velucci, ████████████, DiPalermo Brothers, Sol Bloom, Usche Gelb.

CRIMINAL HISTORY : FBI #1541128. NYCPD B#165513. Arrests since 1938 include vagrancy, counterfeiting, and narcotics. Sentenced 1956 to 19-20 yrs for narcotics, NY, State Court. 1958 sentenced 5 yrs, consecutive to above on Federal narcotic violation.

BUSINESS : No legitimate occupation.

MODUS OPERANDI : Associated with important Mafia members as a partner in the Gelb-Behrman-Velucci organization engaged in smuggling and distributing large consignments of heroin. Payment for heroin arranged thru the manipulation of Swiss bank accounts. Smuggled heroin distributed from NYC to other cities throughout the U.S.

NAME	: Joseph BENDENELLI
ALIASES	: Joe Babs, Tony Russo, Joseph Russo, Joseph Bendinelli
DESCRIPTION	: Born 6-22-10 NYC, 6'2", 185 lbs., brown eyes, grey hair, stoop-shouldered, dark complexion.
LOCALITIES FREQUENTED	: Resides 144-11 Tenth Ave., Malba, Long Island, NY., frequents East Harlem area and race tracks in NYC.
FAMILY BACKGROUND	: Married to Raffaela Malino and has 2 children, father: Denaro, mother: Carmela Orlando (both dead), sisters: Lena and Mrs. Rose Yhlen.
CRIMINAL ASSOCIATES	: Joe Rao, ████████████, Puco brothers, Serpico brothers, Joe Marone, Nick Tolentino, Anthony Mancuso, all of New York City.
CRIMINAL HISTORY	: FBI #296870, NYCPD #B 80775. Arrests since 1930 include robbery and gambling.
BUSINESS	: No legitimate business known.
MODUS OPERANDI	: One of the major narcotic traffickers from East Harlem area, and a trusted Mafia representative in that area.

In 1957, he and Carlo Gambino planned the murder of Albert Anastasia and Biondo became Gambino's under-boss. He died in New York in 1973 of natural causes.

NAME : Joseph BIONDO

ALIASES : "J.B.", Joe Bionda, "Little Rabbitt", Joe Banti, Joe Bondi.

DESCRIPTION : Born 4-16-1897 Barcellona, Sicily. 5'4", 150 lbs., brown eyes, brown-grey hair, naturalized.

LOCALITIES : Resides 77-12 35th Ave.,
FREQUENTED : Jackson Heights, Queens, N.Y. Has summer home at Long Beach, L.I. Frequents area E. 11th St. & 1st Ave. in Manhattan, & makes trips to Italy.

FAMILY : Married to Louise Volpe; brother: John; has a
BACKGROUND : nephew: Vincent Manfredi.

CRIMINAL : Eduardo Aronica, Frank Costello, Vito Genovese,
ASSOCIATES : Steve Armone, Thomas Lucchese, Andrew Alberti, Lucky Luciano, Joe Doto, & Nicola Gentile.

CRIMINAL : FBI#62666. NYC PD-B#50466. Arrests since 1919
HISTORY : include drugs, homicide, revolver, extortion.

BUSINESS : Is Vice-President of See-Boro Forwarding Co., Inc., Queens, N.Y., & operates a real estate office at 84 Oswego Ave., Long Beach, L.I., N.Y.

MODUS : An international drug trafficker who is up among
OPERANDI : the higher echelon members of the Mafia in N.Y.C.

NAME   : Joseph BISOGNO

ALIASES   : None

DESCRIPTION   : Born 12-18-31 NYC, 5'10",
                    180 lbs, brown hair, brown
                    eyes, medium build, olive
                    complexion.

LOCALITIES   : Resides 224-24 Union Turn-
FREQUENTED   pike, Flushing, L.I., N.Y.
                    Frequents Capri Lounge, 2010
                    Williamsbridge Rd., Bronx,
                    Manfredi Rest., 331 E. 108th
                    St., NYC.

FAMILY   : Wife: Caroline; father: Michael; mother: Frances
BACKGROUND   Bambola; brother: Jack, all of New York.

CRIMINAL   : Frank Luciano, Joseph Manfredi, Joseph Valachi,
ASSOCIATES   Tony Lima, Anthony Mirra, Thomas Altamura.

CRIMINAL   : FBI #266750A. NYCPD #B278301. Record dates from
HISTORY   1949 and includes arrests for assault & murder,
                    Federal Narcotic conviction.

BUSINESS   : No known legitimate occupation at the present time.
                    In the past has been in the restaurant & night club
                    business.

MODUS   : Bisogno, called "Mr. East Harlem," is a notorious
OPERANDI   narcotic trafficker of the top echelon. Bisogno
                    reached the top, in his underworld status, at an
                    early age by being a strong arm man in the Mafia
                    organization.

NAME	: Joseph Nicholas BIVONA
ALIASES	: Joe Sciortino, Joe Black
DESCRIPTION	: Born 8-7-20 NYC, 5'10", 160 lbs, medium build, brown eyes, black hair, olive complexion, 1/2 " bullet scar left calf.
LOCALITIES FREQUENTED	: Resides 37 Starr St., Brooklyn, NY. Frequents bars in midtown area, NYC, also Camporeale Social Club, Brooklyn, NY.

FAMILY BACKGROUND	: Wife: Lillian Cusimara, separated since 1950; daughter: Frances; father: Joseph; mother: Frances Mangano.
CRIMINAL ASSOCIATES	: Cristofaro Robino (deceased), Joseph DiGiovanna, Charles LaCascia, Archie Mannarino.
CRIMINAL HISTORY	: FBI #404987A, NYCPD #E15863. Record dates from 1946 and includes arrests for gambling & counterfeit money.
BUSINESS	: Claims employment as painter, admits 20% ownership of Tana Construction Co., Yorktown Heights, NY.
MODUS OPERANDI	: Was an underling of the late Mafia chief Cristofaro Robino and has long been active in illicit operations of all kinds in Brooklyn's Wilson Ave, section.

NAME   : Solomon BLOOM

ALIASES   : Sol Bloom, Saul Berman,
                  Solly, Mutton Head, Sol Rosen,
                  Blubber, Blubberhead.

DESCRIPTION   : Born 9-7-09 NYC, Jewish, 5'8",
                  183 lbs, black greying hair,
                  grey eyes, heavy build, ruddy
                  complexion.

LOCALITIES   : Legal Address is 1120 Brigh-
FREQUENTED   ton Beach Ave, Brooklyn, NY,
                  c/o Mrs. Sarah Berman, sister.
                  Frequents Hotel Olcott, Hotel
                  Bancroft, Westover Hotel, Sidney Garage, Tomaldo
                  Rest., Tony's Bar, all of NYC. Town Pump & Colony
                  Club of Detroit, Mich., also Miami, Fla.

FAMILY   : Father: Julius Bloom (deceased); mother: Fannie
BACKGROUND   Weinstein; sisters: Sarah Berman & Anna Taub of Brook-
                  lyn, NY; brother: Sam Bloom of Brooklyn, NY.

CRIMINAL   : Anthony Teramine, Joe (scarface) Bommarito, Peter
ASSOCIATES   Licavoli, Anthony Giacolone, of Detroit. Florio
                  Isabella, Nathan Behrman, Anthony Vellucci, Harry
                  Stromberg, of NYC.

CRIMINAL   : FBI #198796. Detroit PD #97106. NYCPD #B84213.
HISTORY   Record dates back to 1928 for burglary, grand lar-
                  ceny, assault and robbery, narcotics, violation
                  state gambling laws, stench bombing.

BUSINESS   : No legitimate occupation.

MODUS   : Close associate of important Mafia and other
OPERANDI   narcotic smugglers and traffickers. Engaged in
                  the interstate distribution of narcotics.

NAME	: Cassandros Salvatore BONASERA
ALIASES	: Anthony Bonasera, The Chief, Anthony Buonasera.
DESCRIPTION	: Born 6-1-1897 Vallelunga, Sicily. 5'7", 170 lbs., brown eyes, grey hair, an alien, I&NS file A-5164327.
LOCALITIES FREQUENTED	: Resides 1117 83 Street, Brooklyn, N. Y. Frequents Casa Bianca restaurant and Knock Knock Inn, both in Brooklyn.

FAMILY BACKGROUND	: Married to Sarah Di Carlo & has 1 child, father: Vincenzo, mother: Lucia Spoto, brother: John, sisters: Carmela Milazzo, Ottavia Lodestro, and Rosa Ognibene.
CRIMINAL ASSOCIATES	: Lucky Luciano and Joe Doto of Italy (deportees). John Oddo, Anthony Ricci, Joe Greco, ████████ ████████, all of New York City.
CRIMINAL HISTORY	: FBI #191363, NYCPD-B #57901. Has numerous arrests since 1916 including assault, robbery, burglary, extortion, homicide.
BUSINESS	: Co-owner of Sarah Lee Dress Company, Brooklyn, N. Y. and has interests in J.L.A. Textile Printing Company, Bronx, N. Y.
MODUS OPERANDI	: A Mafia leader in the Bensonhurst-Bathbeach section of Brooklyn who had control of all illegal rackets in that area under the supervision of Joe Doto (now a deportee).

NAME   : Frank BONGIORNO

ALIASES   : Frankie Brown

DESCRIPTION   : Born 5-21-06 NYC, 5'6", 170
                  lbs, black hair, brown eyes.

LOCALITIES   : Resides 135 Audubon Rd, Tea-
FREQUENTED   neck, N.J. Frequents Elizabeth
                  St., area of NYC, usually
                  winters in Florida.

FAMILY   : Married Eve Gottlieb; daugh-
BACKGROUND   ter: Marilyn Levy; son:
                  Joseph; father: Joseph;
                  mother: Marietta Grillo.

CRIMINAL   : James Plumeri, ███████████, █████████████████,
ASSOCIATES   ██████████████, ███████████.

CRIMINAL   : FBI #225874. NYCPD #B90169. Record dates from 1923
HISTORY   and includes arrests for grand larceny, assault,
                  burglary, extortion, criminally receiving and gamb-
                  ling.

BUSINESS   : Production Manager Sea Isles Sportswear, NYC.

MODUS   : With other important Mafiosi finances large scale
OPERANDI   gambling operations in NY, NJ and Fla.

NAME	: Nicholas BONINA
ALIASES	: The Baron
DESCRIPTION	: Born 1-9-28 NYC, 5'4", 165 lbs, stocky build, black hair, brown eyes, sallow complexion.

LOCALITIES FREQUENTED	: Resides 81-20 Dongan Ave, Queens, NY. Frequents Ten Pin Tavern, Throggs Neck Recreation, Tremont Recreation, all in area of Bruckner Blvd & E. Tremont Ave, Bronx, NY; Fountain Blue Bar & Grill, NYC, NY. Currently incarcerated.
FAMILY BACKGROUND	: Married Dorothy Cassidy, two children; father: Salvatore; mother: Giovanna Cambria; brother: Nunzio; sisters: Frances, Anna Filippone.
CRIMINAL ASSOCIATES	: Michael Altimari, Victor Panica, Vincent Squillante, Joseph Quarino, Anthony Pisciotta, Benjamin Indiviglio, ███████████, Frank Borelli.
CRIMINAL HISTORY	: FBI #4803912, NYCPD #B425220. Record dates from 1947 and includes arrests for murder & violation of narcotic laws. Currently incarcerated. Sentenced 10-20-59, term of 12 yrs. for violation of Federal Narcotic Laws. (2nd Federal narcotic conviction).
BUSINESS	: No legitimate employment. Never gainfully employed as an adult.
MODUS OPERANDI	: Gambler and wholesale narcotic trafficker with other Mafia members. Distributed large quantities of narcotics to local and interstate dealers.

NAME	: Salvatore BONITO
ALIASES	: Sal Bonito, Georgie Raft

DESCRIPTION	: Born 3-30-14 Buffalo, NY, 5'3", 159 lbs, medium build, medium complexion, brown eyes, dark brown hair, four moles on left cheek, multiple moles of right neck.
LOCALITIES FREQUENTED	: Resides 233 15th St, Buffalo, NY. Frequents the Dewey Diner, the Allentown Tavern, & the Auto Club Garage, all in downtown Buffalo area.
FAMILY BACKGROUND	: Single. Father: Anthony; mother: Angelina, (born in Sicily), brothers: Peter, Pat, Anthony, John & Victor; sisters: Rose, Angela, and Constance Moore (deceased). He has had common-law relationships with several women, and has three illegitimate children by three of these women. None of the children bear his name or live with him.
CRIMINAL ASSOCIATES	: Fred Randaccio, Eddie Scillia, ▇▇▇▇▇▇▇▇, ▇▇▇▇ ▇▇▇▇▇▇.
CRIMINAL HISTORY	: FBI #349617. Buffalo PD# 26067. Record dates from 1930 and includes arrests for petit larceny, burglary, assault, counterfeiting, grand larceny and violation of parole.
BUSINESS	: No legitimate occupation.
MODUS OPERANDI	: Lower echelon member who works as policy runner for Mafia controllers of gambling in Buffalo, NY area. Engages in every type of underworld activity.

NAME   : Harry BONSIGNORE

ALIASES   : Harry Ponci, Harry Bons

DESCRIPTION   : Born 5-14-03 Bronte, Catania
                   Sicily, 5'6", 164 lbs, med-
                   ium build, black hair, brown
                   eyes, naturalized 1926 in
                   NYC.

LOCALITIES   : Resides 16 Monroe St, NYC,
FREQUENTED   frequents Ganeron Bar, Rue
                   Ganeron #4 Paris, France,
                   also lower East Side, NYC.

FAMILY   : Married Genevieve Reilly, no children; brothers:
BACKGROUND   Joseph & Vincent; sisters: Giovanina, & Jenny
                   Catania; father: Anthony (deceased); mother: Rosalie
                   Di Vincenza, (deceased); both parents were born in
                   Italy.

CRIMINAL   : Joseph Lanza @ Socks, ███████████, Nicholas
ASSOCIATES   Di Stefano @ Salvatore Serago, all of NYC.

CRIMINAL   : FBI #1375991, NYCPD B#202365. Record dates from
HISTORY   1932 & includes arrests for conspiracy & extortion,
                   and violation of Anti Trust Income Tax Laws.

BUSINESS   : Has worked as a salesman, shipyard worker & Mer-
                   chant Mariner.

MODUS   : Gambler, bookmaker & confidence man, affiliated
OPERANDI   with important Mafia criminals.

> Bonventre moved back to Sicily in 1950, ending his association with Bonanno.

NAME : Giovanni BONVENTRE

ALIASES : John Bonventra, Giuseppe Bonanno, Joe Bonventre, John Bonaventure

DESCRIPTION : Born 4-18-01 Castellammare, Sicily, 5'5", 180 lbs, brown eyes, grey hair, naturalized 8-6-46 Brooklyn, N.Y.

LOCALITIES FREQUENTED : Resides 115 Cleveland St., Brooklyn, N.Y. Frequents restaurant-bars at 180 Forsythe St., NYC, 141 Central Ave., & 273 Central Ave., both in Brooklyn.

FAMILY BACKGROUND : Married to Caterina Vitale; brothers; Antonio, Pietro, Ignazio; father: Martino; mother: Carmela Magaddino (both dead).

CRIMINAL ASSOCIATES : Carmine Galante, James Zoleo, Frank Garafolo, Robert Dionisio, Frank Costello, Tom Lucchese, Lucky Luciano, Santo Sorge.

CRIMINAL HISTORY : FBI #8289864C. NYCPD B#215124. I&NS #3301772. Arrests since 1943 include kidnapping & burglary, endangering health of a child.

BUSINESS : Has interests in Levine & Bonventre (ladies coat contractors) 91 Eastern Pkwy & Green Garden Cafe 141 Central Ave., both in Brooklyn.

MODUS OPERANDI : Attended Binghamton Mafia meeting 1956 & Apalachin Mafia meeting 1957. With both his nephew Joe Bonanno & Joe Profaci, he is one of the heads of the Mafia in the U.S.

NAME : Frank BORELLI

ALIASES : Frankie Gooks, Frank the Hawk.

DESCRIPTION : Born 6-19-25, NYC, 5'9", 180 lbs., with black hair (thinning), and brown eyes, wears glasses with thick lenses, is a very dapper dresser.

LOCALITIES FREQUENTED : Frequents the East Harlem section of NYC, and spends some time in Chicago, Ill, resides with his wife at 2042 2nd Ave., Apt #4, NYC.

FAMILY BACKGROUND : Is married to Mary DeGeorge, daughter of Angelo DeGeorge, a convicted East Harlem narcotic violator, his brother-in-law, Mario Colucci, is also a convicted narcotic violator.

CRIMINAL ASSOCIATES : Charles Curcio, Joe Bendenelli, Rocco Mazzie, Nick Tolentino, all narcotic traffickers and racketeers in East Harlem area NYC.

CRIMINAL HISTORY : FBI #3902235, NYC PD# B206594, includes arrests for assault and robbery, burglary, and violation of State and Federal Narcotic Laws.

BUSINESS : None at present.

MODUS OPERANDI : Wholesale trafficker in heroin to associates in NY, Chicago, Ill., and Cleveland, Ohio, and trusted member of the Mafia from East Harlem NYC area.

NAME   : Joseph BOVE

ALIASES   :

DESCRIPTION   : Born 10-20-09 NYC, 5'8", 190
                  lbs, stocky build, grey hair,
                  brown eyes.

LOCALITIES   : Resides 156 E 117th St, NYC.
FREQUENTED   Frequents Newmans Bar &
                  Grill 2243 3rd Ave, Bennys
                  Food Shop 2118 3rd Ave, &
                  Lizzies Clam House 116th St,
                  NYC. Currently incarcerated.

FAMILY   : Wife: Catherine Madiri; has 2 children; brothers:
BACKGROUND   Michael & George; sisters: Sadie, Netti & Millie
                  Porccieri; father: George, (deceased); mother:
                  Caroline Peco (deceased); both born in Italy.

CRIMINAL   : ████████████, ████████████, Alfred Carbonetti @Curly
ASSOCIATES   & ████████████, John Malizia, Stephen Puco.

CRIMINAL   : FBI #251340A, NYCPD #B277718. Record dates from 1949
HISTORY   & includes arrests for counterfeiting, State & Fed-
                  eral Narcotic Law violation. 1959 sentenced to 5
                  years for Federal Narcotics Law violation.

BUSINESS   : No legitimate occupation.

MODUS   : A large scale Mafia narcotic trafficker also
OPERANDI   engages in counterfeiting & gambling.

NAME   : Lorenzo BRESCIA

ALIASES   : Brescio, Chappie, Larry,
                 Chapman

DESCRIPTION   : Born 5-17-1905, Bari, Italy,
                 5'8½", 190 lbs, brown eyes,
                 brown hair greying at temples,
                 stout build, naturalized at
                 NYC 8-20-1929.

LOCALITIES   : Resides 91 Bay Street, Long
FREQUENTED   Beach, L.I., N.Y. and 1545
                 Madison St., Hollywood, Fla.
                 Frequents Alto Knights S.C.,
                 Kenmare & Mulberry Street & La Cava Jr. Restaurant,
                 1122 First Avenue, NYC.

FAMILY   : Wife: Maria; father: John; mother: Anna Novellina.
BACKGROUND

CRIMINAL   : Frank Tieri, Vito Genovese, Michael Mirandi, Carmine
ASSOCIATES   Lombardozzi, Anthony Carillo, Joseph Lanza.

CRIMINAL   : FBI #3445472   NYCPD #B-80823   Record dating from
HISTORY   1930 includes arrests for homicide, extortion and
                 conspiracy. Suspect in murder of Albert Anastasia.

BUSINESS   : Reported to own Saratoga Turf Mineral Waters, 117
                 Chrystie St., NYC. Claims employment with National
                 Waterproofers, 89-30 161 St., Jamaica, N.Y.

MODUS   : Professional Mafia strong arm man and killer. Very
OPERANDI   in Mafia control of labor unions.

NAME	: Angelo BUIA
ALIASES	: Frenchie, Angelo Russo
DESCRIPTION	: Born 7-26-10, Nice, France of Italian parents, became an American citizen through the naturalization of his father. 5'7", 166 lbs, brown eyes, black-grey hair, dark complexion, neat dresser.

LOCALITIES FREQUENTED	: Resided 719 Lexington Avenue, NYC, frequented Greenwich Village area and Lower East Side of NYC.
FAMILY BACKGROUND	: Married to Mary McAvoy; father: Nicholas; mother: Amelia Buia; brother: Matildo.
CRIMINAL ASSOCIATES	: John Stoppelli, Aniello Santagata, Sam Accardi, Thomas and Charles Campisi, Matildo Buia (brother).
CRIMINAL HISTORY	: FBI #161962, NYCPD B#125444. Arrest record dates back to 1934; two convictions for violation of Federal Narcotic Laws, in connection with one of which he is currently (1959) serving a term of 7 years in Federal prison.
BUSINESS	: Machinist.
MODUS OPERANDI	: He and his brother, Matildo, are members of the Accardi-Campisi Mafia organization and distribute heroin in kilogram lots.

NAME   : Matildo BUIA

ALIASES   : Ralph Stella, Frenchie

DESCRIPTION : Born 10-18-08, Trapani,
                  Sicily, 5'4", 147 lbs.,
                  grey hair, brown eyes, tat-
                  too on both arms, fair com-
                  plexion, medium build.

LOCALITIES   : Resides 203 Prince St., NY,
FREQUENTED   NY, frequents Greenwich
                  Village section of NYC.

FAMILY   : Married to Louise Buzzanca,
BACKGROUND   and lives with her and his mother, Amelia Buia at
                  203 Prince St., NYC, his father, Nicholas Buia, (de-
                  ceased); Matildo became an American citizen through
                  the naturalization of his father.

CRIMINAL   : Sam Accardi, John Stoppelli, Aniello Santagata,
ASSOCIATES   Thomas and Charles Campisi, Angelo Buia, (brother).

CRIMINAL   : FBI #683359, NYCPD #B112318, convicted 1933 for
HISTORY   violation of the New York State narcotic laws.
                  Twice convicted and imprisoned for violation of
                  Federal Narcotic Laws in 1938 and 1955, condition-
                  ally released for last conviction on 4-5-59 and on
                  probation until 4-6-60.

BUSINESS   : Employed as a machinist by the Richard Haase Machin-
                  ery Co., 60-15 Waldron St., Corona, Queens, NY.

MODUS   : He and his brother, Angelo Buia, are members of the
OPERANDI   Accardi-Campisi Mafia organization, they distribute
                  heroin in kilogram lots.

NAME	: Fillippo BUZZEO
ALIASES	: Philip Bussero, Buzzero, Buzzio

DESCRIPTION : Born 5-31-17, NYC, 5'8½",
200 lbs, brown eyes, black
hair very thin, high fore-
head, heavy build, medium
complexion.

LOCALITIES : Last address was 446 W 49th
FREQUENTED   St. NYC. Frequented local
racetracks and bars on East
28th St. & East 11th St. in
NYC. Currently incarcerated.

FAMILY : Married Constance Castanga Buzzeo, but when arrested
BACKGROUND   in 1956 was living in common-law with Marion Quinn.
Father: Joseph; mother: Mary Pia; brothers: Louis,
Joseph and Richard, sisters, Laura Cofone, Catherine
Johnson, and Annette Tedesco.

CRIMINAL : ████████████, Charles Vincent Trupia, Joseph Anselmi,
ASSOCIATES   ████████████, ████████████, Joseph Gernie, █████
████, ████████████, Elmer Burke (deceased) and
many other NYC hoodlums.

CRIMINAL : FBI #706372A. NYCPD #B24175. Criminal record dates
HISTORY   from 1946 and includes arrests for conspiracy, forgery
and violation of the Federal Narcotic Laws. 1957 sentenced to 6 yrs in Federal Prison for violation of
Federal Narcotic Laws.

BUSINESS : Bartender - has owned bars.

MODUS : Buzzeo and other Mafia narcotic traffickers were en-
OPERANDI   gaged in smuggling narcotics into the U.S. from Mexico
and Europe and distributing it wholesale.

NAME	: Giuseppe CALATABIANCA
ALIASES	: Joe Castello, Joe Costelli, Joe Alfano, Don Pepino
DESCRIPTION	: Born 7-16-1899, Palermo, Sicily, Italy, 5'10", 165 lbs, blue eyes, thin moustache, grey hair, balding, Naturalized Buffalo, NY, 4-5-1917.

LOCALITIES FREQUENTED : Resides 927 E 227 St,Bronx, NY. Receives mail at beauty parlor, 610 Crescent Avenue, Bronx. Made numerous trips to Europe, but passport expired 1955. Frequents Lower East Side and East Harlem sections of NYC.

FAMILY BACKGROUND : Married first wife in 1922, annulled 1950. Remarried Anna Fodera; son: Giuseppe; daughter: Pietra; father: Antonio (deceased); mother: Pietra Fodera.

CRIMINAL ASSOCIATES : ███████████, Rosario Mancino, Francesco Pirico, ███████████, Angelo DiCarlo, Carlo Gambino.

CRIMINAL HISTORY : No known arrests.

BUSINESS : No legitimate occupation known.

MODUS OPERANDI : Top level Mafioso, specializing in narcotic smuggling and distribution. Recruits unsuspecting elderly Sicilians, travelling to Italy, to carry a suitcase for him on their return trip to the U.S. This suitcase will contain, in a hidden compartment, two to four kilograms of heroin.

NAME   : Ignatius Joseph CANNONE

ALIASES   : Nat Cannone, Sonny Cannone

DESCRIPTION   : Born 11-12-1925, NYC, 5'6",
                  170 lbs, brown hair, brown
                  eyes, V-shaped scar under
                  lower lip.

LOCALITIES   : Resides 210 Madison Avenue,
FREQUENTED   Endicott, NY. Frequents
                  Endicott and Endwell, NY.

FAMILY   : Married Gussie Chiarello;
BACKGROUND   son: David; daughter:
                  Marjorie; father: Diego; mother: Vita DiMateo;
                  godfather: Natale Evola.

CRIMINAL   : Natale Evola, Pasquale Turrigiano, ███████████████,
ASSOCIATES   Emanuel Zicari, Angelo Sciandra, ████████████████,
                  Bartolo Guccia.

CRIMINAL   : FBI #198352-D   Record dating from 1946 includes
HISTORY   arrests for disorderly conduct, resisting arrest
                  and conspiracy to obstruct justice (for which sent-
                  enced (1960) to 3 yrs imprisonment).

BUSINESS   : Formerly owned Nat's Place, Endicott, NY, and the
                  Plaza Lounge, Endwell, N.Y.

MODUS   : Attended 1957 Apalachin Mafia meeting. A younger
OPERANDI   Mafia member who is rising rapidly in the organiz-
                  ation. With Mafia associates he controls illicit
                  alcohol traffic and gambling in central New York
                  State area.

NAME   : Salvatore Antonio CAPIZZI

ALIASES   : Sal, Toto

DESCRIPTION   : Born 5-14-21, Villa Grazia,
                 Palermo, Sicily, 5'8½", 175
                 lbs, brown hair, brown eyes,
                 olive complexion, naturalized
                 NYC in 1958.

LOCALITIES   : Resides 1207 56th St, Bklyn,
FREQUENTED   NY, frequents Garment section
                 of NYC & Lady Grace Fashions,
                 1314 58th St, B'klyn, NY.

FAMILY   : Married: Frances Mangiaracina; sons: Rocco & Salvatore,
BACKGROUND   father: Rocco; mother: Rose Taormina (both Italy);
                 brother: Michele (Italy); sisters: Gesualda, Agata &
                 Anna (Italy).

CRIMINAL   : Giovanni Maugeri, ▆▆▆▆▆▆▆▆▆▆▆▆, Mathew Cuomo,
ASSOCIATES   Corrado Carrubba, Pietro Sorci, Dominique Albertini.

CRIMINAL   : FBI #919877B. Arrested by I&NS 1954 for deportation.
HISTORY   no other arrest record in U.S. Arrested 1945, Palermo,
                 Italy for possession of tobacco without government
                 permit.

BUSINESS   : Part owner of Lady Grace Fashions, 1314 58th St. B'klyn
                 NY.

MODUS   : An important Mafia member, who is engaged in the
OPERANDI   smuggling of large quantities of narcotics into the
                 U.S. through the use of illegal immigrants.

NAME	: Anthony CARILLO

ALIASES : Tony-the-Sheik, Tony Carello
Tony Carilla

DESCRIPTION : Born 9-20-02 San Giuseppe
Vesuviano, Naples, Italy,
5'6½", 135 lbs, slim build,
brown eyes, dark brown hair,

LOCALITIES FREQUENTED : Resides 6837 Yellowstone
Blvd, Forest Hills, NYC.
Frequents Dulce Motor Sales,
4507 63rd St., Queens, NYC,
Ciro's Luncheonette, 698
Liberty Ave., Brooklyn, NYC, vicinity of 348 Liberty
Ave., Brooklyn, NY.

FAMILY BACKGROUND : Wife: Margaret; daughter: Madelaine (changed name to
Dizozza); father: Domenico; mother: Madelina Ambrosio.

CRIMINAL ASSOCIATES : ███████, ██████████, Joseph Rossato,
Michele Miranda, Peter De Feo, ████████████.

CRIMINAL HISTORY : FBI #333810, NYCPD #B87742. Record dates from 1925
and includes arrests for rape, burglary, felonious
assault, robbery with gun.

BUSINESS : Salesman, Dulce Motor Sales & partner of Dominick
Massa in Sun Oil Co., 745 Liberty Ave., Brooklyn,
New York.

MODUS OPERANDI : In his younger days was member of infamous "Murder
Incorporated." Through the years he has been known
as chauffeur delivery man and right hand man of
Michele Miranda.

NAME	: Rosario CARLISI
ALIASES	: Roy Carlisi, Roy Caruso, Rosario Carlise.
DESCRIPTION	: Born 4-10-09 Chicago, Ill., 5'9", 175 lbs, brown eyes, brown-grey hair.
LOCALITIES FREQUENTED	: Resides 20 Anderson Place, Buffalo, NY. Frequents Club 97, Hotel Richmond, & other clubs in downtown Buffalo area; also race tracks.

FAMILY BACKGROUND	: Married to Phillipa Romano & has 3 children; brothers: Carmine & Alfonso; father: Joseph; mother: Calogera Casaro (both dead).
CRIMINAL ASSOCIATES	: Vincent Mauro, Sam Pieri, Stefano Magaddino, Antonio Magaddino, James LaDuca, John C. Montana, Frank Valenti.
CRIMINAL HISTORY	: FBI #1434575. Arrests since 1937 include Federal liquor laws, malicious mischief, gambling, contempt.
BUSINESS	: Owned Club 97 Buffalo, NY till 1958, & has been associated with wholesale sea food markets in the Buffalo area.
MODUS OPERANDI	: Attended Apalachin Mafia meeting 1957 with other members from Buffalo area representing the Mafia controlled rackets in the Buffalo area.

NAME   : Anthony CARMINATI

ALIASES   : Little "T", Tony Pie, Little
                Tony

DESCRIPTION   : Born 2-1-12 Jersey City, NJ,
                5'6", 175 lbs, brown hair,
                brown eyes, medium complex-
                ion, numerous tattoos both
                arms.

LOCALITIES   : Resided 2420 Cambreling Ave,
FREQUENTED   Bronx, NY. Frequented 187
                & Crescent, Bronx, currently
                (1959) incarcerated.

FAMILY   : Wife: Rose Sammano; son: Dominic; daughter: Rose
BACKGROUND   Marie; father: Dominic; mother: Marie Montalto; bro-
                thers: Salvatore, Christopher; sisters: Marian Raimo,
                Mary Ignaro & Lena Ambrosini.

CRIMINAL   : Angelo Loiacano, Anthony Sedotto, Nick DiBene,
ASSOCIATES   Robert Guippone, Anthony Castaldi, ███████████.

CRIMINAL   : FBI #1947698, NYCPD #B207576. Record dates from
HISTORY   1931 and includes arrests for petit larceny, policy,
                possession of gun, violation alcohol laws. Two con-
                victions for violation of Federal Narcotic Laws.
                Sentenced 1957 to 10 years Federal Prison.

BUSINESS   : No legitimate employment known.

MODUS   : One of the leading members of the 187th Street
OPERANDI   Mafia mob. Formerly a Lieutenant of the late
                Frank Scalise. One of the largest heroin whole-
                salers in New York.

NAME	: Dominick CARMINATI
ALIASES	: Dominick Carminate, Chubby.
DESCRIPTION	: Born 4-21-33 NYC, 5'7", 185 lbs, stout, black curly hair, brown eyes, babyfaced.
LOCALITIES FREQUENTED	: Resides at 2424 Beaumont Ave, Bronx, NY. Frequents Monterey Club 4069 Bronxwood Ave. NYC, Copacabana and other midtown NYC night clubs.
FAMILY BACKGROUND	: Married Margaret Mazza; two children; father: Anthony (convicted narcotic trafficker); mother: Rose Samanno.
CRIMINAL ASSOCIATES	: Anthony Carminati (father), Angelo Loicano, Anthony Sedotto, Nicholas Di Bene, Robert Guippone.
CRIMINAL HISTORY	: No criminal record.
BUSINESS	: In partnership with Nick Di Bene. They own the Monterey Club.
MODUS OPERANDI	: With other Mafiosi is running the narcotic distribution and loan shark rackets formerly handled by his father, who is now incarcerated.

NAME   : Corrado CARRUBBA

ALIASES   : Conrad Carrubba

DESCRIPTION   : Born 1-1-1926, Palermo,
                Sicily, Italy. 6'1", 198 lbs,
                heavy build, brown hair, brown
                eyes, heavy Italian accent.
                Naturalized Brooklyn 11-6-52.

LOCALITIES   : Resides 293 Carroll Street,
FREQUENTED   Brooklyn, NY Frequents ILA
                Local 1814, 361 Court St.,
                & Lady Grace Fashions, 1314
                58th St., both Brooklyn, NY,
                and Pier 84, North River, NYC.

FAMILY   : Married Rose Carrera; two children; father: Pio
BACKGROUND   (deceased); mother: Carolina Fiorentino.

CRIMINAL   : Antonio Anastasia, Salvatore Capizzi, ██████████
ASSOCIATES   ██████████, all of NYC, Antonio Sorci of Italy.

CRIMINAL   : No known arrests
HISTORY

BUSINESS   : Employed at freight office of Italian Lines, 24
                State St., NYC, and formerly at Pier 84, North
                River, NYC.

MODUS   : Through his employment with the Italian Lines
OPERANDI   he assists other Mafiosi in smuggling large
                quantities of narcotics into the United States.

NAME	:	Anthony CARUSO
ALIASES	:	Tony Russo, Thomas Costa, & "The Fox".
DESCRIPTION	:	Born 8-19-1898 NYC, 5'6", 175 lbs., grey-black hair, brown eyes, stocky build, olive complexion, small scar over right eye.
LOCALITIES FREQUENTED	:	Resides at 239 Park St., NYC. Frequents the Lower Eastside area.
FAMILY BACKGROUND	:	Wife: Mary Marsillo; sons: Angelo & Joseph; daughter: Margaret; father: Angelo Caruso; mother: Margaret (DiSanta); brothers: John, Nicholas, Joseph, Peter; sister: Mary Caterina.
CRIMINAL ASSOCIATES	:	███████████████, John Brocco, ███████████████, ███████████████, ███████████████, ███████████████.
CRIMINAL HISTORY	:	FBI #1065429, NYCPD #B143340. Record dates from 1935 and consists solely of alcohol law violations.
BUSINESS	:	Secretary-Treasurer of the Full Front Garage, 11 Fulton St., NYC, NY.
MODUS OPERANDI	:	Directs Mafia bootlegging operations in NYC area.

NAME	: Frank CARUSO
ALIASES	: Frankie the Bug, Frank Russo, Frank Ross, Frank Campo.
DESCRIPTION	: Born 2-18-11 N.Y.C., 5'7", 190 lbs., black hair, brown eyes, heavy build.
LOCALITIES FREQUENTED	: Resides 1579 81st Street, Brooklyn, N.Y. Frequents area of Hester & Mulberry St., and Greenwich Village Section, both in Manhattan.

FAMILY BACKGROUND	: Married to Josephine Oddo; son: Frank Jr.; daughter: Mrs. Josephine Anne Morrongiello; father: Frank (dead); mother: Josephine; sister: Nancy; brothers: Joseph & Theodore.
CRIMINAL ASSOCIATES	: Phil Albanese, Joe Marone, John Ormento, Tony Strollo, Saro Mogavero, Tom Lucchese, George Nobile, all of N.Y.C.
CRIMINAL HISTORY	: FBI#187656. NYC PD-B#73604. Arrests since 1928 include robbery, assault, extortion, conviction for Federal Narcotic Laws.
BUSINESS	: Has interests in New York Carting Co., 643 E. 13th St., & Pygmalion Restaurant, 1068 2nd Ave., both in Manhattan.
MODUS OPERANDI	: A trusted Mafia leader in the Tony Strollo organization and a wholesale narcotic trafficker.

NAME   : James Vincent CASABLANCA

ALIASES   : James Costa

DESCRIPTION   : Born 9-29-13 NYC, 5'7½",
                  175 lbs, brown eyes, greying
                  hair bald on top.

LOCALITIES   : Resides 1285 Castle Hill Ave.
FREQUENTED   Bronx, NY. Frequents areas
                  of East Harlem in Manhattan
                  & East Bronx.

FAMILY   : Married to Jean LoPresta;
BACKGROUND   daughters: Phyllis & Jean;
                  sons: Patrick & John; brothers: Benny, Philip, Nino;
                  sister: Mrs. Carmela Ardisona; father: John; mother:
                  Famice Costa.

CRIMINAL   : Anthony Castaldi, Rocco Mazzie, Anthony Carminati,
ASSOCIATES   Angelo Loiacano, Frank Moccardi, Harry Tantillo, all
                  of NYC.

CRIMINAL   : FBI #2154683. NYCPD B#138228. Arrests since 1935
HISTORY   include abduction, assault & robbery, conviction for
                  Federal Narcotic Laws.

BUSINESS   : No legitimate business or employment known.

MODUS   : A major narcotic trafficker, shylock, & bookie who
OPERANDI   works closely with and is trusted by known Mafia
                  traffickers.

NAME	: Anthony CASTALDI
ALIASES	: T.H., Tony Higgins, Tony Bones.
DESCRIPTION	: Born 1-27-13 NYC, 5'10", 219 lbs, brown hair, brown eyes, stocky build.
LOCALITIES FREQUENTED	: Resides 15 Princeton Ave., Yonkers, NY. Frequents Jennie's Rest., 2036 Second Ave., and midtown bars, and racetracks, all NYC.

FAMILY BACKGROUND	: Wife: Jean Penosi (sister of Guido); sons: William & Andrew; father: Andrew; mother: Philomena DeLorenzo; brothers: John N, Lewis, James and Samuel; sisters: Mrs. Lillie DePalma, Mrs. Sadie Blumetti, Mrs. Rose Ciccone.
CRIMINAL ASSOCIATES	: Anthony Strollo, John Ormento, Salvatore Santoro, John Stoppelli, Vincent Mauro, Vincent Squillante, Sam Kass, Carmine & Pete Locascio, Anthony Ciccone, ███████████.
CRIMINAL HISTORY	: FBI #546748. NYCPD #B101443. Arrests since 1932 include assault, robbery, extortion, robbery-gun, and Federal Narcotic Laws.
BUSINESS	: Has interests in Jennie's Rest., 2036 Second Ave., NYC and also in real estate in East Harlem area.
MODUS OPERANDI	: One of the most active Mafia leaders in East Harlem area of Manhattan. A major interstate narcotic trafficker and close associate of most Mafia members in East Harlem area.

NAME   : Paul C. CASTELLANO

ALIASES   : Constantine Castellano

DESCRIPTION   : Born 6-26-1915 Brooklyn, NY, 6'0", 200 lbs, brown eyes, black hair, stocky build.

LOCALITIES   : Resides 1737 E. 23rd St.,
FREQUENTED   Brooklyn, NY, frequents Emcee Meat Market, 140 Ft. Greene Place, Brooklyn, and Manhattan garment district.

FAMILY   : Wife: Mary Beatrice; sons: Joseph, Philip and
BACKGROUND   Paul, Jr.; daughter: Concecca; sister: Mrs. Catherine Gambino (wife of Paul Gambino); father: Joseph; mother: Concettina.

CRIMINAL   : Paolo Gambino, Carmine Locascio, Peter Locascio,
ASSOCIATES   Samuel Kassop, Carmine Galante, Salvatore Maiorana, Giacomo Scarpulla and Ugo Rossi.

CRIMINAL   : FBI #824437 NYCPD #B-125933 Record dating from
HISTORY   1934 includes arrests for robbery with violence, civil contempt and conspiracy to obstruct justice (for which sentenced (1960) to 5 years).

BUSINESS   : Pres. of Allied Retail Butchers Ass'n and operates Emcee Meat Market Co., both Brooklyn, N.Y.

MODUS   : Attended Apalachin Mafia meeting 1957. Is taking
OPERANDI   the place of his aged father in the Mafia and is considered a "strong-arm" man in the organization.

NAME   : Vincenzo CASTORINA

ALIASES   : None

DESCRIPTION : Born 11-16-1896 Riposto,
                        Catania, Sicily, 5'10", 217
                        lbs, brown eyes, dark brown
                        hair (greying and balding),
                        dark complexion, moles on
                        left cheek. Petition for
                        citizenship granted 1954 by
                        Board of Immigration Appeals,
                        Washington, D.C.

LOCALITIES   : Resides 45-05 108th St,
FREQUENTED   Corona, NY.

FAMILY   : Married Rina Mantero Asfodele 1919 in Italy & had
BACKGROUND   one child. Came to U.S. alone 1925 & lived common
                        law with Gladys Moschetto, who bore him two sons,
                        Louis & William; married Moschetto 1952 after
                        learning Asfodele died 1943; father: Salvatore;
                        mother: Rosaria Maccarone.

CRIMINAL   : ████████████████ (brother), ████████████, ████
ASSOCIATES   ██████, Michael Pecorara, ████████████.

CRIMINAL   : FBI #297326. NYCPD #B 129976. Record dates from
HISTORY   1930 and includes arrests for disorderly conduct
                        and counterfeiting.

BUSINESS   : Claims to be importer-exporter, but largely
                        supported by wife.

MODUS   : Confidence man, swindler, arms smuggler and counter-
OPERANDI   feiter. With his Mafia associates will engage in
                        any activity which promises monetary gain.

US TREAS DEPT NY
NAR 9073
5 13 52

NAME   : Joseph CATALDO

ALIASES   : Joe the Wop

DESCRIPTION   : Born 11-16-08 San Fele,
                  Potenza, Basilicata, Italy,
                  naturalized 1-29-34, NYC,
                  5'6½", 180 lbs, brown eyes,
                  black-grey hair balding on
                  top.

LOCALITIES   : Resides 59 West 12th St.,
FREQUENTED   NYC. Frequents Pastor's
                  Club Greenwich Village, &
                  Times Square area of Man-
                  hattan.

FAMILY   : Wife: Thelma West; has one child; brothers: Dan &
BACKGROUND   Carlo; father: Michele; mother: Lucia D'Onofrio.

CRIMINAL   : Tony Strollo, John Stoppelli, Vincent Mauro, Joe
ASSOCIATES   Valachi, Armando Perillo, Frank Caruso, all of NYC.

CRIMINAL   : FBI #5035653, NYCPD #B251041. Arrests include
HISTORY   receiving stolen goods, grand larceny.

BUSINESS   : Owns Pastor's Club at 130 W. 3 Street NYC.

MODUS   : Financier for illegal activities including narcotics.
OPERANDI   An important NYC racketeer and close associate of
                  Mafia leader Tony Strollo.

NAME	: James Calogero CATANIA
ALIASES	: Jimmy the Baker
DESCRIPTION	: Born 10-9-1900 Palermo, Sicily, Italy, 5'8", 157 lbs, brown eyes, brown-grey hair, ruddy complexion. Naturalized NYC 7-20-43.
LOCALITIES FREQUENTED	: Resides 2326 Cambreling Ave, Bronx, NY. Frequents Arthur Murphy Democratic Club, Half Moon Rest., & Catania's Bakery, all Bronx, NY.
FAMILY BACKGROUND	: Married Rose Chodos; son: Anthony (deceased); daughter: Mrs. Frances Scaffidi; father: Anthony; mother: Frances Lascala (both deceased).
CRIMINAL ASSOCIATES	: Lucky Luciano, Frank Caruso, Frank Luciano, Carlo & Paul Gambino, Giacomo Scarpulla.
CRIMINAL HISTORY	: FBI #1122987. NYCPD #B62912. Record dates from 1924 and includes arrests for robbery, assault & vagrancy.
BUSINESS	: Advertising Mgr., for Building Employees Union Newspaper, owns Catania Bakery, 2316 Arthur Ave, Bronx.
MODUS OPERANDI	: Mafia courier and "contact man" closely associated with top Mafiosi in the Crescent Ave, section of Bronx, New York City.

NAME	: Arthur CELI
ALIASES	: Joseph Scal, Joseph Ontario, James Telli.
DESCRIPTION	: Born 2-19-17, NYC, 5'6", 180 lbs, blue eyes, ruddy complexion, dark brown curly hair.
LOCALITIES FREQUENTED	: Resides 179 Mulberry St., NYC, frequents lower East Side and Towncrest Tavern in Manhattan.

FAMILY BACKGROUND	: Married to Mary Scala, children: Joseph and Philip, father, Joseph, mother: Tessie Alferi (both dead), brothers: James and Joseph.
CRIMINAL ASSOCIATES	: ███████████, George Nobile, ████████████, Benny Cinquegrana, Pete and Carmine Locascio, ██████.
CRIMINAL HISTORY	: FBI #1681596, NYC, PD# B129237, arrests since 1934 include robbery, rape and two convictions Federal Narcotic Laws.
BUSINESS	: Truck driver when employed.
MODUS OPERANDI	: Wholesale and interstate narcotic trafficker and trusted associate of Mafia members on lower east side.

NAME   : Anthony CICCONE

ALIASES   : Tony Moon

DESCRIPTION   : Born 7-18-18, NYC, N.Y.,
                  5'9", 170 lbs, medium build
                  black hair, brown eyes, 2"
                  scar left cheek, 3" scar
                  left temple.

LOCALITIES   : Frequents Joe's Bar, 2062
FREQUENTED   1st Ave., Mickey Walkers,
                  1654 Broadway, NYC, present
                  address 11 Center Drive,
                  Whitestone, L.I.

FAMILY   : Married to sister of Anthony Castaldi, has two
BACKGROUND   brothers: Salvatore and Joseph; sisters: Anna and
                  Margaret; father: Sebastian; mother: Gelsamina
                  Piccolla.

CRIMINAL   : Anthony Castaldi, Salvatore Santora, John Ormento,
ASSOCIATES   Rocco Mazzie, Salvatore LoProto, ███████████,
                  Vincent Mauro, and other east Harlem racketeers.

CRIMINAL   : FBI #2526415, NYCPD #B172419, includes arrests and
HISTORY   convictions for violation of State and Federal
                  Narcotic Laws, beginning in 1941.

BUSINESS   : Employed in Fruit Exchange, 1981 1st Ave., NYC.

MODUS   : Is closely associated with most important Mafia
OPERANDI   narcotic traffickers in NYC area, has large sources
                  of supply and sells wholesale quantities of heroin
                  into local and interstate traffic.

NAME   : Benedetto F. CINQUEGRANA

ALIASES   : Vincent Grandi, Radio Red,
                    Benedetto DiPalo, Chink.

DESCRIPTION   : Born 1-6-13 NYC, 5'6", 175
                    lbs, brown eyes, light brown
                    hair, light complexion,
                    wears glasses.

LOCALITIES   : Resides 166 Mulberry St.,
FREQUENTED   NYC. Frequents Mulberry &
                    Grand Sts., (Little Italy
                    area) of Manhattan.

FAMILY   : Married to Lucy DiPalo; son: Louis; daughter:
BACKGROUND   Concetta; brother: Anthony; parents: Luigi &
                    Concetta (both born in Italy).

CRIMINAL   : Frank Caruso, Philip Albanese, ███████████████,
ASSOCIATES   ████████████████, Joe Marone, Tom Lucchese, John
                    Ardito, ████████████, all of NYC.

CRIMINAL   : FBI #444281. NYCPD B#93715. Arrests since 1932
HISTORY   include assault & robbery, criminally receiving
                    stolen property, conviction for Federal Narcotic
                    Laws.

BUSINESS   : Partner in operation of Roma Cafe & Bakery, 385
                    Broome St, NYC.

MODUS   : A major wholesale dealer in narcotics both local
OPERANDI   and interstate. Is a trusted associate of Mafia
                    Traffickers from whom he obtains his supply of
                    narcotics.

NAME	: Vincent James CIRAULO
ALIASES	: Jimmy Second Avenue, Jimmy 92.
DESCRIPTION	: Born 9-8-19 NYC 5'6", 175 lbs, black hair, brown eyes, pronounced bags under eyes, stutters.
LOCALITIES FREQUENTED	: Resides 88 Second Ave, NYC, frequents Stage Bar & Squeeze Inn, 87 & 89 E 4th St, also area of Spring & Elizabeth, NYC.

FAMILY BACKGROUND	: Married Mary San Carlo; daughters: Paula & Rosemary; father: Charles; mother: Paula Giresi (both deceased); brother: Jack; sister: Rose (Mrs. Nick) Alfano.
CRIMINAL ASSOCIATES	: ████████████████, Rocco Mazzie, Joseph Di Palermo, Joseph Bendenelli, ████████████████ (father in law)
CRIMINAL HISTORY	: FBI #1687536. NYCPD #B175085. Record dating from 1938 includes arrests for assault and robbery, felonicus assault and vagrancy.
BUSINESS	: Owns and operates Stage Bar, 89 E 4th St, NYC.
MODUS OPERANDI	: Is a trusted and important member of the Carmine Locascio Mafia narcotics distributing organization, engaged in the local and interstate wholesale narcotic traffic.

NAME   : Joseph CIRELLI

ALIASES   : Cirella, Carroll, Collins

DESCRIPTION   : Born 3-14-1897, NYC, 5'6",
                160 lbs, black-grey hair,
                brown eyes, medium build.

LOCALITIES   : Resides at 115 Ascan Ave.,
FREQUENTED   Forest Hills, L.I. Frequents
                Forest Hills Inn, Bella
                Napoli Bar & Restaurant,
                Westbury, L.I., N.Y., Roose-
                velt Raceway and other NY
                race tracks.

FAMILY   : Single; father: Giovanni, mother: Rosa Menta; bro-
BACKGROUND   thers: Rocco (deceased) & John.

CRIMINAL   : "Lucky" Luciano, Harry Stromberg, Saul Gelb, Joe
ASSOCIATES   Anselmi alias Joe White, Salvatore Spitale, Ugo Rossi,
                Andrew Alberti, Andimo Pappadio, Gaetano Lucchese.

CRIMINAL   : No known criminal record.
HISTORY

BUSINESS   : A former professional prizefighter. Bought the Vil-
                lanova Restaurant, Manhattan, from his brother Rocco
                for whom he had worked as a manager until 1938. A close
                friend of "Lucky" Luciano, he was allegedly backed by
                the latter in his restaurant ventures. In 1956, he
                sold this restaurant and built a $250,000 Villanova
                Rest., in Roslyn, L.I. That restaurant, he sold in
                1958 for $310,000.

MODUS   : Cirelli is not known to have himself engaged in any
OPERANDI   major illegal activities but has undoubtedly been one
                source of income for Luciano. His restaurants were
                notorious as rendezvous for Mafia racketeers

NAME   : Joseph CLEMENTE

ALIASES   : Frank Messina, Joseph Simone,
                 Frank Marino

DESCRIPTION   : Born 6-22-10, Lodi, NJ, 5'6",
                 165 lbs, brown eyes, medium
                 build, 4" scar on forehead.

LOCALITIES   : Resides 20 Suydam St., Brook-
FREQUENTED   lyn, NY. Frequents Wilson
                 Ave, & Bushwick sections of
                 Brooklyn.

FAMILY   : Wife: Mary Piconi; children:
BACKGROUND   Nicholas & Rose; father: Nicholas; mother: Mary
                 Messina; brother: Charles Clemente (Italy).

CRIMINAL   : Vincenzo Morsellino, ███████████, Cristofaro
ASSOCIATES   Robino (deceased), Settimo Accardo, Vincent La Sala,
                 ████████████.

CRIMINAL   : FBI #1801110, NYCPD #E 11602. Record dates from
HISTORY   1937 and includes six arrests for alcohol violations

BUSINESS   : No legitimate employment known.

MODUS   : Mafia still expert. Transports, assembles and
OPERANDI   operates stills for various mobs.

NAME   : Michael CLEMENTE

ALIASES   : Mike Costello, William
                Clemente

DESCRIPTION   : Born 8-29-08 NYC, 5'7", 195
                lbs, heavy build, black hair,
                blue eyes.

LOCALITIES   : Resides 7243 Shore Rd, Brook-
FREQUENTED   lyn, NY. Frequents Local
                #856 I.L.A., 148 Liberty St.,
                NYC, for which association
                he was formerly secretary
                and business agent.

FAMILY   : Married Josephine Tresonte; three daughters; father:
BACKGROUND   Michael; mother: Rosana Chiaffo (both deceased); sis-
                ters: Mrs. Amelia Macio, Mrs. Ida Colangelo;
                brother: Hugo.

CRIMINAL   : Rocco Pellegrino, Rosario Mogavero, Anthony Strollo,
ASSOCIATES   Alex DiBrizzi, ▓▓▓▓▓▓▓▓▓, DiPalermo Brothers.

CRIMINAL   : FBI #2675935 NYCPD #B-321975 Record dating from
HISTORY   1952 includes arrests for rape, assault, disorderly
                conduct, extortion, conspiracy to violate Internal
                Revenue Liquor Laws, Federal & State convictions
                for perjury.

BUSINESS   : Labor organizer, Local #856, I.L.A.

MODUS   : One of chief directors of mob policy on NY water-
OPERANDI   front. As lieutenant of Mafia leader Rocco Pelle-
                grino, uses his position as overlord of NY's East
                Side Piers to facilitate smuggling narcotics into
                U.S. His strong-arm enforcer, Rosario Mogavero,
                personally handles his narcotic transactions.

"Eddie" was convicted of murder and imprisoned in 1967.

NAME : Ettore COCO

ALIASES : Eddie Coco, Killer, Ed Costa

DESCRIPTION : Born 7-12-1908, Palermo, Sicily, Italy, 5'2¼", 161 lbs, dark brown hair, brown eyes, stocky build, fair complexion, I&NS file #A-401-8735 (alien).

LOCALITIES FREQUENTED : Resides 6941 Bay Drive, Miami Beach, Fla., & 2043 Colonial Ave., Bronx, NY; frequents NY, Miami & Chicago

FAMILY BACKGROUND : Wife: Lillian Eppiloto; son: Anthony; father: Anthony; mother: Santina Sapienza; brothers: Thomas & Ludwig.

CRIMINAL ASSOCIATES : Lucky Luciano, Anthony Granza, Thomas Lucchese, Charles Albero, Anthony Corallo, ███████████████,

CRIMINAL HISTORY : FBI #486097, NYCPD #B96208, Miami PD# A-17210. Record dates from 1928 & includes arrests for vagrancy, felonious assault, robbery, gambling & rape. Currently serving life term for murder.

BUSINESS : No strictly legitimate source of income.

MODUS OPERANDI : A lieutenant of underworld boxing czar Frankie Carbo. These two Mafiosi, along with Harry "Champ" Segal, Frank Palermo, James Plumeri and Felix Bocchicchio comprised what was known in the boxing world as "The Combination" an undercover manager's cartel. Coco is a behind-the-scene financier and overseer of large narcotic transactions. Closely associated with top Mafiosi and an intimate friend of Lucky Luciano.

NAME   : Benedetto CONIGLIO

ALIASES   : Saseetz, Sauseetz, Benny
                  Coniglio

DESCRIPTION   : Born 9-9-16 NYC, 5'5", 170
                  lbs, brown eyes, dark brown
                  hair, stocky, dark complex-
                  ion.

LOCALITIES   : Resides 328 E. 107th St,
FREQUENTED   NYC. Frequents East Harlem
                  and lower East Side of NYC.

FAMILY   : Single; father: Nicholas;
BACKGROUND   mother: Mary Zizto; brothers: Gerald and Victor;
                  sisters: none.

CRIMINAL   : ███████████████, █████████████, Salvatore Caneba,
ASSOCIATES   Germaio Anaclerio, Bartolo Ferrigno, John Ormento.

CRIMINAL   : FBI #4883056. NYCPD B#274427. Record dating from
HISTORY   1944 includes arrests for gambling, illegal fire-
                  works and narcotics. State & Federal narcotic convic-
                  tions.

BUSINESS   : Operates candy store at 332 E. 107th St, NYC.

MODUS   : A trusted member of the Mafia narcotic trafficking
OPERANDI   organization wholesaling heroin in the 107th Street
                  area.

On April 1, 1968, Consolo was murdered by his own men for speaking on "friendly terms" with Bill Bonanno in front of a Manhattan courthouse.

NAME : Michael Joseph CONSOLO

ALIASES : Mike Locaso, Anthony Leo, Michael Bruno

DESCRIPTION : Born 4-9-03 Siracusa, Sicily, Italy, naturalized 1944, 5'8", 175 lbs, stout build, black hair, brown eyes.

LOCALITIES
FREQUENTED : Resides 61-05 76 St., Rego Park, Queens, NY, maintains address: 35 E 25th St., Bayonne, N.J. Frequents Mulberry & Worth St., NYC, Club Hoo - Ha, Bayonne, N.J., & Frankie's Auction Market, Lodi, N.J.

FAMILY
BACKGROUND : Wife: Mary Caso; daughter: Catherine; father: Salvatore; mother: Catherine Locaso; sisters: Connie Pagano and Anna Saturno; brother: Anthony.

CRIMINAL
ASSOCIATES : Carmine Galante, Joseph Zicarelli, Vito Genovese, Joseph Bonanno, Salvatore Giglio, Vincent Cotroni.

CRIMINAL
HISTORY : FBI #285487, NYCPD #B59684, NJSP #399012. Record dates from 1915 and includes arrests for juvenile delinquency, vagrancy, robbery, grand larceny, homicide & Federal Alcohol Laws.

BUSINESS : No legitimate employment known.

MODUS
OPERANDI : Active in the leadership of the Galante-Zicarelli Mafia organization which carries on international and domestic narcotic traffic and large scale gambling operations.

NAME   : Thomas CONTALDO

ALIASES   : Tommy Ryan, Stellano, Tough
                  Tommy, Crazy Tommy.

DESCRIPTION   : Born 12-24-13 B'klyn, NY,
                  5'7", 165 lbs, black hair,
                  blue eyes, ruddy complexion,
                  tattoo on both arms.

LOCALITIES   : Resided 825 Union St., Brook-
FREQUENTED   lyn, NY. Frequented 4th Ave,
                  & Union St, B'klyn, Broome
                  & Mulberry Sts, NYC and Budd
                  Lake, NJ. Currently (1960)
                  incarcerated.

FAMILY   : Single; father: Gennaro, mother: Madeline Montalto;
BACKGROUND   sisters: Nancy, Jennie (Mrs. Michael) Zaza.

CRIMINAL   : ████████████, ████████████, August Carfano (de-
ASSOCIATES   ceased), Phillip Albanese, Frank Caruso, George
                  Nobile, Joseph Schipani.

CRIMINAL   : FBI #477828. NYCPD #B-95136. Record dates from 1929
HISTORY   and includes arrests for assault, homicide, kidnap-
                  ping, murder and robbery, Federal narcotic convic-
                  tion. 2-4-57 sentenced to 30 to 60 yrs Brooklyn,
                  for robbery.

BUSINESS   : No legitimate employment known.

MODUS   : Vicious Mafia strong arm man and killer. Headed an
OPERANDI   organization which distributed wholesale quantities
                  of heroin.

NAME : Stephen F. COPPOLA

ALIASES : Steve Cappola

DESCRIPTION : Born 10-28-04 Buffalo, NY,
5'10½", 190 lbs, brown hair,
(receding), brown eyes, medium build, fair complexion,
wears glasses.

LOCALITIES : Resides 324 Hudson St.,
FREQUENTED Buffalo, NY. Frequents San-
tores Restaurant and Park-
edge Restaurant in Downtown
Buffalo, visits Cleveland,
Ohio.

FAMILY : Wife: Josephine Farece; (first wife: Mamie Arrigo,
BACKGROUND deceased); children: James, Joan, Rosalie, Geraldine,
and Rita Ann; brother: Salvatore (deceased); father:
Salvatore; mother: Maria Siccalese (both deceased).

CRIMINAL : Joseph Gallo, ███████, ██████████.
ASSOCIATES

CRIMINAL : FBI #240905, Buffalo PD# 23330. Record dates from
HISTORY 1928 and includes arrests for grand larceny, murder,
& violations of Federal Liquor Laws. Served several
short terms in prison for violations of the Federal
Liquor Laws.

BUSINESS : No legitimate employment known.

MODUS : He is a wholesaler and distributor of illicit alohol
OPERANDI in the Western NY area. Obtains narcotics from other
Mafiosi in NYC and wholesales these drugs in the
Buffalo area. Also engaged in smuggling contraband
across the U.S. - Canadian border. His brother Sal-
vatore (deceased) was highly respected among the
Mafia hierarchy in the western NY-Southern Ontario
area.

He was the longtime leader of the Lucchese family from 1967—1985. He was indicted under the RICO Act and sentenced to 100 years in prison. On August 23, 2000, he died at a medical center for federal prisoners.

NAME : Anthony CORALLO

ALIASES : Tony Ducks, Tony Corralo, Antonio Freno, Antonio Covello.

DESCRIPTION : Born 2-12-13, New York City, 5'6½", 170 lbs., blue eyes, brown hair.

LOCALITIES FREQUENTED : Resides 144-67 North Drive, Queens, N. Y. Frequents New York area race tracks, Little Napoli Restaurant and Tasse Restaurant, both in New York City.

FAMILY BACKGROUND : Married to Ann Ryan, step-daughter: Madeline, son: Jerry, brothers: Joseph & Salvatore, sisters: Carmela, Mary Zogare, Frances Governali, father: Giuseppe, mother, Lucia, (both dead).

CRIMINAL ASSOCIATES : Eddie Coco, Johnny Dio, Andimo Pappadio, John Ormento, Vincent Rao, Carmine Tramunti, Anthony Castaldi, ███ ████, Joe Bendenelli, all of New York City.

CRIMINAL HISTORY : FBI #269969, NYCPD-B #75882. Arrests since 1929 include grand larceny, robbery, violation New York State Narcotic Laws.

BUSINESS : Is vice-president of Local 239, Queens, N. Y. International Brotherhood of Teamsters, and connected with other Teamster locals.

MODUS OPERANDI : Finances large narcotic transactions. Closely associated with most major Mafia narcotic traffickers in New York City. Involved in labor racketeering.

NAME   : Earl CORALLUZZO

ALIASES   : Orlando Coralluzzo, Al
                  Bruno, Al Carbone, Squint

DESCRIPTION   : Born 11-6-15, Fairmount,
                  W. Va., 5'7", 170 lbs, black
                  hair, brown eyes, sallow
                  complexion, medium build,
                  nervous manner, wears silver
                  rimmed glasses.

LOCALITIES   : Resides at 20 Carver Terrace,
FREQUENTED   Yonkers, NY; frequents Nut
                  Club, Capri Bar & Glenview
                  Bar, all NYC, Trade Winds Night Club in Yonkers, NY,
                  Bonfire Club & El Morocco, Montreal, Canada.

FAMILY   : Married Adele Giaccio; children: Earl & Adele;
BACKGROUND   father: Ernest; mother: Hope Orlando, both born
                  in Italy and both deceased; brothers: Harry and
                  Joseph; sisters: Grace Peronia, Anna & Angelina.

CRIMINAL   : John Petrone, Joseph Foti, ███████████, Rocco
ASSOCIATES   and Joseph Barra, Catroni brothers, Anthony Strollo,
                  Michael Coppola, Michele Miranda, Matthew Cuomo.

CRIMINAL   : FBI #464964   NYCPD #B106574   Record dates from
HISTORY   1930 and includes arrests for burglary, criminally
                  receiving, gambling and auto theft.

BUSINESS   : No legitimate occupation known at this time.

MODUS   : International drug trafficker who makes frequent
OPERANDI   trips to Canada arranging for the smuggling of
                  large quantities of heroin into the Unites States
                  for interstate distribution by the Mafia group of
                  which he is a member.

NAME	: Frank CORONA
ALIASES	: Irish, Caruso
DESCRIPTION	: Born 5-15-09 NYC 5'5", 130 lbs, ruddy complexion brown eyes, black hair, birth mark center forehead, always wears glasses.
LOCALITIES FREQUENTED	: Currently (1960) incarcerated. Wife resides 208 E 134th St, NYC. Frequented Merry Cottage S.C., 116th & Paladino; Lizzie's Bar, 116 & 2nd; Tony's Bar, 129 W 72nd St; & Broadway from 96 to 125 St, all NYC.
FAMILY BACKGROUND	: Married Mary Crisco; father: James; mother: Mary Calabrese (both deceased); brothers: Angelo & Samuel; sisters: Mrs. Jennie Mongelli, Mrs. Marie Sherwood, Mrs. Anedina Francia and Mrs. Anna Velluci, wife of narcotic trafficker George Vellucci.
CRIMINAL ASSOCIATES	: Anthony & ████████████, Anthony Castaldi, Matthew Picone, Joseph Marone, Daniel & ███████████.
CRIMINAL HISTORY	: FBI #242674. NYCPD #B 68334. Record dates from 1927 & includes arrests for armed robbery, bookmaking, contempt of court. Federal narcotic conviction 1957 for which now serving 5 yrs.
BUSINESS	: No legitimate occupation known.
MODUS OPERANDI	: Part of an East Harlem, NYC, Mafia drug distribution mob, supplying large quantities of heroin to local and out of state dealers.

NAME   : Vincent CORRAO

ALIASES   : Jimmy the Blonde, Vincent
                 Carrao, Vincent Carreria.

DESCRIPTION   : Born 4-28-09, NYC, 5'11";
                 200 lbs., brown eyes, light
                 brown hair with some grey.

LOCALITIES   : Resides 1564 84 St., Brook-
FREQUENTED   lyn, NY. Frequents area of
                 Mulberry & Grand Sts., in
                 Lower Manhattan.

FAMILY   : Married to Jennie Periver,
BACKGROUND   has 2 sons: Augustus Vincent and Joseph Vincent.

CRIMINAL   : Sam Accardi, Peter Locascio, Phil Albanese, George
ASSOCIATES   Noble, Louis Dio Guardia (deceased), ███████████,
                 Ben Cinquegrana, Arthur Celi, all of NYC.

CRIMINAL   : FBI #1378139, NYCPD B#161697. Arrests from 1937
HISTORY   include receiving stolen goods and conviction for
                 Federal Narcotic Laws.

BUSINESS   : Owns buildings at 210 and 212 Grand St., Manhattan,
                 also operates Casino Trucking Co., Maspeth, Queens,
                 NY.

MODUS   : A Major narcotic trafficker from Mulberry St., area
OPERANDI   of Manhattan, who is closely associated with and
                 trusted by Mafia smugglers.

NAME   : Paul CORREALE

ALIASES   : Paulie Ham, Paul Hamm, Paul
                Hamilton, Paul Hour, Paul
                Mason.

DESCRIPTION   : Born 4-25-11 NYC, 5'11", 185
                lbs, medium build, brown
                hair, brown eyes.

LOCALITIES   : Resides 38 Olive St, Lake
FREQUENTED   Success, L.I., NY. Frequents
                Jefferson Major Club, 242 E
                112th St, 72 Club, 72nd St,
                & 2nd Ave.; Late Edition
                Club, 43rd St, & 2ns Ave.; vicinity of E 56th St, &
                3rd Ave, all NYC.

FAMILY   : Married Ann Gastoni; father: Rosario; mother:
BACKGROUND   Michelina Allarella; sisters: Carmela, Edith &
                Philomenia.

CRIMINAL   : Vincent Alo, Joseph Rao, ██████████████, Patsy
ASSOCIATES   Zaccaro, ██████████████, Carmine Tramunti, Gaetano
                Lucchese, ██████████████, all of New York.

CRIMINAL   : FBI # 177910, NYC PD #B71983. Record dating from 1924
HISTORY   includes arrests for truancy, assault, robbery,
                felonious assault and violation of parole.

BUSINESS   : Has an interest in the Gay Lady Dress Manufacturing
                Co., 1690 Boston Post Rd, Bronx, NY.

MODUS   : Important and trusted member of a Mafia group, with
OPERANDI   headquarters in New York's East Harlem, which engages
                in the wholesale distribution of heroin, both local-
                ly and interstate.

Costiglia became known as the "Prime Minister of the Underworld," because he was one of the most powerful American mafia bosses. In 1957, he was shot in the head by one of Vito Genovese's men, but survived. He retired and, in 1973, died of a heart attack in Manhattan.

NAME : Francisco COSTIGLIA

ALIASES : Francisco Castiglia, Frank Costello, Frank Saverio, Saveria

DESCRIPTION : Born 1-26-1893 Calabria, Italy, 5'7", 155 lbs, brown eyes, black-grey hair, naturalized 9-10-25 NYC.

LOCALITIES FREQUENTED : Resides 115 Central Park West, Apt. 18F, NYC, & has summer home at Sands Point, L.I., frequents Biltmore & Waldorf Astoria Hotels, and most expensive night clubs in Manhattan.

FAMILY BACKGROUND : Married to Loretta Geigerman, have no children; father: Luigi; mother: Mary Sevarrio Aloisa; brother: Edward; sister: Marcellina.

CRIMINAL ASSOCIATES : Michele Miranda, Giuseppe Profaci, Vito Genovese, Frank Erichsen, Phil Kastel, & almost every important racketeer in the U.S.; Giuseppe Doto, Lucky Luciano, Francesco P. Coppola of Italy.

CRIMINAL HISTORY : FBI #936217. NYC PDB#38412. Arrests since 1908 include assault & robbery, concealed weapon, conspiracy, contempt, income tax evasion, deportation proceedings currently pending.

BUSINESS : President of 79 Wall St., Corp., and has numerous other interests in valuable real estate & night clubs in NYC and elsewhere.

MODUS OPERANDI : One of the most influential & powerful Mafia leaders in the U.S. He is one of the controlling factors in all types of commercial vice throughout the U.S.

NAME	: Anthony CRISCI
ALIASES	: Tony Crish
DESCRIPTION	: Born 3-5-11 Beaverdale, Pa., 5'8", 205 lbs, brown hair, brown eyes, dark complexion, stocky build.
LOCALITIES FREQUENTED	: Resides 171 Norfolk St, NYC. Frequents Lower East Side, Lima's Bar & Grill, 58 Clinton St, NYC. Owns summer house, 416 Thompson St, Pt. Jefferson, L.I., NY.
FAMILY BACKGROUND	: Married Pauline Pavlishich; father: Salvatore; mother: Antonia Carluzzo (deceased); sister: Josephine Ciralo.
CRIMINAL ASSOCIATES	: Salvatore Rizzo, Salvatore Pieri, Salvatore Poliafico, Nunzio Romano, Rocco Mazzie, ▮▮▮▮▮▮▮.
CRIMINAL HISTORY	: FBI #995937. NYCPD #74250. Record dates from 1929 and includes arrests for assault & robbery, robbery of truck & merchandise. Federal narcotic conviction 1954 5 years.
BUSINESS	: Delivery truck driver.
MODUS OPERANDI	: An important Mafia narcotic trafficker supplying large amounts of high quality heroin to out-of-state dealers.

NAME   : Alfred CRISCUOLO

ALIASES   : Alfonso Criscuoli, Alphonse
                  Criscolo, Frank Romano,
                  Ralph Esposito, Alfred Rocca,
                  Alfred Tente, Frank Russo,
                  Al, Goodlooking Al.

DESCRIPTION   : Born 1-22-11 NYC, 5'7", 170
                  lbs, brown hair, brown eyes,
                  medium build.

LOCALITIES   : Resides 353 Grove St., New
FREQUENTED   Milford, NJ. Frequents Rex
                  Tavern, Negri Candy Store
                  and taverns on upper 1st Ave., in vicinity of 123rd
                  St., NYC.

FAMILY   : Wife: Gloria Hausa; son: Lewis; father: Francesco;
BACKGROUND   mother: Maria Bello (both born in Italy); brothers:
                  Steve, Larry, Albert; sister: Carmella.

CRIMINAL   : John "Buster" Ardito, Joseph Marone, Al Landi and
ASSOCIATES   Charles Albero, Frank Livorsi, Joseph Vento.

CRIMINAL   : FBI #1529336, NYCPD# B153956. Criminal record dates
HISTORY   from 1934 and includes arrests for burglary, gambling
                  and violations of State and Federal Narcotic Laws.

BUSINESS   : No known legitimate business.

MODUS   : An important member of the old 107th Street Mafia
OPERANDI   group on New York's upper east side. Delivers
                  large amounts of narcotics locally and interstate.

NAME	: Matthew CUOMO
ALIASES	: Joe Cuomo, Matty Cuomo

DESCRIPTION : Born 11-1-05 NYC, 5'6", 130
lbs, bald, grey hair on sides,
blue eyes, fair complexion,
slim build, left leg ¼" short-
er than right, slight limp.

LOCALITIES : Resides 536 E 183rd St,
FREQUENTED   Bronx, NY; frequents Malifran-
do's Stationery Store, 2371
Belmont Ave, Capri Bar, 2010
Williamsbridge Rd, Glenview
Bar & Restaurant, 2491 Southern Blvd, Crescent Ave.
section, all Bronx, New York.

FAMILY : Married Julia Cersoli 1926 & separated 1940; living
BACKGROUND   with Rose Sigiguano; father: Salvatore; mother:
Anna Longobardi, (born Italy and resides Bronx, NY.).

CRIMINAL : Lucien Ignaro, Antoine D'Agostino, ███████████,
ASSOCIATES   ███████████, Giovanni Maugeri, ███████████,
Cotroni Brothers of Canada.

CRIMINAL : FBI #972097, NYCPD #B137826. 1st arrest in 1932
HISTORY   for extortion, numerous subsequent arrests including burglary, vagrancy & gambling.

BUSINESS : A seaman by occupation, U.S. Merchant Mariner's
Document # Z-408139 suspended by the U.S. Coast
Guard 1949 because of his involvement in a smuggling
ring at San Antonio, Texas. No legitimate source of
income.

MODUS : An international smuggler of narcotics between Can-
OPERANDI   ada, U.S., France & Mexico; also active in bootlegging.

NAME : Charles CURCIO

ALIASES : Charlie Mouse, Charles Rossi

DESCRIPTION : Born 7-26-26, N.Y.C., 5'9",
185 lbs., brown eyes, brown
greying hair, medium complexion, heavy build.

LOCALITIES : Resided at 33-18 159th St.,
FREQUENTED Flushing, N.Y., currently
(1959) incarcerated.

FAMILY : Married to Rose Zaccardo,
BACKGROUND children are Diane and
Charles Jr., Father, Anthony, mother, Mary Lemardo
(both dead), brothers, Vincent, Anthony and Louis.

CRIMINAL : Frank Borelli, Rocco Mazzie, Nick Tolentino, Joe
ASSOCIATES and Ben Licchi, and most all narcotic traffickers
in East Harlem NYC.

CRIMINAL : FBI #4226766, NYC, PD# B228844, arrests date from
HISTORY 1944 and include burglary, larceny, state and fed-
eral narcotic laws; sentenced 5-24-57, Hackensack,
N.J., 8 to 10 years, state narcotic violation.

BUSINESS : None.

MODUS : Associated with and received his narcotics from top
OPERANDI echelon Mafia traffickers; a wholesale dealer both
local and interstate, operated a clandestine laboratory.

NAME	: Dominick D'AGOSTINO
ALIASES	: Dominick Dagstino
DESCRIPTION	: Born 12-7-1889 Reggio Calabria, Italy, 5'7", 182 lbs, brown eyes, grey hair, naturalized 3-21-27 N.Y.

LOCALITIES FREQUENTED	: Resides 2226 Ontario Ave., Niagara Falls, N.Y. Frequents Utica, N.Y., & Why Not Bar & Alibi Bar, both in Buffalo, New York.
FAMILY BACKGROUND	: Wife: Domenica Moscato, resides in Italy with children Rosa, Giuseppe & Giuseppa, father: Giuseppe; mother: Dominica Sacca (both deceased).
CRIMINAL ASSOCIATES	: Antonio & Stefano Magaddino, Joseph & Salvatore Falcone, Roy Carlisi, John C. Montana, Bartolo Guccia, Anthony Riela.
CRIMINAL HISTORY	: FBI #332258. Buffalo PD #25668. Arrests since 1930 include Income Tax evasion, contempt & conviction for violation of Federal Narcotic Laws.
BUSINESS	: No current business or employment known. At one time managed the Hilltop Restaurant at Niagara Falls Ontario, Canada.
MODUS OPERANDI	: Attended Apalachin Mafia meeting 1957 with other members from Buffalo-Niagara Falls area. Has long been associated with the international narcotic traffic.

NAME   : John D'ALESSIO

ALIASES   : "Johnny Dee", John D'Andrea

DESCRIPTION : Born 8-6-12 NYC, 235 lbs,
              5'8", brown hair, grey eyes,
              ruddy complexion, stout build
              neat dresser.

LOCALITIES : Resides 151 Jumel St, Great
FREQUENTED   Kills, Staten Island, fre-
              quents bars in the vicinity
              of New Dorp, Staten Island.
              Also is known to frequent
              the water-front hangouts on
              the north shore of Staten Island.

FAMILY   : Father: Michael; mother: Mary DiBrizzi; brothers:
BACKGROUND   Michael, Alexander, Pasquale, & Dominick an attorney;
              sister: Mary DiBrizzi, (married a cousin); nephew of
              the notorious Alexander DiBrizzi, czar of the Staten
              Island underworld.

CRIMINAL   : Anthony Strollo, Alexander DiBrizzi, Lucky Luciano,
ASSOCIATES   and the Anastasia Brothers.

CRIMINAL   : FBI #1789280, NYCPD #B104318. Criminal history dates
HISTORY   from June 6, 1932, and includes arrests for felonious
              assault, policy, bookmaking and evasion of income
              taxes.

BUSINESS   : Owns an interest in the King Vending Machine Co.,
              of Staten Island.

MODUS   : A respected member of the Mafia, who, together with
OPERANDI   his uncle and brothers, controls every illegal
              racket and enterprise in Staten Island. The subject
              is also reputed to play a major role in the long-
              shoremens union which controls the piers of Staten
              Island.

NAME	: John DANIELLO
ALIASES	: Baldy, Joseph O'Neal Daniello
DESCRIPTION	: Born 10-19-21 NYC, 5'7", 145 lbs, thin build, brown eyes, black hair, olive complexion.
LOCALITIES FREQUENTED	:·Resides 1425 Edwards Ave., Bronx, NY. Frequents 107 & 108 Sts., between 1st & 3rd Aves, NYC.
FAMILY BACKGROUND	: Married Bernadette Mancuso; son: Nicholas; father: John; mother: Antoinette Viserto; brothers: Frank, Daniel, Anthony; sisters: Rose, Carolina, Delores & Jeanette.
CRIMINAL ASSOCIATES	: Joseph Manfredi, ██████████, Joseph Pagano
CRIMINAL HISTORY	: FBI #245096A, NYC PD# B272032. Record dating from 1949 consists solely of narcotic arrests. 1952 convicted of Federal Narcotic Law violation, sentence suspended.
BUSINESS	: Occasional construction worker & welder.
MODUS OPERANDI	: A lower level Mafia member who has been delivery man for notorious violators in the East Harlem area.

416

NAME   : Edward D'ARGENIO

ALIASES   : Eddie The Wop

DESCRIPTION   : Born 10-26-1900, Avellino,
                  Naples, Italy, 5'6", 140 lbs
                  dark hair, balding, brown
                  eyes, dark complexion, de-
                  formed left pinky.

LOCALITIES   : Resides 7412 15th Ave.,
FREQUENTED   Brooklyn, NY, frequents
                  lower east side of Manhattan,
                  currently (1959) incarcera-
                  ted.

FAMILY   : Common-Law wife: Rose Pomerantz; son: Edward, Jr.,
BACKGROUND   father: Edward; mother: Carmela Artablo; sisters:
                  Anna Sena, Molly Stranesi, Gloria Mataryli; brothers:
                  Louis and Vincent.

CRIMINAL   : Peter Locascio, Carmine Locascio, ██████████████████,
ASSOCIATES   John Albasi, Michael Picone

CRIMINAL   : FBI #850683, NYCPD #129498, arrest record dates back
HISTORY   to 1917 and includes arrests for burglary, grand
                  larceny, extortion, impersonation of Federal Officer
                  and violations of State and Federal Narcotic Laws.
                  Conviction for the latter 1954. Sentenced to 9
                  years.

BUSINESS   : No legitimate occupation

MODUS   : Is widely known by narcotic dealers in all parts
OPERANDI   of the U.S. Prospective narcotic purchasers con-
                  tact D'Argenio who furnishes them suppliers from
                  among his Mafia associates.

In 1974, Peter was considered a suspect in the Amityville Horror murders, but any involvement was never proved. He died on April 6, 1993.

NAME : Peter DE FEO

ALIASES : Phillip Aquilina

DESCRIPTION : Born 3-4-02 NYC, 5'8", 170 lbs, greying brown hair, brown eyes, large nose.

LOCALITIES FREQUENTED : Resides 130 W 12th St, NYC, frequents Alto Knights Social Club, Patrissey's Rest., Luigi Rest., & Progressivo Rest., all NYC, summers at Orlando's Farm, Hopewell, NJ.

FAMILY BACKGROUND : Married Nunziata (Nancy) Aquilino; son: John Gabriel; father: Giuseppe; mother: Berta Nicolette.

CRIMINAL ASSOCIATES : Vito Genovese, Michele Miranda, Lorenzo Brescia, ███████████, Anthony LaRocca, Anthony Strollo.

CRIMINAL HISTORY : No FBI # assigned. NYCPD #253234. Only arrest was in connection with investigation of a murder.

BUSINESS : Formerly operated Ross Paper Stock Co., 151 Mercer St., NYC.

MODUS OPERANDI : Top echelon Mafioso, closely associated with Vito Genovese, Michele Miranda and Anthony Aperto in control of bookmaking and Italian lottery on NYC's Lower East Side.

418

NAME   : James DE GEORGE

ALIASES   : Jimmy DiGiorgio, Vincent
                 DeGeorge

DESCRIPTION   : Born 2-2-13 NYC 5'4", 158
                 lbs, black hair, brown eyes,
                 olive complexion, 3½" scar
                 right chin, tattoos both
                 arms.

LOCALITIES   : Resides 314 E 100th St, NYC,
FREQUENTED   frequents 100th & 1st Ave,
                 106th & 2nd Ave, 450 E 110th
                 Street.

FAMILY   : Common-law wife: Emily White; father: Angelo;
BACKGROUND   mother: Maria Russo; brothers: Angelo, Joseph and
                 Paul; sisters Jenny DeGeorge Grover and Tillie
                 DeGeorge Otto.

CRIMINAL   : ▓▓▓▓▓▓▓▓, Alfred Criscuolo, ▓▓▓▓▓▓▓▓▓▓,
ASSOCIATES   Charles Curcio, Frank Borelli, ▓▓▓▓▓▓▓▓▓.

CRIMINAL   : FBI #237136. NYC PD# B267662. Record dates from
HISTORY   1939 and includes arrests for grand larceny, bur-
                 glary, possession of narcotics. Convicted of Federal
                 narcotic law violation 1954 - 3 years.

BUSINESS   : No legitimate occupation.

MODUS   : A lower level Mafia member who is associated with
OPERANDI   some of the top Mafia narcotic traffickers, supplies
                 narcotics to dealers in Cleveland, Chicago, Pitts-
                 burgh, Boston and Detroit.

NAME	: Benjamin DE MARTINO
ALIASES	: Benny, Benny the Bum, Ben DeMartini, Benny Martino
DESCRIPTION	: Born 12-21-13 NYC, 5'11", 162 lbs, brown hair, hazel eyes, slender build.

LOCALITIES : Resides Broadway & Lincoln
FREQUENTED   Ave., Rocky Point, L.I., NY,
              frequents Freddie's Barber
              Shop 240 W. 35th St., Man-
              hattan, and Blue Bird Bar in
              Bronx.

FAMILY   : Wife: Emma Purchia, Children: Leona & Martin,
BACKGROUND   mother: Maria Cerrata, father: Leoni (dead), bro-
                thers: Ted, Tony (dead), sister: Dorothy.

CRIMINAL   : Ted DeMartino (brother), ▮▮▮▮▮▮, Joe Ragone,
ASSOCIATES   Joe Tocco, John Ormento, Mike Coppola, Frank
                Fiorello, Michael LiMandri.

CRIMINAL   : FBI #1068509, NYCPD #B106896, arrests since 1932
HISTORY   include assault & robbery, homicide, felonious
                assault.

BUSINESS   : Has interests in Benjamin Vending Corp., and
                National Vending Corp., both in Westbury, L.I., NY.

MODUS   : With brother Teddy is a member of the Mafia organ-
OPERANDI   ization dealing in wholesale narcotic trafficking
                from the East Harlem area NYC.

NAME	: Theodore DE MARTINO
ALIASES	: Teddy, Theodore DeMartini, Teddy the Bum.
DESCRIPTION	: Born 7-3-12 NYC, 5'11", 260 lbs, brown eyes, black hair, stout build.
LOCALITIES FREQUENTED	: Resides 2305 Vance St., Bronx, NY, frequents East Harlem area NYC, has summer home at 170 Edgewater Drive, Shirley, L.I., NY.

FAMILY BACKGROUND	: Wife: Arsanta (Sue), Daughters: Marie, Eleanor, mother: Maria Cerrata, father: Leoni (dead), brothers: Benny, Antonio (dead), sister: Dorothy.
CRIMINAL ASSOCIATES	: Ben DeMartino (brother), Alex Rossi, Joseph Tocco, John Ormento, Frank Fiorello, Michael LiMandri, ▬▬▬▬▬▬▬, Mike Altimare.
CRIMINAL HISTORY	: FBI #1304126, NYCPD #B141109, numerous misdemeanor arrests since 1936 plus conviction of Federal Narcotic Laws.
BUSINESS	: Owns Teddy's Carting Service, 325 E. 117 St., and has interests in Teddy's Service Center and Admiral Trucking Co., both at 2276 1st Ave., all in NYC.
MODUS OPERANDI	: Member of the Mafia organization which controls narcotic trafficking in East Harlem area NYC. Acquainted with other known Mafia traffickers in the United States.

NAME   : Joseph DENTICO

ALIASES   : Joseph Dandia, Joe Bari,
                  Dandio.

DESCRIPTION   : Born 10-5-98, Gioia Del Collo
                  Calabria, Italy, 5'7½", 195
                  lbs., brown eyes, grey hair,
                  wears glasses, alien regis-
                  tration #5348654.

LOCALITIES   : Resides 2355 Prospect Ave.,
FREQUENTED   Bronx, NY, frequents East
                  Harlem section of Manhattan.

FAMILY   : Married to Theresa Romano, Father: Vito Antonio,
BACKGROUND   Mother: Rose (both dead), brothers: Frank & Larry,
                  Sister: Mrs. Grace Doyle.

CRIMINAL   : Charles Albero, Joseph Marone, Joseph Tocco, John
ASSOCIATES   Ardito, Joe Rao, Alfred Criscuolo, all of NYC.

CRIMINAL   : FBI #68636, NYCPD #B45977, numerous arrests since
HISTORY   1916 including assault, grand larceny, burglary,
                  conviction of Federal Narcotic Laws. Currently free
                  on bail pending deportation proceedings.

BUSINESS   : In the past has been interested in radio, phono-
                  graph and "juke box" business.

MODUS   : A member of the Albero - Marone organization which
OPERANDI   has been engaged in the smuggling and distribution
                  of narcotics on a major scale. Is closely associated
                  with most Mafia leaders in East Harlem area NYC.

NAME	: Joseph D'ERCOLE
ALIASES	: Joe Z, Josey, Joe Morelli, Josie Romano.
DESCRIPTION	: Born 11-16-11 NYC, 5'7", 210 lbs, brown eyes, black-grey hair, medium complexion, hoarse voice.
LOCALITIES FREQUENTED	: Resides 428 E 116th St, Apt #18, NYC. Frequents Delightful Luncheonette, NYC.
FAMILY BACKGROUND	: Married Helen Morelli; daughter: Rose Zanfardino; father: Domenico; mother: Rosalia Emanuele; brothers: Anthony, Louis & Ignazio (deceased 1952); sisters: Mary Chionchio, Bessie Dorio, Virginia Derio, and Theresa Ivonelle.
CRIMINAL ASSOCIATES	: Joe Rao, Mike Coppola, Joe Bendenelli, Nicholas Tolentino, John Ardito, Anthony Criscuolo, ███████ ██████, DeMartino Brothers, ████████ & Daniel Lessa.
CRIMINAL HISTORY	: FBI #373891. NYCPD #B82879. Arrests since 1930 include robbery, assault & robbery, grand larceny, Dyer Act & convictions for Federal narcotic laws.
BUSINESS	: Employed as manager & bouncer at Delightful Luncheonette, 116th St, & 1st Ave, NYC.
MODUS OPERANDI	: Is one of the controlling Mafia members in the East Harlem section of NYC, engages in any type of illicit activity, mainly narcotic wholesaling and large scale auto theft.

```
NAME            : Nicholas DiBENE

ALIASES         : Nick, Benny

DESCRIPTION     : Born 3-24-05 NYC, 5'8¼", 182
                  lbs, black-grey wavy hair,
                  brown eyes.

LOCALITIES      : Resides 553 E 183 St, Bronx,
FREQUENTED        NY. Frequents Crescent Ave,
                  section and other parts of
                  Bronx, Monterey Bar, 4069
                  Bronxwood Ave, Bronx, NY.

FAMILY          : Wife: Kathleen
BACKGROUND

CRIMINAL        : Joseph Valachi, Joseph Bisogna, Frank Luciano,
ASSOCIATES        Dominick Carminati, ███████████, Giacomo Scarpulla.

CRIMINAL        : FBI #438428. NYCPD #B62328. Record dating from 1925
HISTORY           includes arrests for robbery, assault, felonious
                  assault, disorderly conduct, sodomy, unlawful entry
                  and illegal gun possession.

BUSINESS        : Owner & Manager Monterey Club, 4069 Bronxwood Ave,
                  Bronx, NY.

MODUS           : Influential Mafioso, closely associated with top
OPERANDI          level Mafia criminals in NYC. Engages in Hi-Jacking,
                  gambling, shylocking, narcotic trafficking & other
                  illicit activities.
```

424

NAME	: Alexander DI BRIZZI
ALIASES	: Al Britton, Alex-The-Ox, Al DiBruzzi, Alexander DiBrisi.
DESCRIPTION	: Born 4-10-1892 NYC, 5'6", 200 lbs, heavy build, grey hair, brown eyes, glasses.
LOCALITIES FREQUENTED	: Resides 120 DeKalb St, Staten Island, NY. Owns Ten Acre Farm, Jamesburg, NJ and other Staten Island & NJ Real Estate; frequents Local 920 I.L.A. 523 Bay St, Stapleton, Staten Island.
FAMILY BACKGROUND	: First Wife: Rose; second wife: Anna; sons: John N. & Alexander C; daughters: Mary, Lillian, Anita, Dorothy & Sandra; father: Joseph; mother: Marie Attardi.
CRIMINAL ASSOCIATES	: Anthony Anastasia, ███████████, John DioGuardi, Anthony Strollo, Anthony Corallo.
CRIMINAL HISTORY	: FBI #787997. NYCPD #B124311. Record dating from 1920 includes arrests for criminal conspiracy, gambling, assault and grand larceny.
BUSINESS	: Past President Local 920 I.L.A.
MODUS OPERANDI	: Top Mafia figure; controls all waterfront operations on Staten Island, New York.

NAME : Calogero Lelio DI CARLO

ALIASES : Lilo Di Carlo

DESCRIPTION : Born 9-19-01 Corleone, Palermo, Sicily, 5'9", 175 lbs, blue eyes, brown hair, naturalized NYC 7-26-51.

LOCALITIES FREQUENTED : Resides 1143 1st Ave, NYC, frequents 12th St., & 1st Ave., & 151 W 40th St., NYC.

FAMILY BACKGROUND : Married Elena Barcia; no children; father: Vincenzo; mother: Maria Santa Castro; brothers: Giovanni, Salvatore, Frank, Giuseppe, Angelo; sisters: Rosina, Catterina, Concettina & Anna (Mrs. Peter LoCascio).

CRIMINAL ASSOCIATES : Annielo De Carlo, Francesco Coppola, Serafina Mancuso, Salvatore Vitale, Lucky Luciano.

CRIMINAL HISTORY : FBI #3492388. 12-28-42 to 5-18-43 interned as enemy alien. No other arrests.

BUSINESS : Owns Di Carlo Travel Agency, 151 W. 40th St., NYC.

MODUS OPERANDI : Operates his travel agency as a cover for transfer of money for illicit enterprises such as narcotic trafficking, counterfeiting and alien smuggling carried on by Di Carlo and other Mafiosi.

NAME	: Joseph DiGIOVANNA
ALIASES	: Joe, Joe Chick, Thomas Rando, Joseph DeJohn
DESCRIPTION	: Born 11-22-04 at NYC, 5'5", 145 lbs, short medium build, brown eyes, brown hair, claims heart condition; has short left leg.
LOCALITIES FREQUENTED	: Resides at 103 Wilson Avenue, Brooklyn, NY, frequents Peoples Democratic Club, 130 Central Ave., Brooklyn, NY.
FAMILY BACKGROUND	: Married to Ethel Novins, no children. Father: Gaetano; mother: Leboria Catallano; brothers: Frank Anthony; sister: Nancy.
CRIMINAL ASSOCIATES	: Joe Sica, ███████████, ████████████, James LaSala, John Stopelli, █████████████, Joe Bruno, Archie Mannerino, ████████████.
CRIMINAL HISTORY	: FBI# 191286, NYCPD# B64753. Dates from 1922 and includes arrests for unlawful entry, robbery, burglary, bootlegging, assault and extortion. National List #121.
BUSINESS	: No legitimate employment known.
MODUS OPERANDI	: An influential Mafia member in the Wilson Ave., Section of Brooklyn. Has direct overseas connections for narcotics which he distributes to dealers from New York to California.

NAME	: Rosario DI MAGGIO
ALIASES	: ZaZa, William Russo, Eddie Cornes
DESCRIPTION	: Born 9-1-05 NYC, 5'4", 155 lbs, black hair, brown eyes, medium build.
LOCALITIES FREQUENTED	: Resides 107 Madison St., NYC, frequents NY's lower east side particularly Broom & Hester Streets.
FAMILY BACKGROUND	: Wife: Henrietta Salatoff; son: Joseph; daughter: Madeline Coppanse; father: Peter; mother: Mary Russo; has four sisters and nine brothers.
CRIMINAL ASSOCIATES	: Frank Prisinzano, Vincent Corrao, Peter LoCascio, Frank Caruso, ███████████.
CRIMINAL HISTORY	: FBI #280623, NYCPD #B62198. Record dates from 1917 and includes over 12 arrests for robbery, bookmaking and State & Federal Narcotic conviction.
BUSINESS	: No legitimate employment known.
MODUS OPERANDI	: Lower echelon Mafia member engaged in narcotic trafficking and bookmaking. Is associated with top level Mafiosi from whom he can obtain any quantity of narcotics.

He aided Jimmy Hoffa's climb to Teamster presidency. While in prison, his cell was on "Mobster's Row." He became increasingly ill in prison and died in the hospital on January 12, 1979.

NAME : John Ignazio DIOGUARDI

ALIASES : Johnny Dio, Diao, Dioguardio, Die, Dioguardia

DESCRIPTION : Born 4-29-1914, NYC, 5'8", 165 lbs, brown eyes, black hair, dark complexion.

LOCALITIES FREQUENTED : Resides 109 Freeport Ave., Pt. Lookout, L.I. Frequents 250 W 57 St, Lower East Side of NYC & NYC night clubs.

FAMILY BACKGROUND : Wife: Ann Chrostek; daughter: Rose; son: Dominick; father Dominick; mother: Rose Plumeri; brothers: Thomas & Frank; uncles: William, Joseph & James Plumeri.

CRIMINAL ASSOCIATES : James Plumeri, ██████████████, Frank Caruso, Lucien Ignaro, Anthony Corallo, ██████████████.

CRIMINAL HISTORY : FBI #665273 NYCPD #B-114267 Record dating from 1932 includes arrests for coercion, extortion, felonious assault, bootlegging, state tax violation, bribery & conspiracy. Indicted in acid blinding of labor columnist Victor Riesel. 1958 sentenced to 15 to 30 years for labor racketeering, conviction reversed on appeal, matter still pending (1960).

BUSINESS : Equitable Research Ass'n, 250 W 57 St, NYC (firm through which he instrumented his labor racketeering).

MODUS OPERANDI : A ranking member of the Mafia. At one time engaged primarily in illicit alcohol operations on a grand scale. Graduated to labor racketeering when, after the death of Louis "Lepke" Buchalter, he, his brothers and James Plumeri gained control of labor racketeering in New York City's garment center.

NAME   : Charles DiPALERMO

ALIASES   : Charlie Beck, Charlie Brody

DESCRIPTION   : Born 2-15-25 NYC, 5'8", 140
                  lbs, slim build, brown eyes,
                  black hair.

LOCALITIES   : Resides 260 Elizabeth St.,
FREQUENTED   NYC, frequents Reno Bar, 168
                  Elizabeth St., & Joy's Rest-
                  aurant, 28 Spring St., NYC,
                  & College Pizzeria, 301 E
                  170th St., Bronx, NY.

FAMILY   : Wife: Marie Cuomo; daughter: Cheryl; son: John;
BACKGROUND   father: John (deceased); mother: Sarah Floria.
                  brothers: Anthony, Steve, Peter, Joseph.

CRIMINAL   : Florio Isabella, Joseph DiPalermo, Carmine Galante,
ASSOCIATES   Vito Genovese, Joseph Bonanno, Natale Evola.

CRIMINAL   : FBI #4532585, NYCPD #B239114. Record dates from
HISTORY   1945 and includes arrests for burglary, perjury,
                  burglary tools, violation of alcohol laws, unlawful
                  entry, forgery; 1959 convicted of narcotic conspiracy
                  and sentenced to 12 years. Now appealing this con-
                  viction.

BUSINESS   : Owner of College Pizzeria, 301 E 170 St., Bronx, NY.

MODUS   : He and his brothers constitute the notorious "Beck
OPERANDI   Brothers," all Mafiosi, led by Joseph Di Palermo.
                  Charles Di Palermo, like his brothers, engages in
                  narcotic trafficking and bootlegging on a major
                  scale.

NAME   : Joseph DI PALERMO

ALIASES   : Joe Beck, Joe Palmer, Joe
                  Palmero, Joe De Palermo.

DESCRIPTION   : Born 6-8-07, NYC, 5'6", 120
                  lbs, slim build, brown eyes
                  light brown hair balding,
                  wears glasses.

LOCALITIES   : Resides 246 Elizabeth St.,
FREQUENTED   NYC. Frequented lower east
                  and west sides of Manhattan
                  also makes trips to Italy.

FAMILY   : Married to Mary Cattone, son: John, daughter: Mrs.
BACKGROUND   Sarah Fiorio, brothers: Peter, Tony, Charles, (all
                  with criminal records).

CRIMINAL   : Carmine Galante, ███████████, Santo Sorge, Vito
ASSOCIATES   Genovese, Joe Bonanno, Natale Evola, all of NYC,
                  Cotroni brothers of Montreal.

CRIMINAL   : FBI #1519166, NYCPD #B 203135, arrests since 1925
HISTORY   include narcotics (state), homicide, convictions for
                  violating Federal Liquor Laws and counterfeiting
                  laws. Sentenced to 15 years on 4-17-59 for Federal
                  Narcotic Laws. He and Carmine Galante suspected of
                  1943 murder of Carlo Tresca in NYC.

BUSINESS   : Has never engaged in any legitimate business.

MODUS   : A most vicious criminal, international drug traff-
OPERANDI   icker, and an "enforcer" for the Mafia in NYC.
                  Attended Binghamton, NY., Mafia meeting in 1956.

NAME	: Peter DI PALERMO
ALIASES	: Petey Beck and Pete Palmer
DESCRIPTION	: Born in 10-18-14, NYC, 5'5", 140 lbs., slender build, hazel eyes, black hair (bald in front), dark complexion.

LOCALITIES FREQUENTED	: Last known address 61 2nd Ave., Apt. #3-B, frequented. Thompson Social Club, 21 Prince St., Nancey's Candy Store, 240 Elizabeth St., all NYC.
FAMILY BACKGROUND	: Married to Frances Lambaisi, has 3 brothers, Joseph, Charles, and Anthony, father's name is John.
CRIMINAL ASSOCIATES	: Joseph Falcone, ██████████, ██████████, Florio Isabella, Joseph, Charles and ██████ ██████████, (brothers).
CRIMINAL HISTORY	: FBI #518878, dates back to 1931 and includes arrests for violation of the liquor laws, receiving stolen goods, burglary and counterfeiting, was sentenced in NYC., to 15 years on 11-29-50 for a counterfeiting violation.
BUSINESS	: No known legitimate business.
MODUS OPERANDI	: Was active in the manufacture of large quantities of alcohol for the illicit market and was also a top member of a counterfeiting organization in the N.Y. area, a feared member of the Mafia, along with his brother Joe.

Di Pietro was murdered by Joseph Galizia in the mid-1970s.

NAME   : Carlo DI PIETRO

ALIASES   : Cosmo, Carlie, Charles

DESCRIPTION   : Born 10-15-1930, NYC, 5'8",
                  140 lbs, black wavy hair,
                  brown eyes, ruddy complexion,
                  scars under right eye and
                  over lip.

LOCALITIES   : Resides 1 Cardinal Hayes Pl.,
FREQUENTED   NYC. Frequents Vivere Lounge,
                  199 2nd Ave., NYC, CIA Club,
                  72 Forsythe St. & entire
                  lower east side area of NYC.

FAMILY   : Married; father: Rocco; mother Rose Palermo; sisters:
BACKGROUND   Mildred Mari (wife of narcotic violator Frank Mari)
                  and Jean Menta; brother: Joseph.

CRIMINAL   : Frank Mari, Anthony Lisi, ███████████, ███████
ASSOCIATES   ███████, ████████████████, Angelo Tuminaro.

CRIMINAL   : FBI #315537A NYCPD #B274644 Record dating from
HISTORY   1936 includes arrests for disorderly conduct,
                  burglary and criminally receiving stolen goods.
                  Federal Narcotic Law conviction.

BUSINESS   : Former professional boxer. Has interest in the
                  Vivere Lounge, 199 2nd Avenue, NYC.

MODUS   : Part of a Mafia narcotic smuggling and distributing
OPERANDI   ring on New York's lower east side. Obtains supplies
                  of heroin from the Cotroni organization in Canada.

NAME   : Vincent Di PIETRO

ALIASES   : Jimmy, James, Vincenzo,
                  De Pietro, Di Pietra, James
                  De Martinie

DESCRIPTION   : Born 5-31-10 NYC, 5'7", 190
                  lbs, stout build, black hair,
                  brown eyes, dark complexion.

LOCALITIES   : Resides 1638 78St., Brook-
FREQUENTED   lyn. Frequents Hester, El-
                  dridge & Mulberry Sts, NYC.

FAMILY   : Wife: Mary Taurrozi; daugh-
BACKGROUND   ters: Theresa & Anna Marie; sisters: Vincenza
                  Colosanto & Margaret Romano; brothers: Carmello,
                  John & Joseph.

CRIMINAL   : Frank Caruso, ████████████████, ███████████,
ASSOCIATES   ███████████, Joseph Falcone.

CRIMINAL   : FBI #1001717, NYCPD #B67789. Arrest record dates
HISTORY   from 1926 and includes arrests for homicide, fel-
                  onious assault, petit larceny, grand larceny & book-
                  making. Federal Narcotic conviction.

BUSINESS   : No legitimate employment known.

MODUS   : Middle echelon Mafioso who engages in narcotic
OPERANDI   traffic in association with top Mafia racketeers.

NAME   : Vincent DI STEFANO

ALIASES   : Jimmy

DESCRIPTION : Born 7-11-05 NYC, 5'9", 175
               lbs, medium build, blue eyes,
               grey hair.

LOCALITIES   : Resides 68 E 3rd St., NYC,
FREQUENTED   frequents barber shop at 149
               E. Houston St., and Knights
               of Ferro Social Club 84 E.
               2nd St., NYC.

FAMILY   : Married to Angelina Saccero,
BACKGROUND   two daughters, Mrs. Marie DiMare and Mrs. Theresa
               Pimpiano, sister, Mrs. Frances Libruzzi, brother,
               Albert.

CRIMINAL   : Joseph Marino, Tom Licata (dead), Carmine Locascio,
ASSOCIATES   Mike Consolo, Carmine Galente, Vito Genovese, Mike
               Miranda.

CRIMINAL   : FBI #1010295, convicted in 1935 in NYC, for smug-
HISTORY   gling narcotics.

BUSINESS   : Operates barber shop at 149 E. Houston St., NYC.

MODUS   : Has been a smuggler and international narcotic traf-
OPERANDI   ficker; is a trusted Mafioso from the Houston-
               Mulberry area NYC.

NAME   : Anthony DONATO

ALIASES   : Tony, Tony Iodine, Tony
                    Russo.

DESCRIPTION   : Born 6-16-14 NYC, 5'7", 155
                    lbs, slim build, brown eyes,
                    black hair, light complexion

LOCALITIES   : Resides 2273 2nd Ave., NYC,
FREQUENTED   frequents the Imperial Candy
                    Store, 118th & 3rd and the
                    Lexington Bar, 116th & Lex-
                    ington, NYC.

FAMILY   : Wife: Madeline Cortozzo; sons: Silvio, Camillo;
BACKGROUND   previously married to Laura Calcero; daughter: (by
                    Laura), Marie; father: Giuseppe; mother: Mira Montara;
                    sister: Mildred Contes (wife of Peter Contes); brother:
                    Frank Donato, (Husband of Marie Vittorino).

CRIMINAL   : Frank Donato, ███████████, ███████████████, ███████
ASSOCIATES   ███████, Anthony Granza, ███████████████████.

CRIMINAL   : FBI #513171, NYCPD #B97765, record dates from 1931
HISTORY   and includes arrests for burglary, criminally carry-
                    ing pistol, murder, parole violation, assault & rob-
                    bery, receiving stolen goods, interstate theft, grand
                    larceny. 1954 sentenced to 4-8 years state narcotic
                    violation.

BUSINESS   : No legitimate occupation.

MODUS   : An important Mafia racketeer who deals in kilo lots
OPERANDI   of heroin.

NAME   : Frank Louis DONATO

ALIASES   : Frank Russo, Frank Iodine

DESCRIPTION : Born 1-7-10 NYC, 5'7", 172
               lbs, stocky build, hazel eyes
               greying hair, ruddy complex-
               ion.

LOCALITIES   : Resides 336 E 117th St. NYC,
FREQUENTED   frequented Lexington Bar,
               116th & Lexington; Imperial
               Candy Store, 118th & 3rd
               Ave., & 107th St. & 2nd Ave,
               all NYC. Currently incar-
               cerated.

FAMILY   : Wife: Marie Vittorino; two children; father: Giuseppe;
BACKGROUND   mother: Mira Montara; sister: Mildred Contes, (wife
               of Peter Contes); brother: Anthony.

CRIMINAL   : ▓▓▓▓▓▓▓▓, Anthony Donato, ▓▓▓▓▓▓▓▓▓▓▓▓,
ASSOCIATES   (wifes brother), ▓▓▓▓▓▓▓▓, Anthony Granza.

CRIMINAL   : FBI #125673, NYCPD #B68319, record dates from 1927
HISTORY   and includes arrests for robbery, assault, hi-jack-
               ing, grand larceny. 1953 convicted of heroin sale,
               state court, sentenced to $7\frac{1}{2}$ - 15 years.

BUSINESS   : No legitimate occupation.

MODUS   : An important Mafia racketeer who deals in kilo
OPERANDI   lots of heroin.

NAME   : Charles DONGARRO

ALIASES   : Rosario Dongarra, Charles
                    Dongarra, Charles Dongara.

DESCRIPTION   : Born 3-20-1896 Palermo,
                    Sicily. 5'6", 150 lbs.,
                    brown eyes, black-grey hair.

LOCALITIES   : Resides 884 54th St.,
FREQUENTED   Brooklyn, N.Y. Frequents
                    area of E. 12th St. & Ave. A
                    in Manhattan, D&L Dress Co.,
                    & J&C Coat Co., both in
                    Brooklyn.

FAMILY   : Is married and has 2 married daughters.
BACKGROUND

CRIMINAL   : Joe Riccobono, Joe Rao, Joe Stracci, Anthony
ASSOCIATES   Bonasera, all of N.Y.C.; Joe Doto & Lucky Luciano
                    of Italy.

CRIMINAL   : FBI#321506. NYC PD-B#56635. Arrests since 1921
HISTORY   include carrying concealed weapons.

BUSINESS   : Has interests in D&L Dress Shop, Troutman Dress
                    Co., J&C Coat Shop, all in Brooklyn, N.Y.

MODUS   : With Mafia associates has been a major narcotic
OPERANDI   trafficker & smuggler who supplied local peddlers
                    in wholesale quantities.

NAME   : Max EDER

ALIASES   : Little Maxie

DESCRIPTION   : Born 6-14-08 South Bend, Ind,
                  Jewish, 5'6", 145 lbs, brown
                  eyes, black-grey hair, med-
                  ium build, fair complexion,
                  glasses.

LOCALITIES   : Resides 86 W 179 St, Bronx,
FREQUENTED   NY. Frequents NY & Florida
                  race tracks, 107th St, & 1st
                  Ave, & Delancey St, area,
                  NYC.

FAMILY   : Married Elizabeth Turrett; no children; father:
BACKGROUND   Morris; mother: Sarah Meinhardt, (both deceased);
                  brothers: Saul, Nathan, Sidney & Cornelius; sister:
                  Sylvia Eder (a call girl involved in the 1949 Minot
                  Jelke trial.

CRIMINAL   : Frank Livorsi, Michael Coppola, Alfred Felice,
ASSOCIATES   Pasquale Erra, Joseph Bendenelli, Mickey Cohen.

CRIMINAL   : FBI #236413. NYCPD #96691. Record dating from 1925
HISTORY   includes arrests for burglary, gambling, vehicular
                  homicide and Federal narcotics conviction.

BUSINESS   : No legitimate occupation known.

MODUS   : Though Jewish he has for many years been affiliated
OPERANDI   with and highly trusted by Mafia racketeers and
                  narcotic traffickers in New York's East Harlem.
                  Narcotic smuggler and wholesale distributor.

439

Embarrato died on February 21, 2001 of natural causes.

NAME : Alfred James EMBARRATO

ALIASES : Alfred Scalisi, Al Walker, Aldo Elvarado.

DESCRIPTION : Born 11-1-09 N.Y.C. 5'7", 165 lbs., black hair, brown eyes, tattoo "AJE" on right arm, wears glasses.

LOCALITIES FREQUENTED : Resides 43 Market St., N.Y.C. Frequents House of Chan, 52nd St., & area of Market & Madison Sts., all in N.Y.C.

FAMILY BACKGROUND : Married to Constance and has 3 children; father: Salvatore; mother: Mary.

CRIMINAL ASSOCIATES : Frank Livorsi, ███████████, Lucky Luciano, Floria Isabella, ████████████, Carmine Locascio, Saro Mogavero, & Anthony Mirra (nephew).

CRIMINAL HISTORY : FBI#776059. NYC PD-B#84812. Arrests since 1930 include felonious assault & conviction for Federal Narcotic Laws.

BUSINESS : Usually employed on piers as a boss loader in N.Y.C.

MODUS OPERANDI : An interstate & local narcotic trafficker closely allied with known Mafia traffickers. A strong arm man who controls the work of stevedores at lower east side piers so that shipping companies have to deal with him.

NAME	: Alfred EPPOLITO
ALIASES	: Freddy, Big Freddy, Ippolito
DESCRIPTION	: Born 9-19-19 NYC, 5'11", 205 lbs, heavy build, black hair, brown eyes, suffers from serious ulcer condition.
LOCALITIES FREQUENTED	: Resides 1727 Troy Ave, Brooklyn, NY. Frequents Gran Mark Bar, Grand & St. Marks Aves, San Chel's Rest., 5000 Kings Highway & Colonial Enterprises, 605 Grand Ave, all in Brooklyn, NY.

FAMILY BACKGROUND	: Married Lorraine Desena; son: Louis; daughters: Lorraine & Marlene; brothers: James, Ralph & Joseph.
CRIMINAL ASSOCIATES	: Andrew Alberti, John Robilotto (deceased); ▇▇▇▇▇ ▇▇▇▇▇, ▇▇▇▇▇▇▇, ▇▇▇▇▇▇▇▇▇.
CRIMINAL HISTORY	: FBI #1824986, NYCPD #B276479. Record dates from 1936 and includes arrests for robbery, counterfeiting, felonious assault and suspected murder. Was prime suspect in murder of John Robilotto a high echelon Mafioso.
BUSINESS	: Owns Colonial Enterprises, 605 Grand Ave., Brooklyn, a jukebox distributing firm.
MODUS OPERANDI	: Finances wholesale smuggling & distribution of narcotics in collusion with the Andrew Alberti organization. Is an important Mafia member and in addition to his narcotic interests is active in loansharking and gambling operations.

NAME	: Frank ERICHSEN
ALIASES	: Frank Erikson, Frank Erickson.
DESCRIPTION	: Born 11-22-95 NYC, 5'9½", 195 lbs, grey hair on sides, bald on top, blue eyes, light complexion, heavy build
LOCALITIES FREQUENTED	: Resides at 610 West End Ave, NYC, Frequents Colony Club Rest., Savoy-Hilton Motel, Waldorf Astoria, and Madison Square Garden, all NYC, Miami, Florida, Cuba.
FAMILY BACKGROUND	: Lives with his wife Amelia; two children, Frank Jr, and Frances (Mrs. James Watson); father: Arthur; mother: Sarah Hackett; brother: Leonard.
CRIMINAL ASSOCIATES	: Charles Fischetti, Gaetano Lucchese, Lucky Luciano, Francesco Costiglia, Giuseppe A. Doto, ███████████, Michele Miranda, William O'Dwyer (past mayor of NYC).
CRIMINAL HISTORY	: FBI #1762258. NYCPD #B179898. Record dating from 1919 includes arrests for gambling, perjury, assault and income tax evasion.
BUSINESS	: Associated with his brother Leonard in the negotiable securities business. Part owner of the retail florist business of Annenburg & Erickson, 1000 Madison Ave, NYC. Has vast undisclosed real estate interests throughout the United States and Cuba.
MODUS OPERANDI	: Top level gambler of world renown. Close and trusted associate of top echelon Mafiosi and other major racketeers in the U.S. & Cuba.

He was one of 20 who were charged with conspiracy at the 1957 Apalachin Convention. He died of cancer while living with his mother in Brooklyn on August 28, 1973.

NAME : Natale Joseph EVOLA

ALIASES : Joe Diamond

DESCRIPTION : Born 1-22-1907, NYC, 5'10", 190 lbs, brown eyes, grey hair, balding.

LOCALITIES FREQUENTED : Resides 972 Bay Ridge Parkway, Brooklyn, NY. Frequents garment center of NYC.

FAMILY BACKGROUND : Single; father: Filippo; mother: Francesca; brothers: Paul & Joseph; sister: Anna.

CRIMINAL ASSOCIATES : Salvatore Santoro, Andimo Papaddio, Cassandros S. Bonasera, Joseph Stracci, James Plumeri, John Ormento.

CRIMINAL HISTORY : FBI #449296 NYCPD #E-8624   Record dating from 1930 includes arrests for coercion, possession of gun, Federal Narcotic Law conviction and conspiracy to obstruct justice, for which sentenced (1960) to 5 years and $10,000 fine.

BUSINESS : Owner of Belmont Garment Delivery and Amity Garment Delivery, both at 240 W. 37th St., N.Y.C.

MODUS OPERANDI : Attended 1957 Apalachin Mafia meeting with other Mafia leaders from NYC. Is a major narcotic trafficker who also engages in labor racketeering in New York City's garment center.

He died around 1988 in Utica, New York.

NAME : Joseph FALCONE

ALIASES : Giuseppe Projetto

DESCRIPTION : Born 1-27-02 Sciacca, Sicily naturalized 2-18-25 Utica, NY., 5'5", 160 lbs., brown eyes, grey hair.

LOCALITIES FREQUENTED : Resides 1623 Mohawk St., Utica, NY., Frequents Utica Rome area of N.Y., NYC, and makes trips to Italy.

FAMILY BACKGROUND : Married to Mary A. Abruzzo; daughters: Mrs. Josephine M. Bronga, Mrs. Mary L. Parisi, son: Anthony J; parents: Antonio and Maria (both dead), brother: Salvatore.

CRIMINAL ASSOCIATES : ███████████████ and Andrew Alberti of NYC, Sam Pieri, Stefano Magaddino and █████████ of Utica-Buffalo area, Nicola Gentile (deportee).

CRIMINAL HISTORY : FBI #1697613, Utica PD# 6722, has arrest for violation of Federal Liquor Laws. Arrested 5-21-59 for 18 USC 371 (pending).

BUSINESS : Is connected with a retail liquor store in Utica, NY.

MODUS OPERANDI : Attended Apalachin Mafia meeting 1957 with his brother Salvatore representing the organization from Utica-Rome NY., area. Both brothers are leaders of the Mafia in this area and control organized gambling and prostitution. Are suspected international drug traffickers.

NAME : Rosario Airo FARULLA

ALIASES : Rosario Farulla, Sausarito

DESCRIPTION : Born 8-25-1882, Villarosa,
Sicily, Italy, 5'6½", 175
lbs, heavy build, ruddy complexion, grey hair (bald on
top).

LOCALITIES : Resided 315 E 48th St., NYC,
FREQUENTED frequented vicinity 40th St,
& 2nd Ave, NYC. Currently
incarcerated.

FAMILY : Single; father: Stefano; mother: Angela Montalbano,
BACKGROUND (both deceased); brother: Michele Airo Farulla, (In-
terpol #1867/53).

CRIMINAL : ███████████, ██████████ & ██████████, (all
ASSOCIATES of France), ██████████, ██████████.

CRIMINAL : FBI #486208B, I&NS #A-5308632. Record dates back to
HISTORY 1908 when he was sentenced to 4 yrs & two months for
murder and possession of weapons. In 1912 sentenced
to 2 yrs 4 months for assault & battery & weapons.
He came to the U.S. and was arrested in 1929 for
bootlegging. In 1935 the Italian courts sentenced
him, in absentia, to life imprisonment for murder &
theft. 1957 sentenced to 5 yrs for violation of
Federal Narcotic Laws.

BUSINESS : No legitimate occupation.

MODUS : Commands great respect in the Mafia having gained
OPERANDI his reputation as a vicious and cold blooded killer.
Engaged in large scale smuggling of narcotics bet-
ween Italy, France and the United States.

NAME	: Bartolo FERRIGNO
ALIASES	: Bartu Lucci
DESCRIPTION	: Born 11-11-04 Palermo, Sicily, 5'6½", 168 lbs, medium build, brown hair, brown eyes. I&N #A5278959 permanent resident alien.
LOCALITIES FREQUENTED	: Resides 1778 63rd St, B'klyn, NY. Frequents vicinity of 11th St, & 1st Ave, NYC.
FAMILY BACKGROUND	: Married Mary Piazza; son: Stephen; father: Gaetano; mother: Santa Schiro (both deceased).
CRIMINAL ASSOCIATES	: Germaio Anaclerio, Benny Coniglio, Salvatore Caneba, Jean Laget, Lucien Ignaro, Salvatore Giordano, ▬▬▬▬▬▬, ▬▬▬▬▬.
CRIMINAL HISTORY	: FBI #1705717, NYCPD #B173085. Record dating from 1927 includes arrests for extortion, felonious assault, illegal possession food ration stamps & violation Federal narcotic laws.
BUSINESS	: Skilled Butcher. Formerly owned a butcher shop at 182 First Ave, NYC.
MODUS OPERANDI	: A trusted member of the Mafia for many years. Former partner in illicit enterprises with East Harlem narcotic violators Benny Coniglio & Salvatore Caneba.

NAME	: Antonio FERRO
ALIASES	: Edward Deipierro, Tony Russo, Anthony Fierra, Buckalo.

DESCRIPTION	: Born 1-24-18 NYC, 180 lbs, 5'7", brown eyes, grey-black hair, heavy build.
LOCALITIES FREQUENTED	: Resides 3033 Roberts Ave, Bronx, NY. Frequents Willow Inn 3077 Westchester Ave, Bronx, Teddy's Barber Shop, 2nd Ave, 118th St, Manhattan, Paddock Bar and Grill 50th Street and Broadway, Manhattan.
FAMILY BACKGROUND	: Single; father: Giuseppe; mother: Maria Santucci; brothers: Louis and Frank.
CRIMINAL ASSOCIATES	: Frank Livorsi, Mike Copolla, ██████████████, ████████████████, ████████████, ████████████.
CRIMINAL HISTORY	: FBI #142209, NYCPD #B165226. Record dates from 1952 and includes arrests for disorderly conduct, policy and dice.
BUSINESS	: No legitimate employment known.
MODUS OPERANDI	: Lower echelon Mafia racketeer who engages in bootlegging, shylocking and narcotic trafficking in NYC's East Bronx area.

NAME : Louis FOCERI

ALIASES : Anthony Falco, Louie Beans

DESCRIPTION : Born 11-21-22 NYC, 5'10",
195 lbs, hazel eyes, sandy
hair, stout build.

LOCALITIES : Resides 2370 93rd St.,
FREQUENTED Corona, NY, frequents East
Harlem section of NYC, part-
icularly 117th & Pleasant
Ave., & Royalites Social
Club, 314 E. 119th St., NYC.

FAMILY : Single; father: Nicholas; mother: Madelaine Pernici,
BACKGROUND (both deceased); brothers: Joseph, Anthony, Vincent
& Dante; sister: Ann.

CRIMINAL : Vincent Ciraulo, Nathan Behrman, Paul Correale, Sam
ASSOCIATES Monastersky, Daniel & ███████████.

CRIMINAL : FBI #2614144, NYCPD #B 189802, record dates from 1940
HISTORY and includes arrests for rape, grand larceny, burglary, felonious assault, policy and illegal possession
of gun.

BUSINESS : No legitimate occupation

MODUS : A respected member of the Mafia engaged in the
OPERANDI numbers racket and narcotic traffic.

NAME : Cosmo FRANCO

ALIASES : Gus Franco, Gus Winters, Harry Stella

DESCRIPTION : Born 10-19-06, NYC; 5'9" 190 lbs, heavy build, brown eyes, black hair, sallow complexion.

LOCALITIES FREQUENTED : Resides 735 Kappock Street, Bronx, N.Y. Frequents the Mulberry St. area & First Ave. & 11th Street, NYC.

FAMILY BACKGROUND : Married to Genevieve Porrazzo; sons: Carmello, Robert Carmello (deceased); mother: Amelia Carito; father: Carmello (deceased); brothers: Joseph, Harry, Basil & Andrew; sisters: Tina (deceased), Mrs. Theresa D'Angelo (deceased), Mrs. Angelina Grandinetti and Mrs. Concetta Verro.

CRIMINAL ASSOCIATES : Andrew Alberti, Eugene Tramaglino, ███████████, Jean Laget, Stephen Armone, Joseph Biondo.

CRIMINAL HISTORY : FBI #1529803   NYCPD #B-169484   Record dates from 1927 and includes five arrests on narcotic charges. Two Federal Narcotic Law convictions.

BUSINESS : Sales Mgr. for North Jersey Cigarette Sales Co., Nutley, N.J.

MODUS OPERANDI : With other Mafiosi, engages in local and interstate narcotic traffic; numbers among his close associates important Mafia members from all sections of NYC.

NAME : August FONTANA

ALIASES : The Champ, August Fontano, Modestino Fontana.

DESCRIPTION : Born 8-9-09 NYC, 5'8", 170 lbs, medium build, brown hair, balding in front, blue eyes.

LOCALITIES FREQUENTED : Resides 123 Mulberry St., NYC. Frequents Mulberry & Hester St., & Jays Restaurant 55 E Houston St., NYC.

FAMILY BACKGROUND : Single; father: Mario; mother: Rosa Marino (both deceased); brother: Anthony; sister: Rosemary.

CRIMINAL ASSOCIATES : Joseph Marino, ███████████, ███████████, ███████████, ███████████ & Angelo Tuminaro

CRIMINAL HISTORY : FBI #257411, NYCPD #70331. Record dates from 1926 and includes arrests for petit larceny, assault & robbery, parole violation, two Federal Narcotic convictions.

BUSINESS : No legitimate occupation.

MODUS OPERANDI : Respected member of the Mafia, part of the "Mulberry Street Mob" directs gambling and wholesale narcotic trafficking.

NAME   : Joseph FOTI

ALIASES   : Chick

DESCRIPTION   : Born 7-21-17 Chester, Pa.,
                      5'8", 150 lbs, medium build,
                      black hair, green eyes, dark
                      complexion.

LOCALITIES   : Resides 1922 Holland Ave,
FREQUENTED   Bronx, NYC, frequents 1st
                      Ave, bet. 109th & 110th Sts,
                      56th, 57th & 58th Sts, bet.
                      Lexington & 1st Aves., all
                      in NYC. The Italian Village,
                      Plattsburg, NY.

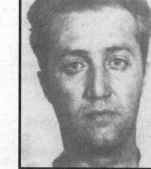

FAMILY   : Father: Carmelo; mother: Concetta Vaccaro, both
BACKGROUND   born in Italy; brothers: Michael and Leonard; sister:
                      Jean.

CRIMINAL   : Nicholas Tolentino, Arnold Barbato, Anthony
ASSOCIATES   Napolitano, Peter Zaccaro, ███████████, all
                      of NYC, and ████████ of Plattsburg, NY.

CRIMINAL   : FBI #2000239, NYCPD #B138369. Record dating from
HISTORY   1935 includes arrests for unlawful entry, assault,
                      assault & robbery, possession of narcotics. Federal
                      narcotic conviction.

BUSINESS   : Laborer.

MODUS   : Trusted Mafia member and was part of an East Harlem,
OPERANDI   NYC, narcotic distribution group, which supplied
                      wholesale quantities of heroin to customers in NYC
                      and Washington, D.C.

NAME   : Paul FRACCACRETA

ALIASES   : Charlie Fraccacreta, Paolo,
                      Charles Montenegro, Charlie
                      The Wop.

DESCRIPTION   : Born 8-13-1898 Naples, Italy,
                      5'3", 185 lbs, stocky build,
                      black-grey hair, black eyes,
                      retired barber, illiterate.
                      Naturalized NY Co., 2-28-27.

LOCALITIES   : Resides 40-18 Junction Blvd,
FREQUENTED   Corona, NY, frequents office
                      of his attorney, Morris
                      Sirofa, 401 B'way, NYC; Fishermans Wharf, 14th St,
                      & Greenwich Village area; all NYC.

FAMILY   : Married Carmela Montenegro; sons: Frank P. & Fred;
BACKGROUND   daughters: Louisa (Mrs. William Watt) & Dolores;
                      father: Frank; mother: Louisa Santina; sister: Ann
                      Scribani.

CRIMINAL   : Anthony Strollo, Vincent Mauro, Michele Miranda,
ASSOCIATES   ███████████, Lorenzo Brescia, Frank Borelli.

CRIMINAL   : FBI #1215348. NYCPD #E6608. Record dating from
HISTORY   1934 includes arrests for doing business under
                      assumed name, state liquor law violation, Inter-
                      nal Revenue violation and burglary.

BUSINESS   : President of Fraccacreta Holding Corp.

MODUS   : "Front" man for Anthony Strollo, Greenwich Village
OPERANDI   Mafia chief. Operates shylock business and the
                      Fraccacreta Holding Corp., which holds mortages on
                      numerous establishments owned by Strollo & other
                      Mafiosi.

NAME	: Anthony FRANCOMANO	
ALIASES	: Tony Franconia, Tony Boots, Thomas Bruno, Dominick Russo	
DESCRIPTION	: Born 4-28-14 NYC; 5'5", 190 lbs, brown eyes, grey hair.	
LOCALITIES FREQUENTED	: Resides 391 Central Park West, NYC; frequents Fordham Road & Grand Concourse, 3rd Avenue & E.149 St., both Bronx, N.Y.	

FAMILY
BACKGROUND   : Wife, Ida Beltrone, deceased;
living with Virginia Kreygen-
baum; son: Joseph; father: Joseph, deceased; mother:
Katherine Muscolino; brothers: Frank, Lawrence,
Pasquale, Thomas and Charles.

CRIMINAL
ASSOCIATES   : Salvatore Santoro, Anthony Napolitano, Nicholas
Tolentino, James Massi, ███████████, Ignazio
and Lorenzo Orlando.

CRIMINAL
HISTORY   : FBI #765907. NYCPD B#379797. Numerous arrests
since 1933 for felonious assault, bookmaking,
violation of N.Y. State narcotic laws.

BUSINESS   : No legitimate business or employment known.

MODUS
OPERANDI   : A close associate of known Mafia narcotic
traffickers, from whom he obtains his supply
of narcotics for re-distribution to smaller
scale traffickers. Also engaged in bookmaking
and policy dealing.

NAME : John FRANZESE

ALIASES : "Sonny", John Francese,
John Frazese, John Carvola

DESCRIPTION : Born 2-6-19 Naples, Italy,
5'10", 180 lbs, black hair,
brown eyes, stocky build,
medium complexion. Derivative
citizenship through parents.

LOCALITIES : Resides 384 Jefferson St,
FREQUENTED   Franklin Square, L.I., NY.
Frequents 769 Club (owned
by brother, Michael) and
Miami Bar, both in Brooklyn, NY.

FAMILY : Divorced from Ann Schiller, who bore him three
BACKGROUND   children; remarried 1959 to Antoinette Capobianco;
father: Carmine "The Lion" (deceased); mother: Maria
Carvola; brothers: Onufrio, Michael & Louis.

CRIMINAL : ████████████, ████████████, Cristofaro Robino,
ASSOCIATES   (deceased), Joseph Vitale, ████████████.

CRIMINAL : FBI #3400301. NYCPD #B164829. Record dates from 1938
HISTORY   and includes arrests for felonious assault, rape,
gambling, disorderly conduct and vagrancy.

BUSINESS : No known legitimate business.

MODUS : Native toughness and deceased father's prestige
OPERANDI   in Mafia are aiding his rise to the top of Brooklyn's
Mafia racketeers controlling narcotics traffic and
other illegal activities.

NAME   : Cosmo FRASCA

ALIASES   : Gus Frasca, Frank Romano

DESCRIPTION   : Born 12-5-07 B'klyn, NY,
                 5'7", 155 lbs, brown hair,
                 brown eyes.

LOCALITIES   : Resides 8850 15th Ave, Brook-
FREQUENTED   lyn, NY. Frequents Endicott
                 Rest., 6908 13th Ave,
                 Frasca's Service Station,
                 1273 66th St, Casa Bianca
                 Bar, 100-05 4th Ave, Larry's
                 Bar, 38 Church Ave, all
                 Brooklyn, New York.

FAMILY   : Wife: Marie; brother: Frank Frasca.
BACKGROUND

CRIMINAL   : Vito Genovese, Michele Miranda, Peter DeFeo,
ASSOCIATES   Giuseppe Profaci, George Smurra, Cassandros
                 Bonasera.

CRIMINAL   : FBI #285760. NYCPD #B82088. Record dating from
HISTORY   1926 includes arrests for rape, grand larceny,
                 assault & robbery, homicide.

BUSINESS   : No legitimate occupation.

MODUS   : Part of a Mafia organization headed by Cassandros
OPERANDI   Bonasera @ The Chief, which controls gambling in
                 the South Brooklyn, Bay Ridge & Bensonhurst sec-
                 tions of Brooklyn and also engages in narcotic
                 smuggling.

He became crime boss when Phillip "Rusty" Rastelli was convicted in 1974 of extortion. When Rastelli got out of jail, he set Galante up and fatally shot him in Brooklyn on July 12, 1979.

NAME : Carmine GALANTE

ALIASES : Camillo Galente, Carmine Galanti, Carmine Galento, Joseph Russell, Louis Volpe.

DESCRIPTION : Born 2-21-10 NYC, 5'5", 168 lbs., grey hair balding, brown eyes.

LOCALITIES FREQUENTED : Resides 274 Marcy Ave., Brooklyn, N.Y., frequents South New Jersey area, Miami Montreal, also makes trips to Sicily.

FAMILY BACKGROUND : Married to Helen Marullo, son: James, daughters: Camilla and Angela, brothers: Sam and Peter, sisters: Mrs. Angela Volpe, Mrs. Josephine Volpe.

CRIMINAL ASSOCIATES : Frank Garofolo, Joe DiPalermo, Vito Genovese, Joe Bonanno, Joe Profaci, Meyer Lansky, all of NYC, Joe Cotroni and ███████████ of Montreal.

CRIMINAL HISTORY : FBI #119495, NYCPD #B 66994, Arrests since 1921 include juvenile delinquent, robbery, assault, homicide, Federal Narcotic Laws. With Joe DiPalermo as an accomplice, believed to have murdered Carlo Tresca in NYC (1943).

BUSINESS : Operates Rosina Costume Co., Brooklyn, N.Y. and Latamer Shipping Co., Manhattan.

MODUS OPERANDI : Attended Binghampton, N.Y., Mafia meeting 1956. An extremely important figure in the international drug traffic, and a ranking Mafia member engaged in terrorist activities. In 1956 he was top representative of American racketeering activities in Montreal.

He started to go straight in 1972 and was working on his memoirs. On his 43rd birthday, April 7, 1972, he was fatally shot five times in Little Italy, NY.

NAME : Joseph GALLO

ALIASES : Joe-the-Blonde

DESCRIPTION : Born 4-6-29 Brooklyn, NY, 5'6", 145 lbs, slim build, brown hair, blue eyes.

LOCALITIES : Resides 639 E 4th St, B'klyn,
FREQUENTED NY. Frequents 108 Beverly Rd, & various sections of Flatbush, Brooklyn.

FAMILY : Single; father: Albert;
BACKGROUND mother: Mary Nunziato; brothers: Ralph & Lawrence; sisters: Carmela Frolera and Jacqueline Meyers.

CRIMINAL : John Oddo, ███████████████, Carmine Lombardozzi,
ASSOCIATES ███████████, ███████████.

CRIMINAL : FBI #120842A. NYCPD #B250889. Record dates from
HISTORY 1947 and includes arrests for dangerous weapon, abduction, possession of gun, burglary, kidnapping and attempted sodomy and felonious assault on police officer.

BUSINESS : Claims to be manager of Jackie's Charcolette, 108 Beverly Rd, Brooklyn, NY.

MODUS : Becoming powerful in the Mafia. A strong-arm man
OPERANDI and labor goon, suspected murderer and trafficker in small arms and narcotics.

NAME	: Lawrence GALLO
ALIASES	: Larry
DESCRIPTION	: Born 11-3-27 Brooklyn, NY, 5'7", 160 lbs, black hair, brown eyes, dark complexion.
LOCALITIES FREQUENTED	: Resides 2031 E 67th St, Brooklyn, NY. Frequents 108 Beverly Rd, B'klyn, NY, and various sections of Flatbush B'klyn, NY.
FAMILY BACKGROUND	: Single: father: Albert Gallo; mother: Mary Nunziato; brothers: Ralph Gallo and Joseph Gallo; sisters: Carmello Frolera, Jacqueline Meyers.
CRIMINAL ASSOCIATES	: ███████████████, Carmine Lombardozzi, ███████ ██████, ███████████████, John Oddo, ████████████, ██████ ███████, Salvatore Pepitone, ███████████.
CRIMINAL HISTORY	: FBI #39253B. NYCPD #B225659. Record dates from 1944 and includes arrests for grand larceny, receiving stolen property, operating a lottery, consorting with criminals, vagrancy, felonious assault & extortion.
BUSINESS	: Claims to work as a counterman in Jackies Charcolette, 108 Beverly Rd, Brooklyn, NY.
MODUS OPERANDI	: With his older brother, Joseph and other Mafia hoodlums, engages in gambling, narcotic trafficking and numerous other illicit enterprises. Strong arm man and suspected murderer.

Galluccio claimed to have given Al Capone the scars on his face. He died around 1966.

NAME : Frank GALLUCCIO

ALIASES : None

DESCRIPTION : Born 4-14-1898 Naples, Italy, 5'2", 130 lbs, small build, blue eyes, grey hair, light complexion.

LOCALITIES FREQUENTED : Resides 264 6th St, B'klyn, NY. Frequents Mike Esposito's Cafe, Union St, & 4th Ave, James Mancarruso's Bar, 216 4th Ave, all B'klyn, NY.

FAMILY BACKGROUND : Married to Sylvia Spear (common-law) in 1930, and they are childless; brothers: Salvatore, Charles, and Robert (deceased); sister: Tessie Minniuccio; father: Vincent; mother: Josephine Baccardi; parents deceased.

CRIMINAL ASSOCIATES : ███████████████, Alfonso Marzano, ███████████, Anthony Carfano (deceased), ███████████, ███████ ███████████, Joseph Schipani.

CRIMINAL HISTORY : FBI #1646961. NYCPD #B50997. Record dates from 1915 and includes arrests for possession of narcotics, receiving stolen property, robbery, burglary and felonious assault.

BUSINESS : No legitimate occupation.

MODUS OPERANDI : A recognized leader in the Mafia. Finances large scale operations in the narcotic traffic.

He took over the family in 1957 and assassinated both Joe Colombo and Joe Gallo. Gambino died of a heart attack on October 15, 1976.

NAME : Carlo GAMBINO

ALIASES : Carlo Gambrino, Carlo Gambrieno, Don Carlo

DESCRIPTION : Born 8-24-02 Palermo, Sicily, an alien, 5'7", 200 lbs., brown eyes, black-grey hair.

LOCALITIES FREQUENTED : Resides 2230 Ocean Parkway, Brooklyn, N. Y. Frequents Carroll Paper Products Co; and Bensonhurst section of Brooklyn; also Italian section of East Bronx, and Miami, Fla.

FAMILY BACKGROUND : Married to his 1st Cousin Vincenza Castellana, son Tom married to Frances Lucchese (daughter of Tom Lucchese), father: Thomas, mother: Felicia Castellana, brother: Paolo, sister: Mrs. Giuseppina Giammona.

CRIMINAL ASSOCIATES : Lucky Luciano and Santo Sorge (deportees), Tom Lucchese, Hugo Rossi, Paolo Gambino (brother), Jack Scarpulla, Meyer Lansky, Scalice brothers, all of New York City.

CRIMINAL HISTORY : FBI #334450, NYCPD-B #128760. Arrests from 1930 include larceny, federal liquor laws, and violation I&NS laws.

BUSINESS : Owns Carroll Paper Products Company, Brooklyn. Is a member of S.G.S. Associates, a labor consultant firm in Manhattan.

MODUS OPERANDI : Attended Apalachin Mafia meeting 1957 as one of the Mafia leaders from NYC. One of the most powerful Mafia leaders in the U. S. With his brother Paolo has been involved in large scale narcotic and alien smuggling.

NAME   : Paolo GAMBINO

ALIASES   : Don Paolo

DESCRIPTION   : Born 11-20-04 Palermo,
                Sicily, naturalized citizen,
                5'7", 210 lbs, brown eyes,
                black-grey hair.

LOCALITIES   : Resides 1219 E. 12th St.,
FREQUENTED   Brooklyn, NY. Frequents
                East Bronx area of NYC and
                Coney Island area of
                Brooklyn. Makes trips to
                Sicily.

FAMILY   : Married to Caterina Castellana (who is his 1st
BACKGROUND   cousin), has 2 sons and 2 daughters, father:
                Thomas, mother: Felicia Castellana, brother:
                Carlo, sister: Mrs. Giuseppina Giammona

CRIMINAL   : Hugo Rossi, Jack Scarpulla, Sam Accardi, Carlo
ASSOCIATES   Gambino (brother), Frank Scalice (dead), Joe
                Profaci, Willie Locascio, all of NYC. Lucky
                Luciano (deportee).

CRIMINAL   : FBI #1667871, Yonkers, NY, PD#F 8164. Arrests
HISTORY   since 1929 include suspicion of a felony and
                conviction for Federal Liquor Laws.

BUSINESS   : Owns Blue Star Meat Market, 40-10 Main Street,
                Flushing, L.I., N.Y.

MODUS   : He and his brother Carlo are high ranking Mafia
OPERANDI   leaders and important large scale narcotic and
                alien smuggling suspects.

```
NAME          : Frank GAROFOLO

ALIASES       : Frank Carroll, Frank
                Garafola, Frank Garofola

DESCRIPTION   : Born 9-10-91, Castellammare,
                Sicily, naturalized 9-8-31
                NYC, 5'7", grey hair, eyes
                brown, wears glasses, dis-
                tinguished looking.

LOCALITIES    : Resides at 339 E. 58th St.,
FREQUENTED      NYC and P.O. Box 1370 Mer-
                ced, Calif.

FAMILY        : Father, Vincent, mother,
BACKGROUND      Caterina Cocco (both dead), brother, Vincent.

CRIMINAL      : Robert Dionisio, Joe DiPalermo, William Tocco, Tom
ASSOCIATES      Lucchese, all Mafia members who attended Apalachin
                Mafia meeting 1957.

CRIMINAL      : NYC PD# B66994, believed to have ordered the murder
HISTORY         of Carlo Tresca at NYC in 1943; arrested 1926 NYC
                for bootlegging.

BUSINESS      : Owner of High Grade Packing Co., Merced, Calif.

MODUS         : Attended Binghampton, N.Y., Mafia meeting in 1956;
OPERANDI        is one of the top ranking Mafia in the U.S. and
                Sicily, and was considered an enforcer and execu-
                tioner.
```

NAME   : Usche GELB

ALIASES   : Solly Gordon, Saul Gelb,
                  Kreisberg, King, Geld,
                  Edward S.A. Jordon.

DESCRIPTION   : Born 3-27-1897 Dembica,
                  Austria. Jewish, 5'7½" 16?
                  lbs, white hair, brown eyes,
                  glasses. Illegal Alien.

LOCALITIES   : Resides 545 West End Ave,
FREQUENTED   NYC. Frequented Lafayette St.
                  machinery center, midtown
                  rest's, & clubs. Summer home
                  Tennanah Lake, NY.

FAMILY   : Married Ethel Egan; father: Tobias Samuel Gelb;
BACKGROUND   mother: Feiger Krantz (both deceased); brother:
                  Hyman; sisters: Mary, Belle & Mrs. Bertha Sterza.

CRIMINAL   : Anthony Vellucci, Nathan Behrman, ██████████,
ASSOCIATES   Joseph Orsini, Morris Taubman, Salvatore Shillitani.

CRIMINAL   : FBI #35989. NYCPD #B53908. Record dates from 1913
HISTORY   and includes arrests for juvenile delinquency, dis-
                  orderly conduct, felonious assault, dangerous weapon,
                  perjury, stolen bonds, federal narcotic conviction.
                  Currently incarcerated for narcotic conspiracy.

BUSINESS   : Machinery Salesman. Owned florist shop.

MODUS   : In association with top level Mafia racketeers, he
OPERANDI   operated a narcotic smuggling and distribution ring
                  which supplied untold quantities of heroin throughout
                  the U.S.; top echelon racketeer & drug trafficker
                  for past thirty years.

NAME   : Pasquale GENESE

ALIASES   : Pat, Patsy Jerome

DESCRIPTION   : Born 3-3-11 NYC, 5'8 3/4",
                 190 lbs, medium build, brown
                 grey hair, brown eyes, dark
                 complexion.

LOCALITIES   : Resides 1219 Colgate Ave.,
FREQUENTED   Bronx, NY, frequents 1961
                 3rd Ave; Garden Pharmacy,
                 50th & Bway; candy store,
                 238 E 116 St, NYC, Roose-
                 velt Raceway, Westbury, L.I.

FAMILY   : Separated from wife Catherine Popp; son: Paul;
BACKGROUND   father: Pasquale; mother: Elizabeth Sarro, (both
                 deceased); brother: Joseph; sisters: Mildred,
                 Josephine.

CRIMINAL   : Alfred Felice, Salvatore Santoro, Frank Luciano,
ASSOCIATES   Nicholas Martello, DeMartino Brothers, Joseph Vento.

CRIMINAL   : FBI #1200745, NYCPD #B 113022. Record dates from
HISTORY   1933 and includes arrests for sodomy, vagrancy,
                 bookmaking and narcotic conspiracy.

BUSINESS   : No legitimate occupation known

MODUS   : Middle Echelon Mafioso who was once quite prominent
OPERANDI   in the narcotic traffic but recently has appeared
                 to confine his activities to gambling.

464

NAME   : Joseph GENNARO

ALIASES   : Pete Russo, Joe-the-Wop

DESCRIPTION   : Born 5-8-10 NYC, 5'9", 198
                  lbs, grey hair, brown eyes,
                  fair complexion, heavy build

LOCALITIES   : Resides 475 Franklin Roose-
FREQUENTED   velt Drive, NYC. Frequents
                  NY racetracks, Elizabeth,
                  Hester, Mulberry & Grand
                  Sts, NYC, NY nightclubs.

FAMILY   : Wife: Nellie Rinaldo; daug-
BACKGROUND   ter: Josephine; father: Dominiano; mother: Josephine
                  Pulpe; brothers: Charles, Anthony, Sam; (all in Italy)
                  sisters: Lucy, Jennie; (all in Italy).

CRIMINAL   : Vincent Carrao, Frank Caruso, Vincent Gigante,
ASSOCIATES   Alfred Guido, ███████████████, Joseph Luparelli.

CRIMINAL   : FBI #1252430, NYCPD B#144909. Record dates back to
HISTORY   1936 includes arrests for vagrancy, and conviction
                  of State & Federal Narcotic violations.

BUSINESS   : Behind-the-scenes owner of several NY night clubs.
                  A leading member of the "Mulberry Street Mob", a
                  Mafia organization which engages in the narcotic,
                  policy, alcohol & other rackets.

NAME   : Anthony S. GENTILE

ALIASES   : Tony

DESCRIPTION   : Born 10-23-05 NYC, 5'6", 210
                  lbs, obese appearance, dark
                  brown hair greying, bald on
                  top. NOTE: Photo taken 1930.

LOCALITIES   : Resides 323 E 108 St, NYC,
FREQUENTED   frequents Mulberry St, area
                  NYC, Lizzi's Restaurant, 116
                  & 1st Ave, NYC, & NY race
                  tracks.

FAMILY   : Married to Rose Quagliato; sons: Thomas, Dominick,
BACKGROUND   Anthony, Robert & Joseph; daughters: Patricia & Mrs.
                  Paul (Mary) Libertelli.

CRIMINAL   : ███████████████, Angelo Tuminaro, ██████████████,
ASSOCIATES   Joseph Russo, Anthony Strollo, Sam Monastersky,
                  Anthony Marchitto.

CRIMINAL   : FBI #1289462, NYCPD #B85098. Has only one arrest,
HISTORY   for grand larceny.

BUSINESS   : Machinist, Oneida Paper Products, Clifton, NJ.

MODUS   : In the past has worked for Mafia chief Anthony
OPERANDI   Strollo in organizing and controlling hiring and
                  racketeering activities on the NJ, waterfront; is
                  currently known as a contact man for more import-
                  ant Mafia members.

NAME : Joseph GERNIE

ALIASES : Joseph Yanni, John Gernie

DESCRIPTION : Born 8-4-21 at N.Y.C.
5'9", 180 lbs, stocky build,
brown hair, brown eyes, dark
complexion, tattoos both arms.

LOCALITIES : Resided at 336 E. 120th St.,
FREQUENTED NYC, frequented vicinity of
76th & Broadway, 86th St. &
3rd Avenue, N.Y.C.

FAMILY : Married to Mary Brancaccio ;
BACKGROUND son: Joseph; daughter: Ann; mother: Erna Manone;
sister: Frances Maresca; half-brother: Thomas
Angelos; half-sister: Pauline Angelos.

CRIMINAL : Anthony Strollo, ████████████, Phillip Buzzeo,
ASSOCIATES Michael Nicoline, Vincent Mauro.

CRIMINAL : FBI #1851322. NYCPD #B167697. Arrests since 1938
HISTORY include felonious assault, burglary, larceny,
gambling and causing explosion with intent to kill.
1957 sentenced to ten years for Federal narcotic
violation at New York City.

BUSINESS : Had wartime employment as longshoreman, but no
recent legitimate employment.

MODUS : An important member of the Mafia narcotic
OPERANDI trafficking and union racketeering organization
in New York City and vicinity. Is a professional
strong-arm man and suspected killer for the Mafia
mob controlled by Anthony Strollo.

NAME : Vincent GIGANTE

ALIASES : "The Chin", "Chin Chin"

DESCRIPTION : Born 3-29-28 in N.Y.C. 5'11", 263 lbs, brown hair and eyes.

LOCALITIES FREQUENTED : Resides 206 Thompson St., NYC Frequents lower East Side and Greenwich Village areas of New York City.

FAMILY BACKGROUND : Married to Olympia Grippa; children: Yolanda, Rose-Ann, Salvatore, Andrew; father: Salvatore; mother: Yolande Scotta; brothers: Pasquale, Mario, Ralph, Louis.

CRIMINAL ASSOCIATES : Vito Genovese, Anthony Strollo, Michael Miranda, Gus Frasca, John Stoppelli, Carmine Galante.

CRIMINAL HISTORY : FBI #5020214. NYCPD-B#231328. Arrests since 1945 include grand larceny, criminally receiving, arson and attempted murder.

BUSINESS : Former professional boxer. No legitimate current employment.

MODUS OPERANDI : A rapidly rising younger member of the Mafia who has gained recognition by carrying out strong-arm assignments for Mafia chief Vito Genovese. In 1957 he was arrested for the attempted murder of the notorious Frank Costello.

NAME : Alexander GIGLIO

ALIASES : Sandrino Giglio, Sandrio
Giglio, Sal Giglio.

DESCRIPTION : Born 7-13-1906 NYC, 5'6",170
lbs, brown hair, brown eyes.
US Passport 267490 issued
2-12-54, renewed 1-9-57.

LOCALITIES : Resides 6414 15 Ave.,B'klyn,
FREQUENTED NY. Frequents Giglio Theater,
277 Canal Street, NYC. Makes
frequent trips to Italy,
Toronto & Montreal, Canada.

FAMILY : Married Louise Pace; daughters: Clementine & Mary
BACKGROUND Gemma; father: Clemente (deceased); mother: Gemma
Cunico; sister: Adele Giglio.

CRIMINAL : Fortunato Papa, Cotroni Brothers of Montreal,
ASSOCIATES Antoine D'Agostino, ▬▬▬▬▬▬, Joseph
Zicarelli, ▬▬▬▬▬▬, Giuseppe Doto.

CRIMINAL : No known criminal record.
HISTORY

BUSINESS : Partner of Salvatore Casolaro in Casolaro Films
Dist. Co. & Giglio Theater, 277 Canal St., N.Y.C.
Also employed by Fortunato Papa's radio station,
WHOM.

MODUS : A highly trusted and influential Mafia member.
OPERANDI Closely associated for many years with the notorious
Cotroni family.

NAME	: Salvatore GIGLIO
ALIASES	: King, Phillips, Gigli, Salvatore Galante
DESCRIPTION	: Born 9-29-06 NYC, 5'5", 140 lbs., black-grey hair, brown eyes, dark complexion.
LOCALITIES FREQUENTED	: Resides 2760 Grand Concourse Bronx, N.Y. Frequents Manhattan News Co., 627 W. 42 St., NYC and Montreal, Canada.

FAMILY BACKGROUND	: Married to Mary Fanale, daughter: Eileen, father is Joseph and mother is Caterina Tonuzzo, brothers: John, Charles, Jack, sister: Mrs. Elizabeth Gioia.
CRIMINAL ASSOCIATES	: Carmine Galante, Joe DiPalermo, John Petrone, Joe Notaro, all of NYC, Joe Cotroni and ███████ ███████ of Montreal, Joe Zicarelli of N.J., Rosario Mancuso of Utica, New York.
CRIMINAL HISTORY	: FBI #1967931, NYCPD #B 154368. Arrests since 1937 include one conviction for violation Federal Narcotic Laws.
BUSINESS	: Official of E. and W. Trucking Co., 131 Varick St., NYC, and Salesman for Theta Electronics Co., Harrisburg, Pennsylvania.
MODUS OPERANDI	: A major local and interstate narcotic trafficker who is closely associated with known Mafia traffickers.

NAME   : Giorgio GIGLIOTTI

ALIASES   : George Gellitte, George C.
                  Gillette.

DESCRIPTION   : Born 12-12-10 Dunmore, Pa.
                  5'8", 203 lbs., brown eyes,
                  black-grey hair, usually has
                  a mustache.

LOCALITIES   : Resides 667 77th St., Brook-
FREQUENTED   lyn, N.Y. and also at 414
                  Arbutus Ave., Staten Island,
                  N.Y. Currently (1959) incar-
                  cerated for violation Federal
                  Liquor Laws.

FAMILY   : Wife: Angelina Doto (sister of Joe Doto); daughters:
BACKGROUND   Georgiana & Mrs. Joan Smith; father: Pasquale;
                  mother: Carmela Mazzola (both deceased).

CRIMINAL   : Salvatore G. Maiorana, Joe DiPalermo, Pete DiPalermo,
ASSOCIATES   Cassandros S. Bonasera, all of NYC; ▮▮▮▮▮▮ & Lucky
                  Luciano of Italy.

CRIMINAL   : FBI #274337. Arrests since 1927 include grand
HISTORY   larceny, assault & robbery, conspiracy & transport-
                  ation forged securities, and convictions for Inter-
                  nal Revenue Laws.

BUSINESS   : Occasionally employed as a butcher.

MODUS   : With other Mafia associates was engaged in operating
OPERANDI   illegal "stills" and dealing in counterfeit secur-
                  ities.

```
NAME          : Salvatore GIORDANO

ALIASES       : Jimmy Costello, Marino,
                Martin, Russo, Pappo

DESCRIPTION   : Born 10-19-11 in NYC, 5'11",
                193 lbs, black hair, brown
                eyes, ruddy complexion, heavy
                build.

LOCALITIES    : Resides 525 E 89th St., NYC,
FREQUENTED      frequents Jim & Andy's Bar,
                116 W 48th St., Towncrest
                Bar, 123 W 49th St., Big
                Dollar Bar, 34th & 3rd all
                NYC.

FAMILY        : Married Geraldine Vincents.  No Children, father:
BACKGROUND      Anthony; mother: Josephine Botecoitti; brother:
                Frank.

CRIMINAL      : Salvatore Santoro, Lucien Ignaro, ███████████,
ASSOCIATES      Joseph DiPalermo, Harold Meltzer.

CRIMINAL      : FBI #394265, NYCPD #B83080, record dates from 1931
HISTORY         and includes arrests for assault & robbery, gun,
                proprietor disorderly house, OPA violation.  Federal
                Narcotic conviction.  As of 10/59 state fugitive
                harboring case pending & Federal Narcotic Case pend-
                ing.

BUSINESS      : Has an interest in Big Dollar Bar, 34th St & 3rd Ave,
                New York City.

MODUS         : With other Mafiosi distributes wholesale quantities
OPERANDI        of heroin locally and interstate.
```

In 1964, he was convicted of conspiracy to help transport heroin into the United States.

NAME : Anthony GRANZA

ALIASES : Tony Skunge, Tony Scallo

DESCRIPTION : Born 3-25-15, Oneida, NY,
5'3", 140 lbs, black hair,
grey eyes, medium build,
medium complexion.

LOCALITIES : Resides 2854 Kingsbridge
FREQUENTED Terrace, Bronx, NY., frequents East Harlem area of
NYC, particularly 107th St.,
& 1st Ave., 104th & 1st Ave.

FAMILY : Wife: Fanny Bifano; daughters: Rosemarie & Theresa;
BACKGROUND father: Joseph; mother: Theresa Bieni (both deceased);
brother: Frank; sisters: Nina Lovino & Mary
Benintendi (wife of Joseph Benintendi).

CRIMINAL : Joseph Benintendi, Joseph Casablanca, Nicholas
ASSOCIATES Corsaro, Benny Coniglio, Rosario Rinaldi.

CRIMINAL : FBI #2042937, NYCPD B#224486. Record dates back to
HISTORY 1940 and includes convictions for violation of state
and Federal Narcotic Laws. On parole until 1961 in
connection with state narcotic conviction.

BUSINESS : Before incarceration in 1951 had no legitimate
source of income. Now, for parole purposes, employed
as general worker by Travel Craft Press, 830 Broadway, NYC.

MODUS : A trusted member of the Mafia who has been engaged
OPERANDI in large scale local & interstate trafficking for
many years. Since release from prison has been
awarded a large area in which to carry on illicit
activities including narcotics and gambling.

473

He died on July 16, 1979 after being shot by Joey Zasa.

NAME   : Frank GRECO

ALIASES   : John Rizzo

DESCRIPTION   : Born 3-4-19 NYC, 5'8", 245
                   lbs, heavy build, black hair
                   brown eyes.

LOCALITIES   : Resides 1057 Brinsmade Ave,
FREQUENTED   Bronx, NY. Frequents Andy's
                   Colonial Tavern, 116th St,
                   & 1st Ave, & East Harlem
                   area in general, NYC.

FAMILY   : Single; father: Gerennaro;
BACKGROUND   mother: Marie Saviola (both born in Italy & now de-
                   ceased); brother: Louis; sister: Antoinette Capozzoli.

CRIMINAL   : Anthony Salerno; Joseph Tortorici, Joseph Rao,
ASSOCIATES   Michael Coppola, Joseph Stracci, Fred Salerno.

CRIMINAL   : No FBI # assigned. NYCPD #E33615. Record dates
HISTORY   from 1940 and includes arrests for policy & U.S.
                   wagering tax violation.

BUSINESS   : Painter by trade.

MODUS   : With other Mafia members operates policy banks
OPERANDI   throughout NY area.

He remained an active member of the Pittston Family into the 1980s.

NAME : Anthony Frank GUARNIERI

ALIASES : "Gov", "Guv", "Guy"

DESCRIPTION : Born 5-1-10, Utica, N.Y. 5'8", 180 lbs, gray hair, bald on top, hazel eyes, ruddy complexion.

LOCALITIES FREQUENTED : Resides 3619 Royal Road, Johnson City, N.Y. Frequents Binghamton, NY, area.

FAMILY BACKGROUND : Married to Ann Longo; no children; four brothers: Joseph, Robert, John, Leo; father: John; mother: Vita Donato Peipoli (both deceased).

CRIMINAL ASSOCIATES : Russell Bufalino, ██████████, Patsy Sciortino, Joseph Profaci, Joseph Barbara, Jr., Angelo Sciandra, James Plumeri, Sam Monachino.

CRIMINAL HISTORY : FBI #5073273. NYCPD-B#319216. Arrests since 1945 include gambling, illegal possession of firearms and felonious assault.

BUSINESS : Has interest in Tri-City Dress Co., Binghamton, N.Y., and Owego Textile Mfg. Co., Owego, N.Y.

MODUS OPERANDI : Attended Apalachin Mafia meeting 1957. Was right-hand man for the late Mafia chief, Joseph Barbara, Sr. Is closely associated with most of the important Mafiosi who are active in garment racketeering in the Binghamton, N.Y., and Pennsylvania areas.

NAME	: Bartolo GUCCIA	
ALIASES	: Bartallo Gucci, Bartalo Vicio, Bartolo Vecia.	
DESCRIPTION	: Born 12-26-91, Castellammare, Sicily. 5'4", 150 lbs, grey hair, brown eyes, wears glasses. Naturalized 1-11-27 at Binghamton, N.Y. I & NS #C-2-478-228.	

LOCALITIES   : Resides 208 Vermont Avenue,
FREQUENTED   Endicott, N.Y. Frequents
                  Endicott, Binghamton and
                  Johnson City, N.Y.

FAMILY   : Married to Vita Scibilia; children: Jennie, Francis,
BACKGROUND   Andrea, Joseph and Vincent; brother: Antonio Vecia;
                  mother: Giovanna Vecia.

CRIMINAL   : Patsy Turrigiano, Emanuel Zicari, Anthony Guarnieri,
ASSOCIATES   Ignatius Cannone, Joseph Barbara, Jr.

CRIMINAL   : FBI #1183087. Binghamton PD #1130. Arrests since
HISTORY   1916 include possession of a revolver, breaking and
                  entering, bootlegging and murder.

BUSINESS   : Operates fish business at Endicott, N. Y.

MODUS   : Attended Apalachin Mafia meeting 1957. Was a boot-
OPERANDI   legger during the prohibition era and is closely
                  associated with all Mafiosi in the Endicott area.

```
NAME          : Alfred GUIDO

ALIASES       : Ralph Petrolli, Iggy, Eggy

DESCRIPTION   : Born NYC 9-26-11, 5'8", 160
                lbs, medium build, black hair
                brown eyes, sallow complex-
                ion, 3" scar right arm.

LOCALITIES    : Resides 2516 Bedford Ave.,
FREQUENTED      Brooklyn, NY, frequents
                Lower East Side, NYC, also
                Turf Bar 51st & Broadway,
                NYC.
```

```
FAMILY        : Wife: Josephine Cuccinello; children: Katherine,
BACKGROUND      Richard, Jessie; father: Angelo; mother: Catherine
                Signetti; father remarried to Rose Isola; half-
                brothers: Albert & Alex; half-sister: Marie.

CRIMINAL      : ████████████, ████████████████, ███████████,
ASSOCIATES      ████████████.

CRIMINAL      : FBI #779756, NYCPD #B121495.  Has a record dating
HISTORY         from 1934 including arrests for violation national
                motor theft act, forgery of U.S. bonds & vagrancy;
                has two State & 2 Federal Narcotic convictions.

BUSINESS      : No legitimate employment.

MODUS         : In association with other Mafiosi wholesales
OPERANDI        heroin on Lower East Side of New York.
```

```
NAME            : Robert Angelo GUIPPONE

ALIASES         : Giapone, "Sonny", "Fat Sonny"

DESCRIPTION     : Born 4-2-30 in N.Y.C.
                  5'8½", 285 lbs, black hair,
                  brown eyes, scar over left
                  eye, mole left side of nose.

LOCALITIES      : Resides 2420 Cambreling Ave.,
FREQUENTED        Bronx,N.Y.  Frequents 187th
                  St. & Cambreling Ave., the
                  Capri Lounge and Southern
                  Blvd. & Fordham Rd., Bronx.

FAMILY          : Unmarried.  Father: Dominick; mother: Mary Cienelli;
BACKGROUND        brother: Daniel; sister: Marie Muschio.

CRIMINAL        : Anthony Carminati, Michael Galgano, Anthony Castaldi,
ASSOCIATES        Rocco Sancinella, Joseph Ambrosini, Rocco Mazzie,
                  Dominick Carminati and Joseph Valachi.

CRIMINAL        : FBI #535872A.  NYCPD B#337619.  Arrests date from
HISTORY           1950, including counterfeiting, assault & battery
                  and N. Y. State narcotic laws.

BUSINESS        : No legitimate business or employment.

MODUS           : A major wholesale interstate narcotic trafficker.
OPERANDI          Is one of the younger Mafia members controlling
                  gambling and narcotics in the Bronx, N.Y., area.
```

NAME : Salvatore HAMEL

ALIASES : Salvatore Ameli, Sam Ameli

DESCRIPTION : Born 10-1-16, Porto Empedocle,
Agrigento, Sicily, Italy,
5'4", 175 lbs, stocky build,
dark complexion, grey-black
hair, brown eyes, small scar
on chin, issued U.S. Passport #137098 on 9-20-46 by
the U.S. Department of State

LOCALITIES : Resides 1235 54th St., Brook-
FREQUENTED lyn, NY, frequents Elizabeth
& Kenmare Sts., Mott St., the Hawaiian Moonlighters
Social Club, 141 Mulberry St., all in NYC.

FAMILY : Wife: Josephine Baio; children: Pasquale & Marianne;
BACKGROUND father: Pasquale; mother: Marianne Zicari, (both de-
ceased); brothers: Paolo & Carlo residing Porto
Empedocle, Sicily; sister: Rosa Valenti residing
Agrigento, Sicily.

CRIMINAL : Vincent Corrao, ███████████████, ███████████████,
ASSOCIATES ████████████████.

CRIMINAL : FBI #830034B, subject's only arrest was in 1954 for
HISTORY violation of Federal Narcotic Laws. 2-3-55 he was
sentenced to $3\frac{1}{2}$ years and 3 years probation. On
probation until 2-3-61.

BUSINESS : Union presser. Employed by Joleo Dress Mfg. Co.,
555 8th Ave., NYC.

MODUS : Part of the Mulberry Street Mafia mob, dealing
OPERANDI in wholesale quantities of heroin.

NAME : Lawrence IAROSSI

ALIASES : Larry Nose

DESCRIPTION : Born 9-18-24 NYC, 5'9½", 210
lbs, brown hair, brown eyes,
heavy build, sallow complexion.

LOCALITIES : Resides 2235 Quimby Ave,
FREQUENTED   Bronx, NY. Frequents social
club 3rd Ave, 116-117th St,
NYC, 145th & Brook Ave.,
Bronx, New York.

FAMILY : Married Mafaldo Tamborino; sons: Vincent, Michael,
BACKGROUND   Nicholas; father: Frank; mother: Concetta Pompeo;
brother: Joseph; sister: Anna Scottozo.

CRIMINAL : Frank Borelli, Anthony Mancuso, Fiore Siano, Arthur
ASSOCIATES   Leo, Vito Panzarino, Joseph Bendenelli.

CRIMINAL : FBI #3567370. NYCPD #218116. Record dates from 1941
HISTORY   and includes arrests for burglary, wayward minor,
burglars tools, possession of narcotics, Federal
narcotic conviction.

BUSINESS : No legitimate occupation.

MODUS : Important East Harlem, NYC, member of the Mafia,
OPERANDI   dealing in wholesale quantities of heroin locally
and interstate.

NAME	: Benjamin INDIVIGLIO
ALIASES	: Benedetto Indiviglia, Benny Indivielia, Benny the Cringe.
DESCRIPTION	: Born 7-16-21 NYC, 5'11", 180 lbs, black hair, brown eyes, has acne marks on both sides of face.
LOCALITIES FREQUENTED	: Resides 353 W 44th St, NYC. Frequents Dell's Cafe & Opera Inn, both in NYC.

FAMILY BACKGROUND	: Father: Giuseppe; mother: Felicia (Fannie) Marino; living with paramour Rose Pizzaro @ Diaz; brothers: Joseph, John and Salvatore.
CRIMINAL ASSOCIATES	: ████████, ██████████████████████████████, ███████████████████████, ███████████████, ███████, ████████, ████████████████, Michael Altimari, Nicholas Bonina.
CRIMINAL HISTORY	: FBI #4333204, NYCPD B#227037. Arrests since 1945 include desertion, assault, felonious assault and conviction for Federal Narcotic Laws.
BUSINESS	: Owns & operates Dell's Cafe, 918 8th Ave, & Opera Inn, 726 8th Ave, both in NYC.
MODUS OPERANDI	: With other Mafia narcotic traffickers engages in narcotic smuggling and interstate distribution.

NAME   : Cirino INDIVIGLIO

ALIASES   : John Indiviglia

DESCRIPTION   : Born 3-6-15 NYC, 5'6", 155
                   lbs, brown eyes, black hair,
                   neat dresser, glasses.

LOCALITIES   : Resides 12 W 4th St, NYC,
FREQUENTED   frequents Silver Rail Rest.,
                   55 W 8th St, & various Green-
                   wich Village (NYC) bars.

FAMILY   : Wife: Rosemary; one child;
BACKGROUND   father: Giuseppe; mother:
                   Felicia (Fannie) Marino; brothers: Salvatore,
                   Joseph & Benjamin; sister: Sally (Mrs. Anthony)
                   Manaco.

CRIMINAL   : ████████████, Paul Zerbo, Anthony Castaldi,
ASSOCIATES   Stephen & ████████ Puco, Charles Curcio.

CRIMINAL   : FBI # 463518A. NYCPD #B288366. Only arrest was in
HISTORY   1950 for grand larceny.

BUSINESS   : Owns Schwab Fashions, 2nd Ave, & 4th St, NYC with
                   brother Benjamin. Former partner allegedly killed
                   by Benjamin.

MODUS   : Mafia narcotic smuggler and distributor. Has
OPERANDI   reputation as dangerous criminal and cold-blooded
                   killer.

He was actor Joe Pantoliano's step-father.

NAME	: Florio ISABELLA
ALIASES	: Flo, Florindo, Fino, William Fino.
DESCRIPTION	: Born 3-30-11 NYC 5'9", 165 lbs, blue eyes, black-grey hair, 1½" scar left forehead.
LOCALITIES FREQUENTED	: Resided 101 Chrystie St, NYC. Frequented Lower East Side & Greenwich Village areas of NYC, Copacabana Night Club, NYC, Grand Mark Bar, St. Marks Ave, & Grand St, B'klyn, NY. Currently (1960) incarcerated.
FAMILY BACKGROUND	: Married Marsha Jones; father: Joseph Angelo (deceased); mother: Elizabeth Fino (remarried, now Mrs. Thomas Pennachio).
CRIMINAL ASSOCIATES	: Joseph & Charles DiPalermo, Anthony Mirra, Alfred Embarrato, ▓▓▓▓▓▓▓.
CRIMINAL HISTORY	: FBI #467320. NYCPD #B105498. Record dates from 1932 and includes arrests for counterfeiting, receiving stolen goods, gambling, interstate theft. Three Federal narcotic convictions. Currently (1960) serving 15 yrs narcotic sentence.
BUSINESS	: Operated luncheonette.
MODUS OPERANDI	: With other important NYC Mafiosi, engaged in large scale local & interstate narcotic traffic. Also had bookmaking & shylocking operations.

NAME : Samuel KASSOP

ALIASES : Sammy the Jew, Sam Cass,
Samuel Kass.

DESCRIPTION : Born 10-26-11 NYC, Jewish,
5'9", 185 lbs, stocky, black
hair, brown eyes.

LOCALITIES : Resides 96-09 66th Ave,
FREQUENTED Queens, NY. Frequents Lower
East Side and Upper East
Harlem areas of NYC. Current-
ly incarcerated.

FAMILY : Married Evelyn Reiss; daughter: Adrianne Sacks;
BACKGROUND father: Isadore Kassop (deceased); mother: Rose
Meshlam; brothers: Dr. Harry Kassop, Benjamin Kassop.

CRIMINAL : John Ormento, Carmine Locascio, Joseph Vento, Frank
ASSOCIATES Borelli, Rocco Mazzie, Arthur Repola, Anthony Ciccone,
Saro Mogavero, Anthony Castaldi.

CRIMINAL : FBI #425901A. NYCPD B#304312. Has been arrested twice
HISTORY for narcotic violation. Currently serving $7\frac{1}{2}$ - 15 yrs
on State narcotic conviction.

BUSINESS : No legitimate employment.

MODUS : Though Jewish he has always associated almost ex-
OPERANDI clusively with East Harlem (NYC) Mafia racketeers.
Distributed wholesale quantities of heroin in NYC
and interstate with assistance of his Mafia associates.

NAME	: Joseph La BARBARA
ALIASES	: Joseph Barone, Joe Labar, Joe LaBarba, Joseph LaBarbera
DESCRIPTION	: Born 8-17-12 Independence, Iowa, 5'7½", 150 lbs, grey eyes, brown hair, medium build.
LOCALITIES FREQUENTED	: Resides 488 West Ave., Buffalo, NY. Frequents the Why Not Bar, Santores Restaurant and the Park Edge Restaurant, all in downtown Buffalo. Visits Chicago, Illinois.
FAMILY BACKGROUND	: Wife: Angelina; son: Michael; father: Dominick; mother: Josephine, (both deceased); brother: Michael.
CRIMINAL ASSOCIATES	: ██████████, ██████████, ██████████, ██████████, Frank Borelli.
CRIMINAL HISTORY	: FBI #383602, Buffalo PD# 25152. Record dates from 1930 and includes arrests for attempted extortion, grand larceny, robbery, assault and violation narcotic laws.
BUSINESS	: He occasionally works on small construction jobs. No steady employment.
MODUS OPERANDI	: He is a hold-up man and a killer for the Mafia. He engages in every type of underworld activity. On occasion obtains heroin and cocaine from Borelli Mob and distributes in wholesale quantities in NY and Chicago.

NAME   : Charles LA CASCIA

ALIASES   : Charles Lo Cascia, Lo Cascio

DESCRIPTION   : Born 2-3-16 Detroit, Mich,
                 5'5½", 136 lbs, slender
                 build, brown eyes, brown
                 hair, olive complexion,
                 small mustache.

LOCALITIES   : Resides 132 Jefferson St,
FREQUENTED   B'klyn, NY. Frequents Pol-
                 izzi's Bar & Grill, Wilson
                 Ave, Lounge Cafe & Enchanted
                 Hour Bar at Myrtle & Wycoff
                 Aves., Peoples Democratic Club, 130 Central, all in
                 Brooklyn, NY.

FAMILY   : Married Patti Francesca; father: Mario La Cascia;
BACKGROUND   mother: Rosa Pecorello (deceased); sisters: Giue-
                 seppa Rubino (wife of Christofaro Rubino), Vincenza
                 Loiacano, Angelina Mucario; mother-in-law: Vita
                 Francesca; father-in-law: Leonard Francesca.

CRIMINAL   : ██████████████, Joseph Di Giovanna, Anthony Strollo,
ASSOCIATES   Settimo Accardo, ██████████████, Christofaro
                 Rubino, (deceased), and ██████████████.

CRIMINAL   : FBI #996427B. Federal narcotic conviction. No other
HISTORY   criminal history.

BUSINESS   : Has worked as tailor, coat manufacturing employee
                 and owned part interest in Purity Cheese Co.

MODUS   : Large scale narcotic trafficker. While he is rel-
OPERANDI   atively unimportant in the Mafia, he assumed great-
                 er stature through his relationship to the late
                 Cristofaro Rubino, his brother-in-law. Was with
                 Rubino when that Mafia leader was shot & killed.

486

NAME : James V. LA DUCA

ALIASES : Vinny La Duca

DESCRIPTION : Born 10-19-12 Buffalo, N.Y.
5'11", 175 lbs, light brown
hair (balding on top), blue
eyes, wears glasses.

LOCALITIES : Resides Dana Drive, Lewiston,
FREQUENTED N.Y. Frequents Magaddino
Funeral Home & Camellia
Linen Supply, both in
Niagara Falls, New York.

FAMILY : Married to Angelina Magaddino; brother: Sam; sisters:
BACKGROUND Mrs. Mary Tormica, Mrs. Sarah Giacarino, Mrs.
Jeanette Verso; father: Giovanni; mother: Giovannina
Bellanca.

CRIMINAL : Stefano Magaddino (father-in-law), Sam Pieri, John
ASSOCIATES C. Montana, Roy Carlisi, Vincent Scro, Joe Stracci,
James Plumeri.

CRIMINAL : FBI #791902C. Record indicates one arrest for con-
HISTORY spiracy to obstruct justice in 1959.

BUSINESS : Financial Secretary & Treasurer of Hotel & Restaurant Employees Union, Local 66, 319 Main St.,
Buffalo, New York.

MODUS : Attended Apalachin Mafia meeting 1957 in place of
OPERANDI his father-in-law Stefano Magaddino, whom he will
eventually replace in the organization controlling
the rackets in the Buffalo-Niagara Falls area.

NAME : Samuel LAGATTUTA

ALIASES : Samuel Lagutta, Lagattuto

DESCRIPTION : Born 4-7-96, Palermo, Sicily
5'6½", 180 lbs, grey hair,
brown eyes, dark complexion.
Naturalized 10-20-19, at
Buffalo, NY.

LOCALITIES : Resides 555 Lafayette St,
FREQUENTED Buffalo, NY. Frequents the
Niagara Frontier Area.

FAMILY : Wife: Jennie; daughter:
BACKGROUND Sophia Alessandria; brother: Frank; father: Nicolo;
mother: Sophia DeMarco.

CRIMINAL : John Montana, Rosario Mancuso, Joseph and Salvatore
ASSOCIATES Falcone, Dominick D'Agostino, Antonio Magaddino,
Stephen Magaddino.

CRIMINAL : FBI #1348437. Buffalo PD #30181. Numerous arrests
HISTORY since 1933 include arson, possession of concealed
weapon and suspicion of murder.

BUSINESS : Painting contractor.

MODUS : Attended Apalachin Mafia meeting 1957. Is a Mafia
OPERANDI member of long standing and closely associated
with all leading underworld figures in the upstate
New York area.

NAME	: Peter LAMONICA
ALIASES	: None
DESCRIPTION	: Born 2-1-04 Brooklyn, NY, 5'8½", 184 lbs, black hair, brown eyes, medium build, dark complexion.
LOCALITIES FREQUENTED	: Resides 610 92nd St, B'klyn, NY. Frequents Vinnie's Rest, 314 Paladino Ave, NYC.
FAMILY BACKGROUND	: Married Josephine Vecchia; father: Giovanni; mother: Maria Guido; sister-in-law is married to John Vitale of St. Louis, National List violator #411.
CRIMINAL ASSOCIATES	: Sebastiano Nani, Nicola Impostato, Joseph Profaci, John Vitale, ▮▮▮▮▮▮▮▮▮▮▮▮▮.
CRIMINAL HISTORY	: No criminal record known.
BUSINESS	: Owns LaMonica Fish Cannery, Cape May, NJ, and has interest in Vecchia Fish Market 7209-13th Ave, Brooklyn, NY.
MODUS OPERANDI	: Influential Mafioso who permits prospective parolees to list his cannery as place of employment. Has sponsored many Italian immigrants who later resorted to crime.

NAME : Albert William LANDI

ALIASES : Big Larry

DESCRIPTION : Born 6-26-11 NYC, 5'6", 231 lbs, heavy build, brown eyes, brown thinning hair, light complexion.

LOCALITIES FREQUENTED : Resides 3244 Paulding Ave., Bronx, NY, (brother's home). Frequents 1537 McDonald Ave, Brooklyn, NY (wife's home); Endicott Bar, 6908 13th Ave, Brooklyn, NY, and Social Club at 1304 67th St., Brooklyn, NY. Currently incarcerated.

FAMILY BACKGROUND : Separated from wife, Frances Padula; sons: Jerry, Michael, Albert; daughter: Mary Anne; father: Giordano (deceased); mother: Clementina Gentile; brothers: Edward, Alfred, Armondo, Anthony & George; sister: Eleanor.

CRIMINAL ASSOCIATES : Charles Curcio, Frank Borelli, Al Criscuolo, James De George, Cosmo Frasca, Frank Tieri.

CRIMINAL HISTORY : FBI #903297B. Only arrest was for Federal Narcotic violation, sentenced in 1955 to 8 years.

BUSINESS : Formerly part owner with Dominic Lentini of Club 124, 2418 2nd Ave., NYC, (now defunct).

MODUS OPERANDI : A middle echelon Mafioso, closely allied with important large scale narcotic traffickers in NYC. Was a main source of supply for narcotics going to Philadelphia, Pa., and also engaged in bookmaking and policy operations.

He was convicted of extortion in the 1940s. Once
released in 1950, he continued to be a part of the
Fulton Fishmarket until his death on October 11, 1968.

NAME : Joseph LANZA

ALIASES : Socks Lanza, Joe Zotz.

DESCRIPTION : Born 8-18-1900 NYC, 5'8½",
200 lbs, brown eyes, black-
grey hair, heavy build.

LOCALITIES : Resides 300 W. 23rd St.,
FREQUENTED Apt. 14 H, NYC. Frequented
Angelo's Neapolitan Restaurant, 146 Mulberry St, &
lower East side dock area
of Manhattan.

FAMILY : Married to Ellen Connor; brothers: Harry, Anthony &
BACKGROUND Salvatore (dead); sisters: Mrs. Sara Guma, Mrs. Rose
Christopher, Mrs. Ann Demeo, Mrs. Frances Viggiano,
Mrs. Eleanor Jannizzi.

CRIMINAL : Frank Costello, Joe Profaci, Mike Clemente, Frank
ASSOCIATES Mancino, Vincent Rao, Vito Genovese, ████████████
████████, all of NYC, Lucky Luciano & Sebastiano
Nani of Italy.

CRIMINAL : FBI #785896. NYCPD B#65346. Arrests since 1917
HISTORY include burglary, extortion, homicide, conspiracy
& extortion.

BUSINESS : Has been affiliated with several Teamster Locals
in NYC.

MODUS : A powerful & feared member of the Mafia in NYC.
OPERANDI Has been one of the most accomplished terrorists in
connection with labor racketeering in the lower
east side Fulton Fish Market area. Received his
weekly "shakedown" from a teamsters local even during his incarceration for extortion.

NAME   : Joseph LAPI

ALIASES   : Joe Beck, Lopi, Lappi

DESCRIPTION   : Born 9-13-10 NYC, 5'11", 185
                 lbs, grey hair, brown eyes,
                 medium build.

LOCALITIES   : Resides 50-39 Francis Lewis
FREQUENTED   Blvd, Bayside, NY. Frequents
                 19 Monroe St, Alto Knights
                 Social Club, Kenmare & Mul-
                 berry Sts, Gotham Health
                 Club, E 54th St, Pygmalian
                 Rest., 1605 2nd Ave, all in
                 NYC; Jays Bar & Grill, 6805 15th Ave, B'klyn, NY.

FAMILY   : Wife: Constance Dispenza; son: Angelo; daughter:
BACKGROUND   Barbara; father: Angelo; mother: Marie Livetchi;
                 brothers: Anthony, Frank & Rosario; sisters: Angelina,
                 Stephannie.

CRIMINAL   : Saro Mogavero, Anthony Corallo, Michael Clementi,
ASSOCIATES   Carmine Tramonti, Joseph Lanza, Frank Caruso.

CRIMINAL   : FBI #846239, NYCPDB# 110003. Record dates back to
HISTORY   1932 and includes arrests for homicide (vehicle),
                 violation Sherman Anti Trust Laws, assault & robbery,
                 violation of parole.

BUSINESS   : Various business interests, including Pygmalian Res-
                 taurant 1605 2nd Ave, NYC, Latona Undertaker, 236
                 Mulberry St, NYC, Jomar Associates Construction Co.,
                 Wilton, Conn.

MODUS   : Important Mafia member in NYC. Currently active in
OPERANDI   many illegal activities, including narcotic traf-
                 ficking with his brother Frank.

492

NAME	: Joseph LATONA
ALIASES	: Joe Laduco, John Russo, Latone, Latonia.
DESCRIPTION	: Born 1-10-1894 Cerda Palermo Sicily, Italy, 5'6½", 160 lbs, medium build, brown eyes grey hair, ruddy complexion, several small scars center of forehead. Naturalized NYC 8-18-25.

LOCALITIES : Resides 464 E. 103 St, B'klyn
FREQUENTED   NY. Frequents Market & Madison St, area; DeVita Pastry Shop, 195 Madison St, Al. E. Smith Dem Club, 49 Market St, & brothers home 10 Catherine Slip, NYC.

FAMILY : Wife: Millie, (deceased); girl friend: Fanny DeVita;
BACKGROUND   father: James; mother: Rose (both deceased).

CRIMINAL : ████████████, Saul Gelb, Nathan Behrman, Anthony
ASSOCIATES   Vellucci, Angelo Tuminaro, ████████████, Joseph DiPalermo.

CRIMINAL : FBI #4553368. Record dates from 1919 and includes
HISTORY   arrests for investigation, attempted larceny and larceny by trick.

BUSINESS : Allegedly has interest in DeVita Pastry Shop, 195 Madison St., NYC.

MODUS : An old time Mafioso, associated with top Mafia
OPERANDI   members in policy, bookmaking, bootlegging, counterfeiting and narcotic trafficking.

NAME	: Carmelo LAZZARO

ALIASES : Carmine

DESCRIPTION : Born 8-8-25 NYC, 5'6", 170 lbs, brown eyes, dark brown hair, stocky build, fair complexion.

LOCALITIES FREQUENTED : Resides 334 E 105th St., NYC, frequents Jennie's Bar, 105th & 2nd; 2025 1st Ave., NYC.

FAMILY BACKGROUND : Single; father: Luigi; mother: Concetta Popalardo; uncles: Benedict & Vincent Macri, (Vincent slain 1954, Benedict currently missing); brother: Salvatore.

CRIMINAL ASSOCIATES : Anthony Castaldi, Danny Carillo, Rocco Mazzie, John Ormento, Salvatore Santoro.

CRIMINAL HISTORY : FBI #4192497, NYCPD #B 215522. Record dates from 1943 and includes arrests for bookmaking & violation State & Federal Narcotic Laws. Sentenced to 5 years on Federal Narcotic Violation, conditionally released 1958.

BUSINESS : No legitimate occupation known.

MODUS OPERANDI : Member of an East Harlem, NYC Mafia organization. Distributes large quantities of heroin locally and interstate.

NAME   : Arthur LEO

ALIASES   : Arthur Rocco, Chink, Mousie

DESCRIPTION   : Born 3-27-24 NYC, 5'10", 195
                      lbs, dark brown hair, brown
                      eyes, ruddy complexion, husky
                      build, considered to be a
                      sexual deviate.

LOCALITIES   : Resides 339 E 105th St, NYC,
FREQUENTED   frequents 2030 2nd Ave, Co-
                      pacabana Night Club; Cicc-
                      one's Bar; 116th St, & 1st
                      Ave., & 105th St, & 2nd Ave,
                      all in New York City.

FAMILY   : Single; father: Jack; mother: Mary Del Rochio; bro-
BACKGROUND   ther: Jack; sister: Mrs. Marie Valenti.

CRIMINAL   : Fred & Angelo Salerno; Vincent Mauro, Anthony Strollo,
ASSOCIATES   Salvatore Santoro, John Ormento, Joseph Vento & ▆▆▆▆
                      ▆▆▆▆▆.

CRIMINAL   : FBI #4520053, NYC PD B#219461. Arrests since 1943
HISTORY   include policy, rape, impairing the morals of a
                      minor, assault with knife, conviction for Federal
                      Narcotic Laws.

BUSINESS   : No legitimate employment.

MODUS   : Associated with other New York Mafiosi in supplying
OPERANDI   narcotics to interstate traffickers.

NAME : Daniel LESSA

ALIASES : Mushky, Monzigi, Minzagee

DESCRIPTION : Born 11-25-15, NYC, 5'5½",
140 lbs, brown wavy hair,
brown eyes, mole on left
cheek, medium build, neat
dresser.

LOCALITIES : Resided at 2885 Sampson Ave,
FREQUENTED Bronx, NY, frequents 117th
St, and Paladino Ave, East
109th St, between Park and
3rd Ave, NYC. Currently
(1960) incarcerated.

FAMILY : Married to Mary Jacobson; children: Lorraine and
BACKGROUND Daniel; father: Frank; mother: Mary (Della Foglia);
sisters: Josephine and Mrs. Mary Wolfson; brothers:
Frank, Louis, Nick and Dominick.

CRIMINAL : Vincent Pacelli, Joseph D'Ercole, John Ardito,
ASSOCIATES ██████████████████████████, ████████ Nick
Tolentino, Steve Puco, Frank Pasqua, Michael Coppola,
Joseph Rao, Rocco Mazzie, Joe DiPalermo, ████████
████████, ████████████████, Ralph Polizano, Frank
Borelli.

CRIMINAL : FBI #1018546. NYCPD #B173869, criminal record
HISTORY includes rape, assault 2nd degree, and violation of
the Federal Narcotic Laws.

BUSINESS : No legitimate employment.

MODUS : A very active interstate narcotic trafficker and a
OPERANDI member of the Mafia in East Harlem area, NYC.

On November 4, 1976, Licata was murdered, perhaps on orders from Sal Catalano.

NAME	: Pietro LICATA
ALIASES	: Pete
DESCRIPTION	: Born 12-9-06 San Cipirello, Palermo, Sicily, Italy, 5'10" 165 lbs, grey hair, brown eyes; naturalized Brooklyn, NY, 1-18-55, #7392500, U.S. Passport #31148.
LOCALITIES FREQUENTED	: Resides 201 Wilson Ave., Brooklyn, NY. Frequents The Bushwick & Ridgewood sections of Brooklyn. Frequent traveler to Italy.
FAMILY BACKGROUND	: Wife: Giuseppa DiGiovanni; father: Castrenzo; mother: Elisabetta LoMonaca (both born & residing Italy).
CRIMINAL ASSOCIATES	: Vincent Todaro, Peter Casella, ███████████, Cristofaro Robino (deceased), Giuseppe DiGiovanni.
CRIMINAL HISTORY	: No FBI # or NYCPD #. Was admonished for criminal activities in Italy prior to coming to the U.S. No known criminal record in U.S.
BUSINESS	: Button hole maker.
MODUS OPERANDI	: A Mafia member and international drug trafficker formerly associated with the late Brooklyn Mafia chief Cristofaro Robino.

NAME	: John LINARDI
ALIASES	: John Gazzola, Chut, John Linarzi
DESCRIPTION	: Born 9-29-08 NYC, 5'5", 160 lbs, black hair, brown eyes, fair complexion.
LOCALITIES FREQUENTED	: Resides 182 Madison Ave, Cresskill, NJ. Frequents the Belvedere Bar, 105th & 1st Ave, the East Harlem area & the lower East Side, NYC.

FAMILY BACKGROUND	: Married Florence Gatti; daughters: Dolores and Beverly; mother: Nunziata Saliceta; father: Raffaele.
CRIMINAL ASSOCIATES	: Pasquale Pagano, Anthony Zangoglia, ████████████, Angelo Tuminaro, John Ormento, Salvatore Santora, Anthony Mirra, Joseph Tortorici.
CRIMINAL HISTORY	: FBI #228346. NYCPD B# 87164. Record dates from 1928 and includes arrests for violation of the Federal Narcotic Laws, felonious assault, robbery, homicide and policy. Federal Narcotics conviction.
BUSINESS	: No legitimate employment.
MODUS OPERANDI	: Bookmaker and policy operator. Is part of a large scale heroin distribution ring in association with other Mafia hoodlums.

NAME : Gaetano LISI

ALIASES : Anthony, Tony, Anthony Leis

DESCRIPTION : Born 7-11-11 Palermo, Sicily, Italy, 5'5", 165 lbs, medium build, brown hair, brown eyes, dark complexion.

LOCALITIES : Resides 154 East Broadway,
FREQUENTED NYC, frequents C.I.A. Club 72 Forsythe St., 81 Mulberry St; Jay's Bar, 49 E Houston St; Madison Bar, 116 Madison St; Holiday Restaurant, 55 Madison St., all in NYC, 2427 W 3rd St., and 382 Ave., W, both Brooklyn, NY.

FAMILY : Wife: Josephine Armano; father: Sebastian; mother:
BACKGROUND Nellie Greco (parents naturalized 1924 & 1927); brothers: Sebastian, Salvatore, Frank; sister: Dorothy DeMartini.

CRIMINAL : ███████████, Frank Mari, Carlo DiPietro,
ASSOCIATES Salvatore Giglio, Frank Caruso, Angelo Tuminaro.

CRIMINAL : FBI #771146, NYC PD #B108091. Record dates from
HISTORY 1932 and includes arrests for grand larceny, possession of deadly weapon, disorderly person, robbery, parole violation, murder and narcotic law violation.

BUSINESS : Has interests in Deeds Transportation, Brooklyn, NY; C.I.A. Club, 72 Forsythe St., NYC, Holiday Inn, 55 Madison St., NYC; Dan & Jay, Accountants, 154 East Broadway, NYC.

MODUS : An important Mafia member and wholesale distributor
OPERANDI of narcotics which he obtains from the Carmine Galante organization which in turn obtains supplies from the Cotroni Mob in Montreal Canada.

NAME	: Frank S. LIVORSI
ALIASES	: Cheech, Ciccio, Frank Livolsi
DESCRIPTION	: Born 11-10-03, Chicago, Ill. 5'7", 170 lbs., brown eyes, brown-grey hair thinning on top, cut-scar over right eye.
LOCALITIES FREQUENTED	: Resides 15 Fulton Ave., Atlantic Beach, Long Island NY, and has winter home in Miami, Fla. Frequents East Harlem area and race tracks, NYC.
FAMILY BACKGROUND	: Married to Dorina Gassola, has 5 daughters: Rosemary (oldest) married to Tom Dio Guardio (brother of notorious Johnny Dio); Dolores, married to Sam Meli (son of notorious Mafiosi Angelo Meli, Detroit); Patricia, married to Tom Ormento (son of John Ormento); father: Bartholomew, mother: Rosaria, has 5 sisters and 3 brothers.
CRIMINAL ASSOCIATES	: John Ormento, Salvatore Santoro, Mike Coppola, Vito Genovese, John Stoppelli, Charles Albero, Sebastiano Vento, Johnny Dio, all of NYC, Meli Family, Tocco family and Rafaele Quasarano of Detroit.
CRIMINAL HISTORY	: FBI #792029, NYCPD B# 74349, arrests since 1927 include assault, homicide, Federal Narcotic Laws, sentenced on 2-18-55 to 15 years NYC for fraudulent Federal Income Tax returns.
BUSINESS	: No legitimate business known.
MODUS OPERANDI	: For over a decade has been the dominating Mafia leader, director & financier of the E. 107 St., mob of narcotic traffickers.

NAME	:	Carmine LoCASCIO

ALIASES	:	Willie the Wop, Willie Orlando, Anthony Corona, Willie Brown, Willie LoCascio
DESCRIPTION	:	Born 9-23-11, NYC., 5'7", 204 lbs., grey black hair, brown eyes, dark complexion, prominent double chin, build stocky.
LOCALITIES FREQUENTED	:	Resides 144-58 10th, Ave., Malba, Queens, frequents Oldtimers Bar, 104th St., and Roosevelt Ave., Corona, Queens, Prince & Sullivan Sts., in Manhattan, One Forty Operating Corp., 140 West 44th St.
FAMILY BACKGROUND	:	Wife, Rose Orlando, Daughter, Rachel, Father, Giuseppe, (deceased), Brother, Peter, Sister, Mrs. Rose Caronia.
CRIMINAL ASSOCIATES	:	John Ormento, Sam Accardi, ██████████████, Peter Locascio, █████████████, █████████, Salvatore Santora, Joe Marone, Charles Albero.
CRIMINAL HISTORY	:	FBI #246742, NYC, PD# 159260, prior arrests since 1929, including robbery, homicide, bribing a Federal Officer, bootlegging, harboring a narcotic fugitive, violation of the Federal Narcotic Laws.
BUSINESS	:	Alleged owner of Peppi's Restaurant, 70-30 Austin St., Forest Hills, Queens and of One Forty Operating Corp., 140 W. 44th St., NYC.
MODUS OPERANDI	:	An important N.Y. Mafia leader, supplier of local and interstate large scale dealers in narcotics. Has direct foreign source of supply.

NAME   : Peter Joseph LoCASCIO

ALIASES   : James Russo, John Russo,
                  Mr. Bread

DESCRIPTION   : Born 6-10-16 NYC, 5'8", 162
                  lbs., black hair, brown eyes.

LOCALITIES   : Resides 216 Audley Court,
FREQUENTED   Copiague, L.I., N.Y. Fre-
                  quents lower east side
                  (Little Italy) section of
                  Manhattan.

FAMILY   : Divorced from first wife
BACKGROUND   Jean Rotandi and has two daughters by her; now
                  married to Anna DiCarlo (sister of Angelo "Gyp"
                  DiCarlo).

CRIMINAL   : Joe and Pete DiPalermo, John Ormento, Carmine
ASSOCIATES   LoCascio (brother), Rocco Mazzie, James Picarelli,
                  Sammy Kass, all of New York City.

CRIMINAL   : FBI #980365. NYC PD B-#180109. Arrests since
HISTORY   1935 include convictions for federal liquor laws,
                  conspiracy and N.Y. State Narcotic Laws.

BUSINESS   : Has interests in Ennis Construction Co., Linden-
                  hurst, L.I., N.Y., and Peppi Restaurant, Forest
                  Hills, Queens, New York.

MODUS   : A trusted associate by high ranking Mafia in NYC.
OPERANDI   Engaged in narcotic trafficking with his brother
                  Carmine. A vicious and feared hoodlum.

NAME	: Frank LOFARO
ALIASES	:
DESCRIPTION	: Born 2-26-1893 Reggio Calabria, Italy, 5'7", 120 lbs, brown eyes, grey hair, slender build, naturalized 7-30-29 at Brooklyn, NY.
LOCALITIES FREQUENTED	: Resides 42-12 76th St., Elmhurst, Queens, NY, frequents dock area in Brooklyn.
FAMILY BACKGROUND	: Wife: Philomena Serrano; daughters: Angela, Vincenza & Giovanna; father: Giovanni; mother: Vincenza Romea.
CRIMINAL ASSOCIATES	: Vincent Randazzo, Salvatore Mezzasalma, Emanuele Cammarata, all of NYC; Sebastiano Nani (deportee); Nicola Impastato (deportee); & ▮▮▮▮▮▮▮▮ of California.
CRIMINAL HISTORY	: FBI #196380, NYCPD B#73137. Arrests since 1923 include grand larceny and felonious assault.
BUSINESS	: Employed as a carpenter by American Stevedores Co., Brooklyn, NY.
MODUS OPERANDI	: Has been one of the Mafia-controlled smugglers and distributors of narcotics from Brooklyn docks.

NAME	: Angelo M. LOIACANO
ALIASES	: Angelo Puggino, Little Puggy.
DESCRIPTION	: Born 6-23-13 N.Y.C., 5'7", 178 lbs., brown eyes, black hair with some grey, wears glasses occasionally.

LOCALITIES FREQUENTED	: Resides 24-48 79th St., Jackson Heights, Queens, N.Y. Frequents area 1st Ave. & E.107th St. in Manhattan.
FAMILY BACKGROUND	: Married to Mary Maccheroni & has 2 sons; sister: Kate; brothers: Stephen & John; father: Carmelo (deceased); mother: Bessie Chabiro.
CRIMINAL ASSOCIATES	: John Ormento, Salvatore Santoro, Anthony Castaldi, Salvatore LoProto, ███████████, Frank Moccardi, all of N.Y.C.
CRIMINAL HISTORY	: FBI#4748953. NYC PD-B#248746. Arrests since 1935 include policy and conviction for N.Y. State Narcotic Laws.
BUSINESS	: Occasional employment as a plasterer.
MODUS OPERANDI	: Wholesale narcotic trafficker who supplies large scale dealers in East Harlem. Obtains his supply from the Mafia narcotic trafficking mob headed by John Ormento. Also engaged in illegal gambling activities.

It is rumored that Lombardo took over as boss of the Genovese family in 1972. In 1981, he retired to Florida and died in April 1987 at the age of 78.

NAME : Philip LOMBARDO

ALIASES : Ben Grasso, Ben Turpin, Benny DeMaio, "Cockeyed" Phil

DESCRIPTION : Born 10-5-08, NYC, 5'6", 155 lbs, black hair, bald on top, brown eyes, small build, sallow complexion, left eye is crossed.

LOCALITIES : Resides 1266 Olmstead Ave.,
FREQUENTED Bronx, NY, frequents East Harlem area of NYC, Miami Beach, Florida.

FAMILY : Single; father: Filipe (deceased); mother: Eleanor
BACKGROUND Rotolo.

CRIMINAL : Charles Albero, Salvatore Santoro, John Ormento,
ASSOCIATES Pasquale Genese, Michael Coppola, Joseph Vento

CRIMINAL : FBI #201426, NYCPD B#90771, Miami PD# 4154, record
HISTORY dates from 1928 and includes arrests for attempted extortion, robbery with gun, possession of stolen car and consorting with known criminals. Two Federal Narcotic convictions.

BUSINESS : No legitimate employment known.

MODUS : A respected & feared member of the Mafia. Active
OPERANDI in the wholesale distribution of narcotics throughout the U.S. A one time bodyguard for Michael Coppola, he has a reputation for violence.

Arrested in 1957 at the Apalachin Convention, he died of natural causes in 1992, at the age of 79.

NAME : Carmine LOMBARDOZZI

ALIASES : Carmelo Lumbata, Carmine Lombardo, Alberto Lombardozzi

DESCRIPTION : Born 12-8-1913, Brooklyn, NY, 5'8", 185 lbs, hazel eyes, black-grey wavy hair.

LOCALITIES FREQUENTED : Resides 114 Stratford Road, Brooklyn, NY. Frequents the Brooklyn dock area & New Corners Restaurant, 7201 8th Avenue, Brooklyn, NY.

FAMILY BACKGROUND : Married Mary Corrolla; brothers: Dominick, John, Paul & Daniel; father: Carmelo; mother: Annunziata Antonelli.

CRIMINAL ASSOCIATES : Anthony Strollo, Salvatore Maiorano, Carmine Galante, Giuseppe DiPalermo, Frank Caruso, Cassandros Bonasera and Philip Albanese.

CRIMINAL HISTORY : FBI #290869 NYCPD #B-82564 Record dating from 1929 includes arrests for homicide, rape, unlawful entry and conspiracy to obstruct justice, for which sentenced (1960) to 5 years and $10,000 fine.

BUSINESS : Has major interests in Monte Marine Corp. & Mobile Marine Power Co., both in Brooklyn, and in Carbal Trading Co., Inc., NYC.

MODUS OPERANDI : Attended 1957 Apalachin Mafia meeting. Is leader of a mob in Brooklyn which is involved in strong-arm tactics, shylocking, trading in stolen merchandise and narcotic trafficking. Is a powerful and feared Mafioso.

NAME : Giuseppe LO PICCOLO

ALIASES : Joseph

DESCRIPTION : Born 8-6-1899, Partinico, Sicily, Italy, 5'8", brown greying hair, grey-blue eyes, medium build. Naturalized Detroit 8-4-1947.

LOCALITIES FREQUENTED : Resides at 796 Middle Neck Rd, Great Neck, Long Island. Formerly at 43 Ixlin Lane, Great Neck, L.I. Frequents business at 714 Middle Neck Rd, Great Neck, L.I., & other sections of Great Neck. From 1923-1947 resided Detroit. In Italy family resides at Via Gallacico, Corleone, Italy.

FAMILY BACKGROUND : Married Giovanna Lunetto; son: Giuseppe; father: Giuseppe; mother: Antonina Noto.

CRIMINAL ASSOCIATES : Michael Pecoraro, Salvatore Settimo, ████████, Lorenzo Orlando, Paul Gambino, Salvatore Missale.

CRIMINAL HISTORY : FBI #513191. Mich., SP D-299. One arrest for violation of National Prohibition Act.

BUSINESS : Operates Kings Point Shoe Shop, 714 Middle Neck Rd, Great Neck, Long Island.

MODUS OPERANDI : An international trafficker in narcotics. Lo Piccolo is an important member of the Mafia and a close associate of Paul Gambino.

His body was discovered on May 21, 1978, in a cemetery on Staten Island, NY, with over fifty stab wounds.

NAME : Joseph Paul LO PICCOLO

ALIASES : Joe

DESCRIPTION : Born 4-28-1918 Chicago, Ill., 5'5½", 218 lbs, brown hair, brown eyes, scar on chin, heavy build.

LOCALITIES FREQUENTED : Resides 233 E 69th St., NYC, & 621 44th St., Miami, Fla., frequented midtown area of NYC. Vesuvio Rest., & Paddock Bar, 50th & Broadway, NYC; also Phila., Chicago and Miami Beach.

FAMILY BACKGROUND : Wife: Carolyn Riggio; sons: Philip, Carl, Joseph; daughter: Margaret; father: Felippo (deceased); mother: Margherita Viso; brothers: Anthony & Frank; sisters: Loretta (Mrs. Dan) Ficarelli & Carmella (Mrs. Nick) Ficarelli.

CRIMINAL ASSOCIATES : Joseph DiPalermo, Santos Trafficante, James Massi, Angelo Loiacano, Vincent Todaro, Ignazio & Lorenzo Orlando.

CRIMINAL HISTORY : FBI #790022C, No NYCPD #, Miami Beach PD# A24278, record consists only of an arrest for investigation in Miami and a Federal Narcotic Conviction. In August 1958 sentenced to 20 years on the Federal Narcotic charge.

BUSINESS : Partner in Rock Creek Fluorspar Mining Co., Hardin County, Illinois.

MODUS ORERANDI : An important member of the Mafia, instrumental in narcotic smuggling and wholesale distribution in association with other top echelon violators.

508

NAME	: Salvatore LO PROTO
ALIASES	: Sally the Blonde, Sally Blue Eyes, Dennis the Menace
DESCRIPTION	: Born 4-22-26 Lodi, N.J., 5'10", 200 lbs., blue eyes, light brown hair, fair complexion.
LOCALITIES FREQUENTED	: Resides 397 Passaic Ave., Lodi, NJ. Frequents area of East Harlem, the Vogue Room The Copacabana, all in NYC.
FAMILY BACKGROUND	: Married to Mildred Pisciotta (killed in auto accident 1958), has 3 children.
CRIMINAL ASSOCIATES	: John Ormento, Salvatore Santoro, Frank Livorsi, Angelo C. Salerno, Fred Salerno, all of NYC.
CRIMINAL HISTORY	: FBI #921798 B, NYCPD #B 355232, arrests include bookmaking, possession of gun (felony), vehicular homicide. Arrested with John Ormento (1955) in possession of two loaded guns concealed in seat of a car, while apparently on their way to commit a Mafia inspired crime.
BUSINESS	: Purportedly employed as dispatcher by Frank Stamato and Co., Lodi, New Jersey.
MODUS OPERANDI	: An important member of the John Ormento Mafia controlled narcotic traffickers from E. Harlem area New York City.

He died on July 13, 1967, of natural causes.

NAME : Gaetano LUCCHESE

ALIASES : Tom Lucchese, Tom Brown, Tom Arra, "Three Finger Brown".

DESCRIPTION : Born 12-1-1899 Palermo, Sicily, 5'5", 150 lbs., brown eyes, grey hair, wears glasses, naturalized 1-25-43 N.Y.C.

LOCALITIES FREQUENTED : Resides 74 Royale St., Lido Beach, L.I., N.Y. Frequents Miami Beach, garment district of Manhattan, various locations in L.I. & N.J.

FAMILY BACKGROUND : Wife: Catherine; sons: Francis & Baldassari; brothers: Anthony & Joseph; sisters: Pietra, Mrs. Rosalie Rosato (wife of Joe Rosato), & Concetta; father: Baldassari; mother: Francesca.

CRIMINAL ASSOCIATES : Joe Biondo, Anthony Corallo, Anthony Strollo, Joe Profaci, Frank Livorsi, Settimo Accardi, Joe Rao, Lucky Luciano, Joe Rosato (brother-in-law).

CRIMINAL HISTORY : FBI#168275. NYC PD-B#68834. Arrests since 1921 include murder, grand larceny, receiving stolen goods.

BUSINESS : Either owns or has interests in Braunell Ltd., Manhattan; Pleasant Coat Co., Pleasant, N.J.; Bob-France Coat Co., Queens, N.Y.; Fordham Hoisting Co., Bronx, N.Y.; & several other businesses.

MODUS OPERANDI : A capable & influential Mafia leader who has developed powerful friends in political circles & has used them at times in behalf of his Mafia associates.

510

NAME : Frank LUCIANO

ALIASES : Frank Miller, Biaggio DeLuca, Gefri Luciano, Gefri DeLuca.

DESCRIPTION : Born 5-5-1900, Salerno, Italy, 5'2", 180 lbs, heavy build, black-grey hair, brown eyes, dark complexion, arrived U.S. 1904, naturalized NYC 12-23-40.

LOCALITIES : Resides 14-24 144 Place,
FREQUENTED Whitestone, Queens, N.Y. Frequents Capri Lounge, 2010 Williamsbridge Road, Flamingo Restaurant, 2694 Jerome Ave., both Bronx, East Harlem Section of NYC.

FAMILY : Married Pauline Magnano; sons: Anthony & Robert;
BACKGROUND daughter: Rita Russo; father: Antonio; mother: Immaculata Della Calce.

CRIMINAL : Paolo & Carlo Gambino, Joseph Bisogna, Joseph
ASSOCIATES Valachi, Joseph Vento, Mike Pecoraro, Jack Scarpulla, Joseph Barra, Mathew Cuomo.

CRIMINAL : FBI #347100, NYCPD #B100676, record dates from 1917
HISTORY and includes arrests for policy, assault, illicit still, attempted grand larceny, fraud & false statements, unlawful possession counterfeit ration coupons.

BUSINESS : Owns Lido Restaurant 1362 Castle Hill Road, Bronx, NY, formerly owned by narcotic trafficker Joseph Valachi.

MODUS : One of the most important Mafiosi in the Bronx, NYC.
OPERANDI Engaged in highjacking, shylocking, bootlegging and narcotic trafficking. Instrumental in smuggling narcotics into the U.S.

511

He died on April 13, 1971.

NAME	: Antonino MAGADDINO
ALIASES	: Antonio Magardino, Tony Lombardo.

DESCRIPTION : Born 7-18-1897 Castellammare, Sicily, 5'9", 200 lbs, brown eyes, black-grey hair, stout build.

LOCALITIES FREQUENTED : Resides 1528 Whitney Ave., Niagara Falls, NY, frequents Magaddino's Memorial Chapel & Camelia Linen Supply Co., both in Niagara Falls, NY.

FAMILY BACKGROUND : Father: Giovanni; mother: Giuseppe Ciaravino; married to Vincenzina Vitale; son: Peter: daughter: Josephine; brother: Stefano.

CRIMINAL ASSOCIATES : Stefano Magaddino (brother), Vincent & ▓▓ Scro, ▓▓▓▓▓▓▓▓▓, Salvatore Pieri, ▓▓▓▓▓▓▓, all of Buffalo-Niagara Falls area.

CRIMINAL HISTORY : FBI #947466. I&NS-A#1086290. Arrested 1935 for violation I&NS Laws. Several arrests in Sicily from 1916 to 1929 including murder, robbery, rape. Fled Sicily when Mafia was being purged. 1959 indicted for conspiracy to obstruct justice, currently a fugitive.

BUSINESS : Is Vice-President & Treasurer of the Magaddino Memorial Chapel, Inc., Niagara Falls, NY.

MODUS OPERANDI : Attended Apalachin Mafia meeting 1957. He and his brother Stefano are the top Mafia leaders in the Niagara Falls area. They control illegal gambling there and have been "muscling" in on legitimate oil and linen supply dealers.

He died on July 19, 1974, of a heart attack.

NAME   : Stefano MAGADDINO

ALIASES   : Stefano Magardino, Don Stefano.

DESCRIPTION : Born 10-10-91 Castellammare, Sicily. 5'6", 200 lbs., grey hair & balding, brown eyes.

LOCALITIES   : Resides Dana Drive, Buffalo,
FREQUENTED   N.Y. Frequents Magaddino's Memorial Chapel & Camelia Linen Supply Co., both in Niagara Falls, N.Y.

FAMILY   : Married; son: Peter; daughters: Josephine, who is
BACKGROUND   married to Charles Montana (nephew of John C. Montana); Angelina, who is married to James LaDuca; & Arcangela, who is married to Vincent Scro; father: Giovanni; mother: Giuseppa (both dead); brother: Antonino.

CRIMINAL   : John C. Montana, James LaDuca, Antonino Magaddino
ASSOCIATES   (brother), Vincent Scro, Salvatore & Joe Falcone, Russell Bufalino, & Ray Carlisi.

CRIMINAL   : FBI#778722C. NYC PD#3080. Arrested in 1921 by
HISTORY   NYC PD for Avon, N.J., PD as a fugitive from justice (homicide).

BUSINESS   : True owner of Magaddino Memorial Chapel, Inc., 1338 Niagara St., Niagara Falls, N.Y.

MODUS   : He & his brother Antonino are the top Mafia leaders
OPERANDI   in the Niagara Falls area. They control illegal gambling in the area and have been "muscling" in on legitimate oil and linen supply dealers.

He died of a heart attack on December 28, 1983.

NAME : Giuseppe MAGLIOCCO

ALIASES : Joe Magliocco, Joe Magliocci

DESCRIPTION : Born 6-29-1898, Portella di Mare, Sicily, 5'9", 245 lbs, brown eyes, brown-grey hair.

LOCALITIES FREQUENTED : Resides 279 Bay 11th Street, Brooklyn, NY. Summer home at Bay View Ave., E. Islip, L.I. Frequents Sunland Beverage Co., Brooklyn, NY.

FAMILY BACKGROUND : Married Rose Angelo: brothers: Anthony, Angelo & Ambrosio; father: Giovanni; mother: Carmela Fontani; sister: Mrs. Ninfa Profaci (wife of Giuseppe Profaci).

CRIMINAL ASSOCIATES : Sebastiano Nani & Lucky Luciano, of Italy, John Balsamo, Emmanuel Cammarata, Paolo Gambino, Frank Livorsi, John Oddo, all of NYC area, Angelo Meli & William Tocco, of Detroit.

CRIMINAL HISTORY : FBI #184224 Cleveland PD #32771 Record dating from 1928 includes arrests for concealed weapon and conspiracy to obstruct justice. 1960 sentenced on latter charge to 5 years & $10,000 fine.

BUSINESS : Owns Sunland Beverage Co., Brooklyn, N.Y.

MODUS OPERANDI : Attended Cleveland Mafia meeting 1928 and the 1957 Apalachin Mafia meeting with brother-in-law Giuseppe Profaci. Is one of the most powerful members of the Mafia in the U.S.

NAME	: Salvatore MAIMONE
ALIASES	: Salvatore Marvone, Sibby Marvone, Saverio Maimone, Saverio Riccardo Mainione.
DESCRIPTION	: Born 4-3-13 NYC, 5'10½", 230 lbs, brown-grey hair, brown eyes, heavy build.
LOCALITIES FREQUENTED	: Resides 1757 58th St., Brooklyn, NY, frequented Corregidor Bar & Vegetable Store both on Columbia St., Brooklyn, NY.

FAMILY BACKGROUND : Married to Mary Mistretta & has 3 children; father: Emmanuel; mother: Gerolina Parise.

CRIMINAL ASSOCIATES : John Ormento, Salvatore Giordano, ███████████, ██████████.

CRIMINAL HISTORY : FBI #905752, NYCPD B# 114691, arrests since 1933 include robbery, assault & robbery, theft from interstate shipment, harboring a fugitive and convictions for Federal Narcotic Laws. Currently (1959) incarcerated for violation Federal Narcotic Laws.

BUSINESS : Owns Manny's Fruit Store, 224 Columbia St., Brooklyn, New York.

MODUS OPERANDI : Has been a Mafia racketeer in Brooklyn's Red Hook section for many years, taking part in all sorts of illicit enterprises, but mainly narcotic trafficking. Obtains narcotics from smuggling groups and distributes to customers in Boston, Washington & Philadelphia.

NAME	: Salvatore Gaetano MAIORANA
ALIASES	: Toddo Marino, Thomas Marino, Toto Marino.
DESCRIPTION	: Born 6-9-1898 Milazzo, Sicily, Alien Reg.#3486560, 6', 210 lbs., brown eyes, black-grey hair, wears glasses.
LOCALITIES FREQUENTED	: Resides 286 19th St., Brooklyn, N.Y. Frequents Dixie Tavern & Cafe DiNapoli in Brooklyn.
FAMILY BACKGROUND	: Married to Marie Procida & has no children; parents are Santo & Rosaria (both dead); brother: Charles; and has 4 sisters.
CRIMINAL ASSOCIATES	: Vito Genovese, Mike Clemente, ███████████, Joe Profaci, all of N.Y.C.; Alfonso Marzano of Florida; Lucky Luciano & Joe Doto of Italy.
CRIMINAL HISTORY	: FBI#1644357. NYC PD-B#45651. Arrests since 1913 include juvenile delinquent, assault & robbery, burglary, Immigration Laws.
BUSINESS	: Engaged in building construction.
MODUS OPERANDI	: A Mafia leader in control of a large segment of the Brooklyn underworld, engaged in the narcotic traffic as smuggler-distributor. Also finances illegal gambling activities.

NAME   : Salvatore J. MAIORINO

ALIASES   : Salvatore Marino, Chubby.

DESCRIPTION : Born 12-12-24 Metuchen, N.J.
                5'8", 176 lbs, brown hair,
                brown eyes, blind in left eye

LOCALITIES   : Resides 417 E. 114th Street,
FREQUENTED   N.Y.C. Frequents vicinity
                of 2nd Avenue & E. 116th
                Street in Manhattan.

FAMILY   : Married to Bessie Euphemia,
BACKGROUND   brothers: Daniel, Michael,
                Anthony, John; sisters: Mrs. Lucy Costello, Rose,
                Helen; father: Anthony; mother: Marie Cachetta.

CRIMINAL   : Charles Curcio, Frank Borelli, Harry Tantillo,
ASSOCIATES   Steve Puco, ██████████████████, ██████████████,
                John Riccardulli, all of NYC area.

CRIMINAL   : FBI# 2738791. NYCPD-B# 207550. Record dates back
HISTORY   to 1935 as a juvenile delinquent, and includes
                larceny, burglary, felonious assault, and convic-
                tion for Federal Narcotic Laws.

BUSINESS   : Operates a Social Club on E. 117th Street be-
                tween 2nd & 3rd Avenues in Manhattan.

MODUS   : A major narcotic trafficker from East Harlem area
OPERANDI   of Manhattan and a trusted associate of known
                Mafia traffickers from whom he obtains his supply
                of narcotics.

NAME	: John Anthony MALIZIA
ALIASES	: Cockeye Benny, one of "Pontiac Brothers"
DESCRIPTION	: Born 4-28-12, NYC, 5'6", 190 lbs, black hair, brown eyes, cast in right eye, heavy build.
LOCALITIES FREQUENTED	: Resides 327 Pleasant Ave., NYC, Frequents the area of Pleasant Ave., and the local NY Race Tracks. Currently incarcerated.
FAMILY BACKGROUND	: Wife: Rose Altobello; father: John (deceased); mother: Gisela Ceroni; brothers: Pasquale & Ernest.
CRIMINAL ASSOCIATES	: ████████, Vincent Pacelli, Joseph Bendenelli, Daniel ████████ Lessa, Steve ████████ Puco, Vincent Panebianco.
CRIMINAL RECORD	: FBI 735314, NYCPD B#114349. Record dates back to 1933 and includes arrests for unlawful entry, assault & robbery, violation of probation, bookmaking, vagrancy, violation of Federal & State Narcotic Laws. Sentenced in 1957 to 9 years for violation Federal Narcotic Laws.
BUSINESS	: No legitimate means of support.
MODUS OPERANDI	: An important NYC East Harlem Mafioso and a large distributor of narcotics to important negro violators in Harlem.

518

NAME : Francesco Joseph MANCINO

ALIASES : Frank Mancino, Chow, Joseph Barbera.

DESCRIPTION : Born 10-25-06 NYC, 5'8", 204 lbs, black-grey hair, brown eyes, heavy build, sloppy dresser.

LOCALITIES FREQUENTED : Resides 44 Marcy Ave, Brooklyn, NY. Frequents Hi-Way Bar, 362 Metropolitan Ave, Orientale Bar 40 Marcy Ave, Mustang Social Club 433 Metropolitan Ave, all B'klyn, NY.

FAMILY BACKGROUND : Common-law wife: Margaret Rodd; previous wives: Angelina Barbera, Beatrice Pulco and Lillian Gershenbaum; daughters: Antoinette McDoagh, Marie Bongiovanni; son: Anthony F.; father: Salvatore; mother: Maria Iolazzolo; sisters: Beatrice, Angelina Degorra, Mary Russo, Vita LaSalle.

CRIMINAL ASSOCIATES : Cotroni Brothers, Frank Moccardi, Salvatore Giglio, ████████████████████, ████████████████.

CRIMINAL HISTORY : FBI #348817. NYCPD #B78209. Record dating from 1929 includes arrests for assault & robbery, grand larceny, robbery, burglary, armed robbery & violation Federal narcotic laws.

BUSINESS : No legitimate occupation.

MODUS OPERANDI : Part of a large scale Mafia narcotic smuggling and distributing group. Acted as Courier for large quantities of heroin furnished by the Cotroni organization in Canada to Mafia mobs in U.S.

NAME   : Anthony MANCUSO

ALIASES   : Tony Nose, Antonio

DESCRIPTION   : Born 12-24-23 NYC, 5'8", 210
                lbs, brown hair, brown eyes,
                heavy build, wears glasses.

LOCALITIES   : Resides 1540 Dwight Place,
FREQUENTED   Bronx, NY. Frequents 428 E.
                116th St, 311 Paladino Ave,
                Social Club on the SW cor-
                ner of 117th St, & Paladino
                Ave, all in NYC.

FAMILY   : Single; father: Michele Mancuso; mother: Lucia Franco.
BACKGROUND   No brothers or sisters.

CRIMINAL   : Joseph Bendenelli, Carmine Paladino, George Palmieri,
ASSOCIATES   Steve Puco, ███████████████, ██████████████████,
                ██████████████████.

CRIMINAL   : FBI #3836361. NYC B#220 226, record dates from 1946
HISTORY   and includes arrests for gambling, burglary and
                veteran's fraud.

BUSINESS   : Operates a fruit stand in the vicinity of Jerome
                Ave., and 161st St., Bronx, NY.

MODUS   : Leader of an East Harlem Mafia Group. Wholesale
OPERANDI   narcotic trafficker on the interstate level. He
                has been engaged in the narcotic traffic for a
                number of years.

NAME : Rosario MANCUSO

ALIASES : Russell Mancuso, Joe Greco, Russell Victor.

DESCRIPTION: Born 1-29-07 Buffalo, NY, 5'5", 235 lbs., brown hair, brown eyes, heavy build.

LOCALITIES : Resides 926 Arthur St.,
FREQUENTED   Utica, NY. Frequents Italian Village Restaurant, Platts- burgh, NY, & Rome-Utica area of NY.

FAMILY : Married to Cora Montemurro; daughter: Carol; father:
BACKGROUND   John; mother: Mary Dispensa.

CRIMINAL : ██████████, ██████████, ██████████,
ASSOCIATES   ██████████ & all major hoodlums in Buffalo-Syracuse- Utica area.

CRIMINAL : FBI# 39238. Buffalo, NYPD# 15940. Numerous arrests
HISTORY   since 1920 including juvenile delinquency, burglary, robbery, assault with intent to kill.

BUSINESS : President of Nuform Concrete Co., Utica, New York.

MODUS : Attended Apalachin Mafia meeting 1957. A notorious
OPERANDI   feared strong-arm and trigger man for the Mafia in the Utica area. Also engaged in labor racketeering, safe-cracking, and disposing of stolen jewelry.

NAME   : Joseph MANFREDI

ALIASES   : JoJo

DESCRIPTION   : Born 1-5-1926, NYC, 5'5",
                 145 lbs, medium build, black
                 hair, brown eyes, medium
                 complexion.

LOCALITIES   : Resided 140 James St., Lodi,
FREQUENTED   NJ. Frequented Manfredi
                 Restaurant, 331 E 108 St.,
                 and Candy Store, 306 E 108
                 St., N.Y.C.

FAMILY   : Married Josephine Lama; father: Fillippio; mother:
BACKGROUND   Josephine Boncorse; brothers: Urbano & Ignacio.

CRIMINAL   : Anthony Castaldi, Joseph Bisogno, Frank Luciano,
ASSOCIATES   ▓▓▓▓▓▓▓▓▓▓▓, John Daniello, ▓▓▓▓▓▓▓▓▓▓,
                 ▓▓▓▓▓▓, ▓▓▓▓▓▓▓, ▓▓▓▓▓▓▓▓, Frank
                 Moccardi and ▓▓▓▓▓▓▓▓▓.

CRIMINAL   : FBI #4354868 NYCPD #B-277340 Record dating from
HISTORY   1946 includes convictions for army desertion and
                 narcotic violation. Sentenced to 7 years, October,
                 1959, for Federal Narcotic Law violation. Is
                 currently (1960) incarcerated.

BUSINESS   : With Urbano & Ignacio Manfredi owned and operated
                 Manfredi Restaurant, 331 E 108 St., NYC.

MODUS   : A trusted Mafia leader and the key man in a Mafia
OPERANDI   narcotic distributing organization operating out
                 of East 108th Street in N.Y.C.'s East Harlem area.

NAME : Richard MANFREDONIA

ALIASES : Diego Manfredonia, Dick, Richard Monroe

DESCRIPTION : Born 1-28-08 Dedham, Mass., 5'6", 200 lbs, heavy build, brown eyes, receding black hair.

LOCALITIES : Resided 590 Southern Blvd.,
FREQUENTED Bronx, NY. Frequented Timpson Bar & Toms Tavern in vicinity of his home & Peacock Bar, 1049 W. Farms Rd, Bronx, NY., also Washington, D.C. Currently (1960) incarcerated.

FAMILY : Married Fannie Dellarca; father: Carmine; mother:
BACKGROUND Carmela; brothers: Anthony & John; sister : Rose (Mrs. Harry) Tantillo.

CRIMINAL : Harry Tantillo, Michael Altimari, John Stopelli,
ASSOCIATES Vincent Mauro, Joseph Valachi, ███████████████.

CRIMINAL : FBI #4061571. NYCPD #B276425. Record dates from
HISTORY 1944 and includes arrests for bootlegging, violation of probation, violation of state narcotic laws. Two Federal narcotic convictions for which currently serving 6-18 years.

BUSINESS : No legitimate occupation known.

MODUS : Was one of a group of Mafia racketeers distributing
OPERANDI wholesale quantities of heroin to various parts of the United States.

NAME   : Giacinto MANNARINO

ALIASES   : Archie Mannarino, Thomas
                  Marino.

DESCRIPTION   : Born 1-1-12 Calaleria,
                  Sicily. 5'6", 165 lbs.,
                  brown eyes, brown-greying
                  hair, has small moles on
                  both cheeks.

LOCALITIES   : Resides 624 Myrtle Ave.,
FREQUENTED   Brooklyn, N.Y. Frequents
                  Frank's Bar & Grill and
                  Lounge Bar & Grill, both in
                  Brooklyn, and the Twenty-One Bar in Manhattan.

FAMILY   : Married to Ann Biondollilo & has 4 children; father:
BACKGROUND   Antonio; mother: Eugenia Brasaccio; brother: Frank;
                  sisters: Angelina, Michelina, & Nora.

CRIMINAL   : Sam Accardi, Vincent Mauro, Charles Albero, ███████
ASSOCIATES   ███████, Pete Tambone, Alexander Amorosa.

CRIMINAL   : FBI#196468. NYC PD-B#73300. Arrests since 1929
HISTORY   include carrying revolver, assault & armed robbery,
                  and conviction for Federal Narcotic Laws.

BUSINESS   : No legitimate business or employment known.

MODUS   : A member of Mafia controlled narcotic traffickers
OPERANDI   in Brooklyn who work through seamen smugglers to
                  obtain their supply of narcotics.

NAME	: Frank MARI
ALIASES	: Frankie T., Frank Russo
DESCRIPTION	: Born 9-3-26 Scilla, Reggio, Calabria, Italy, 5'7", 185 lbs, brown hair, brown eyes, medium build, sharp dresser. Schizophrenic. Derivative citizenship.
LOCALITIES FREQUENTED	: Resides 20 Monroe St, NYC, formerly 68 Forsythe St, & 124 Forsythe St, NYC. Frequents CIA Club, 72 Forsythe St, Vivere Bar, 192 2nd Ave, Sugar Bowl, 305 Broome St, Mott St, & Mulberry St, areas, all NYC.
FAMILY BACKGROUND	: Married Mildred DiPietro (sister of narcotic violator Carli DiPietro); son: Matthew; brother: Rocco; sisters: Antoinette Rando, Adeline Rando (not related to Antoinettes husband) and Minnie Tortorelli; father: Matteo; mother: Concetta DeFranco.
CRIMINAL ASSOCIATES	: ▮▮▮▮▮▮▮▮, Angelo Tuminaro, Salvatore Giglio, Frank Mancino, Anthony Lisi, Carmine Galente.
CRIMINAL HISTORY	: FBI #4371934, NYCPD #233493. Record dates from 1945 and includes arrests for felonious assault, possession of weapons, grand larceny & vagrancy, suspect in two homicide investigations.
BUSINESS	: No legitimate employment.
MODUS OPERANDI	: Large scale Mafia narcotic trafficker obtains narcotics from Tuminaro & DiPasqua, who, in turn obtain their supply from the Cotroni smuggling organization in Canada.

NAME : Joseph Francis MARONE

ALIASES : Maroni, Marrone, Marino

DESCRIPTION : Born 2-11-04 NYC, 5'8", 150
lbs, brown eyes, black-grey
hair, balding.

LOCALITIES : Resides 1815 Grand Concourse,
FREQUENTED Bronx, NY. Frequents vicinity
1st Ave, 123 & 124th Sts, &
107th St, & 2nd Ave, NYC.

FAMILY : Father: Frank; mother:
BACKGROUND Concetta DiPersia; brother:
Rocco Salvatore; cousin: Anthony Gnazzo.

CRIMINAL : ███████████, Charles Albero, Frank Caruso,
ASSOCIATES Alfred Criscuolo, Philip Albanese, James Vintaloro.

CRIMINAL : FBI #318702. NYCPD #B 57799. Record dating from
HISTORY 1919 includes arrests for grand larceny, robbery,
juvenile delinquency, vagrancy, assault & robbery.
Two Federal Narcotic convictions.

BUSINESS : Holds part interest in Melrose Salvage Co., 405
E. 107th St., NYC.

MODUS : One of the leading members of a Mafia narcotic
OPERANDI smuggling & distribution syndicate with headquarters in New York's East Harlem.

NAME : Mariano MARSALISI

ALIASES : Mariano Marsalise

DESCRIPTION : Born 10-21-1879 Palermo,
Sicily, Italy, 5'6¼", 160
lbs, medium build, grey hair
brown eyes.

LOCALITIES : Resides 662 Manida St.,
FREQUENTED Bronx and seldom leaves there
due to his advanced age.

FAMILY : Father: John; mother: Sarah
BACKGROUND Griffo (both deceased) brothers: Luciano, Harry, Charles; sister: Lucy;
children: John, Charles, Ammo, Mary Leonardi, Lucy
Collica, Sarah Caruso, Tina Lynch, Eleanor Terico.

CRIMINAL : Frank Caruso (son-in-law, not "Frankie the Bug"),
ASSOCIATES ▬▬▬▬, Vito Coniglio, ▬▬▬▬▬, Lucien
Ignaro.

CRIMINAL : FBI #455409, no NYC B#, was first arrested in
HISTORY Istanbul, Turkey in 1932 for narcotic smuggling.
In 1942 he was convicted of narcotic conspiracy.

BUSINESS : None

MODUS : Has been a Mafia leader for many years. At one
OPERANDI time he headed what was considered to be the largest heroin smuggling ring in existence. Due to
his advanced age he has apparently retired from
active participation in illegal activities and con-
fines his activities to counseling younger Mafia
members.

527

NAME   : Nicholas MARTELLO

ALIASES   : Bulldog Nick, Nick Marrone

DESCRIPTION : Born 4-7-07, Brooklyn, NY,
                  5'5", 160 lbs., black & grey
                  hair, stocky build, brown
                  eyes, cleft chin.

LOCALITIES   : Resides at 42-06 25th Ave.,
FREQUENTED   Astoria, L.I., NY, frequents
                  Paisano Bar, 304 E. 14th St.,
                  New York, New York.

FAMILY   : Father's name, Sylvester,
BACKGROUND   mother's name, Mary, Wife's maiden name, Alvino;
                  two brothers, Fred and Carmine Martello.

CRIMINAL   : Joe Rao, Mike Rubino, ████████████, ████ & Eugene
ASSOCIATES   ████████, John Ormento, Salvatore Santora, Harry
                  Tantillo.

CRIMINAL   : FBI #54716, NYC PD# B64621 dates from 1926 and in-
HISTORY   cludes arrests for rape, assault, robbery, grand
                  larceny, extortion, conviction for Federal Narcotic
                  Laws; arrested on 10-15-58 for conspiracy to violate
                  Federal Narcotic Laws (pending).

BUSINESS   : Was the owner of the Paisano Bar 304 E. 14th St., NYC,
                  at the present time believed to be in partnership with
                  his father; Martello & Son Shoe Repair, 25-02 Stein-
                  way St., Astoria, Long Island, New York.

MODUS   : An important trafficker in the East Harlem section of
OPERANDI   NY and on the Lower East Side; a leader of the Mafia,
                  in charge of narcotic distribution for a group of
                  these traffickers operating on the Lower East Side and
                  in the East Harlem section of New York City, N.Y.

NAME	: Gaetano MARTINO
ALIASES	: Mimi, Tommo Longo, Tom Long, Thomas Martino.
DESCRIPTION	: Born 9-28-1900, Palermo, Sicily, Italy, 5'11", 235 lbs, brown hair, brown eyes, naturalized NYC 8-30-28.
LOCALITIES FREQUENTED	: Resides 127 Bay 49th St, Brooklyn, NY. Frequents lower East Side of NYC.
FAMILY BACKGROUND	: Wife: Giuseppina; father: Domenico; mother: Rosalia Barbaro; son: Gaetano, Jr; daughter: Carmela Mignose; brother: Charles; stepbrother: Joseph Veneziano; sister: Marguerita DeBlase.
CRIMINAL ASSOCIATES	: ███████, Vito Genovese, Lucky Luciano, Gaetano Maiorano, ███████, ███████.
CRIMINAL HISTORY	: FBI #3136870. NYCPD #B70201. Record dates from 1928 and includes arrests for robbery & traffic violations in U.S., and cigarette smuggling in Italy.
BUSINESS	: No legitimate occupation known at this time.
MODUS OPERANDI	: Allied with other top Mafia criminals in large scale smuggling of aliens, pharmaceuticals and narcotics.

NAME   : James Leo MASSI

ALIASES   : Jimmy Ward, Johnny Martino

DESCRIPTION   : Born 9-23-08 N.Y.C. 5'7",
                  208 lbs, black-grey hair,
                  brown eyes, heavy build.

LOCALITIES   : Resided 1223 Waring Ave.,
FREQUENTED   Bronx, N.Y. Currently(1959)
                  incarcerated in Federal Pen-
                  itentiary.

FAMILY   : Married to Florence Manzi;
BACKGROUND   sons: Michael & James; step-
                  son: Stanley; brothers: Fred, Harry; sisters: Mrs.
                  Rose Botta, Mrs. Lena Casella, Mrs. Fannie DiMonte,
                  Mrs. Antoinette DeMartino; father: Joseph (dead);
                  mother: Mary Loreto.

CRIMINAL   : Ben & Ted DeMartino, Rocco Mazzie, ████████████,
ASSOCIATES   Joe Valachi, Rocco Barra, Frank Pasqua, all of
                  NYC area; ██████████ & Peter Casella of Phila-
                  delphia area.

CRIMINAL   : FBI #495223. NYCPD B#97132. Arrests since 1925
HISTORY   include illegal possession firearms, attempted
                  robbery, conspiracy. Sentenced 7-31-58 to 10
                  years for Federal Narcotic Laws at NYC.

BUSINESS   : No legitimate business or employment known.

MODUS   : A large scale interstate narcotic trafficker
OPERANDI   closely associated with known Mafia international
                  traffickers & smugglers.

NAME : Pasquale MATRANGA

ALIASES : "Patsy" Pasquale Matranca

DESCRIPTION : Born 11-1-1887 Monreale, Palermo, Sicily, Italy, 158 lbs, speaks broken English. No further description available. Naturalized Bronx, NY 3-23-28.

LOCALITIES FREQUENTED : 8733 23rd Ave, Brooklyn, NY. Formerly resided at 125 E. 4th St, NYC, NY. Frequents Bensonhurst Section of Brooklyn and the Lower East Side of Manhattan.

FAMILY BACKGROUND : Wife: Providenza; daughter: Maria; father: Carlo; mother: Carmela Blandino.

CRIMINAL ASSOCIATES : Lucky Luciano, Joseph Profaci, Willie Moretti (deceased), Johnny Russo, ███████████████ ███████.

CRIMINAL HISTORY : No known criminal record here or in Italy.

BUSINESS : Currently self employed as a retail salesman of olive oil from his residence. Formerly owned the Garden State Construction Co., Palisades, NJ.

MODUS OPERANDI : A close associate of Lucky Luciano to whom he brought an Oldsmobile on trip to Italy in 1948. With other Mafiosi has smuggled narcotics from Mexico to U.S. Activities now curtailed because of advanced age.

NAME	: Alfred Vincent MAURIELLO
ALIASES	: Al
DESCRIPTION	: Born NYC 8-14-27; 5'9", 190 lbs, medium build, black hair, brown eyes.
LOCALITIES FREQUENTED	: Last address 2319 Beaumont Ave.,Bronx,N.Y.; frequented 225th & White Plains Road, Capri Lounge & Hi Hat Bar, all in Bronx, N.Y.

FAMILY BACKGROUND	: Married to Ann Pirro; no children; father: Frank; mother: Maria Gianatassio; brothers: Frank, Santos, Thomas & Steve @ Tami.
CRIMINAL ASSOCIATES	: Robert Guippone, Michael & Anthony Sedotto, ███████, ███████, ███████ and ███████.
CRIMINAL HISTORY	: FBI #652540C. NYCPD B#390939. Arrested in 1957 for felonious assault with a bat, in 1957 and 1959 for violation of the Federal narcotic laws. Is currently (1959) serving a five year sentence for Federal narcotic law violation.
BUSINESS	: Sterling Aluminum Company, 3739 Boston Rd.,Bronx.
MODUS OPERANDI	: A wholesal narcotic trafficker and close associate of top Mafia men in the Bronx, N.Y.

NAME	:	Vincenzo Francesco Angelo MAURO

ALIASES : Vincent Murio, Vincent
Maurio, Vincent J. Morrio,
Vinnie Morrow.

DESCRIPTION : Born 2-26-16 NYC, 5'11",
194 lbs., brown eyes, dark
brown hair.

LOCALITIES : Resides 3824 Bronx Blvd.,
FREQUENTED   Bronx, and also at 22 King
St., in Manhattan. Fre-
quents Burke Bar & Ciro's
Bar, both in Bronx, and most night clubs in midtown
Manhattan and in Greenwich Village area.

FAMILY : Single, father: Salvatore, mother: Rafaela Criscuolo,
BACKGROUND sisters: Teresa & Amelia.

CRIMINAL : Anthony Strollo, John Stoppelli, John Ormento,
ASSOCIATES Salvatore Santoro, Patsy Moccio (dead), Anthony
Mirra, Joe Valachi.

CRIMINAL : FBI #760950, NYCPD B#115392. Arrests since 1933
HISTORY   include robbery, burglary, federal income tax
evasion and Federal Narcotic Laws.

BUSINESS : Usually associates himself with some night club or
bar which is under the control of the Strollo
organization.

MODUS : A high ranking member of the Tony Strollo controlled
OPERANDI Mafia organization, which is involved in narcotic
trafficking, shylocking, policy rackets, and after
hours "joints". Considered a merciless and vicious
"killer".

NAME	: Rocco MAZZIE
ALIASES	: Rogie
DESCRIPTION	: Born 2-25-16 Luzerne, Pa., 5'7", 160 lbs, brown eyes, brown-grey hair.
LOCALITIES FREQUENTED	: Resides 2332 Seymour Ave., Bronx, NY. Frequents East Harlem area of Manhattan.
FAMILY BACKGROUND	: Married to Anna Vacchi; daughter: Amelia; brothers: Ralph & James; sister: Mrs. Angelina Branca; mother: Amelia Pecoria; father: Angelo.
CRIMINAL ASSOCIATES	: Frank Borelli, Charles Curcio, John Ormento, Vincent Squillante, Steve Puco, Frank Pasqua, Nick Tolentino, all of NYC, Salvatore Poliafico of Cleveland.
CRIMINAL HISTORY	: FBI #836192. NYCPD B#128301. Arrests since 1934 include robbery, assault & robbery, conviction for Federal Narcotic Laws.
BUSINESS	: No legitimate business or employment known.
MODUS OPERANDI	: A wholesale dealer in narcotics who has supplied many important traffickers throughout the U.S. A close associate of known Mafia traffickers who are his source of supply.

NAME	: Rosario S. MEZZASALMA

ALIASES   : Salvatore Mezzasalma

DESCRIPTION : Born 11-8-1899 Vittoria,
Sicily, 5'5", 200 lbs, brown
eyes, black-grey hair, heavy
build.

LOCALITIES   : Resides 8700 23rd Ave.,
FREQUENTED   Brooklyn, NY. Frequents
Sicilian Cafe 235 Chrystie
St., & Zia Teresa Restaurant
115 W. 49th St., both in NYC.

FAMILY   : Wife's name is Julia; brothers: Salvatore & Thomas;
BACKGROUND   sisters: Mrs. Rose Barone, Mrs. Angela De Angelis;
father: Giovanni; mother: Concetta Salamone.

CRIMINAL   : Steve Armone, Eugene Tramaglino, Vincent Randazzo,
ASSOCIATES   Ugo Rossi, Jean Laget, Paul Gambino, Salvatore
Shillitani, all of NYC area.

CRIMINAL   : FBI #27034, NYCPD E#8448. Arrests since 1923
HISTORY   include counterfeiting, homicide (vehicle), Internal Revenue Laws, and Federal Narcotic Laws.

BUSINESS   : Had interest in Zia Teresa Restaurant, NYC.

MODUS   : A prominent Mafioso from NYC who is a member of
OPERANDI   a group which causes narcotics to be smuggled into
the U.S. and offers it for sale in kilo quantities
only.

NAME	: Thomas Sabbato MILO, JR.
ALIASES	: Sabie, Tommy Jr.
DESCRIPTION	: Born 8-10-23 Bronx, NY, 5'8½", 166 lbs, black hair, brown eyes, fair complexion.

LOCALITIES
FREQUENTED
: Resides 24 Huron Place, Yonkers, NY. Frequents Trade Winds Motel, 1141 Yonders Ave, Yonkers, NY, Rio Steak House, 1187 Yonkers Ave, Yonkers, NY, Glenwood Bar, Riverdale Ave, Bronx, NY, The Yonkers Raceway.

FAMILY
BACKGROUND
: Married Ann Walsh; sons: Thomas & Patrick; daughter: Mary Ann; father: Thomas, Sr., (deceased); mother: Marie Scarfuto; sisters: Josephine Maturi, Mary Maturi.

CRIMINAL
ASSOCIATES
: Anthony Strollo, Joseph Valachi, John & Frank Dio-Guardia, ██████████████, Vincent Mauro, █████████, ██████████, Joseph Barra, ██████████████, ██████████████.

CRIMINAL
HISTORY
: FBI #237349D. March 23, 1959 pleaded guilty to a conspiracy to violate the Federal Housing Act. On May 12, 1959, was sentenced to 18 months and fined $3000.00. He has no previous convictions.

BUSINESS
: Owns and manages the Trade Winds Motel, 1141 Yonkers Ave, Yonkers, NY.

MODUS
OPERANDI
: A Lieutenant for the Anthony Strollo Mafia organization. Successor to his recently deceased father in control of rackets in Westchester County, NY.

NAME : Lester MIRAGLIA

ALIASES : Lefty, Joe Russo

DESCRIPTION : Born 5-16-16 NYC, 5'8", 215 lbs, heavy build, black hair, brown eyes, hard of hearing.

LOCALITIES FREQUENTED : Resided 1082 Morris Park Ave, Bronx, NY. Frequented White Plains Rd, Gun Hill Rd., 187 th & Beaumont, both Bronx, NY.

FAMILY BACKGROUND : Married Marion Greenlaw, formerly married to Patricia Sperano; no children by either woman; father: Alfred J; mother: Katherine Caputo; sister: Gloria; all above reside at 2565 Golden Ave, Bronx, NY.

CRIMINAL ASSOCIATES : ███████████, ███████████, John Stopelli, Robert "Sonny" Guippone, Tony Carminati, Joe Valachi, and Canadian bookmakers ███████████ and Mike Consolo.

CRIMINAL HISTORY : FBI #1967285, NYCPD #B123912, record dates from 4-28-40 and includes arrest for possession of a gun, bookmaking, felonious assault, jostling. Federal Narcotic Law conviction for which sentenced to 6 yrs. in 1957.

BUSINESS : Never known to have legitimate income.

MODUS OPERANDI : A large scale narcotic trafficker on an interstate level in association with other important Mafiosi.

> Miranda retired in 1972 and died of natural causes in 1973.

NAME : Michele MIRANDA

ALIASES : Mike Mirandi, Mr. Big, Frank Russi.

DESCRIPTION : Born 7-26-1896 San Giuseppe Vesuviano, Naples, Italy, 5'5", 160 lbs, brown eyes, black-grey hair, naturalized New York City 5-16-32.

LOCALITIES FREQUENTED : Resides 167 Greenway North, Forest Hills, L.I. Summer home 629 E. Olive St., Long beach, L.I. Frequents Lower East Side and garment district of NYC, travels to Florida, Cuba, Canada and Italy.

FAMILY BACKGROUND : Married Lucy DeLorenzo; son: Anthony Michael; sister: Mrs. Anna Flavio; brothers: Pasquale & Antonio (dead); father: Vincenzo; mother: Carmela Bifulco.

CRIMINAL ASSOCIATES : Lucky Luciano, Giuseppe Doto & Calogero Iacono, of Italy, Francisco Costiglia, Anthony Strollo, Carmine Galante, Joseph Stracci & Meyer Lansky.

CRIMINAL HISTORY : FBI #91524 NYCPD #B-129648 Record dating from 1915 includes arrests for murder, disorderly conduct, vagrancy and conspiracy to obstruct justice (for which sentenced 1960 to 5 yrs & $10,000 fine.

BUSINESS : Cadillac salesman for Huntoon & Raffo, N.Y.C.

MODUS OPERANDI : Attended 1957 Apalachin Mafia meeting as a leader from NYC area. One of the most feared & ruthless Mafiosi in the U.S. Has engaged in narcotic smuggling, murder, extortion and is one of the controlling racketeers in NYC's garment industry.

538

Mirra was killed on February 18, 1982, by his cousins in a parking garage in Lower Manhattan. He was shot at point-blank range in the head. He was shot 4 times in total.

NAME : Anthony MIRRA

ALIASES : Anthony Mirro

DESCRIPTION : Born 7-18-27 NYC, 6'0", 210 lbs., black hair, brown eyes medium build,

LOCALITIES FREQUENTED : Resides 115 Madison St., NYC, frequents LaComedie Restaurant, Manhattan, and 42 College Place, Yonkers, New York.

FAMILY BACKGROUND : Single, father's name Albert mother's name is Millie Embarrato.

CRIMINAL ASSOCIATES : Alfred J. Embarrato (Uncle), ███████████████, Angelo Tuminaro, ███████████████, Joe Latona, Vincent Mauro.

CRIMINAL HISTORY : FBI #393845C, NYCPD #B233768, dates from 1948 and includes arrests for possession of a gun, assault and conviction for Federal narcotic laws.

BUSINESS : Commission salesman for Pure Stone Construction Co., 221 Palisades Ave., Garfield, NJ, alleged owner of LaComedie Restaurant, E. 46th St., NYC., together with Ann Dedon, paramour and owner of record.

MODUS OPERANDI : A wholesaler of narcotics in large quantities. Trusted member of the Mafia. Was purchasing narcotics from the Behrman & Velucci organization in NYC and delivers locally and also into interstate traffic.

539

NAME   : Salvatore MISSALE

ALIASES   : Solly, Big Sol

DESCRIPTION   : Born 11-2-03, Palermo,
                 Sicily, Italy, 5'5", 140 lbs,
                 medium build, brown hair,
                 brown eyes, naturalized
                 Southern Dist., NY, 3-11-36,
                 Cert. #C5678943.

LOCALITIES   : Resides 784 S. Oak Drive,
FREQUENTED   Bronx, N.Y., frequents
                 Willow Inn, Westchester Ave,
                 & Willow St, & Ribbon Inn,
                 East Crosby & Westchester Ave., Bronx, N.Y.

FAMILY   : Wife: Josephine Petrelli; children: Salvatore, Jr.
BACKGROUND   & Rose Florio; father: Salvatore; mother: Rose
                 Collazi, (both deceased).

CRIMINAL   : John Spica & Jack Tocco of Detroit; Paul Gambino &
ASSOCIATES   ▓▓▓▓▓▓▓▓▓▓▓▓ of N.Y.

CRIMINAL   : FBI #1790410, NYCPD #B 168255, arrest record dates
HISTORY   back to 1938 and includes receiving stolen proper-
                 ty, robbery, extortion and policy.

BUSINESS   : Self employed as food salesman.

MODUS   : Closely allied with top Detroit and New York
OPERANDI   Mafia narcotic traffickers.

540

NAME	: Frank MOCCARDI
ALIASES	: Frankie-The-Boss
DESCRIPTION	: Born 12-18-17, NYC, 5'8", 185 lbs, medium build, grey-black hair, brown eyes, neat dresser.

LOCALITIES FREQUENTED	: Resides 277 Bronx River Rd, Yonkers, NY. Frequents Copacabana, 10 E. 60th St, and other midtown NYC night clubs 106th St, between 1st & 2nd Aves, Jennies Bar, 2036 2nd Ave, NYC.
FAMILY BACKGROUND	: Married Rose Imbembo; son: Salvatore; daughter: Rose.
CRIMINAL ASSOCIATES	: John Ormento, Anthony Castaldi, Angelo Loiacano, Salvatore LoProto, Rocco Sancinella, ███████████.
CRIMINAL HISTORY	: FBI #1098685. NYCPD #B 144868. Record dates from 1936 and includes arrests for juvenile delinquency, robbery, bookmaking and gambling.
BUSINESS	: Was reported to have been the actual owner of the now defunct Fontainbleu Rest., 140 E. 53 St, NYC.
MODUS OPERANDI	: A top level Mafia member and one of the most important wholesale heroin dealers in the U.S., obtaining supplies from the Cotroni organization in Canada.

NAME   : Rosario MOGAVERO

ALIASES   : Saro Mogavero, Saro Mogaveno,
                  Saro Mugavero.

DESCRIPTION   : Born 5-2-16 N.Y.C. 5'6",
                  168 lbs., blue eyes, brown
                  hair.

LOCALITIES   : Resides 104 Madison St.,
FREQUENTED   N.Y.C. Frequents area of
                  Madison & Pike Sts., N.Y.C.,
                  and docks on East River.

FAMILY   : Married to Mary Nanetakis &
BACKGROUND   has 4 children; father: Salvatore; mother:
                  Illuminata (both born in Sicily); brother: Joseph.

CRIMINAL   : John Ormento, Salvatore Santoro, Rocco Pellegrino,
ASSOCIATES   Phil Albanese, Sam Kass, Angelo Tuminaro, ███████
                  ████████, Carmine Locascio, Joe Lapi, Angelo
                  Loiacano, all of N.Y.C.

CRIMINAL   : FBI#895630. NYC PD-B#109163. Arrests since 1932
HISTORY   include burglary, felonious assault, harboring a
                  fugitive, extortion.

BUSINESS   : Was vice-president of Local 856 of the International
                  Longshoremen's Union in 1953 when he was sentenced
                  in N.Y.C. for extortion.

MODUS   : A major narcotic trafficker on New York's lower
OPERANDI   east side, and a feared Mafia leader in that area.
                  Close associate of most top Mafia leaders in
                  N.Y.C.

NAME   : Samuel MONASTERSKY

ALIASES   : Sam Manis

DESCRIPTION   : Born 8-1-08 NYC, Jewish,
                 5'10", 210 lbs, black-grey
                 hair, brown eyes, medium
                 complexion.

LOCALITIES   : Resides 2265 2nd Ave, NYC,
FREQUENTED   frequents East Harlem & mid-
                 town areas of NYC.

FAMILY   : Married Helen Pellegrino;
BACKGROUND   son: Robert; daughter:
                 Arlene; father: Harry (deceased); mother: Fannie
                 Crossman, deceased; brothers: Arthur, Irving;
                 sisters: Minnie Farbstein, Arlyne Goldberg.

CRIMINAL   : ███████████████, Giuseppe Pellegrino, Louis
ASSOCIATES   Foceri, Rosario Rinaldi, Marc Orlandino, Joseph
                 Bove.

CRIMINAL   : FBI #270536, NYCPD B#70285. Record dating from
HISTORY   1928 includes arrests for attempted robbery and
                 violations of Federal narcotic laws. Federal nar-
                 cotic conviction.

BUSINESS   : No legitimate occupation.

MODUS   : Wholesale trafficker in heroin. Supplies dealers
OPERANDI   in NYC, and other cities across the U.S. Liaison
                 man between major Mafia and Jewish racketeers.

```
NAME          : Michael MONICA

ALIASES       : Gigs, Gigi, Giggy

DESCRIPTION   : Born 1-12-17 NYC, 5'6", 193
                lbs, brown eyes, brown hair,
                light complexion.

LOCALITIES    : Resides with sister at 3655
FREQUENTED      Willett Ave., Bronx, NY.
                Frequents Sawdust Inn at
                3131 White Plains Rd, Maple
                Tavern at 578 E. Fordham Rd,
                and Burkes Bar 3204 White
                Plains Rd, all in Bronx, NY.

FAMILY        : Single; father: Joseph; mother: Margaret Movigan;
BACKGROUND      brother: Anthony (recently deceased); sisters:
                Mrs. Mary Sassano & Lucille Regante.

CRIMINAL      : Michael Nicoline, Thomas Milo, Joseph Valachi,
ASSOCIATES      Dominick Carminate, Robert Guippone.

CRIMINAL      : FBI #811538. NYCPD #B220924. Record dating from
HISTORY         1934 includes arrests for assault & robbery with
                gun, vagrancy, rape, jostling, policy & felonious
                assault. Currently (1960) defendent in important
                narcotic case.

BUSINESS      : No legitimate occupation.

MODUS         : For many years has operated as "plant man" maintaining
OPERANDI        caches of narcotics for Mafia narcotics distribution
                organizations headed by the late Pasquale Moccio &
                currently Joseph Valachi.
```

NAME : John Charles MONTANA

ALIASES : John Montagna, John Montino

DESCRIPTION : Born 6-30-1893, Montedoro,
Sicily, 5'11", 180 lbs, grey
hair, brown eyes, naturalized 7-7-21, Buffalo, N.Y.

LOCALITIES : Resides 340 Starin Avenue,
FREQUENTED   Buffalo, NY. Frequents
Buffalo-Utica-Rochester area
and makes trips to Italy,
Miami & Hot Springs, Ark.

FAMILY : Married Esther Broom; no children; brothers: Joseph,
BACKGROUND   Salvatore, Angelo, Peter; sisters: Mrs. Arunzi, Mrs.
Sarah Belfonte, Mrs. Vincenza Alfano, all of Sicily;
father: Charles; mother: Rose Valente (both deceased).

CRIMINAL : Lucky Luciano, Russell Bufalino, Antonio & Stefano
ASSOCIATES   Magaddino, James LaDuca, Salvatore & Joseph Falcone,
Giuseppe Profaci.

CRIMINAL : FBI #193791-D Only known arrest was for conspiracy
HISTORY   to obstruct justice, for which sentenced in 1960 to
4 years and $10,000 fine.

BUSINESS : Owns Van Dyke Taxi Co. & Frontier Liquor Corp. in
Buffalo, has horse stables in Ontario, Canada, and
other business interests.

MODUS : Attended the 1957 Apalachin Mafia meeting as leader
OPERANDI   of the Buffalo faction. One of the most influential
Mafia leaders in the U.S. Has used his wealth and
political influence to help the Mafia gain control
of all rackets in the Buffalo area.

NAME   : Samuel MONTEMURRO

ALIASES   : Sam Montemurro

DESCRIPTION   : Born 11-2-17 NYC, 5'3", 133
                 lbs, medium build, black
                 hair, brown eyes, sallow
                 complexion and has crooked
                 right little finger.

LOCALITIES   : Resides 216 E. 114th St,
FREQUENTED   NYC. Frequents the areas of
                 116th St, & Pleasant Ave, &
                 116th St, & 2nd Ave, NYC.

FAMILY   : Married Anna Mezzelini; daughters: Isabella, Jennie,
BACKGROUND   Rosalie; father: Dominio; mother: Isabella; both
                 parents were born in Italy and are now deceased.

CRIMINAL   : ████████████, ██████████████████████
ASSOCIATES   ████████ of NYC & ████████████ of Cleveland, Ohio.

CRIMINAL   : No FBI # assigned. Has never been arrested by the
HISTORY   NYCPD and has no B number. His only arrest was in
                 1952 when he was convicted of Federal narcotic law
                 violation.

BUSINESS   : Has been sporadically employed as porter and labor-
                 er for the Aluminum Co., of America.

MODUS   : Lower echelon member who is employed by higher
OPERANDI   echelon Mafia narcotic traffickers to maintain
                 their caches of narcotics and make deliveries to
                 customers.

NAME   : Vincenzo MORSELLINO

ALIASES   : Charles Adamo, Vincent Adamo,
                 James Mossellino.

DESCRIPTION : Born 9-12-1898 Calatafimi,
                 Trapani, Sicily, Italy, 5'6",
                 170 lbs, heavy build, brown
                 hair, grey eyes, dark com-
                 plexion. Naturalized Brook-
                 lyn, NY 11-16-36, C-6867727.

LOCALITIES   : Resides 4 Locustwood Blvd.,
FREQUENTED   Elmont, NY, frequents Capri
                 Restaurant, 576 Grand St,
                 Brooklyn, Grand St. Bar, 573 Grand St., Wilson &
                 Central Ave, sections of Brooklyn, NY.

FAMILY   : Wife: Anna Verone; no children; father: Giuseppe;
BACKGROUND   mother: Antoinette Adamo (both deceased); brothers:
                 Ignazio, Pietro, Guilio, Sebastian (all in Italy);
                 cousins: Rosario & Vito Morsellino, Settimo Accardo.

CRIMINAL   : Settimo Accardo, Joseph Clemente, Pietro Licata,
ASSOCIATES   Charles LaCascia, Vincent Todaro, ███████████.

CRIMINAL   : FBI #1639120. Record dates from 1931 and includes
HISTORY   one disorderly person and 3 alcohol violation
                 arrests.

BUSINESS   : Chef at Capri Restaurant, has interest in Grand Bar,
                 573 Grand Ave, B'klyn, NY.

MODUS   : Mafia bootlegger, close associate of top level
OPERANDI   Mafiosi; also engaged in large scale narcotic
                 smuggling & distribution.

NAME   : Alfonso MOSCA

ALIASES   : Funzy

DESCRIPTION   : Born 5-14-13 NYC, 5'9", 183
                  lbs, dark brown hair, brown
                  eyes, dark complexion, mole
                  right side of nose.

LOCALITIES   : Resides 99-32 62nd Ave,
FREQUENTED   Forest Hills, NY. Frequents
                  Lighthouse Cafe 76 & Broad-
                  way, Rao's Bar 455 E 114,
                  Dell's Cafe 916 8th Ave,
                  Freddie's Bar 2511 3 Ave,
                  all New York City.

FAMILY   : Married Sadie Oddo; sons: Louis, Alfonso, Jr., and
BACKGROUND   Dennis; daughter: Mary Ann; father: Alfonso; mother:
                  Pasqualina Sabatino; brothers: Raymond, Danny, Romeo
                  and Bianco; sisters; Yolanda Aliberti, Anna Ferrone,
                  Catherine Giamberso and Ida Sandemenro.

CRIMINAL   : Joseph Gernie, Benny Indiviglia, Charles Albero,
ASSOCIATES   Angelo Loiacano, Michael Nicoline.

CRIMINAL   : FBI #517354. NYCPD #B99100. Record dates from 1931
HISTORY   and includes arrests for assault & robbery and
                  violation of state narcotic laws.

BUSINESS   : Over the years has operated a bar, restaurant, gas
                  station and used car business all of which proved
                  to be unsuccessful.

MODUS   : A trusted Mafia member, previously associated with
OPERANDI   the old 106th Street Mob who has been trafficking
                  in narcotics for over 20 years. Handles both whole-
                  sale and retail quantities.

NAME   : Vincent MUMMIANI

ALIASES   : Vinnie, Mummaimi

DESCRIPTION   : Born 2-15-11 NYC, 5'8", 150
                 lbs, brown hair, brown eyes,
                 medium build, prominent
                 tattoos on both forearms.

LOCALITIES   : Resides 428 E 116th St., NYC
FREQUENTED   frequents Mondello Bakery,
                 2265 2nd Ave., & the area
                 of 116th St., & Pleasant
                 Ave., NYC. Now incarcerated.

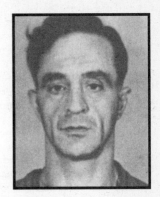

FAMILY   : Single: father: Salvatore; mother: Jennie Lattanzio;
BACKGROUND   brothers: Michael, Pasquale & Frank; sisters:
                 Florence Criscuola, Josephine Saluvene, Connie
                 Garrosi, Millie Salerno & Lucy Mummiani.

CRIMINAL   : ████████████, ███████████, ██████████████,
ASSOCIATES   ██████████, ████████████.

CRIMINAL   : FBI #266549, NYCPD B# 79966. Record dates back to
HISTORY   1930 and includes arrests for counterfeiting, nar-
                 cotic violations, murder, sentenced 1930 to 30 years
                 to life for murder. Given life parole 1951 which
                 revoked 1956 for participation in narcotic case.

BUSINESS   : When gainfully employed, a baker for the Mondello
                 Bakery 2265 2nd Ave., NYC.

MODUS   : A Mafia member of the 116th St., "Mob". A wholesale
OPERANDI   narcotic distributor in the upper East Side area of
                 NYC. Will enter into any illegal venture for mon-
                 Etary gain.

NAME   : Anthony NAPOLITANO

ALIASES   : Tony, Frank, Pal & Tony Naps

DESCRIPTION   : Born 6-7-26 NYC, 5'7", 170
                lbs, brown hair, brown eyes,
                light complexion, medium
                build.

LOCALITIES   : Resides 406 E 120th St., NYC
FREQUENTED   frequents Sally Ann Sports-
                wear Shop, 186 E 117th St.,
                Mary Lou Sportswear Shop,
                176 E 106th St., NYC; Throggs
                Neck Recreation Center, 33-
                57 Tremont Ave., Bronx, NY. Currently incarcerated.

FAMILY   : Wife: Carol Broward (divorced in 1954); father:
BACKGROUND   Anthony; mother: Josephine DeMalo; Brothers: Louis,
                Salvatore Avalino, (half-brother); sisters: Emily
                Altimari, Grace Miano, Mary Tolentino.

CRIMINAL   : Ignazio Orlando, Anthony Tarlentino, ███████
ASSOCIATES   ██████████, Nicholas Tolentino, Benjamin DeMartino,
                John Ormento, ███████████████, James Massi.

CRIMINAL   : FBI #3782486, NYCPDB# 221044. Record dates back
HISTORY   to 1943 and includes arrests for burglary & nar-
                cotics violations. Sentenced in 1959 to 17 years
                for violation of Federal Narcotic Laws.

MODUS   : A young Mafia member of the 107th St., "Mob," who
OPERANDI   were distributing large quantities of narcotics in
                NYC & Interstate.

550

NAME   : Michael NICOLINE

ALIASES   : Nicolini, Nicolino, Ceritello,
                 Mark, Porky

DESCRIPTION   : Born 4-13-13 NYC, 5'7", 180
                 lbs, greying black hair,
                 brown eyes, stocky build.

LOCALITIES   : Resides 61 Bronx River Rd,
FREQUENTED   Yonkers, NY, frequents Burke
                 Bar, Porcaro's A&C Lunch-
                 eonette, Gun Hill Tavern,
                 Castle Hill Diner, Wee Small
                 Hours Bar and Polka Lounge,
                 all Bronx, NY.

FAMILY   : Married Marie DeCarlo; daughter: Marie-Ann; father:
BACKGROUND   John; mother: Marie Conti (both born Italy & now
                 deceased); brothers: Pat & Albert; sisters: Raphaela,
                 Mamie Leone, Viola Pistalici, Millie Guliano.

CRIMINAL   : Michael Monica, Anthony Strollo, Carmine Di Salvo,
ASSOCIATES   John Ormento, Vincent Mauro, Rocco Mazzie.

CRIMINAL   : FBI #481939, NYC PD#B95747. Criminal record dates
HISTORY   from 1930 and includes arrests for grand larceny,
                 burglary, robbery & gambling.

BUSINESS   : Operates private racetrack taxi service.

MODUS   : Since the death of Pasquale Moccio, Nicoline has
OPERANDI   succeeded to the control of narcotics distribution
                 for the Anthony Strollo Mafia organization.

NAME   : George NOBILE

ALIASES   : Georgie Hooks, George Noble,
                 George DeGaetano, Joe Rizzo.

DESCRIPTION   : Born 4-26-10 N.Y.C., 5'7",
                 160 lbs, brown eyes, dark
                 brown hair, small mole on
                 left cheek.

LOCALITIES   : Resided 130 Baxter St, NYC.
FREQUENTED   Frequented area of Mulberry
                 & Hester Sts, Manhattan,
                 made trips to Fla., and Va.

FAMILY   : Married to Isabella DeGaetano & has no children;
BACKGROUND   brother: John; sisters: Mrs. Rose Barniere, Ana,
                 and Mrs. Lena Rapalone.

CRIMINAL   : Vincent Mauro, Frank Caruso, John Stoppelli,
ASSOCIATES   Angelo Tuminaro, ▇▇▇▇▇▇▇▇▇▇▇, ▇▇▇▇▇▇▇▇▇,
                 Philip Albanese, all of NYC, Vincent J. Todaro
                 of Va.

CRIMINAL   : FBI # 1379511. NYCPD-B# 161699. Arrests since 1937
HISTORY   include policy, conspiracy to obstruct justice, &
                 covictions for bothe N.Y. State & Federal Narcotic
                 Laws. Sentenced 5-20-58 to 10 years State Prison,
                 Va., for violation Va. State Narcotic Laws.

BUSINESS   : Has never maintained any legitimate business or
                 employment.

MODUS   : A major local and interstate narcotic trafficker
OPERANDI   and trusted associate of known Mafia traffickers
                 from whom he obtained his supply of narcotics.
                 Working with Mafia associates he acts as chemist
                 in conversion narcotic drugs for the illicit
                 market. Is also known as a "strong-arm" man.

> Notaro died May 17, 1966 of a heart attack at a table at La Scala.

NAME   : Joseph Frank NOTARO

ALIASES   : Joseph Nataro

DESCRIPTION   : Born 1-27-10 NYC, 5'7", 160
                lbs, grey eyes, brown hair,
                slightly bald, light complex-
                ion, reported to have heart
                trouble.

LOCALITIES   : Resides 2885 Harrington Ave,
FREQUENTED   Bronx, NY. Frequents Jew-
                eler's Exchange 37 W 47th
                St, and Moretti's Bar 60 W.
                48th St, both NYC.

FAMILY   : Married Mary Nigro; son: Joseph Jr.; brother: Peter N;
BACKGROUND   sisters: Josephine, Mary Parnepinto, Sophie Polka.

CRIMINAL   : John Petrone, Joseph Orsini, Carmine Galante, ███████
ASSOCIATES   ████████, Lester Miraglia, ██████████████.

CRIMINAL   : FBI #452993A. No NYCPD #. Record consists of only
HISTORY   one arrest - interstate transportation of stolen
                property in 1950.

BUSINESS   : No legitimate employment.

MODUS   : Member of a high level Mafia group engaged in
OPERANDI   varied criminal activities, including the smuggling
                of large quantities of heroin into the U.S. Acts as
                message center for Carmine Galante.

NAME	: Frank OCCHINO

ALIASES   : F.O.

DESCRIPTION : Born 9-1-24 NYC, 5'9", 212
                lbs, black hair, brown eyes,
                medium complexion, husky
                build, scar on left wrist.

LOCALITIES   : Resides 3765 Olinville Ave,
FREQUENTED   Bronx, NY. Frequents Dover
                Bar, 1201 Lexington Ave,
                Campus Bar & Grill, 790 Col-
                umbus Ave, Anchor Bar 1469
                2nd Ave, Open Kitchen 96th
                St, & Lexington Ave, vicinity of 125th & Lexington
                Ave, & 106th St, & 2nd Ave, all in NYC.

FAMILY   : Married Mary Carlino; son: John; daughter: Mary Ann;
BACKGROUND   father: John; mother: Anna; sisters: Lillian Talamone,
                Beatrice Malara and Mary.

CRIMINAL   : John Zoccolillo, Frank, John and Andrew Rasulo,
ASSOCIATES   ████████, ████████████, ████████,
                Frank Borelli.

CRIMINAL   : FBI #465674B. Record consists of one conviction of
HISTORY   Federal Narcotic Law violation.

BUSINESS   : Employed at Highgrade Market, 1582 3rd Ave, NYC.

MODUS   : A young Mafia member, dealing in narcotics in the
OPERANDI   NYC area and interstate.

In May 1975, Oddo died of natural causes.

NAME	: John ODDO
ALIASES	: Johnny Bath Beach, Johnny Bath, Sally the Sheik
DESCRIPTION	: Born 1-8-1904 Palermo, Sicily, Italy, 5'7", 170 lbs, brown hair, brown eyes, stocky build.
LOCALITIES FREQUENTED	: Resides 1402 W 4th St, B'klyn, NY, frequents Bath Beach & Red Hook sections of Brooklyn.
FAMILY BACKGROUND	: Married Anna Esposito; no children; father: Joseph; mother: Maria Tortorici; brother: Joseph (died 1959); sister: Angelina Flavio; brothers-in-law: Joseph Geracitano & John Livotti.
CRIMINAL ASSOCIATES	: Gaetano Maiorana, James Plumeri, Joseph & Lawrence Gallo.
CRIMINAL HISTORY	: FBI #349341. NYCPD #83735. Record dating from 1923 includes arrests for vagrancy, burglary, homicide (gun), assault & robbery, gambling & extortion.
BUSINESS	: Partner with John Villone in Valo Frocks, 1742 86th St, Brooklyn, New York.
MODUS OPERANDI	: One of the top Mafiosi in control of book-making in Brooklyn. Organizer of big money floating dice games.

NAME : Sebastian OFRIA

ALIASES : Buster

DESCRIPTION : Born 7-13-16 NYC 5'6", 145
lbs, slim build, dark brown
hair, brown eyes, ruddy complexion.

LOCALITIES : Resides 1415 66th St, Brook-
FREQUENTED lyn, NY. Frequents Savannah
Club, 66 W. 3rd St, NYC;
Red's Rest., 3714 13th Ave,
Brooklyn; House of Champs,
1654 B'way, NYC; Mulberry &
Houston Sts, NYC; 118th & 1st Ave, NYC.

FAMILY : Married Margaret Gamboli after death of first wife,
BACKGROUND Felicia Difresco, in 1938; daughters: Pauline &
Diane; father: Nunzio (deceased); mother: Pauline
Genovese (now remarried to Frank Rotola); brother:
Dominic Ofria; sister: Nancy Ofria; half-sisters:
Beatrice and Phyllis Rotola.

CRIMINAL : Vincent Mauro, Anthony Strollo, Phillip Albanese,
ASSOCIATES Giacento Mannarino, ▬▬▬▬▬▬▬▬▬▬▬▬▬.

CRIMINAL : FBI #702174. NYCPD #B 117508. Criminal record dates
HISTORY back to 1933 and includes arrests for petit larceny, burglary, unlawful entry, assault & battery
(gun) and gambling.

BUSINESS : No legitimate occupation known.

MODUS : A highly trusted member of Mafia and considered
OPERANDI one of their executioners. Suspect in numerous
Mafia murders.

```
NAME           : Calogero ORLANDO

ALIASES        : Charles

DESCRIPTION    : Born 4-12-06, Terrasini,
                 Palermo, Sicily, Italy; 5'7",
                 190 lbs, heavy build, brown-
                 grey hair, brown eyes, oval
                 face, dark complexion, natur-
                 alized Cleveland, Ohio
                 9-13-34.

LOCALITIES     : Resides 4549 Delafield Ave,
FREQUENTED       Bronx, NY, frequents Orlando
                 Food Co, 99 Hudson St, NYC.

FAMILY         : Married Katherine Vaccaro; son: Carlo; daughter:
BACKGROUND       Frances; father: Nicola; mother: Francesca Bommarito.

CRIMINAL       : ███████████, John Priziola & Ralph Quasarano and
ASSOCIATES       Joe Tocco, of Detroit, Lucky Luciano, Santo Sorge
                 and Francesco Paolo Coppola.

CRIMINAL       : FBI #3201980. Only one arrest for investigation in
HISTORY          1932.

BUSINESS       : Orlando Food Co., 99 Hudson St., NYC.

MODUS          : A long time Mafia member associated in bootlegging
OPERANDI         and narcotic trafficking with the most important
                 Mafiosi in NY., Calif., Detroit and Italy.
```

NAME : Ignazio Lawrence ORLANDO

ALIASES : Big Nose Larry

DESCRIPTION : Born 10-24-24 NYC, 6'1",
195 lbs, black hair, brown
eyes, has large nose.

LOCALITIES : Resided 16 Jacob St., Elmont,
FREQUENTED L.I., N.Y. Currently incarcerated in Federal Penitentiary.

FAMILY : Married to Serafina Rescica;
BACKGROUND daughter: Rose; son: Lawrence
father: Lorenzo; mother: Rose

CRIMINAL : Lorenzo Orlando (father), Nick Tolentino, ▮▮▮▮
ASSOCIATES ▮▮▮▮, James Massi, Angelo Loiacano, Rocco
Sancinella, Joseph Lo Piccolo, all of NYC area,
▮▮▮▮▮▮, Peter Casella of Phila., area,
Vincent Todaro of Virginia.

CRIMINAL : FBI #4369250. Record shows arrest and conviction
HISTORY as army deserter in 1946. Arrested again 1958 &
sentenced to 17 years on 7-31-58 for violation
Federal Narcotic Laws.

BUSINESS : Prior to arrest in 1958 he operated a laundry
truck.

MODUS : A member of a Mafia controlled international
OPERANDI smuggling narcotic ring who acted as a courier and
"plant man" for the ring.

NAME   : Lorenzo ORLANDO

ALIASES   : Lorenzo Rizzo, Lawrence
                          Rizzo

DESCRIPTION   : Born 2-10-01 New Orleans,
                          La., 5'7", 195 lbs, heavy
                          build, black hair, brown
                          eyes.

LOCALITIES   : Resided 164 Hill St., Elmont
FREQUENTED   NY; currently (1959) incar-
                          cerated.

FAMILY   : Married to Rose Orlando
BACKGROUND   (his cousin); son: Ignazio Lawrence Orlando; sisters:
                          Nina, Rosalie; father: Vito; mother: Settima M.
                          Lafuira.

CRIMINAL   : ████████████, Peter Casella, Nicholas Tolentino,
ASSOCIATES   Anthony Napolitano, Joseph LoPiccolo, Angelo Loiacano,
                          Vincent Todaro.

CRIMINAL   : FBI #511557, arrests date back to 1928, largely for
HISTORY.   alcohol violations. In 1958 convicted of Federal
                          Narcotic Law violation and sentenced to a total of
                          17 years.

BUSINESS   : No legitimate occupation known.

MODUS   : Part of a Mafia controlled organization which
OPERANDI   smuggled narcotics into the U.S. and distributed to
                          interstate violators. Orlando was entrusted with
                          the storage of the narcotic drugs and then delivery
                          to the interstate violators.

NAME	: John ORMENTO
ALIASES	: John Ormando, John Forte, Big John, Governor.
DESCRIPTION	: Born 8-1-1912, NYC, 5'10", 240 lbs, black hair, brown eyes, heavy build, sometimes wears glasses.
LOCALITIES FREQUENTED	: Resides 118 Audrey Drive, Lido Beach, L.I. Frequents East Harlem area and various NYC night clubs.
FAMILY BACKGROUND	: Married Carmela Mildred Forte; son: Thomas (married to Patricia Livorsi, daughter of the notorious Frank Livorsi); daughter: Connie.
CRIMINAL ASSOCIATES	: Gaetano Lucchese, Carmine Galante, Salvatore Santoro, Rocco Pellegrino, Frank Livorsi, John DioGuardi, Vincent Squillante, all of NYC, Joseph Ianni of Texas, Rafaele Quasarano & Angelo Meli, of Detroit, the Diecidue brothers, of Tampa, Florida.
CRIMINAL HISTORY	: FBI #1321383 NYCPD #B-158044 Arrests since 1937 include 3 convictions of Federal Narcotic Law violation. 1960 convicted of conspiracy to obstruct justice and sentenced to 5 yrs. & $10,000 fine.
BUSINESS	: Has interest in O & S Trucking Co. & Long Island Garment Trucking Co., both in NYC.
MODUS OPERANDI	: Attended 1957 Apalachin Mafia meeting. Is an important Mafia member and leader of the notorious "107th Street Mob" in NYC, which for many years has been responsible for a large part of the narcotic smuggling & distribution in the U.S.

560

NAME : Theodore Roosevelt ORZO

ALIASES : Freddy, Teddy, Joseph Martine

DESCRIPTION : Born 11-5-04 NYC, 5'7", 151 lbs, medium build, fair complexion, dark brown thinning hair, brown eyes, wears horn rimmed glasses.

LOCALITIES FREQUENTED : Resided 1166 E. 215th St, Bronx, NY. Frequented 96th St & B'way, Parnell Social Club at 109th & 1st Ave, both NYC, vicinity 187th & Cambreling Ave, & Rex Bar at 149th & River Ave, both Bronx, NY.

FAMILY BACKGROUND : Divorced 1937 from Fay Isenberg and 1941 married Mrs. Florence Florio; father: Angelo; mother: Lena Correlli; brothers: Salvatore and Alphonse; sisters: Flora, Connie Giordano and Clara Delarmi.

CRIMINAL ASSOCIATES : Nicholas Tolentino, Joseph Foti, Arnold Barbato, ███████████, ███████████.

CRIMINAL HISTORY : FBI #125775. Metrop, Washington, D.C. PD#133233. Record dates from 1921 and includes arrests for attempted robbery, unlawful entry, operating a still, possession of burglar tools and Federal narcotic conviction.

BUSINESS : Prior to his arrest part-time ship repairer at Brooklyn Navy Yard.

MODUS OPERANDI : A highly trusted Mafioso who carried on large scale interstate narcotic transactions.

561

NAME	: Louis PACELLA	
ALIASES	: Louie Dome	
DESCRIPTION	: Born 10-28-21 NYC, 5'7", 160 lbs, brown eyes, black hair, olive complexion.	
LOCALITIES FREQUENTED	: Resides 322 E 116 St, NYC, frequents Sonny's Bar at 104th & First Ave, Lizzi's Rest., at 116th & Second Ave, and 118th St, & Paladino Ave, all NYC.	
FAMILY BACKGROUND	: Married Jennie Gerardi; no children; father: Anthony; mother: Marie Lamonico.	
CRIMINAL ASSOCIATES	: Joseph D'Ercole, Pasquale Pagano, ████████████, ███████████, Giacomo Reina.	
CRIMINAL HISTORY	: No FBI # assigned. NYCPD #B347933. Only arrest was for grand larceny (automobile) in 1954.	
BUSINESS	: Reported to be employed at Napoli Rest., 141 Rockaway Blvd., Belle Harbor, NY.	
MODUS OPERANDI	: With other important Mafiosi in NY area is engaged in large scale distribution of pure heroin. Has made trips to Europe to further his illicit activities.	

NAME   : Vincent Joseph PACELLI

ALIASES   : Picelli, Bacile, Pacoli,
                    Joe Maci, Anthony Vincent
                    Pacelli

DESCRIPTION   : Born 6-3-21 NYC, 6'0", 175
                    lbs., brown eyes, dark brown
                    hair.

LOCALITIES   : Resides 422 E 118th St., NYC
FREQUENTED   frequents E 117th St. &
                    Paladino Ave., NYC, also
                    makes trips to Los Angeles.

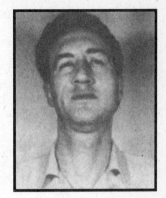

FAMILY   : Wife: Mildred, Father:
BACKGROUND   Michael, Mother: Aureba, Brothers: Frank & Anthony,
                    Sister: Anna.

CRIMINAL   : John Ormento, Edward Sandello, ████████████,
ASSOCIATES   Salvatore Santora, Joe Bendenelli, all of NYC,
                    ███████████████████████ of Los Angeles.

CRIMINAL   : FBI #2084716, NYCPD #B3361, arrest record from
HISTORY   1940 includes burglary and conviction of Federal
                    Narcotic Laws.

BUSINESS   : No Legitimate means of employment

MODUS   : An interstate narcotic trafficker, working directly
OPERANDI   under Mafia associate Joe Bendenelli. Is a trusted
                    member of the organization.

Pagano died at his home in 1989.

NAME	: Joseph Luco PAGANO
ALIASES	: Joe, Joey
DESCRIPTION	: Born 8-28-28 NYC, 5'9", 140 lbs, black hair, brown eyes, slender build, sallow complexion.
LOCALITIES FREQUENTED	: Resides 323 E 115th St, NYC, frequents Santoro's Bar and Grill & Lizzie's Clam House, both in NYC.
FAMILY BACKGROUND	: Wife: Teresa; father: Donato; mother: Antoinette Dimasi; brothers: John & Pasquale.
CRIMINAL ASSOCIATES	: ██████Pasquale Pagano ██████████, Salvatore Mezzasalma, Arthur Repola, Fiore Siano, Joseph Ragone, Peter Contes and Achilles Abbamonte.
CRIMINAL HISTORY	: FBI #4674260. NYCPD #B246200. Arrests since 1946 include attempted robbery, assault & robbery and conviction for Federal Narcotic Laws.
BUSINESS	: Alleged to be manager of Lizzie's Clam House, E 116th St. & 2nd Ave, NYC.
MODUS OPERANDI	: Associated with other important Mafiosi, including the Joseph Valachi organization, which is part of the Anthony Strollo combine, in the local and interstate narcotic traffic.

NAME   : Pasquale Anthony PAGANO

ALIASES   : Big Pat, Patsy Pagano

DESCRIPTION   : Born 2-21-21 NYC, 5'11",
                 202 lbs., black hair, brown
                 eyes.

LOCALITIES   : Resides 3023 Fish Ave.,
FREQUENTED   Bronx, NY., frequented E.
                 Harlem section and night
                 clubs in NYC.

FAMILY   : Father: Donato, mother:
BACKGROUND   Antoinette DiMasi, married
                 to Laura Prete and has two children, brother:
                 Joseph, John.

CRIMINAL   : Tony Strollo, Steve Armone, Fiore Siano, Jack
ASSOCIATES   Scarpulla, Joe Pagano (brother), all of NYC; Pat
                 Erra and Mike Coppola of Miami, Fla., ████████
                 ████████ (France).

CRIMINAL   : FBI #74687 B, Jersey City PD# 13856. Arrests since
HISTORY   1952 include atrocious assault and battery, convic-
                 tion for bribing Federal officer, and conviction
                 (1956) for Federal narcotic laws.

BUSINESS   : Was business agent for Local 59 International Brick-
                 layer's Helpers, A.F.L. prior to narcotic arrest;
                 also a mason contractor, and NJ dock worker for Mafia
                 chief Tony Strollo.

MODUS   : An international and interstate smuggler and dis-
OPERANDI   tributor of narcotics with his own source of supply
                 in France. An up and coming Mafia leader in East
                 Harlem New York City.

NAME   : Carmine PALADINO

ALIASES   : Joseph Palladino, Swatty

DESCRIPTION   : Born 7-14-16 NYC, 5'5", 185
                  lbs, stocky build, grey-
                  black hair, hazel eyes, fair
                  complexion.

LOCALITIES   : Resides 449 E. 116th St.,
FREQUENTED   NYC. Frequents Colonial Tav-
                  ern, 116th & 1st Ave; and
                  Lizzie's Tavern 116th & 2nd
                  Ave, both NYC.

FAMILY   : Married Frances Paladino; son: Richard; daughters:
BACKGROUND   Rose, Annette; father: Annunziato; mother: Rose
                  Vernon; step mother: Angelina; sister: Michelina;
                  half sisters: Anna Petroni, Rose Petriglia.

CRIMINAL   : Anthony Mancuso, ███████████, ███████████,
ASSOCIATES   Joseph Bendenelli, Stephen Puco, Louis Pellechio.

CRIMINAL   : FBI #3289275. NYCPD #139528. Record dates from 1935
HISTORY   and includes arrests for grand larceny, gambling,
                  possession of gun and possession of narcotics.

BUSINESS   : No legitimate employment known.

MODUS   : With other Mafiosi engages in the local & interstate
OPERANDI   narcotic traffic on a large scale.

566

NAME   : George PALMIERI

ALIASES   : Pansy, 3 Finger Pansy

DESCRIPTION   : Born 9-3-21 NYC, 5'4", 145
                lbs, brown eyes, brown hair,
                medium build, dark complex-
                ion.

LOCALITIES   : Resided 32-78 Middletown Rd,
FREQUENTED   Bronx, NY, 238 E. 116th St,
                NYC; frequents various areas
                throughout East Harlem, also
                known to frequent Italian
                area on lower East Side, NYC.
                Currently incarcerated.

FAMILY   : Wife: Angelina Euphemia; son: George; daughter:
BACKGROUND   Debra; father: Frank; mother: Concetta Eliesia;
                brothers: Nunzio, Pasquale, Salvatore, Renato, John;
                sisters: Mary Qualglia, Tillie Illusiato, Josie
                Ferrara.

CRIMINAL   : Joseph Bendinelli, Lucien Ignaro, Ralph Zanfardino,
ASSOCIATES   ███████████████.

CRIMINAL   : FBI #159900C. NYCPD #174946. Record dates from 1938
HISTORY   and includes arrests for assault & battery. A.W.O.L.
                from U.S. Army and possession of narcotics with in-
                tent to sell.

BUSINESS   : Occasionally worked as produce clerk and bakery
                clerk.

MODUS   : With other East Harlem (NYC) Mafiosi engaged in
OPERANDI   large scale narcotic trafficking. Currently serving
                $7\frac{1}{2}$ - 15 yrs on narcotic conviction.

NAME	: Vincent J. PANEBIANCO
ALIASES	: Jimmy Feets, "Sugar".
DESCRIPTION	: Born 12-9-20 N.Y.C., 6'1", 210 lbs., black hair, brown eyes.
LOCALITIES FREQUENTED	: Resides 817 Quincy Ave., Bronx, N.Y. Frequents vicinity E. 116th St. & Palladino Ave., in East Harlem.

FAMILY BACKGROUND	: Married to Josephine Cirillo, has a son Vincent Jr., and a daughter Verna.
CRIMINAL ASSOCIATES	: Rocco Mazzie, ▇▇▇ & Steve Puco, ▇▇▇▇▇▇▇, Joe Bendenelli, ▇▇▇▇▇▇▇▇▇, all of N.Y.C.
CRIMINAL HISTORY	: FBI#1544066. NYC PD-B#157001. Arrests since 1937 include felonious assault, assault & battery, and conviction of Federal Narcotic Laws.
BUSINESS	: Occasional employment as a construction mainten- ance man.
MODUS OPERANDI	: A major distributor of narcotics in East Harlem section of Manhattan, and close associate of all major Mafia traffickers in the area.

He died on January 10, 2005.

NAME   : Victor PANICA

ALIASES   : Vic

DESCRIPTION : Born 4-27-24 NYC, 5'8", 140
               lbs, brown hair, green eyes,
               6" lineal scar on neck below
               left ear.

LOCALITIES   : Resides 141-17 11th Ave,
FREQUENTED   Malba, Queens, NY, frequents
               Westchester & Buhre Aves,
               Bronx, NY, & area of 108 St,
               & 2nd Ave, NYC.

FAMILY   : Married Catherine Matthews; children: Joseph &
BACKGROUND   Marie; father: Victor; mother: Teresa Marchese;
               brother: Paul.

CRIMINAL   : Michael Altimari, Nicholas Bonina, Joseph Valachi,
ASSOCIATES   Vincent Mauro.

CRIMINAL   : FBI # 3986567. NYCPD B#219169. Arrests since 1943
HISTORY   include assault & robbery, gambling, homicide and
               violation Federal narcotic laws.

BUSINESS   : No legitimate employment.

MODUS   : A rapidly rising young Mafia hoodlum who has gained
OPERANDI   a reputation as a triggerman for the underworld in
               NYC. Though it is known that he has been involved
               in gangland killings he has avoided prosecution
               largely through the standard Mafia expedient of
               removing witnesses by one method or another.

NAME	: Vito Anthony PANZARINO
ALIASES	: Pansy, John Casino, Jimmy Santiello
DESCRIPTION	: Born 1-1-21 NYC, 5'5½", 191 lbs, black hair, brown eyes, heavy build, scar right eyebrow.
LOCALITIES FREQUENTED	: Resided 712 Taylor Ave, Bronx, NY & previously 337 E. 114 St., NYC; frequented Riverside Inn & Castle Hill Diner, Stadium Bar & Logan's Bar all Bronx, NY, & East Harlem Section of NYC. Currently incarcerated.
FAMILY BACKGROUND	: Married Marie Gelsomano; daughter: Mary; father: Pasquale; mother: Marie Zacchio; brother: Frank; sisters: Elizabeth Santo and Mary Bottiglieri.
CRIMINAL ASSOCIATES	: Lawrence Iarossi, ███████████, ███████████, Renato Croce, Joseph Valachi.
CRIMINAL HISTORY	: FBI #1380162. NYCPD #B 160113. Record dates from 1937 and includes arrests for unlawful entry, burglary, grand larceny, Federal narcotic conviction for which sentenced 1958 to 10 yrs. Dishonorable army discharge 1945.
BUSINESS	: Owned Wagon Wheel Rest., 373 Brook Ave., Bronx, NY.
MODUS OPERANDI	: Lower echelon Mafia member who used above business as a front for his gambling & narcotic trafficking. Dealt in large quantities of pure and "cut" heroin.

NAME   : Orlando Delli PAOLI

ALIASES   : Bobby London, Robert De Paul

DESCRIPTION   : Born 10-9-12 NYC, 5'6", 179
                  lbs., heavy build, light
                  brown hair, hazel eyes, has
                  tattoo of an eagle on right
                  forearm.

LOCALITIES   : Resides 3153 Waterbury Ave.,
FREQUENTED   Bronx, NY, frequents the
                  lower East Side Italian sec-
                  tion of NYC, also the Lido
                  Bar, 1362 Castle Hill Ave.,
                  Bronx.

FAMILY   : Married to Josephine DePasquale, Daughter: Rose Ann,
BACKGROUND   Son: Andrew, Brothers: Fiorentino, Joseph and Victor,
                  Father's name is Andrew, mother's name is Rose, (both
                  dead).

CRIMINAL   : ███████████████, Joseph Valachi, Edward D'Argenio,
ASSOCIATES   Vincent Panebianco, Michael Monica, Paul Correalle,
                  Joseph Armone, and Angelo Meli, all of NYC.

CRIMINAL   : FBI #1082274, NYCPD #144425, arrests since 1936 in-
HISTORY   clude assault and robbery, transporting Alcohol and
                  possession of untaxed liquor, Internal Revenue Laws,
                  Still Operator, and a conviction in 1954 for the
                  Federal Narcotic Laws.

BUSINESS   : Never permanently employed in any legitimate business.

MODUS   : A high echelon hoodlum who is well respected in
OPERANDI   narcotic traffic circles both in and around the NY
                  area. A close associate of most Mafia traffickers
                  from East Harlem area NYC.

NAME : Fortunato PAPA

ALIASES : Fortune Pope, Fortunato Pope

DESCRIPTION : Born 1-6-1918 West New York, N.J. 6'2", 215 lbs, brown hair, brown eyes.

LOCALITIES FREQUENTED : Resides Club Road, Rye, N.Y. Frequents his places of business, better restaurants & clubs. Travels frequently to Florida, Cuba, Dominican Republic, Italy, etc.

FAMILY BACKGROUND : Married Catherine Mastice 1952 after divorce from Grace Perrotty; father: Generoso, Sr. (dead); mother: Catherine Richichi; brothers: Anthony & Generoso, Jr.

CRIMINAL ASSOCIATES : Frank Costello, Lucky Luciano, Vito Genovese, Giuseppe Doto, Giuseppe Profaci, Vincent Rao.

CRIMINAL HISTORY : 7-19-60 indicted by Federal Grand Jury for diversion of over $375,000 from his companies in connection with fraudulent sales of rock salt to the City of New York.

BUSINESS : Editor of "Il Progresso", Executive V.P. of Colonial Sand & Stone Co., owner of radio station WHOM and has various other enterprises worth millions of dollars.

MODUS OPERANDI : Intimately associated with top Mafiosi in U.S. & Italy, including many who attended 1957 Mafia meeting at Apalachin. Through his newspaper & strong political influence he attempts to refute existence of Mafia and otherwise abets criminal operations of the society. Was with Mafia chief Frank Costello just a few minutes before an attempt was made on Costello's life, in 1957.

On September 24, 1976, Pappadia was killed by shotgun fire in front of his home.

NAME : Andinno PAPPADIA

ALIASES : Andimo Papadio

DESCRIPTION : Born 2-2-14 NYC, 5'10", 202 lbs, grey eyes, brown hair, bald on top, fair complexion, heavy build, one inch scar outside edge of left eyebrow.

LOCALITIES FREQUENTED : Resides Echo Drive, Lido Beach, L.I., NY. Often seen in the vicinity of 108th St, and 2nd Ave., NYC.

FAMILY BACKGROUND : Married Eleanor Rose Atera, (cousin of Mrs. John Ormento); father: Ferdinando; mother: Maria Panica, (both born in Italy).

CRIMINAL ASSOCIATES : John Ormento, Frank Livorsi, Salvatore Santoro, Joseph Vento, Vito Genovese.

CRIMINAL HISTORY : FBI #1331637, NYCPD B# 159069. Record dates from 1936 and includes arrests for gambling, aid & abet member U.S. armed forces to avoid service, Federal narcotic violation.

BUSINESS : Associated with Anna-Lynn Sportswear, Inc., 212 West 35th St., NYC.

MODUS OPERANDI : Important Mafioso and vicious strong-arm enforcer in the Ormento narcotic organization. An intimate friend of Ormento and Santoro. Prominent in labor racketeering.

NAME	: Frank Anthony PASQUA
ALIASES	: Frank Page, Frank Pasquale, Frank Hunt.
DESCRIPTION	: Born 1-13-23 N.Y.C. 6'0", 250 lbs., brown eyes, dark brown hair, heavy build.
LOCALITIES FREQUENTED	: Resides 974 Rhinelander Ave., Bronx, N.Y. Frequented area of East Harlem in Manhattan & Chicago, Ill. Currently (1959) incarcerated for violation Federal Narcotic Laws.

FAMILY BACKGROUND	: Married to Mildred Bartolamucci; sons: Richard & Frank; father: Natale; mother: Rose Comodeo.
CRIMINAL ASSOCIATES	: Jack Scarpulla, John Riccardulli, James Massi, ▒▒▒▒ ▒▒▒▒, Rocco Mazzie, Frank Corona, all of N.Y.C.; Frank Panatera & Jack Rizzo of Chicago, Ill.
CRIMINAL HISTORY	: FBI#241577B. Convicted 4-25-58 to 4 years for violation of Federal Narcotic Laws.
BUSINESS	: Was self-employed in the produce trucking business.
MODUS OPERANDI	: Has been a major interstate narcotic trafficker in association with known Mafia traffickers from East Harlem area of Manhattan.

NAME	: Santo PATTI
ALIASES	: Lloyd, Fats
DESCRIPTION	: Born 4-10-11 in NYC, 5'7", 210 lbs, stocky build, brown hair, brown eyes, dark complexion.
LOCALITIES FREQUENTED	: Resides 396 Seaview Ave., Staten Island, NY., frequents New Dorp section of Staten Island, Mulberry & Mott Sts., & Lower East Side, NYC.

FAMILY BACKGROUND	: Wife: Angela Vail; has two young sons; brother: Paul; father: Vincent; mother: Anna Sardo (deceased), both parents from Sicily.
CRIMINAL ASSOCIATES	: Vincent Corrao, Joseph Gennaro, ██████████████, ████████████, Joseph Marino, August Fontana.
CRIMINAL HISTORY	: FBI #832463C, NYCPDB# 107664, record dating from 1932 includes arrests for homicide, alcohol law violations, bookmaking, vagrancy.
BUSINESS	: No legitimate employment known.
MODUS OPERANDI	: A lower echelon Mafioso, member of the "Mulberry Street Mob". Primarily engaged in gambling & bookmaking.

NAME   : Carmine PELLEGRINO

ALIASES   : Carmine Pell, Carine.

DESCRIPTION : Born 5-18-16, White Plains, N.Y., 5'8", 183 lbs, brown eyes, light brown hair, fair complexion.

LOCALITIES : Resides 21 Park Ave, White
FREQUENTED   Plains, N.Y., frequents Pellegrino's Bakery at 16 Barker Ave, White Plains, and makes trips to Dallas, Texas.

FAMILY   : Wife's name is Catherine, father: Rocco, mother:
BACKGROUND   Elizabeth, brothers: Peter, Salvatore, & Frank.

CRIMINAL   : John Ormento, Saro ▆▆▆▆▆ Mogavero, Richard
ASSOCIATES   Manfredonia, Rocco Pellegrino (father), Peter Pellegrino (brother), all of NYC, Joe Civello, Joe Ianni, both of Dallas, Texas, area.

CRIMINAL   : FBI # 778409C. White Plains, NY, PD # 2277.
HISTORY   Arrests include gambling & disorderly conduct.

BUSINESS   : A musician. Also connected with his father and brother in operation of Pellegrino's Bakery, 16 Barker Ave., White Plains, N.Y.

MODUS   : Looks after the gambling interests of the
OPERANDI   Pellegrino family in Westchester County, NY, and is closely associated with known Mafia narcotic traffickers in NYC and in Dallas, Texas.

NAME   : Peter PELLEGRINO

ALIASES   : Pietro Pellegrino

DESCRIPTION   : Born 2-12-23 White Plains,
                N.Y., 5'8", 190 lbs, brown
                eyes, brown hair, light
                complexion.

LOCALITIES   : Resides 91 Cleveland Street,
FREQUENTED   Valhalla, N.Y. Frequents
                Pellegrino's Bakery at 16
                Barker Ave, White Plains,
                N.Y., also travels to Dallas
                Texas, and Montreal, Canada.

FAMILY   : Married, father: Rocco, mother: Elizabeth, brothers:
BACKGROUND   Carmine, Salvatore, and Frank.

CRIMINAL   : John Ormento, Saro ███████ Mogavero, Richard
ASSOCIATES   Manfredonia, Rocco Pellegrino (father), all of NYC,
                Joseph Ianni, Joseph Civello, ███████████, ██████
                ███████, all of Texas.

CRIMINAL   : FBI # 30429D. White Plains, NY, PD # 9051. Arrests
HISTORY   include gambling and vagrancy.

BUSINESS   : Is associated with his father Rocco in the operation
                of Pellegrino's Bakery, 16 Barker Ave., White Plains,
                New York.

MODUS   : Is one of the younger leaders of the Mafia in West-
OPERANDI   chester County, N.Y., has numerous gambling interests
                in White Plains, N.Y., has been implicated with his
                father Rocco in suspected narcotic dealings with
                known traffickers in Dallas, Texas area.

NAME   : Rocco PELLEGRINO

ALIASES   : The Old Man

DESCRIPTION   : Born 4-13-89, Calabria,
                    Italy, 5'6", 185 lbs, brown
                    eyes, grey hair, stocky
                    build.

LOCALITIES   : Resides 20 Carrigan Ave.,
FREQUENTED   White Plains, NY, frequents
                    Pellegrino Bakery, White
                    Plains, NY.

FAMILY   : Married to Elizabeth Rabasco,
BACKGROUND   4 sons and 4 daughters, Carmine, Sam, Peter, Frank,
                    Mary (wife of Vincent Genari), Cecelia, Elizabeth,
                    Elinore (engaged to son of Saro Magavero); father:
                    Carmine; mother: Maria Violanti.

CRIMINAL   : Saro Magavero, Michael Clemente, ████████████████,
ASSOCIATES   Albert Anastasia (dead), Anthony Strollo, ███████
                    ███████, ██████████, John Ormento, Joe Civello.

CRIMINAL   : NYCPD #E3530, was arrested for assault in 1918 for
HISTORY   which he received a sentence of 1½ years; arrested
                    11-6-22 for violation of Volstead Act, fined
                    $850.00; Deportation proceedings pending against him.

BUSINESS   : Owns Pelligrino Bakery, 16 Barker Ave., White Plains
                    New York.

MODUS   : Head of Mafia in Westchester County; involved in
OPERANDI   gambling and waterfront activities in NYC, with
                    sons was source of supply of narcotics for Italian
                    violators in Dallas, Texas.

NAME : Anthony PELOSO

ALIASES : Tony Pelsa, Tony Pelosa

DESCRIPTION : Born 8-12-07 Italy (city unknown), was brought to U.S. 1908, 5'9", 160 lbs, brown eyes, brown hair, $\frac{1}{2}$" scar over right eye, derived citizenship from mother.

LOCALITIES : Resides 820 Swinton Ave.,
FREQUENTED : Bronx, NY. Frequents 909 Beck St, 1225 Washington Ave, & 652 Southern Blvd, all Bronx, NY, East Harlem & Lower East Side areas of NYC.

FAMILY : Married Virginia Navarro; daughter: Norma; father:
BACKGROUND : Dominick; mother: Carmella (both deceased); mother came to U.S. after fathers death with sons Joseph, Frank, John (deceased) & Anthony. Remarried Gilio Galossa & had daughter, Fannie.

CRIMINAL : ███████████, ███████████, ███████████,
ASSOCIATES : Vincent Panebianco, ███████████, ███████████.

CRIMINAL : FBI #60360. NYCPD #B65577. Record dating from 1924
HISTORY : includes arrests for felonious assault, attempted burglary, robbery, homicide (gun), gambling & abduction and Federal narcotics violation.

BUSINESS : No legitimate employment known;has worked as electrician.

MODUS : Lower echelon Mafioso who has overseas sources for
OPERANDI : narcotics and distributes heroin in the interstate traffic.

On December 28, 1983, Petillo died in Spain.

NAME : David PETILLO

ALIASES : Joe Rose, Herbert Quello,
Little Davy, David Rosa,
David Rosen, Anthony Ferrara

DESCRIPTION : Born 3-11-08 NYC, 5'6", 155
lbs, ruddy complexion, brown
hair, brown eyes, slim build.

LOCALITIES : Resided 246 W 48th St., NYC,
FREQUENTED frequented New York's lower
East Side and bars along
Lexington Ave., from 50th
St. to 60th St. Currently
incarcerated.

FAMILY : Wife: Madeline Poparlardo (deceased); no children;
BACKGROUND father: Anthony; mother: Mary Lomberdi; brother:
Roland; sisters: Anna, Clara Penna, Florence Elia
and Lavenia Santulli.

CRIMINAL : Frank Caruso, Tony Mirra, Lucky Luciano, Vincent
ASSOCIATES Mauro, Anthony Strollo, Vito Genovese.

CRIMINAL : FBI #360387, NYCPD #B65556, record dates from 1924
HISTORY and arrests include attempted grand larceny, gambling, compulsory prostitution & violation of
parole. 1936 sentenced to 20-40 yrs, paroled
4-6-55. Returned for violation 8-4-55, not again
eligible until 1962.

BUSINESS : Alleged to have interest in several bars vicinity
of 50th & Lexington Ave., including Chicks Showplace

MODUS : High ranking Mafia leader, deals in narcotics and
OPERANDI big time robberies.

NAME   : John Michael PETRONE

ALIASES   : John Bennett, John Michael,
                 John Carrila.

DESCRIPTION   : Born 2-4-96 N.Y.C. 5'8",
                 175 lbs., blue eyes, grey
                 hair, left index finger
                 amputated.

LOCALITIES   : Resides 1500 Rowland St.,
FREQUENTED   Bronx, N.Y. Frequents
                 Pastry Shop, Elizabeth &
                 Prince Sts., Michael Angelo
                 Jewelry Shop, 37 W. 47th St.,
                 both in N.Y.C., and Gondolfo Motors, Bronx, N.Y.

FAMILY   : Married to Mary Rose Cerrita; son: John; daughter:
BACKGROUND   Annette Marie Mirrando.

CRIMINAL   : Salvatore Shillitani, Anthony D'Agostino, Charles
ASSOCIATES   & Joseph DiPalermo, Carmine Galanti, Mike Consolo,
                 ████████████, Paul Gambino, Joseph Notaro, &
                 ████████████.

CRIMINAL   : FBI#1474964. NYC PD-B#408659. Arrests since 1938
HISTORY   include concealing assets in bankruptcy &
                 conviction for counterfeiting.

BUSINESS   : Has interests in Michael Angelo Jewelry Shop,
                 37 W. 47th St., N.Y.C.

MODUS   : An international narcotic trafficker who also deals
OPERANDI   in gold smuggling and counterfeiting. A close and
                 trusted associate of high ranking Mafia in N.Y.C.

NAME   : Peter John PIACENTI

ALIASES   : Pete Nimo, Pete Gallo

DESCRIPTION   : Born 8-26-21 NYC, 5'7", 190
                 lbs, brown eyes, black curly
                 hair, medium complexion.

LOCALITIES   : Last known address was 20D
FREQUENTED   Wilklow Ave, Hempstead, NY.
                 Frequents Rickey's Rest.,
                 and Bonnander's Drive In,
                 both in Palo Alto, Calif.,
                 7513 17th Ave, Brooklyn, NY.

FAMILY   : Father: Vincent Piacenti; mother: Rosalie Oliva;
BACKGROUND   brothers: Frank, Salvatore, and Joseph; sister: Sara
                 Razzagone; brother Frank Piacenti arrested with
                 Sebastiano Nani on attempted bribery of Federal
                 Agent.

CRIMINAL   : Sebastiano Nani, ██████████████, ██████████, ██████
ASSOCIATES   ██████████, John Stopelli, ███████████████.

CRIMINAL   : FBI #561015A, NYCPD #B252724. Record dates from
HISTORY   1947 and includes arrests for conspiracy, theft,
                 felonious assault, and violation of the Federal
                 narcotic laws.

BUSINESS   : House painter.

MODUS   : A large scale narcotic distributor who has close
OPERANDI   ties with top level Mafia members in NY and Calif.

NAME	: James PICCARELLI
ALIASES	: Rushe, Rellie, Pucciarelli, Jimmy Rush
DESCRIPTION	: Born 9-28-06 NYC, 5'6", 180 lbs, medium-heavy build, grey hair, brown eyes, olive complexion.
LOCALITIES FREQUENTED	: Resides 100 Ocean Parkway, Brooklyn, NY. Frequents Water, Madison, James & Elizabeth Sts., NYC, Sam Woo's & Wo Ping Restaurants, Mott & Pell Sts., NYC.
FAMILY BACKGROUND	: Wife: Mary Alavera; no children; father: Ralph; mother: Mary Sanganese; brother: Ralph; sister: Mary.
CRIMINAL ASSOCIATES	: Vincent Mauro, Salvatore Santoro, John Ormento, Anthony Strollo, George Nobile.
CRIMINAL HISTORY	: FBI #619767, NYCPD #B 110176. Record dates from 1926 and includes arrests for grand larceny (auto), Federal Narcotic Law violation & illegal possession gas ration stamps.
BUSINESS	: No legitimate occupation known.
MODUS OPERANDI	: A top level Mafioso who is said to have been elected to the position in the Mafia held by the late Joseph Bernava alias Joe Bedelli: arranges smuggling and distribution of huge quantities of narcotics.

NAME : Joseph Charles PICCARELLI

ALIASES : Charlie Rivera, Charlie
Relli, Charlie Bull.

DESCRIPTION : Born 3-18-01 Brooklyn, NY,
5'10", 220 lbs, heavy build,
grey balding hair, dark complexion.

LOCALITIES : Resides 119-18 178th Place,
FREQUENTED St. Albans, NY. Frequents
Rivera Pin-up Co., 39 W 46th
St, Ace Billiard Parlor 43rd
& 7th Ave, and Hectors Cafe-
teria, B'way & 46th St, all NYC.

FAMILY : Married Angelina Brindise 1921 died 1924, no child-
BACKGROUND ren; remarried 1926 to Blanche Fusari; sons: Joseph
& Charles; daughter: Antoinette (Mrs. Paul) Sicone;
father: Ralph; mother: Antoinette (both deceased);
brother: Victor (deceased); sister: Katherine
Monachio.

CRIMINAL : ████████████, ████████████, ████████████
ASSOCIATES and ████████████, all of NYC. ████████████ of
Columbus, Ohio.

CRIMINAL : FBI # 3618478. Record dates from 1943 and includes
HISTORY arrests for alcohol violations, interstate commerce
violations & mailing pornography.

BUSINESS : Co-owner of Rivera Pin-up Co., also part-time dis-
patcher for Anthony Guariglia Trucking Co., 158
Clay St., Brooklyn, NY.

MODUS : Lower echelon Mafia racketeer, former bootlegger,
OPERANDI now chiefly engaged in distribution of pornographic
literature.

NAME	: Michael PICONE

ALIASES   : Matthew Picona, Slim, Matty

DESCRIPTION : Born 11-3-04, NYC, 5'10",
205 lbs, heavy build, black-
grey hair, blue eyes.

LOCALITIES : Resides 205 E 124 St., NYC,
FREQUENTED   frequents barber shop, Lexington Ave., between 124 &
125 St., Cancro Ash Removal
428 E 108th St., NYC.

FAMILY   : Wife: Isabelle Pastore;
BACKGROUND   children: Florence, Matty, Anna & Lucille; father:
Matthew; mother: Fannie La Puma.

CRIMINAL   : Sammy Cass, Frank Corona, Anthony Castaldi, Alfredo
ASSOCIATES   Felice, Anthony Ciccone, John Dio Guardio

CRIMINAL   : FBI #344490 B, NYC PD# 326064. Record includes only
HISTORY   one arrest - violation of NY State Narcotic Laws sentenced to 1-2 years Sing Sing.

BUSINESS   : Owns all or part Cancro Ash Removal, 428 E 108th St.,
New York City.

MODUS   : A highly trusted Mafia racketeer, engaged in the
OPERANDI   wholesale narcotic traffic and carting racket.

Pieri died on July 24, 1981.

NAME : Salvatore PIERI

ALIASES : Sam Pieri, Samuel Johns

DESCRIPTION : Born 1-29-11, Buffalo, NY, 5'7", 165 lbs, brown eyes, brown hair, medium build, neat dresser.

LOCALITIES FREQUENTED : Resided 63 Claremont Ave, Buffalo, NY. Frequented Ciro's Bar, Buffalo and Niagara Falls, NY area. Currently incarcerated.

FAMILY BACKGROUND : Wife: Carol; daughter: Shirley (Mrs. Samuel Amoia); father: Giovanni; mother: Anna Ciriese, (both deceased); brothers: John, Stephan, Horace; sisters: Genevieve, Mrs. Adelaide Fina & Mrs. Elise DiCarlo.

CRIMINAL ASSOCIATES : Anthony and Steve Maggadino, Jos. DiCarlo, Sal & Angelo Rizzo, ███████████████, ███████████, John Ormento, Rocco Mazzie, Anthony Strollo.

CRIMINAL HISTORY : FBI #182971, Buffalo PD #20699, several arrests since he was a juvenile, including burglary, possession firearms, robbery, grand larceny and conviction (1954) Federal Narcotic Laws (sentenced to 10 years imprisonment).

BUSINESS : No legal source of income known.

MODUS OPERANDI : A well known interstate narcotic trafficker, a trusted Mafioso from the Buffalo-Niagara Falls area.

```
NAME          : Stephen Thomas PIGNETTI

ALIASES       :

DESCRIPTION   : Born 1-2-22, NYC 5'7", 155
                lbs, medium build, brown
                hair, brown eyes, fair com-
                plexion.

LOCALITIES    : Resides 313 E 104th St., NYC,
FREQUENTED      also maintains address at
                94 Keesler Ave., Lodi, NJ,
                frequents East Harlem Area,
                NYC, particularly 2nd Ave,
                102-104 St.
```

```
FAMILY        : Single; father: James; mother: Albina; sister: Eva.
BACKGROUND

CRIMINAL      : ████████████, ████████████, ████████████,
ASSOCIATES      ████████████, ████████████.

CRIMINAL      : FBI #3549889, NYCPD #B207905.  Record dates from
HISTORY         1950 & includes arrests for violation State & Federal
                Narcotic Laws.  Federal narcotic conviction.

BUSINESS      : No legitimate occupation known.

MODUS         : With other East Harlem (NYC) Mafiosi has for at
OPERANDI        least the past ten years engaged in the wholesale
                narcotic traffic.
```

NAME   : Anthony PINTO

ALIASES   : Tea Bags

DESCRIPTION   : Born 10-27-26 NYC, 5'7½",
                  156 lbs, brown eyes, black
                  curly hair, rough complexion.

LOCALITIES   : Most recent address of record
FREQUENTED   is 163 E. 104 St, NYC, fre-
                  quents Knobby's Bar & Grill,
                  2012 2nd Ave, and Jennies
                  Rest., 2036 2nd Ave, NYC,
                  also Rex Stationary, 2035
                  1st Ave, NYC.

FAMILY   : Father: Michael Pinto, owner of Rex Stationary;
BACKGROUND   brother: Joseph Pinto, known narcotic violator.

CRIMINAL   : Anthony Castaldi, ███████████, John Ormento,
ASSOCIATES   Salvatore Santoro, ███████████.

CRIMINAL   : FBI #373818A. Only arrests were for violation of
HISTORY   narcotic laws and gambling.

BUSINESS   : No legitimate occupation known.

MODUS   : Narcotic delivery man for the East Harlem NYC Mafia
OPERANDI   group headed by Anthony Castaldi. This group dis-
                  tributes large quantities of narcotics locally and
                  throughout the United States.

NAME	: Anthony PISCIOTTA
ALIASES	: Tony
DESCRIPTION	: Born 2-16-23 NYC, 5'11", 210 lbs, heavy build, brown hair, brown eyes.

LOCALITIES FREQUENTED	: Resides 288 Brinsmade Ave., & 1923 3rd Ave., both NYC. Frequents Skyway Bar, East Elmhurst, NY, Barge Restaurant, Ten Pin Bar & Jacks Restaurant, all Bronx, NY, Copacabana Club, NYC, Roosevelt & Yonkers Raceways.
FAMILY BACKGROUND	: Wife: Rose DeCaro; sons: Anthony & Charles; father: Nicholas; mother: Geraldine Passanondi; brother: Rosario; sisters: Rose Luceretta, Vivian Milazzo.
CRIMINAL ASSOCIATES	: ███████████, Salvatore LoProto, Frank Borelli, Michael Altimari, ███████████, ███████.
CRIMINAL HISTORY	: FBI #592746A, No NYCPD #. Criminal record consists of two arrests by Federal Narcotic Bureau. 5-25-51 sentenced to 9 years followed by 5 years probation. On probation until 1965. Second case now (1959) pending.
BUSINESS	: Has an interest in the Skyway Bar, East Elmhurst, New York.
MODUS OPERANDI	: Is engaged, with other important Mafiosi, in the wholesale narcotic traffic, supplying heroin to dealers from all sections of the United States.

NAME   : Rosario PISCIOTTA

ALIASES   : Sally, George

DESCRIPTION   : Born 5-12-20 NYC, 6'1", 175
                   lbs, medium build, brown
                   hair, hazel eyes, fair com-
                   plexion.

LOCALITIES   : Resides 75-08 Bell Blvd,
FREQUENTED   Queens, NY & 1937 3rd Ave,
                   NYC. Frequents Skyway Bar,
                   Barge Rest., Ten Pin Club,
                   all in NYC; Yonkers & Roose-
                   velt Raceways.

FAMILY   : Unmarried. Lives with Bridget Carroll wife of Wm. P.
BACKGROUND   Carroll, who is currently serving 10-15 yr prison
                   term; father: Nicholas; mother: Geraldine Passanondi;
                   brother: Anthony; sisters: Rose Luceretta & Vivian
                   Milazzo.

CRIMINAL   : ██████████, ██████████, Salvatore LoProto,
ASSOCIATES   ██████████, Anthony Pisciotta.

CRIMINAL   : FBI #731531A. His criminal recrod consists solely of
HISTORY   Federal Narcotic Law conviction in 1951 for which he
                   received a 7 year sentence.

BUSINESS   : Has worked as laborer for DD-EE Plastering Co., 391
                   E 149 St., Bronx, NY & Anthony Cotrone, Contractor,
                   160 Tallamore Rd, Garden City, L.I., NY.

MODUS   : With other NY Mafiosi engages in distribution of
OPERANDI   wholesale quantities of heroin in NYC and mid-west-
                   ern states.

NAME	: Ralph POLIZZANO	
ALIASES	:	
DESCRIPTION	: Born 5-16-22 NYC, 5'10", 210 lbs, medium build, black hair, brown eyes, fair complexion.	
LOCALITIES FREQUENTED	: Resides 57 E 4th St, NYC, frequents Squeeze Inn Bar 57 E 4th St, NYC, also the Club 82, E 4th St, NYC. Currently incarcerated.	

FAMILY
BACKGROUND
: Wife: Marion Labarbera; son Charles; father: Charles; mother: Mary Antonelli; brothers: Carmine & Charles; sisters: Frances & Rose.

CRIMINAL
ASSOCIATES
: ▆▆▆▆▆▆▆▆▆, Joseph DiPalermo, ▆▆▆▆▆▆▆, Vito Genovese, Charles DiPalermo, Jack Russo, Charles Barcellona.

CRIMINAL
HISTORY
: FBI # 736566C, NYCPD #B397206. Record commenced 1957 with an arrest and conviction for State Narcotic Law violation. 1959 convicted of Federal Narcotic Law violation & sentenced to 7 years.

BUSINESS
: Owns Squeeze Inn Bar, 57 E 4th St., NYC.

MODUS
OPERANDI
: Part of the Vito Genovese-Joseph DiPalermo Mob. Distributes large quantities of illicit heroin.

NAME	: Angelo PRESINZANO
ALIASES	: Little Moe, Moey

DESCRIPTION : Born 1-25-1908 NYC, 5'4"
153 lbs, black hair, brown
eyes, dark complexion,
medium build.

LOCALITIES : Resides 53 S 10th St., B'klyn,
FREQUENTED   NY. Frequents 96 Henry St.,
NYC, and NYC's Lower East
Side, particularly the vic-
inity of Canal, Market &
Catherine Streets.

FAMILY   : Father: Angelo; mother: Jennie; sisters: Mary and
BACKGROUND   Sadie; brothers: Frank and Epifano; cousin:
Carmine Galante.

CRIMINAL   : Carmine Galante, ███████████████, Angelo Tuminaro,
ASSOCIATES   ████████████████████, Thomas Marino and ████████
████████, ███████████████████████.

CRIMINAL   : FBI #187717   NYCPD #B71432   Record dating from
HISTORY   1927 includes arrests for rape, homicide and violation of narcotic laws. At present (1960) on $5000
bail from Federal District Court, Newark, NJ, on a
charge of harboring fugitive Carmine Galante.

BUSINESS   : Owns business at Fulton Fish Market, NYC.

MODUS   : Finances Mafia racketeers and narcotic traffickers
OPERANDI   on the Lower East Side of NYC. Has interests in
varied underworld activities in association with
top Mafiosi.

NAME   : Frank PRISINZANO

ALIASES   : Frankie, Frangino, Pardini

DESCRIPTION   : Born 8-2-02 NYC, 5'3", 158
                  lbs, medium build, black-
                  grey hair, brown eyes.

LOCALITIES   : Resides 167 Mott St., NYC,
FREQUENTED   frequents Madison & Cather-
                  ine St., Forsythe & Henry,
                  and Fulton Fish Market, all
                  New York City.

FAMILY   : Married Mary Esposito; no
BACKGROUND   children; father: Salvatore; mother: Rosa Cozentino;
                  (both deceased); brothers: Joseph, Epifano, Anthony,
                  Angelo; sister: Mary.

CRIMINAL   : Carmine Galante, ███████████, Angelo Tuminaro,
ASSOCIATES   ████████████, ███████████.

CRIMINAL   : FBI #229423, NYC PD# 59155. Record dates from 1919
HISTORY   and includes arrests for burglary tools, revolver,
                  petit larceny, assault & robbery, conviction for vio-
                  lation of State & Federal Narcotic Laws.

BUSINESS   : Claims employment as fish loader for John Plock,
                  150 Beekman St., New York City.

MODUS   : A long time Mafia member who engages in narcotic
OPERANDI   traffic together with his brother Angelo & Carmine
                  Galante. Also believed to be a "Boss" in the
                  Fulton Fish Market.

NAME : Anthony J. PRIVATERA

ALIASES : Anthony Privateer, Albert
Battaglia

DESCRIPTION : Born 1-22-05 Buffalo, NY,
5'5", 150 lbs, black hair,
brown eyes, medium build,
dark complexion, small scar
on bridge of nose which is
broken to the left side.

LOCALITIES : Resides at 29 Busti St, Buf-
FREQUENTED falo, NY. Frequents West Side
of Buffalo.

FAMILY : Divorced from Catherine Kandra, has one son Frank;
BACKGROUND father: Francesco; mother: Rosalia Granata, both
born in Italy and now deceased; step-father:
Dominick Battaglia (deceased), was born in Italy.

CRIMINAL : ████████████, ██████████, ██████████,
ASSOCIATES ████████████, Roy Carlisi, Magaddino brothers.

CRIMINAL : FBI #338604, Buffalo PD #26117. Criminal record
HISTORY dates from 1927 and includes arrests for assault,
murder, concealed weapon (revolver) and counterfeiting gas stamps. Served 15 yr sentence at Auburn
State Prison for Manslaughter (reduced from murder).

BUSINESS : He has no legitimate occupation.

MODUS : Engages in every type of underworld activity.
OPERANDI Known as a distributor of illegal alcohol.

NAME : Frank PROFACI

ALIASES : Frankie

DESCRIPTION : Born 4-15-07 Villabate,
Sicily, 5'7", 160 lbs, brown
hair, brown eyes, naturalized U.S. 2-8-44.

LOCALITIES : Resides 3801 Ave P, B'klyn,
FREQUENTED NY, Newburg Coat Co., 1578
86th St, B'klyn, NY.

FAMILY : Married Vinenza Costello;
BACKGROUND sons: Salvatore, Ignazio,
Emmanuel; father: Salvatore; mother: Rosaria Schillaci;
brothers: Salvatore, Andrew, Joseph; sisters:
Josephine Tipa & Sister Madelina of the Dominican
Sisters of NYC.

CRIMINAL : Joseph Profaci (brother), Frank Costello, Nicolo
ASSOCIATES Gentile, Joseph Rinaldi, Frank Scalici (deceased).

CRIMINAL : No criminal record known.
HISTORY

BUSINESS : Associated with brother Joseph in Olive Oil Co.,
and clothing companies. Owns Newburg Coat Co., 1578
86th St, B'klyn, NY.

MODUS : An underling of his brother Giuseppe Profaci, who
OPERANDI is a top level international narcotic violator and
high ranking Mafioso.

On June 6, 1962, Profaci died of cancer.

NAME : Giuseppe PROFACI

ALIASES : Joe Proface

DESCRIPTION : Born 10-1-1897, Villabate,
Sicily, 5'6", 180 lbs, grey
hair, brown eyes, glasses,
naturalized Brooklyn 9-27-27.

LOCALITIES : Resides 8863 15th Avenue,
FREQUENTED   Brooklyn, NY. Frequents
his places of business.

FAMILY : Married Nina Magliocco
BACKGROUND   (sister of Giuseppe Magliocco); daughters: Carmela
(married to Anthony Tocco, son of Wm. Tocco, Detroit),
Rosalie (married to Anthony Zerilli, son of Joseph
Zerilli, Detroit); sons: John, Dominick & Joseph;
brothers: Frank & Andrew; sisters: Mrs. Josephine
Tipa, Mrs. Providence LoCastro, Mrs. Paolina Savone
and Sister Marie Madelena, a nun; father: Salvatore;
mother: Rosaria Schillaci.

CRIMINAL : Lucky Luciano, Sebastiano Nani, Nicholas Impastato
ASSOCIATES   (all deportees), Francisco Costiglia, Joseph Stracci,
John Oddo, Gaetano Lucchese, Frank Livorsi.

CRIMINAL : FBI #362142-A NYCPD #B-13328 Record in U.S. dating
HISTORY   from 1928 includes arrests for gun, suspicion of
murder, income tax evasion & conspiracy to obstruct
justice (on which sentenced 1960 to 5 years and
$10,000 fine. Also has criminal record in Italy.

BUSINESS : Owns Carmela Mia Packing Co. & many other firms.

MODUS : Attended 1928 Cleveland & 1957 Apalachin Mafia meet-
OPERANDI   ings. One of most powerful Mafia leaders in U. S.

NAME	: Stephen Martini PUCO
ALIASES	: Daniel Puco, Steve the Bug
DESCRIPTION	: Born 4-12-18 N.Y.C. 5'10", 160 lbs., brown thinning hair, brown eyes, has a large nose.
LOCALITIES FREQUENTED	: Resides 323 Paladino Ave., Apt. 2-B, N.Y.C. Frequented DeMartino Restaurant, 320 E. 117th St.; 326 E. 117th St.; 325 Paladino Ave.; 2nd Ave. between 109th & 110th Sts.; 501 E. 116th St.; all N.Y.C.
FAMILY BACKGROUND	: Married to Rose Catapano; sons: Anthony & Stephen; father: Antonio; mother: Caterina Quillo; brothers: Andrew, Albert, & Philip; sisters: Mary Bruno, Anna DeStefano, & Tessie Perrie.
CRIMINAL ASSOCIATES	: Rocco Mazzie, Salvatore Barbato, Nicholas Tolentino, John Ormento, Joe Bruno, Joe Bendenelli, ███████ ███████.
CRIMINAL HISTORY	: FBI#971099. NYC PD-B#137105. Arrests since 1935 include assault & robbery, robbery, possession of gun, & convictions for Federal Narcotic Laws. Currently (1959) incarcerated for Federal Narcotic Laws.
BUSINESS	: Formerly employed by father at Puco Manufacturing Co., 583 E. 189th St., Bronx, N.Y.
MODUS OPERANDI	: A member of the Mafia controlled narcotic traffickers from the East Harlem section of Manhattan. A major local & interstate wholesale narcotic dealer.

NAME   : Lawrence QUARTIERO

ALIASES   : Larry Quartiero

DESCRIPTION   : Born 5-24-23 NYC, NY, 5'7",
                  189 lbs, black hair, brown
                  eyes, medium stocky build,
                  dark complexion.

LOCALITIES   : Resides at 410 W 54th St.,
FREQUENTED   NYC, frequents waterfront
                  areas on west side of NYC.

FAMILY   : Married to Nora Berry; child-
BACKGROUND   ren: Michael, Noreen, Cath-
                  leen and Larry Jr; sisters: Charlotte LaRosa,
                  Josephine Grosso, Camille Kendell, Joanna Quartiero;
                  brother: Frank; father: Michael, (deceased); mother:
                  Rosetta Catugna, (deceased).

CRIMINAL   : Pasquale Pagano, Steve Armone, Anthony Strolla,
ASSOCIATES   Vincent Mauro.

CRIMINAL   : FBI #2117032, NYCPD #194107. Arrest record dating
HISTORY   back to 1940 includes petty larceny, unlawful
                  entry, felonious assault, gambling, burglary &
                  conviction of conspiracy to violate narcotic laws
                  for which sentenced to 5 years in 1956.

BUSINESS   : No known business but is associated with long-
                  shoremen and other shipping and waterfront activ-
                  ities.

MODUS   : Member of International Longshoremen Association
OPERANDI   who supplies seaman narcotic couriers to Anthony
                  Strolla. A prominent figure in Mafia internation-
                  al smuggling. Also, is an expert jewlry and fur
                  thief and fence.

NAME   : Joseph RAGONE

ALIASES   : Joe Ragone

DESCRIPTION   : Born 9-4-18 NYC, 5'7½", 155
                  lbs, medium build, brown
                  eyes, brown hair,

LOCALITIES   : Resides 1639 Colden Ave,
FREQUENTED   Bronx, NY. Frequents Parma
                  Cafe, 364 W. 57th St., 2067
                  2nd Ave., NYC, 2nd Ave, &
                  136th St. all NYC, Capri Bar,
                  Ten Pin Bar and Fordham Sec-
                  tion of the Bronx; owns Blue-
                  bird Bar on Buhre Ave, in the Bronx.

FAMILY   : Married Helen DeLuca; father: Emilio; mother: Mary
BACKGROUND   Ippolito, (both deceased); brothers: Gaspare, Albert,
                  Michael, Anthony.

CRIMINAL   : ███████████, Paul Zerbo, ████████████, Joe
ASSOCIATES   Valachi & ████████████.

CRIMINAL   : FBI #688161B. Arrested 8-2-54 for violation of the
HISTORY   Federal Narcotic Laws; sentenced on 11-27-54 to
                  serve 3½ yrs in prison and 5 yrs probation. No other
                  arrests.

BUSINESS   : Works with brother Gaspare Ragone in vending machine
                  business and has interests in Bluebird Bar on Buhre
                  Ave, in the Bronx, NYC.

MODUS   : Ragone is a large scale narcotic violator and an
OPERANDI   influential Mafia member in the NYC area.

NAME	: Calogero RAO
ALIASES	: Charles Rao
DESCRIPTION	: Born 1-2-1889 Corleone, Palermo, Sicily, Italy, 5'3", 145 lbs, brown-grey hair, brown eyes, naturalized NYC 9-15-1920.
LOCALITIES FREQUENTED	: Resides at 2 Hillside Pl., Bronxville, NY, summer home 134 Wilson Ave, Long Beach, NY. Frequents the area of E. 106th & 116th Sts, in the East Harlem section of NYC.
FAMILY BACKGROUND	: Married Maria Conzonerie, has two daughters, Liboria and Mary; father: Antonio; mother: Liboria Colletti; brother: Vincent; sister: Mary Speciale.
CRIMINAL ASSOCIATES	: Vincent Rao, Joseph Lanza, ███████████████, Frank Borelli, ████████████.
CRIMINAL HISTORY	: No known criminal record.
BUSINESS	: Owns and operates a Real Estate and Insurance firm, at 218 East 116th St, NYC.
MODUS OPERANDI	: Is reputed to be a trusted member of the Mafia in NYC though not as important as his brother Vincent, who attended 1957 Apalachin meeting.

On May 10, 1962, Rao died of a stroke.

NAME	: Joseph RAO
ALIASES	: Joseph Cangro, Joe Raio, Joe Cangero
DESCRIPTION	: Born 3-12-01, NYC. 5'7", 200 lbs., brown eyes, black-grey hair thinned out on top, wears glasses.
LOCALITIES FREQUENTED	: Resides 337 E.116 Street, NYC. Frequents area of E. 116 Street between 1st & 2nd Avenues.

FAMILY BACKGROUND	: Married to Lena Stracci (sister of Joe Stracci), daughter: Frances, sons: Charles & Robert, father: Charles, mother Frances, (both dead), brothers: Vincent & Louis.
CRIMINAL ASSOCIATES	: Mike Coppola, Joe Stracci, ▓▓▓▓▓▓, Charles Albero, Frank Livorsi, Patsy Erra, Alfred Felice, Joe Bendenelli.
CRIMINAL HISTORY	: FBI #283669, NYCPD-B #65991. Numerous arrests since 1920 include burglary, robbery, homicide, felonious assault.
BUSINESS	: Believed to operate parking lot on E. 107 St., near 1st Ave., in Manhattan.
MODUS OPERANDI	: A well known and feared member of the East Harlem Mafia narcotic trafficking organization. Reputed "boss" of all rackets in area of 1st Ave., & E. 116 St., and receives income from persons in these rackets.

Rao died on September 25, 1988, of natural causes, in
Florida.

NAME **:** Vincenzo John RAO

ALIASES **:** Vinny Rao

DESCRIPTION **:** Born 6-21-1898 Palermo,
Sicily, 5'5", 180 lbs, brown
eyes, black-grey hair. Naturalized NYC 12-5-21.

LOCALITIES **:** Resides 192 Dunwoodie St.,
FREQUENTED Yonkers, NY. Frequents area
E. 116th St, & 1st Ave, in
Manhattan.

FAMILY **:** Married to Carmelina Alberti,
BACKGROUND daughters: Mrs. Nina Pancoldo, Mrs. Liegria Vento;
brother: Charles; sister: Mrs. Mary Speciale;
father: Antonio; mother: Liboria Colletti.

CRIMINAL **:** Frank Costello, Lucky Luciano, John Ormento, Frank
ASSOCIATES Livorsi, Joseph Vento (son-in-law), John DioGuardi,
Anthony Corallo.

CRIMINAL **:** FBI #792086C. NYCPD #E4857. Arrests since 1919
HISTORY include grand larceny, homicide, possession of a
gun.

BUSINESS **:** Has interests in Five Boro Hoisting Co., Rao
Realty Co., Rao Parking Lot, all at 218 E. 116th
St., also in Vin-Sons Paints, Inc., Bronx, NY.

MODUS **:** Attended Apalachin Mafia meeting 1957 as a leader
OPERANDI from East Harlem area NYC. A powerful & influential
Mafia leader who has engaged in all types of illegal
rackets including narcotic smuggling.

> He was murdered not long after the 1957 Apalachin
> Convention due to his alliance to Albert Anastasia.

NAME : Armand Thomas RAVA

ALIASES : Thomas RAVO, Armand RAVO

DESCRIPTION : Born 1-7-1911, NYC, 5'7", 180 lbs, black hair, brown eyes, heavy build.

LOCALITIES FREQUENTED : Resided 1180 Ocean Avenue, Brooklyn, NY, & frequented vicinity of 7201 8th Ave., Brooklyn. Whereabouts unknown since 11-14-57, and his wife has moved to 490 Audubon Ave., Bronx, N.Y.

FAMILY BACKGROUND : Married Florence DelBono 1929, divorced 1939 and married Dorothy Bloom 1940; son: David; father: Angelo; mother: Marie; brothers: James, John, Joseph and Jerry; sister: Marie.

CRIMINAL ASSOCIATES : Carlo Gambino, Paul Castellano, ██████████████, ████████████████, Giuseppe Profaci, ██████████ ████████.

CRIMINAL HISTORY : FBI #1773203 NYCPD #B-73155 Record dating from 1929 includes arrests for extortion, policy, bootlegging, vagrancy and narcotic law violation.

BUSINESS : Owns New Corners Restaurant, 7201 8th Avenue, Brooklyn, N.Y.

MODUS OPERANDI : Attended Mafia meeting at Apalachin, N.Y., 11-14-57, and hasn't been seen since that time. He has been a leader of the Mafia in Brooklyn and a powerful influence in the narcotic and illicit alcohol traffic.

NAME	: Giacomo REINA

ALIASES : Jack Reina, Jack Ricca,
Henry Reina

DESCRIPTION : Born 9-21-09 NYC, 5'8½",
155 lbs., brown eyes, black
hair with grey streaks.

LOCALITIES : Resides 152 Kearny Ave.,
FREQUENTED Kearny, NJ., frequents bar
at 49 Market St., and 121
Mulberry St., both in NYC.

FAMILY : Wife: Phyllis, brothers:
BACKGROUND Henry, Sam, John & Bernard,
Sisters: Anna, Mildred Valachi (wife of Joe Valachi),
Rose Bongrieco, Lucy Sterling, Father: Gaetano,
Mother: Angelina Olivera.

CRIMINAL : Frank Caruso, Anthony Strollo, Vincent Mauro, Joe
ASSOCIATES Orsini, Joe Valachi, all of NYC, Marius Ansaldi,
██████████████, Francois Spirito, all of France.

CRIMINAL : FBI #193805, NYCPD #B73123, arrests from 1928 in-
HISTORY clude felonious assault, robbery, conviction of Federal Narcotic Laws.

BUSINESS : No legitimate business known.

MODUS : Wholesale smuggler - distributor of heroin with
OPERANDI sources of supply in France. Has connections with
most leading Mafia members of NYC.

NAME   : Arthur REPOLA

ALIASES   : Fat Artie

DESCRIPTION   : Born 8-5-27 N.Y.C. 5'9",
                  230 lbs., brown eyes, brown
                  hair, stout build.

LOCALITIES   : Resides 1040 Rosedale Ave.,
FREQUENTED   Bronx, N.Y. Frequented area
                  E. 116th St. & Paladino Ave.,
                  Manhattan.

FAMILY   : Married to Florence
BACKGROUND   Scotorchio; father: Cosimo;
                  mother: Matilda Marroti; brothers: Anthony, Albert,
                  & Armando; sisters: Mrs. Josephine Sinno, Mrs.
                  Pearl Diluro.

CRIMINAL   : John Ormento, Salvatore Santoro, Frank Borelli,
ASSOCIATES   Charles Curcio, Rocco Mazzie, ███████████,
                  & Sammy Kass.

CRIMINAL   : FBI#3969481. NYC PD-B#223028. Arrests since 1944
HISTORY   include possession of revolver, burglary warehouse,
                  attempted burglary & burglary tools, & conviction
                  of New York State Narcotic Laws for which he is
                  still (1959) incarcerated.

BUSINESS   : No legitimate business or employment known.

MODUS   : A major narcotic trafficker who was associated with
OPERANDI   other Mafia traffickers in the E. 116th St. and
                  Paladino Ave. area of Manhattan.

NAME   : John J. RICCARDULLI

ALIASES   : Johnny Schlitz, Slits,
                  Freddie, Ronnie.

DESCRIPTION   : Born 1-29-12 NYC, 5'2", 144
                  lbs, brown eyes, brown hair,
                  medium stocky build.

LOCALITIES   : Resides 974 Rhinelander Ave,
FREQUENTED   Bronx, NY. Frequents 3rd
                  Ave, 102nd to 105th St, Har-
                  lem Social Club, 222 E 104th
                  Jim's Bar, 309 E 104 & 336
                  E 119 St, all in NYC.

FAMILY   : Single; father: Leonard (deceased); mother: Maria
BACKGROUND   Vito; sisters: Anna & Virginia Riccardulli, Frances
                  Velliare; brothers: Paddy & Tony.

CRIMINAL   : ██████████████, Frank Pasqua, ██████████████,
ASSOCIATES   Anthony Castaldi, Stephen Puco.

CRIMINAL   : FBI #2453962, NYCPDE# 12678. Has only one arrest
HISTORY   which was for violation of Federal Narcotic Laws.
                  He was convicted and served 2 years in Federal
                  prison.

BUSINESS   : No known legitimate employment at this time.

MODUS   : Has been a large scale local and interstate nar-
OPERANDI   cotic trafficker for over 20 years in close asso-
                  ciation with important Mafiosi.

NAME	: Anthony RICCI
ALIASES	: Tony Gobel, Gaetano Ricci, Antonio Ricci.
DESCRIPTION	: Born 1-1-1893 Vieste, Foggia, Italy, 6'1", 215 lbs, medium build, brown-grey hair, brown eyes. Naturalized Brooklyn, NY, 11-20-44.
LOCALITIES FREQUENTED	: Resides 125 Ocean Parkway, Brooklyn, NY. Frequents Nathan Outfitters, 1135 Broadway, Brooklyn, NY, and Bars in Ridgewood section of Brooklyn.
FAMILY BACKGROUND	: Married Florence Lorenz 1915, divorced 1944; three children; father: Jerome; mother: Jennie Faustina; lives with Anna Friedman, a business associate.
CRIMINAL ASSOCIATES	: Gaetano Maiorana, John Roselli, Giuseppe Doto, Vito Genovese.
CRIMINAL HISTORY	: FBI #276249A. NYCPD #B-261555. Record dates from 1915 and includes arrests for assault, gun, grand larceny & abandonment.
BUSINESS	: In partnership with Anna Friedman in Nathan Outfitters, 1135 Broadway, Brooklyn, NY, and in operation of several apartment buildings.
MODUS OPERANDI	: An international drug trafficker and a top ranking member of the Mafia. Disciplinarian for the Mafia in the eastern United States.

He died in May 1975 in Staten Island, NY.	

NAME   : Joseph S. RICCOBONO

ALIASES   : Joe Riccobona, Joe Ricciardi
                 Joe Bono

DESCRIPTION   : Born 4-23-1894 Palermo,
                 Sicily, 5'11", 150 lbs, brown
                 eyes, grey hair (balding),
                 naturalized 6-7-22 NYC.

LOCALITIES   : Resides 781 Pelton Ave.,
FREQUENTED   Staten Island, N.Y. Fre-
                 quents Bay Ridge section of
                 Brooklyn and garment center
                 of Manhattan.

FAMILY   : Married to Christine Gumpman & has no children;
BACKGROUND   sisters: Mrs. Mary Bono, Mrs. Rosalie Passallo,
                 Mrs. Speranza Vassalo, Mrs. Carmela Pinzola; brother:
                 Salvatore; father: John; mother: Rosalia D'Aleo.

CRIMINAL   : Joe Profaci, Joe Bonanno, ███████████████, ██████████
ASSOCIATES   Natale Evola, John Bonventre, Paul Castellano, Jean
                 Laget.

CRIMINAL   : FBI #321523. NYCPD B#228590. Arrests since 1930
HISTORY   include concealed weapon, conspiracy & extortion.

BUSINESS   : Owns Christine Dresses & Toni-Bell Dresses, both
                 in Brooklyn, New York.

MODUS   : Attended Apalachin Mafia Meeting 1957 as one of the
OPERANDI   more influential leaders in NYC. A powerful racket-
                 eer in garment industry which has been infiltrated
                 with wealthy Mafiosi. Is a former member of the
                 Lepke-Buchalter mob of NYC.

NAME   : Rosario RINALDI

ALIASES   : Sammy, Samuel Rinaldi,
                 Rinaldo

DESCRIPTION   : Born 3-7-17 NYC 5'8", 138
                 lbs, black hair, brown eyes,
                 slim build, dark complexion

LOCALITIES   : Resides 1760 Watson Ave.,
FREQUENTED   Bronx, NY, frequents Belved-
                 ere Bar, 2056 2nd Ave., NYC;
                 Tivoli Bar, Westchester Ave,
                 & Bronx River Parkway, Bronx;
                 163rd & Bruckner, Bronx, NY.

FAMILY   : Married Anna Russo; sons: Ross, Robert; father:
BACKGROUND   Rosario; mother: Catherine Marthola.

CRIMINAL   : Anthony Granza, Vincent Squillante, Samuel Monastersky,
ASSOCIATES   Vincent Mauro, Anthony Corallo.

CRIMINAL   : FBI #1504259, NYCPD #B-119879. Record dates from
HISTORY   1932 and includes arrests for grand larceny & vio-
                 lation of Federal Narcotic Laws. Sentenced 10/55
                 for Federal Narcotic violation, released 5/59.

BUSINESS   : No legitimate occupation known.

MODUS   : With other Mafiosi in East Harlem area of NYC is
OPERANDI   active in local and interstate wholesale narcotic
                 traffic.

NAME   : Angelo RIZZO

ALIASES   : Tony Rizzo, Frank Rizzo

DESCRIPTION   : Born 10-8-17 Buffalo, NY,
                  5'7", 142 lbs, medium build,
                  fair complexion, brown eyes,
                  black hair.

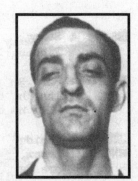

LOCALITIES   : Resides 12 Brayton St, Buf-
FREQUENTED   falo, NY. Frequents Santores
                  & Parkedge Rests., in Buf-
                  falo; visits Cleveland,
                  Toronto, Montreal & NYC.

FAMILY   : Single; father: Pietro; mother: Concettina Augello
BACKGROUND   (both deceased, were born in Italy); brother:
                  Salvatore (Sam) Rizzo; sister: Mary C. Rizzo.

CRIMINAL   : Sam Pieri, the Magaddino brothers, John C. Montana,
ASSOCIATES   and the subject's brother, Salvatore (Sam) Rizzo.

CRIMINAL   : FBI #3048101. Buffalo PD #43211. Record dates from
HISTORY   1937 and includes arrests for robbery, possession of
                  narcotics, counterfeiting, receiving stolen goods,
                  gambling & bookmaking. Paroled 6-29-59 after serving
                  8 years of 5-10 yr sentence for state narcotic vio-
                  lation.

BUSINESS   : Construction worker for the Railroad Waterproofing
                  Co., Niagara Falls, NY.

MODUS   : Important Mafia member and wholesale distributor of
OPERANDI   narcotics in the Buffalo area. He engages in every
                  type of underworld activity, in association with
                  his brother, Salvatore, and other Mafiosi.

NAME   : Salvatore Peter RIZZO

ALIASES   : Sam Rizzo

DESCRIPTION   : Born 8-14-13, Buffalo, NY.,
                  5'6", 156 lbs, black hair,
                  brown eyes, medium build.

LOCALITIES   : Resides 12 Brayton St, Buf-
FREQUENTED   falo, NY. Frequents Santores
                  Rest., and Park Edge Rest.,
                  in downtown Buffalo, Crystal
                  Beach, Ontario, Canada,
                  Cleveland, Ohio and Roches-
                  ter, NY.

FAMILY   : Marriage annulled 1947, no children. Father: Pietro;
BACKGROUND   mother: Concettina Augello (both deceased), were
                  born in Italy; brother: Angelo; sister: Miss Mary C.
                  Rizzo.

CRIMINAL   : Salvatore (Sam) Pieri, Maggadino brothers, John C.
ASSOCIATES   Montana, ▊▊▊▊▊▊▊▊▊, Papalardo brothers, Angelo
                  Felicia.

CRIMINAL   : FBI #4449035. Buffalo PD #46193. Record dates from
HISTORY   1942 and includes arrests for larceny, robbery,
                  gambling and violation of the Federal narcotic
                  laws.

BUSINESS   : Silent partner of the Huron Smoke Shop, 86 W.
                  Huron St., Buffalo, NY.

MODUS   : An important Mafia member and wholesaler of narcotics
OPERANDI   supplying upstate New York and Midwest cities. Oper-
                  ates with other Mafiosi in Cleveland, Ohio and Buf-
                  falo, NY. Has sources of supply for pure heroin in
                  NYC.

NAME	: Anthony RIZZUTO
ALIASES	: Tony, Nino
DESCRIPTION	: Born 6-21-02 Camporeale, Trapani, Sicily, Italy, 5'5½", 210 lbs, stocky build, brown hair, bald front, brown eyes, ruddy complexion, wears glasses.

LOCALITIES FREQUENTED	: Resides 266 Throop Ave, Brooklyn, NY. Frequents Wilson Ave, & East NY sections of Brooklyn, East Harlem section of NYC.
FAMILY BACKGROUND	: Wife: Anna Pipitone; father: Philip; mother: Nina Gianimalvo (both deceased); sister: Eva Breglio; brothers: Frank, Jack (New Orleans).
CRIMINAL ASSOCIATES	: ███████████, ███████████, Vincenzo Morsellino, Charles LaCascia, Pietro Licata.
CRIMINAL HISTORY	: FBI #1564155. Record dates from 1928, arrests include burglary, possession stolen auto, transporting illicit alcohol, operating unregistered still.
BUSINESS	: No legitimate occupation known.
MODUS OPERANDI	: Member of the Wilson Ave, Brooklyn, group of Mafiosi engaging in large scale bootlegging narcotic smuggling & distribution.

NAME   : Nunzio ROMANO

ALIASES   : "Fats", "Arthur Casino",
                  "Charles Ross"

DESCRIPTION   : Born 11-24-09 NYC, 5'8", 190
                  lbs, black-greying hair,
                  hazel eyes, ruddy complexion,
                  stocky build.

LOCALITIES   : Resides 341 E 104th St, NYC
FREQUENTED   Frequents Cleveland, Ohio.

FAMILY   : Wife: Mary Sgro; father:
BACKGROUND   Domenico Romano (born in
                  Italy); mother: Consiglia; sister: Josephine Corrada.

CRIMINAL   : Michael Erra, Rocco Mazzie, ████████████████
ASSOCIATES   ██████, Pasquale Erra.

CRIMINAL   : FBI #671118. NYCPD #B78413. Record dates from 1928
HISTORY   and includes arrests for extortion, robbery, homicide,
                  Federal narcotic conviction.

BUSINESS   : Longshoreman.

MODUS   : Is a leading Mafia trafficker in narcotics in
OPERANDI   NYC and on an interstate level.

NAME   : Joseph ROSATO

ALIASES   : Joe Palisades

DESCRIPTION   : Born 1-4-04 Palermo, Sicily,
                  5'7", 175 lbs., brown eyes,
                  black-grey hair

LOCALITIES   : Resides 34-31 81 St.,
FREQUENTED   Jackson Heights, L.I., N.Y.
                  Frequents Fort Lee, N.J.,
                  garment area of Manhattan,
                  & Miami, Florida

FAMILY   : Married to Rosalie Lucchese
BACKGROUND   & has no children; father: Joseph; mother: Angela
                  Puccio.

CRIMINAL   : Tom Lucchese (brother-in-law), ███████, Harry
ASSOCIATES   Stromberg, Joe Stracci, James Plumieri, Natale Evola,
                  Joe Riccobono, Tony Strollo, Tony Corallo.

CRIMINAL   : FBI #4165533. NYCPD B#8732. Record since 1928
HISTORY   includes homicide, disorderly conduct.

BUSINESS   : Has interests in S&R Trucking Co., 460 W. 35th St.,
                  New York City.

MODUS   : Attended Apalachin Mafia meeting 1957 as a leader
OPERANDI   from NYC and also representing Tom Lucchese. With
                  other Mafia associates he gradually "muscled in"
                  the garment industry in NYC. A powerful and feared
                  Mafia leader.

NAME	: Solomon ROSEN
ALIASES	: Solly Kaplan, Solly Rothman, Solly Cohen.
DESCRIPTION	: Born 5-8-08 NYC, Jewish, 5'8" 170 lbs, cleft chin, blue eyes, brown-grey hair, balding.
LOCALITIES FREQUENTED	: Resides 115 Essex St, NYC. Frequents Essex & Rivington St, area & other parts of NY's Lower East Side.
FAMILY BACKGROUND	: Married Ruth Litchman; son: Arnold Rosen; father: Morris; mother: Anna Alpert; brothers: Michael, Nathan & David; half-sister: Pauline Rosen.
CRIMINAL ASSOCIATES	: ███████████, ███████████, ███████, ███████████, ███████████.
CRIMINAL HISTORY	: FBI #2089439. NYCPD #B97260. Record dating from 1928 includes arrests for robbery, assault and Federal narcotic conviction.
BUSINESS	: No legitimate occupation.
MODUS OPERANDI	: Large scale smuggler and distributor of narcotics. Skilled clandestine narcotic chemist. Operates in alliance with Mafia narcotic traffickers.

NAME   : Ugo ROSSI

ALIASES   : Hugo Rossi, Mr. Hugo

DESCRIPTION: Born 12-10-01 Palermo,
              Sicily, 6'3", 210 lbs.,
              brown eyes, black-grey hair
              thinning out on top, natur-
              alized 1951 NYC.

LOCALITIES   : Resides 128 St. Marks Place,
FREQUENTED   NYC. Frequents area of E 11
              St. & 1st Ave., & Pizzeria
              at 279 1st Ave., NYC.

FAMILY   : Living with one May Salamone; father: Roberto;
BACKGROUND   mother: Matilda Paterno (both dead); sisters: Olga,
              Ada, Letizia, and Ellena, all in Italy.

CRIMINAL   : Giacomo Scarpulla, Andrew Alberti, Jean Laget,
ASSOCIATES   Paolo Gambino, John Ormento, Salvatore Santoro,
              John Sperandeo.

CRIMINAL   : FBI #346645B. Only arrest in U.S. in 1953 when con-
HISTORY   victed for Federal Narcotic Laws. Prior arrests in
              Sicily between 1919 & 1929 include aggravated theft,
              brawling, delinquent association.

BUSINESS   : Was sales representative for Terrenia Trading Co.,
              wholesale grocers, 263-265 Stanhope St., Brooklyn,
              NY.

MODUS   : One of the most important Mafia international drug
OPERANDI   traffickers in NYC, who has direct sources of supply
              in Italy & France, and who deals only in kilogram
              lots.

NAME   : Gaetano RUSSO

ALIASES   : Tommy Russo, Guy Russo

DESCRIPTION   : Born 4-24-1891 Palermo,
                  Sicily, Italy, 5'5", 160 lbs,
                  white hair, brown eyes, na-
                  turalized 12-18-24 B'klyn,
                  New York.

LOCALITIES   : Resides 2145 East 5th St,
FREQUENTED   Brooklyn, NY. Is the Funeral
                  Director at Cusimano & Russo,
                  2111 West 6th St, B'klyn, NY.

FAMILY   : Wife: Louise; father: Cosmo; mother: Antonina
BACKGROUND   Pietaresa.

CRIMINAL   : ██████████, Joseph Profaci, Joseph Magliocco, Albert
ASSOCIATES   Anastasia, ████████████, Lucky Luciano, ███████
                  ██████, ████████████████, Sebastiano Nani, Carlo
                  Gambino.

CRIMINAL   : No criminal record known.
HISTORY

BUSINESS   : Owns Cusimano and Russo Funeral Home, 2111 West
                  6th St., Brooklyn, New York.

MODUS   : Obstensibly a well known and respected business man,
OPERANDI   Russo is reportedly the Mafia leader of the Benson-
                  hurst area. He is the intimate of virtually every
                  major hoodlum in this country. In 1955, he visited
                  Italy with the purpose of setting up narcotic de-
                  liveries through Lucky Luciano. His name was found
                  on a seaman narcotic courier at the time of the
                  couriers arrest.

NAME : James SABELLA

ALIASES : Jimmy, Vincent Tobozzi, Vincenzo Sabella

DESCRIPTION : Born 2-18-1900 NYC, 5'7", 180 lbs, black-grey hair, brown eyes, good dresser, heavy drinker, gambler.

LOCALITIES : Resides 1338 85th St, B'klyn,
FREQUENTED NY, frequents Bensonhurst & Bath Beach sections of Brooklyn, better night clubs & garment center in NYC. Vacations at Hot Springs, Arkansas.

FAMILY : Married Guilia Addis; father: Antonio; mother: Caola
BACKGROUND Catanzaro.

CRIMINAL : Sebastiano Nani, Francesco Costiglia, Giuseppe Doto,
ASSOCIATES John Dioguardi, Joseph Profaci, Joseph Magliocco, the late Albert Anastasia.

CRIMINAL : FBI #703841. NYCPD B#173309. Arrests since 1923 for
HISTORY grand larceny, illegal possession of a gun, attempted rape and assault in the 3rd degree. Obtained a pistol permit in 1945 in NYC.

BUSINESS : Silent partner in several garment factories.

MODUS : A top underworld figure, feared and respected by all
OPERANDI echelons of the Mafia. Reputed financier of underworld activities including narcotic transactions. Associated with underworld garment unions.

NAME   : Angelo Charles SALERNO

ALIASES   : Charley Four Cents, Angelo
                  Sasso.

DESCRIPTION   : Born 11-11-02 N.Y.C. 5'6",
                  190 lbs., brown-grey hair,
                  brown eyes, stocky build.

LOCALITIES   : Resides 1420 Grand Concourse,
FREQUENTED   Bronx, N.Y. Frequents area
                  of E. 107th St. & 1st Ave.

FAMILY   : Married; son: Fred (a known
BACKGROUND   narcotic trafficker); reputed
                  to be brother-in-law of Charles Albero.

CRIMINAL   : John Ormento, Salvatore Santoro, Charles Albero,
ASSOCIATES   Fred Salerno (son), Joe Marone, Anthony Ciccone,
                  Tom Lucchese, all of N.Y.C.; Mike Coppola &
                  Pat Erra of Miami Beach.

CRIMINAL   : FBI#490193. NYC PD-B#85969. Arrests from 1924
HISTORY   include assault & robbery, and conviction for
                  Federal Narcotic Laws.

BUSINESS   : Owns Ciccone's Bar on 1st Ave. between E. 106th
                  & E. 107th Sts. in Manhattan.

MODUS   : A major local & interstate narcotic trafficker and
OPERANDI   a trusted member of the Ormento controlled Mafia
                  trafficking organization.

On July 27, 1992, Salerno died of a stroke while in police custody.

NAME : Anthony Michael SALERNO

ALIASES : Fat Tony, Punchy, Tony

DESCRIPTION : Born 8-5-13 NYC, 5'8", 180 lbs, black hair, brown eyes, part of left ring finger missing.

LOCALITIES FREQUENTED : Resides 344 E 116th NYC, frequents Lizzi's Bar, 116th & 2nd Ave, parking lot 111th & 1st Ave., NYC.

FAMILY BACKGROUND : Father: Alfio; mother: Mary Corroccio; brothers: Alfred & Angelo.

CRIMINAL ASSOCIATES : Michael Coppola, Joseph Stracci, Joseph Rao, Charles Albero

CRIMINAL HISTORY : FBI #574465, NYCPD B#101580, record dates from 1932 and includes arrests for robbery, policy, assault & coercion & conviction for Federal Narcotic Law violation.

BUSINESS : Parking lot, 111th & 1st Ave., NYC.

MODUS OPERANDI : With other East Harlem Mafiosi engages in policy, bookmaking and narcotic trafficking.

NAME   : Ferdinando Joseph SALERNO

ALIASES   : Fred, Fat Freddie

DESCRIPTION   : Born 5-2-24 NYC, 6'0", 210
                   lbs, heavy build, black hair,
                   brown eyes, medium complex-
                   ion, artificial left eye.

LOCALITIES   : Resides 1540 Pelham Parkway,
FREQUENTED   Bronx, NY, frequents Engle-
                   wood, N.J., Copacabana Nite
                   Club, 10 E 60th St, Ciccones
                   Bar, 2062 1st Ave., NYC.

FAMILY   : Wife: Donna; two children; father: Angelo; mother:
BACKGROUND   Rosina Camerato.

CRIMINAL   : Arthur Leo, Joseph Vento, John Ormento, Salvatore
ASSOCIATES   Santoro, Michael Pecoraro, Harold Meltzer.

CRIMINAL   : No FBI # assigned, NYCPD #B250452, record dates
HISTORY   from 1947 & includes arrests for felonious assault,
                   rape, policy & bookmaking.

BUSINESS   : Interests in Young Distributors, 375 11th Ave.,
                   Runyon Sales Corp., 593 10th Ave., & Atlantic-
                   New York Corp., 843 10th Ave., all NYC. These are
                   vending machine companies.

MODUS   : A trusted member of the John Ormento Mafia organ-
OPERANDI   ization, engaged in distribution of heroin in kilo-
                   gram lots.

NAME : Salvatore SALLI

ALIASES : Sam Salli

DESCRIPTION : Born 11-5-09 Racalmuto,
Agrigento, Sicily, 5'10",
200 lbs, brown eyes, black
hair, stocky build. Derived
citizenship through naturali
zation of father, Indiana,
Penna., 1924.

LOCALITIES : Resides 342 No. Division St,
FREQUENTED Buffalo, NY. Frequents San-
tore's & Parkedge Rests.,
Buffalo, Cleveland,O., Ontario & Montreal, Canada.
Currently (1960) fugitive.

FAMILY : Wife: Hilda Frederick (deceased); daughters: Joan
BACKGROUND & Judy; son: Thomas; father: Luigi; mother: Jennie
DiLiberto; brothers: Louis & Charles; sisters:
Catherine Morganti, Mary Tromba (sister-in-law of
Salvatore Rizzo), Angelina & Josephine.

CRIMINAL : Salvatore Pieri, Salvatore Rizzo, Magaddino brothers,
ASSOCIATES ██████████████████████, ███████████████████████.

CRIMINAL : FBI #1185619. Buffalo PD #22446. Record dating
HISTORY from 1929 includes arrests for grand larceny, gambling, assault, bootlegging & counterfeiting. Federal
narcotic conviction. Wanted for interstate theft.

BUSINESS : Occasional construction worker.

MODUS : One of the most active Mafia racketeers in the Buf-
OPERANDI falo area. Principal source of supply for alcohol &
narcotics in that area. Will engage in any type of
crime.

NAME   : Battisto SALVO

ALIASES   : John B. Salvo, Bart Salvo,
                 Battisimo Salvo

DESCRIPTION   : Born 2-23-06 NY, NY, 5'9",
                 180 lbs, medium build, is
                 balding with grey hair on
                 sides of head, brown eyes
                 dark complexion.

LOCALITIES   : Resides 195 Townsend Ave,
FREQUENTED   Pelham, NY. Frequents Park
                 Inn Rest., Bronx, NY, and
                 Del Rio Bar and Grill, Yon-
                 kers, NY.

FAMILY   : Wife: Sadie Lesnick; daughter: Merle Linda; father:
BACKGROUND   Paul (dead); mother: Angelina Salvo (nee Salvo).

CRIMINAL   : Joe Doto, Thomas Milo (deceased), Vito Genovese,
ASSOCIATES   Lucky Luciano, Frank Costello, Joe Valachi, Frank
                 Scalici (deceased), Morris Barra.

CRIMINAL   : FBI #297699, NYCPD #79837, arrests since 1927 in-
HISTORY   clude attempted rape, felonious assault, armed
                 robbery, kidnapping, suspicion of felony.

BUSINESS   : Partner with brother-in-law Pete Federico in Plaster-
                 ing firm, P.J. Federico, Inc., 30 Stevens Ave, Mt.
                 Vernon, NY, also connected with Nulite Standard
                 Lighting Co, 309 E 47th St, NYC.

MODUS   : Bookmaker, makes trips to Italy to see deportee
OPERANDI   Joe Doto; and also believed to negotiate narcotic
                 transactions while there. A top Mafia member from
                 the Bronx, NY, area.

NAME	: Rocco SANCINELLA
ALIASES	: None
DESCRIPTION	: Born 5-6-19 NYC, 5'9", 185 lbs, brown hair, brown eyes, dark complexion.

LOCALITIES FREQUENTED	: Resides 421 W. 260 St, Bronx, NY. Frequents Anchor Bar at 76th & 2nd Ave, Green Open Kitchen, 77th & 1st Ave, Wright's Coffee Shop, 86th & Lexington, all NYC, Hi-Way Bar, 362 Metropolitan Ave, Brooklyn, New York.
FAMILY BACKGROUND	: Married Virginia Donofrio; father: Frank; mother: Carmela D'Orio (both born Italy).
CRIMINAL ASSOCIATES	: Ignazio Orlando, Angelo Loiacano, Vincent Todaro, Charles Albero, Frank Moccardi, Salvatore Santoro, Cotroni Brothers (Canada).
CRIMINAL HISTORY	: FBI #5132291, NYCPD #B213629. Record dates from 1943 and includes arrests for assault & robbery and violation of the narcotic laws.
BUSINESS	: Operates a luncheonette at 4533 3rd Ave, Bronx, NY.
MODUS OPERANDI	: Member of major Mafia group engaged in counterfeiting and in distributing huge quantities of heroin obtained from the Cotroni organization in Canada.

NAME   : Carmelo SANSONE

ALIASES   : Michel Nasone, Schnozzola.

DESCRIPTION   : Born 9-10-12 N.Y.C. 5'9",
                  160 lbs, brown eyes, black
                  hair, nose scars due to plas-
                  tic surgery, tattoo of man's
                  head on right forearm, tattoo
                  of woman's head on left fore-
                  arm.

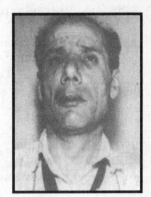

LOCALITIES   : Resides 163 W. 71 Street,
FREQUENTED   NYC. Frequented French Res-
                  taurants in vicinity 8th Ave
                  & W. 47th St in Manhattan.

FAMILY   : Single; brothers: Joseph & Chalo; sister:
BACKGROUND   Mrs. Angelo Ouvar; mother: Josephine Kanela (dead);
                  father: Carmelo.

CRIMINAL   : Eugene Giannini (dead), Jean Laget, Lucien Ignaro,
ASSOCIATES   Giovanni & Corrado Maugeri, Francisco Pirico,
                  Antoine D'Agostino, Francois Spirito.

CRIMINAL   : FBI# 780875A. NYCPD-B# 299646. Arrests since 1951
HISTORY   include convictions for Federal Narcotic Laws. Cur-
                  rently (1959) awaiting trial for violation Federal
                  Narcotic Laws at N.Y.C.

BUSINESS   : No legitimate business of employment known.

MODUS   : An important Mafia narcotic trafficker who has
OPERANDI   direct sources of supply from international
                  Corsican Mafia traffickers.

In 2000, at the age of 87, Santoro died while in prison.

NAME   : Salvatore T. SANTORO

ALIASES   : Tom Mix, Salvatore Santora,
                  Arthur Ricco

DESCRIPTION   : Born 11-18-15, 5'9", 200 lbs
                  black hair, brown eyes,
                  stout build.

LOCALITIES   : Resides 132 Longview St.,
FREQUENTED   Leonia, NJ, frequents East
                  Harlem area and midtown
                  Manhattan.

FAMILY   : Married to Mary Zangaglia
BACKGROUND   and has one child, father:
                  Antonio, mother: Teresa Borgio.

CRIMINAL   : John Ormento, Sal LoProto, Frank Livorsi, Charles
ASSOCIATES   Albero, Joe Marone, Angelo C. Salerno, Joe Rao,
                  all of New York City.

CRIMINAL   : FBI #838426, NYCPD #B 128622. Arrests since 1933
HISTORY   include attempted grand larceny, 1897 PL of NY, and
                  2 convictions for Federal narcotic laws.

BUSINESS   : Associated with John Ormento in trucking concern,
                  and a produce salesman.

MODUS   : A notorious Mafia associate of John Ormento in the
OPERANDI   smuggling and distributing of narcotics from the
                  East Harlem area of New York City.

NAME   : Giacomo SCALICI

ALIASES   : Jack, Scalise, Scalice

DESCRIPTION : Born 1-21-1902, Palermo,
Sicily, Italy, 5'5", 140 lbs,
black hair, brown eyes.

LOCALITIES : Resides 678 E. 225th Street,
FREQUENTED   Bronx, NY, frequents Crescent
Avenue section of Bronx.

FAMILY   : Married Josephine LaPorte;
BACKGROUND   father: Giacomo; mother:
Giovanna Caviglia; sister:
Providenza; brothers: Giuseppe (missing), Salvatore,
Francisco (deceased) and Giovanni.

CRIMINAL   : Lucky Luciano, Salvatore Scalici, Giacomo Scarpulla,
ASSOCIATES Matteo Cuomo, Morris Barra, Frank Luciano.

CRIMINAL   : No known criminal record in U. S. or Italy.
HISTORY

BUSINESS   : Owns and operates Jack's Candy Store, 597 Crescent
Avenue, Bronx, N.Y.

MODUS   : Was a member of a large scale narcotic smuggling
OPERANDI   and distribution ring headed by his late brother
Francesco (murdered in connection with a narcotic
transaction). Uses his store as a front for
gambling, bootlegging, extortion and other illicit
activities in which he engages with his Mafia
associates.

NAME	: Salvatore SCALICI

ALIASES : Torrido, Sam, Scalisi,
Scalise, Scalice

DESCRIPTION : Born 2-19-1886, Palermo,
Sicily, Italy, 5'8", 150 lbs,
medium build, black hair,
brown eyes, medium complexion

LOCALITIES : Resides 276 Hickory St.,
FREQUENTED   Burlington, N.J. Frequents
Jacks Candy Store, 597 Cres-
cent Ave., Bronx, NY.

FAMILY : Married; father: Giacomo; mother: Giovanna Caviglia;
BACKGROUND   brothers: Frank (deceased), Joseph (missing),
Giacomo, Giovanni (Italy); sister: Providenza Polizzi.

CRIMINAL : Lucky Luciano, ████████████████, Giovanni Maugeri,
ASSOCIATES   ███████████████, Matthew Cuomo, Giacomo Scarpulla.

CRIMINAL : FBI #1442929, NYCPD #B165240. Record in Italy dates
HISTORY   from 1915 when he was arrested on a charge of
double homicide. In the U.S. was arrested for attempted swindle, extortion (fake murder racket), &
violation of immigration laws.

BUSINESS : Wholesale egg business, Burlington, N.J.

MODUS : Was engaged with his brother the late Mafia Chief
OPERANDI   of the Bronx, NYC in the narcotic and alcohol
traffic. Continues to supply alcohol to distributors in the Bronx, N.Y.

NAME	: Michele Giacomo SCARPULLA
ALIASES	: Giacomino, Jack Scarpulla
DESCRIPTION	: Born 5-16-1899 Palermo, Sicily, Italy, 5'8", 185 lbs, stout build, dark complexion, brown eyes, brown hair turning white.
LOCALITIES FREQUENTED	: Resides 77 Winter St., Bronx, NY. Frequents New Prosperity Meat Market, 284 5th Ave, Brooklyn, NY, and Crescent Ave, section of Bronx, NY.

FAMILY BACKGROUND	: Married Rosa Scalici (sister of late Francesco); son: Angelo; daughter: Maria Anna; father: Giacomo; mother: Marion Quadrini; Angelo married Rosemary Lapi, daughter of convicted counterfeiter Vincent Rocco Lapi.
CRIMINAL ASSOCIATES	: Frank Luciano, Carlo & Paul Gambino, Joseph Bisogno, Salvatore Caneba, Sebastiano Bellanca.
CRIMINAL HISTORY	: FBI #983998. NYCPD #B113221. Record dates from 1933 and includes arrests for grand larceny and bootlegging.
BUSINESS	: He and son Angelo own & operate New Prosperity Meat Market, 284 5th Ave, Brooklyn, NY.
MODUS OPERANDI	: High echelon Mafioso. Key member of the large scale narcotic smuggling ring formerly headed by his brother-in-law the late Francesco Scalici.

```
NAME          : Giovanni SCHILLACI

ALIASES       : Frank Coniglio, Thomas
                Coniglio, John Lanza, Frank
                Lanza, John Longo, Frank
                Long, Al Brown, Frank
                Alberto.

DESCRIPTION   : Born 10-29-01, Corleone,
                Sicily, 5'5", 175 lbs., eyes
                brown, stocky build, brown-
                grey hair, partially bald,
                dark complexion.
```

```
LOCALITIES    : Deported to Italy in 1947,
FREQUENTED      present whereabouts unknown, believed in U.S.

FAMILY        : Mother, Maria Concetta Coniglio (dead), father,
BACKGROUND      Biagio (dead), brothers, William, Angelo, Louis,
                sisters: Catherine Zangari and Maria Lanza.

CRIMINAL      : Charles Albero, Frank Livorsi, Salvatore Santora,
ASSOCIATES      Philip Lombardo, Lucky Luciano, John Ormento.

CRIMINAL      : FBI #202010, NYC, PD# B-58457, since 5-4-21, 11
HISTORY         arrests for assault and robbery, burglary, robbery
                and conviction of Federal Narcotic Laws; deported to
                Italy on 4-2-47; in 1951 believed to have illegaly
                re-entered the U.S.

BUSINESS      : Prior to deportation to Italy, he was reported to be
                part owner of Butler's Top Hat Room, Columbus Ave.,
                and 83rd St., NYC.

MODUS         : He was one of the leaders of the upper east side
OPERANDI        Mafia group of NYC which financed the wholesale dis-
                tribution and smuggling of opium and heroin from
                Mexico.
```

NAME   : Joseph F. SCHIPANI

ALIASES   : Little Joe

DESCRIPTION   : Born 3-1-12 NYC, 5'7", 165
                  lbs, brown eyes, hair-grey
                  mixed with black, butterfly
                  tattoo on right arm.

LOCALITIES   : Resides 165 East 19th St,
FREQUENTED   B'klyn, NY. Frequents Bay
                  Ridge section of B'klyn and
                  lower East Side of NYC.

FAMILY   : Married Anna DeLuca; son:
BACKGROUND   Joseph Schipani, Jr.; father: Frank (deceased);
                  mother: Serafina Gigliotti (deceased).

CRIMINAL   : Giuseppe Doto, Frank Caruso, Gaetano Maiorana,
ASSOCIATES   Michael Clementi, Anthony Anastasia.

CRIMINAL   : FBI #571946. NYCPD B#102663. Record dates from 1932
HISTORY   and includes robbery and vagrancy.

BUSINESS   : No legitimate employment known.

MODUS   : Brooklyn Lieutenant of deported Mafia chief
OPERANDI   Giuseppe Doto. Narcotic smuggler and wholesale dis-
                  tributor, controls "policy" and bookmaking in
                  South Brooklyn and Bay Ridge.

NAME : Pasquale SCIORTINO

ALIASES : Pat Sciortina

DESCRIPTION : Born 3-5-15 Cattolica
Eraclea, Sicily, 5'6",
140 lbs., brown eyes, brown
hair, naturalized 9-18-39
Auburn, New York

LOCALITIES : Resides 58 Holley St.,
FREQUENTED Auburn, N.Y. Frequents
Buffalo-Rochester area of NY.

FAMILY : Married to Josephine Rizzo;
BACKGROUND daughters: Donna & Josephine; father: Amedeo;
mother: Giuseppina

CRIMINAL : Sam & Patsy Monachino, Emanuel Zicari, Salvatore &
ASSOCIATES Joe Falcone, Vincent Scro, Roy Carlisi, Ignatius
Cannone.

CRIMINAL : FBI #769201A. White Plains NYPD #6952. Only arrest
HISTORY in 1951 for violation Immigration Act. Currently
under investigation by I&NS.

BUSINESS : Operates Diana Bleach Co., 44 Jefferson Ave.,
Auburn, New York

MODUS : Attended Apalachin Mafia meeting 1957. Member of
OPERANDI upper New York State Mafia group which controls
gambling, illegal alcohol, & other illegitimate
rackets in the area.

NAME	: Michael SEDOTTO
ALIASES	: LaRocco, Sedetto, Mike-the-Geep
DESCRIPTION	: Born 2-22-20 NYC, 5'8½", 185 lbs, medium build, grey hair (bald), blue eyes.
LOCALITIES FREQUENTED	: Resides 2715 DeWitt Place, Bronx, NY, frequents 187th & Crescent, 187th & Cambreling, Bronx, NY.
FAMILY BACKGROUND	: Married Dorothy Lauer; sons: Michael & Salvatore; father: Joseph; mother: Anna LaRocco, (both deceased); brothers: Joseph, Patrick & Anthony; sister: Mary Acvino.
CRIMINAL ASSOCIATES	: Alfred Mauriello, ███████████████, Joseph Barra, Rocco Mazzie, Vincent Panebianco, ████████████████.
CRIMINAL HISTORY	: FBI #3242790, NYCPD #B246243, record dates from 1937 and includes arrests for possession of burglary tools, felonious assault, perjury & violation of probation Federal Narcotic case pending.
BUSINESS	: Self-employed dress contractor.
MODUS OPERANDI	: A powerful Mafioso who controls policy and Italian lottery rackets in the East Bronx area of NYC. Also controls a wholesale narcotic trafficking combine.

NAME   : Salvatore Speciale SETTIMO

ALIASES   : Toto, S_al, Sam

DESCRIPTION   : Born 9-1-1900 Partinico,
                  Palermo, Sicily, Italy, 5'7",
                  185 lbs, heavy build, black
                  hair, brown eyes, ruddy com-
                  plexion, Alien registration
                  # 3927981.

LOCALITIES   : Resides at 62 Chestnut Rd.,
FREQUENTED   Centereach, L.I., NY. Fre-
                  quents Lower East Side &
                  mid-town areas NYC.

FAMILY   : Wife: Josephine Calagna; children: Josephine Angela,
BACKGROUND   Angela Rose, Rose Marie, and Paul; 2 brothers: Frank
                  & Thomas; sisters: Rose & Anafrio (in Partinico,
                  Italy); father: Salvatore (deceased); mother:
                  Josephine Speciale, (born in Italy).

CRIMINAL   : Leonard Accardo, ███████████, ████████,
ASSOCIATES   Michael Pecoraro, ██████████, ██████████,
                  Salvatore Mezzasalma, Mimi Limandri, ███████████,
                  Steve Armone, Carmine Locascio, Paul Gambino, Carlo
                  Gambino.

CRIMINAL   : FBI #251035, NYCPD #B74266. Record dates from 1926
HISTORY   and includes arrests for concealed weapon, forgery
                  and counterfeiting.

BUSINESS   : Salesman with the Carrol Paper Products, 410 3rd
                  Ave, Brooklyn, NY. Owned by Carlo Gambino.

MODUS   : An international drug trafficker and trusted Mafia
OPERANDI   member with the notorious Gambino brothers, Paul &
                  Carlo, wholesales large quantities of narcotics to
                  major traffickers in the NY area.

Siano was last seen with three men in the Spring of 1964.

NAME : Fiore SIANO

ALIASES : Fiore Sanguino

DESCRIPTION : Born 6-22-27, N.Y.C., N.Y.,
5'10½", 163 lbs., black hair
brown eyes, ruddy complexion
two vertical scars on bridge
of nose.

LOCALITIES : Resides at 2881 1st Ave.,
FREQUENTED   N.Y.C., N.Y. (1954), currently (1959) incarcerated.

FAMILY : Father, Michael, Mother,
BACKGROUND   Filomena, Sisters, Emily
Buchanan and Mary Seaton, brother, Dominick.

CRIMINAL : Joseph Pagano, ██████████████, Joseph Ragone,
ASSOCIATES   Joe Valachi, ████████, ████████, ████████
████████, Anthony Mancuso, all narcotic traffickers
in East Harlem area NYC.

CRIMINAL : FBI #109492, NYC, PD# 268897, 1st arrested for
HISTORY   burglary in 1948, subsequent arrests include assault
and robbery with a gun, sentenced 11-27-54 to 8
years for violation of the Federal Narcotic Laws.

BUSINESS : None.

MODUS : A wholesale dealer in heroin and cocaine to traf-
OPERANDI   fickers in NYC and in interstate traffic, A main
source of supply for negro narcotic traffickers.
A trusted associate of important Mafia leaders
in the East Harlem area NYC.

NAME	: David SMITH

ALIASES : John Payne, Pop Smith.

DESCRIPTION : Born 5-28-08 NYC, 5'8", 200
lbs, stout build, black hair,
brown eyes, ruddy complexion,
tip left index finger missing.

LOCALITIES : Resides 92-40 Queens Blvd.,
FREQUENTED Rego Park, NY. Frequents
100th St, and First Ave,
1885 Third Ave, 1618 Westchester Ave, Bronx, all in
New York City. Visits Phoenix, Arizona.

FAMILY : Married Wanda Klein; has one child; father: Joseph,
BACKGROUND born in England; mother, deceased.

CRIMINAL : Rosario Rinaldi, Anthony Corallo, ███████████,
ASSOCIATES ██████████, Solly Kaplan.

CRIMINAL : FBI #747793, NYCPD B#121211. Record dating from 1934
HISTORY includes arrests for felonious assault and violation
of State and Federal narcotic laws. Federal narcotic
conviction.

BUSINESS : Co-owner with Joseph Costa of the New Third Avenue
Bakery Shop 1909 Third Ave, NYC.

MODUS : Wholesaler of narcotics to interstate violators.
OPERANDI Engages in the conversion of opium and morphine
base. Though non-Italian he is accepted and trusted
by top NYC Mafia violators.

He died in January 1981.

NAME : George SMURRA

ALIASES : George Sumirre, George Blair
George Smarra, George Small,
"Blah-Blah".

DESCRIPTION : Born 1-1-10 Brooklyn, N.Y.
5'7½", 196 lbs., brown eyes,
black hair, stocky build.

LOCALITIES : Resides 1627 78th St.,
FREQUENTED   Brooklyn, N.Y. Frequents
Club 1717, Elegante Night
Club, Pompeii Restaurant,
Surburban Night Club,
Endicott Bar & Grill, all in Brooklyn, N.Y., and
also Miami Fla.

FAMILY : Married to Helen Palamarro; son: Ambrose; father:
BACKGROUND   Ambrose; mother: Angelina (both deceased); sisters:
Marion, Julia, & Mrs. Helen LaRocca; brothers: Henry
& William.

CRIMINAL : Mike Miranda, Vito Genovese, ▮▮▮▮▮▮▮, John Oddo,
ASSOCIATES   Anthony Bonasera, Carmine Lombardozzi, Gus Frasca,
Pete DeFeo, & ▮▮▮▮▮▮▮▮▮▮▮▮▮▮.

CRIMINAL : FBI#183755. NYC PD-B#70645. Arrests since 1928
HISTORY   include burglary, felonious assault, assault &
robbery, & murder.

BUSINESS : Has interests in Balinese Supper Club, Washington
Ave., Brooklyn, N.Y.

MODUS : Assists Mafia associates Vito Genovese & Mike
OPERANDI   Miranda in controlling illegal gambling and
narcotic trafficking in Brooklyn, N.Y. A "strong-
arm" man and "killer" for the Mafia.

> He is one of the great "Unknowns" of the mafia in the
> United States.

NAME : Santo SORGE

ALIASES : None

DESCRIPTION : Born 1-11-1908, Mussomeli,
Caltanissetta, Sicily, Italy
5'10", brown hair, brown eyes.
Immigrated to U.S. 2-3-41.
Naturalized NYC 6-7-48.

LOCALITIES : Resides 222 E 57th St., NYC.
FREQUENTED Frequents exclusive clubs
and restaurants in NYC.

FAMILY : Married Bertha Kretschmer;
BACKGROUND father: Salvatore (deceased); mother: Rosena Gange,
resides in Mussomeli, Sicily, Italy.

CRIMINAL : Lucky Luciano, Carmine Galante, Calogero DiCarlo,
ASSOCIATES Vito Genovese, Giuseppe Bonanno, Giuseppe DiPalermo,
John Balsamo.

CRIMINAL : No record in U.S. Expelled from France 1932. 1939
HISTORY Italian Govt convicted him, in absentia, of espionage
and falsification of documents, arrested 1948 in
connection with this and later released.

BUSINESS : Managing Director Rimrock Int'l Oil Co., 680 5th Ave.,
NYC, member of Foreign Economic Research Ass'n.

MODUS : One of the most important Mafia leaders. Travels
OPERANDI extensively between Italy & U.S. in furtherance of
ostensibly legitimate international ventures which
probably cover for liaison duties between highest
ranking Mafiosi in U.S. and Italy. Has considerable
political influence in Italy.

NAME   : Joseph SPADARO

ALIASES   : None

DESCRIPTION   : Born 2-5-06 NYC, 5'5", 160
                  lbs, brown eyes, brown hair,
                  neat dresser.

LOCALITIES   : Resides 199-52 Keno Ave,
FREQUENTED   Hollis, NY. Frequents 111
                  Himrod St; Gondola Rest., 20
                  Lafayette Ave, & Monterey
                  Club, 1251 Flatbush Ave, all
                  in Brooklyn.

FAMILY   : Married Rose LaBruzzo; father: Giuseppe; mother:
BACKGROUND   Angelina; brother: Larry; wife's sister married to
                  Joseph Bonanno one of 1957 Apalachin delegates.

CRIMINAL   : Joseph Bonanno, Vito Genovese, John Bonventre,
ASSOCIATES   Joseph Profaci, Frank Garafola.

CRIMINAL   : No known criminal record.
HISTORY

BUSINESS   : Owns Joe Spadaro & Co., Suit Manufacturers and he
                  & brother Larry own Perfect Suit & Coat Co., both
                  located 111 Himrod St, Brooklyn, NY.

MODUS   : An underling of his brother-in-law Mafia leader
OPERANDI   Joseph Bonanno for whom he collects extortion fees
                  from businessmen who are seeking to avoid labor
                  troubles. Is closely associated with top level Mafia
                  members responsible for the importation & distribution
                  of untold quantities of illicit narcotics.

NAME   : Salvatore SPECIALE

ALIASES   : Benny, Sal-the-Beak

DESCRIPTION   : Born 3-12-16 NYC, 5'3", 170
                  lbs, black hair, brown eyes,
                  dark complexion, stocky build

LOCALITIES   : Resides 213 E 107 St., NYC,
FREQUENTED   frequents 116th St., & 1st
                  Ave., Regal Wine & Liquor
                  Store, 2010 3rd Ave, NYC.

FAMILY   : Wife: Nettie Belluscio;
BACKGROUND   father: Salvatore; mother:
                  Mary Rao (sister of Vincent Rao).

CRIMINAL   : Vincent Rao, Carlo Gambino, Carmine Lombardozzi,
ASSOCIATES   Natale Joseph Evola, Vito Genovese, Michele Miranda,
                  Dominick Oliveto, John Ormento, Thomas Luchese.

CRIMINAL   : FBI #996765, NYCPD B#126550. Criminal record dates
HISTORY   back to 1934 and includes arrests for Grand Larceny,
                  Rape, Policy, Vagrancy, Bookmaking, violation of the
                  Federal Narcotic Laws.

BUSINESS   : Employed by the Regal Wine & Liquor Corp., 2010 3rd
                  Ave., NYC. This corporation investigated by the
                  U.S. Rackets Grand Jury in 1958 and 1959.

MODUS   : Speciale has for many years been associated with
OPERANDI   the most important Mafiosi in the country in the
                  narcotic traffic and the control of gambling on
                  the upper east side of New York City.

NAME : Pasquale SPINA

ALIASES : Patsy

DESCRIPTION : Born 6-25-22 Naples, Italy,
5'4", 165 lbs, brown hair,
brown eyes, stocky build,
derivative citizenship.

LOCALITIES : Resides at 3203 Park Ave.,
FREQUENTED   Oceanside, L.I. Frequents
the Monterey Club, located
at 1251 Flatbush Ave, B'klyn,
NY.

FAMILY : Married to Madeline Bifucco, daughter:Vincenza;
BACKGROUND   father: Anthony; mother: Vivian Sarno; brothers:
Victor, Anthony, Phillip, Archie; sisters: Florence,
Cora, Phyliss.

CRIMINAL :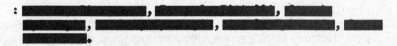
ASSOCIATES

CRIMINAL : FBI #321888A. Arrested in 1949 in NYC and charged with
HISTORY   being a fugitive from NJ and Penna. Sentenced in 1949,
in Scranton, Pa. to 5 to 14 yrs for burglary (safe-
cracking.) Paroled in 1954 from State Prison in Gra-
terford, Pa. and is now under the supervision of the
NY State Parole Board.

BUSINESS : Employed as a laborer for his father in law, Frank
Bifucco, a sub-contracter whose offices are located
in his home at 3203 Park Ave., Oceanside, L.I.

MODUS : Lower echelon Mafia burglar and narcotic trafficker.
OPERANDI

NAME : Salvatore SPITALE

ALIASES : Salvy, Sam Salvin, The Greek, James Martin

DESCRIPTION : Born 1-2-1897 Petralia, Sicily, Italy, 5'8", 200 lbs heavy build, grey hair, brown eyes, medium complexion.

LOCALITIES FREQUENTED : Resides 27 Hull St., Grant City, Staten Island, NY. Frequents Hotel Richmond, NY, NY, Lindy's Rest., NYC, Fan and Bill's Rest., Miami Beach, Fla., Shore Park Hotel, Miami Beach, Fla.

FAMILY BACKGROUND : Married Irene Fiamen Salvin; daughter: Mrs. Jane Marcouecchio; son: Salvatore, Jr.,; father: Joachimo Spitale (deceased); mother: Josephine Sabatino; brothers: Gaetano (Guy); and Joseph Spitale.

CRIMINAL ASSOCIATES : Irving Bitz, ███████████, ███████████) ███████, ███████████, ███████████, ███████, James Plumeri, ███████████.

CRIMINAL HISTORY : FBI #583515, NYCPD #B104206. Record dating from 1912 includes arrests for delinquent child, bootlegging, burglary, homicide (gun), felonious assault, concealed weapon, grand larceny and parole violation.

BUSINESS : Claims to be Real Estate Broker. Former owner of the Richmond Hotel, NYC, Count Casino Night Club, Miami, Fla, & Hotel Belmont, Newark, NJ. President of Lucarini Products Inc, NYC, owner of Richmond Ideal Homecraft Corp., Staten Island, NY.

MODUS OPERANDI : A trusted member of the Mafia. He and former partner Irving Bitz were go-betweens with the underworld in the Lindbergh kidnapping investigation.

He was last seen alive on September 23, 1960. His body was never found. Some speculate that he was shot in the head, put into a car trunk, and that the car went through an automobile crusher.

NAME : Vincent James SQUILLANTE

ALIASES : Jimmy Jerome

DESCRIPTION : Born 6-17-17 NYC, 5'2", 130 lbs, black hair, brown eyes, slight build, large horn rimmed glasses, natty dresser.

LOCALITIES : Resides 1962 Narragansett
FREQUENTED Ave, Bronx, NY. Frequents 106th St & 1st Ave, Jennie's Rest., at 2036 2nd Ave, & midtown night clubs, all in Manhattan, 187th & Cambreling Ave, & Bluebird Rest., at 2890 Burke Ave, Bronx, New York.

FAMILY : Married Theresa Scialabba 1949 & had one child,
BACKGROUND Bedilia; divorced 1951 & married Olivia Hughes, by whom two daughters: Donna & Olivia; father: Louis; mother: Euthalia Alberti; brother : Nunzio; nephew: Jerry Mancuso; has seven sisters.

CRIMINAL : Rocco Mazzie, Frank Borelli, Charles Curcio, ▮▮▮▮
ASSOCIATES ▮▮▮▮▮▮▮, ▮▮▮▮▮▮▮▮▮▮▮▮, Anthony Sedotto.

CRIMINAL : FBI #297633B. NYCPD #B323484. Record dating from
HISTORY 1953 includes arrests for income tax violation, state narcotic laws, violation of probation and extortion.

BUSINESS : Holds positions in numerous unions and has interests in several garment & surplus companies.

MODUS : Has risen from small time narcotics peddler to top
OPERANDI racketeer and labor extortionist; is feared by lesser racketeers because of his powerful position in the Mafia. Finances narcotic smuggling ventures and controls garbage collection business in greater NY, through Mafia tactics. Claims to be god-child of the late Mafia leader Albert Anastasia.

NAME : Innocenzio STOPELLI

ALIASES : John Stoppelli, Johnny the Bug.

DESCRIPTION : Born 4-10-07 NYC, NY, 5'7", 160 lbs, medium build, black greying hair, brown eyes, dark complexion.

LOCALITIES : Resides: 153 Madison St.,
FREQUENTED NYC, frequents 191 Prince St. Prince & Sullivan Sts, Bleecker & Sullivan Sts., Milady's Bar, 167 Bleecker St, Tony Pastor's Club 130 W 3rd St., Tommy's Bar, 171 Bleecker St., all New York City.

FAMILY : Wife: Marion Groger; father: Rocco; mother: Carmela
BACKGROUND Miraglio; brother: Caeser; sister: Margaret.

CRIMINAL : Anthony Strollo, Joseph Marone, Vincent Mauro, Frank
ASSOCIATES Caruso, Charles Albero, Joseph Valachi, Harry Tantillo.

CRIMINAL : FBI #67649, NYCPD #B 67307. Record dates from 1924
HISTORY to 1948, and includes arrest for possession of a gun, robbery, bribing a government officer & violation of Federal Narcotic Laws.

BUSINESS : Alleged to be in partnership with Tommy Annichiario, owner of Tommy's Bar, 171 Bleecker St., NYC., N.Y.

MODUS : Trusted inner-circle Mafia Leader in the Anthony
OPERANDI Strollo Organization. One of the most active large scale wholesale narcotic traffickers in the U.S.

NAME   : Joseph STRACCI

ALIASES   : Joe Stretch, Joseph Street, Joe Russo.

DESCRIPTION   : Born 1-6-06 NYC, 5'8", 165 lbs, brown eyes, black hair, slightly heavy build.

LOCALITIES   : Resides 80 S Woodland St.,
FREQUENTED   Englewood, NJ., frequents Dunhill Restaurant, 1440 Broadway, NYC, Alto Knights, 86 Kenmare St., NYC, Colonial Tavern, 116th St., NYC, NY.

FAMILY   : Wife: Cecilia Rao (sister of Joseph Rao); Son:
BACKGROUND   Joseph Thomas; father Anthony Stracci; mother: Marie Lobalbo.

CRIMINAL   : Joey Rao, Raymond Patriarca, Charles Albero, Thomas
ASSOCIATES   Luchese, Frank Livorsi, James Plumeri, Joseph Bendenelli, Johnny Dio, Anthony Corallo, Natale J. Evola, Philip Lombardo.

CRIMINAL   : FBI #72208, NYCPD #B64304. Arrests date back to 1923
HISTORY   and include rape, burglary, assault & robbery, robbery, attempted grand larceny and violation of the Federal Narcotic Laws.

BUSINESS   : Secretary & Treasurer of D. Zimit Inc., 500 7th Ave., NYC, NY. (Manufacturer of Ladies wear), believed to have interest in several other organizations in garment industry.

MODUS   : Active together with other Mafiosi in labor racket-
OPERANDI   eering in garment industry and related trucking operations.

Strollo disappeared from his home in NJ on April 8, 1962. His murder has never been solved, though it's been rumored that he faked his own death to avoid arrest.

NAME : Anthony C. STROLLO

ALIASES : Tony Benda, Tony Bender

DESCRIPTION : Born 6-18-1899 NYC 5'7½", 156 lbs., brown hair, brown eyes, wears glasses.

LOCALITIES FREQUENTED : Resides 1015 Palisades Ave., Fort Lee, NJ, frequents Greenwich Village section of Manhattan and dock area in Newark and Hoboken, NJ.

FAMILY BACKGROUND : Married to Edna Goldenberg and has 3 children, father: Leone, mother: Giovannina Nigro, brothers: Emilio and Dominick (both dead).

CRIMINAL ASSOCIATES : Frank Costello, Joe Adonis, Vito Genovese, Vincent Mauro, Pat Pagano, Joe Valachi, Anastasia brothers, and most top racketeers in NYC and U.S.

CRIMINAL HISTORY : FBI # 4282858, NYCPD #B 64086, arrests from 1926 include possession of a gun, conspiracy to contrive a lottery.

BUSINESS : Claims to be a real estate broker.

MODUS OPERANDI : One of most powerful racketeers in U.S., having control of northern NJ Dock area. A recognized Mafia leader and head of a narcotic smuggling-distributing organization with several of his criminal associates who handle the distribution of narcotics.

NAME   : Harry STROMBERG

ALIASES   : Nig Rosen, Harry Rosen,
                 Hyman Stromberg, Chaim
                 Stromberg, The Mahoff,
                 Joseph Bloom, Hyman Chaim

DESCRIPTION   : Born 7-15-1903, Sorokov,
                 Russia, Jewish, 5'8", 190
                 lbs, grey hair, balding,
                 brown eyes, dark complexion,
                 neat, conservative dresser.
                 Naturalized NYC 8-6-1945.

LOCALITIES   : Resided 420 E 55th St., NYC,
FREQUENTED   & 5196 Pine Tree Drive, Miami Beach. Frequented
                 NYC garment district & better night clubs, Miami
                 Beach & Philadelphia. Currently (1960) incarcerated.

FAMILY   : Divorced Silvia Cohen; adopted son: Joseph; remarried
BACKGROUND   Gretchen Gershon; father: Harry; mother: Netti Cohen.

CRIMINAL   : Lucky Luciano, Francesco Costiglia, Giuseppe Doto,
ASSOCIATES   Gaetano Lucchese, Meyer Lansky, Mickey Cohen.

CRIMINAL   : FBI #786309 NYCPD #57333   Arrests include robbery,
HISTORY   illegal lottery, burglary, possession of a gun,
                 violation of Federal liquor and narcotic laws.
                 1958 sent. to 5 yrs on Federal narcotic conspiracy.

BUSINESS   : Has been connected with the following garment houses:
                 Studio Frocks, Dearest Miss, Jay & Lou Mfg. Co.,
                 LouJay Dress Co., Judy Lee Fashions.

MODUS   : Though non-Italian he is allied with top Mafia crim-
                 inals in all types of illicit activity, including
                 labor racketeering, gambling & narcotic trafficking.

NAME	: Peter Salvatore TAMBONE

ALIASES : Pete - Little Pete

DESCRIPTION : Born 11-23-20 Brooklyn, NY, 5'1", 170 lbs, brown eyes, dark brown hair, dark complexion, neat dresser.

LOCALITIES FREQUENTED : Resides at 134 Warren St., Brooklyn, N.Y. Frequents the Bay Ridge section of Brooklyn, Court & Carroll St., Brooklyn, NY, Columbia & Sackett St., Naples Restaurant 151 Montague St., Brooklyn, NY.

FAMILY BACKGROUND : Single; father: Carmelo; mother: Catherine; brother: Alfred.

CRIMINAL ASSOCIATES : Cristoforo Robino (murdered Mafia chief), Frank Di Gregorio, Alexander Amarosa, Anthony Annichiarico, Giacento Mannarino.

CRIMINAL HISTORY : FBI #1708930, NYCPD E# 14993. Criminal record dates back 1939 and includes arrests for policy, assault & battery and violation of the Federal Narcotic Laws. Tambone is currently (1959) serving a 5 year sentence for violation of the Federal Narcotic Laws, imposed in 1956.

BUSINESS : No legitimate employment.

MODUS OPERANDI : Tambone, up until the time of his incarceration, was an underling of Mafia Chief Cristofaro Robino, since murdered. Tambone handled narcotic transactions for Robino who was too cautious to handle such deals himself.

NAME	: Enrico Nicolo TANTILLO
ALIASES	: Harry Tantillo, Blackie, Coco, Harry Cantillo
DESCRIPTION	: Born 1-28-16, NYC, NY, 5'6", 160 lbs, medium build, black hair, brown eyes, dark complexion.
LOCALITIES FREQUENTED	: Resides 4303 Furman Ave., Bronx, NY, frequents Florence Lingerie Shoppe, 4148 White Plains Rd, Bronx & vicinity 106th & 2nd Ave., New York City.
FAMILY BACKGROUND	: Wife: Matilda Manfredonia; father: Giuseppe; mother: Genoveffa Salerno (both born Italy); brother: Alfred Tantillo; half brother: Frank Tantillo; sister: Mary Lucchese; brothers-in-law: Richard, John & Anthony Manfredonia.
CRIMINAL ASSOCIATES	: Joseph Marone, John Stoppelli, Vincent Mauro, Nicholas Tolentino, Fred Salerno, John Ormento.
CRIMINAL HISTORY	: FBI #1024285, NYCPD #137405, record dates from 1935 and includes arrests for possession of revolver, obstructing justice, influencing witness & conviction for violation of Federal Narcotic Laws.
BUSINESS	: Owns Dominick's Pastry Shop, 2058 2nd Ave., NYC.
MODUS OPERANDI	: A trusted member of the Mafia inner circle. Supplies wholesale quantities of heroin to local & out of town customers.

NAME   : Moische TAUBMAN

ALIASES   : Morris Tennenbaum, M. Stein,
                Morris Gold, Morris Galloway

DESCRIPTION   : Born 9-16-03, Biola, Russia,
                Jewish, 5'9", 195 lbs, brown
                eyes, black hair-balding,
                stocky build. Deportable
                alien, but no country will
                accept. I&NS #A-10256576.

LOCALITIES   : Resides 63-60 102 St, Queens,
FREQUENTED   NY. Frequents brother's home
                325 E 23 St, NYC; Copacabana
                & Harwyn Clubs in NYC; Miami Beach & Chicago; re-
                ceives mail c/o Rashkin, 1491 Grand Concourse, Bronx,
                NY.

FAMILY   : Lives common-law with woman named Mildred & young
BACKGROUND   son; father: Joseph; mother: Anna Rosoff; sisters:
                Hilda Field, Sarah Geller, Rachel Solowitz & Esther
                Frank; brothers: Solomon & Samuel.

CRIMINAL   : Usche Gelb, ████████████, ██████████, Samuel
ASSOCIATES   Monastersky, Charles Schiffman, ██████████,
                Francisco Costiglia.

CRIMINAL   : FBI #19874. NYCPD #B59828. Chicago PD #C86356.
HISTORY   Record dating from 1919 includes arrests for burglary,
                assault & battery, robbery. Two Federal narcotic con-
                victions.

BUSINESS   : Silent interest in several NY garment manufacturing
                companies.

MODUS   : Top level wholesaler of narcotics in NYC, Chicago
OPERANDI   and elsewhere. Though non-Italian he is affiliated
                with and respected by important Mafiosi.

```
NAME          : John J. TERRANOVA

ALIASES       : Michael Catrone

DESCRIPTION   : Born on 10-4-23 B'klyn, NY,
                5'6", 195 lbs, brown eyes,
                brown hair, stocky build.

LOCALITIES    : Resides 48 Bonneilo Drive,
FREQUENTED      Mahopac Falls, NY. Frequents
                Nino's Rest., Jefferson Val-
                ley, NY; Lounge Cafe & the
                Ridgewood-Bushwick section of
                Brooklyn, NY.
```

```
FAMILY        : Married Blanche Lane; sons: Michael, Thomas, John Jr,
BACKGROUND      Philip and Edward; father: Santo; mother: Margarita
                Catrone; sister: Mrs. William Lang; brother: Fred.

CRIMINAL      : Frank Di Gregorio, Charles Campisi, Vincent Mauro,
ASSOCIATES      Charles LaCascia, Peter Tambone, ███████████████,
                █████████████, Giancento Mannarino, Alexander Amarosa.

CRIMINAL      : Never arrested.
HISTORY

BUSINESS      : Owner of Yampa Construction Co., Jefferson Valley,
                NY. From 1946 to present, either formed, owned, or
                was an officer in eight construction companies.

MODUS         : Due to his educational and professional talents, he
OPERANDI        has "fronted" for Mafia elements in various legit-
                imate enterprises established from funds derived
                from illegal sources. He is also known to have used
                these same enterprises for various underworld uses
                such as harboring fugitives and rendering legitimate
                aspects to strictly illegal activities.
```

NAME	: James TESSALONE
ALIASES	: Vincent Tessalone, Vincenzo Tessalona, James Curley, Jimmy, Silk Shirt Jimmy
DESCRIPTION	: Born 7-9-99 NYC, 5'9", 170 lbs, grey hair, brown eyes, light complexion.
LOCALITIES FREQUENTED	: Resides 212 Grand St., NYC, frequents Elizabeth & Broome St., on lower east side of NY. Also frequents Grand & Mulberry St., NYC.

FAMILY BACKGROUND	: Married Rose LaRocca; son: Michael; daughters: Anna and Marie; father: Michael; mother: Anna, both deceased; brothers: Frank, Joseph, John, Anthony; sisters: Marie and Angelina.
CRIMINAL ASSOCIATES	: ███████████, ███████████, Alfonso Marzano, ██████████, ██████████, Vincent Corrao.
CRIMINAL HISTORY	: FBI #532386, NYCPD B#100575. Record dates from 1923 and includes arrests for robbery, grand larceny, assault, possession of counterfeit gasoline ration stamps, and violation of the Federal Narcotic Laws. Sentenced 1944 to 3 years for Federal Narcotic violation.
BUSINESS	: Operates the Albert Tessitore Trucking Company, 40 Harrison Street, NYC, NY.
MODUS OPERANDI	: With other Mafiosi operates in and around the lower east side area of NY, supplying large amounts of heroin to Italian violators.

Tieri died on March 31, 1981 of natural causes. He was the first mobster to be convicted under the RICO Act.

NAME   : Frank Alfonso TIERI

ALIASES   : Funzi, Funzuola

DESCRIPTION   : Born 2-22-04 Naples, Italy,
                 5'7", 170 lbs, grey hair,
                 brown eyes, medium build,
                 pock marked, ruddy complex-
                 ion; Alien Reg # A-5263294.

LOCALITIES   : Resides 68 Bay 28th St,
FREQUENTED   Brooklyn, NY. Frequents Cafe
                 Royal & Knotty Pine Rest's.,
                 NYC, Rio Grande Social Club,
                 Crown Rest., Brooklyn, NY, &
                 Sorrentino's Restaurant, Newark, New Jersey.

FAMILY   : Married America Lucia; daughters: Antoinette Villani
BACKGROUND   & Carmela Alaimo Bern; father: Agostino Tieri; mother:
                 Carmela Taufano.

CRIMINAL   : Vito Genovese, ▮▮▮▮▮▮▮▮▮▮▮▮, Anthony Carillo,
ASSOCIATES   Carmine Lombardozzi, Gaetano Maiorano, Gus Frasca.

CRIMINAL   : FBI #4372673. NYCPD #B415324. Record dating from
HISTORY   1945 includes arrests for vagrancy and violation
                 alcohol laws.

BUSINESS   : President, Amerfrank Holding Corp.; Vice Pres. Jayvee
                 Sportswear, Hoboken, NJ., partner in Broadway Glove
                 Co., 1412 69th St., B'klyn (formerly operated by
                 Vincent Squillante).

MODUS   : High echelon Mafioso. Has been host to several
OPERANDI   important Mafia meetings. Part of a Mafia group
                 engaged in the smuggling of narcotics from France.

NAME   : Giuseppe TIPA, Jr.

ALIASES   : Joseph Tipa

DESCRIPTION   : Born Villabate,Sicily,Italy
                  on 11-11-11; 5'10", 180 lbs
                  medium build, black hair,
                  brown eyes. Naturalized
                  May 25, 1945.

LOCALITIES   : Resides 8205 14 Ave,B'klyn,NY
FREQUENTED   Frequents garage at 1901
                  Cropsey Ave., Brooklyn, NY

FAMILY   : Married Adele Mangano;
BACKGROUND   father: Giuseppe,Sr., mother: Josephine Profaci
                  (sister of Joseph Profaci); sister: Rosaria.

CRIMINAL   : Joseph Profaci, Salvatore Mezzasalma, Joseph
ASSOCIATES   Bonnano, Vito Genovese, Anthony Anastasia

CRIMINAL   : FBI #4829597   NYCPD #B-252723
HISTORY   Record dates from 1944 and includes arrests
                  for narcotic investigation and lottery.

BUSINESS   : No legitimate occupation known.

MODUS   : An important member of the Mafia, closely
OPERANDI   associated with top echelon members; allegedly
                  controls policy and lottery in Brooklyn, N.Y.

Tocco died on May 3, 1938.

NAME : Joseph TOCCO

ALIASES : "The Eye"

DESCRIPTION : Born 7-13-02 N.Y.C. 5'6", 160 lbs., brown eyes, fair complexion, brown-grey hair.

LOCALITIES FREQUENTED : Resides 401 E. 116th St., N.Y.C. Frequents Hofbrau Bar, 2nd Ave. & E. 120th St.; Turf Bar, Broadway & W. 50th St.; both in Manhattan. Also makes trips to Detroit and San Francisco.

FAMILY BACKGROUND : Married and has no children; brother: Salvatore.

CRIMINAL ASSOCIATES : Antonio Campagna & Salvatore Maugeri of California; Frank Caruso, Joe Marone, Charles Albero, John Ormento, & Salvatore Santoro, all of N.Y.C.

CRIMINAL HISTORY : FBI#1948493. Detroit PD#40439. Arrests since 1931 include suspicion of murder & conviction for Federal Narcotic Laws.

BUSINESS : Salesman for specialty food items, covering the Middle-Atlantic States.

MODUS OPERANDI : Has been a major interstate narcotic trafficker closely associated with known Mafia traffickers from East Harlem area of Manhattan. Also allied with known Mafia traffickers in California.

NAME : Nicholas TOLENTINO

ALIASES : Nick Tollentino

DESCRIPTION : Born 2-10-09 N.Y.C. 5'8",
165 lbs., brown eyes, medium
build, black-grey balding
hair, wears glasses.

LOCALITIES : Resides 350 Pleasant Ave.,
FREQUENTED   Apt. 9, N.Y.C. Frequents
Parnell Social Club, 224
E. 112th St.; Square Deal
Pet Shop, 2133 1st Ave.;
Mollie's Restaurant, 2126
1st. Ave.; all in N.Y.C.

FAMILY : Married to Mary Avalino; brothers: Anthony, James,
BACKGROUND   Martin, & Thomas; sister: Lucy; father: Anthony;
mother: Rose Canzoni.

CRIMINAL : Joseph Foti, Arnold Barbato, Theodore Orzo, John
ASSOCIATES   Ormento, Frank Borelli, Charles Curcio, & Harry
Tantillo.

CRIMINAL : FBI#1352699. NYC PD-B#68336. Arrests since 1920
HISTORY   include robbery, assault & robbery, & convictions
for Federal Narcotic Laws.

BUSINESS : No legitimate business or employment known.

MODUS : Wholesale dealer in interstate narcotic traffic
OPERANDI   and is closely associated with Mafia traffickers
in East Harlem section of Manhattan.

NAME	: Andrea TORREGROSSA
ALIASES	: Andrew Torregrossa
DESCRIPTION	: Born 3-26-1892, Licata, Agrigento, Sicily, 5'7", 190 lbs, brown eyes, grey hair, balding. Naturalized Brooklyn, NY, 6-7-1920.
LOCALITIES FREQUENTED	: Resides 1305 79th St, B'klyn, NY. 345 Avenue U; Ridgehill Club, 8301 Ridge Blvd, all B'klyn. Greenwich Village area of NYC.
FAMILY BACKGROUND	: Married Pietrina D'Angelo; sons: Angelo, Andrew, John, Antonio; daughters: Rose & Mary; father: Angelo; mother: Rosa Bonvessuto.
CRIMINAL ASSOCIATES	: Gaetano Lucchese, Anthony Anastasia, Giuseppe Profaci, Joseph Magliocco, Michele Miranda, Carlo Gambino, Carmine Galante, Vito Genovese, Carmine Lombardozzi, Lucky Luciano.
CRIMINAL HISTORY	: No known criminal record.
BUSINESS	: President of Andrew Torregrossa and Sons Inc. Funeral Homes, also owns a parking lot and numerous real estate parcels.
MODUS OPERANDI	: In the 1930's was active in the Italian lottery racket in NYC but was forced out and became a mortician. Is the owner of record of two pretentious funeral homes which are said to be actually owned by the Mafia and in which numerous Mafia meetings have been held.

NAME   : Joseph TORTORICI

ALIASES   : Joe Stutz

DESCRIPTION   : Born 5-14-09, NYC, 5'6", 170
                  lbs, brown eyes, brown-grey
                  hair.

LOCALITIES   : Resides 2276 Second Ave.,
FREQUENTED   NYC, frequents area of E
                  116th St. & 1st Ave., in
                  Manhattan.

FAMILY   : Wife: Joy Terrio; daughter:
BACKGROUND   Camille; father: Carmelo;
                  mother: Mary Geraci; brother: Frank; sister:
                  Johanna.

CRIMINAL   : Joseph Rao, Mike Coppola, Joseph Bendenelli, Joseph
ASSOCIATES   Stracci, Charles Albero, Vincent Squillante, John
                  Ormento.

CRIMINAL   : FBI #623052, NYCPD B#76307. Was a suspect in
HISTORY   political murder of Joe Scottoriggio in NYC in 1946.
                  Arrests since 1927 include bootlegging, homicide,
                  robbery, felonious assault.

BUSINESS   : Has interests in Tortorici Blouse Co., 285 Paladino
                  Ave., NYC.

MODUS   : Affiliated with the most important Mafia racket-
OPERANDI   eers in NY. Illicit interests include narcotics,
                  gambling and labor racketeering. Believed to con-
                  trol Local 222, Jewelry Employees Union.

He died in 2008 of natural causes. He was 81 years old.

NAME : Charles TOURINE, JR.

ALIASES : Chuck, Charlie White, Jr.,
name legally changed to
Charles Del Monico 3-20-53.

DESCRIPTION : Born 3-20-27, Matawan, N.J.,
5'7", 170 lbs, brown hair,
blue eyes, heavy build,
ruddy complexion, scar on
right cheek.

LOCALITIES : Resides 420 E 64th St., NYC,
FREQUENTED frequents 120 Central Park,
South, NYC and 4120 Pine Tree
Drive, Miami, Florida; Latin Quarter & Copacabana
in NYC.

FAMILY : Unmarried. Father: Charles Tourine, Sr., alias
BACKGROUND Charlie-the Blade; stepmother: Erena Victoria Perera,
a Cuban citizen.

CRIMINAL : Vito Genovese, Anthony Strollo, Frank Costello,
ASSOCIATES ████████████, ████████████, ████████.

CRIMINAL : FBI #587385B, NYCPD #B408243. Record consists of
HISTORY arrests for possession of a concealed weapon, vagrancy and lottery.

BUSINESS : Salesman for Central Art Gallery 100 Central Park,
S., NYC.

MODUS : Is following in the footsteps of his father, a
OPERANDI prominent Mafioso and is active with him in narcotic
smuggling and gambling operations in New York, New
Jersey, Florida and Cuba.

NAME : Giuseppe TRAINA

ALIASES : None

DESCRIPTION : Born 1-5-1883 San Giuseppe
Jato, Palermo, Sicily, 5'5",
160 lbs, brown eyes, grey
hair.

LOCALITIES : Resides 1778 73rd St, B'klyn,
FREQUENTED NY. Frequents Empire Yeast
Co., Manhattan, & Concord
Luncheonette, Brooklyn.

FAMILY : Wife's name is Mary; sons:
BACKGROUND Joseph & Mario, daughter: Mary; father: Domenico;
mother: Providenza Termina (both deceased); sister:
Mrs. Annina Motisi; brothers: Vincenzo and Antonio.

CRIMINAL : Joe Profaci, Joe Magliocco, ██████████████████
ASSOCIATES ████, Emanuel Cammarata, Frank Livorsi, all of NYC
area, Lucky Luciano, Joe Adonis, Sam ████ Accardi,
of Italy.

CRIMINAL : FBI #455744, NYCPD B#106400. Arrests since 1928
HISTORY include homicide, investigation as a suspicious
person.

BUSINESS : President of Empire Yeast Co., 159 Chrystie St.,
Manhattan, & has interest in C&M Coat Co., 1778
73rd St., Brooklyn, N.Y.

MODUS : Attended the Cleveland Mafia meeting 1928 and was
OPERANDI a powerful & influential Mafia leader during his
younger years. Is now in semi-retirement & his
activities are limited due to his age.

NAME   : Eugene TRAMAGLINO

ALIASES   : Genoa, Joseph Mariono,
              Eugene Romano, Eugene
              Traumaglino, Gino

DESCRIPTION : Born 11-5-15 NYC; 5'9½",
              150 lbs, black hair, brown
              eyes, sallow complexion,
              scar over left eye, plastic
              surgery straighten nose (1950)

LOCALITIES : Resides 1621 St. Marks Place,
FREQUENTED   Brooklyn, frequents 13th St.
              & 2nd Avenue, NYC.

FAMILY   : Parents Lorenzo and Amalia deceased; brothers Victor,
BACKGROUND   Alemondo, John and George; sister Margaret; wife
              Madeline Wojtowiez; daughters Barbara & Delores.

CRIMINAL   : Stephen Armone, ████████████, ████████████, Cosmo
ASSOCIATES   Franco, Joseph Valachi████████████.

CRIMINAL   : FBI #588015. NYCPD B#147997. Criminal record
HISTORY   dates back to 1932 and includes numerous arrests
              for grand larceny, counterfeiting, intimidation
              of witnesses, Federal Liquor Laws and conviction
              for violation of Federal Narcotic Laws.

BUSINESS   : Operates Margene's Lunch Room, 193 2nd Ave., NYC,
              owned by his wife, Madeline.

MODUS   : A key member of the Arnold Romano Mafia gang
OPERANDI   which distributes wholesale quantities of heroin
              in New York and interstate.

He died of natural causes on October 15, 1978 while in prison for his part in a heroin distribution ring.

NAME : Carmine Paul TRAUMUNTI

ALIASES : Gribbs, Tramunti

DESCRIPTION : Born 10-1-10 Naples, Italy, arrived U.S. 1913, 5'10", 200 lbs, brown eyes, dark brown hair, heavy build.

LOCALITIES FREQUENTED : Resides 145-79 6th Ave., Whitestone, L.I., N.Y., frequents Carmela Mia, 1406 65th St., Brooklyn and Lauritano's Restaurant 335 E 149th St., NYC.

FAMILY BACKGROUND : Wife: Lillian Anelli; daughter: Rosalie; sons: Louis (deceased) and Robert; father: Luigi; mother: Rosa DeRosa; sister: Ermiland Fioranventi.

CRIMINAL ASSOCIATES : Joseph Profaci, Joseph Bendinelli, John Dio Guardio, James Plumeri, ▬▬▬▬▬▬▬▬.

CRIMINAL HISTORY : FBI #471313, NYCPD B#87534, record dates from 1922 and includes arrests for robbery, felonious assault, assault & robbery and gambling.

BUSINESS : Until recently operated Imperial Trucking Co., 37th St., NYC., now owns Rosalie's Florist, 645 Lexington Ave., NYC.

MODUS OPERANDI : A strong arm man for the Mafia and at one time bodyguard for John DioGuardio, now believed in control of the greater New York Cartmen's Association.

NAME	: Charles Vincent TRUPIA
ALIASES	: Carlo Trupia
DESCRIPTION	: Born 11-26-23 NYC, 5'6", 155 lbs, medium build, black hair, brown eyes.
LOCALITIES FREQUENTED	: Resides 377 Broome St, NYC. Frequents Towncrest Rest., 123 W. 49 St, NYC.
FAMILY BACKGROUND	: Single; resides with parents at 377 Broome St, NYC; father: Vincenzo; mother: Carmela Celeste; brothers: Vincent & Angelo; sisters: Grace, Josephine (Mrs. Joseph) Dattalio.
CRIMINAL ASSOCIATES	: Joseph DiPalermo, Santo Sorge, Francesco Pirico, Peter DiPalermo.
CRIMINAL HISTORY	: FBI #4293745. NYCPD #305423. Record dates from 1945 when arrested for army desertion. Convicted of narcotic trafficking in Italy & mail theft in U.S.
BUSINESS	: Automobile mechanic, taxi driver.
MODUS OPERANDI	: Trusted Mafia courier for money and narcotics.

NAME	: Angelo TUMINARO
ALIASES	: "Little Angie", Angelo Tumensio
DESCRIPTION	: Born 2-22-10 NYC 5'2", 135 lbs., brown hair, brown eyes, cut-scar near left eye.
LOCALITIES FREQUENTED	: Resides 24 Rutgers St., NYC, frequents area of Madison and Pike Sts., in lower Manhattan.

FAMILY BACKGROUND	: Married to Bella Stein, father: Pasquale, mother: Mary Presenzano, has 7 brothers and 5 sisters.
CRIMINAL ASSOCIATES	: ██████████████, Saro Mogavero, Al Embarrato, Frank Mari, Carli DiPietro, Nathan Behrman, all of NYC, Joe Cotroni of Montreal.
CRIMINAL HISTORY	: FBI #270010, NYCPD #B 80192, several arrests since 1929 including grand larceny, assault and robbery, NY State narcotic laws.
BUSINESS	: Has interest in Apollo Barber Shop, 144 Clinton St., New York City.
MODUS OPERANDI	: Together with Anthony DiPasqua, is one of the largest wholesale narcotic traffickers in NYC, dealing with known Jewish traffickers, and having Mafia traffickers as a source of supply. Is suspected in some unsolved homicides in Manhattan.

NAME	: Giuseppe TURRIGIANO
ALIASES	: Giuseppe Torregiano, Paul Bongiorno, "Lucky Joe"

DESCRIPTION : Born 8-13-04 Palermo, Sicily, Italy, 5'4", 166 lbs, black-grey-balding hair, brown eyes, fair complexion, Alien No. #A-4294895. Has petition for citizenship under number 584910 with Immigration Department.

LOCALITIES FREQUENTED : Resides at 1775 78th St, Brooklyn, NY. Frequents Flatbush and Atlantic Aves., 18th Ave, & 65th St, both Brooklyn, NY.

FAMILY BACKGROUND : Married Fillippa Scalfidi, father: Giuseppe; mother: Vincenza Bongiorno.

CRIMINAL ASSOCIATES : ███████████, ████████████████, George Gillette.

CRIMINAL HISTORY : FBI #1099339. No NYCPD #. First arrest in 1936 for operator of illegal still and since then was arrested numerous times for unregistered stills.

BUSINESS : Was employed during 1940 to 1950 by the JT Provision Co., and the Pack & Wheel Moving Co. Did own and operate a farm located in Marlboro, NY.

MODUS OPERANDI : Mafia "still" expert and important persistent interstate trafficker in illegal whiskey.

NAME	: Pasquale TURRIGIANO
ALIASES	: Pasquale Turriciano
DESCRIPTION	: Born 8-7-1906, Castellammare, Sicily, 5'4", 165 lbs, grey hair, bald pate, hazel eyes, glasses, naturalized 9-1-39 at Binghamton, N.Y.

LOCALITIES FREQUENTED	: Resides 3015 Watson Blvd., Endicott, NY. Frequents Society of Concordia, Castellammare del Golfo, Inc., 109 Odell St., Endicott, NY.
FAMILY BACKGROUND	: Married Josephine Catalano; daughters: Vincenza and Maria; father: Vincenzo; mother: Vincenza Randesi (both parents deceased).
CRIMINAL ASSOCIATES	: Emanuel Zicari, Bartolo Guccia, John Bonventre, James Colletti, Natale Evola, Vito Genovese.
CRIMINAL HISTORY	: FBI #145499A Record dating from 1928 includes arrests for larceny, assault, violation prohibition laws and conspiracy to obstruct justice (for which sentenced 1960 to 5 years).
BUSINESS	: Has interest in grocery store, 3013 Watson Blvd., Endicott, N.Y.
MODUS OPERANDI	: Attended 1957 Apalachin Mafia meeting, representing interests of the Mafia-controlled rackets in the Endicott area.

NAME	:	Anthony VADALA
ALIASES	:	Anthony Grio, Tony Grio
DESCRIPTION	:	Born 10-11-1899 Torre DiFaro, Messina, Sicily, Italy, 5'8", 175 lbs, brown hair, balding, brown eyes, naturalized U.S. I&NS # C-4392484.
LOCALITIES FREQUENTED	:	Resides 7-02 144th St., Malba Queens, NY. Frequents Bentivegna's Restaurant, Houston St., & Mulberry St., area of NYC.
FAMILY BACKGROUND	:	Wife: Frances; daughter: Concetta; father: Vincenzo; mother: Concetta Grio; sister: Mrs. Angelina Vassolo.
CRIMINAL ASSOCIATES	:	Gaetano Lucchese, Colagero Lelio Di Carlo, Salvatore Schillitani, Raffaele Quasarano.
CRIMINAL HISTORY	:	FBI #4917260, NYCPD #B252438. Only arrest was in 1947 for contriving a lottery.
BUSINESS	:	Owns Grio Press, 292 Lafayette St., NYC. President of Malba-Park, Inc., 1065 Morris Park Ave., NYC.
MODUS OPERANDI	:	Influential Mafioso and close associate of Gaetano Lucchese. Prints lottery tickets and runs lottery with Lucchese.

Valachi died on April 3, 1971 from a heart attack. He
was at an El Paso correctional institute at the time
of his death.

NAME   : Joseph VALACHI

ALIASES   : Joe Cago, Joe Cargo, Joe
                  Kato, Joseph Siano.

DESCRIPTION   : Born 9-22-1903, NYC, 5'5",
                  195 lbs, brown eyes, grey
                  hair, dark complexion.

LOCALITIES   : Resides 45 Shawnee Avenue,
FREQUENTED   Yonkers, NY, frequents the
                  Belmont Ave. section of Bronx,
                  NY, & Yonkers (NY) Racetrack.

FAMILY   : Wife: Mildred; son: Donald;
BACKGROUND   father: Dominick; mother: Mary Casale; (both deceased);
                  girl friend: Carol Jacobs Cuccuru.

CRIMINAL   : Anthony Strollo, John Stoppelli, Vincent Mauro,
ASSOCIATES   ████████████, Salvatore Santoro, John Batista
                  Salvo, John Ormento, Giuseppe Doto, Fiore Siano
                  and Giacomo Reina.

CRIMINAL   : FBI #544 NYCPD #B-58458 Record dating from
HISTORY   1921 includes arrests for concealed weapon,
                  burglary, robbery. Pleaded guilty to Federal
                  Narcotic Law violation (1960).

BUSINESS   : Formerly owned Lido Bar, 1362 Castle Hill Ave.,
                  Bronx, NY. Has part interest in juke box firm
                  and in several race horses.

MODUS   : A trusted Mafia member and part of the Anthony
OPERANDI   Strollo narcotic smuggling and distributing organ-
                  ization. Wholesales heroin to major Mafia narcotic
                  traffickers on the Upper East Side of NYC.

NAME   : Costenza Peter VALENTI

ALIASES   : Stanley P. Valenti,
              Stanley Valente

DESCRIPTION: Born 2-8-26 Rochester, NY.
             6'2", 160 lbs, brown eyes,
             brown hair, slim build.

LOCALITIES : Resides 79 Bellevue Drive,
FREQUENTED   Rochester, NY. Frequents
             Rochester area and also
             Pittsburgh, Pa., area.

FAMILY   : Married to Catherine N.
BACKGROUND   Ripepi, brothers: Paul, Tony, Sam, John, & Frank;
              sisters: Rose, Mary, Bessie, Lillian, Josephine, &
              May Lawrence; father: Joseph; mother: Rosalia
              Inserra.

CRIMINAL   : Joseph & Salvatore Falcone, Andrew Alberti,
ASSOCIATES   Sebastiano Nani, Joe Biondo, Frank Valenti (brother)
              Michael J. Genovese.

CRIMINAL   : Has no criminal history with FBI or Rochester PD.
HISTORY

BUSINESS   : Is a partner in Valenti Brothers Wholesale Produce,
              202 Hamilton St., Rochester, New York.

MODUS   : Attended Apalachin Mafia meeting 1957. Engaged in
OPERANDI   illegal gambling & other rackets in Rochester area
              under supervision of his brother Frank.

NAME : Frank Joseph VALENTI

ALIASES : Frank Valente, Larry Costello Frank Ross, Joe Jackson.

DESCRIPTION: Born 9-14-11, Rochester, NY. 5'10", 168 lbs., brown eyes, grey hair.

LOCALITIES : Resides 1410 Highland Ave.,
FREQUENTED Rochester, NY. Frequents Rochester area & Pittsburgh, Pennsylvania.

FAMILY : Married to Eileen Barefoot
BACKGROUND (2nd wife), daughters: Ramona, Karen, Nancy; brothers: Paul, Tony, Sam, John, Stanley; sisters: Rose, Mary, Bessie, Lillian, Josephine, May Lawrence (a nun); father: Joseph; mother: Rosalie Inserra.

CRIMINAL : Andrew Alberti, Sam Mannarino, ███████████,
ASSOCIATES Michael Genovese, Stanley Valenti (brother), Joe & Salvatore Falcone, Vincent Scro.

CRIMINAL : FBI# 752390. Pittsburgh PD# 27741. Numerous arrests
HISTORY since 1933 include counterfeiting, extortion, assault & battery, murder, liquor laws.

BUSINESS : Part owner of Valenti's Restaurant 123 State St., Rochester, New York.

MODUS : Attended Apalachin Mafia meeting 1957 as a leader
OPERANDI of the Mafia in the Rochester area and representing the interests of the Mafia controlled illegal rackets there. A vicious hoodlum who has operated as a strong arm man & killer for the Mafia.

NAME   : Alarico VALLE

ALIASES   : None

DESCRIPTION   : Born 9-29-1884 Rome, Italy,
                  5'5", 170 lbs, brown eyes,
                  sparse black-grey hair,
                  heavy build, bulbous nose.

LOCALITIES   : Resides 2229 Clove Rd,
FREQUENTED   Staten Island, NY. At Rome
                  resided Largo Berchet #4;
                  former NYC addresses 403 E.
                  8th St, and 47 W. 42nd St.

FAMILY   : Father: Filippo; mother: Felicetta Ilari; son:
BACKGROUND   Philip, Kalamazoo, Mich; nephew: Spartaco Cionci;
                  niece: Eliana Cionci; both Cionci's reside Largo
                  Berchet #4, Rome.

CRIMINAL   : ███████████████, ████████, ██████████████,
ASSOCIATES   Aniello Santagata, ███████████.

CRIMINAL   : FBI #666814B. Arrested 1951 in connection with a
HISTORY   Federal narcotic investigation and 1956 for counter-
                  feiting.

BUSINESS   : Salesman, mechanic, engineer.

MODUS   : Although not of Sicilian birth or descent he is
OPERANDI   intimately associated with, and respected by, top
                  Mafia criminals in both U.S., and Italy. Engages
                  in large scale narcotic trafficking and counter-
                  feiting.

NAME	: Anthony J. VELLUCCI
ALIASES	: Tony Velluci, Anthony Velluccia, Tony Miserable

DESCRIPTION : Born 12-18-24 NYC, 5'9", 185 lbs, black hair, brown eyes, 2 small scars on fore-head, stocky build.

LOCALITIES FREQUENTED : Resides 310 E. 112th St., NYC, frequents East Harlem area of NYC, currently in-carcerated.

FAMILY BACKGROUND : Wife: Jennie Spada; daughters: Valerie & Janet; father: Vincent; mother: Clementine Ogero (now re-married to Angelo Cordona); uncle: George Vellucci @ Jumbo.

CRIMINAL ASSOCIATES : Nathan Berman, ▬▬▬▬▬▬▬, Anthony Mirra, Anthony Ciccone @ Tony Moon, ▬▬▬▬▬ ▬▬▬▬▬.

CRIMINAL HISTORY : FBI #2858768, NYCPD B#208187. Arrests since 1939 include juvenile delinquency, unlawful entry, attempted grand larceny, violation and conviction of State & Federal Narcotic Laws, 1955 sentenced to 14-15 years for State narcotic violation.

BUSINESS : No legitimate employment known.

MODUS OPERANDI : An important member of the Mafia in the East Harlem Section of NYC. Was the key figure in a multi-million dollar ring that smuggled narcotics into the U.S. and Canada from Europe and Cuba from 1950 to 1955.

NAME	: Joseph A. VENTO

ALIASES : Babo, Sebastiano Vento

DESCRIPTION : Born 2-8-13 NYC, 5'6½",
165 lbs., medium build,
brown hair, brown eyes.

LOCALITIES : Resides at 168-01, 12th Ave
FREQUENTED   Queens, NY, frequents E.
Harlem area and vicinity
of 50th St., and Broadway
both in NYC. Helen Mar Hotel
Golden Nugget Motel, Eden
Roc Hotel, all in Miami, Fla.

FAMILY : Married to Mary Messina, has one daughter, brothers:
BACKGROUND   Benjamin, Frank and Jack, sisters: Nancy and
Elizabeth, father: Louis, mother: Edmonda Schiletti.

CRIMINAL : Salvatore Santoro, John Ormento, Salvatore LoProto,
ASSOCIATES   Alfred Felice, Pasquale Genese, ▮▮▮▮▮▮▮▮▮▮,
Harold Meltzer.

CRIMINAL : FBI #1432959, NYC PD# B103810, National List #408.
HISTORY   Arrest record dates from 1932, and includes arrests
for burglary, robbery violation of Liquor Laws and
conviction for Federal Narcotic Laws.

BUSINESS : Salesman for Irving Lazarus Jewelers, 32 W. 42nd
St., New York City.

MODUS : A trusted member of the Mafia organization which
OPERANDI   controls the distribution of heroin in large quantities on the upper East Side of NYC. As a smuggler-
distributor has been interested in clandestine laboratories.

NAME : James VINTALORO

ALIASES : James Vitalora, Jimmy the Sniff, James Vintalora.

DESCRIPTION : Born 6-30-11 NYC, 5'4", 200 lbs, black hair, brown eyes, heavy build.

LOCALITIES FREQUENTED : Resides 4606 Richardson Ave, Bronx, NY. Frequents Lindy's Rest., in NYC; Half-moon Pizzeria & Vigo Social Club both in Bronx, NY.

FAMILY BACKGROUND : Married to Evelyn Alvera and has 2 children; father: Joseph; mother: Jessica Formano, (both deceased).

CRIMINAL ASSOCIATES : Thomas Lucchese, Carmine Tramunti, Joseph Profaci, Joseph Bonnano, Vincent Rao, Charles Rao, all of NYC; Angelo Meli, Mike ▇▇▇▇▇ Polizzi, of Detroit, Michigan.

CRIMINAL HISTORY : FBI #296926. NYCPD B#94144. Arrests since 1928 include felonious assault, assault & robbery, murder and conviction for NY State Narcotic Laws.

BUSINESS : Claims to be salesman of salad oil & cheese.

MODUS OPERANDI : Key figure in a group of Mafia racketeers operating in Bronx, Westchester & Putnam Counties, NY, controlling bookmaking, shylocking and narcotic trafficking.

NAME   : Michaelangelo VITALE

ALIASES   : Michael Angelo Vitale

DESCRIPTION   : Born 1-6-19, Castellammare
                  De Golfo, Trapani, Sicily,
                  Italy; 5'11", 225 lbs, brown
                  eyes, brown hair, fair com-
                  plexion, naturalized 4-15-58
                  at Brooklyn, NY.

LOCALITIES   : Resides 1636 81st St., Brook-
FREQUENTED   lyn, NY. Frequents Demo-
                  cratic Political Club, Wilson
                  Ave., Brooklyn, NY.

FAMILY   : Wife: Angelica Domingo; son: Vito; daughter: Mary
BACKGROUND   Anne; father: Vito; mother: Maria Bologna; (parents
                  reside Corso Regina Maria, Pia 210, Ostia, Rome,
                  Italy); brother: Giuseppe (Partinico, Sicily).

CRIMINAL   : Raphael Quasarano, ▮▮▮▮▮▮▮▮▮▮, Giuseppe
ASSOCIATES   Calatabianca, Frank Garofolo, and father Vito Vitale

CRIMINAL   : FBI #22232B. Criminal record consists only of an
HISTORY   arrest for deportation in 1950. Re-entered legally
                  in 1954.

BUSINESS   : Butcher and electronics mechanic.

MODUS   : With other important Mafia members engages in the
OPERANDI   smuggling and wholesale distribution of narcotics.
                  Occasionally participates as a Mafia "Executioner".

NAME   : Salvatore VITALE

ALIASES   : Sam, Salvadore, Vitole

DESCRIPTION   : Born 4-10-03, Cinisi, Sicily
                 Italy, 5'3", 200 lbs, black
                 straight hair, grey temples,
                 blue eyes, olive complexion,
                 stocky build, round face.
                 Alien #A-4254663.

LOCALITIES   : Resided 40-48 98th St.,
FREQUENTED   Corona, Queens, NY, frequent-
                 ed 44 Delancey St, 510 E 13th
                 St, 9 Prince St, and Mario &
                 DiBono Plastering Co., 40-03 National Ave, all NYC,
                 currently (1959) a fugitive. Believed to be in
                 Cinisi, Italy.

FAMILY   : Wife: Josephine Palazzola; no children; father:
BACKGROUND   Pietro; mother: Marie Concetta Comercio; sisters:
                 Rosalia & Concetta (parents & sisters reside in
                 Cinisi).

CRIMINAL   : Carlo & Paul Gambino, ███████████, ██████
ASSOCIATES   ██████████████████████████ of Detroit.

CRIMINAL   : FBI #461979, NYCPD #B107032, record dates from 1930
HISTORY   and includes arrests for suspicion of murder, lar-
                 ceny by trick, fraud and Federal Narcotic Law viola-
                 tion. In 1957 after being indicted on 5 counts of
                 grand larceny, he fled and is currently on NYCPD's
                 list of 13 most wanted criminals.

BUSINESS   : No legitimate occupation.

MODUS   : Was involved with other Mafiosi in supplying whole-
OPERANDI   sale quantities of narcotics to dealers in Kansas
                 City, Missouri. Also a confidence man and swindler.

NAME : Patsy ZACCARO

ALIASES : Little Patsy, Patsy White,
John Trotta, Pat Della

DESCRIPTION : Born 3-16-12 NYC, 5'4¼",
150 lbs, medium build, black
hair, brown eyes, sallow
complexion, dark red birth
mark left cheek.

LOCALITIES : Resides 224 E 112th St.,
FREQUENTED NYC, frequents 2nd Ave., &
112th St., Broadway & 50th
St., Thistle Inn, 154 W 54th
St., Bazaar Nite Club, 49th St., & 3rd Ave., all in
New York City.

FAMILY : Single; father: Frank; mother: Marie Corengo; bro-
BACKGROUND thers: Anthony, Louis, Peter,& Joseph; sisters:
Angelina, Julia & Rose.

CRIMINAL : ███████████████, Salvatore Caneba, Morris Taubman,
ASSOCIATES Carmine Locascio, Paul Correale, Vincent Foceri.

CRIMINAL : FBI #2312795, NYCPD# B201388. Record dates from 1940
HISTORY & includes arrests for bookmaking, possession of a
gun and unlawful possession gasoline coupons, State
and Federal Narcotic conviction.

BUSINESS : Operates the Quickie Lunchonette, 239 E 115th St.,
New York City.

MODUS : With other Mafiosi engages in narcotic traffic
OPERANDI with headquarters in East Harlem, supplies kilogram lots of heroin to local and out of state
dealers.

677

NAME : Anthony F. ZANGOGLIA, Jr.

ALIASES : "T.Z.", Tee Zee.

DESCRIPTION : Born 5-16-25 N.Y.C. 5'8",
200 lbs., brown eyes, dark
brown hair, heavy build,
wears glasses.

LOCALITIES : Resides 136 Longview Ave.,
FREQUENTED Leonia, N.J. Frequents area
of E. 107th St. & 1st Ave.
in Manhattan.

FAMILY : Wife: Eleanor; brother:
BACKGROUND Charles; father: Anthony F. Sr.; his aunt Mary is
married to Salvatore Santoro.

CRIMINAL : John Ormento, Salvatore Santoro, Harry Tantillo,
ASSOCIATES Anthony Ciccone, Fred & Angelo Salerno, Charles
Schiffman, Harold Meltzer, Abe Chapman.

CRIMINAL : FBI#846936A. Sheriff's Office Jersey City #37274.
HISTORY Arrests since 1951 include harboring a fugitive.

BUSINESS : When employed works as a bartender.

MODUS : A member of the E. 107th St. John Ormento
OPERANDI controlled Mafia narcotic traffickers.

NAME	: Paul ZERBO
ALIASES	: Ippolito Zerbo, Paulie Legs
DESCRIPTION	: Born 11-15-12 NYC, 6'1", 180 lbs, slender build, grey hair brown eyes, dark complexion, circular scar on center of forehead.
LOCALITIES FREQUENTED	: Resides at 240 E 106th St., NYC. Frequents East Harlem section of NYC, in particular 106th St., & 2nd Ave.
FAMILY BACKGROUND	: Married Jenny Abate; has two children; brother: Joseph; father: Castrenge; mother: Rose Arnetta, both born Italy.
CRIMINAL ASSOCIATES	: Joe Ragone, John Ormento, ███████████, ████████ ████████, ████████████████, ██████████████████, ████████ ████████, ██████████████████████, all of East Harlem, NYC. Wille Comforte of New Haven, Conn.
CRIMINAL HISTORY	: FBI #2447703, NYCPD B#12338, Stamford, Conn., PD# 3288. Record dates from 1941 and includes arrests for armed robbery, possession of a gun, disorderly person.
BUSINESS	: With co-owners Florence & Joseph Morriale, he operates the M&M Novelty Co., at 106 East 126th St., NYC.
MODUS OPERANDI	: An interstate drug trafficker, who deals in large quantities of heroin, for distribution to New England and upstate NY. A trusted member of the Mafia 107th St., organization, in the East Harlem section of NYC. On occasion obtains heroin from seaman smugglers.

NAME   : Emanuel ZICARI

ALIASES   : None

DESCRIPTION   : Born 2-10-1900, Siculiana,
                  Agrigento, Sicily, Italy.
                  5'8", 200 lbs, brown eyes,
                  glasses, black-greying hair.
                  Naturalized 11-6-1925 at
                  Binghamton, N.Y.

LOCALITIES   : Resides 103 Squires Avenue,
FREQUENTED   Endicott, NY. Frequents the
                  Societa Concordia Castell-
                  ammare del Golfo, 109 Odell
                  St., Endicott, N.Y.

FAMILY   : Divorced from Frances Grisafi; current wife: Nancy
BACKGROUND   Micari; son Pasquale C.; sisters: Rosa & Giuseppina;
                  brothers: Giovanni & Onofrio.

CRIMINAL   : Pasquale Turrigiano, Pasquale Monachino, Dominick
ASSOCIATES   Alaimo, Angelo Sciandra, Russell Bufalino, Pasquale
                  Sciortino, Anthony Guarnieri.

CRIMINAL   : FBI #777025 Binghamton PD #2328 Arrested in 1934
HISTORY   for counterfeiting.

BUSINESS   : Works at Endicott-Johnson Shoe Co., Endicott, N.Y.

MODUS   : Attended Apalachin Mafia meeting 1957. Member of
OPERANDI   a Mafia group operating in the tri-city area of
                  northern Pennsylvania and New York State.

OHIO

NAME   : Gasparo AIELLO

ALIASES   : Fats, Joe Joseph Aiello

DESCRIPTION   : Born 8-9-13, St. Louis, Mo.,
                  5'8½", 137 lbs, slender
                  build, dark complexion, dark
                  brown hair, brown eyes.

LOCALITIES   : Resides 26 Four Mile Run Ave,
FREQUENTED   Youngstown, Ohio. Frequents
                  15 Oak Hill Ave, the Ohio
                  Hotel, and various gambling
                  establishments in the Youngs-
                  town, Ohio area.

FAMILY   : Wife: Rose; father: Antonio; mother: Giuseppa Lusso;
BACKGROUND   alleged to be a distant cousin of Alfred Polizzi
                  @ Al Polizzi.

CRIMINAL   : Joseph DiCarlo, Charles Cavallaro, Nick Constantino,
ASSOCIATES   ███████████, and ███████████████, all of
                  Youngstown, Ohio; Al Polizzi of Miami, Fla., and
                  Cleveland, Ohio.

CRIMINAL   : FBI #665 723, Youngstown PD #9158. Has criminal
HISTORY   record dating from 1932 for violation of liquor
                  laws, burglary, larceny, carrying concealed weapons,
                  shooting to kill, receiving stolen property, and
                  issuing a fraudulent check.

BUSINESS   : Operates National Cigarette Service, 15 Oak Hill
                  Ave., Youngstown, Ohio, with Anthony Dellessandro.

MODUS   : Is the "contact man" for Mafiosi and other criminals
OPERANDI   in the Youngstown area. Closely associated with the
                  gambling element operating "clubs" in the Youngstown,
                  Ohio area.

In February 1934, after escaping to Italy, Amato turned himself into Sicilian police and was found guilty of murder. He was sentenced to 30 years of hard labor.

NAME : Angelo A. AMATO

ALIASES : Enso Bruno, Enzo Bruno, Bruno Enzo, Andrew Camara, Carl Cauravana.

DESCRIPTION : Born 11-18-10, Licata, Sicily, naturalized, 5'7", 165 lbs, black hair, brown eyes, ruddy complexion, has a small mole on each cheek.

LOCALITIES FREQUENTED : Resides 16615 Throckley Ave, Cleveland, Ohio, frequents night clubs on Short Vincent St, & Captain Frank's Restaurant, Cleveland, Ohio.

FAMILY BACKGROUND : Married to Lillian Angela Orteca, sister of Joe Orteca (a known narcotic trafficker); children: Angelo Joseph & Serena Marie; father: Salvatore; mother: Sarah Lauria (deceased).

CRIMINAL ASSOCIATES : Anthony Castaldi & Carlo Gambino of NYC, Joseph Orteca, Sylvester Papalardo, & Frank Liosi of Cleveland, Sam Signore of Chicago.

CRIMINAL HISTORY : FBI #1189758. Cleveland PD #58105. Arrests since 1936 include violations of the Internal Revenue Laws, theft from Interstate Commerce, conviction for Federal Narcotic Laws.

BUSINESS : Self employed as a grocer.

MODUS OPERANDI : An interstate narcotic trafficker; is considered one of the high ranking Mafia in the Cleveland, Ohio, area.

NAME   : Nicholas BIBBO

ALIASES   : Nick

DESCRIPTION   : Born 6-22-23 Bronx, NY, 5'4",
                 120 lbs, black hair, grey
                 eyes, tattoo left arm,
                 marine corps emblem "1943-
                 1946 USMC."

LOCALITIES   : Resides 15802 Mandalay Ave.,
FREQUENTED   Cleveland, Ohio. Frequents
                 Blue Grass Bar, Libby &
                 Northfield Roads, Cleveland,
                 Ohio.

FAMILY   : Married Mary Vaccaro, NYC, 1946; sons: John Nicholas,
BACKGROUND   Joseph; father: Giovanni; mother: Assuntia Ziolla,
                 (both residing Bronx, NY), sisters: Josephine Nero
                 and Cecelia Rosano; brothers: Angelo, Anthony, Louis
                 and Frank (all NYC).

CRIMINAL   : ████████████ and ████████ of Cleveland, Ohio,
ASSOCIATES   Lester Miraglia and ██████████ of NYC.

CRIMINAL   : FBI #537601B, Cleveland PD #77485. Record consists
HISTORY   of one arrest and conviction for violation of
                 narcotic laws.

BUSINESS   : Salesman for Home Asphalt & Improvement Co.,
                 Cleveland, Ohio.

MODUS   : Lower level Mafioso who obtains heroin from NYC
OPERANDI   sources and distributes in Cleveland, Ohio area.

NAME	: Giuseppe Thomas BLUMETTI
ALIASES	: Frank Rose, Little Joe, Joseph Blumetti.
DESCRIPTION	: Born 8-6-13 Youngstown, Ohio, 5'6", 170 lbs, dark hair, brown eyes, wears dark tinted glasses.

LOCALITIES FREQUENTED	: Resides 3923 Shelby Rd, Youngstown, Ohio. Frequents Vending Machine & Teamsters Union Headquarters.
FAMILY BACKGROUND	: Married Rose G. Blumetti 1932, divorced 1937. Married Elizabeth Adams 1938; father: Frank (Deceased); mother: Mary Dechime; brothers: Albert, Frank & Charles.
CRIMINAL ASSOCIATES	: ▮▮▮▮▮▮▮▮▮▮▮▮ & William Presser of Cleveland, Gasparo "Fats" Aiello, Charles Vizzini and Charles Cavallaro of Youngstown, Ohio.
CRIMINAL HISTORY	: FBI #1625158. Record dates from 1938 and includes arrests for counterfeiting, selective service violation and white slavery.
BUSINESS	: Business agent for various labor unions, including Vending Machine Local #410, Teamsters Local #377 and International Brotherhood of Electrical Workers.
MODUS OPERANDI	: Closely allied with other Youngstown, Ohio Mafiosi. He formerly engaged in counterfeiting, narcotic trafficking and other crimes but has now graduated to the field of labor racketeering.

NAME : Amato Angelo BUCCI

ALIASES : Tuttie

DESCRIPTION : Born 7-4-27, Cleveland, Ohio
5'5", 160 lbs, brown hair,
blue eyes, stocky build, cut
scars on forehead & right
cheek.

LOCALITIES : Resides 2568 E 110 St.,
FREQUENTED Cleveland, O; frequents
area of E 124th & Mayfield
Road, Cleveland, O.

FAMILY : Wife: Pearl M. Fucas; daughters: Beverly Ann &
BACKGROUND Christine; father: Cesidio (deceased); mother: Mary;
brother: Umberto.

CRIMINAL : ████████, Frank Ciccarello, Joseph Orteca, Sam
ASSOCIATES Poliafico, all of Cleveland, Ohio.

CRIMINAL : FBI #88828A, Cleveland PD# 66790. Record dates
HISTORY from 1948 and includes arrests for delinquency,
burglary, larceny & possession of burglar tools,
Federal Narcotic Law conviction.

BUSINESS : Driver for Tri-County Beverage Dist., 3961 Jennings
Road, Cleveland, Ohio.

MODUS : A minor Mafia racketeer who engages in the narcotic
OPERANDI traffic and participates in burglaries and strong-
arm robberies.

NAME	: Anthony BUFFA
ALIASES	: Tony
DESCRIPTION	: Born 1-14-21 Cleveland, Ohio, 5'5", 183 lbs, black hair, receding, brown eyes, dark complexion, stocky build, violent temper.
LOCALITIES FREQUENTED	: Resides 4562 Joyce Ave., Warrensville Heights, Ohio. Frequents East 9th St. & Short Vincent St., area of Cleveland, Ohio. Currently (1959) incarcerated.
FAMILY BACKGROUND	: Married Shirley Raitz; daughters: Sharon & Deborah; father: Salvatore; mother: Anna.
CRIMINAL ASSOCIATES	: Frank Liosi, ██████████, ██, Alex Calarco, ████ ████████.
CRIMINAL HISTORY	: FBI #2152228, Cleveland PD# 88243. Record dates from 1937 and includes arrests for robbery, burglary, larceny, O.P.A. violation receiving stolen property (for which incarcerated since 1958).
BUSINESS	: Occasional construction worker & salesman.
MODUS OPERANDI	: Lower echelon Mafioso who is noted more for brawn than brains and is called on by more important Mafia members to carry out strong-arm assignments.

He was the mafia boss in the Youngstown, Ohio area until his assassination. On October 11, 1968, Cavallaro was blown up by a car bomb and his son was shotgunned in his home's driveway.

NAME : Charles CAVALLARO

ALIASES : Charles DiFrancesco, Charles Cavalier, Joe Tropicano.

DESCRIPTION : Born 2-2-02 Agrigento, Sicily. 5'6", 167 lbs., brown eyes, dark brown & grey hair, I&NS#A5261277.

LOCALITIES FREQUENTED : Resides 164 Roslyn Drive, Youngstown, Ohio. Frequented gambling houses in Youngstown and poolroom at 26 Champion St.

FAMILY BACKGROUND : Divorced 1st wife, presently married to Helen Mae Boila, has 3 children, Rowana, Charles Jr., & Thomas.

CRIMINAL ASSOCIATES : Charles Vizzini, Marino Paolacci, Joe DiCarlo, ███████████████, all of Youngstown; Angersola brothers and Al Polizzi of Miami area.

CRIMINAL HISTORY : FBI#1144812. Youngstown PD#9987. Arrests since 1934 include Internal Revenue Laws, extortion, concealed weapons. Currently (1959) awaiting deportation proceedings.

BUSINESS : Lists occupation as self-employed trucker.

MODUS OPERANDI : Has been one of the influential Mafia members in the Youngstown area for many years, and has been active in all types of gambling rackets.

He was a consigliere for the Cleveland, Ohio crime family. He died on October 25, 1972, of natural causes.

NAME : John Anthony De MARCO

ALIASES : Martin L. O'Donnell, Baron, John O'Brien, John King, Joe Pacino.

DESCRIPTION : Born 2-14-03, Licata, Sicily naturalized 8-24-26, Cleveland, 5'3", 165 lbs, short, stocky build, black-grey hair, brown eyes, neat and conservative dresser.

LOCALITIES FREQUENTED : Resides 3536 Hildana St., Shaker Heights, Ohio, frequents LaMarco Barber shop, Mount Pleasant Turkish Bath, LiPuma Spumoni Co., all of Cleveland, Ohio.

FAMILY BACKGROUND : Married Mary Poliafico, (sister of Sam Poliafico, major interstate narcotic trafficker); father: Angelo; mother: Rosaria Leonardo (both deceased).

CRIMINAL ASSOCIATES : John T. Scalish, Sam Poliafico, ███████████, ██████████████, all of Cleveland; is associated with major racketeers throughout the U.S., but present health limits travel.

CRIMINAL HISTORY : FBI #1783102, Cleveland PD #36154, criminal record dates back to September, 1930; has convictions for robbery, extortion, unlawful flight, threats of personal violence and blackmail; arrested 5-21-59 for 18 USC 371 (pending).

BUSINESS : No legitimate occupation known.

MODUS OPERANDI : One of the controllers of the policy racket and all gambling in Cleveland area; attended Apalachin Mafia meeting (1957) representing the Cleveland area Mafia interests.

NAME   : Mariano. PAOLACCI

ALIASES   : Marian Palacci, Frank Bruno

DESCRIPTION   : Born 3-12-1892, Alvito,
                  Frosinone, Italy, 5'5½", 135
                  lbs, slender build, dark
                  brown hair, brown eyes,
                  glasses. Naturalized Cleve-
                  land, Ohio 4-11-58, I&NS #C-
                  7996299.

LOCALITIES   : Resides 619 Marlin Ave,
FREQUENTED   Youngstown, Ohio. Frequents
                  Youngstown & Akron.

FAMILY   : Married Jane Milner in 1925 after divorce from first
BACKGROUND   wife, who had borne him daughter Isabelle (Castor);
                  father: Vincent; mother: Isabel DiFico; brother:
                  Vincent.

CRIMINAL   : Charles Vizzini & Charles Cavallaro, of Youngstown.
ASSOCIATES

CRIMINAL   : FBI #1876936. Youngstown PD #7779. Record dating
HISTORY   from 1939 includes arrests for counterfeiting,
                  blackmail and extortion.

BUSINESS   : Retired.

MODUS   : Old time Mafia racketeer. Because of advanced age
OPERANDI   apparently no longer takes active part in Mafia
                  affairs, though retaining his contacts with im-
                  portant Mafiosi.

NAME	: Sam PAPALARDO
ALIASES	: Sam Papp
DESCRIPTION	: Born 8-23-09 Cleveland, Ohio 5'7", 150 lbs., black hair, brown eyes, sallow complexion, sharp weasel features, medium build, wears sport clothes.
LOCALITIES FREQUENTED	: Resides 4119 East 176th St., Cleveland, Ohio, frequents Victory Lounge Bar, 6605 Detroit Ave., and night clubs on Short Vincent St.
FAMILY BACKGROUND	: Single. Father is Rosario, sister is Mrs. Josephine Rini, widow of Gus J. Rini, brother Sylvester @ Studo.
CRIMINAL ASSOCIATES	: Sylvester Papalardo, ███████████████, John DeMarco, Sam Poliafico, ███████████, Frank Liosi, Anthony ███████████ Spitalieri, all of Cleveland; Frank Borelli, Charles Curcio, Rocco Mazzie, Vincent Squillante, all of N.Y.C., Salvatore Pieri, Salvatore Rizzo, Nicholas Tutino, all of Buffalo; ███████████, of Detroit.
CRIMINAL HISTORY	: FBI #118998, Cleveland PD #28652, criminal record dates back to 1927. Sentenced in May, 1927 for rape, to 8-10 years; has been picked up numerous times in connection with murder and narcotics; was acquitted on 2-13-58 at N.Y.C., for Conspiracy to Violate the Federal Narcotic Laws.
BUSINESS	: Owns and manages, by proxy, the Victory Lounge Bar, W. 65th St., and Detroit Ave., Cleveland, Ohio.
MODUS OPERANDI	: Major interstate narcotic trafficker, alleged to be the "bankroll" for the John Montana organization; considered to be an important member of the Mafia at Cleveland, Ohio.

NAME	: Sylvester PAPALARDO
ALIASES	: Studo
DESCRIPTION	: Born 11-27-10 Cleveland, Ohio, 5'7½", 188 lbs, brown hair, brown eyes, stocky build, small moles on both sides of face.

LOCALITIES FREQUENTED	: Resides 17620 Walden Ave., Cleveland, Ohio, frequents Victory Lounge Bar and various night clubs on Short Vincent St., Cleveland.
FAMILY BACKGROUND	: Married Katherine Frisina; sons: Russell and Fred; father: Rosario; brother: Sam; sister: Mrs. Josephine Rini.
CRIMINAL ASSOCIATES	: Sam Papalardo, Sam Poliafico, ███████████, Frank Liosi, ███████████, ███████████, all of Cleveland; Rocco Mazzie, Vincent Squillante, of NYC, Salvatore Rizzo, Salvatore Pieri, all of Buffalo, New York.
CRIMINAL HISTORY	: FBI #463957, Cleveland PD #39941, record dating from 1932 includes arrests for burglary, robbery, narcotics and homicide, currently incarcerated at the U.S. Penitentiary, Leavenworth, Kansas, having been sentenced on 8-14-53 to 15 years for violation of Federal Narcotic Laws.
BUSINESS	: No legitimate occupation. Derives income from narcotic trafficking and gambling.
MODUS OPERANDI	: Major interstate narcotic trafficker, large scale gambler and ranking member of the Mafia in Cleveland, Ohio

NAME	: Salvatore F. POLIAFICO
ALIASES	: Sylvester Poliafico, Sam Polo.
DESCRIPTION	: Born 6-7-11 Cleveland, Ohio, 5'7", 150 lbs., medium build black hair, brown eyes,
LOCALITIES FREQUENTED	: Residence 3309 Milverton Rd., Shaker Heights, Ohio, frequented Khoury's Night Club and various other night clubs on Short Vincent St., Cleveland, Ohio.

FAMILY BACKGROUND	: Married to Judy Lascko on 9-9-35 at Cleveland, Ohio, has two sons, Joseph and Dominic, sister Mary is married to John DeMarco, father, Joseph, resides with John DeMarco in Cleveland.
CRIMINAL ASSOCIATES	: Anthony Crisci, ███████████, █████████, ███████████, Nunzio Romano, all of New York City; Salvatore Pieri, Salvatore Rizzo, all of Buffalo, N.Y., John DeMarco, Sam and Sylvester Papalardo, all of Cleveland, Ohio.
CRIMINAL HISTORY	: FBI #1482222, Cleveland PD #36451, arrest record dates back to 1930, when he was acquitted of murder, incarcerated at U.S. Penitentiary, Leavenworth, Kansas on 4-23-57 in connection with a 15 year sentence received for violation of the Federal Narcotic Laws.
BUSINESS	: Night club manager, operator of T.V. repair service shop, with partner David L. Zallan.
MODUS OPERANDI	: A major interstate drug trafficker, operating from Cleveland, Ohio; brother-in-law of John DeMarco; a "strongarm" member of the Mafia in the Cleveland area.

> He died during open heart surgery on May 26, 1976.

NAME   : Giovanni SCALICI

ALIASES   : John Scalish, John Scalich,
                  John Scalise.

DESCRIPTION   : Born 9-25-1913, Cleveland, O.
                  5'11", 185 lbs, brown eyes,
                  black-grey hair, medium build,
                  neat dresser.

LOCALITIES   : Resides 11706 Farringdon Ave.,
FREQUENTED   Cleveland, O. Frequents the
                  Theatrical Grill, LeMarco
                  Barber Shop, Mt. Pleasant
                  Turkish Bath, all in Cleveland.
                  Also makes trips to Las Vegas, Nevada.

FAMILY   : Married Matilda Rockman; sons: Frank & John; daughters:
BACKGROUND   Margherita & Francine; brothers: Frank & Salvatore;
                  father: Frank; mother: Margherita Fito.

CRIMINAL   : ███████████, Salvatore Poliafico, ███████,
ASSOCIATES   all of Cleveland; Angersola brothers & Al Polizzi, of
                  Miami; Meyer (Mickey) Cohen, of California.

CRIMINAL   : FBI #348011 Cleveland PD #37141 Record dating from
HISTORY   1930 includes arrests for burglary, robbery and con-
                  spiracy to obstruct justice (for which sentenced in
                  1960 to 5 years & $10,000 fine).

BUSINESS   : Co-owner Buckeye Cigarette Vending Machine Co., Cleve-
                  land; also has interests in night clubs in Las Vegas,
                  Nevada, and Newport, Kentucky.

MODUS   : Attended 1957 Apalachin Mafia meeting with John
OPERANDI   DeMarco, representing the interests of the organiza-
                  tion in the Cleveland area. Is an important figure
                  in labor racketeering.

NAME   : Anthony J. SPITALIERI

ALIASES   : Tony Spit

DESCRIPTION   : Born 3-12-22, Cleveland, O.
                  5'11", 218 lbs, stocky build,
                  black hair, blue eyes, dark
                  complexion.

LOCALITIES   : Resides 2815 Division Street,
FREQUENTED   Cleveland, O. Frequented
                  Terminal Bar, Woodland Ave.,
                  Cleveland. Incarcerated.

FAMILY   : Married Doris Porter 1944 &
BACKGROUND   subsequently divorced; 1948 married Gloria Cisanin;
                  sons: Anthony & Mark; brothers: Charles and Salvatore.

CRIMINAL   : Charles Spitalieri & Julius Weizer, of Cleveland;
ASSOCIATES   Salvatore Pieri, of Buffalo, NY, Joseph Amato, Frank
                  Borelli, Charles Curcio, of NYC.

CRIMINAL   : FBI #2973566 Cleveland PD #57081 Criminal record
ASSOCIATES   dating from 1939 shows convictions for attempted
                  burglary, army desertion and violation of the Federal
                  Narcotic Laws. Currently incarcerated at Atlanta
                  Penitentiary, having been sentenced in 1955 to nine
                  years for Federal Narcotic Law violation.

BUSINESS   : No legitimate occupation.

MODUS   : Interstate narcotic trafficker and member of the Mafia
OPERANDI   at Cleveland, Ohio. Also involved in gambling rackets
                  in the Cleveland area.

694

NAME   : Frank VISCONTI

ALIASES   : Captain Frank

DESCRIPTION   : Born 7-4-1899, Palermo,
                  Sicily, 5'5½", 165 lbs, black
                  grey hair, brown eyes, olive
                  complexion, naturalized
                  12-3-26 at Cleveland, Ohio.

LOCALITIES   : Resides 3636 E 151st St,
FREQUENTED   Cleveland, Ohio. Frequents
                  Captain Frank's Seafood House,
                  E 9th St, Pier, and Fulton
                  Fish Market, 411 Bolivar Ave,
                  Cleveland, Ohio.

FAMILY   : Married Rose Bartolino (or Certolino); son: Russell
BACKGROUND   Visconti, operator of Fulton Fish Market, 411 Bolivar
                  Ave.; daughters: Rose Marie Ferrara, Ida LaGatta &
                  Mary Anne Rabek; father: Rosco; mother: Mary Ann
                  (both deceased).

CRIMINAL   : ▆▆▆▆▆▆▆▆▆▆, John DeMarco, John Scalish, Joseph
ASSOCIATES   Orteca, all of Cleveland, Ohio.

CRIMINAL   : FBI #946462, Cleveland PD #44479. Record dates from
HISTORY   1931 and includes arrests for bootlegging, vagrancy,
                  counterfeiting and Federal narcotics conviction.

BUSINESS   : Operates Captain Frank's Seafood House, E 9th St,
                  Pier, and owns Fulton Fish Market, 411 Bolivar Ave,
                  Cleveland, Ohio.

MODUS   : Important Cleveland Mafia figure, his restaurant is
OPERANDI   frequented by both high echelon Mafia hoodlums and
                  politicians with whom he wields great influence.

NAME : Calogero VIZZINI

ALIASES : Charles Vizzini

DESCRIPTION : Born 9-6-1894 Agrigento,
Sicily, Italy. 5'6½", 170
lbs, brown-grey hair, brown
eyes, dark complexion. Naturalized Battle Creek, Mich.,
1-7-1919.

LOCALITIES : Resides 845 5th Ave., Youngs-
FREQUENTED town, O. Frequents gambling
houses Youngstown & Florida.

FAMILY : Married Frances Pironi; father Alfonso; mother:
BACKGROUND Concetta Turano.

CRIMINAL : ███████████, ██████████████, Charles Cavallaro,
ASSOCIATES Frank Cammarata, ████████████.

CRIMINAL : FBI #1225912   Youngstown PD #10145   Record dating
HISTORY from 1919 includes arrests for armed robbery,
murder, counterfeiting and carrying concealed
weapons.

BUSINESS : No legitimate occupation.

MODUS : Mafia leader in control of rackets & gambling
OPERANDI in the Youngstown area. Reputed to have considerable political influence.

NAME   : Joseph ZINGALE

ALIASES   : None

DESCRIPTION : Born 4-7-22, Cleveland, Ohio,
               5'8½", 225 lbs, black hair,
               brown eyes, dark complexion,
               stocky build.

LOCALITIES   : Resides 4429 Warner Road,
FREQUENTED   Cleveland, Ohio.

FAMILY   : Married to Lucille C.
BACKGROUND   D'Alessio; daughter: Mary
               Ann; sisters: Angela and
               Lucille; brothers: Thomas and Frank; father:
               Salvatore William; mother: Marianne Srzozurello.

CRIMINAL   : ██████████, ██████████, ██████████, Sam
ASSOCIATES   Poliafico, all of Cleveland, Ohio.

CRIMINAL   : FBI #352422B, Cleveland PD #66551. Record dates from
HISTORY   1948 and includes arrest for homicide. Federal Nar-
               cotic conviction.

BUSINESS   : Truck driver for the Hunkin-Conkey Co., Cleveland,
               Ohio.

MODUS   : Lower echelon Mafioso. Considered a prime suspect
OPERANDI   for burglaries, strong arm robberies and gambling
               in the Cleveland area.

NAME   : Thomas Joseph ZINGALE

ALIASES   : None

DESCRIPTION : Born 6-3-30 Cleveland, Ohio,
               5'8", 180 lbs, dark complex-
               ion, black hair, brown eyes,
               medium build, three black
               moles on left cheek, one
               mole on right side of chin.

LOCALITIES   : Resides 9310 Murray Rd,
FREQUENTED   Valley View, Ohio. Frequents
               Boathouse Bar, Valley View,
               Ohio. Also Italian bars &
               restaurants in the Mayfield Road area.

FAMILY   : Wife: Lucille; father: William; mother: Josephine
BACKGROUND   Lonero; sister: Josephine; brother: Vincent.

CRIMINAL   : ███████████, ███████████, Anthony Spitalieri,
ASSOCIATES   ███████████████████████████, all of Cleveland,
               Ohio.

CRIMINAL   : FBI #904512A. Cleveland PD #72478. Record consists
HISTORY   solely of Federal narcotic conviction in 1951.

BUSINESS   : Occasionally employed as a short order cook and bar-
               tender.

MODUS   : A lesser figure of the Cleveland Mafia hoodlum
OPERANDI   element. He is a prime suspect for burglaries and
               reputed to have some ability as a "safe man".

NAME   : Dominick ALAIMO

ALIASES   : Dominick Aliamo, Alimo,
Nick Alimao.

DESCRIPTION : Born 1-28-10 Montedoro,
Sicily; 5'6", 165 lbs,
brown eyes, light brown
and grey hair.

LOCALITIES : Resides 6 Cherry Street,
FREQUENTED   Pittston, Pa. Frequents
Jane Hogan Dress Co., in
Pittston, and all major
boxing matches in the East.

FAMILY   : Married to Carrie Falcone; son: Dominick Jr.;
BACKGROUND   daughter: Josephine; brothers: Charles, Gregory,
Sam; sisters: Rose & Mrs. Kate Bellania; parents:
John and Josephine (both deceased).

CRIMINAL   : Harry Stromberg, Nick Benfante, ████████, Sam
ASSOCIATES   DeBella, Modesta LoQuasto, Sam Alaimo (brother),
all from Penna. area, James Plumeri of NYC.

CRIMINAL   : FBI# 727127. Wilkes-Barre PD# 2487. Arrests since
HISTORY   1932 include robbery, federal liquor laws, and
labor laws.

BUSINESS   : Owns Jane Hogan Dress Co., Pittston, Pa. Also
part owner with Angelo Sciandra and Russell
Bufalino of the Alaimo Dress Co., Pittston, Pa.

MODUS   : Attended Apalachin Mafia meeting 1957 with other
OPERANDI   Mafia associates from Pittston area.A prominent
leader of the Mafia in the Pittston-Wilkes Barre
area, regarded as an "enforcer". Engaged in labor
racketeering and gambling operations with his
brother Sam.

699

Alaimo was murdered in 1985.

NAME : Salvatore ALAIMO

ALIASES : Sam Alaimo, Sam Aliamo

DESCRIPTION : Born 1-2-14 Pittston, Pa.
5'5½", 144 lbs., brown eyes,
dark brown hair.

LOCALITIES : Resides 45 Elizabeth St.,
FREQUENTED   Pittston, Pa. Frequents
Jane Hogan Dress Co;
Pittston & Pittsburgh area.

FAMILY : Married to Rose Rallo & has
BACKGROUND   daughter Josephine; father:
John; mother:Josephine Falcone (both dead); brothers:
Charles, Gregory, Dominick; sisters: Rose & Mrs.
Kate Bellania.

CRIMINAL : Dominick Alaimo (brother), Nick Benfante, Modesta
ASSOCIATES Loquasto, William Medico, Russell Bufalino, James
Osticco, Angelo Sciandra, all of Pittston, Pa.,
area.

CRIMINAL : FBI#2878224. Pa. State Police #B-19463. Arrests
HISTORY   since 1942 include pandering and gambling.

BUSINESS : Is connected with Jane Hogan Dress Co., Pittston,
Pa., with his brother Dominick.

MODUS : A "strong arm" Mafia member in the Pittston, Pa.,
OPERANDI   area. Engaged in gambling and labor racketeering
with his brother Dominick.

Amato was the Pittsburgh family boss starting in 1937. He died in 1973.

NAME : Frank AMATO

ALIASES :

DESCRIPTION : Born 2-15-1893 Roccarainola, Sicily, 5'8½", 177lbs., blue eyes, brown-grey hair, naturalized 6-19-22 Pittsburgh, Pa.

LOCALITIES FREQUENTED : Resides 430 2nd St., Braddock, Pa. Frequents Laetus Club, New Kensington, Pa.

FAMILY BACKGROUND : Wife: Ernestine; daughters: Attilia, Mrs. Gina Mannarino, Mrs. Minnie Lettier; son: Frank Jr; father: Domenico; mother: Attilia Miele.

CRIMINAL ASSOCIATES : Gabriel Mannarino, Sam Mannarino (son-in-law), John LaRocca, ███████████, ███████████, all of Pittsburgh area; Nicola Gentile of Italy; James J. Lanza of California.

CRIMINAL HISTORY : FBI #1689858, Pittsburgh PD# 28197. Arrests since 1929 include murder & suspicion of murder.

BUSINESS : Owner-distributor of pinball machines, juke-boxes, & vending machines in the Pittsburgh-Braddock, Pa., area.

MODUS OPERANDI : One of the leaders of the Mafia in the Pittsburgh area, who, with other Mafia associates, controls most gambling & gambling devices in the Westmoreland County, Pa., area.

NAME	: Nicholas BENFANTI
ALIASES	: Nick Benfante, Nick Benfonto Nick Bonfonte, Nick Belfonte
DESCRIPTION	: Born 8-24-06 Soldier, Pa. 5'7½", 165 lbs, brown eyes, black hair.
LOCALITIES FREQUENTED	: Resides 17 Landon Street, Pittston, Pa. Frequents Northeastern Penna., Workers Association in Pittston, & Air Port Hotel, Avoca, Pa.

FAMILY BACKGROUND	: Married to Gertrude Richardson; brothers: Anthony and Joseph; father: Sam; mother: Sarah Angello.
CRIMINAL ASSOCIATES	: Russell Bufalino, Dominick Alaimo, Sam DeBella, Angelo Sciandra, William Medico, Dave Osticco, Casper Guimento, Modesta Loquasto, all of Pittston, Pa., area.
CRIMINAL HISTORY	: FBI# 703753. Penna. State Police #B-4058. Arrests since 1931 include robbery, rape, disorderly con- duct, state liquor law violation.
BUSINESS	: Owner of Air Port Motel, Avoca, Pa., & president of Northeastern Penna. Workers Association, Kehoe Building, Pittston, Pa.
MODUS OPERANDI	: An important member of the Mafia in the Pittston area; who has engaged in labor racketeering, arson, and illicit alcohol traffic.

> "The Gentle Don" ran the Philadelphia crime family for about 20 years. On March 21, 1980, Bruno was murdered by his own consigliere with a shotgun blast to the back of the head. He was in his car at the time.

NAME : Angelo BRUNO

ALIASES : Ange Bruno, Angelo Annaloro

DESCRIPTION : Born 5-21-10 at Villalba, Italy, 5'8", 198 lbs, heavy build, dark brown hair, brown eyes, dark complexion.

LOCALITIES FREQUENTED : Resides 934 Snyder Ave., Phila., Pa., frequents Atlas Extermination Co., Trenton, N.J., Aluminum Products Sales Corp., Hialeah, Fla., Iezzi Bar, 8th and Washington Sts., Phila., Pa.

FAMILY BACKGROUND : Wife: Sue Maranca; has two children; father: Michael Bruno Annaloro; mother: Vincenzina Cumella; brother: Victor Bruno; sisters: Josephine, Lena Maggio; Lena married to Peter Maggio, son of late Mike Maggio prominent Philadelphia Mafia leader.

CRIMINAL ASSOCIATES : Felix DeTullio, Joseph Rugnetta, Harry Riccobene, Peter Casella, Dominick Pollino, Frank Palermo, ▓▓▓▓▓▓▓▓, all of Phila., Pa., Louis Campbell, Pasquale Massi, ▓▓▓▓▓▓▓▓ all of Camden, NJ.

CRIMINAL HISTORY : FBI #1045098, Phila., PD #85869, 1st arrest in 1928 for reckless driving, numerous subsequent arrests including violations of fire-arms Act, operation of illicit still, gambling, receiving stolen goods.

BUSINESS : Owns and operates the Atlas Extermination Co., Trenton, NJ, and the Aluminum Products Sales Corp., Hialeah, Fla., he is reported to own an interest in a casino in the Plaza Hotel, Havana Cuba.

MODUS OPERANDI : Considered one of the upper echelon of the Mafia organization in the Phila., area, he is in a policy making position with the Mafia.

NAME : Russell A. BUFALINO

ALIASES : Ross Bufalino, Rosario Bufalino, Buffalino.

DESCRIPTION : Born 10-29-1903, Montedoro, Sicily, 5'8", 166 lbs, medium build, grey hair, hazel eyes, sallow complexion, left thumb & index finger amputated.

LOCALITIES FREQUENTED : Resides 304 E. Dorrance St., Kingston, Pa. Frequents the Medico Electric Motor Co., Pittston, Pa. & attends most championship prizefights.

FAMILY BACKGROUND : Married Carolina Sciandra; brother: Charles; sister: Josephine; father: Angelo; mother: Maria Cristina Buccolliere (both deceased).

CRIMINAL ASSOCIATES : Modesto Loquasto, William Medico, Santo Volpe, Sam Mannarino, ███████████, James Plumeri, Al Polizzi, John Dioguardi, William Bufalino (cousin).

CRIMINAL HISTORY : FBI #691589 Buffalo PD #18580 Arrests since 1927 include vagrancy, petty larceny, criminally receiving stolen property and conspiracy to obstruct justice, for which sentenced (1960) to 5 yrs & $10,000 fine.

BUSINESS : Owns Penn Drape & Curtain Co., Pittston, Pa. Interest in other Pittston & NYC dress manufacturing companies.

MODUS OPERANDI : Arranged and attended the 1957 Apalachin Mafia meeting. One of the most ruthless and powerful leaders of the Mafia in the U.S. Also engaged in narcotic trafficking, labor racketeering and dealing in stolen jewels and furs.

NAME   : Antonio CALIO

ALIASES   : Nino

DESCRIPTION   : Born 4-14-1889, Castro-
                  Giovanni, Italy, entered
                  U.S., 8-6-06, N.Y.C.

LOCALITIES   : Resides 6628 Torresdale Ave.
FREQUENTED   Philadelphia, Penna., fre-
                  quents Olive Oil and Italian
                  Cheese Co., 820 Watkins St.,
                  Phila., Pa.

FAMILY   : Wife's name Mary, married
BACKGROUND   1926, father's name Joseph,
                  mother's name Barbara, both of whom were born in Italy.

CRIMINAL   : Joseph Rugnetta, Mike Maggio (dead), Dominick Pollino,
ASSOCIATES   Angelo Bruno, Felix DeTullio, was a close associate
                  of Harry Riccobene's father, who is dead.

CRIMINAL   : No criminal record.
HISTORY

BUSINESS   : Operates the Olive Oil and Italian Cheese Co.,
                  820 Watkins Street, Philadelphia, Penna.

MODUS   : Is an important member of the Mafia in the Phila-
OPERANDI   delphia area.

NAME	: Samuel DeBELLA
ALIASES	: Steven DeBella, Salvatore DeBella, Swimmy DeBella.

DESCRIPTION	: Born 9-1-18, Pittston, Pa., 5'10", 160 lbs, medium build black hair, brown eyes.
LOCALITIES FREQUENTED	: Resides 25 East Oak St., Pittston, Pa., frequents Penn Drape and Curtain Co., 161 S. Main St., Pittston, and the S and B Machine Co., 112 S. Main St., Pittston, Pa.
FAMILY BACKGROUND	: Married to Jennie Cumbo, has one daughter Mary Anne, father's name Patsy, deceased 1939; stepmother's name Carrie, brother Ignatius DeBella.
CRIMINAL ASSOCIATES	: Russell Bufalino, Angelo Sciandra, Santo Volpe, Dominick Alaimo, Nicholas Benfanti, Louis Pagnotti, Modesta Loquasto, Casper Guimento, Dave Osticco, all of Pittston area. Gabriel Mannarino, New Kensington, Pa.
CRIMINAL HISTORY	: Pa., State Police #B11937, 1st arrest in 1938 for breaking, entering and larceny, numerous subsequent arrests including robbery, gambling, carrying a concealed deadly weapon, disorderly conduct.
BUSINESS	: Owns part interest with Russell Bufalino in the Penn Drape Co., 161 S. Main St., Pittston and the S and B Machine Co., 112 S. Main St., Pittston.
MODUS OPERANDI	: Considered an important Mafia member in the Pittston area of Pa; known strongarm man and "enforcer" for the Mafia organization in the Pittston area.

NAME : Michael James GENOVESE

ALIASES : Antonio Genovese

DESCRIPTION : Born 4-19-19 Pittsburgh, Pa. 5'6½", 175 lbs, brown eyes, black hair, dark complexion.

LOCALITIES FREQUENTED : Resides RD 2, Box 149B, Gibsonia, Pa. Frequents Red Eagle Athletic Club in Pittsburgh, Club 30 on Rte 30 in Chester, W. Virginia, Holiday House, Monroeville, Pa.

FAMILY BACKGROUND : Divorced (1945) from Carmela Napoletano; now living with Alice Gray Rohbacker; daughters: Kathleen, Yvonne, Alice-Jo; brothers: Felix & Fiore; sister: Angelina; father: Antonio; mother Ursula DiAngelo.

CRIMINAL ASSOCIATES : William Medico, Nick Stirone, Sam Mannarino, Sam Alaimo, Frank Amato, ███████████████████, ██████████████, all of Pittsburgh area.

CRIMINAL HISTORY : FBI# 4373362. Pa. State Police #185296. Arrests since 1936 include assault & battery, carrying concealed weapon, robbery. Has been a suspect in some killings in the Pittsburgh area.

BUSINESS : Part owner of Archie's Automatic Car Wash, 850 Bennett St., Pittsburgh, Pa.

MODUS OPERANDI : Attended Apalachin Mafia meeting 1957 with other Mafia members representing the interests of the Mafia controlled rackets in the Pittsburgh area. Has control of a "numbers" racket in East Liberty District of Pittsburgh. Is considered a dangerous and feared hoodlum in the Pittsburgh area.

NAME   : Casper GUIMENTO

ALIASES   : Cappy Guimento

DESCRIPTION   : Born 9-15-14 Dunmore, Pa.
                  5'5½", 133 lbs, brown eyes,
                  black-grey hair, has scar
                  on right cheek.

LOCALITIES   : Resides 209 Willow Street,
FREQUENTED   Dunmore, Pa. Frequents
                  Purple Cow Restaurant and
                  Tony Harding's Diner, both
                  in Scranton, Pa., and Reds
                  Restaurant in Dunmore, Pa.

FAMILY   : Married to Catherine Van Luvander and has daughter
BACKGROUND   Angela; father: Ross; mother: Angeline (both dead).

CRIMINAL   : Russell Bufalino, Dominick Alaimo, Nick Benfanti,
ASSOCIATES   Angelo Sciandra, James Osticco, William Medico,
                  Sam DeBello, Modesta Loquasto, all of Pittston,
                  Pa., area.

CRIMINAL   : FBI# 183432B. Pa. State Police #B-32649. Record
HISTORY   shows only two arrests, both for gambling.

BUSINESS   : No legitimate business or employment known.

MODUS   : Close associate of all Mafia members in the
OPERANDI   Scranton-Pittston area. A professional gambler
                  who operates illegal games controlled by Mafia
                  leader Russell Bufalino.

He was the head of criminal operations in Pittsburg, PA. Rocca died of natural causes on December 3, 1984.

NAME : Sebastian John LA ROCCA

ALIASES : John S. LaRocco, Lester LaRock, Lester LaRocca.

DESCRIPTION : Born 12-12-02 Villarosa, Sicily. 5'10", 210 lbs, grey hair, brown eyes, stocky build, I&NS #A5537570.

LOCALITIES FREQUENTED : Resides 6426 Apple Street, Pittsburgh, Pa. Frequents the Bloomfield & East Liberty area of Penna., also attends most major prize fights.

FAMILY BACKGROUND : Married to Mary Semilk & has an adopted son John; brothers: Joseph, Anthony, John; sisters: Mrs. Rose Conti, Mrs. Leona Rose, Mrs. Angeline Zito; father: Ignazio; mother: Rosaria Scancarella (both dead).

CRIMINAL ASSOCIATES : Nick Stirone, Gabriel & Sam Mannarino, Patsy & Sam Monachino, Frank Amato, Michael Genovese, Frank Valenti, Russell Bufalino.

CRIMINAL HISTORY : FBI# 96725. Penna. State Police # 20782. Arrests since 1922 include aggravated assault, perjury, liquor laws, carrying concealed weapons.

BUSINESS : Has interests in North Star Cement Block Co., Standard Dryer Distribution Co., Fayette Novelty Co., Rock-O-La Music Machine Co., all in the Greater Pittsburgh area.

MODUS OPERANDI : Attended Apalachin Mafia meeting 1957 as a leader from the Pittsburgh area. Operates a "numbers" ring in the East End Section of Pittsburgh; also engaged in labor racketeering.

NAME	: Modesta LOQUASTO
ALIASES	: Murph Loquasto, Murphy Loquasto, Modeste Loquasto.
DESCRIPTION	: Born 9-23-11, Pittston, Pa, 5'6", 165 lbs, medium build, dark complexion, dark brown hair, brown eyes.
LOCALITIES FREQUENTED	: Resides 372 S. Main St., Pittston, Pa., frequents Medico Electric Motor Co., 11 Tomkins St., Pittston, Pennsylvania.
FAMILY BACKGROUND	: Married Angeline Leedock, three children.
CRIMINAL ASSOCIATES	: Russell Bufalino, Angelo Sciandra, Nicholas Benfanti, Dave Osticco, Sam DeBella, William Medico, Dominick Alaimo, Casper Guimento, Santo Volpe, Angelo Polizzi, all of the Pittston area of Pa.
CRIMINAL HISTORY	: FBI #389359. Pa. State Police #B-2444, record dates from 1929 and includes arrests for larceny of auto, robbery, disorderly conduct, gambling, violation Mann Act, armed robbery, assault and battery.
BUSINESS	: No legitimate occupation.
MODUS OPERANDI	: Mafia member in the Pittston area of Pa., his position in the Mafia has always been that of a strongarm man; he was Russell Bufalino's constant companion and body guard in the early 1940's.

NAME   : Gabriel MANNARINO

ALIASES   : Kelly Mannarino, Gabriel
                  Manerine, Gabriel Rugiero,
                  Gabriel Mannerino.

DESCRIPTION   : Born 10-31-16 New
                  Kensington, Pa., 5'5½",
                  170 lbs., brown eyes,
                  black hair.

LOCALITIES   : Resides 540 Charles St.,
FREQUENTED   New Kensington, Pa. Fre-
                  quents Miami Beach, Fla.,
                  and Havana, Cuba.

FAMILY   : Married, has daughter Georgenne, brothers:
BACKGROUND   Salvatore & Joseph, father: George, mother:
                  Domenica Politano.

CRIMINAL   : Frank Amato, Nick Stirone, Sam Alaimo, Sam
ASSOCIATES   Mannarino (brother), all of Pittsburgh area;
                  Joe Massei, Mike Coppola, Patsy Erra, Charles
                  Tourine, Meyer Lansky all of Miami Beach area.

CRIMINAL   : FBI #854850, Pa. State Police #115122. Arrests
HISTORY   since 1933 include gambling, liquor laws, uniform
                  arms act, obstruction of justice.

BUSINESS   : With brother Sam operates Ken Iron & Steel Company
                  and Nu-Ken Novelty Company both in New Kensington;
                  also has interests in night clubs in Miami Beach
                  and New Kensington.

MODUS   : Attended Apalachin Mafia meeting 1957 as a leader
OPERANDI   from the New Kensington, Pa., area. Both he and
                  brother Sam are considered "strong arm" Mafia
                  hoodlums and control all forms of gambling in
                  New Kensington area.

NAME   : Salvatore MANNARINO

ALIASES   : Salvatore Rugiero, Sam
                 Mannarino

DESCRIPTION   : Born 1-1-06, Pittsburgh,
                 Pa. 5'2", 162 lbs., brown
                 eyes, brown hair, stocky
                 build.

LOCALITIES   : Resides 201 Highland Ave.,
FREQUENTED   New Kensington, Pa. Fre-
                 quents Miami Beach, Fla.,
                 and Havana, Cuba.

FAMILY   : Married to Jean Amato (daughter of Frank Amato)
BACKGROUND   and has a married daughter (Mrs. R. Carlucci);
                 father: Giacinto, mother: Domenica Politano,
                 brothers: Gabriel and Joseph.

CRIMINAL   : Gabriel Mannarino (brother), Frank Amato (father-
ASSOCIATES   in-law), John S. La Rocca, Michael Genovese, all
                 of Pittsburgh area; Charles Tourine, Patsy Erra,
                 Santos Trafficante, all of Miami Beach area.

CRIMINAL   : FBI #115840. Arrests since 1927 include
HISTORY   impersonating a U. S. Officer, operating a
                 gambling house, fraud.

BUSINESS   : With his brother Gabriel operates Ken Iron & Steel
                 Co; and Nu-Ken Novelty Co; both in New Kensington,
                 Pa. Also believed to have interests in a hotel and
                 night club in Miami Beach with brother Gabriel.

MODUS   : Both he and brother Gabriel are "strong arm" Mafia
OPERANDI   hoodlums and they control all forms of gambling in
                 the New Kensington, Pa., area.

712

NAME	: William MEDICO
ALIASES	: Burgio Medico
DESCRIPTION	: Born 3-6-09, Pittston, Pa., 5'5½", 170 lbs, heavy build, dark complexion, grey-brown hair, brown eyes, has a mustache, scar on palm of right hand near wrist.
LOCALITIES FREQUENTED	: Resides 204 Montgomery Ave., Pittston, Pa., frequents Medico Electric Motor Co., Pittston, Pa., and Medico Industries, Pottsville, Pa.

FAMILY BACKGROUND	: Married; father: Cataldo; mother: Gaetana Gelsa; one daughter who is married to Santo Volpe's son.
CRIMINAL ASSOCIATES	: Russell Bufalino, Angelo Sciandra, Dominick Alaimo, Nicholas Benfanti, Louis Pagnotti, Samuel DeBella, Modesto Loquasto, Santo Volpe, Casper Guimento, Dave Osticco, all of Pittston area; Santo Trafficante, Havana, Cuba.
CRIMINAL HISTORY	: FBI #376599, Penna., State Police #36475, 1st arrest in 1928 for assault and battery, subsequent arrests for suspicion of murder, state liquor violations, and larceny.
BUSINESS	: Owns and operates the Medico Electric Motor Co., 11 Tomkins St., Pittston, Pa., Medico Industries, Inc., 108 N. Centre St., Pottsville, Pa., President of Greater Pittston Chamber of Commerce.
MODUS OPERANDI	: Considered an important Mafia leader in the Pittston area; his legitimate enterprises operate as "Fronts" for illegal activities of the Mafia in the Pittston area of Penna.

713

NAME	: Luigi PAGNOTTI
ALIASES	: Louis Pagnotti
DESCRIPTION	: Born 7-13-1894 Old Forge, Pa, 5'7", 160 lbs, medium build, grey hair, brown eyes, dark complexion.
LOCALITIES FREQUENTED	: Resides 603 Moosic Rd, Old Forge, Pa., frequents New Recreation Center, Old Forge, Pa., Pagnotti Enterprise Coal Mines, Luzerne Co. area.
FAMILY BACKGROUND	: Married Mary Tedesco; 3 daughters & 2 sons; father: Rosario; mother: Maria Gnatza.
CRIMINAL ASSOCIATES	: Santo Volpe, █████████████, Russell Bufalino, Angelo Sciandra, Angelo Polizzi, █████████, █████████, █████████, Nicholas Benfanti, all of the Pittston, Pa., area.
CRIMINAL HISTORY	: No criminal record.
BUSINESS	: Owns New Recreation Center, Old Forge, Pa., and several coal mining companies in Old Forge, Tremont and Jolliet, Pa.
MODUS OPERANDI	: A ranking member of the Mafia in the Pittston, Pa., area; illicit still operator, slot machine owner and distributor in 1930's.

```
┌─────────────────────────────────────────────────────────────────┐
│  Palermo died in May 1996.                                        │
└─────────────────────────────────────────────────────────────────┘
```

NAME   : Frank PALERMO

ALIASES   : Blinky Palermo

DESCRIPTION   : Born 1-26-05, Philadelphia,
                Pa., 5'5", 169 lbs, heavy
                build, dark brown hair,
                chestnut eyes.

LOCALITIES   : Resides 800 N. 64th St.,
FREQUENTED   Philadelphia, Pa., frequents
                Sansom Delicatessen, 111 S.
                39th St., Phila., Pa., the
                500 Club, Atlantic City, NJ.

FAMILY   : Married; sons: Fred and Frank Jr., daughter: Violet;
BACKGROUND   brother: John in Philadelphia.

CRIMINAL   : Felix Bocchicchio, Angelo Bruno, Felix DiTullio,
ASSOCIATES   Peter Casella, Dominick Pollino, Pasquale Massi,
                Louis Campbell, all of the Philadelphia-Camden area;
                ██████████████, ████████████████, William Brown,
                Columbus, Ohio; ███████████, N.Y., ████████████
                █████████, Baltimore, Md.

CRIMINAL   : FBI #626755, Philadelphia PD #241909, 1st arrest
HISTORY   in 1933 as a suspicious person, numerous subsequent
                arrests including lottery, operating without boxing
                manager's license, reckless use of firearms.

BUSINESS   : Boxing promotor, fight manager, has managed such
                fighters as Johnny Saxton, Joey Giardello; owns
                Sansom Delicatessen, 111 S. 39th St., Phila.,
                operated by his son-in-law.

MODUS   : Alleged to operate a numbers bank in Phila., gambler
OPERANDI   in Phila., underworld; considered head man in fight
                "racketeering" in Philadelphia area.

NAME	: Gioacchino PARISI
ALIASES	: Jack Parisi, Jack Parise, Jackina Parisi, "Dandy Jack".
DESCRIPTION	: Born 3-19-99 Bagnara, Reggio Calabria, Italy. 5'6", 160 lbs., grey hair, brown eyes, dark complexion. I&NS-A# 8196736.

LOCALITIES FREQUENTED	: Resides 672 Monges St., Hazelton Pa. Frequents Nuremberg Dress Co., Nuremberg, Pa., & Madison Dress Co., Wilkes-Barre, Pa.
FAMILY BACKGROUND	: Married to Theresa Alampi; father: Francesco; mother: Rosa; is a brother-in-law to Vincent Mangano (deceased).
CRIMINAL ASSOCIATES	: Angelo Sciandra, Sam Alaimo, Dominick Alaimo, Russell Bufalino, the late Vincent Mangano, & the late Albert Anastasia.
CRIMINAL HISTORY	: FBI#244372. NYC PD-B#124301. Arrests since 1926 include extortion, possession of gun, grand larceny, murder, & conviction for Federal Narcotic Laws. Deportation proceedings have been pending since 1953.
BUSINESS	: Production Manager of Nuremberg Dress Co., Nuremberg, Pa., & Supervisor at Madison Dress Co., Wilkes-Barre, Pa.
MODUS OPERANDI	: At one time reputed to have been a paid professional killer for the Mafia in Brooklyn, N.Y. Currently reputed to be engaged in labor racketeering in the dress manufacturing industry in the Hazelton, Pa., area.

NAME	: Dominick POLLINO
ALIASES	: Nick Pollino, Antonio Pollina Dominick Pollina.
DESCRIPTION	: Born 9-20-1892 Caccamo, Sicily, 5'7", 179 lbs, medium build, grey-black hair, chestnut eyes, dark complexion. Naturalized Phila., Pa, 7-12-44 #C6326783.

LOCALITIES FREQUENTED	: Resides 2515 S. 21st St, Phila., Pa, frequents Maggio Cheese Co., 11th & Washington Ave, Phila., Pa.
FAMILY BACKGROUND	: Married Mary Rodia; father: Francesco; mother: Giovanna Cecala; brother: Phillip Pollino.
CRIMINAL ASSOCIATES	: Joseph Rugnetta, Angelo Bruno, Harry Riccobene, Peter Casella, Felix DeTullio, Frank Palermo, ███████ ██████, Pasquale Massi & Louis Campbell.
CRIMINAL HISTORY	: FBI #1672301, Phila., PD #74786. Record dates from 1927 & includes arrests for murder, concealed weapons, untaxed liquor, assault & battery.
BUSINESS	: Employed as a salesman for Maggio Cheese Co., 11th & Washington Ave, Phila., Pa, formerly owned by late gangster Mike Maggio who left it to his criminal associate sons Mario, Joe & Tony.
MODUS OPERANDI	: One of the top leaders of the "Greaser Gang," the Mafia organization in Phila., Pa. Known as "Mr Big" to other Mafia members. Controls loan shark corporation which operates within the "Greaser Gang".

NAME   : Harry RICCOBENE

ALIASES   : Anthony DeMarco, Little
                   Harry, Hunchback Harry.

DESCRIPTION   : Born 7-27-09 Enna, Sicily,
                   5'1", 136 lbs, medium build,
                   dark brown hair and greying,
                   (bald in front), brown eyes,
                   wears glasses.

LOCALITIES   : Resides 728 Carpenter St.,
FREQUENTED   Philadelphia, Pa., currently
                   in jail (Pa., State)

FAMILY   : Separated from wife Evelyn,
BACKGROUND   half-brother Mario, father Mario, mother Anna
                   Cimmarri (both dead).

CRIMINAL   : Felix DeTullio, Pete Casella, Tony Calio, Joe
ASSOCIATES   Rugnetta, Anthony Crisci, Sam Papalardo, Salvatore
                   Poliafico, ███████████.

CRIMINAL   : FBI #470924, Phila., P.D. #89592, numerous arrests
HISTORY   since 1929 including, concealed deadly weapons,
                   larceny, Federal Narcotic Laws (conviction), poss-
                   ession narcotics (state law); currently serving $7\frac{1}{2}$
                   to 15 years (Penna., State Narcotic Laws).

BUSINESS   : Operated Quaker T.V. Tube and Service Co., 728
                   Carpenter St., Phila., Pa., has interests in T.V.
                   tube companies in Yonkers, N.Y., and Richmond, Va.

MODUS   : For many years has been an interstate narcotic
OPERANDI   trafficker and is connected with all the known Mafiosi
                   in the Phila., Camden area.

NAME	: Giuseppe RUGNETTA
ALIASES	: Joseph Rugnetti, "Joe the Boss".
DESCRIPTION	: Born 3-16-96 Sinopoli, Calabria, Italy, naturalized 12-19-22, Phila., Pa., 5'5", 160 lbs, medium build, grey hair, chestnut eyes, wears glasses, dark complexion.
LOCALITIES FREQUENTED	: Resides 703 Annin St., Phila., Pa., frequents S. Philly Bar and Grill, 2026 S. 12th St., Phila., Pa.
FAMILY BACKGROUND	: Married to Lina Latorre, 3-18-19, wife died 1945; father's name Rocco, mother's name Maria both of whom were born in Italy.
CRIMINAL ASSOCIATES	: Angelo Bruno, Felix DeTullio, Harry Riccobene, Peter Casella, Dominick Pollino, all of Phila.; Dominick Oliveto and Pasquale Massi, Camden, N.J.
CRIMINAL HISTORY	: Phila., P.D. #35894, arrested twice in Phila., Pa., 1st arrest 5-21-17 for carrying concealed weapons, disposition-discharged 6-14-17; arrested 11-14-20 for assault and battery, assault to kill by shooting, found not guilty 1-5-21.
BUSINESS	: With co-owner Charles Scarcelli operates the S. Philly Bar, 2026 S. 12th St., Phila., Pa.
MODUS OPERANDI	: Considered a powerful figure in the Mafia in the Philadelphia area, he is an old "enforcer" in the Mafia; at present he acts as the referee in settling disputes; he also operates a loan shark business.

NAME   : Angelo Joseph SCIANDRA

ALIASES   :

DESCRIPTION   : Born 11-26-1923, Pittston, Pa.
                6'0", 215 lbs, brown eyes,
                dark brown hair, dark com-
                plexion, stocky build.

LOCALITIES   : Resides 101 Dorrance Street,
FREQUENTED   Wyoming, Pa. Frequents Ann-
                Lee Frocks, Gramercy Restaur-
                ant, Twin Restaurant, all in
                Pittston.

FAMILY   : Married Helen Driscoll; sons: John, Thomas, Patrick
BACKGROUND   & Angelo, Jr.; brothers: John & Joseph; sister: Mrs.
                Eleanor Malacco; father: John; mother: Josephine.

CRIMINAL   : Nicholas Benfante, William Medico, Modesto LoQuasto,
ASSOCIATES   Salvatore Alaimo, all of Pennsylvania area, James
                Plumeri & ▨▨▨▨▨▨, of NYC and Miami.

CRIMINAL   : FBI #796092-C Only known arrest was for conspiracy
HISTORY   to obstruct justice, for which sentenced in 1960 to
                5 years and $10,000 fine.

BUSINESS   : Owns Ann-Lee Frocks in Pittston, Pa. and has other
                interests in women's coat and dress factories in
                Pennsylvania & NYC.

MODUS   : Attended 1957 Apalachin Mafia meeting with associates
OPERANDI   from the Pittston area. Is taking the place of his
                deceased father, who was one of the leaders of the
                Mafia in Pittston. Is a strong-arm man for the Mafia-
                controlled garment industry in Pittston.

NAME	: Vincenzo STICCO
ALIASES	: James Anthony Osticco, Dave Osticco, Dave Ostico, Dave Osticko, James Ostico.
DESCRIPTION	: Born 4-22-1913 Pittston, Pa. 5'9", 175 lbs, black-grey hair, bald, sometimes wears glasses & moustache.
LOCALITIES FREQUENTED	: Resides 156½ Elizabeth St., Pittston, Pa. Frequents the Pittston area and makes trips to Miami & Cuba.
FAMILY BACKGROUND	: Married Helen Gushock; seven children, Cecilia, Mary Ellen, Patrina, twins Anita & Anthony, twins Dorina & Helen; father: Antonio; mother: Maria Antonia DeBlasi.
CRIMINAL ASSOCIATES	: William Medico, Salvatore Alaimo, Salvatore Mannarino, Modesto LoQuasto, Nicholas Benfante, Salvatore De Bella, all of Pa., James Plumeri of NYC & Miami, Fla.
CRIMINAL HISTORY	: FBI #376451 Penna. State Police #B-24124 Record dating from 1931 includes arrests for prohibition law violation and conspiracy to obstruct justice. On the latter charge sentence 1960 to 5 yrs and $10,000 fine.
BUSINESS	: Transportation manager for Wm. Medico Industries, Pittston, Pa. Interest in Ann Lee Frocks & Connie Frocks, both in Pittston, Pa.
MODUS OPERANDI	: Attended 1957 Apalachin Mafia meeting with other members from Pittston area. Formerly a bootlegger and now strong-arm man for the Mafia-controlled garment Industry in Pittston & Vicinity.

NAME : Nicholas STIRONE

ALIASES : Joseph Stirone

DESCRIPTION : Born 5-23-02 Berdifuma, Italy, 5'8", 174 lbs, brown eyes, fair complexion, brown hair, medium build.

LOCALITIES FREQUENTED : Resides Bigelow Apts., 1506 Bigelow Square, Pittsburgh, Pa., frequents 2155 Centre Ave., Pittsburgh, International Hod Carriers Union.

FAMILY BACKGROUND : 1st wife was Angelina Falcone, has two daughters by her, 2nd wife is Anastasia; brothers are Frank and Joseph, sisters are May and Louise, parents are Olimpio and Mary.

CRIMINAL ASSOCIATES : John La Rocca, Frank Amato, ███████████, ███████ ██████████████, all of Pittsburgh, Frank Valenti of Rochester.

CRIMINAL HISTORY : FBI #1685221, 1st arrest 1934 Newark, N.J., for threat with intent to kill; arrested 1957 Pittsburgh for Hobbs Anti-Racketeering Act.

BUSINESS : President of Local 1058 International Hod Carriers Bldg., and Common Laborers Union and of Heavy Engineer, Railroads Contracting and Highway Construction Council, both of Pittsburgh.

MODUS OPERANDI : Uses his position in labor unions to extort money from employers to insure labor peace; considered a high ranking Mafia in the Pittsburgh area.

NAME : John CANDELMO

ALIASES : John Condelmo, "Candy"

DESCRIPTION : Born 3-28-05 Providence, R.I.
5'6¼", 170 lbs., blue eyes,
black-grey hair, stocky
build.

LOCALITIES : Resides 141 Pocassett Ave.,
FREQUENTED Providence, R.I. Frequents
Coin-o-matic Distributing
Co., 168 Atwells Ave.,
Providence & bars in that
same area.

FAMILY : Father: Luigi; mother: Vincenzina Darezza; wife:
BACKGROUND Frances Coviello (deceased); brothers: William,
Anthony, & Ernest.

CRIMINAL : Ray ██████ Patriarca, ██████████, all of
ASSOCIATES Providence; ████████████, █████████, █████████
█████████, all of N.Y.C.

CRIMINAL : FBI#944077. Providence PD#12266. Arrests since
HISTORY 1922 include holdup, burglary, breaking & entering,
murder, possession of guns and narcotics.

BUSINESS : Has interests in Federal Dairy Co., 83 Greenwich
St., and business property at 198 Atwood St., both
in Providence.

MODUS : A strong-arm man. Is closely associated with other
Mafia leaders in the Boston-Providence area, and
they control all rackets & gambling in the area.

On July 11, 1984, Patriarca died from a heart condition and diabetes.

NAME : Raymond PATRIARCA

ALIASES : John Roma, Raymond L.S. Patriaca, Raymond E. Patriaca

DESCRIPTION : Born 3-17-08, Worcester, Mass., 5'6", 175 lbs., stocky build, dark chestnut hair, brown eyes, dark complexion, scar under right cheek bone.

LOCALITIES FREQUENTED : Resides 165 Lancaster St., Providence, R.I. frequents Giro's Cafe and Paddock Bar, Boston, Miami, Fla.

FAMILY BACKGROUND : Married, wife's name is Helen, father is Eleutrio (deceased), mother is Mary Jane DeNubile.

CRIMINAL ASSOCIATES : Philip Buccola, ████████, Albert Santaniello, ████████, Henry Selvitella, Frank Cucchiara, Rocco Palladino.

CRIMINAL HISTORY : FBI #191775, Mass. State Police #30408, 1st arrest in 1926, subsequent arrests for violation of Mann Act, white slavery, assault with dangerous weapon, larceny, armed robbery.

BUSINESS : Owns Coinamatic Distributing Co., D & H Construction Co., Miehle Fabric Co., Cadillac City (Cadillac Agency) all of Providence, R. I.

MODUS OPERANDI : Is a leader of Mafia in New England area; one of the heads of all gambling rackets in New England.

NAME   : Biagio ANGELICA

ALIASES   : Biaggio Angelico, Blasco
                  Moscato, Big Angelo

DESCRIPTION   : Born 5-18-1907, NYC, 5'7½",
                  192 lbs, brown eyes, wears
                  glasses, black-grey hair,
                  balding.

LOCALITIES   : Resides 3925 Avenue R,
FREQUENTED   Galveston, Texas. Frequents
                  Galveston and Houston, Texas

FAMILY   : Married; son: Vincent;
BACKGROUND   father: Vincenzo; mother: Theresa.

CRIMINAL   : Louis Marino, Vitor Maddi, Joseph Lucca, Joseph
ASSOCIATES   Civello, Vincent A. D'Ingianni, all of Texas, Alfonso
                  Attardi, of NYC, and ██████████████, of Italy
                  (deportee).

CRIMINAL   : FBI #541336 Houston PD #16323 Record dating from
HISTORY   1930 includes arrests for armed robbery, extortion,
                  kidnapping and conviction for violation of Federal
                  Narcotic Laws.

BUSINESS   : Operates M & M Music Co., 2114 Market Street, Gal-
                  veston, Texas, in partnership with Louis Marino.

MODUS   : An influential and feared member of the Mafia in
OPERANDI   the southeast Texas area. Member of a large scale
                  narcotic trafficking ring which smuggled heroin into
                  the U.S. and distributed it in Texas and other
                  southern states

NAME   : Joseph F. CIVELLO

ALIASES   : Joe Civillo

DESCRIPTION   : Born 2-3-1902 Port Allen, La.
                5'11", 163 lbs, blue eyes,
                grey hair, wears glasses,
                slender build.

LOCALITIES   : Resides 5311 Denton Drive,
FREQUENTED   Dallas, Texas. Frequents
                Civello's Fine Foods, Dallas,
                & makes trips to N.Y.C.

FAMILY   : Wife: Mary; father: Joseph;
BACKGROUND   mother: Catherine; brother: Charles; sisters: Mrs.
                Frances Musso, Mrs. Anna Cangelosi, Mrs. Phyllis
                Ginestra, Mrs. Margaret Polito.

CRIMINAL   : Rocco & Peter Pellegrino, of NYC, ███████████,
ASSOCIATES   Biagio Angelica, Joe Ianni & ████████ of Texas,
                Nicholas Impastato (deportee), Joseph Filardo &
                Joseph DeLuca, of Kansas City, Mo.

CRIMINAL   : FBI #1222605 Dallas PD #7265   Record dating from
HISTORY   1928 includes conviction for Federal Narcotic Law
                violation and conspiracy to obstruct justice (for
                which sentenced (1960) to 5 years).

BUSINESS   : Operates Civello's Fine Foods & Liquor, 4236 Oak
                Lawn Avenue, Dallas, Texas.

MODUS   : Attended the 1957 Apalachin Mafia meeting as the
OPERANDI   leader from the Dallas area. Controls all rackets
                in Dallas and vicinity.

NAME   : Vincent Anthony D'INGIANNI

ALIASES   : Vincent Dingianni

DESCRIPTION   : Born 6-20-16 Scalea, Italy,
                 5'9", 132 lbs, brown eyes,
                 black wavy hair. Derived
                 citizenship from father who
                 naturalized New Orleans 4-7-
                 1927.

LOCALITIES   : Resides 4609 Bellaire Blvd,
FREQUENTED   Houston, Texas. Frequents
                 Galveston, Texas, and New
                 Orleans, La.

FAMILY   : Married Mary Maude Dossett; daughter: Dorothy;
BACKGROUND   father: Amerigo; mother: Cersosimo Annunziata;
                 brother: Amerigo.

CRIMINAL   : Biaggio Angelica, Joe Lucca, Louis Marino, Victor
ASSOCIATES   Maddi, all of Texas area, Carlos Marcello and
                 Anthony S. Carolla of New Orleans, Silvestro
                 Carolla of Italy (deportee).

CRIMINAL   : FBI #903043, New Orleans PD #24365, arrests since
HISTORY   1925 include breaking and entering, transportation
                 of firearms, possession of stolen property.

BUSINESS   : Owns and operates two Smile's Restaurants in
                 Houston, Texas.

MODUS   : Considered a member of the Mafia in the southeast
OPERANDI   area of Texas, a major figure in the prostitution
                 racket and suspected of being involved in the drug
                 traffic.

NAME	: Joseph IANNI
ALIASES	: Giuseppe Ianni.
DESCRIPTION	: Born 8-23-13 Calabria, Italy, 5'6", 146 lbs, brown eyes, black-grey hair, naturalized 2-10-45 Dallas, Texas.
LOCALITIES FREQUENTED	: Resides 5024 W. Stanford, Dallas, Texas. Frequents Vesuvio Restaurant in Dallas, Texas.
FAMILY BACKGROUND	: Wife: Marie Elizabeth Pinto; one daughter; sisters: Mrs. Frances Vallone, Mrs. Evelyn Carcelli; father: Frank (deceased); mother: Marianna Calabro.
CRIMINAL ASSOCIATES	: Joseph Civello, ███████, Biagio Angelica, & Louis Marino of Texas; Rocco & Peter Pellegrino of NYC.
CRIMINAL HISTORY	: FBI #3426142, Dallas, Texas PD# 21660. Arrests since 1946 include Federal Liquor Laws, bookmaking, murder.
BUSINESS	: Operates Vesuvio Restaurant, 5120 West Lovers Lane, Dallas, Texas.
MODUS OPERANDI	: A Mafia member from Dallas area who has taken over the position of his deceased father Frank. Associated with the Pellegrino Family of NYC, in interstate gambling & narcotic trafficking.

728

NAME	: Joseph LUCCA
ALIASES	: Joe Peter Luke, Joe Luke, Joe Rando
DESCRIPTION	: Born 8-3-01, New Orleans, La., 5'9 3/4", 165 lbs., brown eyes, black-grey hair.
LOCALITIES FREQUENTED	: Resides 3755 Childress St., Sunset Terrace Addition, Houston, Texas. Frequents Embassy Lounge, Houston, and Miami, Fla.

FAMILY BACKGROUND : Has parents believed to be residing in Miami, Fla.

CRIMINAL ASSOCIATES : Biaggio Angelica, Louis Marino, Victor Maddi, ████████, Vincent A. D'Ingianni, all of Texas.

CRIMINAL HISTORY : FBI #82535, Houston PD# 6338, arrests since 1925 include grand larceny, assault and robbery, liquor laws, conviction for Federal narcotic laws.

BUSINESS : Operates Embassy Lounge, 1508 Texas Ave., Houston, Texas.

MODUS OPERANDI : A major Mafia figure in narcotics and gambling in the southeast Texas area.

NAME   : Victor MADDI

ALIASES   : Victor Maddie, James Debrow,
                 Joseph Debro.

DESCRIPTION   : Born 4-25-05 Kansas City, Mo.
                 5'9", 170 lbs., brown eyes,
                 black hair balding on top.

LOCALITIES   : Resides 8518 Glen Valley Dr.,
FREQUENTED   Houston, Texas. Frequents
                 Swanky Inn, Boulevard Hotel,
                 & M&M Music Co., all in
                 Galveston, Texas.

FAMILY   : Wife's name is Jacqueline; sister: Josephine;
BACKGROUND   parents are deceased.

CRIMINAL   : Biagio Angelica, Louis Marino, Joe Lucca,
ASSOCIATES   & Vincent D'Ingianni, all of Houston-Galveston
                 area.

CRIMINAL   : FBI#213247. Houston PD#74099. Arrests since 1924
HISTORY   include suspicion stickup, prohibition laws,
                 interfering with Federal Officer, assault & robbery.

BUSINESS   : Associated with All Brands Beer Distributing Co.,
                 Galveston, Texas.

MODUS   : Considered an "enforcer" for the Mafia in the
OPERANDI   Houston-Galveston area. Close associate of narcotic
                 trafficker Biagio Angelica.

NAME   : Louis MARINO

ALIASES   : Louis Mariano, Louis Marano,
                  Louis Marion.

DESCRIPTION   : Born 12-25-13 Lake Charles,
                  La., 5'7", 160 lbs., blue
                  eyes, brown hair balding on
                  top.

LOCALITIES   : Resides Boulevard Hotel,
FREQUENTED   Galveston, Texas. Frequents
                  Swanky Inn, Galveston,
                  Texas, & Houston, Texas
                  area.

FAMILY   : Is separated from wife Rosalie; has 2 sons.
BACKGROUND

CRIMINAL   : Biagio Angelica, Victor Maddi, Joseph Lucca,
ASSOCIATES   Vincent D'Ingianni, all of Texas.

CRIMINAL   : FBI#743589. Houston, Texas PD#13535. Arrests
HISTORY   since 1932 include burglary, burglary & theft,
                  murder.

BUSINESS   : Associated with Biagio Angelica in operating the
                  M&M Music Co. and the H&M Music Co., both in
                  Galveston. Also operates the Swanky Inn Bar in
                  Galveston.

MODUS   : Closely associated with international drug
OPERANDI   trafficker Biagio Angelica in illegal dealings;
                  is also considered an enforcer for the Mafia in
                  the Galveston-Houston area.

NAME : Vincent James TODARO

ALIASES : Charles Todaro, Frank Todaro

DESCRIPTION : Born 1-8-14 Palermo, Sicily, naturalized NYC, 6'1", 195 lbs., black hair, brown eyes

LOCALITIES FREQUENTED : Resides Herndon, Va., (P.O. Box 23, Merrifield), currently (1959) incarcerated.

FAMILY BACKGROUND : Wife is Helen Fay, has 2 children, father is Andrea and mother is Filippina Ruoppolo (both in Italy)

CRIMINAL ASSOCIATES : George Nobile, James Massi, Ignazio and Lorenzo Orlando, Joe LoPiccolo and Frank Moccardi of NYC, also Frank Coppola, Peter Licata, Antoine Cordoliani and ▮▮▮▮▮▮▮▮ of Europe.

CRIMINAL HISTORY : FBI #534748, Extensive criminal record since 1932, including robbery, concealed weapon, receiving stolen goods, counterfeiting O.P.A. stamps, sentenced 5-20-58 to 10 years in Fairfax County, Va., violation Va., State Narcotic Laws.

BUSINESS : Landscaping and real estate dealer.

MODUS OPERANDI : An international narcotic trafficker with Mafia associates in Italy.

WISCONSIN

NAME : James Ralph CAPONE

ALIASES : "Bottles", Ralph Capper

DESCRIPTION : Born 1-12-1894, Naples,
Italy, 5'10½", 210 lbs,
brown eyes, brown & grey
hair, dark complexion and
stout build. Derivative cit.

LOCALITIES : Resides with sister at
FREQUENTED   Martha Lake near Mercer,
Wis. Frequents the Am-
bassador Hotel, Polly Valley
Motel and Fazio's Restaurant,
all in Milwaukee, Wisconsin.

FAMILY : Separated from wife Velma Pheasant. They have one son,
BACKGROUND   Francis. Father: Gabriel; mother: Theresa Rialo,
(Parents deceased); brothers: Alfonse "Al" (deceased),
Albert, Mathew & Ermino John; sisters: Mary Capone &
Malfalda Maritote, the latter residing at Mercer, Wisc.

CRIMINAL : Tony Accardo, Sam Giancana and Felice DeLucia, all of
ASSOCIATES   Chicago, Ill., ████████████, Milwaukee, Wis., and
████████████ of Mercer, Wis.

CRIMINAL : FBI #145581, Milwaukee PD #81646. First arrest
HISTORY   October, 1929, numerous other arrests for evasion
of taxes, etc. No felony convictions.

BUSINESS : Owns interest in a vending machine business in
Western Chicago.

MODUS : One of the survivors of the old "Al Capone" gang
OPERANDI   and an important member of the successor Mafia
faction in Chicago area now headed by Tony Accardo.
Gambling & prostitution interests in Mercer & Hurley,
Wisconsin.

NAME : Giuseppe COTRONI

ALIASES : Pepe, Joe Catrone, Catroni

DESCRIPTION : Born 2-22-20, Reggio Calabria Italy, 5'6½", 200 lbs,
brown eyes, brown hair balding on top.

LOCALITIES : Resides 3615 Ridgewood St.,
FREQUENTED   Apt 104, Montreal, Canada.
Frequents Metropole Club,
Bonfire Rest., Jacques Cart-
ier Motel, all in Montreal,
also Vivere Lounge on 2nd
Ave, and Hotels Edison & Lexington in NYC.

FAMILY : Single, father: Giuseppe, mother: Maria Rosa Michelotti;
BACKGROUND   brothers: Vincent, Frank, Michael; sister: Mrs. Mar-
guerite Luca.

CRIMINAL : Vincent Cotroni, ███████, ███████████, ███
ASSOCIATES   ██████, ████████████, of Montreal; Carmine Galante,
Salvatore Giglio, Angelo Tuminaro, ███████████,
Frank Moccardi, Frank Mari of NYC.

CRIMINAL : FBI #164790 D, RCMP #608. Arrests since 1937 in-
HISTORY   clude theft and receiving, theft by breaking into,
theft with violence, possession of stolen bonds.
Convicted 1959, violation Canadian Narcotic Laws.

BUSINESS : Restaurant operator in Montreal, Canada.

MODUS : Head of the largest and most notorious narcotic
OPERANDI   syndicate on the North American Continent. A
supplier of major Mafia traffickers in the U.S.
has direct French-Corsican sources of supply. Is
a terrorist and vicious hoodlum in the Montreal
area.

Known as the "Montreal Godfather," Cotroni sued Maclean's for being so dubbed, but only awarded $2. He died of cancer on September 19, 1984.

NAME	: Vincenzo COTRONI
ALIASES	: Vincent Cotroni, Catroni, Catrone, Vic Cotroni.
DESCRIPTION	: Born 11-10-10 Marina, Reggio Calabria, Italy, 5'5", 170 lbs, blue-green eyes, black hair, stocky build, dark complexion. Naturalized Canadian.
LOCALITIES FREQUENTED	: Resides 4800 Pie Neux Blvd, Montreal, Canada. Frequents Chez Paree, Montreal; Sea Gull Hotel, Miami; Hotel Nacional, Havana.
FAMILY BACKGROUND	: Married Maria Brisciani; daughter: Rosina (Mrs. Frank Guzzo); father: Giuseppe; mother: Maria-Rosa Michelotti; brothers: Giuseppe, Frank, Michael; sister: Mrs. Marguerite Luca.
CRIMINAL ASSOCIATES	: Giuseppe Cotroni, ███████████, Carmine Galante, █████████, Salvatore Giglio, Frank Moccardi.
CRIMINAL HISTORY	: FBI #415374D. Montreal Police FPS 183003. Record dates from 1928 and includes arrests for rape, false pretenses, counterfeiting, theft, receiving, felonious assault and narcotic conspiracy.
BUSINESS	: Owns Chez Paree and Vic's Cafe. Vice Pres. of Servet Agencies, Ltd., Pharmaceutical importing firm.
MODUS OPERANDI	: He and his brother head the largest & most notorious narcotic syndicate in North America. Supplies major Mafia traffickers in U.S., with heroin obtained from French-Corsican sources. A vicious hoodlum who engineers varied major crimes.

NAME : Dante GASBARRINI

ALIASES : Daniel Gasbarrini, Daniel
Basbarini, Daniel Gesberini

DESCRIPTION : Born 2-11-21 Fontechio,
L'Aquila, Italy, 5'5", 135
lbs, dark brown hair, hazel
eyes, slight build, naturalized Canadian.

LOCALITIES : Resides 749 King Rd., Bur-
FREQUENTED   lington, Ontario, Canada.
Frequents Hamilton, Burling-
ton & Guelph all in Ontario,
Canada.

FAMILY : Married Pasqualina Sylvestro (daughter of his
BACKGROUND   sister and Antonio Sylvestro; father: Luigi; mother:
Antonia Vecchioni; sisters: Celia (Claire) and
Angelina.

CRIMINAL : Antonio Sylvestro, ███████████, ███████████,
ASSOCIATES   ██████████, ████████ & ████████.

CRIMINAL : R.C.M.P. #FPS 480017. Record dates from 1939 and
HISTORY   includes arrests for receiving, theft, false pre-
tenses and narcotic law violations.

BUSINESS : Has interest in Escarpment Realty Co., and
Gasberini Construction Co.

MODUS : Taking over gradually from Antonio Sylvestro the
OPERANDI   Mafia leadershop of Ontario, Canada. Large scale
narcotic smuggler and distributor.

NAME   : Pasquale MONACHINO

ALIASES   : Pat Monachino

DESCRIPTION: Born 1-3-08 Realmonte, Sicily
                5'7", 150 lbs, brown eyes,
                brown-grey hair, I&NS #
                C-4807761, naturalized 2-8-41
                Auburn, NY.

LOCALITIES :   Resided 14 Orchard St.,
FREQUENTED   Auburn, NY, moved early in
                1959 to Ontario, Canada, &
                became Canadian citizen.

FAMILY   : Married to Josephine Zupardo; Son: Joseph; daughters:
BACKGROUND   Matilda, Lillian; father: Giuseppe; mother: Mattea
                Piazza; brother: Saverio.

CRIMINAL   : ████████, Anthony Guarnieri, Patsy Sciortino,
ASSOCIATES   Emanuel Zicari, Joe & Salvatore Falcone, Saverio
                Monachino (brother) all from up state NY area.

CRIMINAL   : No criminal history identified in FBI files or
HISTORY   Utica PD files.

BUSINESS   : Has interest in Super Beverage Co., 229 W. Genessee
                St., Auburn, New York.

MODUS   : Attended Apalachin Mafia meeting 1957 with other
OPERANDI   Mafia associates from Utica area. Engaged in Mafia
                controlled illegal rackets in the Utica area.

NAME   : Saverio MONACHINO

ALIASES   : Sam Monachino, Salvatore
                Monachino

DESCRIPTION   : Born 2-18-1893 Realmonte,
                Sicily, 5'6", 190 lbs, brown
                eyes, grey hair, heavy build,
                naturalized 5-28-27 Auburn,
                New York.

LOCALITIES   : Resided 14 Orchard St.,
FREQUENTED   Auburn, N.Y. Moved early in
                1959 to Ontario, Canada, &
                applied for Canadian citizen-
                ship.

FAMILY   : First wife deceased; present wife is Giovanna; son:
BACKGROUND   Joseph; brother: Pasquale. Father Giuseppe,mother Mattea
                Piazza.

CRIMINAL   : Patsy Monachino (brother), Salvatore & Joe Falcone,
ASSOCIATES   Patsy Sciortino,   , Emanuel Zicari,
                Anthony Guarnieri, all from up state New York area;
                Nicolo Gentile from Italy.

CRIMINAL   : FBI #771133C. This number assigned in connection
HISTORY   with prints submitted by I&NS. Has no known crim-
                inal record.

BUSINESS   : Has interests in Super Beverage Co., 229 W. Genessee
                St., Auburn, New York.

MODUS   : Attended Apalachin Mafia meeting 1957 with other
OPERANDI   Mafia associates from Utica area. Engaged with
                brother Patsy in Mafia controlled illegal activities
                in Utica area.

NAME : Antonio SYLVESTRO

ALIASES : Tony Ross

DESCRIPTION : Born 5-14-1892 St. Giorgio Morgeto, 5'7", 180 lbs, black-grey hair, brown eyes, stout, naturalized Canadian.

LOCALITIES
FREQUENTED : Resides 749 King Rd, Burlington, Ontario, Canada. Frequents Hamilton, Burlington & Guelph, all in Ontario Canada.

FAMILY
BACKGROUND : Married Angelina Gasbarrini; daughter: Pasqualina (married to Daniel Gasbarrini, brother of Angelina); brother: Frank Sylvestro @ Ross, apparently suicide 1949, but rumored to have been murdered by Antonio; nephew: Frank Sylvestro; father: Francesco; mother: Pasqualina Capra.

CRIMINAL
ASSOCIATES : Daniel Gasbarrini, ████████████, ███████████, ████████, ████████████, all of Canada, and ████████████ of New Haven, Conn.

CRIMINAL
HISTORY : R.C.M.P. #FPS 121738. Record dating from 1924 consists of arrests for assault.

BUSINESS : No legitimate occupation. Has some legitimate income from real estate.

MODUS
OPERANDI : Mafia leader in Ontario, Canada. Large scale narcotic smuggler and trafficker, closely allied with important Mafia racketeers in the U.S., Canada and Italy. Gradually turning authority over to Daniel Gasbarrini.

NAME   : Dominique ALBERTINI

ALIASES   : Charles Albert Albertini

DESCRIPTION   : Born 4-2-08 Loretto DiGascin-
                  ca (Corsica) France; French
                  (Italian descent) 5'6" 180
                  lbs, dark brown hair, brown
                  eyes, stocky build.

LOCALITIES   : Resides Boulevard DeLaCabane,
FREQUENTED   Villa Pierreverte #15, St.
                  Julien, Marseilles, France.
                  Frequents Paris & other French
                  cities, Milan, Ventimiglia,
                  San Remo & other Italian cities.

FAMILY   : Wife: Catherine Mastromauro; children: Anna Marie,
BACKGROUND   Charles Albert, Richard, Dominique; father: Charles
                  Albert; mother: Annetti Paoli; father-in-law:
                  Dominique Mastromauro.

CRIMINAL   : ████████████, ████████████, ████████████,
ASSOCIATES   ████████████, ████████████, ████████████, Jean
                  Baptiste Croce, Ignazio Bracco, Peter Gaudino.

CRIMINAL   : FBI #190608   Convicted 1952 for illegal entry into
HISTORY   U.S. & attempted bribery. Sentenced 1 yr & 1 day.

BUSINESS   : Broker, Industries-Diffusion, 118 LaCanabiere,
                  Marseilles, France.

MODUS   : One of Europe's largest narcotic smugglers and
                  wholesale dealers. Has operated heroin processing
                  laboratories in Marseilles and other French cities.
                  Source of supply for U.S. Mafia narcotic distributors.

NAME   : Marius Jacques ANSALDI

ALIASES   : None

DESCRIPTION : Born 9-9-01 Toulon, France,
                French citizen.

LOCALITIES   : Resides 8 Alle de L'Alma,
FREQUENTED   Perreux, Seine, France, fre-
                quents Hotel California,
                Cafe Murat, San Francisco
                Rest., & Carol Club all
                Paris, France.

FAMILY   : Married Jeanne Masson; no
BACKGROUND   children; father: Pierre; mother: Dominique Delfino.

CRIMINAL   : In U.S. Usche Gelb, ███████████████████, Nathan
ASSOCIATES   Behrman and Joseph Orsini; in Europe, ████████████
                ██████, ███████████████, ███████████████,
                ██████████.

CRIMINAL   : Never in U.S. 1953 was sentenced to four years im-
HISTORY   prisonment and one million francs fine for operating
                a clandestine heroin laboratory in Paris, France.
                Appealed sentence, but lost and started serving
                2-6-1957.

BUSINESS   : When gainfully employed, works as a Wine Broker.

MODUS   : Large scale illicit heroin manufacturing labora-
OPERANDI   tory operator. Supplies heroin to Mafia and other
                racketeers. Was the prime source for the Gelb-
                Behrman and Orsini-Shillitani organizations.

NAME   : Marius Antoine ARANCI

ALIASES   :

DESCRIPTION   : Born 4-16-1886, Marseilles,
                  France, Corsican descent.
                  5'6", 170 lbs, grey hair,
                  wears glasses, carries cane.

LOCALITIES   : Resides 37 Allees Leon Gam-
FREQUENTED   betta, Marseilles. Frequents
                  Bar La Daurade, rue Fortia,
                  Marseilles, France.

FAMILY   : Married Cesarine Benaglia; daughter: Jeanne (Mrs.
BACKGROUND   Raoul Battestini); father: Sauvoir; mother: Jeanne
                  Cristofini; brother: George Joseph.

CRIMINAL   : Antoine Cordoliani, ██████████████, Salvatore Man-
ASSOCIATES   cuso, ████████████; ████████████████.

CRIMINAL   : Arrested in France 1929 in possession of 5 kilos of
HISTORY   opium, 1934 in connection with 3000 kilos of opium
                  smuggled into France from Istanbul and 1959 in
                  possession of 5 kilos of heroin.

BUSINESS   : Retired merchant mariner. From time to time has
                  operated bars on the Marseilles waterfront.

MODUS   : Over the past thirty-five years or more has supplied
OPERANDI   huge quantities of heroin to Mafia associates and
                  other narcotic traffickers in the U.S. In his
                  younger days, while employed as a seaman, he acted
                  as a courier. Now he and his organization operate
                  their own laboratories for the conversion of morphine
                  base to heroin.

NAME	: Ansan Albert BISTONI
ALIASES	: Monsieur Albert, Aga Khan, Albert Bistoni, Joseph Bistoni
DESCRIPTION	: Born 11-21-1911, Marseilles, France. Corsican descent, 5'7¼", 175 lbs, dark brown hair, pale eyes.

LOCALITIES FREQUENTED	: Sometimes resides 35 rue Victor Masse, Paris, and sometimes with mother at Marseilles. Frequents Bar Villa D'Esaste & Bar Washington, Paris, also Cuba, Mexico & Canada.
FAMILY BACKGROUND	: Father: Attilion; mother: Ida Buonchristiani; mistress: Simone Prevost.
CRIMINAL ASSOCIATES	: Roger Coudert, Paul Mondoloni, Jean Baptiste Croce, ████████████, Cotroni brothers of Montreal.
CRIMINAL HISTORY	: Interpol Secretariat file #841/52 Arrested three times for narcotic trafficking. 1956 convicted of narcotic trafficking and sentenced to 3 yrs imprisonment & 5 yrs restricted residence.
BUSINESS	: Believed to have interests in the "Eve", "Cupidon" and "Pigalle" night clubs, Havana, Cuba.
MODUS OPERANDI	: Head of a large narcotic trafficking organization which smuggles morphine base into France and converts it to heroin, which is sent to the U.S. and Canada. Supplies several Mafia narcotic distributing organizations.

NAME	: Antoine CORDOLIANI
ALIASES	: Cordolerini, Cordelliano
DESCRIPTION	: Born 2-22-1890, Brando, Corsica, France. French citizen, 5'6", 150 lbs, grey hair, balding.
LOCALITIES FREQUENTED	: Resides 150B rue Paradis, Marseilles, France. Frequents Bar "La Daurade", rue Fortia, and other bars frequented by the underworld in Marseilles.
FAMILY BACKGROUND	: Married; daughters: Marthe and Mrs. Antoine Cinti; son: Emile; father: Barthelemy; mother: Catherine Causti; both parents deceased.
CRIMINAL ASSOCIATES	: Marius Aranci, ▇▇▇▇▇▇▇▇▇▇, Salvatore Mancuso.
CRIMINAL HISTORY	: Several arrests in France, dating back to the 1930's, including two narcotic trafficking convictions, 1938 and 1959.
BUSINESS	: No legitimate occupation. Former merchant seaman.
MODUS OPERANDI	: For the past thirty years or more has been supplying heroin to Mafia and other narcotic traffickers. In his early days, when employed as a seaman, he acted as courier for narcotics, but more recently he and his associates have operated their own laboratories for the conversion of morphine base to heroin.

NAME	: Roger Antoine COUDERT
ALIASES	: Charles Conte, Paul Brown, Joseph Mireault, Roy Roger, Roger Davis, Pierre Arnault.
DESCRIPTION	: Born 8-23-95 Cognac, Charente, France. French citizen, 6'2" 189 lbs, grey hair, hazel eyes, ruddy complexion, burn scars above upper lip.
LOCALITIES FREQUENTED	: Since 1954 incarcerated at Federal Penitentiary, Atlanta, Ga. Previously frequented French quarter of NYC and travelled between NYC, Canada, France, Mexico and California.
FAMILY BACKGROUND	: Married Jessie Kenmuir; father: Alexandre; mother: Lucie Nexon; no known brothers or sisters.
CRIMINAL ASSOCIATES	: Antoine D'Agostino, Paul Mondoloni, Antonino Farina, Ansan Bistoni, ▬▬▬▬▬▬▬, Cotroni brothers.
CRIMINAL HISTORY	: FBI #959779 NYCPD #E32883 Record dating from 1911 includes arrests for theft, vagrancy, fraud, assault, desertion, procuring and conspiracy. 1954 sentenced to 10 yrs & $16,000 fine for violation Federal Narcotic laws. Currently (1960) incarcerated.
BUSINESS	: Has operated several cafes in Montmartre section of Paris.
MODUS OPERANDI	: Part of a large scale narcotic smuggling organization which supplied huge quantities of heroin to Mafia racketeers in the United States and Canada.

NAME   : Jean Baptiste CROCE

ALIASES   : None

DESCRIPTION   : Born 4-9-20 Olmeto di Tuda,
                Bastia, Corsica, France,
                5'7", 185 lbs, black hair,
                stocky build.

LOCALITIES   : Resides at Marseille, France,
FREQUENTED   also 15 rue de Perre, Paris,
                France. Travels by air to
                Montreal and Havana, Cuba.
                Owns two night clubs in
                Havana, Cuba.

FAMILY   : Married; mistress: Catherine Maestracci; father:
BACKGROUND   Dominique; mothers maiden name: Annonciade.

CRIMINAL   : Joseph Albert Bistoni, Dominique Albertini, Paul
ASSOCIATES   Mondolini of Marseille, Cotroni Mob of Montreal.

CRIMINAL   : FBI #394-335C. RCMP File #57HQ1180-4-Q7. Arrested
HISTORY   in France for murder, in U.S. for immigration vio-
                lation & smuggling investigation.

BUSINESS   : Night club operator. Owns two night clubs in Havana,
                Cuba.

MODUS   : Top member of a group of French-Corsican narcotic
OPERANDI   traffickers who obtain large quantities of heroin
                from illicit laboratories in France and smuggle it
                to Mafia racketeers in the U.S., and Canada.

NAME	: Antoine D'AGOSTINO

ALIASES : Michel Sisco, Louis Floris, Antoine Scarfoni, Alberto Blasis, Albert Dujardin, Lunettes.

DESCRIPTION : Born 12-8-14 Bone, Algeria, French citizen, 5'7", 177 lbs, heavy build, dark brown hair, brown eyes.

LOCALITIES FREQUENTED : Marseille, Paris & Evereaux, France; Montreal, Canada; French rests., in NYC; Mexico City. Currently 1960 incarcerated Canada.

FAMILY BACKGROUND : Married Suzanne Filleau; daughter: Michele Theresa; wife & daughter have taken name Filleau & reside Mexico City; brothers: Albert & Stephen; father: Joseph; mother: Theresa Scarfoni. Both parents born Naples, Italy.

CRIMINAL ASSOCIATES : Joseph Orsini, Carmelo Sansone, Francois Spirito, Paul Mondoloni, Marius Ansaldi, ████████████.

CRIMINAL HISTORY : FBI #409989A. Record dates back to 1935 with arrests in Algeria & France for theft & treason. Federal narcotic conviction in U.S., & narcotic conviction Canada for which sentenced to 3 yrs in 1958.

BUSINESS : No legitimate occupation.

MODUS OPERANDI : A persistent large scale narcotic trafficker. Closely allied with top Mafia members of Europe & North America and has supplied them with huge amounts of heroin, gold & stolen jewelry.

NAME	: Jean DAVID
ALIASES	: Jean Laget, Silver Fox, Whitey

DESCRIPTION : Born 8-29-1898, Arles Bouches Du Rhone, France, 5'11", 193 lbs, white wavy hair, grey eyes, ruddy complexion, French accent. I&NS #A-465-2328.

LOCALITIES FREQUENTED : Resided at 312 W 56th St, NYC, frequented French restaurants in NY's midtown area. Currently (1960) incarcerated.

FAMILY BACKGROUND : Married Simone Alice Marcelli; no known children; annulled 12-6-43, in NYC; father: Pierre; mother: Marie Vidal; brothers: Vincent, Joseph, Marcel.

CRIMINAL ASSOCIATES : Lucien Ignaro, Ugo Rossi, Andrew Alberti, Joseph Orsini, Antoine D'Agostino, ███████████, Paul Mondoloni, John Sperandeo, ███████████, ████████; ████████████, Roger Coudert.

CRIMINAL HISTORY : FBI #3654908. Arrests since 1921 include burglary, contempt of court and narcotics. Wanted for murder in France committed in 1937. Currently serving a 10 year sentence at Leavenworth Prison. Eligible for parole at end of 1960. Subject to deportation.

BUSINESS : Was formerly a partner in Felice's Rest., 330 W 46th St, NYC, and a partner of Alfred Letourneur in Letourneur Sulky Wheels Inc., NY.

MODUS OPERANDI : Is an important member of a group which for years has smuggled large quantities of heroin into the U.S. for sale to top level Mafia narcotic traffickers.

NAME	:	Gabriel ███████████
ALIASES	:	Gaby
DESCRIPTION	:	Born ███████████████████████ ████████████, 5'5", 145 lbs, medium build, black hair, brown eyes, scar over right temple. I&NS #V-1832105.
LOCALITIES FREQUENTED	:	Resides ███████████, ████████████████████████ ████████ Travels frequently between the U.S., Canada, South America and Europe.
FAMILY BACKGROUND	:	████████████████████████████ ████████████████████████
CRIMINAL ASSOCIATES	:	Antramick Paroutian, ████████████, Jean-Baptiste Croce, ███████████, ███████████, ███████████, Andre Quendane, all of France. Giuseppe Cotroni, Joseph DiPalermo, Carmine Galante.
CRIMINAL HISTORY	:	FBI # 864135C. No record in U.S. In 1958 was arrested in Switzerland while trying to negotiate stolen Canadian securities. He was released when Canada failed to extradite.
BUSINESS	:	████████████████████████████ ███████████████████ Also owned a grocery and a coffee roasting shop. Coppersmith by trade.
MODUS OPERANDI	:	An international drug trafficker; closely associated with and trusted by top level members of the Mafia. A courier for the Croce-Nicoli-Paroutian smuggling group. Travels frequently to major cities in the U.S., Canada, South & Central America & Europe making contacts for the organization.

NAME	: Lucien IGNARO
ALIASES	: Lucian Vincent Ignaro Lucien Collonna, Frenchy
DESCRIPTION	: Born 5-10-1903, Maurice, Constantine, Algeria, 5'4", 115 lbs, black hair, blue eyes.
LOCALITIES FREQUENTED	: Resides Algiers, Algeria. 1953 deported from USA where resided 112 W. 82 St., NYC,& 46 Vine St., Roxbury, Mass.

FAMILY BACKGROUND	: Married Antoinette Navarro; no known children; father: Giro, born Algeria, de- ceased; mother: Angelina Califano, born Italy, de- ceased; sisters: Carmen Francisco, Mary Gentile, Vincenza Duquor, Daisire Perez; brother: Charles.
CRIMINAL ASSOCIATES	: ███████, ████████, Jean David, D'Agostino Brothers, Frank Tornello, Salvatore Giordano, Ugo Rossi, Andrew Alberti, ████████, Matthew Cuomo.
CRIMINAL HISTORY	: FBI #1009068 NYCPD #B139387 Record dating from 1935 includes arrests for narcotic trafficking, immigration law violation and parole violation. Two Federal Narcotic convictions and deported from U.S. three times.
BUSINESS	: No recent legitimate employment.
MODUS OPERANDI	: Has for many years been closely associated with top Mafia members in the international narcotic traffic. Has caused untold quantities of heroin to be smuggled into the United States.

NAME	: Ange Dominique LUCIANI
ALIASES	: L'Ange, Mario Luciani
DESCRIPTION	: Born 6-4-1916 Afa, Corsica, France. French citizen, 5'8", 220 lbs, stout build, black hair, brown eyes.
LOCALITIES FREQUENTED	: Resides 63 Rue deLodi, Marseilles, France. Frequents Au Drap D'Or, Fouquet's and other bars in Paris. Has visited Canada.
FAMILY BACKGROUND	: Separated from wife.
CRIMINAL ASSOCIATES	: Lucien Ignaro, ███████████, ██████████, ██████ ██████, ████████████, ███████████, █████████.
CRIMINAL HISTORY	: No arrests in the United States or Canada. Arrested for various offenses in France.
BUSINESS	: Has an interest in Au Drap D'Or, rue Bassano, Paris. Alleged to be part owner of a large hotel in Paris.
MODUS OPERANDI	: A most important international narcotic trafficker who has allied himself with top level Mafiosi. His operations cover the whole scope of narcotic trafficking, from the purchase of morphine base in Lebanon & conversion to heroin in France to the smuggling and delivery in the United States and Canada. Also engages in counterfeiting and other major crimes.

NAME   : Paul Damien MONDOLONI

ALIASES   : Paul Marie Bejin, Eduardo
                  Dubian Chabolla, Jacques
                  Desmarais, Paul Mondolini,
                  Paul Madraleni, Jean Kraeber

DESCRIPTION   : Born 9-27-1916 Sartene,
                  Corsica, France. French
                  citizen, 5'6", 140 lbs,
                  brown hair, blue eyes.

LOCALITIES   : Frequents Paris, Montreal,
FREQUENTED   Mexico City and gambling
                  casinos in Havana, Cuba.

FAMILY   : Mistress: Marcelle Senesi; father: Antoine;
BACKGROUND   mother: Marie Giacomini.

CRIMINAL   : Jean Baptiste Croce, Roger Coudert, ███████████,
ASSOCIATES   Nathan Behrman, ███████████, Giuseppe Cotroni,
                  Antoine D'Agostino.

CRIMINAL   : FBI #564009B   Arrested in U.S. for immigration
HISTORY   violation and narcotic conspiracy, in France for
                  aggravated theft and armed attack and in Mexico
                  (1960) for immigration violation.

BUSINESS   : No legitimate occupation.

MODUS   : Internationally known narcotic trafficker with
OPERANDI   associates in Canada, Mexico, Cuba, France, U.S.
                  and elsewhere. Originally became notorious as a
                  jewel thief. Closely associated with top Mafia
                  racketeers.

NAME   : Joseph ORSINI

ALIASES   : Joseph Casabianca, Joe
                  Dorney, Francois.

DESCRIPTION   : Born 3-19-03 Bastia, Corsica,
                  France, French citizen, 5'8",
                  170 lbs, brown eyes, grey
                  hair, partly bald, medium
                  build, tattoos on left arm.

LOCALITIES   : Now resides in France. For-
FREQUENTED   merly resided at 26 W. 85th
                  St, NYC and frequented
                  French Rests., in the Mid
                  Town area of NYC.

FAMILY   : Mistress: Marcelle Ansellem; father: Louis; mother:
BACKGROUND   Maria Leonetti.

CRIMINAL   : Antoine D'Agostino, Francois Spirito, Jean Laget,
ASSOCIATES   ████████, Marius Ansaldi, ████████████, Saul
                  Gelb, ████████████, Carmelo Sansone, Vincent
                  Randazzo, Salvatore Shillitani.

CRIMINAL   : FBI #708363A. He has been convicted in France for
HISTORY   fraud & robbery and collaboration with the Germans
                  during World War II. Federal narcotic & counterfeit-
                  ing convictions in U.S., for which sentenced to 10
                  years 1951. Deported from U.S., 1958.

BUSINESS   : Ex-seaman. No legitimate occupation.

MODUS   : He was the Canadian-American representative for the
OPERANDI   Ansaldi group which operated a clandestine labora-
                  tory in France and smuggled heroin in large quantities
                  to Mafia racketeers in the U.S.

NAME : Antronik PAROUTIAN

ALIASES : Andre

DESCRIPTION : Born 4-30-25 Gardonne (Bouches du Rhone), France.
French-Armenian, 5'8", 190
lbs, dark brown wavy hair,
brown eyes, stocky build,
round face.

LOCALITIES : Resides 211 Promenade de la
FREQUENTED Corniche & frequents Place de
L'Opera, both Marseilles,
France.

FAMILY : Unmarried; father: Ohannes (deceased); mother:
BACKGROUND Boyzar Armandjan (resides with Paroutian); brother:
Sauren.

CRIMINAL : Joseph DiPalermo, Carmine Galante, Ernesto Barese,
ASSOCIATES ████████████, Giuseppe DiGiorgio, Jean Baptiste
Croce, Paul Mondoloni.

CRIMINAL : Arrested 1947 for violation of the French Price
HISTORY Control Act and 1949 as a violator of the French
Economic Law. 1960 Federal narcotic conspiracy (U.S.)

BUSINESS : Purports to be in the Grocery business, operating
under the name of Gabriel & Cie, #6 Rue Bussy,
l'Indien, Marseilles, France.

MODUS : Large scale narcotic trafficker who obtains morphine
OPERANDI base in Turkey, Syria & Lebanon for conversion in
illicit laboratories in France. Smuggles furnished
heroin by way of Canada to Mafia Traffickers in the
U.S.

NAME : Pierre Dominique SIMONI

ALIASES : Nique

DESCRIPTION : Born 9-24-04 Bastia, Corsica,
France, French citizen, 5'6",
175 lbs, brown eyes, brown
hair, dark complexion, heavy
build.

LOCALITIES : Resides Hotel Les Pieds
FREQUENTED Dans L'Eau, Sanary Sur Mer,
Department of Var, France.
Paris, Marseille and other
cities in France, also Milan,
San Remo and other cities in Italy.

FAMILY : Wife: Honorine Confortini; step-son: Emilien Dallest;
BACKGROUND father: Pierre; mother: Angele Zanzauchi.

CRIMINAL : ███████████, ███████████, ███████████,
ASSOCIATES Paul Mondoloni, ███████████, ███████████,
███████████, ███████.

CRIMINAL : Record dates from 1938 and includes arrests for
HISTORY theft and trafficking in gold. In 1957 convicted
for trafficking in narcotics in Italy and sentenced
to 1 year and 4 months.

BUSINESS : Hotel Owner.

MODUS : Owned his own speed boat which he used in the
OPERANDI clandestine smuggling of gold, cigarettes and
narcotics. These he later sold to other violators
in Italy and France which was later smuggled into
the U.S., for distribution by Mafia narcotic traffickers.

NAME   : Francois SPIRITO

ALIASES   : Charles Henri Faccia,
                    Le Grand, Big Frank, Charles
                    Lamoss.

DESCRIPTION   : Born 1-23-1900 Marseilles,
                    France, French citizen, 6'0",
                    170 lbs, grey hair, brown
                    eyes, olive complexion,
                    slender build.

LOCALITIES   : Resides Marseilles, France.
FREQUENTED   In U.S. resided midtown NYC
                    and Greenwood Lake, NY. Fre-
                    quented NYC's French section, visited Montreal,
                    Canada and Cranston, Rhode Island.

FAMILY   : Son: Paul; daughter: Maria; father: Dominick; mother:
BACKGROUND   Rosina DeNola; brother: John; sister: Angelina Corona,
                    nephew: Anthony Palumbo, Cranston, R.I.

CRIMINAL   : ▮▮▮▮▮▮▮▮▮▮, Joseph Orsini, ▮▮▮▮▮▮▮▮▮▮▮▮▮▮▮,
ASSOCIATES   Carmelo Sansone, ▮▮▮▮▮▮▮▮▮▮ & Antoine D'Agostino.

CRIMINAL   : FBI #837850A. Lengthy record in France includes
HISTORY   arrests for assault & battery, theft, smuggling,
                    using false civil status & attempt against security
                    of state. Federal narcotic conviction in NYC 1951.

BUSINESS   : Bar owner & men's shop operator.

MODUS   : Well known international narcotic violator and member
OPERANDI   of one of the largest smuggling rings in France.
                    Major source of narcotics for the Joseph Orsini
                    narcotic smuggling organization.

NAME	:	Pietro AMATO
ALIASES	:	None
DESCRIPTION	:	Born 4-19-1915 at Cinisi, Palermo, Sicily, Italy, 5'6", 120 lbs, black hair, brown eyes, slender build.
LOCALITIES FREQUENTED	:	Resides Villa Archimiendi #53, Cinisi, Italy. In the U.S. resided at Chicago, Ill.
FAMILY BACKGROUND	:	Married Maria Tocopelli; father: Santo (deceased); mother: Rosalia Vitale.
CRIMINAL ASSOCIATES	:	Vito LaFata, Giuseppe Mazzella, Nicolo Maniscalco, ████████████, ████████████, ████████ █████████, █████████, Nicola Impastato and ████████████.
CRIMINAL HISTORY	:	FBI #4288748 Arrested in the United States for illegal entry and deported to Italy in 1953. Criminal record in Italy.
BUSINESS	:	Barber.
MODUS	:	Is a trusted courier for the Mafia. At the time he clandestinely immigrated to the United States he and his associates are known to have carried in with them a large quantity of pure heroin for distribution by their Mafia associates in the United States.

NAME	: Giuseppe AMORUSO
ALIASES	: Antonio Cirillo
DESCRIPTION	: Born 1-14-20 Torre Annun- ziata, Naples, Italy, 5'7½", 200 lbs, bald, brown eyes.
LOCALITIES FREQUENTED	: Resides Corso Vittorio Emanuele III, #314, Naples, Italy.
FAMILY BACKGROUND	: Father: Luciano; mother: Caterina Angrisano.
CRIMINAL ASSOCIATES	: ██████████, ████████, ██████████, ██████████, ██████████, ██████████.
CRIMINAL HISTORY	: Has been arrested and imprisoned in Italy for vio- lation of the narcotic laws and possession of fire- arms.
BUSINESS	: Shipping Agent.
MODUS OPERANDI	: Obtains heroin and/or morphine base from Beirut, Lebanon through Vitiello who has a motor-boat for this purpose. The morphine base is shipped to Marseille where it is converted to heroin and sold to Mafia racketeers in the U.S.

NAME   : Giuseppe ANZALONE

ALIASES   : None

DESCRIPTION : Born 5-25-1898 Ventimiglia
di Scilia, Prov. of Palermo,
5'6", 140 lbs, grey eyes,
black hair, thin build, dark
complexion.

LOCALITIES   : Resides at Via Umberto 77,
FREQUENTED   Ventimiglia di Sicilia. Frequents Bonito, Palermo, Montelepre, Acqua Santa (Palermo) Partinico, Monreale all
in Sicily.

FAMILY   : Father: Rosario; mother: Maddalena Bandi, (both
BACKGROUND   deceased).

CRIMINAL   : Antonio Caruso, Giorgio Misuraca, Giorgio Venezia,
ASSOCIATES   Vincenzo Cottone and ▮▮▮▮▮▮▮▮▮▮▮▮▮.

CRIMINAL   : Palermo Police #887/8 687 76 7/64. With other Mafiosi
HISTORY   Anzalone was arrested by the Palermo police in 1956.
He was exiled on the Island of Ustica for a period
of 5 years. This sentence was imposed on him by the
Palermo Exile Commission on September 8, 1956, for
his participation in the Mafia produce market war in
Sicily during 1955-56.

BUSINESS   : Farmer - owns 5 hectares of land and cultivates same.

MODUS   : Anzalone is considered by the Italian Police auth-
OPERANDI   orities as a dangerous element of the underworld, a
Mafia strong arm man and an assassin used to eliminate
recalcitrant produce merchants through shotgun "Lupara"
assassination. On November 17, 1957, he ceased to be
subject of Special Surveillance of the Public Security
authorities.

NAME : Vincenzo ATTRAENTE

ALIASES : Vincenzo Attrenti

DESCRIPTION : Born 3-25-1888, Naples, Italy
5'6", 135 lbs, thin, bald,
brown eyes, sickly looking,
always wears hat.

LOCALITIES : Resides Via Canneto il Lungo
FREQUENTED #14, Genoa, Italy. Frequents
Milan, Torino, Rome, Naples
and other Italian cities.

FAMILY : Father: Luigi; mother: Chiara Iesu.
BACKGROUND

CRIMINAL : Dominique Albertini, ███████████, ██████████████,
ASSOCIATES ████████████████, ███████████████.

CRIMINAL : Never known to be in the U.S. Criminal record
HISTORY unknown.

BUSINESS : Bar Tender.

MODUS : A top member of the Albertini gang. Obtains heroin
OPERANDI from Albertini's laboratories and disposes of it to
Mafia narcotic traffickers in the United States.
Considered on of the largest wholesale narcotic
dealers in Italy.

NAME : Gaetano BADALAMENTI

ALIASES : Tannino, Tano

DESCRIPTION : Born 9-14-23 Cinisi, Prov. of Palermo, Sicily, 5'10", 165 lbs, thin build, black hair, brown eyes, dark complexion.

LOCALITIES FREQUENTED : Resides at Via San Badalamenti #1, Cinisi, Prov. of Palermo, Sicily. Frequents Palermo, Partinico, Alcamo, Trapani, Montelepre and other Mafia strongholds in Sicily.

FAMILY BACKGROUND : Father: Vito (deceased); mother: Giuseppa Spitaleri; brothers: Vito and Giuseppe (deceased).

CRIMINAL ASSOCIATES : Vito Badalamenti, Paolo Greco, Silvestro Carollo, ██████████████, ████████████████████, ████████████, Giuseppe Indelicato, ████████████, ████████████.

CRIMINAL HISTORY : Has been arrested for various crimes including extortion, kidnapping and contraband cigarettes.

BUSINESS : Land owner and farmer.

MODUS OPERANDI : He and the other members of the notorious Badalamenti family are the ruling members of the Cinisi Mafia, dealing in narcotics and cigarettes and enforcing Mafia decrees regarding the control of the Fruit and Produce market in the Provinces of Palermo and Trapani.

765

NAME   : Vito BADALAMENTI

ALIASES   : None

DESCRIPTION   : Born 9-16-13 Cinisi, Sicily, Italy.

LOCALITIES   : Resides at Via Salvatore
FREQUENTED   Badalamenti #24, Cinisi,
                Sicily, Italy. Frequents
                Palermo, Partinico, Alcamo,
                Trapani, Montelebre and
                other Mafia strongholds in
                Sicily.

FAMILY   : Father: Vito; mother: Giuseppa Spitaleri; brothers:
BACKGROUND   Gaetano, Giuseppe (deceased); cousin: Cesare
                Badalamenti.

CRIMINAL   : Gaetano Badalamenti, ███████████, Silvestro
ASSOCIATES   Carollo, ███████, ███████, Giuseppe
                Indelicato, ███████, ███████,
                ███████, ███████.

CRIMINAL   : No known criminal record.
HISTORY

BUSINESS   : Farmer.

MODUS   : He and other members of his family are the ruling
OPERANDI   members of the Mafia in Cinisi dealing in narcotics
                and black market cigarettes and enforcing Mafia
                decrees regarding the control of the fruit and
                produce markets in the Provinces of Palermo and
                Trapani.

```
NAME          : Ugo BALZARINI

ALIASES       : None

DESCRIPTION   : Born 1-7-03, Milan, Italy,
                5'4", 160 lbs, brown hair,
                balding, brown eyes, medium
                build, light complexion.

LOCALITIES    : Resided at Via Giulio Romano
FREQUENTED      #15, Milan, Italy. Frequented
                Rome, San Remo, Genoa & other
                cities in Italy.

FAMILY        : Father: Pietro; mother:
BACKGROUND      Ester Negri.

CRIMINAL      : ██████████████, Giovanni Barilla, Armando Fiume,
ASSOCIATES      ██████████████, ██████████████.

CRIMINAL      : Has been arrested for trafficking in narcotics.
HISTORY

BUSINESS      : No legitimate occupation known.

MODUS         : With other Mafiosi he conducted a large scale
OPERANDI        narcotic traffic in Italy, obtaining the narcotics
                from French violators which was in turn sold to
                trusted U.S., customers.
```

NAME   : Giovanni BARILLA

ALIASES   : None

DESCRIPTION   : Born 10-21-10 Archi, Reggio
                 Calabria, Italy, 5'9", 175
                 lbs, brown eyes, brown hair
                 greying, medium build, dark
                 complexion.

LOCALITIES   : Resided at Via Nazionale,
FREQUENTED   Reggio Calabria, frequented
                 the cities of Milan, San
                 Remo, Naples, Rome, Genoa
                 in Italy.

FAMILY   : Father: Giuseppe; mother: Margherita Saracemo.
BACKGROUND

CRIMINAL   : ████████████, ████████████, Armando Fiume, ████████
ASSOCIATES   ████████████, Ugo Balzerini.

CRIMINAL   : Has been arrested for trafficking in narcotics.
HISTORY

BUSINESS   : Wholesale fruit and vegetable dealer.

MODUS   : Part of a Mafia group which conducted a large scale
OPERANDI   narcotic traffic in Italy, obtaining same from
                 French violators and disposing of it to trusted U.S.,
                 customers.

NAME   : Enzo BERTI

ALIASES   : None

DESCRIPTION   : Born 8-7-18 Pisa, Italy.
                 5'9", 180 lbs, brown hair,
                 brown eyes.

LOCALITIES   : At present in prison in
FREQUENTED   Switzerland. (1960)

FAMILY   : Wife: Maria Giannullo;
BACKGROUND   mother: Bruna Macchia;
                 father: Luigi Enrico.

CRIMINAL   : Costantino Gamba, Francesco Saverino, Francesco
ASSOCIATES   Pirico, ███████████, ███████████, Salvatore
                 Caneba, Ugo Caneba, Armando Fiume, ███████████.

CRIMINAL   : 1958 convicted of narcotic trafficking in Switzerland.
HISTORY

BUSINESS   : Merchant - Doctors Degree in Philosophy.

MODUS   : Together with Costantino Gamba, purchased morphine
OPERANDI   base from Turkish violators and converted same to
                 heroin. This heroin was sold to Pirico and Savarino
                 who then re-sold it to traffickers in the U.S.
                 Gamba and Berti were two of the largest clandestine
                 laboratory operators in Europe.

NAME : Francesco ████████████

ALIASES : None

DESCRIPTION : Born ████████ Palermo, Sicily, Italy. 5'7", 165 lbs, medium build, black hair, brown eyes, heavy beard, dark complexion.

LOCALITIES FREQUENTED : Resides ████████████████ ████████████. Frequents Palermo, Milan, Naples and other Italian cities, also Austria and Germany.

FAMILY BACKGROUND : ████████████████████████ ████████████████.

CRIMINAL ASSOCIATES : ████████████, Pietro Davi, ████████████, ████████████.

CRIMINAL HISTORY : Has never been in U.S. Convicted in Italy for cigarette smuggling.

BUSINESS : Textile merchant.

MODUS OPERANDI : A trusted member of the Mafia. Member of a group which supplies large quantities of heroin to distributors in the United States.

Buccola died at the age of 101 in 1987.

NAME : Philip BUCCOLA

ALIASES : Philip Bucollo, Phil Bucalo,
Filippo Bruccola.

DESCRIPTION : Born 8-6-86 Palermo, Sicily
5'7", 167 lbs, medium build,
brown-grey hair, brown eyes,
dark complexion, naturalized
Boston, Mass., in 1927,
holds American passport
#31902 as Filippo Bruccola.

LOCALITIES : Resides Azienda Agraricola
FREQUENTED Sicilone, Via Magni 9,
Pallavecino, Palermo, Sicily. When in Boston Frequents
Giro's Cafe and the European Restaurant.

FAMILY : Father Vincent, mother Nina Blandino, both dead,
BACKGROUND married to Rosena McDonough, has nephew Joseph Buccola
and wife's nephew Richard Hogan both pin-ball machine
operators Boston.

CRIMINAL : Salvatore Lucania, Joseph Doto, Frank Cucchiara,
ASSOCIATES Raymond Patriarca, Henry Selvitella, ███████████,
Albert Santaniello, Joseph Lombardo, and all top
ranking hoodlums in the Boston area.

CRIMINAL : FBI #847638, Mass. State Police #138536, 1st arr-
HISTORY est in 1923 for carrying a loaded weapon, paid $100
fine. Additional arrests for gambling and suspicion
of murder.

BUSINESS : Owns shares Revere dog track, has money invested
in Hotel Bostonian.

MODUS : Went to Sicily in 1954. In Boston was head of New
OPERANDI England Mafia, came to Boston 2 weeks before Apalachin
meeting (1957), returned to Sicily shortly thereafter.

NAME	: Egidio CALASCIBETTA
ALIASES	: None
DESCRIPTION	: Born 2-10-1898 Alimena, Palermo, Sicily, 5'9", 180 lbs, brown eyes, brown hair-greying, dark complexion, tinted glasses.

LOCALITIES FREQUENTED	: Resides Via Vittorio Pisani #12 Milan, Italy. Travels to Naples, Torino, Trieste and Rome, Italy.
FAMILY BACKGROUND	: Father: Pietro; mother: Lucia D'Amico.
CRIMINAL ASSOCIATES	: Lucky Luciano, Joseph Biondo, Joe Pici, Francesco Pirico, Francesco Paolo Coppola.
CRIMINAL HISTORY	: Never in the U.S. Record in Italy, dating from 1931 includes arrests for bankruptcy and criminal use of rubber stamps, tobacco smuggling, fraud, forgery & narcotic law violation.
BUSINESS	: An important business man who, with Prof. Guglielmo Bonomo, owned Sace, a chemical corp., in Milan. Also headed an organization which included at least six pharmaceutical companies.
MODUS OPERANDI	: Was responsible for the diversion of 716 kilograms of heroin from the Schiapparelli Company to the Lucky Luciano mob which then smuggled it into the U.S. He has continued close association with the Luciano mob and is therefor still a strong threat in the narcotic traffic.

NAME	: Francesco CAMMARATA

ALIASES : Commarata, Commarats, Sam
Morecia

DESCRIPTION : Born 5-16-1898 San Cataldo,
Caltanissetta, Sicily, 5'11",
160 lbs, grey-black hair,
hazel eyes, dark complexion.

LOCALITIES : When in the U.S., frequented
FREQUENTED Detroit, Mich, Warren &
Youngstown, Ohio. In December 1958 he left U.S. for
Cuba to avoid deportation,
then proceeded to Lisbon & Rome. Present location
unknown.

FAMILY : Married Grace Licavoli, sister to notorious Peter
BACKGROUND Licavoli; three children, came to U.S. as an orphan
in 1913.

CRIMINAL : Peter ▆▆▆▆ Licavoli, Jos "Scarface" Bommarito,
ASSOCIATES Joseph "Long Joe" Bommarito, Giuseppe Catalanotte,
▆▆▆▆▆▆▆.

CRIMINAL : FBI #9739. Detroit PD#19408. I&NS #A-6-337-006.
HISTORY Record dates from 1922 and includes arrests for
armed robbery, disorderly person, possession offen-
sive weapon, bond jumping, violation immigration
laws, etc.

BUSINESS : No legitimate employment.

MODUS : Mafia killer, holdup man and narcotics distributor.
OPERANDI In the 1920's was a bootlegger and a member of
Detroits notorious "Purple Gang".

NAME   : Salvatore CANEBA

ALIASES   : Toto, John Sperandeo

DESCRIPTION   : Born 10-24-01 Palermo, Sicily
                5'6", 180 lbs, heavy build,
                black-greying hair, balding,
                brown eyes; poor english,
                fluent Italian-French.

LOCALITIES   : Resides via Priscioan #69,
FREQUENTED   Rome, Italy, frequently
                travels to Palermo & Milan,
                Italy, also Germany, France
                & Switzerland. Before de-
                portation resided 3425 89th St, Jackson Heights, NY,
                and frequented vicinities of 1st Ave & 11th St, 2nd
                Ave & 106th St, NYC.

FAMILY   : Married Irene Pluber (last reported living NYC with
BACKGROUND   their son); father: Giuseppe; mother: Marianna Ania
                (sister of late Pasquale Ania former head of Mafia
                in Italy); brothers: Giosue, Giovanni & Ugo.

CRIMINAL   : William LoCascio, Samuel Kass, ▓▓▓▓▓▓▓▓▓, Sorci
ASSOCIATES   brothers (Palermo), Rosario Mancini, ▓▓▓▓▓▓▓
                ▓▓▓▓▓▓▓, Lucky Luciano, and Ugo Caneba (brother).

CRIMINAL   : FBI # 611860B. European record dates from 1918 and
HISTORY   includes arrests for theft, criminal conspiracy,
                armed assault, receiving, etc., in Italy & France.
                Expelled from France 1936. Record in U.S. dates from
                1950 & includes arrests for violation of Immigration
                and Federal Narcotic Laws; deported from U.S. 1954.

BUSINESS   : Claims to be in finance & loan business.

MODUS   : A prominent Mafia member. One of the largest narcotic
OPERANDI   smugglers & wholesale dealer in Italy, in partnership
                with his brother, Ugo, purchases pure heroin from
                major Corsican gangsters in Marseilles & Paris, France
                & ships it to customers in the U.S.

NAME	: Ugo CANEBA
ALIASES	:
DESCRIPTION	: Born 3-18-10 Palermo, Sicily, Italy, 5'4", 140 lbs, brown eyes, brown hair, balding, dark complexion, medium build skin discoloration right temple.
LOCALITIES FREQUENTED	: Resides via Priscioano #69, Rome, Italy, frequently travels to Palermo & Milan, Italy.
FAMILY BACKGROUND	: Married; father: Giuseppe; mother: Marianna Anea, (sister of late Pasquale Anea the former head of Mafia in Italy); brothers: Salvatore, Giosue and Giovanni.
CRIMINAL ASSOCIATES	: William LoCascio, Lucky Luciano, Serafino Mancuso, Rosario Mancino, ███████████, Sorci Brothers.
CRIMINAL HISTORY	: No FBI #. Arrested in Italy 1955 for traffic in contraband and 1957 in connection with the Berti-Gamba narcotic case.
BUSINESS	: Claims to be in finance & loan business.
MODUS OPERANDI	: Prominent Mafioso. Was the Italian agent for his brother, Salvatore Caneba, while the latter was in U.S. Now, in partnership with his brother, purchases pure heroin from Corsican gangsters in France and ships it to U.S. customers.

NAME   : Silvestro CAROLLO

ALIASES   : Sam Caroua, Silva Carollo,
                   Sylvestre Carollo, Sam
                   Carolla.

DESCRIPTION   : Born 6-17-1896, Terrasini,
                   Palermo, Sicily, 5'6", 170
                   lbs, black hair sparse,
                   brown eyes, dark complexion,
                   scar left upper lip.

LOCALITIES   : Resides Terrasini, Palermo,
FREQUENTED   Sicily. Frequents the cities
                   of Palermo & Cinisi in
                   Sicily.

FAMILY   : Married Caterina; sons: Anthony & Salvatore (New
BACKGROUND   Orleans, La.); father: Michel; mother: Serafina
                   Bommarito.

CRIMINAL   : Francesco Coppola, Jack Ancona, ███████████████,
ASSOCIATES   Gaetano Badalamenti, Salvatore (Sam) Vitale.

CRIMINAL   : FBI # 84223. New Orleans PD #13819.
HISTORY   Record dates back to 1923 and includes arrests for
                   violation of the alcohol & Federal narcotic laws,
                   attempt murder of a narcotic agent. Deported in
                   1947 and again in 1951. In Italy arrested in 1952
                   for swindling, trafficking in drugs.

BUSINESS   : Has legitimate investments in the New Orleans, La,
                   area. Owns & operates a cafe at Terrasini, Sicily.

MODUS   : Top level Mafioso. Has been active for many years
OPERANDI   in large scale narcotic trafficking and arms smug-
                   gling.

Carrollo was imprisoned in 1940 for tax evasion, among other offenses. He was released from prison in 1954 and died in 1979, at the age of 77, from natural causes.

NAME : Charles Vincenzo CARROLLO

ALIASES : None

DESCRIPTION : Born 8-25-02 Santa Cristina, Gela, Sicily, Italy, 5'8½", 237 lbs, brown eyes, black hair, balding.

LOCALITIES FREQUENTED : Last reported living at Palermo, Sicily. Lived in Kansas City, Mo., before deportation in 1954. I&NS # A-5548437.

FAMILY BACKGROUND : Married Carolina DiMaggio; son: Anthony Charles; daughters: Mrs. Rose Marie Falco, Mrs. Anna Marie Arnone, Mrs. Antoinette Cipolla, Carol and Kathy; father: Anthony; mother: Rose; brothers: Salvatore, Peter, John, Frank, Joseph and Carlo.

CRIMINAL ASSOCIATES : Lucky Luciano, ███████████, Nicola Impastato, Joseph DeLuca.

CRIMINAL HISTORY : FBI #70586. Kansas City S.O. #8780. Record dating from 1921 includes arrests for grand larceny, bootlegging, misuse of U.S. Mails, income tax evasion, perjury, gambling and immigration violation.

BUSINESS : Owned and still has income from grocery & drug stores at Kansas City, Missouri.

MODUS OPERANDI : High ranking Mafia criminal. Engaged in narcotic trafficking, bootlegging and other illicit activities in U.S. Also known as a "fixer" with strong political connections.

NAME   : Antonino CARUSO

ALIASES   : None

DESCRIPTION   : Born 6-7-1897 Palermo,
                 Sicily, 5'9", 165 lbs, med-
                 ium build, brown eyes, grey
                 hair, dark complexion.

LOCALITIES   : Resides at Cortile Casalini
FREQUENTED   #8, Palermo, Sicily. Fre-
                 quents Partinico, Monreale,
                 Montelepre, San Giuseppe
                 Iato all in Sicily.

FAMILY   : Father: Rosario; mother: Grazia Rubino (both de-
BACKGROUND   ceased); relatives in the U.S.: Antonino Caruso,
                 Francesco Caruso and Carolina Caruso, all living in
                 Madison, Wisconsin.

CRIMINAL   : Giorgio Misuraca, Vincenzo Cottone, Giorgio Venezia,
ASSOCIATES   Giuseppe Anzalone.

CRIMINAL   : Palermo, Italy Police #345 308 3444. With other
HISTORY   Mafiosi, Caruso was arrested by the Palermo police
                 during 1956. He was exiled on the Island of Ustica
                 for a period of 1 year. This sentence was imposed on
                 him by the Palermo Exile Commission on September 29,
                 1956, for his participation in the Mafia produce mar-
                 ket war in Sicily during 1955-56.

BUSINESS   : Fruit vendor, lives modestly.

MODUS   : Caruso is considered by the Italian police authori-
OPERANDI   ties as a dangerous element of the underworld, a
                 Mafia strong arm man and an assassin used to elimin-
                 ate recalcitrant produce merchants through shotgun
                 "lupara" assassination.

NAME	: Vincenzo CATALANOTTE
ALIASES	: Vincenzo Cantalonoti, Jimmy

DESCRIPTION	: Born 8-24-1896 Alcamo, Trapani, Sicily, 5'7", 160 lbs, brown eyes, black-grey hair, balding.
LOCALITIES FREQUENTED	: Resides Via Stefano Polizzi & Via T. Tasso, Alcamo, Sicily. Frequents Palermo, Trapani, Castellammare del Golfo, Partinico & other cities in Sicily.
FAMILY BACKGROUND	: Married Marie Taormina (separated & she lives in the U.S.); father: Liberio; mother: Vincenza Giacolone; brothers: Benedetto (Alcamo) & Giuseppe (Detroit).
CRIMINAL ASSOCIATES	: Giuseppe ████████ Catalanotte (████████), ██████ ████████, Giuseppe Manino, Serafino Mancuso and Salvatore Vitale (missing).
CRIMINAL HISTORY	: FBI #292994 Detroit PD #22883 Record in U.S. dates from 1924, when arrested for disorderly conduct. Federal narcotics conviction 1930 & deported to Italy 1934. 1940 sentenced in Italy to 13 yrs for aggravated theft, pardoned 1944. Several other arrests in Italy.
BUSINESS	: Wine merchant.
MODUS OPERANDI	: Catalanotte, his brothers and other Mafia criminals smuggled into the U.S. large amounts of heroin. At the present time he is a large scale cigarette smuggler, obtaining cigaretts in Tangiers and bringing them to Italy for resale on the black market.

NAME : Joseph CATALANOTTO

ALIASES : Joe Contelanotte, Joe
Catalanotte, Joe Catalanote,
Joe Catonoa, Cockeyed Joe,
The old man.

DESCRIPTION : Born 8-8-01 Salemi, Sicily,
5'7", 160 lbs., black hair,
brown eyes, medium build,
wears glasses.

LOCALITIES : Former resident Detroit,
FREQUENTED   Mich., deported 1957 to Italy
returned clandestinely to
U.S., and Cuba, deported to
Italy again 1959 from Cuba.

FAMILY : Married to Mary Ann Ruisi who lives in Windsor, Canada;
BACKGROUND   two daughters, Virginia and Angela Marie, brother,
Benedict, father, Liborio, mother Vincenza Ciacalone.

CRIMINAL : William Tocco, John Priziola, Peter Lombardo, Peter
ASSOCIATES   Gaudino, Paul Cimino, John Ormento, Rafaele Quasarano,
Frank Coppola.

CRIMINAL : FBI #3825453, Detroit PD# 15556, numerous arrests
HISTORY   since 1921 including assault with intent to kill,
murder, extortion, and conviction for Federal Narcotic
Laws.

BUSINESS : No known legitimate sources of income.

MODUS : An international trafficker of illicit drugs; a very
OPERANDI   important member of the Detroit Mafia, who is expected
to work with other Mafia deportees in Italy in the
International traffic.

NAME : Francesco Paolo COPPOLA

ALIASES : Frank Cappola, Jim Barbero, Frank Loicono, Angelo Vota, Frank Lomonde, Don Ciccio

DESCRIPTION : Born 10-6-1899, Partinico, Sicily, 5'2", 150 lbs, blue eyes, brown-grey hair, ring & little fingers of left hand amputated.

LOCALITIES FREQUENTED : Resides Localita San Lorenzo, Ardea, Rome, Italy, also Partinico, Sicily. Has resided Detroit, Kansas City, Los Angeles, Rock Island, Ill, also Mexico. Deported from U.S., 1-9-48.

FAMILY BACKGROUND : Wife: Leonarda Chimenti; daughter: Pietra; father: Francesco; mother: Pietra Loicano; son-in-law: Giuseppe Corso, Jr.; Fay Tavolacci, his ex-mistress, lives in Detroit, Mich.

CRIMINAL ASSOCIATES : Lucky Luciano, Phil Kastel, Carlos Marcello, ███████ ████████, ███████████████, Giuseppe Corso, Sr.

CRIMINAL HISTORY : FBI # 549933. Suspect in several Mafia murders, fled Sicily in 1926 to avoid prosecution. Record in U.S. dates from 1931 and includes arrests for murder & bootlegging. Narcotic convictions U.S., & Italy.

BUSINESS : Claims to be a farmer and exporter-importer. Still receives money from illicit interests in the U.S.

MODUS OPERANDI : Dangerous criminal and killer. In the narcotic traffic for many years and an important link in the international narcotic traffic. High Mafia leader who hears grievances, then orders restitution or assassination.

```
NAME         : Giuseppe CORSO JR.

ALIASES      : None

DESCRIPTION  : Born 6-10-27 Partinico,
               Trapani Sicily, brown eyes,
               black hair, dark complexion,
               medium build.
```

```
LOCALITIES   : Two residences, one at
FREQUENTED     Partinico, Sicily and the
               other at the home of his
               father-in-law, Francesco
               Paolo Coppola, at localita
               San Lorenzo, Ardea, Rome.
               Frequents Alcamo and Palermo, Sicily.

FAMILY       : Wife: Pietra Coppola (daughter of Francesco Coppola);
BACKGROUND     father: Giuseppe, Sr.; mother: Antoinetta Nania.

CRIMINAL     : Frank Coppola, Giuseppe Corso, Sr., Vito Vitale,
ASSOCIATES     ████████████████, Raphael Quasarano and Lucky
               Luciano.

CRIMINAL     : He was arrested in 1952 along with Coppola for
HISTORY        being involved in the seizure of 6 kilograms of
               heroin, at Alcamo, Sicily. Has never been to USA.

BUSINESS     : He claims to be a farmer and salesman.

MODUS        : Underling of his father and Francesco Paolo Coppola,
OPERANDI       both important Mafia figures. He makes contact for
               Coppola with other members of the Mafia when it is
               inopportune for Coppola to personally be involved.
```

```
NAME         : Giuseppe CORSO, SR.

ALIASES      : None

DESCRIPTION  : Born 4-10-1899, Partinico,
               Sicily, Italy, 6'0", 200 lbs,
               brown eyes, brown hair, dark
               complexion, small vertical
               scar on his left cheek.

LOCALITIES   : Resides at Partinico, Sicily
FREQUENTED     and frequents the farm of
               Francesco Paolo Coppola at
               Localita San Lorenzo, Ardea,
               Rome. Visits Alcamo & Paler-
               mo area of Sicily.
```

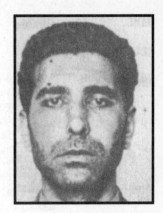

```
FAMILY       : Married Maria Antoinetta Nania; son: Giuseppe, Jr.,
BACKGROUND     (who married Frank Coppola's daughter); father:
               Giuseppe; mother: Margherita Tortorici.

CRIMINAL     : Francesco Paolo Coppola, Raphael Quasarano, Lucky
ASSOCIATES     Luciano, ███████████, G. Manini.

CRIMINAL     : Never in U.S.  Has criminal record in Italy com-
HISTORY        mencing before 1930. Because of his Mafia activities
               was proposed for exile by the old Italian government.

BUSINESS     : Claims to be farmer and salesman.

MODUS        : Silent partner of Francesco Paolo Coppola. Highly
OPERANDI       respected in Mafia circles and has raised his son in
               the Mafia tradition.
```

```
NAME          : Giuseppe COTTONE

ALIASES       :

DESCRIPTION   : Born 9-6-16 Villabate, Pal-
                ermo, Sicily, 5'7", 170 lbs,
                brown eyes; black hair; flat
                nose with large nostrils;
                square face, bushy & arched
                eyebrows; dark complexion.
```

```
LOCALITIES    : Villabate, Montelepre; Alta-
FREQUENTED      fonte; all Prov. of Palermo,
                Sicily.

FAMILY        : Father: Antonino; mother: Maria Fontana; brothers:
BACKGROUND      Vincenzo & Antonino.

CRIMINAL      : Michele Bruno, ████████████, ████████,
ASSOCIATES      ████████████, ████████████, ████████████,
                ████████████, and his brother Vincenzo Cottone.

CRIMINAL      : Palermo, Sicily Police #894684-3648, photo #32995.
HISTORY         With other Mafiosi Cottone was arrested by the Pal-
                ermo Police 9-11-56, was exiled on the Island of
                Ustica for a period of 4 years.  This sentence was
                imposed on him by the Provincial Commission for
                Provision of Exile for his participation in the
                Mafia produce market war in Sicily during 1955-56.

BUSINESS      : Salesman.

MODUS         : Is considered by the Italian Police Authorities as
OPERANDI        a dangerous element of the underworld.  This hood-
                lum is considered a Mafia strong arm man, an assa-
                sin used to eliminate recalcitrant produce mer-
                chants through shotgun "lupara" assasination.
```

NAME   : Vincenzo COTTONE

ALIASES   :

DESCRIPTION   : Born 8-21-10, Villabate,
                  Palermo, Sicily, 5'5", 165
                  lbs, dark brown hair-bald
                  top, brown eyes, heavy build
                  square face, large mouth,
                  thick eyebrows, dark com-
                  plexion, 10 stitches over
                  heart area, appendectomy.

LOCALITIES   : Villabate; Montelepre;
FREQUENTED   Altafonte; all Prov. of
                  Palermo, Sicily.

FAMILY   : Father: Antonino; mother: Maria Fontana; brothers:
BACKGROUND   Antonino, Guiseppe.

CRIMINAL   : Michele Bruno; ███████████; ███████████;
ASSOCIATES   ███████████; ███████████; ███████████
                  ███████; and his brother Guiseppe Cottone.

CRIMINAL   : Palermo, Sicily Police #226-354-3634. With other
HISTORY   Mafiosi, Cottone was arrested by the Palermo
                  police on September 7, 1956. He was exiled to the
                  Island of Ustica for a period of 5 yrs. This
                  sentence was imposed on him by the Palermo Exile
                  Commission on October 5, 1956 for his participation
                  in the Mafia produce market war in Sicily during
                  1955-56.

BUSINESS   : Cattle merchant

MODUS   : This hoodlum is considered a Mafia strong arm man,
OPERANDI   an assassin used to eliminate recalcitrant produce
                  merchants through shotgun "lupara" assassination.

NAME : Pietro DAVI

ALIASES : None

DESCRIPTION : Born 10-24-1907, Palermo, Sicily, Italy, 5'6", 175 lbs, black hair, brown eyes, medium build, medium complexion.

LOCALITIES FREQUENTED : Resides Via Salvatore Mettio #25, Palermo. Frequents all parts of Sicily, Northern Italy, Mexico & Canada.

FAMILY BACKGROUND : Father: Francesco; mother: Natalia LaBarbaria.

CRIMINAL ASSOCIATES : ███████████████, Lucky Luciano, ███████████, ███████████████, Nicola Gentile, Joseph Biondo, ███████████, ███████████, ███████████████, ███████, ███████████ & Rosario Mancino.

CRIMINAL HISTORY : Convicted in Italy for trafficking in contraband cigarettes & sentenced to 3 years & 3 months in jail.

BUSINESS : Large property holdings.

MODUS OPERANDI : Large scale cigarette and narcotic smuggler who uses fast motorboats for his smuggling activities in Italy. The smuggled cigarettes are sold on the black market in Italy and the narcotics sent to Mafia narcotic traffickers in the U.S. He is part of a group which in 1950 engineered the diversion of 200 kilograms of German Army cocaine to illicit markets, chiefly in the United States.

In 1970, Di Carlo was arrested for extortion and sentenced to twelve years, but was pardoned by President Nixon after serving a year and a half. He died on October 20, 1973, at the age of 82. His death came five days before a deadline to pay a $20,000 fine from his 1970 conviction.

NAME : Angelo DI CARLO

ALIASES : Anniello Di Carlo, U Capitano, The Captain.

DESCRIPTION : Born 2-8-1891, Corleone, Palermo, Sicily, 5'10", 180 lbs, grey hair, brown eyes, heavy build.

LOCALITIES FREQUENTED : Resides Corleone, Sicily, Italy. Lived in the U.S., from 1926 to 1947, then deported to Italy.

FAMILY BACKGROUND : Father: Vincenzo; mother: Luisa Castro; brothers: Calogero (Lelio), Giovanni, Giuseppe, Francesco and Salvatore; sisters: Rosina Castro and Marianni Piazza.

CRIMINAL ASSOCIATES : Francesco Paolo Coppola, ████████████, Francesco Pirico, Lucky Luciano.

CRIMINAL HISTORY : FBI #3804752. Has criminal record in Italy for murder, extortion, assault and narcotic law violation. In the U.S. he was interned from 1943 to 1947 as enemy alien.

BUSINESS : At various times has been engaged in travel agency business with his brothers.

MODUS OPERANDI : DiCarlo and his brothers utilized their travel agency to facilitate the smuggling of gold, counterfeit money, narcotics, pharmaceuticals and aliens between Italy and U.S. and the exchange of funds for underworld interests. Was a killer in his youth and now directs assassinations for the Mafia.

```
NAME          : Giovanni DI PIETRO

ALIASES       : John DiPietro

DESCRIPTION   : Born 5-20-1906, Licodia
                Eubia, Catania, Sicily,
                Italy, 5'2½", 148 lbs, black
                hair, brown eyes, stocky.

LOCALITIES    : Resides Catania, Sicily.
FREQUENTED      Frequented Naples, Rome,
                Palermo and other Italian
                cities, but since 1953 has
                been confined to live within
                the limits of the city of
                his birth.
```

```
FAMILY        : Father: Gaetano (deceased); mother: Teresa Pandoro;
BACKGROUND      brothers: Vincenzo, Joseph; sisters: Francesca Cola-
                sante and Vincenza; brother-in-law: Dominick Cola-
                sante; uncle: Carmelo Aliotta; aunt: Concetta Aliotta.

CRIMINAL      : Lucky Luciano, Giuseppe Pici, ███████████████,
ASSOCIATES      ████████████████, Vincenzo DiPietro (brother).

CRIMINAL      : FBI #202014   Record in U.S. dating from 1924 in-
HISTORY         cludes arrests for grand larceny, burglary and vio-
                lation of probation.  Federal narcotic conviction
                1942.  Deported from U.S. on 6-24-49.

BUSINESS      : No legitimate occupation.

MODUS         : Is a trusted member of the Mafia.  In the past he
OPERANDI        has been involved in large scale narcotic trafficking
                between the U.S. and Italy.  Upon being deported
                from the U.S. he became the bodyguard of Lucky
                Luciano.
```

Doto died of natural causes in the town of Acona, Italy on November 26, 1971. His remains were sent to the U.S. and buried on December 6, 1971, in Fort Lee, NJ.

NAME : Giuseppe Antonio DOTO

ALIASES : Joe Adonis, Joe DeMio, Joe Arrosa, Joe Arressa, "Doto", James Arrosa.

DESCRIPTION : Born 11-22-02, Montemarano, Avellino, Naples, Italy, 5'9½", 175 lbs, brown eyes, dark brown hair, greying. Voluntarily left the U.S. 1-3-56, for Italy while deportation proceedings still pending against him.

LOCALITIES FREQUENTED : Resides, Via Albricci 2, Milano, Italy. Owns a villa at Lake Como, Italy. Frequents the better restaurants and night clubs in Milan, also the Hotel Francia and Excelsior Gallia Palace in Milan.

FAMILY BACKGROUND : Married Jean Montimorano; son: Joseph A. Doto, Jr.; daughters: Maria Dolores, Ann Marie and Elizabeth; father: Michele; mother: Maria DeVito; brothers: Antonio, Ettore and Genesio.

CRIMINAL ASSOCIATES : Willie Moretti, Albert Anastasia, Philip Mangano, Frank Scalice all of whom died by violence, Lucky Luciano, Anthony Strollo, Meyer Lansky, John Bart Salvo, Vito Genovese.

CRIMINAL HISTORY : FBI #500203. NYCPD B#64766. Record dates from 1926 & includes arrests for grand larceny, robbery, liquor smuggling, carrying a concealed weapon, kidnapping, extortion, assault and others.

BUSINESS : Numerous business enterprises in U.S. Haiti & Italy.

MODUS OPERANDI : Powerful Mafia figure, became wealthy through bootlegging, gambling & narcotic trafficking, then put money and Mafia tactics into legitimate and semi-legitimate enterprises. American Mafiosi going to Italy contact Doto for advice and assistance. Also bring him large sums of money obtained from his enterprises in U.S.

NAME : Antonio FARINA

ALIASES : Nino, Antonio Farina Bono

DESCRIPTION : Born 6-3-12 Palermo, Sicily, 5'9½", 221 lbs, black hair, (bald), brown eyes, heavy build, speaks only Italian, 4" scar on right side of face from ear to neck.

LOCALITIES FREQUENTED : Resided Via Antonio Scioscia #1 Palermo, Italy until the middle of 1959 when he disappeared. He is suspected of having clandestinely emigrated to Canada, South America or Mexico. Before 1953 arrest, resided Paseo De la Reforma #489 Mexico City and travelled frequently to the U.S. Present whereabouts unknown.

FAMILY BACKGROUND : Wife: Rosa resides Sicily with their four children, Gioia, Bina, Massimo and Elvira; in Mexico had paramour Lina D'Orlando DiBello; father: Antonino; mother: Lucia Bono.

CRIMINAL ASSOCIATES : Roger Coudert, Antoine D'Agostino, Paul Mondoloni, John Sperandeo, Antonino Sorci, Antoine Cordoleani, ████████████ & Paolo Greco, all of Italy.

CRIMINAL HISTORY : FBI #525025B. USM NY# C-1652-53. Arrested in 1953 for violation Federal Narcotic Laws, sentenced April 1954 to serve 5 yrs & fined $10,000.00. In Italy has arrests since 1928 for living off profits of prostitution, violence, carrying a knife & fraud.

BUSINESS : Owns Real Estate in Sicily. In Mexico operated dry goods store.

MODUS OPERANDI : Important Mafia narcotic trafficker. Acts as middle man between French & Italian sources of supply & customers in the U.S.

NAME	: Armando FIUME
ALIASES	: None
DESCRIPTION	: Born 7-7-07 Villa San Giovanni, Reggio Calabria, Italy, 5'6", 165 lbs, brown hair, greying, brown eyes, medium build, light complexion.
LOCALITIES FREQUENTED	: Resides at Via Petrella #8, Milan, Italy. Frequents Genoa, San Remo, Rome & other cities in Italy.
FAMILY BACKGROUND	: Father: Giuseppe, mother: Carolina Cimino.
CRIMINAL ASSOCIATES	: Enzo Berti, ███████████, ███████████, Giovanni Barilla, ███████████, ███████████.
CRIMINAL HISTORY	: Has been arrested for narcotic trafficking.
BUSINESS	: Clothing Salesman.
MODUS OPERANDI	: Part of a Mafia group which obtained heroin from French sources and disposed of it to trusted customers in the U.S.

NAME   : Costantino GAMBA

ALIASES   : None

DESCRIPTION   : Born 2-14-15 Flumeri, Avel-
                lino, Italy, 5'7", 185 lbs,
                brown eyes, dark brown hair,
                dark complexion.

LOCALITIES   : Resided at Via Brocchi #3,
FREQUENTED   Milan, Italy. Frequented,
                Milan, Rome, Genova, Italy
                and Zurich, Switzerland.

FAMILY   : Father: Giuseppe; mother:
BACKGROUND   Maria Grella.

CRIMINAL   : Francesco Pirico, Francesco Savarino, Dr. Enzo Berti,
ASSOCIATES   ██████████, ██████████████.

CRIMINAL   : Never in United States. Record dates from 1950, when
HISTORY   he was arrested in Italy for trafficking in narcotics.
                At present is a fugitive from Swiss justice for the
                violation of their narcotic laws.

BUSINESS   : Owned a pharmaceutical laboratory in Milan, Italy.

MODUS   : Together with Dr. Enzo Berti, purchased morphine
OPERANDI   base from Turkish violators and converted same to
                heroin. This heroin in turn was sold to Pirico and
                Savarino who then re-sold it to traffickers in the
                U.S. Gamba and Berti were two of Europe's largest
                converters of morphine base to heroin.

NAME : Francesco GASSISI

ALIASES : Vincenzo Massi

DESCRIPTION : Born 6-2-02 Contessa Entellina, Prov. of Palermo,
Sicily, 5'9" 180 lbs, brown
eyes, bald, large build,
light complexion.

LOCALITIES : Resides at Via Morea #71,
FREQUENTED Contessa Entellina. Frequents Palermo, Monreale,
Partinico and other cities
in Sicily.

FAMILY : Father: Giuseppe (deceased), mother: Giovanna Foto
BACKGROUND (deceased); brother: Giuseppe. A sister (name unknown) is married to one Antonino Cuccia and lives
in Venezuela.

CRIMINAL : ██████████████(████████), ██████████████, ████████
ASSOCIATES ██████, ████████████████████, ██████████████████,
████████████████████.

CRIMINAL : Never in U.S. Has a lengthy criminal record in Italy,
HISTORY including aggravated robbery, conspiracy, kidnapping
and other violent crimes.

BUSINESS : Unemployed, though in fairly good financial condition.

MODUS : As far back as 1925 was a member of a Mafia group in
OPERANDI Sicily engaged in cattle rustling, pillaging, kidnapping, armed robbery & extortion. Has continued
his criminal activities to the present date and is
feared by his townsmen because of his violent nature
and past record.

He recieved an "underworld death sentence" after publishing his Mafia experiences in his 1963 memoirs, but managed to escape the sentence and and died of natural causes on November 6, 1966.

NAME   : Nicola GENTILE

ALIASES   : Zio Cola, Nick, Don Cola, Cola Gentile

DESCRIPTION   : Born 6-12-1895 Siculiana, Agrigento, Sicily, 5'6", 160 lbs, chestnut eyes, grey hair, bald top.

LOCALITIES   : Resides Via Ammiraglio Grav-
FREQUENTED   ina #2, Palermo, Italy. Occasionally visits Rome & Naples. Formerly resided in U.S. at NYC, Pittsburgh, Detroit, New Orleans and Houston.

FAMILY   : Married and has several grown children, however,
BACKGROUND   he now lives alone. Son is married to the daughter of Pietro Davi notorious Palermo Mafioso. Father: Antonio; mother: Maria Zarbo.

CRIMINAL   : Joseph Biondo, ███████████████, Pietro Davi,
ASSOCIATES   ████████████████, ████████████, ███████████.

CRIMINAL   : FBI #1383119. Record in both Italy & U.S. dating from
HISTORY   1915 includes arrests for assault & battery, murder, extortion and narcotic trafficking.

BUSINESS   : Claims to be sales representative, but in reality receives money from Pietro Davi & various American racketeers.

MODUS   : Was an important smuggler & distributor of narcotics
OPERANDI   when in the U.S. Was an adjudicator for the Mafia in U.S. and is still highly regarded by both Italian and U.S. Mafiosi.

NAME	: Filippo GIOVE
ALIASES	: Filippo Giova, Philip Giova, Tony Padro, Philip Gioia, Philip Goia, Philip Gieava, Philip Calleo.
DESCRIPTION	: Born 4-24-13 Canneto (Adelfia),Bari, Italy, 5'7", 200 lbs, brown eyes, brown hair, balding, dark complexion.
LOCALITIES FREQUENTED	: Resides Via P. Toselli 11/3 Genoa, Italy. In USA resided 5922 Hereford Ave, Los Angeles, Cal. Frequents Genoa, Naples, Roma and Torino, all in Italy.
FAMILY BACKGROUND	: Married Lina Smaldino; two children; father: Giovanni (deceased); mother: Agnes Nigra.
CRIMINAL ASSOCIATES	: ███████████, ███████████, ███████████.
CRIMINAL HISTORY	: FBI #377708. I&N Alien Registration Card #A506525. Record dates from 1931 and includes arrests for cashing stolen checks, illegal entry into the U.S., narcotics, grand larceny, rape, robbery & wife-beating. Arrested in Italy in 1949 in possession of 3.6 kilos of opium.
BUSINESS	: In Genoa, Italy works as bar manager and bouncer on Genoa waterfront. In USA, worked for Ace Auto Sales, 114 South Ford Blvd, Los Angeles, Calif.
MODUS OPERANDI	: Part of an Italian-Swiss gang of smugglers in Genoa, dealing in stolen and black-market jewelery, cigarettes and narcotics. Persistently enters the USA, illegally.

NAME   : Manlio Giuseppe GRECO

ALIASES   : None

DESCRIPTION   : Born 2-3-22 Palermo, Sicily,
                 Italy.

LOCALITIES   : Resides Via Ciostra #1,
FREQUENTED   Palermo, Italy. Frequents
                 the cities of Milan, Genoa,
                 Rome, Naples & other cities
                 in Italy.

FAMILY   : Father: Giuseppe (deceased);
BACKGROUND   mother: Maria Stella
                 Pattavina; uncle: Sebastiano Pecoraro.

CRIMINAL   : Giuseppe Greco (father-deceased), ███████████████,
ASSOCIATES   Egidio Calascibetta.

CRIMINAL   : Arrested in Italy 1951 for narcotic trafficking.
HISTORY

BUSINESS   : Drug store clerk.

MODUS   : A highly trusted Mafioso. He inherited a large scale
OPERANDI   narcotic business established by his late father who
                 had a previous narcotic conviction in Italy.
                 Obtained over 40 kilos of heroin from the Calasci-
                 betta mob for sale to U.S. customers.

NAME	: Paolo GRECO

ALIASES : None

DESCRIPTION : Born 4-1-12 Palermo, Sicily,
Italy, 5'10", 185 lbs, light
brown hair, blue eyes, grad-
uate of University of Palermo

LOCALITIES : Resides Via Rosario Sante Fe,
FREQUENTED #26, Torino, Italy. Frequents
Palermo, Partinico, Alcamo & ·
other cities in Sicily.
Travels frequently to North-
ern Italy.

FAMILY : Father: Giuseppe; mother: Santa Greco; cousin:
BACKGROUND Salvatore Greco.

CRIMINAL · : Francesco Coppola, Antonio Sorci, Serafino & Giuseppe
ASSOCIATES Mancuso, Giuseppe Corso, Salvatore Greco, (cousin),
Angelo DiCarlo, ███████████ of Italy; Antoine
Cordoleani of France; Raffaele Quasarano, John
Priziola of the U.S.

CRIMINAL : Has been arrested in Italy many times for murder,
HISTORY extortion and narcotics.

BUSINESS : Fruit & Vegetable merchant.

MODUS : With the Mancuso Brothers, Coppola & Salvatore Greco,
OPERANDI conducted large scale narcotic business, supplying
Quasarano & Priziola with heroin obtained from
Cordoleani and from Yugoslav violators. Was a
principal in the 1956 Palermo Produce Market War.
Strong-arm man & vicious killer.

NAME : Peter GRECO

ALIASES : Peter Grieco

DESCRIPTION : Born 12-18-1887 Amantea,
Cosenza, Calabria, Italy,
5'9", 165 lbs, brown eyes,
white hair, olive complexion,
cut scar left cheek.

LOCALITIES : Deported 10-22-58 & now be-
FREQUENTED lieved living at Amantea; in
U.S. resided 54-30 65th Pl,
Maspeth, L.I., & frequented
Green Parrot Cafe, 1806 3rd
Ave, NYC.

FAMILY : Wife: Rosalie; daughter: Mildred; son: Mario; father:
BACKGROUND Antonio; mother: Maria Cannella (both born Italy &
now deceased).

CRIMINAL : Carmine LoCascio, ███████████████, ████████
ASSOCIATES ██████, ████████████████.

CRIMINAL : FBI #98201. NYCPD #B66031. I&NS #A-11524233. Record
HISTORY dates from 1917 & includes arrests for grand larceny,
possession of loaded revolver & immigration violation. Deported 10-22-58.

BUSINESS : No legitimate employment known; formerly a barber.

MODUS : For many years participated with other Mafiosi in
OPERANDI numerous illegal enterprises and crimes of violence.
Due to his advanced age his active participation in
such crimes had diminished by the time he was deported.

> Greco has been on the run since 1963, and was rumored to still be alive in 2001.

NAME : Salvatore GRECO

ALIASES : Sam Greco, Salvatore Turridu, Toto L'Ingegnere, Sal Creco, Toto.

DESCRIPTION : Born 5-12-24 Palermo, Sicily, Italy, 6'0", 185 lbs, brown eyes, brown hair, medium build, light complexion.

LOCALITIES FREQUENTED : Resides 216 Via Ciaculli, Palermo, Sicily, frequents Partinico, Alcamo & other cities in Sicily; travels frequently to large northern Italian cities.

FAMILY BACKGROUND : Father: Pietro; mother: Antonia Greco; cousin: Paolo Greco.

CRIMINAL ASSOCIATES : Vincenzo Rimi, Francesco Coppola, Paolo Greco, (cousin), ███████████████, Antonio Sorci, Serafino and Giuseppe Mancuso, Giuseppe Corso, Salvatore Vitale, Angelo DiCarlo, ███████████, Raffaele Quasarano, John Priziola, Paolo Cimino.

CRIMINAL HISTORY : Record dates from 1948 when he was arrested in Palermo, Sicily for illegally carrying war weapons, arrested Rome 1953 for conspiracy to violate Italian narcotic laws.

BUSINESS : Fruit and vegetable merchant.

MODUS OPERANDI : With Francesco Coppola, Serafino Mancuso, Paolo Greco & other Mafiosi supplied large amounts of heroin to Quasarano and Priziola in the U.S., using a Sicilian ship captain as a courier. This heroin was obtained from French & Yugoslav violators. Is also a large scale smuggler of American cigarettes from Tangiers to Italy.

He was deported to Sicily following a release from prison. He died in Sicily in September 1979.

NAME : Nicolo IMPASTATO

ALIASES : Nick Impastato, Nicolene, Frank Impostato, Migolene

DESCRIPTION : Born June 1, 1900 Cinisi, Sicily, Italy; 5'5½", 160 lbs, brown eyes, grey hair, almost bald, dark complexion.

LOCALITIES FREQUENTED : Now residing in his home town, Cinisi, Sicily; was in USA from 1927 to 1955, residing in NYC, Kansas City & New Orleans. In 1955 deported to Mexico, thence to Italy the same year.

FAMILY BACKGROUND : Married in September, 1958; father: Giacomo; mother: Marianna Beretta; three brothers and two sisters, living in Sicily.

CRIMINAL ASSOCIATES : Sam Vitale, ███████████████, Anthony Carolla, Silvestro Carolla, Carlo & Paolo Gambino.

CRIMINAL HISTORY : FBI #2716692. Kansas City PD #52296. Has a criminal record in Italy, dating back to 1920's, including homicide and attempted murder; in the USA convicted of violation of Federal narcotic laws.

BUSINESS : Is a landowner and farmer in Sicily.

MODUS OPERANDI : Is high in Mafia circles, a trusted and respected member; trafficks in narcotics and has been known to use violence, including murder, to maintain his organization; though deported in 1955 he still has an income from rackets in the U. S.

800

NAME : Vincenzo ITALIANO

ALIASES : None

DESCRIPTION : Born 2-14-1911 Partinico,
Palermo, Sicily, Italy.
5'11", 195 lbs, grey-black
hair, brown eyes.

LOCALITIES : Resides in Partinico, Sicily,
FREQUENTED and frequents Palermo,
Alcamo, Trapani and other
cities in Italy.

FAMILY : Father: Vito; mother:
BACKGROUND Ninfa Russo.

CRIMINAL : ▮▮▮▮▮▮▮▮, ▮▮▮▮▮▮▮▮▮▮▮, Salvatore
ASSOCIATES Vitale, ▮▮▮▮▮▮▮, Rosario Mancino, Francesco
Coppola, Giuseppe Mannino, Vincenzo Rimi, ▮▮▮▮▮
▮▮▮▮, Vito Mazzanobile.

CRIMINAL : Has been arrested for kidnapping, murder and
HISTORY trafficking in narcotics.

BUSINESS : Merchant

MODUS : Acts as front man for Francesco Coppola and partic-
OPERANDI ipates in the narcotic business of Coppola, supplying large amounts of heroin to Mafia narcotic
traffickers in the United States.

NAME   : Salvatore LAFATA

ALIASES   :

DESCRIPTION   : Born 3-13-09 Palermo, Sicily,
                  Italy, 5'6", 170 lbs, brown-
                  grey hair, balding, brown
                  eyes, medium build, dark com-
                  plexion, moustache, good
                  dresser.

LOCALITIES   : Palermo, Villabate, Montele-
FREQUENTED   pre, Altafonte, Partinico,
                  Bagheria all in Sicily, Italy.

FAMILY   : Father: Pietro, mother: Rosalia Gennaro.
BACKGROUND

CRIMINAL   : Antonio Cottone (dead), ███████████████, Vincenzo
ASSOCIATES   & Giuseppe Cottone, ███████████████, ███████████████,
                  ███████████████.

CRIMINAL   : Palermo, Italy, Police #855-758-5435. With other
HISTORY   Mafiosi Lafata was arrested by the Palermo Police
                  1956 and exiled on the Island of Ustica for a period
                  of 4 years. Sentence imposed for his participation in
                  the Mafia produce market war in Sicily during 1955-
                  1956.

BUSINESS   : Is listed as a fruit merchant.

MODUS   : He is considered by the Italian Police authorities
OPERANDI   as a dangerous element of the underworld. This
                  hoodlum is considered a Mafia strong arm man, an
                  assassin used to eliminate recalcitrant produce
                  merchants through shotgun assassination("lupara").

NAME : Vito LAFATA

ALIASES : None

DESCRIPTION : Born 7-1-1926, Cinisi,
Palermo, Sicily, Italy.
5'8", 145 lbs, black hair,
brown eyes, dark complexion.

LOCALITIES : Resides at Via Nuova #28,
FREQUENTED Cinisi, Italy.

FAMILY : Wife: Vincenza; father:
BACKGROUND Filippo; mother: Francesca
(last name unknown); uncle:
Paul LaFata

CRIMINAL : Pietro Amato, ███████████████, Nicola Impastato,
ASSOCIATES Nicola Maniscalco, Giuseppe Mazzella.

CRIMINAL : FBI #446582B   Deported from the United States in
HISTORY 1953 for illegal entry.

BUSINESS : Clerk.

MODUS : At the time he immigrated to the United States he
OPERANDI was part of a group which is known to have brought
a large shipment of narcotics. Is a trusted
courier for the Mafia.

NAME	: Giuseppe LAGONARO
ALIASES	: Giacomo Giarrusso, Salvatore Mercadante.
DESCRIPTION	: Born 11-27-13 Palermo, Sicily Italy, 5'10", 175, dark brown hair, brown eyes, medium build, sometimes wears moustache, poor teeth.
LOCALITIES FREQUENTED	: Resides Via Cirinioni #40, Palermo, Sicily; Frequents Naples, Reggio Calabria & Southern France, currently (1960) Fugitive from Palermo Carabinieri Police.
FAMILY BACKGROUND	: Father: Giovanni Batista; mother: Vincenza Intartaglia.
CRIMINAL ASSOCIATES	: ███████████, ███████████, ███████████.
CRIMINAL HISTORY	: Record dates from 1947 and includes arrests for swindling, theft against Italian State Railways, theft and false oaths, criminal investigation and narcotic trafficking.
BUSINESS	: No legitimate occupation known.
MODUS OPERANDI	: One of the leaders of a Mafia group in Sicily, highly respected by his fellow members for his daring exploits and his connections with top French gangsters. He traffics in narcotics and counterfeit money on a large scale.

NAME   : Francesco LA MANTIA

ALIASES   : None

DESCRIPTION   : Born 3-12-25, Monreale, Prov.
                  of Palermo, 5'9", 175 lbs,
                  brown eyes, brown hair, med-
                  ium build, light complexion.

LOCALITIES   : Resides at Via Sciafino 16,
FREQUENTED   Monreale. Frequents Palermo,
                  Partinico, Altafonte, San
                  Giuseppe Iato all in Sicily.

FAMILY   : Father: Giuseppe; mother:
BACKGROUND   Carmela Cappello.

CRIMINAL   : Giorgio Venezia, Antonino Caruso, Giuseppe Anzalone,
ASSOCIATES   Giuseppe Cottone, ███████████ and ███████████.

CRIMINAL   : Palermo Police #465 254 4444. With other Mafiosi
HISTORY   La Mantia was arrested by the Palermo Police in
                  September 1956. He was exiled on the Island of Ustica
                  for a period of 5 years. This sentence was imposed on
                  him by the Palermo Exile Commission for his partici-
                  pation in the Mafia produce market war in Sicily
                  during 1955-56.

BUSINESS   : Agricultural laborer.

MODUS   : Considered by the Italian Police as a dangerous
OPERANDI   hoodlum, Mafia strong arm man and assassin. Carries
                  out shotgun "lupara" assassinations of recalcitrant
                  produce merchants under the direction of higher
                  echelon Mafiosi.

NAME   : Pietro LENA

ALIASES   : None

DESCRIPTION   : Born 10-29-1900, Altafonte,
                Palermo, Sicily, 5'5", 150
                lbs, black hair, brown eyes,
                medium build, light complex-
                ion, heavy eyebrows, surgical
                scar on right side of neck.

LOCALITIES   : Resides Altofonte, Palermo,
FREQUENTED   Sicily. Frequents Balestrate,
                Palermo, Alcamo, Trapani,
                all Sicily.

FAMILY   : Father: Giovanni Battista; mother: Pietra Castellesi.
BACKGROUND

CRIMINAL   : ██████████████, ██████████████, ██████████████,
ASSOCIATES   ██████████████, ██████████████, ██████████████.

CRIMINAL   : Palermo Police #353-357-5343. With other Mafiosi he
HISTORY   was arrested in 1956 for the murder of Ignazio Tafuri,
                Altofonte, Palermo, Sicily, in connection with the
                citrus fruit wars. The Provincial Commission on Exile
                on September 11, 1956 sentenced Lena to 3 yrs. exile.

BUSINESS   : Manual laborer.

MODUS   : This Mafioso strong-arm bandit was one of the 50
OPERANDI   persons exiled as the results of a wave of murders
                perpetrated in Sicily in the year 1956 and carried on
                by the Mafia to bring the citrus fruit markets under
                their control.

NAME   : Francois LICARI

ALIASES   : Francesco Licari, Il Tunisino

DESCRIPTION   : Born 5-21-15 Tunis, North
                Africa.

LOCALITIES   : Resides at Via Gafurio #5,
FREQUENTED   Milan, Italy. Frequents
                Torino, Rome, Genova, Naples
                and other cities in Italy.

FAMILY   : Father: Salvatore; mother:
BACKGROUND   Francesca Cucinella.

CRIMINAL   : ██████████████, Dominique Albertini, Joe Pici,
ASSOCIATES   ██████████████, Francesco Severino, ████████
                ██████, Roger Coudert, Antoine D'Agostino, Giovanni
                Maugeri, Sebastian Bellanca (fugitive U.S.A.).

CRIMINAL   : Denounced by the French for collaboration with the
HISTORY   Germans and also wanted for murder by the French
                authorities.

BUSINESS   : No known legitimate occupation.

MODUS   : Leading figure in a Mafia group which obtains
OPERANDI   heroin from the Albertini organization in Marseille
                and smuggles it via seamen and airline personnel,
                to the U.S. A major source of heroin for U.S.
                narcotic traffickers.

```
NAME            : Raffaele LIGUORI

ALIASES         : Ralph Liguori, Ralph-the-
                  Pimp.

DESCRIPTION     : Born 3-17-10 Rome, Italy,
                  5'7" tall, 175 lbs, brown
                  eyes, brown hair, heavy
                  build, dark complexion.

LOCALITIES      : Resides Hotel della Lunetta,
FREQUENTED        Piazza del Paradiso #68,
                  Campo di Fiore Trastevere,
                  Rome, Italy. Frequents nite-
                  clubs & hotel Nord in Rome.
                  Visits Naples, Milan & other major cities in Italy.

FAMILY          : Father: Giuseppe (deceased), mother: Agnes Ruggeri,
BACKGROUND        divorced from Eveline Nelson, has one son Giuseppe;
                  brothers: Alfredo & Armando.

CRIMINAL        : Salvatore Lucky Luciano,
ASSOCIATES
```

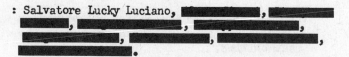

```
CRIMINAL        : FBI #274732, NYCPD #B-95853. He was sentenced to
HISTORY           15 years for compulsory prostitution in 1936 to-
                  gether with Lucky Luciano. Deported to Italy and
                  arrested in 1956 for compulsory prostitution, con-
                  victed in Rome 1959 of same violation.

BUSINESS        : Operates Auto Rental and acts as tourist guide.

MODUS           : Handles the prostitution business for Luciano, pro-
OPERANDI          cures girls with the inducement of becoming famous
                  dancers and sends them off to countries in Africa
                  and Asia, where the girls are forced into white
                  slavery. Handles large narcotic operations for
                  Luciano using young tough hoodlums to deliver the
                  narcotics to customers.
```

He died January 26, 1962 of a heart attack at the Naples
Airport in Italy. He was planning to meet a movie producer
who wanted to make a movie about his life. He was buried in
Queens, NY in 1972, ten years after his death. The delay was
caused by the terms of his 1946 deportation from the U.S.

NAME : Salvatore C. LUCANIA

ALIASES : Lucky Luciano, Charles Reid,
Charles Luciano, Charles
Lucania, Charles Ross.

DESCRIPTION : Born 11-24-1897 Lercara Fridi
Sicily; 5'10", brown eyes,
black-grey hair, 140 lbs,
wears glasses.

LOCALITIES : Resides 464 Via Tasso, Naples;
FREQUENTED frequents Zia Teresa, San
Francisco & Giacomino's restaurants, all in Naples,
also the Agnano Race Track in Naples.

FAMILY : Single; father: Antonio; mother: Rosalia Cafarella;
BACKGROUND (both deceased), brother: Bartolo (living in N.Y.C.)

CRIMINAL : Vito Genovese, Joe Biondo, Joe Profaci, Joe Bonanno,
ASSOCIATES Frank Costello, Meyer Lansky, all of US, Joe Doto,
Joe Pici, Pietro Davi, Frank Pirico, all of Italy.

CRIMINAL : FBI# 62920. NYCPD-B# 72321. Arrests since 1916 in-
HISTORY clude assault & robbery, grand larceny, conviction
of Federal Narcotic Laws. Sentenced NYC 1936 to 30
to 50 years for compulsory prostitution; paroled
and deported to Italy in 1946.

BUSINESS : Has interests in San Francisco Cafe & is secret
owner of apartment building at 464 Via Tasso, both
in Naples; also interested in a clinic at Cercola,
a suburb of Naples.

MODUS : Is one of the highest ranking Mafia both in Italy
OPERANDI & the US. From Italy he participates in directing
of American rackets & regularly receives his share
of the profits through Mafia couriers.

```
NAME            : Francesco MAGLIOCCO

ALIASES         : None

DESCRIPTION     : Born 2-10-03 Misilmeri, Prov.
                  of Palermo, Sicily, 5'8",
                  160 lbs, brown eyes, grey
                  hair, medium build, dark
                  complexion.

LOCALITIES      : Misilmeri, Bisacquino, Prov.
FREQUENTED        of Palermo, Sicily; Torino,
                  Italy.

FAMILY          : Father: Simone; mother:
BACKGROUND        Maria Grano (both deceased); brothers: Salvatore and
                  Pietro.

CRIMINAL        :
ASSOCIATES
```

```
CRIMINAL        : Italian Police #755-988-6484. 1929 was convicted of
HISTORY           participating in a gigantic Mafia conspiracy to
                  carry out numerous crimes, including cattle rustling,
                  pillaging, kidnapping, extortion & robbery. Several
                  subsequent criminal arrests, the most being in 1955.

BUSINESS        : Claims to be farm laborer.

MODUS           : Lower echelon member of the Mafia in Sicily. Member
OPERANDI          of Mafia conspiracy as far back as early 1920's.
```

NAME : Rosario MANCINO

ALIASES : Saro, Sauro Mancino

DESCRIPTION : Born 1-14-1915, Palermo, Sicily, Italy, 5'9", 200 lbs, black hair, bald, brown eyes.

LOCALITIES FREQUENTED : Resides Via Ugdulena #10, Palermo, Italy. Frequents Rome, Milan & other Italian cities, Lebanon, Mexico, Canada & United States.

FAMILY BACKGROUND : Married Rosa Marino; children: Gaetano, Nunzia, Ignazio, Domenica Silvana; father: Gaetano; mother: Nunzia Castelli; brothers: Pietro, Salvatore, Vincenzo; uncle: Enrico Marino (Lodi,NJ).

CRIMINAL ASSOCIATES : Lucky Luciano, Francesco Pirico, ████████████, ████████ ████████, Salvatore Greco, ████████████████, ████████████ ████████████, Francesco Saverino, ████████████, ████████, ██████████████████████, Pietro Davi.

CRIMINAL HISTORY : No known arrests.

BUSINESS : Large Real Estate holdings. Has operated tomato canning factories. Owns Maritime Agency Impressi and Imbarco & Sbarco, Via Ammiraglio Gravina #34, Palermo, Sicily, Italy.

MODUS OPERANDI : Large scale heroin smuggler, concealing the contraband in cans of tomato paste. Operated heroin laboratory in Lebanon under guise of a tomato canning factory. He and his brothers own a boat which is used for smuggling activities.

NAME	: Giuseppe MANCUSO

ALIASES	: Francois Di Stefano, Frank Stefano, Joseph Mancuso, Marzucco.

DESCRIPTION : Born 4-30-1900 Alcamo, Trapani, Sicily, 5'8", 145 lbs, black hair, brown eyes, dark complexion, speaks poor English.

LOCALITIES
FREQUENTED : Resides with his brother Serafino Mancuso at 52, Piazza Umberto I, Alcamo.
He travels to Rome, Naples, Milan, Trieste, Paris & Marseille. He lived in NY from about 1930 to 1935 & resided in Paris before World War II.

FAMILY
BACKGROUND : Father: Francesco Paolo; mother: Vincenza Ferrara; brothers: Serafino & Salvatore.

CRIMINAL
ASSOCIATES : Antoine Cordoleani, Francesco Coppola, his brothers Serafino & Salvatore Mancuso, Giuseppe Corso Jr, & Senior.

CRIMINAL
HISTORY : FBI #872905. Deported to Italy 1935, for illegal entry into the USA. Arrested in U.S. for kidnapping and illegal entry; in Italy for narcotic violation and other crimes.

BUSINESS : With his brother Serafino he operates a large farm near Alcamo.

MODUS
OPERANDI : This man is a well known Mafioso. He is an excellent heroin and morphine base chemist. He has worked in the past with his brothers and other well known Italian, French and American narcotic violators.

812

NAME   : Salvatore MANCUSO

ALIASES   : Sal DiStefano

DESCRIPTION   : Born 5-27-06 Alcamo, Trapani,
                 Sicily, 5'6", 160 lbs, brown
                 eyes, dark brown hair, dark
                 complexion, scar on chin.

LOCALITIES   : Resided in Brooklyn, NY, from
FREQUENTED   1929 to 1949 then deported
                 to Italy. Brought to U.S.
                 1951 to testify in kidnapping
                 case, he disappeared. Present
                 whereabouts unknown.

FAMILY   : Married Nellie Mancuso; son: Frank; father: Francesco
BACKGROUND   Paolo; mother: Vincenza Ferrara; brothers: Serafino
                 and Giuseppe.

CRIMINAL   : Francesco Paolo Coppola; Serafino & Giuseppe Mancuso
ASSOCIATES   and others in Palermo, Sicily. Peter Gaudino and
                 other Detroit gangsters.

CRIMINAL   : FBI #825483. NYCPD #B126876. Record dating from 1934
HISTORY   includes arrests for kidnapping & Federal Narcotic
                 Law violation. Currently (1960) a fugitive.

BUSINESS   : No legitimate occupation known.

MODUS   : With his brothers was a member of a large scale
OPERANDI   narcotic smuggling ring. Now believed to be in
                 Canada and probably still engaged in smuggling
                 operations.

Mancuso went into hiding after being brought to the
U.S. to be a witness for a government case.

NAME   : Serafino MANCUSO

ALIASES   : Pier DeStefano, Pierre
                 De Stefano, Sam, Pierre
                 Stefano

DESCRIPTION   : Born 4-5-11, Alcamo, Sicily,
                 5'7½", 162 lbs, medium build,
                 medium complexion, black
                 hair, dark hazel eyes, ver-
                 tical scar 3/4" left temple,

LOCALITIES   : Deported from the USA (NYC,
FREQUENTED   N.Y.) in 1947 and establis-
                 hed residence in Alcamo. He
                 has traveled much and has worked as a seaman on
                 ocean going ships.

FAMILY   : Father: Francesco Paolo; mother: Vincenza Ferrara;
BACKGROUND   brothers: Salvatore & Giuseppe Mancuso, well known
                 Mafia hoodlums and narcotic traffickers.

CRIMINAL   : ████████████, Francesco Paolo Coppola, Vincenzo Rimi,
ASSOCIATES   Giuseppe Corso Sr., Giuseppe Corso Jr.,

CRIMINAL   : FBI #1191423, arrested in 1936 for smuggling narcotics
HISTORY   into the USA and served 10 years in the Federal Pen-
                 itentiary. He was paroled and deported to Italy in
                 February of 1947. Arrested and convicted in 1952 at
                 Alcamo for possession of trunk containing 6 kilos of
                 heroin he was shipping to U.S. for Frank Coppola.

BUSINESS   : With his brother Giuseppe, he operates a large farm
                 near Alcamo, Sicily.

MODUS   : With his brother Giuseppe he maintains close ties
OPERANDI   with French heroin suppliers furnishing to Mafia
                 associates in the U.S. and Italy heroin which he
                 obtains from the French.

NAME : Nicolo MANDALA

ALIASES : None

DESCRIPTION : Born 11-12-06 Villabate, Palermo, Sicily, 5'2", 110 lbs, brown eyes, brown hair-greying, dark complexion, large nose; deep set eyes.

LOCALITIES FREQUENTED : Villabate, Montelepre, Alta-fonte, all Prov. of Palermo, Sicily.

FAMILY BACKGROUND : Married; father: Antonino; mother: Maria Antonia Terranova.

CRIMINAL ASSOCIATES : Francesco Rizzo, ████████████, ████████ ████████, ████████████, ████████ ████.

CRIMINAL HISTORY : Palermo Police #545-295-453 (4) 5. Arrested Palermo 1956 & exiled for 4 years for his participation in the 1955-56 produce market war in Sicily. Never in United States.

BUSINESS : Claims to be farmer.

MODUS OPERANDI : Mafia strong arm man and assassin. Carries out shotgun "lupara" assassinations of those who refuse to submit to Mafia demands.

NAME : Salvatore Charles MANERI

ALIASES : Salvatore ^Manera, Salvatore
Piazza, Antonio Magana

DESCRIPTION : Born 8-15-1912 Marineo, Palermo,
Sicily, 5'5", 140 lbs, brown
eyes, black hair, dark complexion, medium build.

LOCALITIES : Resides Palermo, Italy. Be-
FREQUENTED   fore deportation from U.S.
resided in Brooklyn and
Staten Island, N.Y.

FAMILY : Married Jennie Morello; son: Michael; father:
BACKGROUND   Michaelangelo; mother: Maria Gippetto; sisters:
Celia Collecta & Anna Scorsone; brothers: Joseph
& Philip.

CRIMINAL : Ernesto Barese, Giuseppe DiGiorgio, Michael
ASSOCIATES   Spinella, ███████████████, ████████████████.

CRIMINAL : FBI #495856   NYCPD #B-97217   Record dating
HISTORY   from 1924 includes arrests for juvenile delinquency, truancy, petit larceny, grand larceny,
burglary tools, theft from foreign shipment and
immigration violation.

BUSINESS : No legitimate occupation.

MODUS : Though himself a narcotic addict, Maneri engaged
OPERANDI   in large scale narcotic smuggling, personally re-
moving drugs from ships in N.Y. harbor and also
acting as contact man between French sources and
the Joseph DiPalermo narcotic smuggling organization.

NAME   : Nicolo MANISCALCO

ALIASES   : None

DESCRIPTION   : Born 7-12-1916, Burgio,
                  Agrigento, Sicily, Italy.
                  5'4", 145 lbs, brown hair,
                  blue eyes, medium dark
                  complexion.

LOCALITIES   : Resides Via Coriticillo #8,
FREQUENTED   Burgio, Agrigento, Sicily,
                  Italy.

FAMILY   : Father: Giuseppe Antonio;
BACKGROUND   mother: Maria Vitale; uncle: Domenico Maniscalco
                  (living in the United States).

CRIMINAL   : ████████████████, ████████████████, ████
ASSOCIATES   ████████, Pietro Amato, Giuseppe Mazzella, Vito
                  LaFata

CRIMINAL   : FBI #443966B USI&NS #E-125635 Deported from the
HISTORY   United States in 1953 for illegal entry.

BUSINESS   : Butcher and bricklayer.

MODUS   : At the time he immigrated clandestinely to the
OPERANDI   United States he was part of a group which is
                  known to have carried in a large shipment of
                  heroin. Is a trusted courier for the Mafia.

```
NAME          : Giuseppe MANNINO

ALIASES       : Giuseppe Manino, Giuseppe
                Manini

DESCRIPTION   : Born 1-28-07 Carini, Palermo,
                Sicily, Italy.

LOCALITIES    : Resides at Via Monastero #3,
FREQUENTED      Carini, Sicily, Italy. Fre-
                quents Palermo, Partinico,
                Alcamo, Trapani and other
                cities in Italy.

FAMILY        : Father: Antonino; mother:
BACKGROUND      Vita Cucci; nephew: Francesco Cicala.

CRIMINAL      : ███████████, ███████████, Francesco
ASSOCIATES      Coppola, Vincenzo Italiano, ███████████, Paul
                Cimino, ███████████, Salvatore Vitale, Giuseppe
                Corso Senior and Junior.

CRIMINAL      : No known criminal record.
HISTORY

BUSINESS      : Citrus Fruit merchant.

MODUS         : A large scale narcotic trafficker. Obtains heroin
OPERANDI        from Corsican laboratory operators and disposes of
                it to Mafia associates in Sicily, who then ship it
                to Mafia violators in the U.S.
```

NAME	: Corrado MAUGERI
ALIASES	: Corrado Mauceri
DESCRIPTION	: Born 4-5-02 Bizerte, Tunisia, 5'8", 170 lbs, black hair, (greying), brown eyes, stout build, Italian national, speaks fluent French.
LOCALITIES FREQUENTED	: He lives in Milan, Italy but travels extensively in Italy and other parts of Europe.
FAMILY BACKGROUND	: Father: Luigi; mother: Corradina Aparo; brother: Giovanni Maugeri.
CRIMINAL ASSOCIATES	: Dominique Albertini, ███████████, Joe Pici, Giovanni Maugeri, ██████████, Sebastiano Bellanca.
CRIMINAL HISTORY	: Never in the United States. He has a criminal record in Italy for thefts, swindles, assault, counterfeiting.
BUSINESS	: No legitimate occupation.
MODUS OPERANDI	: With his brother Giovanni and other Mafiosi has been supplying heroin to traffickers in the U.S. for many years. Obtains supplies of heroin from French-Corsican mobs in France.

NAME   : Giovanni MAUGERI

ALIASES   : Giovanni Mauceri, John,
                  Johnny.

DESCRIPTION   : Born 8-15-06, Tunis, Tunisia,
                  5'11", 180 lbs, hazel eyes,
                  black-grey hair, speaks
                  Italian, French, Spanish,
                  Arabic and poor English.

LOCALITIES   : He lives in Milan, Italy.
FREQUENTED   He was deported from the USA
                  (NYC), in April of 1957 for
                  illegal entry. He travels
                  over most of Italy and southern France.

FAMILY   : Married, but separated; has one daughter; father:
BACKGROUND   Luigi; mother: Corradina Aparo; brother: Corrado.

CRIMINAL   : Dominique Albertini, Corrado Maugeri, Joe Pici,
ASSOCIATES   ██████████████████, ████████████, Pietro Sorci,
                  Matthew Cuomo, Sebastiano Bellanca.

CRIMINAL   : FBI #468582C. Has a long criminal record in Italy for
HISTORY   murder, assault, theft, counterfeiting and narcotics.
                  He was deported from the USA in 1957 for illegal
                  entry.

BUSINESS   : No legitimate occupation.

MODUS   : With his brother, Corrado and other Mafiosi, has
OPERANDI   been for many years supplying heroin to U.S., traf-
                  fickers. Obtains supplies of heroin from French
                  Corsican mobs in France. Italian national.

NAME   : Vito MAZZANOBILE

ALIASES   : None

DESCRIPTION : Born 2-15-06 Partinico,
Palermo, Sicily, 5'9", 150
lbs, thin build, brown eyes,
brown hair, dark complexion,
birthmark on right cheek.

LOCALITIES : Via Valloni #40, Partinico,
FREQUENTED   Sicily. Frequents Alcamo,
Montelepre, Cinisi Castella-
mare del Golfo, Palermo,
Rome and Milan all in Italy.

FAMILY   : Father: Michaelangelo (deceased); mother: Isabella
BACKGROUND   Inghilleri.

CRIMINAL   : Francesco Coppola, ████████████, Vincenzo
ASSOCIATES   Italiano, Vincenzo Rimi, ████████, ████████,
████████.

CRIMINAL   : Has been arrested for kidnapping, murder and pro-
HISTORY   tecting fugitives from justice. Was last arrested
in 1953, together with Francesco Coppola, for murder,
and was sentenced to 5 years in exile.

BUSINESS   : Land owner and wine merchant.

MODUS   : This man is a leading Mafioso of Partinico, closely
OPERANDI   associated with Francesco Coppola in narcotics. In
the past he has been involved in Mafia extortions
and black-marketeering.

NAME   : Giuseppe MAZZELLA

ALIASES   : None

DESCRIPTION   : Born 10-17-28 Ponza, Latina,
                  Italy, 5'5½", 120 lbs, black
                  hair, blue eyes, small build.

LOCALITIES   : Resided at Ponza, Italy.
FREQUENTED

FAMILY   : Married Ida Santoro; father:
BACKGROUND   Giuseppe; mother: Teresa
                  Virginia D'Arco (living in
                  U.S.); brother: Tobia (Liv-
                  ing in U.S.); brother: Luigi (Italy).

CRIMINAL   : ██████████, ██████████, ██████████,
ASSOCIATES   ██████████.

CRIMINAL   : FBI #447294B. USI&NS #E125633. Deported from the
HISTORY   U.S., 1953 for illegal immigration.

BUSINESS   : No legitimate employment.

MODUS   : At the time of his original immigration to the U.S.,
OPERANDI   he was part of a group which is believed to have
                  carried a large quantity of heroin into the U.S.
                  Is believed to have again clandestinely immigrated
                  to the United States.

NAME   : Carlo MIGLIARDI

ALIASES   : None

DESCRIPTION   : Born 7-5-10 Alice Bel Colle,
                  Prov. of Alessandria, Italy,
                  5'10", 180 lbs, brown eyes,
                  light brown hair, robust
                  build, fair complexion.

LOCALITIES   : Resided at Corso Raffaello
FREQUENTED   #25, Turin, Italy. Frequent-
                  ed Milan, Bologna, Rome &
                  other cities in Italy.

FAMILY   : Father: Giovanbattista (dead), mother: Teresa Sitto
BACKGROUND   (dead).

CRIMINAL   : Egidio Calascibetta, Lucky Luciano, Giuseppe Pici,
ASSOCIATES   Francesco Pirico, ████████████████████.

CRIMINAL   : On April 22, 1955 in Turin, Italy, he was sentenced
HISTORY   to 11 years and fined 270,000 Lire and forbidden to
                  work in any civil service capacity. Released from
                  prison on July 14, 1959 by Presidential Pardon.

BUSINESS   : Formerly directing chemist of Schiapparelli Mfg.,
                  Co., and professor of Chemistry, both Turin, Italy.

MODUS   : Migliardi, Calascibetta and Bonomo were responsible
OPERANDI   for the diversion of 716 kilos of heroin into the
                  illegal traffic for the Luciano mob, which then
                  arranged for the smuggling of this contraband into
                  the United States.

NAME	: Giorgio MISURACA

ALIASES   : None

DESCRIPTION : Born 4-9-25 San Cipirello,
              Palermo, Sicily, 5'5", 145
              lbs, brown eyes, brown hair,
              medium build, dark complex-
              ion.

LOCALITIES : Resides at Via Di Giovanni
FREQUENTED   #17, San Cipirello. Fre-
              quents Palermo, Monreale,
              Partinico, Montelepre, Al-
              camo all in Sicily.

FAMILY   : Father: Giuseppe (deceased); mother: Serafina Vicari.
BACKGROUND

CRIMINAL   : Giorgio Venezia, Salvatore Giuliano (dead), Giuseppe
ASSOCIATES   Anzalone, Vincenzo Cottone, Francesco LaMantia.

CRIMINAL   : Palermo Police #265 68 4/5 1 4/5 14. Has lengthy
HISTORY   criminal record in Italy including conviction of
              participation in 1955-56 Sicilian produce market war,
              for which sentenced to 2 years in exile.

BUSINESS   : Works for the "Cantiere Scuola of San Cipirello.
              Very poor financial condition.

MODUS   : Carries out Mafia ordered shotgun "lupara" assassin-
OPERANDI   ations of those who refuse to submit to Mafia demands.

NAME : Sebastiano NANI

ALIASES : Benny Nani, Peter Nani

DESCRIPTION : Born 8-15-06 Pozzalo, Sicily
Italy, 5'8" 185 lbs, brown
eyes, grey hair, stout build,
dark complexion.

LOCALITIES : Formerly resided 1888 Troy
FREQUENTED Ave., Brooklyn, NY. Frequented NY and Calif. Ex-
pelled from U.S. 2-8-58 &
returned to Pozzalo, Sicily.

FAMILY : Married Theresa Volpone; son: Peter; daughter: Tina;
BACKGROUND father: Pietro; mother: Alicia Ignazia (both dead);
brother: Salvatore (Montreal).

CRIMINAL : Vincent Randazzo, ███████████, Joseph Profaci, (of
ASSOCIATES NY); Joseph & Frank DeLuca (of Kansas City).

CRIMINAL : FBI #3347865, NYCPD B#108235. Arrest record dates
HISTORY from 1932, includes auto theft, murder, extortion,
sale of narcotics and bribery of federal officer.

BUSINESS : Formerly owned butcher shop in Brooklyn; no
legitimate occupation in Italy known.

MODUS : Close associate of Lucky Luciano, was an important
OPERANDI figure in the Mafia control of the Brooklyn, NY,
waterfront. A top echelon international narcotic
trafficker.

NAME	: Giuseppe PELLEGRINO
ALIASES	: Joseph Pelligrino, Joe Hardy, Frank Sciallo, Louis Carbonetti, Anthony Pellegrino.
DESCRIPTION	: Born 11-3-02 Teggiano, Campagna, Salerno, Italy, 5'8", 200 lbs, brown eyes, straight black hair, dark complexion.
LOCALITIES FREQUENTED	: Deported from U.S. 1947. Resides via Alfaro #27, Salerno, Italy.
FAMILY BACKGROUND	: Father: Vincenzo; mother: Maria Tropiano; brothers: Anthony & Charles Pellegrino @ Tropiano; sisters: Mrs. Sam Monastersky & Mrs. Eugene Giannini.
CRIMINAL ASSOCIATES	: Eugene Giannini (deceased), Sam Monastersky, Giacomo Reina, ▮▮▮▮▮▮▮▮▮▮▮▮▮▮, Francesco Saverino.
CRIMINAL HISTORY	: FBI #42935. NYCPD #B63160. Record dating from 1921 includes arrests for concealed weapon, robbery, homicide, assault & robbery, grand larceny and violation Federal narcotic laws.
BUSINESS	: Claims to be manager Brazil Bar, Salerno, Italy.
MODUS OPERANDI	: Was a member of the Mafia narcotic smuggling & distributing ring headed by the late Eugene Giannini. His task was to receive heroin from the suppliers, safeguard it and turn it over to couriers for delivery to the U.S.

826

NAME   : Armando PERILLO

ALIASES   : Pete Herman, John Burns,
                  Anthony Valente, Herman
                  Perillo, Frank Ernano.

DESCRIPTION   : Born 11-22-02 Carrara, Italy,
                  5'6", 160 lbs, hazel eyes,
                  brown hair, dark complexion,
                  tip of left little finger
                  missing.

LOCALITIES   : Deported to Italy from NYC
FREQUENTED   1-28-53, on SS Independence.
                  Present whereabouts unknown.

FAMILY   : Father: Salvatore; mother: Elisa Granito.
BACKGROUND

CRIMINAL   : Anthony Strollo, John Stoppelli, Joseph Cataldo,
ASSOCIATES   Vincent Mauro.

CRIMINAL   : FBI #2668435. Record dating from 1918 includes ar-
HISTORY   rests for burglary, violation of immigration laws
                  and Federal Narcotic conviction.

BUSINESS   : No known legitimate occupation.

MODUS   : Before his deportation was an important member of
OPERANDI   the Anthony Strollo Mafia narcotic trafficking or-
                  ganization, and though he cannot be located it is
                  almost certain he is still engaged in some phase
                  of the international narcotic traffic.

NAME   : Giuseppe PICI

ALIASES   : Joe Picci, Peach, Pacey,
                Pisano, Chester Ricardi.

DESCRIPTION   : Born 4-27-11 Bovino, Foggia,
                Italy, 5'7", 165 lbs, brown
                eyes, black hair.

LOCALITIES   : Resided Via Aurelia #47,
FREQUENTED   Bogliasco, Genoa, Italy.
                Before deportation from U.S,
                in 1946 lived in Turtle
                Creek, Pa., & made frequent
                trips to Pittsburgh, Kansas
                City and NYC. Currently (1959) incarcerated.

FAMILY   : Wife: Enrica; two children of his deceased former
BACKGROUND   wife, Joseph & Janet, live in Turtle Creek, Pa.,
                father: Santo; mother: Teresa Carletto.

CRIMINAL   : Lucky Luciano, ███████████████, ███████████,
ASSOCIATES   ███████████, Gaetano Ciofalo(deceased)

CRIMINAL   : FBI #639336. Pittsburgh PD# 26793. Record in U.S.,
HISTORY   dates from 1932 and includes arrests for violation
                firearms act, white slavery, conspiracy, suspicious
                person and violation immigration laws.

BUSINESS   : Claims to be landowner & frequently invests in
                restaurant & bar enterprises.

MODUS   : Important Mafia figure and wholesale supplier of
OPERANDI   heroin to smugglers. Organizes & finances other
                criminal activities, principally alien smuggling.

NAME   : Francesco PIRICO

ALIASES   : Don Ciccio, Cheech

DESCRIPTION   : Born 6-1-01 Palermo, Sicily,
                5'10", 180 lbs, brown eyes,
                lt. brown hair, small mouth,
                usually wears glasses and
                moustache, has droopy right
                eye lid.

LOCALITIES   : Resides via Vincenzo Monte
FREQUENTED   #34, Milan, Italy.

FAMILY   : Father: Giovanni; mother:
BACKGROUND   Angela Pirico (both deceased); son: Gianni.

CRIMINAL   : Lucky Luciano, Giuseppe Pici, Nicola Gentile,
ASSOCIATES   Joseph Di Palermo, Albert Bistoni, ███████████████,
                Francesco Saverino, Egidio Calascibetta.

CRIMINAL   : Never in United States. Record in Italy dating back
HISTORY   many years includes arrests for theft, gambling,
                fraud and narcotic trafficking.

BUSINESS   : Claims to be a business man and tradesman.

MODUS   : Important Mafia figure, 1948 to 1951 was distributor
OPERANDI   of large quantities of diverted heroin from the
                Schapparelli Pharmaceutical Co., supplying U.S.
                customers Frank Scalise, Joseph Di Palermo, Eugene
                Giannini and others. When diversion ceased he ob-
                tained French heroin for his American customers.

NAME	: Francesco RESTUCCIA
ALIASES	: Antonio Francesco Messina, Frank.
DESCRIPTION	: Born 3-25-1887 Savoca, Messina, Sicily, Italy, 5'9", 150 lbs, slim build, thinning grey hair, hazel eyes, fair complexion.
LOCALITIES FREQUENTED	: Resides in Santa Theresa, Sicily, Italy, formerly 501 W 51St, NYC & 184 Tenafly Rd., Tenafly, NJ. Frequented mid-town area of NYC. Also lived for several years at Caracas, Venezuela.
FAMILY BACKGROUND	: Widower; daughters: Carmella Garufi & Theresa Mannina; father: Vincenzo; mother: Carmella Tonrantola.
CRIMINAL ASSOCIATES	: ███████████, Mariano Marsalisi, Vincenzo Randazzo, Agatino Garufi, ███████████.
CRIMINAL HISTORY	: No FBI #assigned. I&NS #A 10942130. Only known arrest was one in 1939 by Italian police at request of U.S. Customs for conspiracy in connection with the seizure of 6 lbs, of smuggled opium.
BUSINESS	: At one time operated money exchange in NYC.
MODUS OPERANDI	: Known to have, in the past, participated with Eduardo Aronica and other Mafia leaders in the smuggling of large quantities of opium and morphine base. Travels extensively and may act as courier.

NAME   : Vincenzo RIMI

ALIASES   : Don Vincenzo

DESCRIPTION   : Born 3-5-01 Alcamo, Trapani,
                 Sicily, 5'9", 160 lbs, large
                 forehead, brown eyes, pro-
                 truding ears, dark brown
                 hair, greying.

LOCALITIES   : Alcamo, Partinico, Palermo,
FREQUENTED   Trapani, all Sicily; also
                 Rome, Italy.

FAMILY   : Father: Filippo; mother:
BACKGROUND   Anna Cusumanio; son: Filippo.

CRIMINAL   : Salvatore and Paolo Greco, ██████████████, ██████████
ASSOCIATES   ████████, ████████████████, Vito Vitale, Frank Coppola,
                 ████████████████████, Giuseppe and Serafino Mancuso.

CRIMINAL   : Never in U.S. Has a lengthy criminal record in
HISTORY   Italy including arrests in connection with Black
                 Marketeering, murders and kidnappings.

BUSINESS   : Land owner and farmer.

MODUS   : Is the head of the Mafia in Alcamo, Sicily and
OPERANDI   exerts great influence in the Mafia councils of
                 Palermo, Partinico, other parts of Italy and the
                 United States.

NAME   : Domenico ROBERTO

ALIASES   : Dominic Ruberto, Dan Roberts

DESCRIPTION   : Born 2-16-1896 Sambiase,
                 Calabria, Italy, 5'2", 165
                 lbs, grey hair, bald, heavy
                 build, olive complexion,
                 wears glasses.

LOCALITIES   : Resides at Viale Stazione
FREQUENTED   #14, Nicastro, Calabria,
                 Italy. Frequents Rome, Milan,
                 Naples, Taranto, Palermo &
                 other major cities of Italy.

FAMILY   : Father: Giuseppe; mother: Caterina Falvo; brothers:
BACKGROUND   Francesco, Antonio, Giovanni and Michael.

CRIMINAL   : ███████████████, ███████████, ██████████████,
ASSOCIATES   ██████████████, ██████████████, Anthony Accardo.

CRIMINAL   : FBI #445245. Record dates from 1921 and includes
HISTORY   arrests for robbery, concealed weapon, suspected
                 murder, violation of Prohibition Act and perjury
                 in regard to naturalization proceedings. Sentenced
                 to 2 years in prison and deported to Italy 1935.

BUSINESS   : Land and Property owner, living off his income and
                 is considered very wealthy.

MODUS   : Prior to his deportation he was a member of the
OPERANDI   Capone gang. Was very important in Chicago, run-
                 ning the gambling, prostitution and bootlegging
                 for Capone. Still wields great influence in Mafia
                 circles.

NAME   : John ROBERTO

ALIASES   : John Ruberto, Giovanni
                 Ruberto

DESCRIPTION   : Born 1-9-04 Sambiase, Catan-
                 zaro, Italy, 5'7", 230 lbs,
                 blue-grey eyes, grey hair,
                 stout build, light complex-
                 ion.

LOCALITIES   : Resides at Sambiase, Catan-
FREQUENTED   zaro, Italy, frequents Rome,
                 Naples, Palermo, Catania &
                 other important cities in
                 Italy. Is a U.S. citizen with a valid passport and
                 may return to Chicago or the U.S. at anytime. Pass-
                 port #1682063.

FAMILY   : Wife: Isabelle Strangis; father: Giuseppe; mother:
BACKGROUND   Katherine Falvo; both born & living in Italy; bro-
                 thers: Domenico and Michael.

CRIMINAL   : Domenico Roberto, brother: ███████████████████
ASSOCIATES   ████████████, ███████████, Anthony Accardo,
                 █████████████.

CRIMINAL   : In 1928 arrested by U.S. Prohibition Agents for
HISTORY   violation of the Prohibition Act. Arrests in
                 Italy for inflicting injuries & desertion.

BUSINESS   : Owns land and property in Sambiase, Italy. Owned
                 and operated the Co-operative Music Co., (Music
                 Supplies) 1728 Halsted St., Chicago, Ill.

MODUS   : This Mafioso was activily engaged in organized
OPERANDI   crime in Chicago for many years. He was an im-
                 portant power in the juke box racket through his
                 operation of the Co-operative Music Co. Still
                 maintains his associations with top level Mafia
                 members in Italy and U.S.

NAME	: Calogero ROBINO
ALIASES	: Caliddu, Calogero Rubino
DESCRIPTION	: Born 1-25-1917, Salemi, Trapani, Sicily, Italy. 5'9", 175 lbs, brown hair, brown eyes, dark complexion, deep cleft chin.

LOCALITIES FREQUENTED	: Resides Via Marcona #9, Salemi, Italy. Frequents Palermo, Trapani, Alcamo & other Italian cities.
FAMILY BACKGROUND	: Father: Santo; mother: Caterina Caruso; cousin: Cristofaro Robino, the notorious narcotic trafficker who was slain in N.Y.C. in 1958.
CRIMINAL ASSOCIATES	: ███████████, Pietro Sorci, ███████████, Lucky Luciano.
CRIMINAL HISTORY	: Not known to have ever been in the United States. Arrested for non-political crimes in Palermo and Trapani, confined and proposed for exile.
BUSINESS	: Fruit and produce merchant.
MODUS OPERANDI	: He and other Mafiosi in Italy comprise an organization which supplied twenty kilos of heroin per month to a distributing organization in the U.S., headed by his cousin, the late Cristofaro Robino.

```
NAME            : Francesco Paolo SAVERINO

ALIASES         : Don Ciccio, F. SEVERINO

DESCRIPTION     : Born 8-5-11 Salemi, Trapani,
                  Sicily, 5'6", 155 lbs, black
                  hair, brown eyes, thin build
                  moustache, very good dresser.

LOCALITIES      : Lives at Viale Papignao #28,
FREQUENTED        Milan, Italy, frequents
                  better night clubs in Milan
                  and also the cities of Rome,
                  San Remo in season & other
                  major cities of Italy &
                  Sicily.

FAMILY          : Father: Salvatore; mother; Alonza Gaspare both born
BACKGROUND        in Italy.

CRIMINAL        : Frank Pirico, Ugo Caneba, Sal Caneba,██████████
ASSOCIATES        ████████████, Frank Coppola, Paolo Greco, Serafino
                  Mancuso, Joe Pici, Joe Pellegrino, Eugene Giannini
                  (dead), ████████████████, Constantino Gamba, Dr. Enzo
                  Berti & all other major narcotic violators,inItaly.

CRIMINAL        : Dates from 1938. At one time he was arrested for
HISTORY           resisting a police officer.  Arrested in 1949 for
                  possession of 2 kilos of cocaine and convicted in
                  1950 Palermo.  In 1958 arrested in Milan in connec-
                  tion with the Enzo Berti et al laboratory case.

BUSINESS        : Operated a textile business on Via V. Hugo #2,
                  Milan, Italy.

MODUS           : Operates clandestine heroin laboratories in Italy.
OPERANDI          Is also supplied by Corsican gangsters in France.
                  Distributes kilo lots of heroin to many important
                  American gangs.
```

NAME	: Giovanni SCALICI

ALIASES : Giovanni Scalise, John
Scalise, John Scalice

DESCRIPTION : Born 2-28-1899, Palermo,
Sicily, Italy, 5'4", 135
lbs, brown-grey hair, brown
eyes. Alien Reg. #5283103.

LOCALITIES : Resides Via Francesco Maggio
FREQUENTED   15, Palermo, Sicily; former-
ly resided 1066 Rhinelander
Ave., NYC, frequented Crescer_
Avenue section of Bronx, N.Y.

FAMILY : Married Theresa D'Amico, an American citizen, who
BACKGROUND   resides in NYC; father: Giacomo; mother: Giovanna
Caviglia; brothers: Francesco (murdered), Giuseppe
(missing), Salvatore, Giacomo, Antonio & Domenico;
sister: Rosa (Mrs. Giacomo Scarpulla).

CRIMINAL : Lucky Luciano, Anthony Strollo, Giacomo Scarpulla,
ASSOCIATES   Matteo Cuomo, Vincent Squillante, Sebastiano
Bellanca (missing).

CRIMINAL : FBI #323762 NYCPD #B-86503   Record dating from
early 1920's includes arrests in Italy for theft,
counterfeit money, resisting arrest, dangerous
weapon, fraud & bribery, and in U.S. for gun, grand
larceny, felonious assault & bootlegging.

BUSINESS : Operates gasoline station at Palermo, Sicily.

MODUS : Was part of a large scale Mafia narcotic smuggling
organization headed by his brother, the late
Francesco Scalici, who was murdered in connection
with a narcotic transaction.

NAME   : Gaspare SILVESTRI

ALIASES   : None

DESCRIPTION   : Born 6-13-37 Palermo, Sicily.
                5'6", 140 lbs, eyes brown &
                deep set, medium build, brown
                hair, dark complexion, bushy
                eyebrows and meeting over
                bridge of nose, scars on
                forehead.

LOCALITIES   : Palermo, Sicily.
FREQUENTED

FAMILY   : Father: Giovanni; mother: Angela Baresi.
BACKGROUND

CRIMINAL   : Giuseppe Cottone, Salvatore Piazza, ███████████,
ASSOCIATES   ████████████, █████████████, ██
                ████████, ████████████.

CRIMINAL   : Palermo, Italy Police #143-154-111. 1956 arrested
HISTORY   and exiled for one year for participation in the
                Mafia's produce market war in Sicily.

BUSINESS   : Butcher

MODUS   : Dangerous young Mafia strong arm man and shotgun
OPERANDI   "Lupara" assassin.

NAME   : Antonino SORCI

ALIASES   : Nino

DESCRIPTION   : Born 3-21-04 Palermo, Sicily,
                  Italy, 5'8", 165 lbs, medium
                  build, brown eyes, brown
                  hair, dark complexion.

LOCALITIES   : Palermo, Milan, Naples,
FREQUENTED   Genova, Partinico, Alcamo,
                  Trieste and all other major
                  cities in Italy.

FAMILY   : Married Susanna DiBella;
BACKGROUND   father: Francesco; mother: Maria Levantino, brother:
                  Pietro.

CRIMINAL   : Lucky Luciano, Dominique Albertini, Giovanni Maugeri,
ASSOCIATES   Antoine Cordoleani, Salvatore Caneba, ███████████,
                  Francesco Coppola, Joe Pici, Francesco Pirico,
                  Salvatore Greco, Rosario Mancino, Calogero Robino,
                  Serafino, Salvatore and Giuseppe Mancuso.

CRIMINAL   : Ministry of Interior Police #596788 6494. In 1938
HISTORY   he was arrested and confined to his home town by
                  the Palermo Court. Has never been in USA.

BUSINESS   : Fruit merchant.

MODUS   : He and his brother, Pietro, are among the top
OPERANDI   Mafiosi in Italy and have supplied huge quantities
                  of heroin to the U. S. market. These brothers are
                  believed to have instigated the Palermo produce
                  market war of 1956.

NAME   : Pietro SORCI

ALIASES   : None

DESCRIPTION   : Born 7-23-11 Palermo, Sicily,
                  Italy, 5'8", 165 lbs, brown
                  hair, brown eyes, medium
                  build, dark complexion.

LOCALITIES   : Resides Via Viviani #10,
FREQUENTED   Milan, Italy. Frequents Rome,
                  Trieste, Taranto, Naples,
                  Palermo, Genova & other
                  major cities in Italy. Also
                  Marseille, France & other
                  cities on the French Riviera.

FAMILY   : Father: Francesco; mother: Maria Levantino; brother:
BACKGROUND   Antonino.

CRIMINAL   : Lucky Luciano, Dominique Albertini, Giovanni Maugeri,
ASSOCIATES   Antoine Cordoleani, Salvatore Caneba, ███████████,
                  Francesco Coppola, Joe Pici, Francesco Pirico,
                  Salvatore Greco, Rosario Mancio, Calogero Robino,
                  Serafino, Salvatore and Giuseppe Mancuso.

CRIMINAL   : Ministry of Interior Police #494395 4343. In 1950
HISTORY   Sorci was detained in Milan, Italy by the Italian
                  Ministry of Interior for criminal investigation,
                  suspected of trafficking in narcotics.

BUSINESS   : Owns a fruit business on via Boiardo #6, near the
                  Porta Vittoria, Milan, Italy.

MODUS   : He and his brother Antonino are among the top
OPERANDI   Mafiosi in Italy and have supplied huge quantities
                  of heroin to the U.S., Market. These brothers are
                  believed to have instigated the 1956 produce mar-
                  ket war in Palermo.

NAME   : Michael SPINELLA

ALIASES   : Martin Steel

DESCRIPTION   : Born 3-3-94 Sicily, 5'8",
                165 lbs, white hair, blue
                eyes (pupil missing from
                one eye), ruddy complexion,
                not U.S. citizen, I&NS #A7-
                463519.

LOCALITIES   : Last known to be living on
FREQUENTED   the Island of Capri; he has
                lived in Naples and Palermo.
                In the USA lived in Paramus,
                NJ, and Miami, Fla.

FAMILY   : His wife is in the USA. Married 4 times and had 4
BACKGROUND   children. Has a son, Matthew, about 20 years old
                who lives in NY and Fla. A daughter, Rosanne, is
                married to Frank Caughey. They run a rest., called
                Caughey's Pine Room at 64 Hoboken Rd, E. Rutherford,
                New Jersey.

CRIMINAL   : Lucky Luciano, Francesco Costiglia, Vito Genovese,
ASSOCIATES   Giuseppe Profaci.

CRIMINAL   : FBI #738966. Record dating from 1933 includes
HISTORY   arrests for vagrancy, disorderly house, assault
                & battery, robbery, assault to kill and murder.

BUSINESS   : No known legitimate business in Italy. He is re-
                ported to still be receiving money from various
                enterprises, legitimate and illegal, in the USA,
                including the Arcola, NJ, Motor Lodge.

MODUS   : Mafia hoodlum and killer; a one-time member of
OPERANDI   the infamous "Purple Gang". Engages in large scale
                narcotic traffic in addition to other illicit ac-
                tivities.

NAME   : Giorgio VENEZIA

ALIASES   : None

DESCRIPTION   : Born 9-20-25 Caccamo,
                Palermo, Sicily, 5'6", 155
                lbs, brown eyes, brown hair,
                medium build, light complex-
                ion.

LOCALITIES   : Resides Via della Rocca #12,
FREQUENTED   Caccamo, Sicily. Frequents
                Palermo, Monreale, Partinico,
                San Giuseppe Iato all in
                Sicily.

FAMILY   : Father: Fortunato; mother: Domenica Sanfratello.
BACKGROUND

CRIMINAL   : Giuseppe Anzalone, Vincenzo Cottone, Francesco
ASSOCIATES   LaMantia, Giorgio Misuraca.

CRIMINAL   : Palermo Police #99955554 4/53. Convicted 1956 for
HISTORY   participation in the produce market war in Sicily.

BUSINESS   : No legitimate occupation.

MODUS   : Dangerous Mafia killer. Assigned to carry out
OPERANDI   shotgun "lupara" assassinations of produce mer-
                chants who refuse to comply with Mafia demands.

NAME   : Vito VITALE

ALIASES   : Don Vito

DESCRIPTION   : Born 8-24-1885, at Castel-
                    lammare, Trapani, Sicily,
                    5'2", 135 lbs, brown-grey
                    hair, brown eyes, dark com-
                    plexion, medium build (photo
                    over 30 years old).

LOCALITIES   : Resides Corso Regina Maria
FREQUENTED   Pia #21C, Ostia, Italy.
                    Frequents Rome and suburbs
                    Ostia & Ardea. Also Palermo
                    Castellamare, Partinico & Alcamo, in Sicily; all
                    Italy.

FAMILY   : Father Antonino; mother: Giovanna Giaravino; son:
BACKGROUND   Michaelangelo; daughter: Giovanna (married to
                    Raffaele Quasarano of Detroit).

CRIMINAL   : Francesco Coppola, ███████████████, Giuseppe
ASSOCIATES   Maninni, Vincenzo Rimi, Giuseppe Corso, Serafino &
                    Giuseppe Mancuso.

CRIMINAL   : Has never been in America. Criminal record in Italy
HISTORY   dates back to 1918 and includes arrests for alien
                    smuggling, bootlegging and murder.

BUSINESS   : Owns property in Rome and Palermo areas.

MODUS   : Regarded as a top leader and arbitrator of Mafia in
OPERANDI   Italy and arranges money transfers from America to
                    Italy regarding narcotic and other illicit trans-
                    actions. Introduces American gangsters to Sicilian
                    and Corsican narcotic suppliers.

842

MEXICO

NAME	: Jaspere J. MATRANGA
ALIASES	: Gaspare Matranga, Joseph Vitale
DESCRIPTION	: Born 5-28-98 at Palermo, Sicily; 5'6", 190 lbs.; eyes brown, black hair, medium complexion, stout build and scar on upper lip.
LOCALITIES FREQUENTED	: Reported to be residing at 950 Ave., Negrete, Tijuana, Mexico.
FAMILY BACKGROUND	: Wife is named Maria. They have two daughters, Vita and Concetta (now Mrs. Angelo Polizzi), subject is the son of Matteo and Concetta Matranga, both of whom are residents of Sicily.
CRIMINAL ASSOCIATES	: ███████████ (son-in-law) and the Matranga Family of San Diego, the Dippolito Family of San Bernardino, Calif., Joseph Aiello of Springfield, Ill., and Nicolo Impostato of Italy.
CRIMINAL HISTORY	: FBI #4508829, criminal history includes a series of arrests at Chicago, Ill., from 1932 to 1939 under name of Joseph Vitale, was arrested by immigration authorities on 6-4-53 at Los Angeles, Calif., and deported to Italy 6-18-54.
BUSINESS	: Reported to be in the produce business at Tiajuana, Mexico.
MODUS OPERANDI	: From 1932 to 1945 was an enforcer and professional "Killer" for the Mafia at Chicago, Ill., in 1945 moved to San Diego, Calif., where he controlled the organizations gambling interests until his deportation in 1954.